Lecture Notes in Computer Science 15174

The series Lecture Notes in Computer Science (LNCS), including its subseries Lecture Notes in Artificial Intelligence (LNAI) and Lecture Notes in Bioinformatics (LNBI), has established itself as a medium for the publication of new developments in computer science and information technology research, teaching, and education.

LNCS enjoys close cooperation with the computer science R & D community, the series counts many renowned academics among its volume editors and paper authors, and collaborates with prestigious societies. Its mission is to serve this international community by providing an invaluable service, mainly focused on the publication of conference and workshop proceedings and postproceedings. LNCS commenced publication in 1973.

Alexis Quesada-Arencibia · Michael Affenzeller ·
Roberto Moreno-Díaz
Editors

Computer Aided Systems Theory – EUROCAST 2024

19th International Conference

Las Palmas de Gran Canaria, Spain, February 25 – March 1, 2024

Revised Selected Papers, Part III

Editors
Alexis Quesada-Arencibia
Universidad de Las Palmas de Gran Canaria
Las Palmas de Gran Canaria, Spain

Michael Affenzeller
FH OÖ Studienbetriebs GmbH
Hagenberg, Austria

Roberto Moreno-Díaz
Universidad de Las Palmas de Gran Canaria
Las Palmas de Gran Canaria, Spain

ISSN 0302-9743 ISSN 1611-3349 (electronic)
Lecture Notes in Computer Science
ISBN 978-3-031-83887-3 ISBN 978-3-031-83885-9 (eBook)
https://doi.org/10.1007/978-3-031-83885-9

This Springer imprint is published by the registered company Springer Nature Switzerland AG
The registered company address is: Gewerbestrasse 11, 6330 Cham, Switzerland

Preface

The EUROCAST conference is particularly unique among the European Scientific Technical Congresses because it is one of the few periodic meetings promoted and organized exclusively by university and socio-cultural institutions, without the tutelage, direction or funding of associations, professionals or companies. It is currently the oldest of those. It is celebrated every two years, initially alternating Las Palmas de G.C. and a university in continental Europe, and since 2001, always in Las Palmas de G.C.

The idea of the first EUROCAST was developed in 1988 by Franz Pichler of the University of Linz and Roberto Moreno at a meeting in Vienna promoted by the past Honorary President, the late Werner Schimanovich. The first meeting, EUROCAST 1989, took place in February of that year, at Las Palmas School of Industrial Engineers, promoted by the Faculty of Informatics of Las Palmas and the Institute of Systems of the University of Linz. The Opening Session took place in the town of Gáldar, on February 26th, 1989.

Science, and especially technology, have moved in an almost vertiginous way, driven by the need for the promotion of consumerism, which is associated with the change of values that has taken place in recent generations. And EUROCAST, within what we understand as a certain freedom, and with prudence, has been adapting the profile of its organization from a meeting of very specific specialists, to a practically multidisciplinary, flexible and changing conference, which in each event tries to attract experts and especially young researchers, facilitating the interaction between them, which is a generator of creativity.

The key to the success of EUROCAST for 35 years has been in the quality of the contributions of its participants. This has to be recognized in the first place. They have made possible, with the help of the Springer publications in Computer Science, the worldwide distribution of the most important effect of EUROCAST: bringing together for many years scientists and engineers of different ages, training, interests and from very different European and non-European institutions. And they could share their experiences in the design and analysis of systems using the most advanced mathematical methods to make efficient models and algorithms in computers. And this from the socio-economic, biological, medical technologies and sciences and information and communication engineering topics. All in a multidisciplinary atmosphere, which has facilitated the appearance and discussion of new and creative ideas and developments.

Selected papers from previous editions have been published as Springer Lecture Notes in Computer Science volumes 410, 585, 763, 1030, 1333, 1798, 2178, 2809, 3643, 4739, 5717, 6927, 6928, 8111, 8112, 9520, 10671, 10672, 12013, 12014 and 13789 and in several special issues of Cybernetics and Systems: An International Journal. EUROCAST and CAST meetings are consolidated, as shown by the number and quality of the contributions over the years.

In this open multidisciplinary spirit, the 2024 Conference was composed of three plenary lectures by distinguished international Professors and 14 major thematic workshops, which covered a broad spectrum of cutting-edge research in Systems Theory, Applications, Pioneers, and Landmarks, Theory and Applications of Metaheuristic Algorithms, Mechatronic Product Development, Model-Based System Design, Verification and Simulation, Applications of Signal Processing Technology, Applied Data Science and Engineering for Intelligent Transportation Systems and Smart Mobility, Computer and Systems-Based Methods and Electronic Tools in Clinical and Academic Medicine, Systems in Industrial Robotics, Automation and IoT, Systems Thinking: Applications in Technology, Science, and Management, Data Science in Medical and Bio-Informatics, Modeling, Simulation, and Optimization in Production and Logistics, "Green AI" and SW-Tools for Sustainable Energy and Materials Consumption, Stochastic Models, Statistical Methods, and Applied Systems Simulations.

In this conference, as in previous ones, most of the credit for the success lays in the quality of proposals of subjects for Workshops, their resonance and impact, their diffusion and their strict selection of the many intended contributions. From 150 proposals, 104 revised papers were selected to be included in these volumes. The reviews of papers and their selection was made by the agreement of at least two members of the Program Committee, listed in the following pages, by a double open peer review process.

The editors would like to express their thanks to all the contributors, many of whom have already been EUROCAST participants for years, particularly in the considerable interaction of young and senior researchers, as well as to the invited speakers, Manuel Maynar from the University of Las Palmas de Gran Canaria; Ryszard Klempous from Wrocław University of Technology; and Dirk Jacob from Kempten University of Applied Sciences. We would also like to thank the director of the Elder Museum of Science and Technology, José Gilberto Moreno, and the museum staff. Special thanks are due to the staff of Springer for their valuable support.

October 2024

Alexis Quesada-Arencibia
Michael Affenzeller
Roberto Moreno-Díaz

Organization

Workshops

Systems Theory, Applications, Pioneers, and Landmarks

Chairpersons

F. Pichler, Linz, Austria
R. Moreno-Díaz, Las Palmas, Spain

Theory and Applications of Metaheuristic Algorithms

Chairpersons

M. Affenzeller, Hagenberg, Austria
S. Wagner, Hagenberg, Austria
G. Raidl, Vienna, Austria

Mechatronic Product Development

Chairpersons

M. Jungwirth, Wels, Austria
T. Schlechter, Wels, Austria

Model-Based System Design, Verification and Simulation

Chairpersons

J. Nikodem, Wrocław, Poland
Ito, A., Chuo, Japan
Nikodem, M., Wrocław, Poland

Applications of Signal Processing Technology

Chairpersons

Zagar, MULeoben, Austria
Lunglmayr, Linz, Austria

Applied Data Science and Engineering for Intelligent Transportation Systems and Smart Mobility

Chairpersons

J. Sanchez-Medina, Las Palmas, Spain
J. del Ser, Bilbao, Spain
H. B. Celikoglu, Istanbul, Turkey
R. Rossetti, Lisboa, Portugal
L. Acosta, La Laguna, Spain

Computer and Systems Based Methods and Electronic Tools in Clinical and Academic Medicine

Chairpersons

J. Rozenblit, Tucson, USA
M. Maynar, Las Palmas, Spain
R. Klempous, Wroclaw, Poland
L. Kovacs, Budapest, Hungary

Systems in Industrial Robotics, Automation and IoT

Chairpersons

D. Jacob, Kempten, Germany
R. Stetter, Munich, Germany
E. Markl, Vienna, Austria

Systems Thinking: Applications in Technology, Science, and Management

Chairpersons

M. Schwaninger, St. Gallen, Switzerland
S. Groesser, Bern, Switzerland

Data Science in Medical and Bio-informatics

Chairpersons

M. Giretzlehner, RISC Software, Hagenberg, Austria
M. Geiß, Software Competence Center, Hagenberg, Austria
S. Winkler, FH OÖ, Hagenberg, Austria

Modeling, Simulation, and Optimization in Production and Logistics

Chairpersons

S. Wagner, Hagenberg, Austria
F. Longo, Calabria, Italy
A. Padovano, Calabria, Italy

"Green AI" and SW-Tools for Sustainable Energy and Materials Consumption

Chairpersons

D. Jacob, Kempten, Germany
R. Stetter, Munich, Germany
E. Markl, Vienna, Austria

Stochastic Models, Statistical Methods, and Applied Systems Simulations

Chairpersons

E. Pirozzi, Napoli, Italy
V. Giorno, Salerno, Italy

Systems Cybersecurity Technologies and Quantum Approaches Potentials

Chairpersons

P. Caballero, La Laguna, Spain
A. Quesada-Arencibia, Las Palmas, Spain

Invited Plenary Lectures

Towards the Technologically Intelligent Hospital

Manuel Maynar Universidad de Las Palmas de Gran Canaria

Eurocast from the 1990s: Personal Perspective and Contributions

Ryszard Klempous Wrocław University of Technology

Programs for Motivation of Science and Technology Among Youngsters

Makeathon Green Island

Dirk Jacob	Kempten University of Applied Sciences

Ciberlandia Canarias

Alexis Quesada-Arencibia	Universidad de Las Palmas de Gran Canaria

Program Committee

Acosta, L.	Univ. of La Laguna, Spain
Affenzeller, M.	Univ. of Applied Sciences, Upper Austria, Austria
Berk Celikoglu, H.	Istanbul Technical University, Turkey
Caballero, P.	Univ. of La Laguna, Spain
del Ser, J.	Univ. of Bilbao, Spain
Geiß, M.	SCCH, Austria
Giorno, V.	Univ. di Salerno, Italy
Giretzlehner, M.	RISC Soft, Austria
Groesser, S.	Univ. of Applied Sciences, Bern, Switzerland
Jacob, D.	Univ. of Applied Sciences, Kempten, Germany
Jungwirth, M.	Univ. of Applied Sciences, Wels, Austria
Klempous, R.	Wrocław University of Science and Technology, Poland
Kovacs, L.	Univ. of Obuda, Hungary
Longo, F.	Univ. of Calabria, Italy
Ito, A.	Univ. of Chuo, Japan
Lunglmayr, M.	JKU, Linz, Austria
Markl, E.	Univ. of Applied Sciences, Vienna, Austria
Maynar, M.	Univ. of Las Palmas de Gran Canaria, Spain
Moreno-Díaz, R.	Univ. of Las Palmas de Gran Canaria, Spain
Nikodem, M.	Wrocław University of Science and Technology, Poland
Nikodem, J.	Wrocław University of Science and Technology, Poland
Padovano, A.	Univ. of Calabria, Italy
Pichler, F.	JKU, Linz, Austria
Pirozzi, E.	Univ. di Napoli, Italy

Quesada-Arencibia, A.	Univ. of Las Palmas de Gran Canaria, Spain
Raidl, G.	TU Wien, Austria
Rossetti, R.	Univ. of Lisbon, Portugal
Rozenblit, J.	Univ. of Arizona, USA
Sanchez-Medina, J.	Univ. of Las Palmas de Gran Canaria, Spain
Schlechter, T.	Univ. of Applied Sciences, Wels, Austria
Schwaninger, M.	Univ. of St Gallen, Switzerland
Stetter, R.	Munich, Germany
Wagner, S.	Univ. of Applied Sciences, Upper Austria, Austria
Winkler, S.	FH OÖ, Hagenberg, Austria
Zagar, B.	Montan univ. Leoben, Austria

Program Committee Chairs

R. Moreno Díaz	Las Palmas de Gran Canaria
M. Affenzeller	Hagenberg
A. Quesada-Arencibia	Las Palmas de Gran Canaria

Conference Chairs

Founder and Honorary

F. Pichler, Linz

General

R. Moreno Díaz
Las Palmas de G.C.

Program

M. Affenzeller, Hagenberg

Logistics

A. Quesada-Arencibia, Las Palmas de G.C.

Conference Web

https://eurocast2024.fulp.ulpgc.es.

Supporter Institutions

Instituto Universitario de Ciencias y Tecnologías Cibernéticas
Universidad de Las Palmas de Gran Canaria

Johannes Kepler University Linz

University of Applied Sciences Upper Austria

MUSEO DE LA CIENCIA
Y LA TECNOLOGÍA

Museo Elder de la Ciencia y la Tecnología

Fundación Universitaria de Las Palmas

Contents – Part III

Modeling, Simulation, and Optimization in Production and Logistics

Age-Layer-Population-Structure with Self-adaptation in Optimization 3
Kaifeng Yang, Bernhard Werth, and Michael Affenzeller

Machine Learning Update Strategies for Real-Time Production Environments 12
Philipp Neuhauser, Philipp Fleck, Sebastian Leitner, and Stefan Wagner

Online Machine Learning for the Estimation of Process Times in Dynamic Scheduling 25
Michael Heckmann, Bernhard Werth, Johannes Karder, and Stefan Wagner

Concurrent Evolution of Dynamic Single and Dual-Crane Scheduling Scenarios 38
Johannes Karder, Bernhard Werth, Stefan Wagner, and Michael Affenzeller

Learning-Based Algorithm Selection for a Multiprocessor Scheduling Problem 50
Roland Braune

Using the Pilot Method as a Problem-Independent Metaheuristic for Multi-objective Beam Search 61
Oliver Bindreiter, Bernhard Werth, and Stefan Wagner

Solving Two-Machine Sum-Cost Flow Shop Problem on D-Wave Quantum Annealer 69
Wojciech Bożejko, Ryszard Klempous, Mariusz Uchroński, and Mieczysław Wodecki

Integrating Optimization Techniques and Live Tracking Software in Maritime Logistics 79
Bruno Lorenzo Arroyo-Pedraza, Sergio Leopoldo Benítez-Delgado, Airam Expósito-Márquez, Christopher Expósito-Izquierdo, and Israel López-Plata

Incrementally Solving the Dynamic Stacking Problem 87
Sebastian Leitner, Stefan Wagner, and Michael Affenzeller

Predicting the Processing Effort for Block Relocation Problems 98
Roland Braune and Michael Raunig

Modelling Electric Vehicle Routing Problem with Heterogeneous Fleet for Simultaneous Pickup and Delivery 107
Prateek Gupta, Devanand, Antonio Ken Iannillo, Jorge Augusto Meira, Radu State, and Danilo D'Aversa

"Green AI" and SW-Tools for Sustainable Energy and Materials Consumption

A Predictive Maintenance Concept for Sustainable Lubricant Oil Usage Based on Federated Learning 119
Hadi Ghaeni, Ferdinand Heinrich, Florian Rieger, Franz Wenninger, Tim Egger, and Benjamin Kormann

Introduction to Circular System Design and First Use Cases for Sustainable Product Development in Smart Meter Remanufacturing and Robotics 132
Nathanael Nafz, Bernhard Höfig, Markus Glück, and Niclas-Alexander Mauß

Elegant Architectures: Sustainability in Information Technology 147
Enrique Ismael Mendoza Robaina, José María Silva Bravo, Alberto García Cabrera, and Diego Ambite Varona

Surrogates for Fair-Weather Photovoltaic Module Output 154
Dominik Falkner, Michael Bögl, Ines Langthallner, Jan Zenisek, and Michael Affenzeller

How Digital Twins Can Help to Accelerate the Transition to a Carbon-Neutral System 167
Tobias Rodemann and Christiane Attig

Performance and Computation Time Gains Caused by Sampling Rate Reduction in Time Series Deep Anomaly Detection 176
Dominik Wiesner and Frank Schirmeier

Exploring the Green AI Potential of Adapter Tuning for Language Models 187
Dennis Mustafić and Frank Schirmeier

Stochastic Models, Statistical Methods, and Applied Systems Simulations

Disease Incidence in a Stochastic SVIRS Model with Waning Immunity 199
M. J. Lopez-Herrero and D. Taipe

A Spreaders-Ignorants-Skeptics Model for the Spreading of Fake News and a Related Finite Birth-Death Process 213
Paola Paraggio and Serena Spina

Comparing Some Simulation Strategies for First Passage Times of Time-Changed Brownian Motion 228
Luigia Caputo, Maria Francesca Carfora, and Enrica Pirozzi

Numerical Evaluations for Fractional Stochastic Differential Equations in Neuronal Dynamics 243
Enrica Pirozzi

Handling Uncertainties on the Right-Hand Side of a Classical Transportation Model by Stochastic Optimisation and a Matheuristic Approach 252
Abtin Nourmohammadzadeh and Stefan Voß

Unified Formulations of Entropy and Extropy 268
Maria Longobardi

Time-Inhomogeneous Diffusion Process for the SI Epidemic Model 277
Virginia Giorno and Amelia G. Nobile

A Vasicek-Type Model with Structural Breaks in the Drift 286
Giuseppina Albano and Virginia Giorno

Estimating a Time-Inhomogeneous Hyperlogistic Diffusion Process 295
G. Albano, A. Barrera, V. Giorno, and F. Torres-Ruiz

Systems Cybersecurity Technologies and Quantum Approaches Potentials

A Federated Learning-Based Android Malware Detector Through Differential Privacy 307
Christian Peluso, Giovanni Ciaramella, Francesco Mercaldo, Antonella Santone, and Fabio Martinelli

A Generative Model Based Honeypot for Industrial OPC UA Communication ... 320
Olaf Sassnick, Georg Schäfer, Thomas Rosenstatter, and Stefan Huber

Theoretical Approach to Backdoor Attack on CRYSTALS-Dilithium ... 335
É. Pérez-Ramos and P. Caballero-Gil

An IoT Lab Dedicated to Cybersecurity – Teaching, Learning and Research ... 344
Georg Hackenberg and Mario Jungwirth

Author Index ... 359

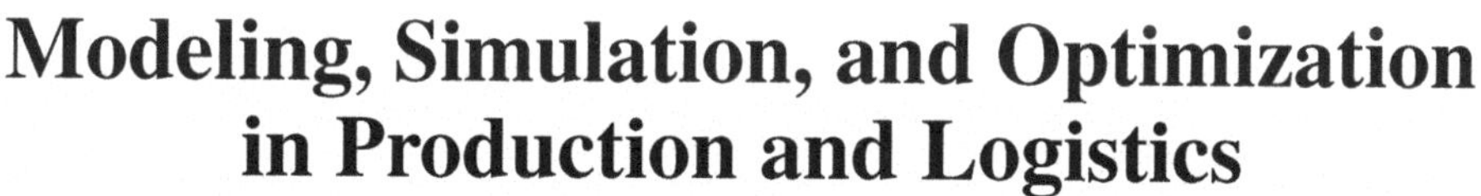

Modeling, Simulation, and Optimization in Production and Logistics

Age-Layer-Population-Structure with Self-adaptation in Optimization

Kaifeng Yang(✉), Bernhard Werth, and Michael Affenzeller

Heuristic and Evolutionary Algorithms Laboratory, University of Applied Sciences Upper Austria, 4232 Hagenberg, Austria
{Kaifeng.Yang,Bernhad.Werth,MichaelAffenzeller}@fh-hagenberg.at

Abstract. Dynamic optimization problems are a class of optimization problems where the objective function, constraints, or both can change over time. In this work, we address the dynamic travelling salesman problem (TSP) by using the age-layered population structure (ALPS). To enhance different layer's behaviour, we introduce the self-adaptation strategies to adjust the mutation and crossover rate in each layers, which are stationary in the conventional ALPS. The proposed strategies are compared with the stationary strategy over 7 different dynamic TSPs. The experimental results shows that the proposed strategy, *convex* strategy, yields much better results than the stationary strategy on complex problems.

Keywords: Evolutionary Algorithms · ALPS · Self-adaptation

1 Introduction

Population diversity in dynamic optimization problems is vital as it enables the algorithm to explore various regions of a changing solution landscape, preventing premature convergence to suboptimal solutions. A diverse population ensures adaptability, resilience, and the ability to track and adapt to shifting optima, essential for effectively addressing the dynamic nature of the problem. Several methods have been devised to sustain diversity in such contexts. Dynamic adaptation of parameters, such as mutation rates or selection pressures, based on the changing landscape, allows the algorithm to dynamically adjust to new optima. Niching methods, including crowding or fitness sharing, explicitly encourage the maintenance of diverse solutions by penalizing similarity. Besides, restart mechanisms, such as Bipop-CMA-ES [6], also keep the population diversity by reinitializing the population. Additionally, hybridization techniques and multi-population strategies introduce diverse genetic pools that can exchange information, facilitating a broader exploration of the altered problem space. These methods collectively enable evolutionary algorithms to effectively navigate dynamic environments by preserving diversity, ensuring adaptability, and facilitating the discovery of high-quality solutions amidst changing conditions.

A. Quesada-Arencibia et al. (Eds.): EUROCAST 2024, LNCS 15174, pp. 3–11, 2025.
https://doi.org/10.1007/978-3-031-83885-9_1

Age-layered population structure (ALPS) [7] in evolutionary algorithms involves organizing the population into layers based on the "age" of individuals, typically representing the number of generations they have survived or the time of creation within the algorithm. Each layer might have distinct characteristics and roles. Younger layers often represent exploration, bringing in fresh solutions, while older layers emphasize exploitation by retaining promising solutions that have survived multiple generations.

ALPS stands out for its exceptional features, notably its continuous integration of new genetic material without necessitating resource-intensive restarts due to fully converged population states. Furthermore, the system adeptly retains genetic information from earlier problem epochs implicitly within higher layers. These distinctive traits not only foster a harmonious balance between exploration and exploitation, but also confer robustness against premature convergence, rendering ALPS highly efficient for navigating dynamic environments.

Nonetheless, a notable drawback of ALPS lies in its demand for meticulous parameterization. Establishing optimal age gaps, mutation rates, and crossover rates proves challenging, given the inherent limitation of a "one-size-fits-all" paradigm, where constant rates are applied across diverse layers. To address this challenge, we advocate for a more tailored evolution approach across different layers, each representing populations of varied ages and convergence states. To avoid exacerbating the complexity of parameterization with additional factors, we revisit the concept of self-adaptation, originally introduced for evolutionary strategies [1]. This approach aims to enhance adaptability and performance without introducing an undue burden of additional parameters.

In this work, we propose a self-adaptive mechanism inspired by evolutionary strategies [1], wherein hyperparameters (including age gap, aging scheme, mutation rate, crossover rate) dynamically adjust based on the evolving problem landscape. Specifically, we utilize individual stepsize adaption strategy [10] for mixed-integer optimization problems. The age gap, aging scheme, and crossover rate are automatically tuned by population similarity, inherent building blocks, and other evolution behaviors. This self-adaptation ensures that ALPS remains responsive to changes, allowing for an automatic fine-tuning of hyperparameters during runtime. By integrating self-adaptation, ALPS gains the flexibility needed to navigate dynamic environments without the need for constant manual intervention, thereby enhancing its adaptability and overall optimization performance. In addition, we will compare the proposed self-adaptive ALPS with various fixed instances of ALPS, in order to gauge both resilience against miss-parameterization as well as classic performance, using dynamizised versions of the classic TSPLib [13] instances. We will utilize the empirical attainment function [11] to statistically analyze the dynamic features of algorithm's behavior, such as probabilistic distribution of the outcomes and convergence behavior. Population diversity in dynamic optimization problems is vital as it enables the algorithm to explore various regions of a changing solution landscape, preventing premature convergence to suboptimal solutions. A diverse population ensures adaptability, resilience, and the ability to track and adapt to shifting optima, essential for effectively addressing the dynamic nature of the problem. Several methods have been devised to sustain diversity in such contexts. Dynamic adaptation of parameters, such as mutation rates or selection pressures, based on the changing landscape, allows the algorithm to dynamically adjust to new optima. Niching methods, including crowding or fitness sharing, explicitly encourage the maintenance of diverse solutions by penalizing similarity. Besides, restart mechanisms, such as Bipop-CMA-ES [6], also keep the population diversity by reinitializing the population. Additionally, hybridization techniques and multi-population strategies introduce diverse genetic pools that can exchange information, facilitating a broader exploration of the altered problem space. These methods collectively enable evolutionary algorithms to effectively navigate dynamic environments by preserving diversity, ensuring adaptability, and facilitating the discovery of high-quality solutions amidst changing conditions.

2 Dynamic Traveling Salesman Problem

As a basis for the following experiments a dynamizised version of the well-known Travelling Salesman Problem (TSP). The static TSP is defined as minimizing the length of a cyclic tour through a network of cities where every city has to be visited once (i.e. finding the minimum Hamiltonian circle in a graph). The TSP therefore features a very intuitive solution encoding as a permutation of cities. In order to transform the static TSP into a dynamic variant, only a subset of cities is considered to be *active* at any point i.e. only active cities can be and need to be visited. Whenever the problem changes its *epoch*, a number of cities are chosen uniformly random from the active and inactive cities, respectively, that switch their activation state. This procedure has the benefit of keeping the length of the encoding constant during the optimization and avoids introducing inactive cities into the solution candidate, which would create introns (genetically irrelevant information).

2.1 Dynamics in TSP

- The *epoch length* of the dynamic TSP defines the number of evaluations between changes. A note has to be made here that since the number of active layers in ALPS is dynamically adjusted, one can opt to apply any change during the evaluation of a layer, between layers or between iterations of ALPS main loop. Naturally, shorter epoch lengths lead to more perturbed and presumably difficult dynamic optimization problems. In this work, an immediate update approach was chosen.
- The *activation severity* denotes the percentage of cities that are considered active at any moment and therefor directly influence the size of the solution candidates in ALPS. <TODO Kaifeng mention your AS here, I believe it is 90%>
- The*swap severity*, conversely, denotes the percentage of cities that are activated/deactivated when the problem epoch changes and controls how strong individual epoch changes are. In this work, the swap severity is set to 50%.

2.2 Additional Remarks

A considerable advantage of using the well-known and well-studied TSP problem is the possibility to obtain global optimal solutions via the application of exact solvers like Concorde[1], which allows for normalized fitness values that are given as the relative error to the current global optimum. Thus, partially negating the effects of one epoch, allowing for significantly shorter routes than others. Furthermore, test instances can be created by adapting existing static TSP instances; in this paper, instances are based on a subselection of the well-known TSPLIB[2].

3 Methodologies

3.1 Framework of ALPS

Age-layered population structure (ALPS) was proposed by Hornby [7] to promote diversity via niching and periodic reinitialization. ALPS achieves this by introducing a new property, age, for every individual. A set of simple age update rules define how individuals age:

- A new, randomly initialized individual is assigned an age of zero.
- Offspring produced through crossover or mutation inherit the age of their oldest parent.
- An individual's age increases by one after each fitness evaluation.

ALPS restricts competition for survival to individuals within the same *age layer* to prevent young individuals from being driven to extinction by older, more evolved individuals. This form of niching promotes diversity by making competition for survival fairer.

The pseudocode of ALPS is described in Algorithm 1. The parameter *AgeGap* specifies the maximum allowed age in each layer, which typically increase with each layer according to different strategies (e.g., linear, Fibonacci, polynomial or exponential). The hierarchy of layers is organized from bottom to top, with the youngest age layer at the bottom and the oldest at the top. The entire population in ALPS comprises the union of the populations across all active layers.

Initially, there is a single age layer, but age update rules soon create a heterogeneous distribution of age values. When an individual's age exceeds the maximum for its current layer, the individual is moved to the next layer, and a new individual is inserted in its place, either transferred from the previous layer or randomly initialized. Additionally, the bottom layer is periodically reinitialized with new individuals every *AgeGap* generations. This ensures a continuous influx of new genetic material, maintaining diversity throughout the evolutionary process.

As a result, ALPS forms a unidirectional hierarchical structure that pushes individuals from the bottom layer to the top layer. This approach differs from

[1] https://www.math.uwaterloo.ca/tsp/concorde.html(lastaccessedMay2024).

[2] http://comopt.ifi.uni-heidelberg.de/software/TSPLIB95/(lastaccessedMay2024).

the Hierarchical Fair Competition structure (HFC) [8], which uses fitness information to segregate layers. Age segregation in ALPS is considered fairer as it does not consider fitness.

Algorithm 1: Pseudocode of ALPS

```
Input: parameters of any EA $para_{EA}$, objective function $f(.)$, age gap for
       ALPS $AgeGap$, global similarity $Sim_g$, layer similarity $Sim_l$ ;
Output: optimal solution $\mathbf{x}^*$
$n_{\text{alps}} = 1$;                                        ▷ Number of active layers
$Layer(0) \longleftarrow$ InitializePopulation($para_{EA}$) ;
$idx = 0, t = 0$;
while not terminate do                                        ▷ Main loop
    for $i = 0, i < n_{alps}, i++$ do                         ▷ Updating layers
        $Layer(i)' = \emptyset$;                   ▷ Offspring population for the $i$-th layer
        for $j = 0; j < n_{pop}; j++$ do                      ▷ Updating one layer
            $para_{EA} \longleftarrow$ UpdateParameter($para_{EA}, i, Sim_g, Sim_l$);
            $operator \longleftarrow$ SelectGeneticOperator($para_{EA}$);
            $\mathbf{x}_1, \mathbf{x}_2 \longleftarrow$ MateSelection($Layer(i)$) ;
            $\mathbf{x}' \longleftarrow operator(\mathbf{x}_1, \mathbf{x}_2)$ ;
            UpdateAge($\mathbf{x}'$) ;
            if $Age(\mathbf{x}') > AgeGap(i)$ then
                if $|Layer(i+1)| < n_{pop}$ then
                    $idx = idx + 1$ ;
                    $Layer(i+1) \longleftarrow Layer(i+1) \cup \{\mathbf{x}'\}$;
                else                                          ▷ The next layer is active
                    $Layer(i+1) \longleftarrow Layer(i+1) \cup \{\mathbf{x}'\}$;
                    $\mathbf{x}_d \longleftarrow \arg\min_{\mathbf{x} \in Layer(i+1) \wedge f(\mathbf{x}) > f(\mathbf{x}')} [Age(\mathbf{x})]$ ;
                    $Layer(i+1) \longleftarrow Layer(i+1) \setminus \{\mathbf{x}_d\}$;
                    if $Age((\mathbf{x}_d) < Age(\mathbf{x}')$ then
                        $Layer(i+1) \longleftarrow Layer(i+1) \setminus \{\mathbf{x}_d\}$;
                        $Layer(i+1) \longleftarrow Layer(i+1) \cup \{\mathbf{x}'\}$;
                Add a newly randomly generated $\mathbf{x}'$ to $Layer(i)'$ ;
            else
                $Layer(i)' \longleftarrow Layer(i)' \cup \{\mathbf{x}'\}$;
            if $idx = n_{pop} - 1$ then
                $n_{alps} = n_{alps} + 1$ and $idx = 0$;      ▷ Activate the next layer
        Select($Layer(i) \cup Layer(i)'$);
    $t = t + 1$;
    if ($t \mod AgeGap(0) = 0$) then
        $Layer(0) \longleftarrow$ InitializePopulation($para_{EA}$) ;
$\mathbf{x}^* \longleftarrow \arg\min f(\mathbf{x})$ where $\mathbf{x} \in \{Layer(0) \cup \cdots \cup Layer(n_{alps})\}$;
```

3.2 Dynamic Strategy for Layer Parameters in ALPS

Inspired by self-adaptation in ES [2], the proposed self-adaptation strategy in this paper focouses on mutation rate and crossover rate. The main philosophy of the self-adaptation is the commonly accepted argument in EA field, that is: balancing exploration and exploitation is essential and can be achieved by adjusting mutation and crossover rate.

To adjust the mutation and crossover rate, we utilizes the population diversity (in the genotype) as the indicator, including *global similarity* (Sim_g) and the *local similarity*(Sim_l) to represent the all populations' similarity and each layer's population similarity, respectively. Local and global similarities are computed using the Hamming distance metric [3]. Six different strategies are proposed and shown in Algorithm 2, where n_l, n_x, and $\mathcal{N}(0,1)$ represent the active number of layers, the length of a decision vector, and a random real number that follows a normal distribution, respectively.

Algorithm 2: Update Parameters

Input: global similarity Sim_g, layer similarity Sim_l, ALPS layer i, number of layers n_l ;
Output: crossover rate $p_c(i)$, mutation rate $p_m(i)$

switch *Method* **do**
  case *'Linear'* **do**
    $\delta = 1/n_l \times Sim_g \times Sim_l$;
  case *'Concave'* **do**
    $\delta = 2 \times Sim_l \times \log(i+1)/\log(n_l)$;
  case *'Convex'* **do**
    $\delta = 0.2 \times Sim_l \times 10^{(i+1)/n_l} - 0.2$;
  case *'Exponential'* **do**
    $\delta = Sim_g \exp(Sim_l - 1)$;
  case *'ES'* **do**
    $\delta = \mathcal{N}(0,1) + \mathcal{N}(0.5, 0.5)/\sqrt{2n_x} Sim_g + \mathcal{N}(0.5, 0.5)/\sqrt{2n_x^2} Sim_l$;
  case *'Multiplication'* **do**
    $\delta = Sim_l \times Sim_g$;
$p_c\{i\} = p_c\{i\} - \delta$;
$p_m\{i\} = p_m\{i\} + \delta$;

4 Experiments

4.1 Algorithm Parameter Settings

The parameter settings include: $\mu = 10$, $\lambda = 10$, $AgeGap = 20$, initial $p_m = 0.1$. The parent selection operator is *tournament* [12] selector. The dynamic rate strategies covers all the operators mentioned in Alg. 2. The statistical results are concluded from 25 independent runs.

4.2 Performance Metrics

Offline fitness [4] is traditionally computed as an average of the cumulative minimal objective value encountered by the algorithm. Grefenstette [5] extended this notion to report always the current best objective in the current population as not to inadvertently compare objectives obtained from different epochs. Since the dynamic TSP could change epochs during a generation, making it impossible to effectively sort the population without reevaluations, we opt assume that the epoch changes are known to the performance evaluator and reset the cumulative minimum whenever a change happens. Additionally, in many dynamic decision scenarios the shape of the convergence curve is of less importance than the quality of the one solution that is going to be implemented we report the *pre-shift fitness* which is the [9] best found fitness just before the epoch changes. The *online error* which is usually named in conjuction with the other two measures denotes the average of *all* fitness evaluations, favoring highly converged algorithms, which runs counter to the main idea of alps to retain solution diversity and is therefore excluded from further results. To quantify the offline error over all the epochs, we also use the average offline fitness over all the epochs in this paper.

Problem	Metric	Concave	Convex	ESmethod	Exp	Linear	Multiplication	None
Berlin52	mean	0.1081	0.1041	0.1056	0.1058	0.1436	0.1197	0.1027
	std	0.0156	0.0181	0.0244	0.0300	0.0179	0.0398	0.0130
	50%	0.1026	0.1021	0.1022	0.1024	0.1418	0.1062	0.1013
KroA100	mean	0.8761	0.7641	0.7806	0.8027	0.9908	0.7836	0.7807
	std	0.0686	0.0506	0.0553	0.0642	0.0867	0.0561	0.0620
	50%	0.8587	0.7676	0.7842	0.7971	0.9853	0.7696	0.7621
KroA150	mean	1.7269	1.6517	1.6721	1.6969	1.9200	1.6745	1.6782
	std	0.0987	0.1079	0.1095	0.0922	0.1158	0.0885	0.0860
	50%	1.7356	1.6537	1.6460	1.6710	1.9175	1.6803	1.7010
KroA200	mean	1.6211	1.5637	1.6218	1.6452	1.7386	1.6397	1.6507
	std	0.5572	0.4997	0.4995	0.5446	0.6332	0.5534	0.5661
	50%	1.2887	1.2314	1.2681	1.2553	1.2811	1.2660	1.2896
KroB100	mean	0.6838	0.6269	0.6378	0.6382	0.7584	0.6248	0.6353
	std	0.1914	0.1846	0.1740	0.1780	0.2364	0.1654	0.1827
	50%	0.7493	0.6885	0.7109	0.7250	0.8428	0.6750	0.6867
KroB150	mean	1.4989	1.4762	1.4921	1.5133	1.6476	1.4853	1.4742
	std	0.3627	0.3777	0.3503	0.3671	0.4038	0.3595	0.3607
	50%	1.6398	1.6147	1.6605	1.6571	1.8077	1.6326	1.6280
KroB200	mean	2.2694	2.1696	2.2525	2.2788	2.3535	2.2296	2.2625
	std	0.1735	0.1812	0.1596	0.1857	0.1858	0.1864	0.2288
	50%	2.2665	2.2175	2.2491	2.2955	2.3831	2.2764	2.3237

Fig. 1. Offline fitness in the last epoch. The entries are color-coded relative to the corresponding ones (e.g., we take all the mean values in a column) in the same column/problem, where a more greenish color indicates better performance and vice versa.

4.3 Empirical Experimental Results

Figures 1 and 2 shows the statistical results w.r.t. *offline fitness* and *average offline fitness* over all the epochs, respectively. From these two figures, it is clear

Problem	Metric	Concave	Convex	ESmethod	Exp	Linear	Multiplication	None
Berlin52	mean	0.3974	0.3908	0.3921	0.3871	0.4383	0.3918	0.3795
	std	0.0261	0.0256	0.0209	0.0238	0.0246	0.0268	0.0250
	50%	0.3951	0.3896	0.3943	0.3811	0.4356	0.3942	0.3773
KroA100	mean	1.4716	1.3872	1.4107	1.4205	1.5457	1.4184	1.4012
	std	0.0681	0.0543	0.0662	0.0598	0.0926	0.0533	0.0484
	50%	1.4708	1.3823	1.4093	1.4172	1.5361	1.4228	1.4005
KroA150	mean	2.5420	2.4872	2.4888	2.5302	2.6779	2.4929	2.5195
	std	0.1074	0.0786	0.1097	0.0754	0.0806	0.0779	0.0831
	50%	2.5356	2.4903	2.5008	2.5433	2.6925	2.5007	2.5152
KroA200	mean	2.7006	2.6709	2.6775	2.7132	2.8210	2.6267	2.6654
	std	0.5628	0.4581	0.4922	0.5330	0.5357	0.5738	0.5236
	50%	2.4239	2.5354	2.5819	2.6322	2.7216	2.3325	2.5768
KroB100	mean	1.2322	1.2140	1.2175	1.2216	1.3175	1.1817	1.2099
	std	0.2425	0.2166	0.1792	0.2042	0.2535	0.2266	0.2049
	50%	1.3228	1.2881	1.2862	1.2976	1.4173	1.2696	1.2938
KroB150	mean	2.3525	2.2894	2.3071	2.3286	2.4745	2.2977	2.3252
	std	0.3686	0.3869	0.3235	0.4026	0.3990	0.3933	0.3764
	50%	2.5025	2.4386	2.4601	2.4868	2.6247	2.4286	2.4674
KroB200	mean	3.2374	3.1840	3.2391	3.2646	3.3617	3.2285	3.2280
	std	0.1158	0.0919	0.1284	0.1142	0.1144	0.1031	0.1002
	50%	3.2177	3.1859	3.2438	3.2690	3.3672	3.2208	3.2148

Fig. 2. The average offline fitness over all the epochs. The entries are color-coded relative to the corresponding ones (e.g., we take all the mean values in a column) in the same column/problem, where a more greenish color indicates better performance and vice versa.

to see that the dynamic self-adaptation strategy of Convex yields better results w.r.t. *offline fitness* all over the test problems, except for the 'Berlin52' problem. On the 'Berlin52' problem, the best results are achieved by without applying any dynamic self-adaptation strategy. This is because the 'Berlin52' problem is the most simplest test problem, as its dimensionality of the search space is just 52.

The effectiveness of different combinations of μ, λ, parent selector, mutation/crossover operators is not analyzed in this paper, due to the limitation of the pages.

5 Conclusions and Future Work

In this paper, six different self-adaption strategies for ALPS' mutation and crossover rate are proposed. The proposed strategies are compared with conventional fixed hyperparameters on 7 different dynamic TSP problems. The experimental results indicate that the conventional strategy (stationary crossover and mutation rates) only yields better results on simple test problem with low dimentionality in a search space. For complex problems with higher dimentionality of a search space, the performance of the proposed self-adaptation strategies varies, but the convex strategy yields the best results all over the other strategies. For dynamic TSP problems, we recommend to use 'Convex' strategy under the framework of ALPS, due to its good statistical performance.

For future works, it is interesting to investigate the behaviour of the different combination of more hyperparameters of ALPS, such as μ, λ, crossover operators, mutation operators, and the proposed self-adaptation strategies.

Acknowledgement. This work is supported by the Austrian Science Fund (FWF – Der Wissenschaftsfonds) under the project (I 5315, 'ML Methods for Feature Identification Global Optimization). The authors would like to thank the anonymous reviewers and the editor for their insightful comments.

References

1. Beyer, H.G.: Toward a theory of evolution strategies: Self-adaptation. Evol. Comput. **3**(3), 311–347 (1995)
2. Beyer, H.G., Schwefel, H.P.: Evolution strategies-a comprehensive introduction. Nat. Comput. **1**, 3–52 (2002)
3. Bookstein, A., Kulyukin, V.A., Raita, T.: Generalized hamming distance. Inf. Retriev. **5**, 353–375 (2002)
4. De Jong, K.A.: An analysis of the behavior of a class of genetic adaptive systems. University of Michigan (1975)
5. Grefenstette, J.J.: Evolvability in dynamic fitness landscapes: a genetic algorithm approach. In: Proceedings of the 1999 Congress on Evolutionary Computation-CEC99 (Cat. No. 99TH8406). vol. 3, pp. 2031–2038. IEEE (1999)
6. Hansen, N.: Benchmarking a bi-population CMA-ES on the BBOB-2009 function testbed. In: Proceedings of the 11th Annual Conference Companion on Genetic and Evolutionary Computation Conference: Late Breaking Papers, pp. 2389–2396 (2009)
7. Hornby, G.S.: Alps: the age-layered population structure for reducing the problem of premature convergence. In: Proceedings of the 8th Annual Conference on Genetic and Evolutionary Computation, pp. 815–822 (2006)
8. Hu, J.J., Goodman, E.D.: The hierarchical fair competition (HFC) model for parallel evolutionary algorithms. In: Proceedings of the 2002 Congress on Evolutionary Computation. CEC 2002 (Cat. No. 02TH8600), vol. 1, pp. 49–54 (2002)
9. Kramer, G.R., Gallagher, J.C.: Improvements to the* CGA enabling online intrinsic evolution in compact eh devices. In: Proceedings of NASA/DoD Conference on Evolvable Hardware, 2003, pp. 225–231. IEEE (2003)
10. Li, R., et al.: Mixed integer evolution strategies for parameter optimization. Evol. Comput. **21**(1), 29–64 (2013). https://doi.org/10.1162/EVCO_a_00059
11. López-Ibáñez, M., Paquete, L., Stützle, T.: Exploratory analysis of stochastic local search algorithms in biobjective optimization. In: Bartz-Beielstein, T., Chiarandini, M., Paquete, L., Preuss, M. (eds.) Experimental Methods for the Analysis of Optimization Algorithms, pp. 209–222. Springer, Heidelberg (2010). https://doi.org/10.1007/978-3-642-02538-9_9
12. Miller, B.L., Goldberg, D.E., et al.: Genetic algorithms, tournament selection, and the effects of noise. Complex Syst. **9**(3), 193–212 (1995)
13. Reinelt, G.: TSPLIB–a traveling salesman problem library. ORSA J. Comput. **3**(4), 376–384 (1991)

Machine Learning Update Strategies for Real-Time Production Environments

Philipp Neuhauser[1,2](✉), Philipp Fleck[1,2], Sebastian Leitner[1,2], and Stefan Wagner[1,2]

[1] Heuristic and Evolutionary Algorithms Laboratory, University of Applied Sciences Upper Austria, Wels, Austria
philipp.neuhauser@fh-hagenberg.at

[2] Josef Ressel Center for Adaptive Optimization in Dynamic Environments, University of Applied Sciences Upper Austria, Wels, Austria

Abstract. Modern application scenarios in the dynamic industrial, financial, and economic sectors increasingly require quick and agile machine learning solutions. Instead of waiting hours for batch processing systems to deliver results, these systems should ideally adapt and make decisions as soon as new data comes in. As the demand for real-time machine learning solutions using streaming data is steadily increasing, this paper explores a software architecture that efficiently combines the Apache Kafka ecosystem with Microsoft's machine learning framework ML.NET for reliable data processing and model adaptation. The research addresses the complexity of deciding when to re-train these models in an unbounded data stream context. Various update strategies, including periodic, and performance-based model training, are evaluated for effectiveness under different conditions. The goal of this paper is to propose a completely autonomous machine learning pipeline that is capable of keeping models updated while minimizing computational costs required for re-training and ensuring prediction accuracy.

Keywords: Data Streaming · Machine Learning · Update Strategies

1 Introduction

In recent years, especially in times of Industrial IoT, a shift in paradigm from a traditional batch processing approach of large datasets towards a modern event-processing of unbounded, infinite data streams can clearly be observed. An event is something that happened at a certain point in time, for example a message, a measurement, an observation or a database record. These events are continuously extracted from a wide variety of data sources, pre-processed accordingly and then stored in a central Big Data platform in order to ultimately obtain new information from them using modern Data Science methods or techniques from the field of artificial intelligence, like machine learning (ML) [8]. The idea is, that decisions and analyses should be made as soon as new data points arrive.

A. Quesada-Arencibia et al. (Eds.): EUROCAST 2024, LNCS 15174, pp. 12–24, 2025.
https://doi.org/10.1007/978-3-031-83885-9_2

Waiting for the results of a batch processing system is inconceivable, and in many cases also involves certain economic costs. In fact, it is not only important that trained machine learning models can be used in real-time (e.g., for forecasting or prediction scenarios), but also that they can be quickly adapted to the current data situation in order to maintain a high degree of accuracy. Detecting the right point in time for a model update can be a challenging task, especially for unbounded streaming data. To ensure rapid adaptability, it is important to train models with as little human interaction as possible. The increasingly popular discipline of automated machine learning (AutoML) [6] addresses precisely this problem and is capable of adapting ML algorithms independently through automated hyperparameter tuning.

Section 2 provides a step-by-step explanation of the central software components that comprise a modern, real-time-capable data pipeline. Building on this, a machine learning infrastructure based on infinite data streams is presented. Various model update strategies are explained in Sect. 3 and then tested for their practical suitability in Sect. 4 using a benchmark dataset. A summary and an outlook on possible future extensions conclude this paper in Sect. 5.

2 Machine Learning on Unbounded Data Streams

Machine learning on unbounded streaming data has two fundamental requirements. On the one hand, a real-time capable software architecture must be set up in order to transfer and react to events at high-speed. On the other hand, a powerful and real-time capable machine learning pipeline is responsible for gaining new insights by applying common Data Science techniques.

2.1 Real-Time Stream Processing with Apache Kafka

Over the past few years, Apache Kafka [2] has clearly established itself as the de facto standard for real-time processing of massive data streams in almost all industrial, economic and financial sectors. The underlying distributed server-client architecture, as shown in Fig. 1, efficiently combines the concepts of a high-throughput message broker system with a reliable underlying data storage. Events (messages) are organized in so-called topics that consists of a key, a value, a timestamp and an optional header for metadata. Numerous extensions also ensure a comprehensive data stream processing. Messages can be extracted from common data sources by using appropriate plugins (Kafka Connect), modified and joined accordingly with a stream processing API (ksqlDB [3]), and ultimately transferred to other systems, like a long-term data storage. Furthermore, the aspect of a central schema management with an integrated version control (Confluent Schema Registry [4]) and serialization mechanisms is also taken into account in order to handle a variety of different message formats (e.g., JSON, Google Protocol Buffers, Apache Avro) that are constantly evolving over time. All these components around Apache Kafka fit together seamlessly to form a sophisticated Kappa architecture [7], which serves as a central starting point for further Data Science tasks and ML applications in dynamic, mission-critical production environments [9].

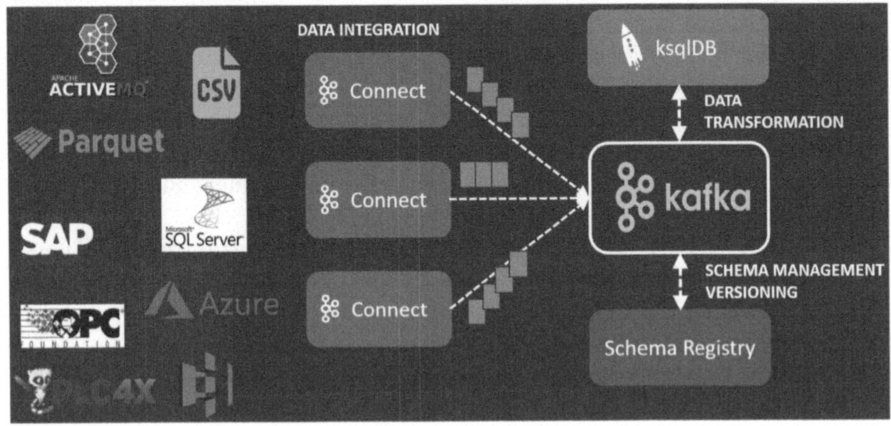

Fig. 1. Real-time stream processing with Apache Kafka technology stack

2.2 Stream ML Pipeline

The architecture in Fig. 2 provides a general overview of how stream machine learning (Stream ML) works. As it is not desirable to trigger and evaluate the ML pipeline with every single consumed event (blue rectangles), micro batches have to be formed, meaning a set or collection of messages that is consumed from the data source (e.g., Apache Kafka) at hand. The data may then need to be pre-processed, if not already done, with a powerful stream processing ETL engine such as ksqlDB. The next step is to split the data into a training and test partition. Alternatively, the latest micro batches (data frames/windows) can also be cached, or relevant data points can be filtered out in order to obtain a type of "super dataset" that contains representative data points (events/messages) to solve the actual machine learning task. Once the data provision aspect has been satisfied, a re-training strategy (see Sect. 3) decides whether a machine learning model needs to be updated or not. Manual model-training can be a quite cumbersome trial and error process and requires the knowledge of a domain expert or data scientist. AutoML can tackle these problems by automatically learning a model, given a certain computational and time budget. Updated models must then be rolled out for subsequent application to new data. It is also advisable to annotate the models with appropriate metadata. This includes, for example, analyses of the training dataset, or quality values achieved (MAE, accuracy, R^2, etc.). Finally, one must carefully decide where to continue with consuming the unbounded data stream. Should be started over with the next (unseen) event, should one continue with the latest (newest) one or might be started somewhere in between – the answer to this question depends on the scenario at hand. Nevertheless, it must be kept in mind, that model training takes some time, e.g. several minutes or hours, and it is probably not sufficient to continue with the first unseen (oldest) element as this behavior would make the Stream ML pipeline to permanently fall back in time and train on an obsolete data basis. Extracting new insights from real-time data streams requires the use of a reliable machine learning framework. Besides well-established ML libraries like TensorFlow, H2O.ai or Scikit-learn, Microsoft's ML.NET [1] has proven to be a suitable candidate for solving common ML tasks. It offers a variety of different machine learning algorithms as well as a wide range of functions for data pre-processing and feature engineering. Ultimately, the integrated AutoML API also enables autonomous training of machine learning models due to several exchangeable hyperparameter tuners [10]. Especially for real-time applications, it is of enormous importance that accurate models are updated as quickly as possible with a minimum amount of human interaction. Often, there is not much time for comprehensive manual fine-tuning, which is why AutoML can certainly be an advantage.

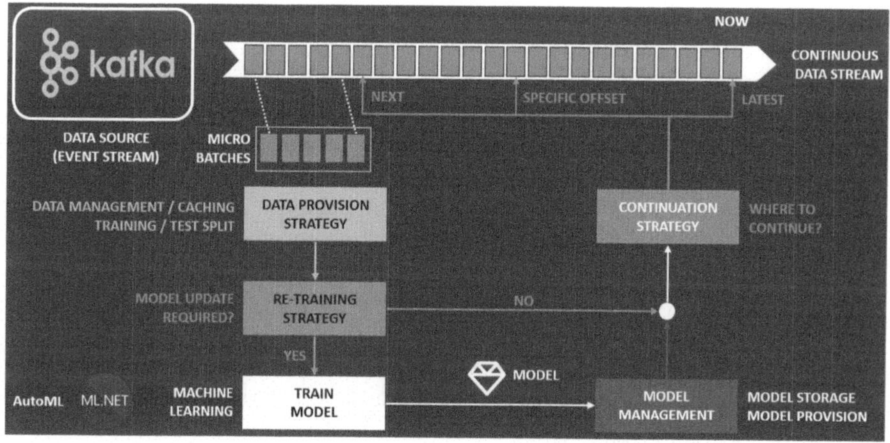

Fig. 2. Basic machine learning workflow on unbounded data streams

3 Machine Learning Update Strategies

When applying machine learning methods to unbounded data streams, the question inevitably arises as to when exactly a model needs to be re-trained. The right time has to be chosen carefully, because the training phase can be very time-consuming and resource-intensive. Temporary outliers, data drift or concept drift [5] must be reliably recognized within the data stream in order to keep the model's accuracy (quality) at a constant high level at all times. On the one hand, it would be possible to use an online (continuous) learning approach, which updates the model with every new data point or micro batch. However, one of the biggest problems is that the pool of algorithms suitable for online learning is limited. Many traditional machine learning algorithms are not designed for use in online environments, which limits the possibilities. As of today, e.g., the only available method for linear regression tasks in ML.NET is the Online Gradient Descent Trainer. Therefore, alternatives are needed that can be realized with any ML framework.

- **Periodic Re-training:** One popular mechanism is a periodic re-training strategy, as shown in Fig. 3. The designed Stream ML pipeline is triggered at fixed times or after a certain amount of data points (micro batches) have been consumed. Some major advantages are that the models are more resilient to temporary noise and that they can adapt to new patterns after a while. Moreover, the resource usage is manageable, meaning that hardware capacities can be efficiently used, e.g. overnight. Nevertheless, choosing the right update-interval can be quite cumbersome. If the interval is too long, the model may perform poorly; if it's too short, it may be computationally expensive or over-reactive to noise (overfitting).
- **Performance-based Re-training:** Another common re-training approach is to continuously monitor the model's performance (R^2, MSE, F1 score, etc.) on the current/latest micro batch. As depicted in Fig. 4, whenever the quality drops below a predefined threshold, the model will be updated. Determining appropriate performance thresholds is very challenging. If they are set too high, re-training might be done too frequently. If they are too low, performance might drop noticeably before a model update is triggered. Unfortunately, this strategy is also very sensitive to abnormal data. Because this methodology can nonetheless prove to be very efficient and intuitive, it has been expanded over time to include additional aspects and considerations.
- **Moving Average Re-training:** Instead of relying on a single quality value, a more stable but still simple approach is to monitor multiple performance measures within a sliding window and then calculate the moving average, as illustrated in Fig. 5. Taking the mean quality of the currently trained model helps to reduce temporary fluctuations and highlight the underlying trend or pattern. If there are complex patterns or subtleties in the data stream beyond a general shift up or down, moving averages may not adequately capture them. However, this strategy is particularly problematic for those trends where quality begins to decline slowly or insidiously. Moreover, an equally weighted view of historical and current quality measurements should be treated with caution.
- **Exponential Smoothing Re-training:** A technique called exponential smoothing (see Fig. 6) can be more responsive to recent changes in data streams than the previously mentioned update strategies, because it assigns greater weight to the latest observations (quality measures). By changing a smoothing factor (α) balances the sensitivity to new data against the risk of

overreacting to random noise. Specifying an appropriate value for α can be a non-trivial task and may require expertise. Moreover, the smoothing factor not only determines the weightings for observations but is indirectly controlling the "length" of the moving average. Despite being more reactive to recent changes, like moving averages, exponential smoothing still introduces some lag, and may be slow to respond to sudden shifts in the data stream.

- **N-Times-Below Re-training:** The previously mentioned threshold-based variant is relatively susceptible to temporary outliers, but is much more robust against slowly developing data or concept drift, because re-training is triggered immediately as soon as a certain performance value is undercut. Figure 7 depicts the so-called N-Times-Below update strategy that involves waiting for several consecutive measurements/evaluations that surpass the predetermined threshold before initiating the model update process. This introduces a sort of buffer to prevent overreaction to temporary fluctuations, which maintains a higher degree of stability. Nevertheless, the choice of a suitable buffer size N and a proper quality threshold can be challenging.

4 Experiments and Results

The next step is to evaluate and compare the performance of the aforementioned model update strategies. A generated regression benchmark dataset will be used to check their practical suitability and identify possible limitations. In addition, the impact of anomalies and noise within the data stream on the model quality and the number of executed re-training runs will be examined.

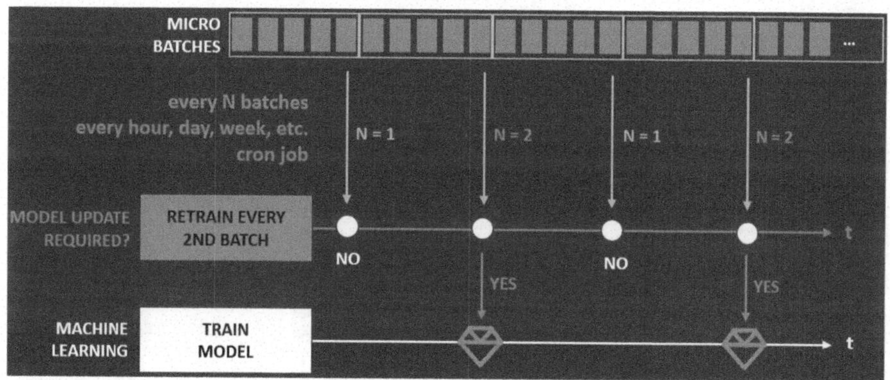

Fig. 3. Periodic re-training after every second micro batch

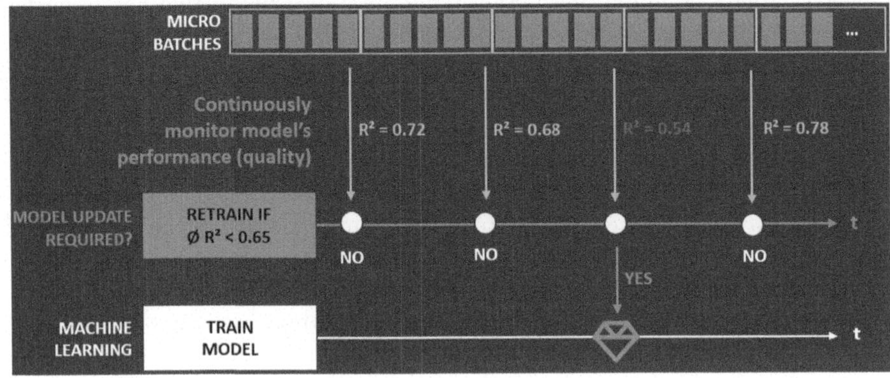

Fig. 4. Performance-based re-training when quality R^2 is below 0.65

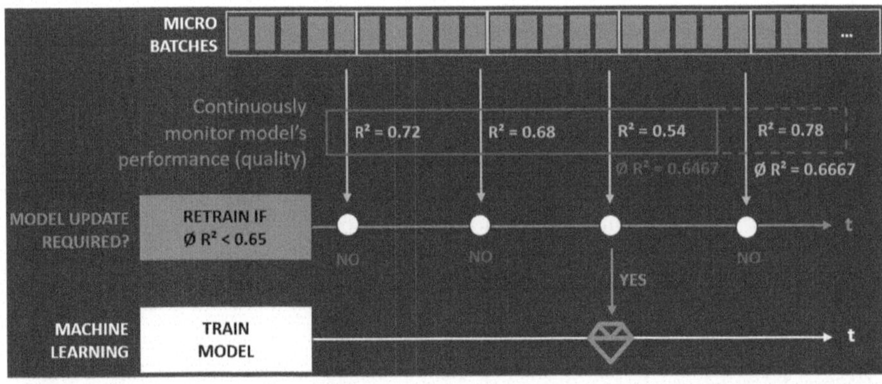

Fig. 5. Moving average re-training with window size of 3 and min. R^2 of 0.65

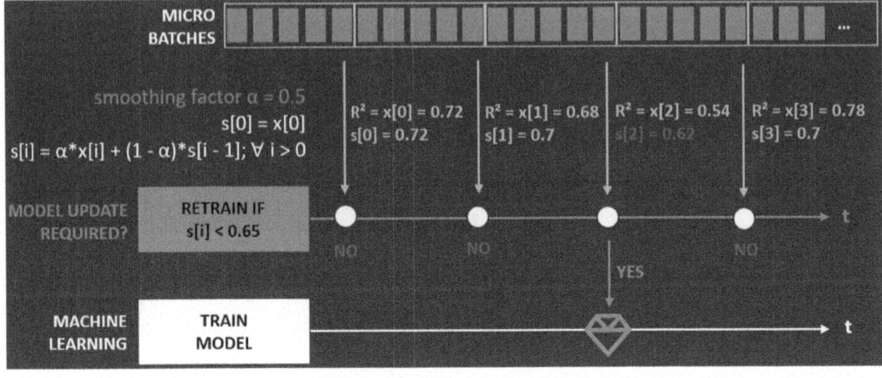

Fig. 6. Exponential smoothing re-training with α of 0.5 and min. R^2 of 0.65

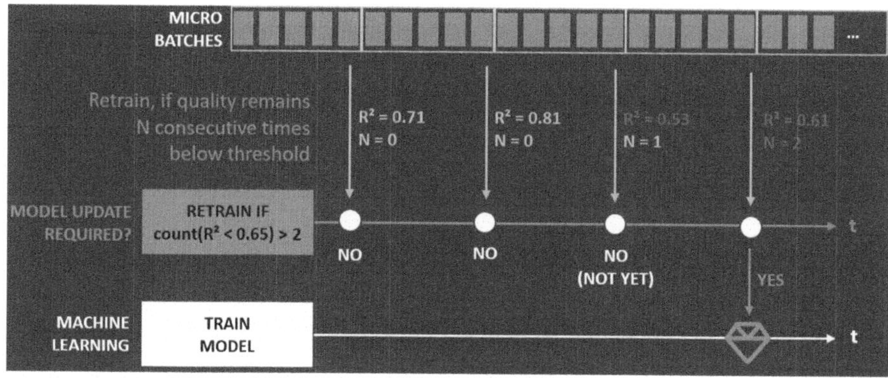

Fig. 7. N-Times-Below re-training with N of 2 and min. R^2 of 0.65

4.1 Experiment Setup

For testing the individual update strategies, a regression benchmark dataset with 8 feature columns and 2 million data points was created using Pythons `make_regression` function and then stored in an Apache Kafka topic. The resulting data stream, as illustrated in Fig. 8, consists of 4 types of areas, which can be described as follows. There are several regions, e.g., right at the beginning, with 100000 data points that represent regular data and that should offer ideal conditions for model training. Then, single anomalies in form of mathematical functions (e.g., sin, cos, exponential, square, and logarithm) were included in the range [100000 - 750000] to different feature columns. Within the [750000 - 1500000] range, the outliers become increasingly dense and the anomaly phases progressively longer. The last 500000 data points are characterized by increasingly strong and longer noise components. In between, there are parts with regular data. The ML.NET-based Stream ML pipeline was then configured to consume the corresponding data stream and to form micro batches with a size of 2000 messages. The latest (newest) 75 batches were cached locally for subsequent machine learning process. 70% of the data were then used for training, and the remaining 30% were used to evaluate the performance (quality) of the updated models. The machine learning process itself was entirely automated by using the automated model builder API (AutoML) from ML.NET [10]. As the only data pre-processing step, all features were min-max normalized. The training time for solving the regression ML task was limited to 30 s in order to simulate a real-time-critical scenario. For better comparability, the continuation strategy was set to always continue with the next unread data point in order to finally consume the entire data stream.

4.2 Benchmark Results

Different observations can be made for each of the mentioned update strategies. The upper part of the following diagrams shows the quality curve achieved

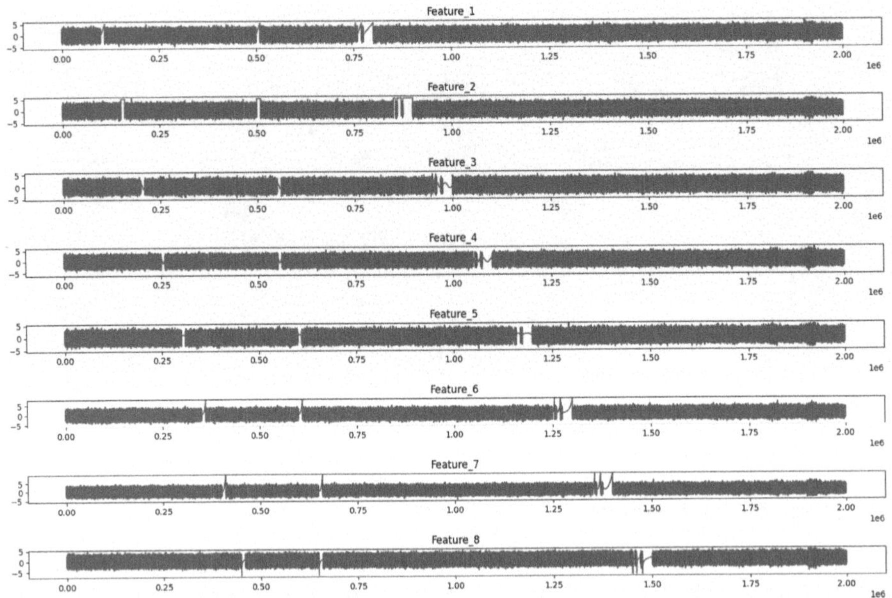

Fig. 8. Regression benchmark dataset with 2 million data points, including anomalies

with the respective re-training mechanism over the entire data stream consumed (x-axis). The closer a quality value (R^2) is to 1.0 (y-axis), the better/more performant the (updated) model can be considered. The black vertical bars in the lower part of the diagram show at which point (micro batch) a re-training call has taken place. A high quality curve with minimal required model update phases is therefore desirable.

Figure 9 shows the results of the periodic re-training strategy. A model update was triggered after every 25th consumed micro batch (50000 data points). It is noticeable that a deteriorating model quality moves at least slightly upwards again after each model update. In performance-based re-training with a quality threshold R^2 of 0.7 (see Fig. 10), the machine learning model was updated comparatively frequently, especially at those points with a high proportion of anomalies or noise. In the worst case, however, this behavior can lead to the Stream ML pipeline lagging behind the real-time data. Nevertheless, the quality curve appears more stable in direct comparison to periodic updating. As expected, the addition of a moving average approach (see Fig. 11) with a window size of 15 and a quality threshold R^2 of 0.7 led to fewer re-training calls. However, the quality curve is much more unsteady compared to the two strategies mentioned above. The exponential smoothing approach, as shown in Fig. 12, with a quality threshold R^2 of 0.7 and a smoothing factor α of 0.25 appears much more stable than the moving average variant. Nevertheless, training was carried out comparatively frequently at those points with high noise components. The N-Times-Below strategy (see Fig. 13) with a buffer size N of 10 significantly reduced the number of performed re-training runs. Above all, this approach was less susceptible in the noisy areas of the data stream, which significantly reduces the risk of overfitting. However, it must be noted that the quality sometimes fell towards or even below 0.0, which illustrates the difficulty of choosing a suitable buffer size N. The evaluations in Table 1 show that the model qualities (median R^2) of all update strategies are very close to each other. The best results were achieved by the periodic re-training mechanism with an median quality of 0.80, which is one of the faster variants with a number of only 40 models (training time 21 min). The performance-based strategy, including its extensions moving average and N-Times-Below re-training, all achieved a quality value of 0.78, but they differed in the number of model learning phases. The N-Times-Below variant only required 28 training runs and clearly stands out from the other strategies. The moving average method required the fewest updates to the model with only 27 runs and was therefore the most economical for the benchmark dataset used. However, the worst quality of R^2 0.76 was achieved with this methodology.

Table 1. Evaluation results of model update strategies

Strategy	Mean R^2	Median R^2	Runs	Runtime
Periodic	0.78	0.80	40	21 min
Performance-based	0.78	0.78	96	51 min
Moving Average	0.76	0.76	27	15 min
Exponential Smoothing	0.78	0.78	101	53 min
N-Times-Below	0.75	0.78	28	16 min

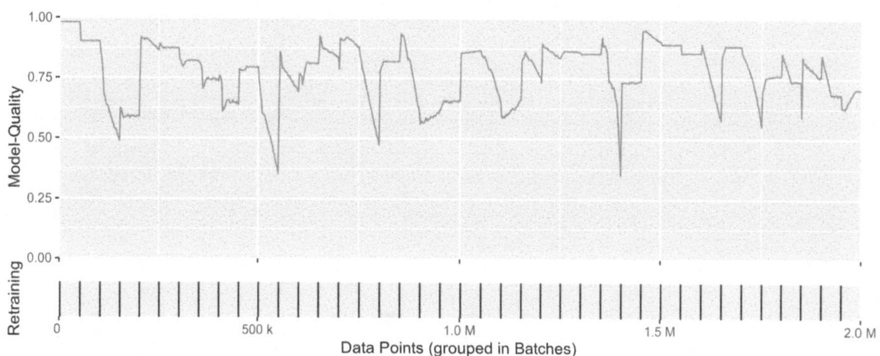

Fig. 9. Periodic re-training after every 25th consumed micro batch

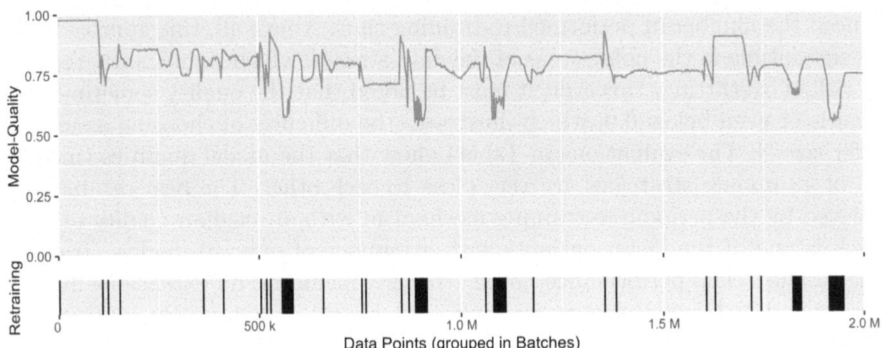

Fig. 10. Performance-based re-training when quality $R^2 < 0.7$

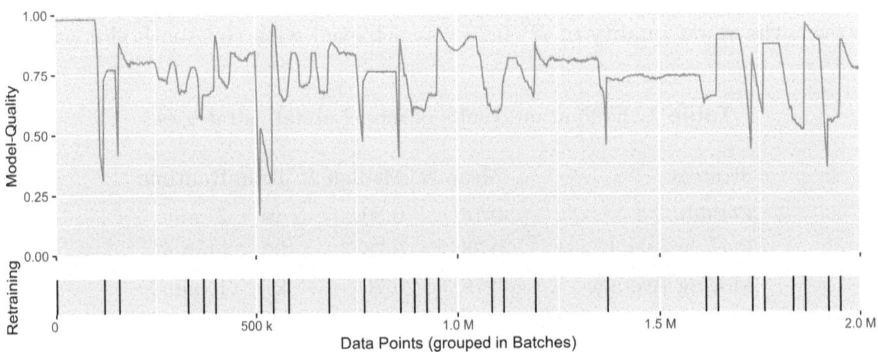

Fig. 11. Moving average re-training with window size of 15 and min. $R^2 = 0.7$

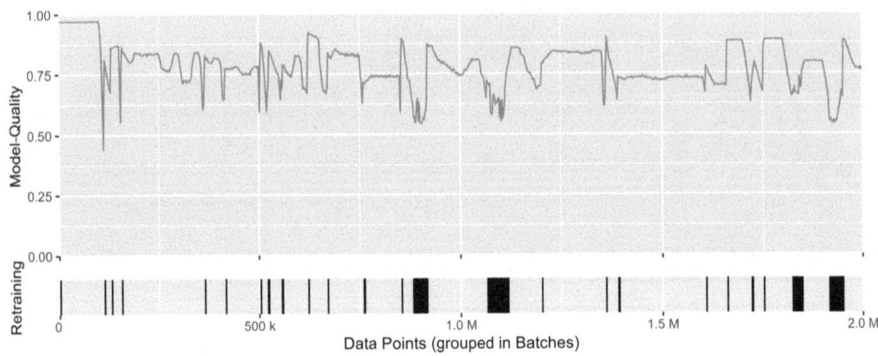

Fig. 12. Exponential smoothing re-training with $\alpha = 0.25$ and min. $R^2 = 0.7$

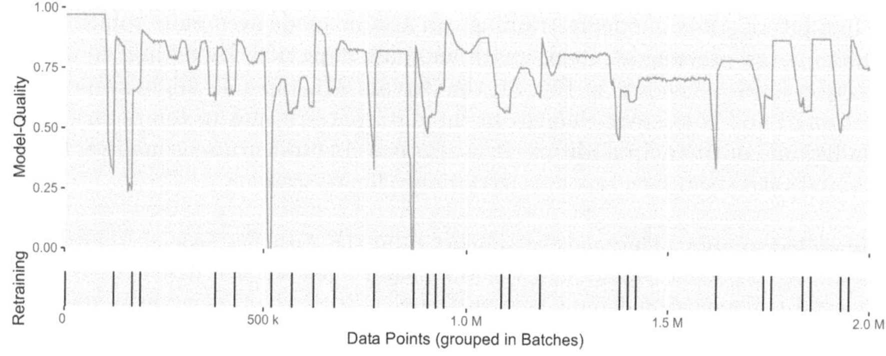

Fig. 13. N-Times-Below re-training with buffer size N = 10 and min. $R^2 = 0.7$

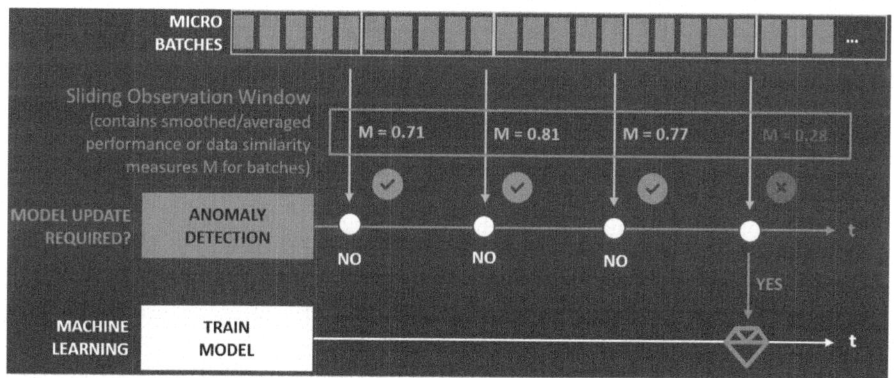

Fig. 14. Outlook: anomaly detection-based re-training strategy

5 Conclusion and Outlook

Within this paper, a software architecture for machine learning with real-time data streams based on Apache Kafka and ML.NET was presented. The designed Stream ML pipeline served as a starting point for the integration and evaluation of different model update strategies. A regression benchmark dataset was used to investigate the performance of various re-training mechanisms and their handling of different types of anomalies and increasing levels of noise. The goal of these strategies was to recover from a loss of quality and to restore the ability to make reliable predictions on new data points. It was noted that if the number of training runs and thus the risk of overfitting is to be reduced, the use of the periodic, N-Times-Below and moving average re-training strategy is recommended. If one is not aware of the characteristics of the data situation (anomalies, noise components, etc.) in advance, the periodic re-training strategy is the first choice. This is also the only method whose required resources and exact execution times (when using AutoML) can be fully controlled by the data scientist.

In a future study, model re-training can also be made even more robust when combining the previous strategies with anomaly detection. By adding an outlier detection layer, as shown in Fig. 14, the Stream ML pipeline might respond to substantial and consistent changes in the data pattern, not to temporary noise or individual outliers. In addition, it is also possible to learn seasonalities in the data and take them into account accordingly for re-training.

Acknowledgments. The financial support from the Austrian Federal Ministry for Digital and Economic Affairs and the National Foundation for Research, Technology and Development and the Christian Doppler Research Association is gratefully acknowledged.

Disclosure of Interests. The authors have no competing interests to declare that are relevant to the content of this article.

References

1. Ahmed, Z., et al.: Machine learning at Microsoft with ML. NET. In: Proceedings of the 25th ACM SIGKDD International Conference on Knowledge Discovery & Data Mining, pp. 2448–2458 (2019)
2. Apache Software Foundation: Apache Kafka (2024). https://kafka.apache.org/
3. Confluent, Inc.: KSQLDB - The database purpose-built for stream processing applications (2024). https://ksqldb.io/
4. Confluent, Inc.: Schema Registry Overview (2024). https://docs.confluent.io/platform/current/schema-registry/index.html
5. Gama, J., Žliobaitundefined, I., Bifet, A., Pechenizkiy, M., Bouchachia, A.: A survey on concept drift adaptation. ACM Comput. Surv. **46**(4), 1–37 (2014). https://doi.org/10.1145/2523813
6. Hutter, F., Kotthoff, L., Vanschoren, J.: Automated Machine Learning. Springer Nature, Cham (2019). https://doi.org/10.1007/978-3-030-05318-5
7. Kreps, J.: Questioning the Lambda Architecture (2024). https://www.oreilly.com/radar/questioning-the-lambda-architecture/
8. Mitchell, T.M.: Machine Learning, vol. 1. McGraw-hill, New York (1997)
9. Neuhauser, P.: Real-time Machine Learning for Product Quality Prediction. Master's thesis, University of Applied Sciences Upper Austria, Hagenberg (2022)
10. Neuhauser, P., Wagner, S.: Performance comparison of Microsoft's AutoML API. In: 35th European Modeling and Simulation Symposium, EMSS 2023. Proceedings of the 35th European Modeling and Simulation Symposium (EMSS 2023) (2023)

Online Machine Learning for the Estimation of Process Times in Dynamic Scheduling

Michael Heckmann[1(✉)], Bernhard Werth[1,2], Johannes Karder[1,2], and Stefan Wagner[1]

[1] Josef Ressel Center for Adaptive Optimization in Dynamic Environments, Heuristic and Evolutionary Algorithms Laboratory, University of Applied Sciences Upper Austria, 4232 Hagenberg, Austria
michael.heckmann@fh-hagenberg.at

[2] Symbolic Artificial Intelligence, Johannes Kepler University, 4040 Linz, Austria

Abstract. This paper presents a study on applying online machine-learning models to estimate the processing times of different production tasks for dynamic scheduling problems. Specifically, various machine-learning approaches and their impact on the schedule quality are evaluated. A discrete event simulation of a production process was created, with different functions determining processing time. This production simulation was optimized with the OERAPGA optimization algorithm. Based on the experiments, the performance of different machine learning models was assessed. Moreover, the speed and prediction quality of these models and their resulting optimization quality were evaluated. Results showed that the speed of evaluation plays a more significant role in optimization quality than prediction accuracy, as the optimizer seems to be focused on optimizing macroscopic aspects of the production schedule.

Keywords: dynamic production scheduling · online machine learning · genetic algorithms

1 Introduction

Dynamic scheduling is a popular research topic and has many applications, such as crane scheduling and production and manufacturing planning [9]. Unlike static optimization of schedules, dynamic scheduling has to react to changes that are coming from the real-world environment. Those changes may impact the current solution [11]. In many academic static scheduling problems, the processing times are known. In many real-world applications, the processing times of the individual steps may be unknown but can be estimated by machine learning models. The training data format may also differ for dynamic scheduling, as training data about the current processing times is continuously generated. This makes dynamic scheduling an ideal use case for online models. The area of online

A. Quesada-Arencibia et al. (Eds.): EUROCAST 2024, LNCS 15174, pp. 25–37, 2025.
https://doi.org/10.1007/978-3-031-83885-9_3

machine learning is relatively new. It is gaining traction in the machine learning community [3], but compared to static machine learning models, the amount of research is still underrepresented and several challenges remain open.

This paper aims to apply online machine learning models to approximate processing times for production tasks. The tasks are processing steps, to be completed by various machines, with processing times influenced by factors like the processed materials, setup time, human interaction, and additional unidentified components. A good approximation of the processing time enables the optimization algorithm to create solutions close to the real-world processes. Research indicates that accurate predictions are highly beneficial for static scheudling [2].

In many problem instances the behavior of processing times may change over time and is not tracked, which does not provide ideal conditions for static models as they lack the flexibility required in such cases [4]. Online machine learning models may mitigate the lack of data and the potential change in processing time behavior. These models are designed to continuously train on small amounts of new data, and predict based on the already observed data. The ability to phase out old training data in favor of more current observations is another crucial advantage of online machine learning models.

This paper focuses on two aspects. The first aspect is the comparison of several machine-learning approaches, based on the prediction speed and accuracy. The second considered aspect is the correlation between the schedule quality and the model quality. Besides the online models, some other models are tested as a baseline. For example, a basic online median model is a baseline model used in this paper. River [7], the library from which the more sophisticated online machine learning models are used, provides online machine-learning implementations for decision trees, forests, linear regression, and neural networks.

A discrete event simulation of a production process was created to evaluate the model quality and its effect on the optimization. Applying such simulation-based techniques usually allows for much more complex and detailed scenarios than closed-form mathematical models [10] but almost prevents the use of specific optimization heuristics. Therefore, using black-box optimizers like genetic algorithms is common [8]. To test a broad range of processing time behaviors, the machines in the simulation use different functions to determine the processing time. These machine processing time behaviors contain factors for the type of work step, material features, random noise, and effects of wear on the tools. During the simulation, orders are periodically added to the production environment for the optimizer to consider. The simulation sends events to the twin of the production environment which keeps track of the current simulation state. Based on this, the order of required steps is optimized using the OERAPGA [5] optimization algorithm.

The optimized solution is then applied to the production simulation, which follows the processing plan. When a machine completes processing, the required processing time and the corresponding processing information are captured and supplied to the online machine-learning model.

Section 2 describes the setup of the case study, detailing the problem statement, the implemented simulation model, the applied optimization algorithm, and all evaluated machine learning models. The obtained results are discussed in Sect. 3, including the learned model's prediction speed and quality, and focus on optimization quality. Finally, the paper concludes with Sect. 4, summarizing the gained insights and giving an outlook on future work.

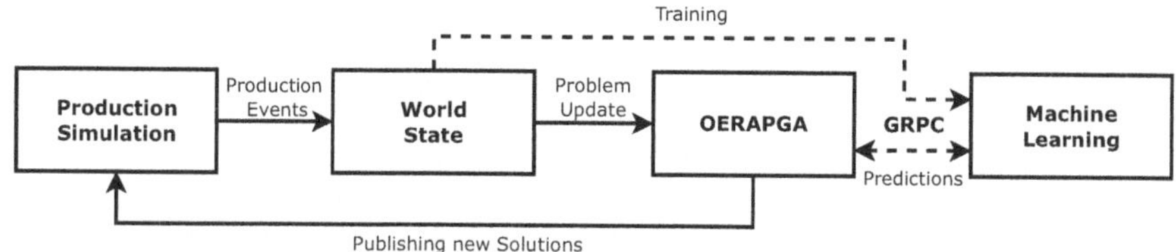

Fig. 1. Experiment architecture showing the four main components of the simulation optimization cycle.

2 Methods

The prediction quality and the resulting optimization performance are compared using a dynamic production scheduling problem to evaluate the performance of different machine learning models. A system of four components is set up, shown in Fig. 1. At the core of the experiment is the production simulation, an asynchronous simulation of a production facility. In the presented case, it is asynchronous and progresses independently of the optimizer. Connecting the simulation with the optimizer is the world state. The world state is a twin of the simulation, based on events from the simulation. Based on this world state, a population-based optimizer, in this case, the OERAPGA optimizes the order and assignment of the tasks. Machine learning models are used to evaluate the solutions in the optimizer. These models are trained by events from the simulation which are processed by the world state.

2.1 Problem

Before discussing the exact problem instance used for the experiments, the general problem has to be addressed. In general, the problem can best be described as flexible job shop scheduling [6]. A material and its sub-materials must be processed in a fixed order throughout the production facility. It is possible that some work steps can be done on alternative machines. In our case, the machines are not identical and thus have different processing times. Additionally, material storage areas, also called buffers are utilized between the machines. This problem can be split into two parts: the optimization of the assignment of tasks to machines and the optimization of the order of tasks.

A production facility shown in Fig. 2 with nine machines was set up for the experiments. In this facility, three general types of work steps are defined. The initial step introduces the materials into the simulation. These materials can be further processed in a processing step or immediately combined in the finalizing step. The finalizing step marks the end of the simulated material.

Each machine has a process timing behavior listed in Table 1. Some processing behaviors also consider the previously processed material. Additionally, all processing times have Gaussian noise added.

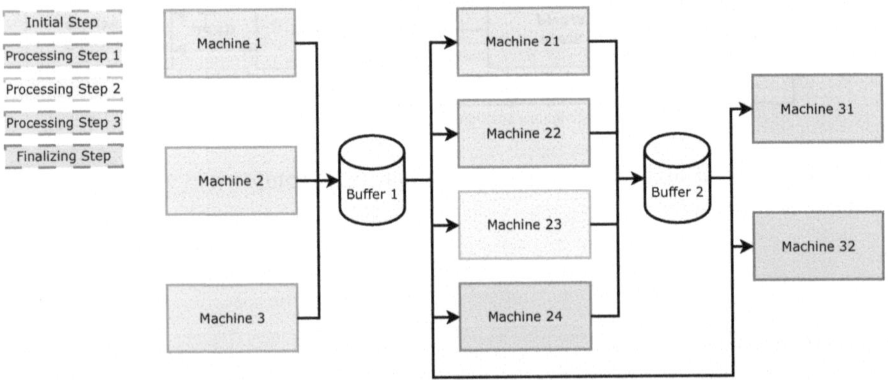

Fig. 2. Production setup used for the conducted experiments. The colors of each machine indicate the type of step and the connections show the material flow.

Table 1. The factors influencing the machine processing times.

Machine	Behavior based on
1	Size and thickness, getting slower for each task until reset
2	Plate count and thickness
3	Plate count
21	Weight, extremely slow for thick plates
22	Weight, faster for consecutive plates of the same thickness
23	Size
24	Area
31	Size and weight, slower each task until reset, exponential by size if too large
32	Size and weight

2.2 Simulation

The simulation uses SimSharp[1] which allows running pseudo-realtime discrete-event simulations [1]. The simulation strictly processes the tasks in the order and assignment specified in the last received solution. When a machine completes a task, the simulation creates an event for the world state to process. Furthermore, it is possible to set a speed-up factor compared to real-time in the SimSharp simulation. As the simulation runs detached from the optimizer, speeding up the sim reduces the time available to the optimizer. The speedup is fixed for all runs to have comparable results.

2.3 World State

The world state is the connecting part between the simulation and the optimizer. It keeps track of the current state of the simulation, by holding information about the current state of the materials, the state of orders, and the contents of the buffers. This information is made available to the optimizer which uses it to generate solutions and evaluate them in the optimization process.

Furthermore, the world state also tracks the work done by the simulated machines. With this information and information about the materials processed the training data for the processing time machine-learning models is constructed. Each time the world state receives an event regarding the completion of a work step, the corresponding machine learning model is updated with the new training data.

2.4 Optimizer

To optimize the assignment and order of the tasks, an OERAPGA [5] is used. OERAPGA is a genetic algorithm that iteratively improves the quality of the population by selection, crossover, and mutation. Each generation contains a synchronization step to enable the GA to adjust to dynamic changes. In this step, the current population is updated to the current world state by removing tasks reported as done by the simulation and adding new tasks from new orders. Furthermore, the algorithm is open-ended by restarting it with a new population when it has converged.

To evaluate the quality of the solutions in the population, the solution gets simulated starting with the state of the simulation of the last update. This is not SimSharp a simulation, but rather just a sequential application of the tasks of the solution. To estimate the machine processing times, machine learning models are used.

From the history of applied tasks, the quality criteria are calculated. For the experiments, a list of hierarchical quality criteria is used. When comparing two solutions the first quality criterion is compared and, if equal, the next criteria are compared in order to decide which solution is better. The first metric handles

[1] https://github.com/heal-research/SimSharp accessed on 6 June 2024.

the buffer utilization. Solutions can contain task orders where removing anything from the buffer is impossible before adding another material. This can result in cases where the buffers are overfilled. To fix this, the number of materials that do not fit in the buffer anymore is minimized. The next metric is the makespan, the time required to process all tasks. Finally, orders have a fixed due date, so reducing the overdueness is the last metric.

2.5 Models

To evaluate the solutions, the processing times are required. As the actual timing behavior is unknown, it is estimated by machine learning models. As the inference speed of the model is a factor, the overhead for all models is kept the same. This also applies to the exact model which represents the exact machine behavior. For the online models, the Python library River[2] is used. As the simulation and the optimizer are implemented in C#, a communication framework is required. For this work, the communication is done via gRPC[3], as it is available in both languages and is easy to set up.

The features must be defined before the different model types can be considered. The features use information about the current and previously processed materials and are listed below.

- Total size of all materials in step
- Total weight of all materials in step
- Average thickness of all materials in step
- Is one material in step laminated
- Is one material in step soft-coated
- How much time has passed since the last step on this machine
- How long did the last action on this machine take
- Did the thickness change since the last action on this machine

To evaluate the online model performance, the error is calculated by making the initial prediction and comparing with the processing times from the production simulation.

2.6 Constant Value

As a baseline, a constant value of 30 s is used. This value is fixed for all machines and does not change throughout a run.

2.7 Online Statistics

Online implementations for mean and median are tested, as a robust approximation of the processing times. For both variants, the River implementation is used.

[2] https://riverml.xyz accessed on 7. June 2024.
[3] https://grpc.io accessed on 7. June 2024.

Linear Model Scikit-learn's[4] linear regression implementation is used as the non-online linear model. The standard scaler is applied, as a preprocessing step to the linear regression.

Random Forrest Regression. As with the linear model, the random forest implementation of Scikit-learn was used, and the standard scaler was applied.

Online Linear Model. The River linear regression is used as the online linear model variant. This implementation is based on minibatch updating of the coefficients. Such an implementation calls for a standard scaler to improve the convergence behavior.

Adaptive Random Forest Regression. The River implementation of adaptive random forest regressor is used, as the online counterpart to the random forest regression of scikit-learn. For this model, the inputs are also prepared by the standard scaler.

2.8 Experiment Setup

To achieve reproducible, stable, and comparable results for all experiment settings, some aspects of the experiment setup are worth mentioning:

For all runs, the orders converted into the scheduled tasks are the same, eliminating the random order generation as a factor for the model and optimization quality. However, the time when new orders are added to the simulation differs, as new orders are only added when the number of scheduled materials falls below 50.

As the optimizer is not deterministic, the simulation is run ten times for each machine learning model. To conduct the experiments in a manageable timeframe, the simulation is sped up 20 times. This increases the interval between the optimizer updates and reduces the optimization quality.

3 Results

Within this section, the speed of the used machine learning model is compared first. Secondly, the prediction error in the simulation runs for the machine learning models is compared. Finally, the resulting optimization quality is discussed and compared.

[4] https://scikit-learn.org accessed 7 June 2024.

3.1 Model Speeds

Figure 3 shows the speed of the tested machine learning models in training and prediction inclusive gRPC overhead. Looking at the training speed, the difference between the model types is clear. The training of the random forest regression especially shows the linear correlation between training data and training time. The non-online linear regression also shows this behavior. The online models only add one data point each time, so the time is constant and overall faster. The prediction does not show the same linear trend for the prediction of single data points but also shows the improved speed of the online model implementations as they are designed to predict single points.

Depending on the prediction speed of the models, the optimizer calculates more or fewer generations throughout one run. Figure 4 shows the number of generations calculated for the different models. As expected, the two non-online models take the most time to evaluate and thus produce about 30% fewer generations. Noteworthy is that despite the slower predictions of the online random forest, it produced about 100 generations more than the online linear regression. This may have to do with the stability of the prediction in combination with the OERAPGA. The exact model is also shown to confirm that it is in a similar ballpark as the other models.

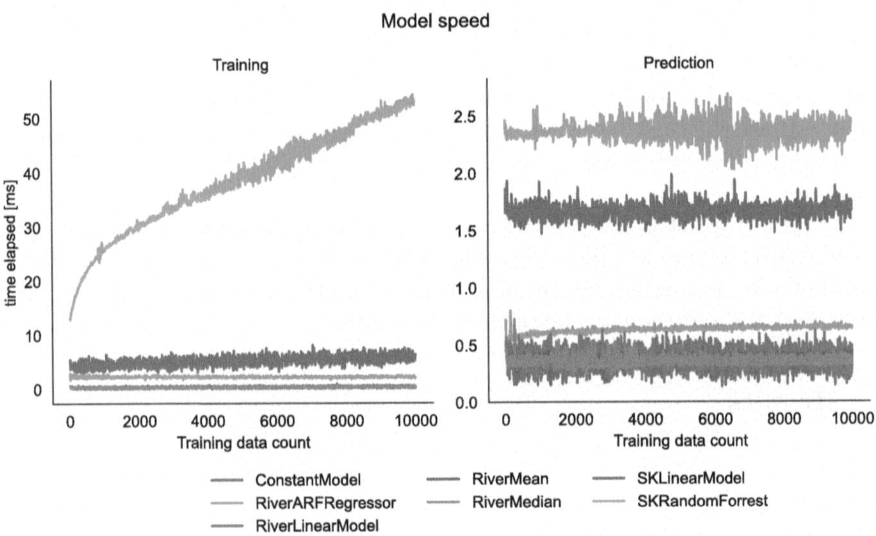

Fig. 3. Comparison of the training and prediction speeds of the applied models. For each training iteration, the online models use one data point to train. For the non-online models, each iteration with additional training data results in complete retraining with all data.

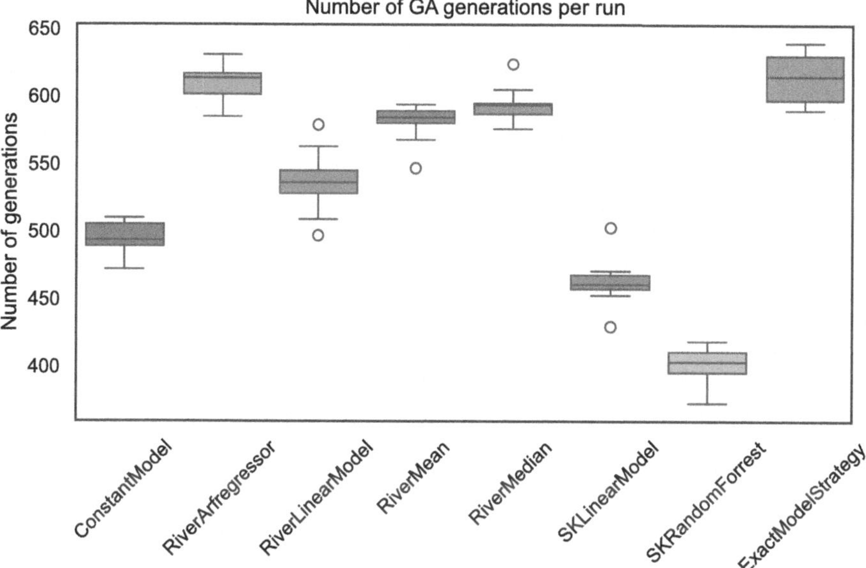

Fig. 4. A comparison of the number of GA generations over ten runs for model type. The color of each model matches the colors in Fig. 3.

3.2 Model Prediction Quality

Figure 5 compares the *Mean Absolute Error* (MAE) for all models. Unsurprisingly, the more simplistic linear models perform worse than their compatriots within the same packages with the constant model performing worse. Additionally, it must be noted that the River linear model performs rather poorly compared to its scikit-learn counterpart in terms of MAE, indicative that the online variant sacrifices a bit of accuracy for increased training speed. This trade-off is assumedly more significant when very few data points are available. The poor performance of the River linear model compared to the River mean and the median is potential because learning the coefficients using a minibatch takes more than one iteration.

Figure 6 displays the enormous drawback of a delayed reaction by the optimization system. The significantly longer training times of the Scikit-learn random forest delay the optimizer so much that updates arrive faster than the system can respond.

3.3 Optimization Quality

Figure 7 on the other hand provides an image of a much faster model allowing for a significantly higher number of optimizer generations at the same time, although even in this scenario the number of tasks increases faster than the optimizer-simulation system can work through, the overall utilization of the production

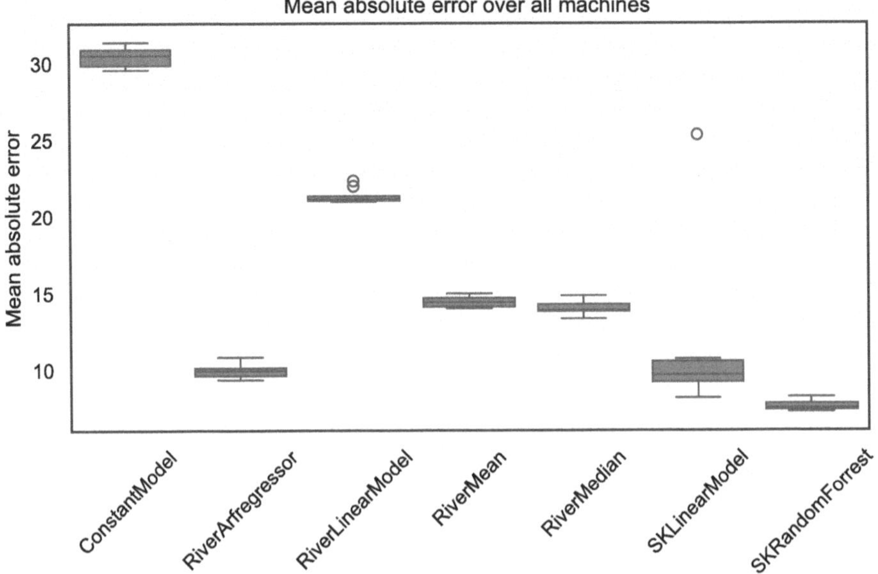

Fig. 5. Comparison of the absolute error rates for the models over all machines over ten simulation runs.

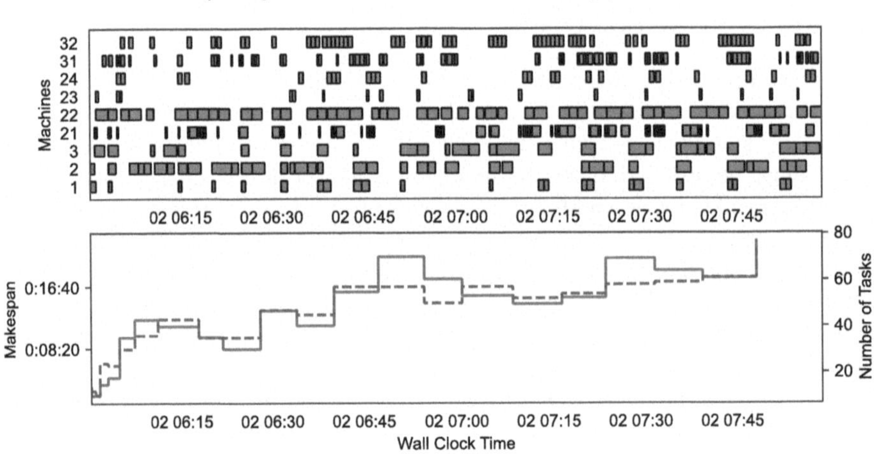

Fig. 6. The visual representation of a simulation run with the non-online random forest model as a Gantt chart. The lower plot half shows the makespan as the blue line and the number of tasks in the solution as the green dashed line. (Color figure online)

machines is significantly higher. Since in terms of error, the Scikit-learn random forest outperforms its dynamic counterpart from River in terms of MAE,

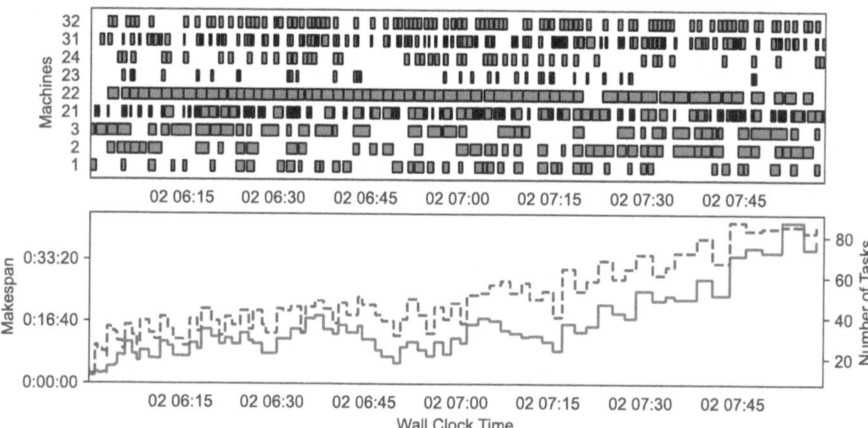

Fig. 7. The visual representation of a simulation run with the online random forest model as a Gantt chart. The lower plot half shows the makespan as the blue line and the number of tasks in the solution as the green dashed line. (Color figure online)

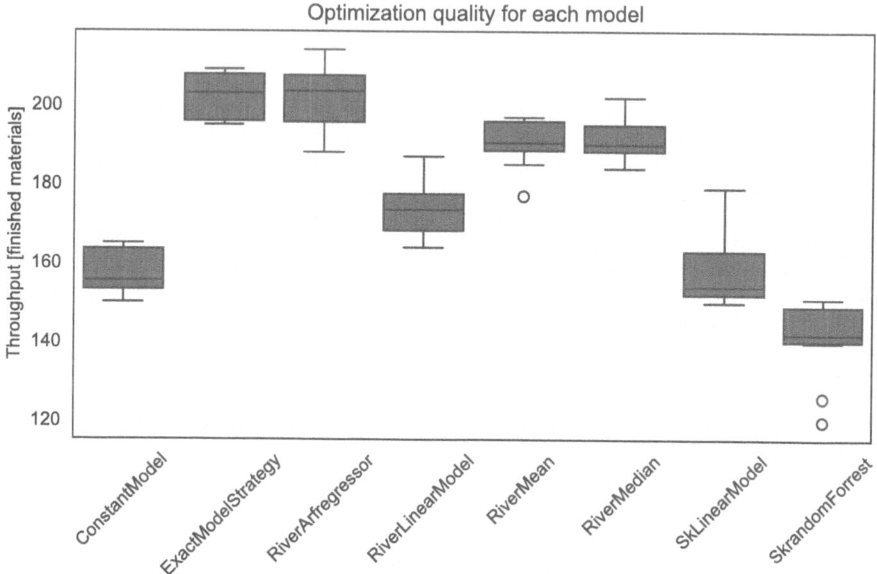

Fig. 8. Comparison between the optimization quality indicated by the throughput throughout the simulation runs.

this indicates that at a certain speed ratio between modeling, optimization and production, it may be beneficial to prefer faster models over more accurate ones.

Figure 8 underlines this assessment. Here the number of finished tasks is reported as the quality of the overall system. The River random forest model performs very similarly to its upper bound (the *exact model*) with the River mean and mean models close behind. The Scikit-learn models, although superior in model quality, perform significantly worse in terms of overall system performance. Overall, the extremely high correlation between model speed and system performance has to be noted.

4 Conclusion

This work aims to evaluate the performance of online machine-learning models compared to other machine-learning models, regarding the model speed, prediction quality, and resulting optimization quality. For this, an experiment with a production simulation, an OEPRAPGA optimizer, and several models, is set up. The results show that the most important factor in the optimization quality is the evaluation speed of the models. The prediction accuracy only plays a minor role. In the experiment setup, the optimizer is primarily occupied by optimizing the overall solution and does not get to finetuning the solution. Likely giving the optimizer more time by reducing the speedup of the simulation would shift the importance to the model quality, as it is important to finetuning the solution.

In further work, it would be interesting to reduce the speedup of the simulation to give it more time for finetuning. Additionally, testing more models and optimizing their hyperparameters to better fit the use case could further improve the quality.

Acknowledgments. The financial support by the Austrian Federal Ministry for Digital and Economic Affairs and the National Foundation for Research, Technology and Development and the Christian Doppler Research Association is gratefully acknowledged.

References

1. Beham, A., et al.: Integrated simulation and optimization in heuristiclab, pp. 418–423 (2014)
2. Chirkin, A.M., Belloum, A.S., Kovalchuk, S.V., Makkes, M.X., Melnik, M.A., Visheratin, A.A., Nasonov, D.A.: Execution time estimation for workflow scheduling. Futur. Gener. Comput. Syst. **75**, 376–387 (2017)
3. Hoi, S.C., Sahoo, D., Lu, J., Zhao, P.: Online learning: a comprehensive survey. Neurocomputing **459**, 249–289 (2021)
4. Im, S., Kumar, R., Qaem, M.M., Purohit, M.: Non-clairvoyant scheduling with predictions. ACM Trans. Parallel Comput. **10**(4), 1–26 (2023)
5. Karder, J., Werth, B., Beham, A., Wagner, S., Affenzeller, M.: Analysis and handling of dynamic problem changes in open-ended optimization. In: Moreno-Díaz, R., Pichler, F., Quesada-Arencibia, A. (eds.) Computer Aided Systems Theory - EUROCAST 2022, pp. 61–68. Springer Nature Switzerland, Cham (2022). https://doi.org/10.1007/978-3-031-25312-6_7

6. MacCarthy, B., Liu, J.: Addressing the gap in scheduling research: a review of optimization and heuristic methods in production scheduling. Int. J. Prod. Res. **31**, 59–79 (1993). https://doi.org/10.1080/00207549308956713
7. Montiel, J., et al.: River: machine learning for streaming data in python. J. Mach. Learn. Res. **22**, 1–10 (2021)
8. Nili, M.H., Taghaddos, H., Zahraie, B.: Integrating discrete event simulation and genetic algorithm optimization for bridge maintenance planning. Autom. Constr. **122**, 103513 (2021)
9. Priore, P., Gómez, A., Pino, R., Rosillo, R.: Dynamic scheduling of manufacturing systems using machine learning: an updated review. AI EDAM **28**(1), 83–97 (2014). https://doi.org/10.1017/S0890060413000516
10. Ramadan, M., Salah, B., Othman, M., Ayubali, A.A.: Industry 4.0-based real-time scheduling and dispatching in lean manufacturing systems. Sustainability **12**(6), 2272 (2020)
11. Xiong, H., Shi, S., Ren, D., Hu, J.: A survey of job shop scheduling problem: the types and models. Comput. Oper. Res. **142**, 105731 (2022)

Concurrent Evolution of Dynamic Single and Dual-Crane Scheduling Scenarios

Johannes Karder[1,2](✉), Bernhard Werth[1,2], Stefan Wagner[1], and Michael Affenzeller[1,2]

[1] Josef Ressel Center for Adaptive Optimization in Dynamic Environments, Heuristic and Evolutionary Algorithms Laboratory,University of Applied Sciences Upper Austria, 4232 Hagenberg, Austria
johannes.karder@fh-hagenberg.at

[2] Institute for Symbolic Artificial Intelligence, Johannes Kepler University, 4040 Linz, Austria

Abstract. Various approaches can be used to solve dynamic optimization problems. For example, on the one hand, optimization algorithms can be restarted every time the problem changes. As this results in a loss of optimization progress, algorithms can on the other hand also be implemented in an open-ended way, and to adapt to changing problem data during the run. Some problem updates cause fundamental changes to the optimization scenario. This paper describes different strategies to evolve solutions for such problems with scenario changes in the context of crane scheduling operations. It shows that simply ignoring such changes has negative effects on optimizer convergence, and compares the convergence behavior of five different strategies that can be applied when switches between different scenarios occur.

Keywords: open-ended optimization · dynamic optimization · single-crane scheduling · dual-crane scheduling

1 Introduction and Related Work

An optimization problem is defined by a problem formulation and instantiated with problem data. When both the problem formulation and problem data remain constant, we consider the problem to be a static optimization problem. However, when either is subject to change over time, we classify the problem as dynamic optimization problem. These problems can be approached using common optimization algorithms. Depending on the complexity of the problem, exact algorithms or metaheuristics can be utilized. The latter include, for example, population-based approaches such as genetic algorithms [6] or evolution strategies, or trajectory-based metaheuristics such as simulated annealing or local search. These algorithms are designed to deal with static optimization problems, but can also be applied to dynamic optimization problems by simply starting a new algorithm instance (or restarting an existing instance) when

A. Quesada-Arencibia et al. (Eds.): EUROCAST 2024, LNCS 15174, pp. 38–49, 2025.
https://doi.org/10.1007/978-3-031-83885-9_4

the optimization problem updates. However, this leads to a loss of optimization progress, as algorithms have to start their search from scratch. Therefore, these algorithms can be changed to run in an open-ended way, which results in two fundamental changes: algorithms (i) run until stopped manually and (ii) update their problem data and solutions when the optimization problem changes.

Open-ended optimization has been promoted in previous work [9]. In the context of crane scheduling, Karder et al. (2022) [7] describe how dynamic problem changes affect open-ended optimization algorithms and how these changes can be handled by extending algorithms to automatically adapt specific algorithm parameters. In the context of production scheduling, Werth et al. (2021) [8] enrich open-ended optimization algorithms with machine learning models to learn the system behavior of a dynamic manufacturing system over time, and as a result are able to outperform restarting construction heuristics up to 24% in high-load scenarios.

Regarding crane scheduling literature, two surveys on single-crane and multi-crane scheduling scenarios have been published by Boysen et al. (2016, 2017) [3, 4]. The latter introduces a classification scheme, the notation of which is also used within this paper. Furthermore, they list a total of 82 papers, out of which only six deal with a dynamic set of jobs.

In this paper, an open-ended version of a *relevant alleles preserving genetic algorithm* (RAPGA) [1], henceforth written as OERAPGA, is used to optimize crane schedules for an academic logistics warehouse setup. The dynamic optimization problem at hand switches between two different scenarios, depending on how many cranes are active at a given point in time. As a change in the number of available cranes has a significant impact on optimized crane schedules, five strategies that aid OERAPGA to evolve solutions for multiple scenarios are presented.

The rest of this paper is structured as follows. Section 2 presents the crane scheduling problem and open-ended optimization approach. Section 3 lists five strategies to deal with multi-scenario optimization problems. The experimental setup and obtained results are presented in Sect. 4. Finally, conclusions and an outlook on future work are given in Sect. 5.

2 Open-Ended and Multi-scenario Optimization

This section describes the simulated warehouse, as well as the open-ended optimization algorithm applied to solve the multi-scenario crane scheduling problem.

2.1 Simulated Warehouse

The presented optimization scenario is an abstracted, academic version of a real-world crane scheduling application. Using Boysen et al.'s notation [3], it is defined as follows:

$$[\mathrm{2D^{top}, 2|M, mv}^{XZ}\mathrm{, dy, prec, pos|C}^{max}] \tag{1}$$

A visual representation of the setup is depicted in Fig. 1. The top shows a front view of the warehouse. Two gantry cranes (shown in orange) must transport stacked items (shown in gray) between storage locations. Only the top item of each stack can be accessed by a crane at any time. The bottom shows the ground view. Both cranes can access all warehouse locations (shown as rectangles in different shades of gray). Storage locations are shown in lighter gray, while input/output (IO) locations are shown in darker gray. These IO locations are used by transporters, and items that need to be stored inside the warehouse or dispatched are either picked up or dropped off at these locations, resulting in pickup or dropoff transport orders, shown in red and green, respectively. In the simplified scenario that is optimized later on, only the x- and z-axis of the crane movements are considered. As the warehouse is much longer (x-axis) than wide (y-axis), the movements along the y-axis are neglected. However, picking up and dropping off items takes time, therefore service times are simulated and represent movements along the z-axis. The cranes share a single lane (shown in brown) and cannot overtake each other.

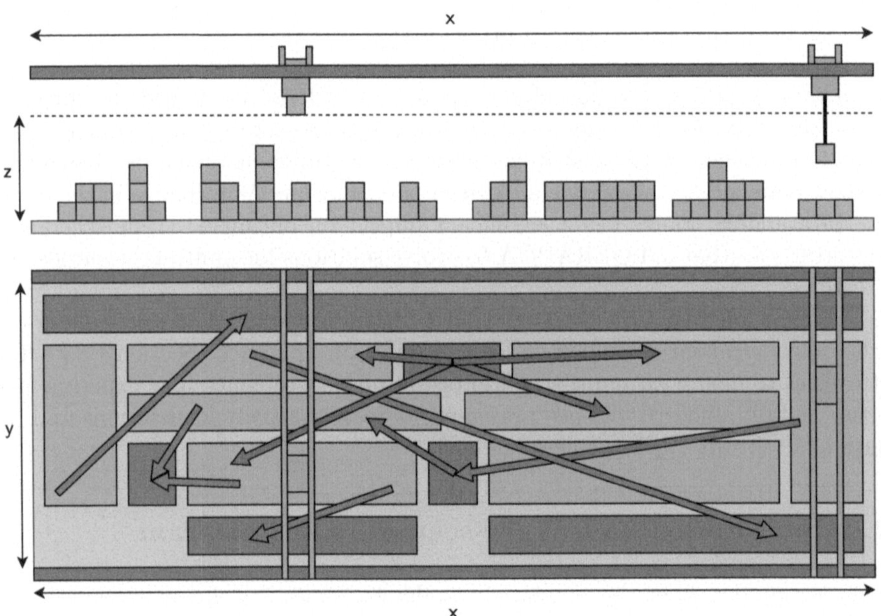

Fig. 1. An overview of the crane scheduling scenario.

A Sim#[1] [2] simulation is implemented to model the respective warehouse operations. Crane agents execute crane schedules that are provided to the simulation from external optimizers. During a simulation run, transport orders (i.e.

[1] https://github.com/heal-research/SimSharp (last accessed June 2024).

pickups and dropoffs) are generated as transporters arrive at IO locations. Transport orders describe which items must be moved to which target locations, and are converted to corresponding crane moves. These moves are split into three categories: (i) pickup moves, (ii) dropoff moves and (iii) relocation moves, the latter being necessary to access items with other items stacked above. Relocation moves also introduce precedence constraints.

In addition to the periodically changing move set, cranes become (in-)active at certain points in time. This simulates crane operators taking breaks or crane breakdowns. The simulation model is implemented so that one crane is always operational at any point in time. Therefore, the simulation switches between a single- and dual-crane scenario. Moves assigned to a deactivated crane must be reassigned to the other active crane in order to be processed.

2.2 Open-Ended Optimization

When solving static optimization problems, algorithms usually run until specific termination criteria are met. These criteria often include a fixed number of generations/iterations, time restrictions, or convergence states. In dynamic optimization, problems change over time, and algorithms must be able to handle these changes and update existing solutions accordingly. This is where open-ended optimization comes into play, as open-ended algorithms are able to handle dynamic problem changes, adapt existing solutions and run until stopped manually. Within this paper, OERAPGA, as depicted in Fig. 2, is used to optimize crane schedules. It extends the well-known RAPGA by two additional steps: (i) it synchronizes its internal problem data with the system to be optimized and (ii) reseeds its population once it converged. Synchronization is done with the last known world state that was published by the simulation, and leads to an update of all relevant data points in the algorithm's problem data, e.g., existing crane moves are updated. Reseeding happens once no successful offspring could be created within the current generation, and respects possibly configured elitism.

3 Concurrent Evolution

This section explains the different optimization strategies that have been implemented to deal with changes between single- and dual-crane scenarios.

3.1 Strategy 0: Ignorance

When optimizing dual-crane scenarios, genetic material is lost as soon as the scenario changes from a dual-crane to a single-crane scenario, henceforth notated as 2c and 1c, respectively, because all individuals are adapted to form valid solution candidates for the 1c scenario, as can be seen in Fig. 3a.

At the top, the figure shows a number of individuals in a single population. It also shows the actual genotype of the first individual within this population for

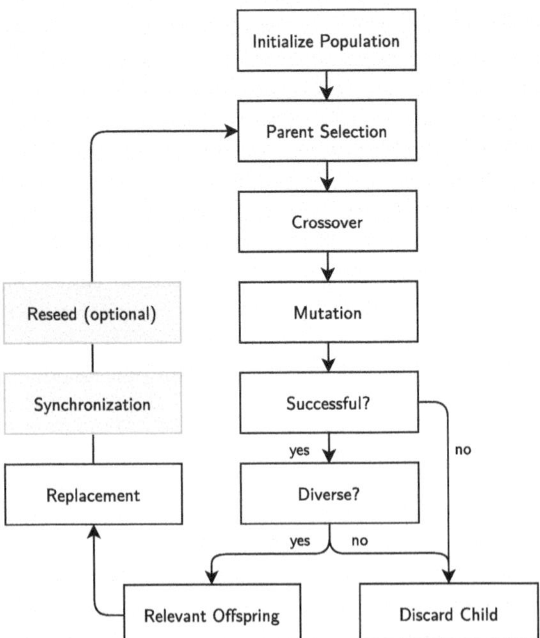

Fig. 2. The generational cycle of OERAPGA.

a 2c scenario. M and C mark the permutation for the schedule and the binary vector for crane assignment, respectively. Joining the permutation and binary vector results in a list of (move $= m$, crane $= c$) tuples, where $m \in \mathcal{M}$ and $c \in \mathcal{C}$, $\mathcal{M}$ and $\mathcal{C}$ being the move and crane sets. When the scenario changes from 2c to 1c, all assignments to a second crane, represented by 1 in the binary vector, are overridden by 0, i.e. all moves are assigned to a single crane. A conventional genetic algorithm evolves a single population and introduces new genetic material by chance. *Unwanted* mutation can happen during crossover when two individuals are combined to form a new one. The crossover operation might destroy some of the parents' genetic material and (re-)introduce schemas that were not present in the parent's population. The GA explicitly mutates created offspring with a certain probability, which is usually set rather low. In its conventional form, the algorithm does not react to scenario changes. This leads to a massive loss of genetic information when the assignment is changed to only reference a single crane. The gravity of this loss becomes apparent when a change from 1c to 2c happens later on during the search process. There is no immediate way for the GA to make assignments to the second crane, as these genes are not present in the population anymore.

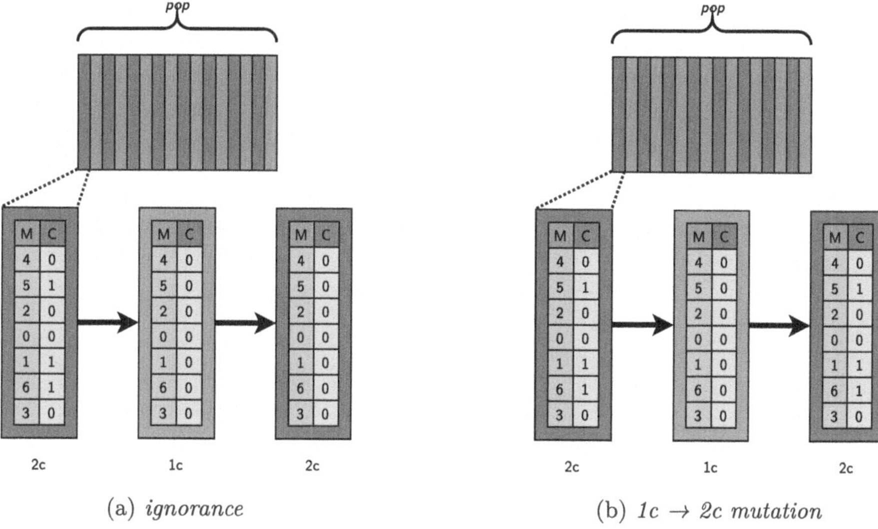

Fig. 3. The *ignorance* and *1c → 2c mutation* strategies.

3.2 Strategy 1: Reintroduction of Genetic Material

A logical next step is to reintroduce genetic material if required, depending on the scenario change. Figure 3b shows the same scenario changes as before. This time when the scenario changes from 1c to 2c, the assignment vector is mutated on purpose to reintroduce genetic material. Assignments to the second crane are present again and can be used in subsequent generations.

3.3 Strategy 2: Reuse of Genetic Material

As observed in strategy 1, present genetic information is simply thrown away when the scenario changes from 2c to 1c. All assignment vectors that have been optimized so far are zeroed, meaning that all assignment optimization work done so far is void. When applying strategy 2, optimized assignment vectors are saved when not applicable, but reused once they become applicable again. Figure 4a showcases this approach. When a change from 2c to 1c occurs, the optimized assignment vector (shown in lighter green coloring) is stored in addition to the correct 1c vector. The entries of both assignment vectors are tied to the schedule permutation, i.e. if the move order changes, the order in the assignment vector changes too. Finally, when a change from 1c to 2c occurs, the 2c assignment vector is activated again.

3.4 Strategy 3: Concurrent Evolution

The first truly concurrent evolution of individuals is implemented in strategy 3. This approach splits the GA's population into two subpopulations for

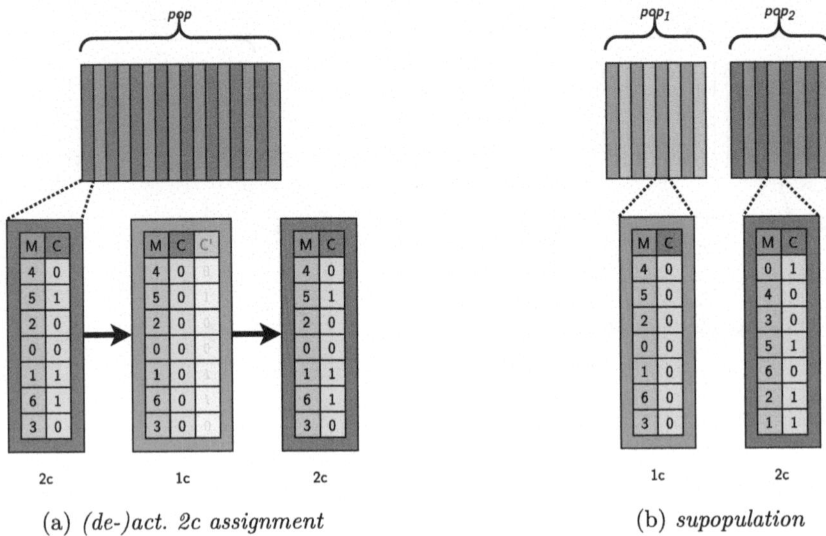

(a) *(de-)act. 2c assignment* (b) *supopulation*

Fig. 4. The *(de-)act. 2c assignment* and *supopulation* strategies.

each scenario that should be considered. Individuals in each subpopulation are evolved independently, but within one generation of the GA. Parent selection, crossover, mutation and replacement happen within these subpopulations only, which therefore cannot get mixed up. Figure 4b depicts this approach. Once a subpopulation has converged, as no successful offspring could be generated, it is reseeded, respecting elitism settings.

3.5 Strategy 4: Transformation

In the second to last evaluated strategy, transformation functions are applied in between scenario changes. These functions are explained below and respectively depicted in Fig. 5a.

- $\tau_a(\mathbf{2c}) \rightarrow \mathbf{1c}$: A transformation function τ_a transforms a 2c solution into a 1c solution. In case of the presented single- and dual-crane scenarios, it first groups the (move, crane) tuples by crane and then concatenates the two groups.
- $\tau_b(\mathbf{2c}) \rightarrow \mathbf{1c}$: A transformation function τ_a transforms a 1c solution into a 2c solution. In case of the presented single- and dual-crane scenarios, the first step is to assign cranes depending on the center of the move. For both cranes, the corresponding half of the warehouse is assigned as their primary area of operation. For a given move, the center of the move between pickup and dropoff locations is calculated, and the move is assigned to that crane whose area of operation contains the move center. These (move-crane) tuples are then enqueued in one move queue per crane. The resulting schedule is obtained by dequeuing from all move queues in a round-robin fashion.

The performance of this strategy heavily depends on the performances of the used transformation functions.

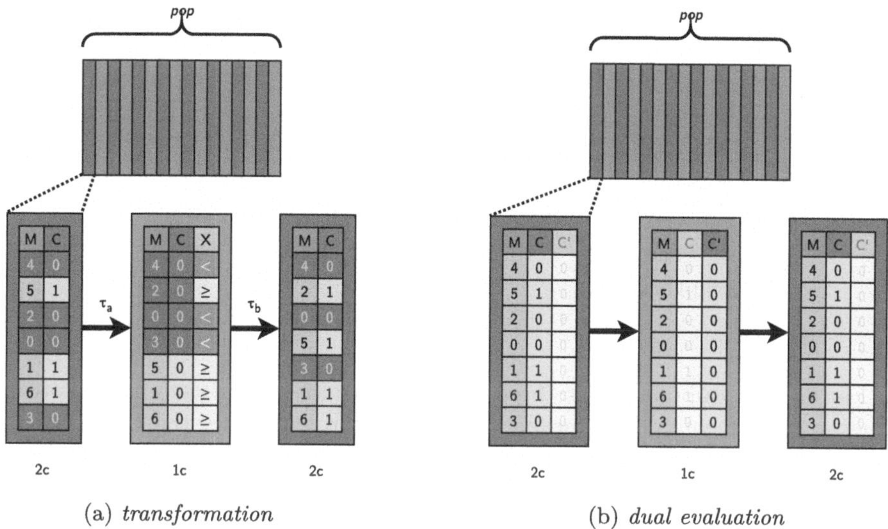

(a) *transformation* (b) *dual evaluation*

Fig. 5. The *transformation* and *dual evaluation* strategies.

3.6 Strategy 5: Multi-evaluation

The last strategy is to evaluate each individual for each possible scenario, and combine these evaluations into a single objective value. In the presented case, each individual is evaluated for the 1c and 2c scenario, one of which is currently active. The goal is to combine these evaluations in such a way that the algorithm prefers solutions that more geared towards the currently active scenario. Two objective functions are used and combined in the following way:

$$f(\boldsymbol{x}, \omega) = \omega \cdot f_a(\boldsymbol{x}) + f_i(\boldsymbol{x}) \tag{2}$$

$f_a(\boldsymbol{x}) \rightarrow \mathbb{R}$ and $f_i(\boldsymbol{x}) \rightarrow \mathbb{R}$ evaluate the individual in the currently active and inactive scenarios, respectively, and ω scales the impact of the individual's fitness in the active scenario as determined by $f_a(\boldsymbol{x})$. Figure 5b shows that an individual always has a 1c and 2c representation that can be evaluated.

4 Experiments and Results

All aforementioned strategies have been evaluated using OERAPGA instances configured with the algorithm parameters specified in Table 1. The convergence behavior of these algorithm instances when using either strategy can be observed

Table 1. Algorithm configurations defined per strategy.

Strategy	1,2,4,5	3
Parameter	Value	
PopSize	500	$2 \cdot 250 = 500$
Effort	1000	$2 \cdot 500 = 1000$
Elites	1	
Selector	Proportional	
Crossover	PMX [5] for (move, crane) tuples	
Mutator	Swap2 for (move, crane) tuples, BitFlip for C	
MutProb	0.05	
CompFact	0.0	

in Fig. 6. Each subplot hosts three axes. The x-axis shows the current world timestamp in seconds. The primary y-axis on the left shows the current best total makespan in seconds, and the respective line series is shown in blue. This makespan is the sum of time required to execute all open moves using the planned schedule and the time that already passed since the simulation and optimization were started, the reason being that this value remains constant if the scenario progresses as planned. When plotting only the time required to finish all open moves, this value would decrease as moves are consecutively executed by the cranes, making it difficult to differentiate this from actual quality improvements. The secondary y-axis on the right shows the current number of moves that have to be executed, and the line series is dotted and green. Special attention should be given to the subplot in the upper right, which displays the results obtained using the subpopulation strategy. In this case, both makespans of the two subpopulations are plotted. Blue indicates the current best total makespan found in pop_1 which contains only 1c individuals, whereas the makespan found in pop_2 which contains only 2c individuals is shown in orange. Therefore, the progress of the effective makespan (depending on which scenario is active) is plotted in red.

The following observations and interpretations can be made when looking at the results in Fig. 6:

- Ignoring these scenarios changes negatively impacts the search. As genetic material is lost, the algorithm gets stuck and can only reintroduce necessary genetic material by chance via its mutation operators. This is apparent in the convergence behavior shown in the upper left subplot. The algorithm is not able to improve the makespan after the first switch from a 1c to 2c scenario. Only once it receives new moves to execute, the presence of another crane is detected, as random cranes are assigned to new moves.
- Strategy 1, shown in the upper right corner, is able to mitigate the loss of genetic material that occurs when changing from 2c to 1c scenarios. When

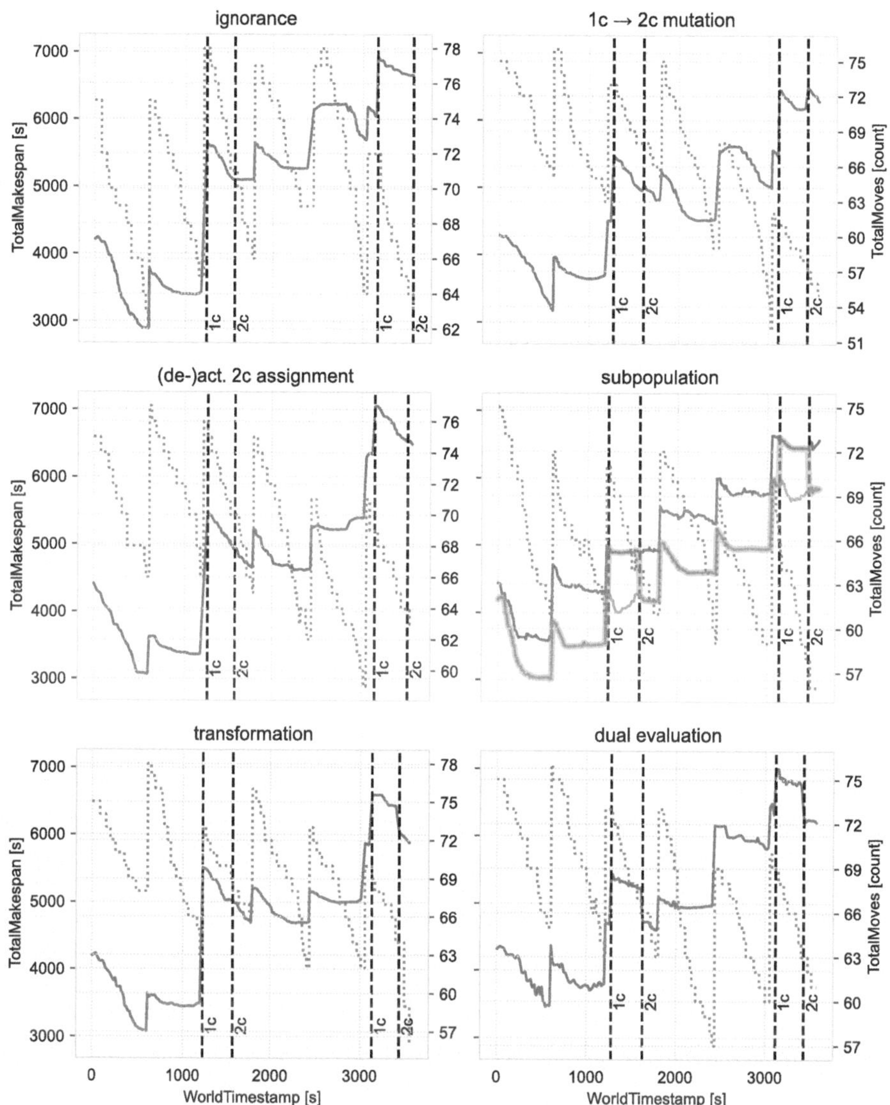

Fig. 6. Test run showing the algorithm behavior of all OERAPGA versions.

needed, new genetic material is introduced, which enables the GA to further improve the makespan after changes from 1c to 2c scenarios.

- A similar effect is observed when looking at strategy 2, depicted by the middle left subplot. The algorithm is able to improve the makespan by reusing previously optimized assignments, as can be seen right after the change from 1c to 2c.

- When looking at the subpopulation strategy, both scenarios seem to be optimized as expected. Once changes to the move set occur, both subpopulations converge. When the scenario changes, the algorithm switches between these subpopulations. Note that in the later halves of the 1c scenarios, the makespan of pop_2 increases, although the number of moves decreases. This is due to the fact that the simulation effectively applies 1c solutions during this phase, which would be suboptimal if both cranes were operational. In a 2c scenario, two cranes would execute (more) moves in parallel, however, such a 2c schedule cannot be executed in a 1c scenario. Solutions in pop_2 are evaluated with the assumption that both cranes are operational and moves are executed in parallel. When computing the observed and planned makespan, the observed part becomes larger and larger, as parts of the schedule take longer than anticipated, and therefore the makespan increases.
- When using the transformation strategy, the algorithm's convergence behavior is akin to the behaviors obtained using strategies 1 and 2.
- The dual evaluation strategy shows a convergence behavior that closely resembles the one seen in the subpopulation approach. However, the achieved solution qualities are lower, meaning the achieved makespans are higher. This is due to the fact that dual evaluation is not able to combine the best 1c and 2c solution as one, but rather optimizes solutions that are good for both scenarios. It therefore trades specialization for generalization.

5 Conclusion and Outlook

Within this paper, various strategies for multi-scenario crane scheduling optimization via an open-ended version of RAPGA (OERAPGA), have been described. As the optimization problem dynamically switches between scenarios, genetic material ist lost when a crane is deactivated and only one crane remains active. As a consequence, essential building blocks necessary to construct optimal solutions in a dual-crane scenario are lost. The only way for a conventional GA to reintroduce these building blocks is by means of mutation, which greatly depends on the specified mutation probability. In a multi-scenario application, we suggest to at least manually reintroduce genetic material on purpose if required, or remember and reuse (pre-)optimized genetic material. Another approach is to concurrently evolve multiple subpopulations, where each population consists of individuals optimized for a specific scenario. When these subpopulations are optimized (independently of the currently active scenario), the algorithm is able to immediately switch to high quality solutions when a scenario change occurs. The fourth suggested strategy is to transform solutions between scenario changes. This, however, is a problem-specific operation. Finally, a dual evaluation approach, in which each individual is evaluated in every scenario, and the individual's fitness is a linear combination of these fitness evaluations, trades solution specialization for generalization.

In a future study, the effects of the implemented strategies should be quantified in order to gain insights into the optimization potential that arises when applying the proposed approaches. Implementing and evaluating these multi-scenario extensions in the context of dynamic real-world crane scheduling applications is especially interesting. Improved algorithm convergence and thus a reduction of time required to generate valid, efficient schedules when switching scenarios should also positively affect the crane operators' acceptance of the created schedules.

Acknowledgments. The financial support by the Austrian Federal Ministry for Digital and Economic Affairs and the National Foundation for Research, Technology and Development and the Christian Doppler Research Association is gratefully acknowledged.

References

1. Affenzeller, M., Wagner, S., Winkler, S.: Self-adaptive population size adjustment for genetic algorithms. In: Moreno Díaz, R., Pichler, F., Quesada Arencibia, A. (eds.) EUROCAST 2007. LNCS, vol. 4739, pp. 820–828. Springer, Heidelberg (2007). https://doi.org/10.1007/978-3-540-75867-9_103
2. Beham, A., et al.: Integrated simulation and optimization in heuristiclab. In: Proceedings of the 26th European Modeling and Simulation Symposium EMSS, pp. 418–423 (2014)
3. Boysen, N., Briskorn, D., Meisel, F.: A generalized classification scheme for crane scheduling with interference. Eur. J. Oper. Res. **258**(1), 343–357 (2017)
4. Boysen, N., Stephan, K.: A survey on single crane scheduling in automated storage/retrieval systems. Eur. J. Oper. Res. **254**(3), 691–704 (2016)
5. Fogel, D.B.: An evolutionary approach to the traveling salesman problem. Biol. Cybern. **60**(2), 139–144 (1988)
6. Holland, J.H.: Adaptation in Natural and Artificial Systems: An Introductory Analysis With Applications to Biology, Control, and Artificial Intelligence. MIT Press, Cambridge (1992)
7. Karder, J., Werth, B., Beham, A., Wagner, S., Affenzeller, M.: Analysis and handling of dynamic problem changes in open-ended optimization. In: Moreno-Díaz, R., Pichler, F., Quesada-Arencibia, A. (eds.) Computer Aided Systems Theory – EUROCAST 2022. EUROCAST 2022. LNCS, vol. 13789, pp. 61–68. Springer, Cham (2022). https://doi.org/10.1007/978-3-031-25312-6_7
8. Werth, B., Karder, J., Beham, A., Wagner, S.: Dynamic landscape analysis for open-ended stacking. In: Proceedings of the Genetic and Evolutionary Computation Conference Companion, pp. 1700–1707 (2021)
9. Yazdani, D., Cheng, R., Yazdani, D., Branke, J., Jin, Y., Yao, X.: A survey of evolutionary continuous dynamic optimization over two decades–part a. IEEE Trans. Evol. Comput. **25**(4), 609–629 (2021)

Learning-Based Algorithm Selection for a Multiprocessor Scheduling Problem

Roland Braune[1,2,3](✉)

[1] University of Applied Sciences Upper Austria, Operations Management, Wels, Austria
roland.braune@univie.ac.at

[2] Department of Business Decisions and Analytics, University of Vienna, Vienna, Austria

[3] Josef Ressel Center for Adaptive Optimization in Dynamic Environments, University of Vienna, Vienna, Austria

Abstract. This paper addresses a multiprocessor scheduling problem with real-world-inspired constraints. A learning-based prediction approach is proposed to support an effective algorithm selection during problem-solving. Classifiers are trained to predict whether a particular solver should be employed. The core of the contribution is the selection and engineering of features based on the structural properties of problem instances. These features are used as predictors in several well-known binary classification approaches. Computational experiments based on randomly generated problem instances reveal accuracy scores of up to 90% and indicate the potential time savings when embedding the proposed classifiers into the overall solution procedure.

Keywords: Multiprocessor scheduling · Algorithm selection · Machine learning · Classification · Feature engineering

1 Introduction

The scope of multiprocessor scheduling is certainly not limited to information technology. Rather, many real-world production-related scenarios actually fit this type of scheduling problem. The industrial setting that provides the background and motivation for the work presented in this paper originates from the petrochemical industries. A company-internal research laboratory for product development performs material tests on different types of resources. The development of a decision support tool for automated scheduling of those test activities was the goal of a research project conducted in cooperation with the company. A bucket-based scheduling approach was adopted, with the time horizon discretized into daily or weekly periods and the resources' capacities aggregating according to the chosen bucket size. The material tests can be divided into subtasks, but the latter cannot be processed independently of each other.

A. Quesada-Arencibia et al. (Eds.): EUROCAST 2024, LNCS 15174, pp. 50–60, 2025.
https://doi.org/10.1007/978-3-031-83885-9_5

In fact, they are subject to precedence constraints involving minimum and maximum time lags, resulting in a special form of task malleability [2]. The reader is referred to [6] for further details on the industrial scenario. On a single resource level, the underlying scheduling problem can be considered as a multiprocessor scheduling problem [8].

For solving problems of this kind with special precedence constraints, a two-stage procedure has recently been proposed [5]. The first stage consists of a subset-sum heuristic, which is highly effective if the optimal schedule exhibits a particular resource allocation profile. The second stage is a custom branch-and-bound algorithm, which is generic enough to tackle the problem under all circumstances but gets very inefficient due to excessive combinatorics if all tasks are very "small", meaning that they require only a small amount of resource units (= processors). The main contribution of this paper is a machine learning-based approach to predict whether the first stage is likely to succeed, i.e., whether the corresponding (optimal) resource allocation profile exists or not. An accurate prediction effectively allows for an algorithm selection and a reduction of the required computation time.

Problem features are extracted, engineered and selected to serve as the independent variables of several classifiers known from machine learning. The efficacy of the classifiers is finally evaluated based on randomly generated problem instances. Prediction accuracies of around 90% are achievable for test sets exhibiting the same structural properties as the training set. When extrapolating to unseen instances with different properties, the scores drop to around 70%, which is still considerably better than the baseline.

2 Problem Statement

The subject of this contribution is a particular kind of multiprocessor scheduling problem. A set of n tasks $T = \{1, \ldots, n\}$ is to be processed on a set of m identical parallel processors. Each task $i \in T$ consists of n_i subtasks or task "slices". Such a sub-task is identified by a pair (i, j), with $i \in T$ and $j \in \{1, \ldots, n_i\}$. The number of processors to be allocated simultaneously for the execution of a task slice is denoted by $size_{i,j}$, also commonly known as the *width* of a task (slice) [8]. All slices (i, j) that make up a task $i \in T$ have unit processing time, that is, $p_{ij} = 1$, $i \in T$, $j \in \{1, \ldots, n_i\}$, and share the same width, hence, $size_{i,1} = size_{i,2} = \ldots = size_{i,n_i}$. Consequently, it is possible to specify the width on the level of outer tasks $i \in T$, yielding $size_i = size_{i,1} = \ldots = size_{i,n_i}$. The slices of a task are organized into chain-like structures by defining appropriate, generalized precedence constraints. Those constraints are enforced by imposing minimum time lags (delays) on every two sub-tasks of one and the same outer task. Since preemption of tasks is not allowed, all slices of a task are also subject to maximum time lags. Chain precedence constraints have already been discussed in the multiprocessor scheduling literature [3], but not in conjunction with maximum time lags.

Figure 1a shows a multiprocessor schedule for $m = 14$ processors, based on three different task chains, with 6, 4 and 4 slices (sub-tasks), respectively.

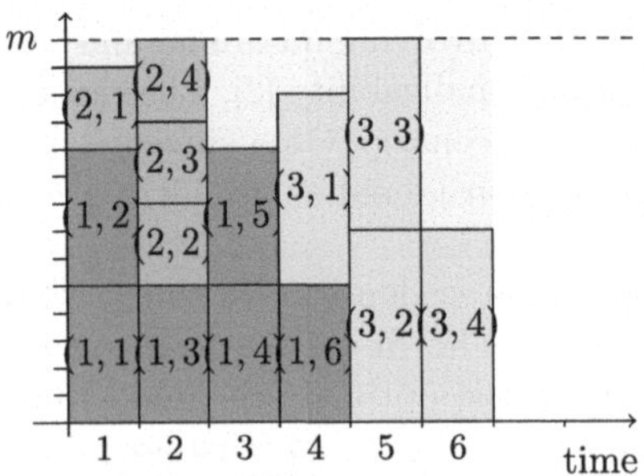

(a) Scheduling multiprocessor task chains s.t. minimum and maximum time lags

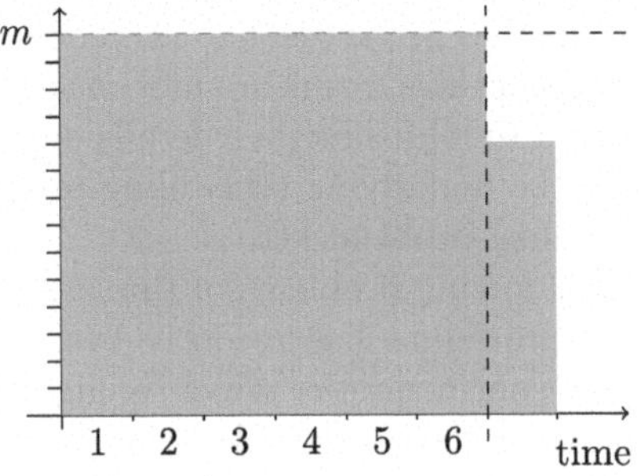

(b) "Ideal" resource allocation profile for the WCT objective

Fig. 1. Different resource profiles for the considered discrete malleable multiprocessor scheduling problem

The widths are given as $size_1 = 5$, $size_2 = 3$, and $size_3 = 7$. It can be seen that the processor allocation changes three times for chain one, once for chain two, and twice for chain three. The number of sub-tasks of a particular chain that are processed simultaneously is not limited, but at least one sub-task has to be processed at any time during the processing time window of a chain because of the implicit non-preemption constraint.

Let C_{ij} denote the completion time of a task slice in a feasible schedule S and w_{ij} its corresponding weight, where $w_{ij} = size_{ij} = size_i$, and thus the weights are proportional to the size of a task (slice). The optimization objective considered in this paper is the minimization of the total weighted completion time (TWCT) of all task slices, i.e., $\sum w_{ij}C_{ij}$. Using the common three-field notation of Graham et al. [11], the problem at hand can be classified as $P \mid chains(l); size_{ij}; p_{ij} = 1; w_{ij} = size_{ij} \mid \sum w_{ij}C_{ij}$, where $chains(l)$ refers to the fact that the chain precedence constraints are subject to constant delays.

Note that the objective function leads to a schedule which is *left-shifted*, meaning that the resource load is higher in earlier time periods and tends to decrease towards the future. This is exactly the behavior that is desired in the underlying real-world setting because it is preferred to "freeze" the schedule for the near future and to leave some space for further dated time periods. Figure 1b depicts what is referred to as an "ideal" schedule in the remainder of this paper, exhibiting maximum resource loads in all but the last (rightmost) time period.

Problem $P \mid chains(l); size_{ij}; p_{ij} = 1; w_{ij} = size_{ij} \mid \sum w_{ij}C_{ij}$ is a generalization of $P \mid size_i; p_i = 1; w_i = size_i \mid \sum w_iC_i$, which has been shown to be NP-hard in the strong sense in [4]. Therefore, the discrete malleable task scheduling problem is also NP-hard in the strong sense.

3 Solution Algorithms

An advanced branch-and-bound (B&B) algorithm has recently been proposed for this specific problem [5], based on a packing-based reformulation. Although it makes use of sophisticated techniques like dominance rules and custom constraint propagation, it still struggles with combinatorics in the case of very small task sizes. The number of feasible sets increases exponentially, and many dominance rules known from bin packing cannot be used because of the precedence constraints. On the other hand, computational experiments have shown that the smaller the (maximum) task size, the more likely the existence of an ideal schedule for a given instance. Consequently, for scenarios with small task sizes only, i.e., when all $w_{ij} \leq 0.4\,\mathrm{m}$, it can be beneficial to focus on the generation of feasible sets that fully utilize a multiprocessor's capacity. This can be achieved by solving a series of *subset-sum* problems, one for each time period. The subset-sum problem is a well-known NP-complete decision problem and answers the question of whether there exists a subset of a given set of integer numbers that sum up to a target value T. It is also known as a special case of the knapsack problem [13]. In the context of the problem under consideration, it is, however, not only the decision version that matters. One is rather interested in the composition of the subset that fulfills the above criterion, and hence, the optimization version of the subset-sum problem is also required here. For this reason, a limited enumeration algorithm has been devised [5], which determines subset-sum solutions in consecutive time periods under consideration of minimum and maximum time lags. It is basically an enumeration algorithm, but the number of branches at each level is limited. The resulting approach is a heuristic and is also commonly known as "Beam Search" [10].

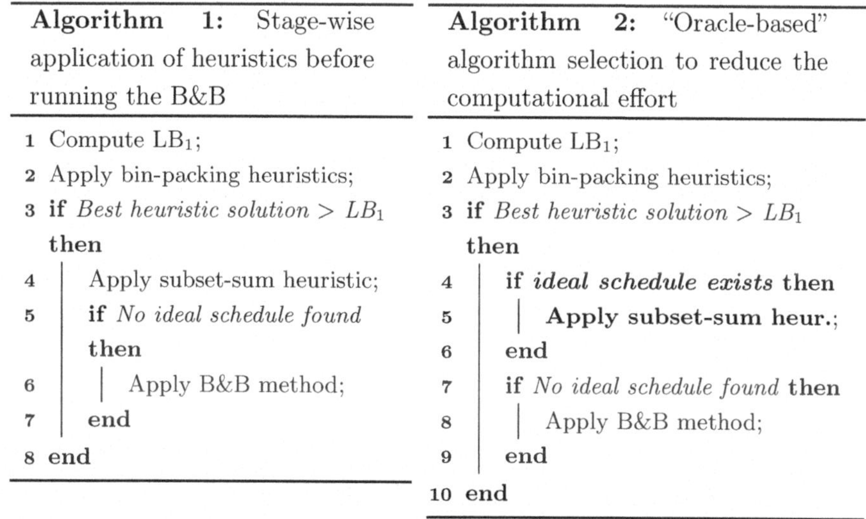

Algorithm 1: Stage-wise application of heuristics before running the B&B

```
Compute LB1;
Apply bin-packing heuristics;
if Best heuristic solution > LB1 then
    Apply subset-sum heuristic;
    if No ideal schedule found then
        Apply B&B method;
    end
end
```

Algorithm 2: "Oracle-based" algorithm selection to reduce the computational effort

```
Compute LB1;
Apply bin-packing heuristics;
if Best heuristic solution > LB1 then
    if ideal schedule exists then
        Apply subset-sum heur.;
    end
    if No ideal schedule found then
        Apply B&B method;
    end
end
```

The idea of the overall solution approach is to run the subset-sum heuristic before the B&B, as shown in Algorithm 1. However, this pre-optimization step is performed for every instance, regardless of whether an ideal solution exists or not. Although the occurrence of ideal solutions becomes more likely with decreasing task sizes, there might still exist a substantial amount of instances that are not ideally solvable since other instance properties (besides the task size) also have an impact in this context. In other words, it is difficult to "guess" whether an ideal solution actually exists for a particular instance. On the other hand, if one had an oracle providing an instance classification, the perfect overall approach could be outlined as shown in Algorithm 2. As can be seen in the pseudo-code notation, the subset-sum heuristic would only be executed if an ideal schedule existed, essentially introducing an algorithm selection aspect. Note that both displayed flow structures comprise a further pre-optimization step involving the application of bin-packing heuristics. The output of both pre-optimization phases is compared to the simplest lower bound for that problem, referred to as LB_1. This lower bound always yields an ideal resource allocation profile by assuming tasks to be splittable (fractional). It is clear that if one succeeds in constructing a feasible schedule with the same profile but with tasks considered non-splittable, an optimal solution has been found, and the overall procedure can terminate. It is also clear that, in absence of an oracle, one has to think about ways to effectively predict whether an ideal schedule exists or not. An approach to accomplish this with a reasonable accuracy is presented in the remainder of this paper.

4 Feature Selection and Engineering

Trying to predict whether an ideal schedule exists for a given problem instance basically boils down to solving a classification problem. The field of machine learning offers a broad range of classification approaches that can be employed in this context. Before using one of these, one has to identify, extract, and potentially engineer features that then serve as the independent variables. Since the problem setting at hand represents a single-class classification problem, there is only one dependent (target) variable, indicating a yes/no answer to the question posed further above.

The features that were extracted, engineered, and tested in the context of the work presented in this paper can be summarized as follows:

- *Relative task sizes* (in relation to m):
  Minimum, maximum, average, quartiles, frequency information (histogram)
- *Chain lengths:*
  Average, coefficient of variation
- *Subset sums:*
  Subset sums in the range $[1, m]$ were enumerated using a recently proposed, near linear-time pseudo-polynomial algorithm [7]. The idea behind this approach was to analyze the concentration of subset sums around particular target values. If subset sums are most frequently observed around values close to m, this might indicate a higher probability of encountering an ideal schedule. Besides the concentration, the coefficient of variation of these subset sums is used as a measure of dispersion.
- *Maximal feasible sets:*
  A maximal feasible set is a set of tasks that can be processed at the same time on m processors without leaving room for any additional task. Despite the analogy to bin packing, classical procedures for generating those maximal

feasible sets (e.g. [12]) are not suited in this particular case. Instead, the focus lies on feasible sets that use up *all* of the available capacity m. For this purpose, the well-known dynamic programming algorithm for knapsack problems [13] was extended such that feasible sets of the above type could easily be generated. However, this algorithm runs in pseudopolynomial time with a worst-case complexity of $O(n \cdot m)$. This fact might render it prohibitive for instances with excessive numbers of processors. On the other hand, the number of feasible sets that allocate exactly m processors might be correlated with the probability of encountering an ideal schedule because this kind of schedule consists almost entirely of such feasible sets.

- *Residual load:*
  In an ideal schedule, there might be some residual load left to be allocated during the last time period (see also Fig. 1b). This residual load can easily be computed as $\sum_{i=1}^{n} w_i - \lfloor \sum_{i=1}^{n} w_i / m \rfloor$. If there is a feasible set that exactly amounts to the residual load, the last time period of an ideal schedule can theoretically be filled. Contrary to that, if there is no matching feasible set, it is clear that the ideal schedule cannot be assembled for the instance in question. Note that both the subset-sum and the maximal feasible set generation approach (with a target value equal to the residual load) could be used to verify the existence of such a feasible set.

5 Experimental Setup

To evaluate the performance of machine learning-based classifiers in conjunction with the features described in Sect. 4, randomly generated instances of the considered multiprocessor scheduling problem were used. The goal of the instance generation process was to produce large amounts of training instances in a reasonable amount of time. Clearly, for effective training, provably optimal solutions are required for each of those instances to provide the labels for the learning algorithms. Therefore, the problem parameters were chosen such that the solution approach from [5], as roughly outlined in Algorithm 1, should not require more than 60 s to reach an optimal solution.

Table 1. Parameter settings for instance generation

Parameter	Values
# of chains	$\{8, 10, 12, 14\}$
# of task slices per chain	$[3, 8]$
# of processors (m)	$\{50, 100, 250, 500, 1000\}$
Task size upper bounds	$\{0.25m, 0.3m, 0.35m, 0.4m\}$

Table 1 provides an overview of the chosen parameter settings. The number of chains was held fixed at the stated values, whereas the number of tasks/slices per chain was varied uniformly within the range [3, 8]. On average, this led to a total number of tasks ranging between 40 and 70. The task size upper bounds are given relative to the number of processors, implying a potential range between 1 and the respective upper bound for a particular task's size to be drawn from. The value ranges for the parameters resulted in 20 instance sets per task size upper bound, hence 80 instance sets in total. Per instance set, 1000 problem instances were randomly generated.

The code for training and testing the classifiers was implemented in Python 3, using the popular open-source machine learning library `scikit-learn` [14] (version 1.5.0). The following classification approaches were applied in the context of this work:

- *Logistic regression*
- *Decision tree*
- *Random forest*
- *AdaBoost* [9], a meta-estimator that iteratively fits a classifier (a decision tree by default) on a dataset, where in each iteration, weights of incorrectly classified instances are modified to effectively "steer" the classifier to the more difficult cases (see also [1]).
- *Extremely randomized trees* (extra-trees) as another ensemble method. Similar to random forests, randomness is introduced in the classifier construction, but extra trees differ in the way the discriminative thresholds are determined. The goal is to further reduce the variance of the model while slightly increasing the bias [1].

All experiments were conducted on an Intel Core i7-4770 workstation (3.4 GHz) with 16 gigabytes of RAM, running Windows 11 as an operating system.

6 Computational Results

Before actually covering the prediction results, an analysis concerning the frequency of occurrence of ideal schedules for the randomly generated problem instances shall be presented. Figure 2 gives an overview of these percentages for two different task size upper bounds. As expected, smaller task sizes in fact lead to a considerably higher portion of ideal schedules (see Fig. 2a), especially when the number of chains ($\approx$ number of distinct task sizes) is large, since it is easier to form maximal feasible sets exhausting the multiprocessor capacity. It is also worth noting that the percentages drop significantly when the number of processors increases. However, this is also conclusive because a range of [0, 1000] leads to a much finer granularity with regard to task sizes than a range of [0, 50]. Independently of that, the observed percentage of ideal solutions gets notably smaller as tasks get larger and thus "bulkier" (see Fig. 2b).

Since the task size upper bounds obviously have a major impact on the probability of occurrence of ideal solutions, the computational evaluation is based on obtaining separate classifiers for each task size upper bound. Within each

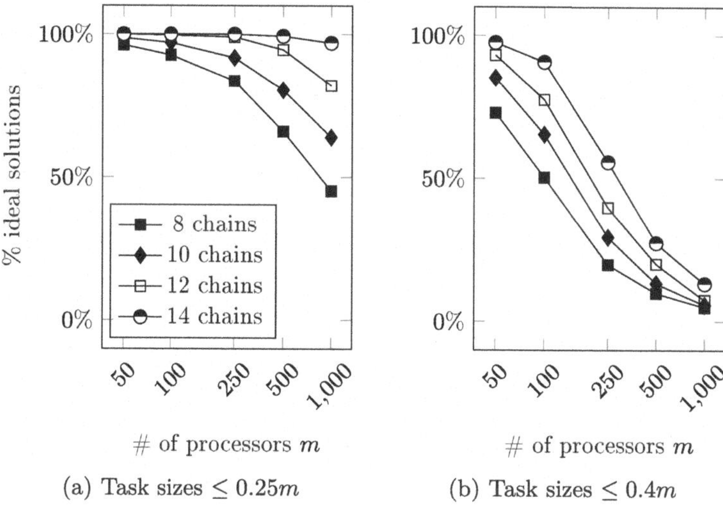

Fig. 2. Percentage of ideal solutions observed for increasing numbers of multiprocessors and chains

resulting group of instances, the goal was to train a classifier on one out of the 20 instance sets. The selected instance set was considerably boosted in its size (10000 instances) before a train/test split in a 60:40 manner was applied. The instance sets used for this purpose were all made up of 50 tasks, 10 chains, and processor counts ranging between 100 (for task sizes $\leq 0.4\,\mathrm{m}$) and 1000 (for task sizes $\leq 0.25\,\mathrm{m}$). The parameters were selected with the goal of obtaining almost balanced data sets, i.e., there is no distinct bias with regard to instances with or without ideal solutions. Small imbalances were resolved by applying a simple downsampling procedure before applying the train/test split.

Table 2. Prediction accuracies achieved by classifiers on test instances with the same characteristics as the training instances.

Max. task size	m	Log. regr.	Dec. tree	Rand. forest	AdaBoost	Extr. trees
0.25 m	1,000	0.87	0.91	0.90	0.91	0.90
0.3 m	500	0.89	0.89	0.89	0.88	0.89
0.35 m	250	0.86	0.87	0.87	0.87	0.87
0.4 m	100	0.87	0.86	0.86	0.88	0.87

Table 2 shows the accuracy scores obtained for the respective test set, which then had the same basic characteristics as the training set. The obtained scores were consistently high and close to 90% across all instance groups and classifiers, indicating that the learning approaches were able to successfully capture the target concept. Note that these results were achieved by using only a subset of the features described in Sect. 4. Using both the recursive feature elimination (RFE) approach and the extra trees' feature importances provided by `scikit-learn`, the original feature set could be reduced to three features of central importance, i.e., the average relative task size, a boolean value indicating the existence of a subset sum equal to the residual load in the last time period of an ideal schedule and finally the relative share of maximal feasible sets that completely use up all of the multiprocessor's capacity. It has to be remarked that no normalization or scaling was necessary with these three features since all of them are relative values.

Table 3. Prediction accuracy achieved by various different classifiers on test data

Max. Task Size	Log. regr.	Dec. tree	Rand. forest	AdaBoost	Extr. trees
0.25 m	0.91	0.69	0.67	0.67	0.82
0.3 m	0.75	0.67	0.61	0.66	0.70
0.35 m	0.76	0.70	0.69	0.69	0.72
0.4 m	0.70	0.67	0.68	0.69	0.68

The next step was to analyze the extrapolation capabilities of the trained classifiers, but still within the four groups. Table 3 reveals insights into the obtained accuracy scores, which are expectedly lower. Instances with task sizes smaller than 0.25 m appear to be the easiest to classify, and in this context, the difference between the classifiers themselves becomes more apparent. The logistic regression approach seems to perform best across all four groups of instances, with scores still ranging between 70% and 90%.

Table 4. Potentially achievable time savings (in percent) for various task counts and relative task sizes

# of tasks	# of chains	Max. task size			
		0.25 m	0.3 m	0.35 m	0.4 m
40	8	12.95	16.87	18.35	18.79
50	10	4.34	6.17	7.51	9.21
60	12	3.77	3.11	3.75	4.86
70	14	4.38	3.93	2.93	3.18

Finally, the question remains in how far the proposed prediction approaches can improve the overall solution process of problem $P \mid chains(l); size_{ij}; p_{ij} = 1; w_{ij} = size_{ij} \mid \sum w_{ij} C_{ij}$. At the current stage of this research work, this question can be answered at least partly. When comparing Algorithms 1 and 2, it becomes clear that a computational advantage might arise from skipping the subset-sum heuristic when its application would be useless. Therefore, an analysis was conducted to quantify the potential time savings under the assumption of a perfect prediction or algorithm selection. The results reported in Table 4 for each maximum task size and grouped by the number of tasks were obtained by putting the runtime of the subset-sum heuristic (using a maximum aperture size window of 500) in relation to the runtime of both the subset-sum and the B&B algorithm executed in sequence. Accordingly, computation time reductions of up to 19% are possible. Clearly, these results reflect best-case scenarios, imposing upper bounds on the "real" time savings achievable when applying one of the learning-based prediction approaches.

7 Conclusion and Outlook

A learning-based algorithm selection approach for a special kind of multiprocessor scheduling problem has been presented, with feature selection and engineering as the core components of the contribution. Although some of these features include subset sum-related considerations, which would basically fit the target concept much better, the systematic feature selection and elimination facilities provided by `scikit-learn` identified a small set of relatively simple yet crafted features as the most effective ones. Extensive computational experiments give evidence for a solid performance of the custom feature-driven classifiers, yielding accuracy scores of up to 90% on problem instances with similar structural properties while still exhibiting reasonable accuracies in extrapolation scenarios.

Future work will be concerned with the potential derivation of additional and even more effective features with regard to the extrapolation performance. Furthermore, the actual embedding of the trained classifiers in the overall solution procedure will be one of the next steps, aiming to quantify the actual computational advantage arising from the proposed algorithm selection approach.

Acknowledgments. The financial support by the Austrian Federal Ministry for Digital and Economic Affairs, the National Foundation for Research, Technology and Development, and the Christian Doppler Research Association is gratefully acknowledged.

References

1. Scikit-learn user guide, ensemble methods. https://scikit-learn.org/stable/modules/ensemble.html. Accessed 31 May 2024
2. Blazewicz, J., Kovalyov, M., Machowiak, M., Trystram, D., Weglarz, J.: Preemptable malleable task scheduling problem. IEEE Trans. Comput. **55**(4), 486–490 (2006)
3. Blazewicz, J., Liu, Z.: Scheduling multiprocessor tasks with chain constraints. Eur. J. Oper. Res. **94**, 231–241 (1996)
4. Braune, R.: Lower bounds for a bin packing problem with linear usage cost. Eur. J. Oper. Res. **274**(1), 49–64 (2019). https://doi.org/10.1016/j.ejor.2018.10.004

5. Braune, R.: Packing-based branch-and-bound for discrete malleable task scheduling. J. Sched. **25**, 675–704 (2022). https://doi.org/10.1007/s10951-022-00750-w
6. Braune, R., Doerner, K.F.: Real-world flexible resource profile scheduling with multiple criteria: learning scalarization functions for MIP and heuristic approaches. J. Oper. Res. Soc. **68**(8), 952–972 (2017). https://doi.org/10.1057/s41274-017-0239-y
7. Bringmann, K.: A near-linear pseudopolynomial time algorithm for subset sum. In: Proceedings of the 2017 Annual ACM-SIAM Symposium on Discrete Algorithms (SODA), pp. 1073–1084. https://doi.org/10.1137/1.9781611974782.69
8. Drozdowski, M.: Scheduling for Parallel Processing. Computer Communications and Networks. Springer Verlag, London (2009)
9. Freund, Y., Schapire, R.E.: A decision-theoretic generalization of on-line learning and an application to boosting. J. Comput. Syst. Sci. **55**(1), 119–139 (1997). https://doi.org/10.1006/jcss.1997.1504, https://www.sciencedirect.com/science/article/pii/S002200009791504X
10. Frohner, N., Gmys, J., Melab, N., Raidl, G., Talbi, E.G.: Parallel beam search for combinatorial optimization. In: Workshop Proceedings of the 51st International Conference on Parallel Processing. ICPP Workshops 2022, Association for Computing Machinery, New York, NY, USA (2023). https://doi.org/10.1145/3547276.3548633
11. Graham, R.L., Lawler, E.L., Lenstra, J.K., Rinnooy Kan, A.H.G.: Optimization and approximation in deterministic sequencing and scheduling: a survey. Ann. Oper. Res. **5**, 187–326 (1979)
12. Korf, R.E.: An improved algorithm for optimal bin packing. In: Proceedings of the 18th International Joint Conference on Artificial Intelligence, pp. 1252–1258. IJCAI 2003, Morgan Kaufmann Publishers Inc., San Francisco, CA, USA (2003). http://dl.acm.org/citation.cfm?id=1630659.1630838
13. Martello, S., Toth, P.: Knapsack Problems: Algorithms and Computer Implementations. John Wiley and Sons, New York (1990)
14. Pedregosa, F., et al.: Scikit-learn: machine learning in python. J. Mach. Learn. Res. **12**, 2825–2830 (2011)

Using the Pilot Method as a Problem-Independent Metaheuristic for Multi-objective Beam Search

Oliver Bindreiter(✉), Bernhard Werth, and Stefan Wagner

Heuristic and Evolutionary Algorithms Laboratory, University of Applied Sciences Upper Austria, 4232 Hagenberg, Austria
oliver.bindreiter@fh-hagenberg.at

Abstract. This paper proposes a combination of multi-objective beam search and the pilot method. The idea is to use the pilot method as a problem-independent metaheuristic to guide the search process of multi-objective beam search. Through this combination, the newly created search algorithm is less dependent on problem specific heuristics, which would otherwise be required to guide the search process. Especially when dealing with problems where no well-known heuristic functions exist this approach can be feasible. It must be noted, that in this situation, the design of the required heuristic functions is a challenging task because a deep understanding of the underlying problem as well as the chosen search algorithm is required. The proposed methodology does not use multiple heuristic functions to evaluate nodes. Instead, a sub search process in the form of the pilot method is started to obtain an estimation for the node's quality. This sub search process is a single target search process and can only provide an estimation for one of the problems target functions. Therefore, the target functions are now also used as heuristic functions. Applying this new search algorithm to well-known benchmark problems yielded promising results and generates high quality solutions compared with current state-of-the-art algorithms.

Keywords: metaheuristic · multi-objective optimization · multi-objective beam search · beam search · pilot method

1 Introduction and Related Work

As part of an ongoing project in the field of scheduling, preliminary experiments showed that multi-objective beam search combined with the pilot method as metaheuristic can yield high quality results and compete with other methodologies to solve the underlying problem.

The effect of the chosen heuristic functions on the overall performance as well as the achieved quality of the solutions when using multi-objective beam search is presented in [2]. Furthermore, the authors explore the limits associated with problem specific heuristic functions and their impact on the efficiency of

A. Quesada-Arencibia et al. (Eds.): EUROCAST 2024, LNCS 15174, pp. 61–68, 2025.
https://doi.org/10.1007/978-3-031-83885-9_6

the search process. However, these insights focus only on integer multi-objective optimization problems. A different method through a backtracking approach was proposed in [6].

The overall usefulness of a tree encoding with a subsequent solving through beam search was shown in [9] where the authors used beam search to solve scheduling problems and achieved high quality results. A filtering approach to further improve the quality of obtained solutions when using beam search was proposed in [7]. Also solving a container loading problem proved to be feasible using beam in search in [1].

More recently beam search also proved to be a viable methodology in combination with Large Language Models like the authors of [8] showed. The authors used beam search in combination with gradient descent to achieve promising results in the field of Automatic Prompt Optimization. In the domain of puzzle solving, a combination of beam search with Monte Carlo tree search was able to match the performance of existing solving mechanism. This was shown in [4].

Overall beam search is a versatile tool for solving different problems. The proposed combination aims to make beam search even more applicable in the fields of multi-objective optimization as well as highly custom problem instances where good heuristics functions are not always available.

2 Multi-Objective Beam Search and Pilot Method Look-Ahead

Beam search extends breadth first search by a heuristic function and an additional parameter called beam width. It was first presented in [3]. The beam width parameter limits the number of nodes that are considered by the search process at each layer of the tree. To determine which nodes should be considered and which should be discarded, the heuristic function is used. Estimating the quality of a given node and its corresponding subtree by using the heuristic function makes it possible to order all the expanded nodes in each layer by their respective heuristic values. Given this order the best nodes per layer are selected for expansion while the remaining nodes will be discarded. This means that beam search is not exhaustive and depends on the heuristic function to guide it as well as a reasonable choice for the beam width to prune unfavorable parts of the tree. However, it is only applicable for single target optimization problems.

To make beam search applicable to multi-objective optimization problems more heuristic functions are required to estimate a nodes quality for each target function. Additionally, the selection of the best nodes per layer must be adapted, since there are now multiple heuristic values for each node that must be considered for the order. Inspired by NSGA-II (as described in [5]), the best nodes are determined by non-dominated sorting. Additionally, after choosing the best nodes from a set of Pareto optimal fronts a crowding factor is used to establish an order within a single front should the beam width limit make it impossible to select all nodes on a given front.

In contrast to beam search, the pilot method proposed in [10], uses a look-ahead to steer the search process in desirable subtrees. To obtain an estimation for a node's quality, a simple depth first search is performed until a terminal state is reached. The value of the target function of this terminal state is then used as a heuristic estimator for the entire subtree in question. Once all successor nodes have an estimated quality value assigned to them, the best one is chosen and the process repeats. Overall, the pilot method performs a heuristic depth first search where the target function is also used as a heuristic function. This characteristic is beneficial if no suitable heuristic functions are available.

When combining multi-objective beam search and the pilot method, the heuristic functions required by beam search are replaced by the pilot method. Every time the quality of a node is estimated a single target pilot method search process is started instead. This not only combines breadth first search with depth first search elements, but also removes the necessity for heuristic functions completely. Moreover, the final set of Pareto optimal solutions now also consists of nodes expanded through the look-ahead and not only of the best nodes per layer. The beam width parameter remains unchanged and is still required. However, given that a pilot method look-ahead is performed for every target function, the beam width can be set to lower values resulting in a narrower search.

3 Experiments and Results

The evaluation of the proposed combination was carried out by solving multiple instances of the knapsack problem. To adapt this well-known standard problem for multi-objective optimization, a new profit value was added to all the items. This change yields a binary knapsack problem. Additionally, a second target function was added, which is identical to the original target function as it also dictates a maximization of the newly added profit values. The capacity constraint and the weights associated with the items remained unchanged. All of the problem instances were randomly generated. The generated profit and weight values are sampled from a normal random distribution. To ensure that most of the sampled values lie within the range of 10 to 100 the mean of the normal random distribution was set to be 55 with a standard deviation of 22.5. If values outside of this range were sampled, they were disregarded, and a new value was sampled. This correcting behavior was chosen to prevent possible issues when using clipping methods or other correcting measures. Furthermore, no correlation between the profits or weights was added to prevent possible effects on performance due to the correlation. It must be noted that the profit values and weights are integer values and therefore rounding is required. Moreover, the generated problem instances are chosen to be very restrictive in terms of the size of the knapsack. The chosen capacities range from 0.2% to 10% of the total weight of all the items. This decision was made to show the potential of the algorithms on problem instances where state-of-the-art algorithms like NSGA-II show poor performance. The reason for this poor performance lies in the rather large search space, which hosts only a small number of valid solutions due to the restrictive nature of the problem instances. Figure 1 depicts this poor performance of the NSGA-II compared to beam search and the combination of beam search and the pilot method. The used problem instance for this comparison can be found in Table 1 as 'Problem 1'. The beam width of beam search and the combination of beam search and the pilot method was set to 2. The population size of NSGA-II was set to 100 with a maximum number of generations of 1000. The mutation probability was set to 5% using a single bit flip mutation operator. Crossover was performed with a probability of 90% by randomly choosing either n-point crossover, single point crossover or uniform crossover. Due to the non-deterministic nature of NSGA-II 5 repetitions were carried out.

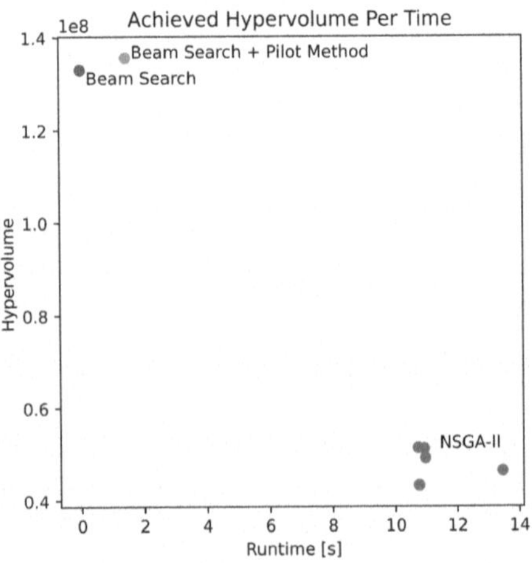

Fig. 1. Achieved hypervolume per runtime for beam search, beam search & the pilot method and NSGA-II

A factor that influences the effectiveness and achieved quality of a tree search algorithm is the structure of the traversed search space or search tree in this case. Two fundamental decisions have to be made when generating the search space. First is the order of the layers in the tree. For the knapsack problem this corresponds to the order in which decision for and against certain items are made. The second ordering that impacts the search behavior is the order of the successor nodes of a given node. In case of the knapsack problem, this corresponds to whether the choice to put a given item in the knapsack is the left or right successor of a node. The pilot method is especially affected by this choice, since it has an inherent left drift and always expands nodes that are further left in any given tree. To maximize the effectiveness of the look-ahead, it is therefore beneficial that the greediest successor is the leftmost successor. For the conducted experiments the left successor always represents the choice to put an item in the knapsack, whereas the right successor represents the decision against this item. The order of the layers is part of the analysis but will be fixed to the highest summed profit per weight to lowest if not stated otherwise. Also, the generated search spaces do not contain any invalid solutions in the form of overfull knapsacks which limits the size of the tree to some extent. This is possible through an validation step when expanding a given node.

Another relevant aspect for the evaluation of the algorithms is the chosen heuristic function for beam search. To guide the search process of beam search in the most promising parts of the search tree, the following heuristic function was utilized. For any given node, be it a terminal node or an internal node, sum up the profits of all the chosen items so far and divide the result by the number of chosen items. This steers the search process towards solutions with a high profit to item ratio. Throughout all of the conducted experiments, this heuristic function remained unchanged. Since both targets functions of the binary knapsack problem are identical, the heuristic functions are also chosen to be identical. The only differences are the profits, which are used to calculate the total profit so far. Meaning either the original profit values or the newly added profit values are taken into account, but never both at the same time.

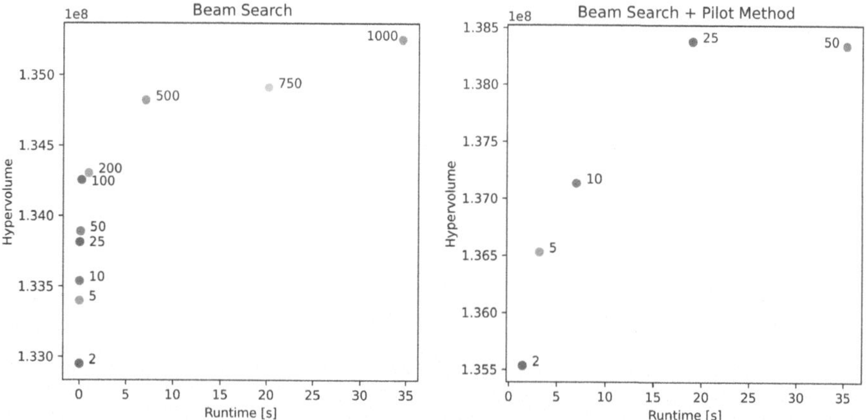

Fig. 2. Achieved hypervolume per runtime for different beam width settings of beam search (left) and beam search & the pilot method (right)

To determine suitable beam width parameters for beam search and the combination of beam search and the pilot method, different values for the beam width were tested on a single problem instance. The achieved hypervolume of the final set of Pareto optimal solutions and the runtime for every beam width can be seen in Fig. 2. The results for the beam width tests can be seen on the left side, whereas the right side depicts the combination of beam search and the pilot method. A runtime limit of 35 s was introduced as an upper bound. It can be clearly stated that even with significantly smaller beam widths, the pilot method look-ahead achieves better results in the form of higher hypervolumes compared to beam search without the pilot method look-ahead. Both algorithms however reach a point where an increased beam width primarily effects the runtime but not the achieved hypervolume. This point is reached at 500 for beam search and 25 for the combination of beam search and the pilot method. Therefore, for all the following tests, the beam widths were fixed to equal those values respectively.

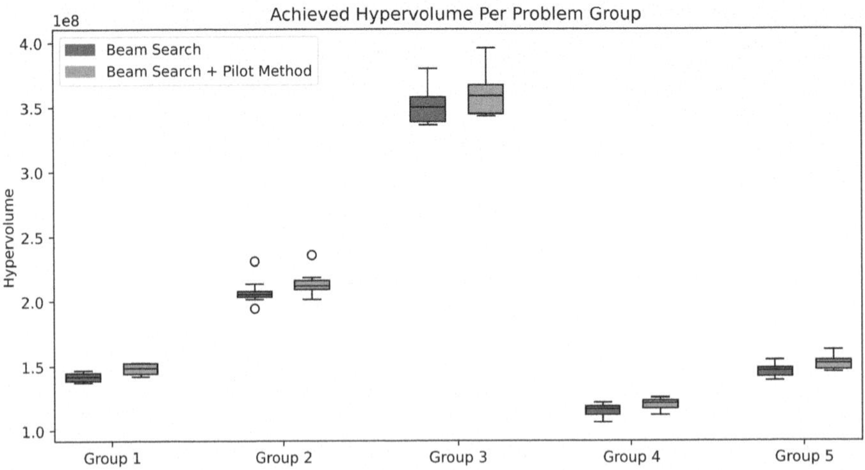

Fig. 3. Achieved hypervolume per algorithm and problem group

Table 1. Properties of the problem groups

Problem Group #	Number of Items	Size of Knapsack (relative)	Size of Knapsack (total)
1	1.000	10%	~ 5500
2	2.000	5%	~ 5500
3	5.000	2%	~ 5500
4	10.000	0.4%	~ 2200
5	20.000	0.2%	~ 2200

To analyze the performance of the algorithms when confronted with problem instances of different sizes and properties, 5 groups of problem instances were created. These groups differ in the number of items and capacity, as well as the ratio of items to capacity. Each group consists of 10 different problems with the same properties. The properties of the problem groups can be found in Table 1. It must be noted that the relative size of the knapsack refers to the percentage of the sum of all the weights, which can fit into knapsack, and the total size of the knapsack refers to the actual capacity value. Figure 3 depicts the achieved hypervolume of the final set of Pareto optimal solutions for both algorithms for all 5 problem groups. It can be stated that for all problem groups the achieved hypervolume of the combination of beam search and the pilot method are significantly higher than the achieved hypervolume of beam search alone. Moreover, the proposed combination of beam search and the pilot method acts as a black box algorithm since no knowledge of the underlying knapsack problem is used to guide the search process, whereas the used heuristic of beam search utilized problem specific details to guide the search process. This indicates a successful replacement of the problem dependent heuristic functions with the problem independent pilot method.

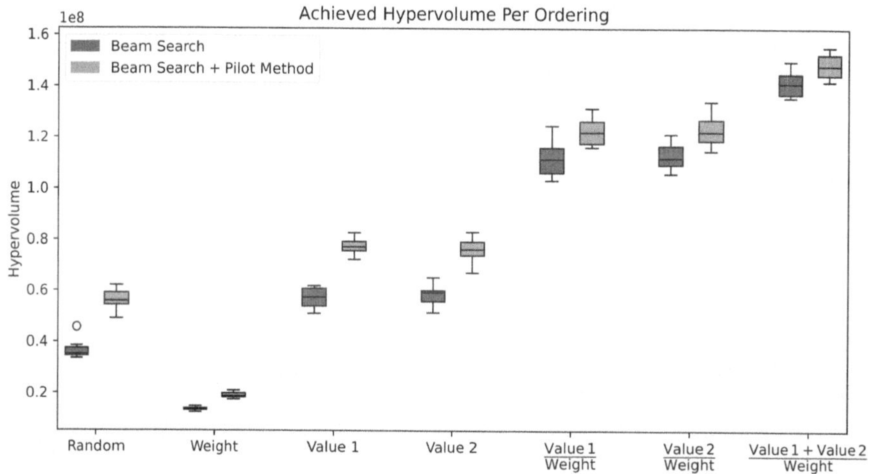

Fig. 4. Achieved hypervolume per algorithm and ordering of items

As previously mentioned, the overall structure of the search tree greatly effects the search process. While the order of the successor nodes greatly impacts the results, the same is true for the order in which decisions for the items are made. Since the best order of choices is often unknown and identifying it requires deep insight in the underlying problem, a certain resilience of the algorithm regarding the order of choices and the overall structure of the tree is desirable. Therefore, 7 possible orderings of the items in the knapsack problem were tested. Figure 4 shows the achieved hypervolume per algorithm for those orderings. For each combination of algorithm and ordering, 10 problem instances were tested. It can be stated that regardless of the used ordering, the combination of beam search and the pilot method always achieves significantly better values for the hypervolume than beam search alone. This indicates a more robust algorithm for black box solving.

4 Conclusion and Outlook

Overall, it could be shown that the replacement of the problem dependent heuristic functions with the problem independent pilot method led to a more resilient and better performing algorithm when compared to the original beam search. It could also be shown that state-of-the-art algorithms can be beaten in certain scenarios. However, a drawback of the proposed algorithm is runtime. With an increasing number of target functions more and more look-ahead search processes have to be started at each layer in the tree. Combined with the fact that heuristic functions are typically fast to evaluate this leads to overall higher runtimes. One possibility to mitigate this issue to some degree would be to never expand a subtree twice by caching look-ahead values of previous look-ahead runs and reusing them on lower layers in the tree. It must be emphasized that the idea of this proposed combination is not to outperform state-of-the-art algorithms but to create an algorithm which can be used when no good heuristic functions are available.

Acknowledgments. The work described in this paper was done within the project Adaptive scheduling in multi-stage production systems with sensor-based predictions for reducing energy consumption (SCHED-ENERGY), #891173 within the funding program Production of the Future, 41st call - by the Austrian Research Promotion Agency (FFG) and funded by the Republic of Austria.

References

1. Araya, I., Riff, M.C.: A beam search approach to the container loading problem. Comput. Oper. Res. **43**, 100–107 (2014)
2. Barthelemy, T., Parragh, S.N., Tricoire, F., Hartl, R.F.: Beam search for integer multi-objective optimization (2015)
3. Bisiani, R.: Encyclopedia of Artificial Intelligence, pp. 56–58. Wiley & Sons, Hoboken (1987)
4. Cazenave, T.: Monte Carlo beam search. IEEE Trans. Comput. Intell. AI Games **4**(1), 68–72 (2012)
5. Deb, K., Pratap, A., Agarwal, S., Meyarivan, T.: A fast and elitist multiobjective genetic algorithm: NSGA-II. IEEE Trans. Evol. Comput. **6**, 182–197 (2002)
6. Honda, N.: Backtrack beam search for multiobjective scheduling problem. In: Tanio, T., Tanaka, T., Inuiguchi, M. (eds.) Multi-Objective Programming and Goal Programming. Advances in Soft Computing, vol. 21, pp. 147–152. Springer, Berlin, Heidelberg (2003). https://doi.org/10.1007/978-3-540-36510-5_19
7. Ow, P.S., Morton, T.E.: Filtered beam search in scheduling. Int. J. Prod. Res. **26**(1), 35–62 (1988)
8. Pryzant, R., Iter, D., Li, J., Lee, Y.T., Zhu, C., Zeng, M.: Automatic prompt optimization with "gradient descent" and beam search (2023)
9. Sabuncuoglu, I., Bayiz, M.: Job shop scheduling with beam search. Eur. J. Oper. Res. **118**(2), 390–412 (1999)
10. Voss, S., Duin, C., Fink, A.: Looking ahead with the pilot method. Ann. Oper. Res. **136**, 225–242 (2005)

Solving Two-Machine Sum-Cost Flow Shop Problem on D-Wave Quantum Annealer

Wojciech Bożejko[1(✉)], Ryszard Klempous[1], Mariusz Uchroński[1,2], and Mieczysław Wodecki[1]

[1] Wrocław University of Science and Technology, Janiszewskiego 11-17, 50-372 Wrocław, Poland
{wojciech.bozejko,ryszard.kelmpous,mariusz.uchronski, mieczyslaw.wodecki}@pwr.edu.pl

[2] Wroclaw Centre for Networking and Supercomputing, Wybrzeże Wyspiańskiego 27, 50-370 Wrocław, Poland

Abstract. The work concerns the use of D-Wave's quantum cloud service to solve the NP-hard flow shop scheduling problem with due dates and with the criterion of maximizing the weighted number of tasks performed on time. Constrained Quadratic Model, Binary Constrained Quadratic Model, and Binary Unconstrained Quadratic Model were proposed. Load experiments were carried out in a hybrid D-Wave *LeapHybridCQMSampler* environment using a combination of metaheuristics and quantum annealing, and *DWaveSampler* natively implementing quantum annealing. Calculations in the *DWaveSampler* environment are performed very quickly, but their practical application is currently limited due to the relatively small number of available qubits.

Keywords: Scheduling · Discrete optimization · Quantum computing

1 Introduction

Quantum computers can already be successfully used to solve NP-hard discrete optimization problems. However, in the case of practical problems, due to the small number of qubits currently available, they are not competitive with traditional computations on CPUs. In anticipation of significant increases in the computational power of quantum computers, computations are limited to small-sized examples. Despite this, there is great interest in research on methods for constructing new algorithms that take into account the specificity of quantum computing. For many problems, this is a big challenge. However, the results of current research will make it possible in the future to significantly shift the barrier, which limits the size of examples that can be solved in an acceptable time.

In the two-machine flow shop problem with profit maximization considered in this paper, a set of tasks and two machines are given. Every task must be performed on the first machine and then on the second machine, with the order

A. Quesada-Arencibia et al. (Eds.): EUROCAST 2024, LNCS 15174, pp. 69–78, 2025.
https://doi.org/10.1007/978-3-031-83885-9_7

in which the tasks are performed on both machines is the same. The duration times for tasks and their due dates (on the second machine) are also given as the weight resulting from completing the task on time. One should determine the order in which tasks are performed that minimizes profit: a weighted number of tasks performed on time. The problem under consideration belongs to the NP-hard class, as it is a generalization of the NP-hard single-machine problem with this criterion (Karp [6]).

In this paper, we present a new method for solving this scheduling problem. We formulate three mathematical models: The constrained Quadratic Model (CQM), the Constrained Binary Quadratic Model, and the Quadratic Unconstrained Binary Optimization model (QUBO). The CQM and QUBO models were implemented and run in the D-Wave quantum annealer environment. Computational experiments were performed to compare the effectiveness of both approaches. The results indicate limited applicability of the QUBO model due to the relatively small number of available qubits in existing quantum machines. The paper c is a continuation of the authors' work on constructing computational models of difficult optimization problems for quantum machines, see Bożejko et al. [2–5].

2 Description of the Problem and Its Mathematical Model

Permutational flow shop problem on two machines with maximization the total weight of tasks performed on time can be formulated as follows:
TT2FS Problem: Let a set of tasks

$$\mathcal{J} = \{1, 2, \ldots, n\},$$

and a collection of machines

$$\mathcal{M} = \{1, 2\}.$$

Task $j \in \mathcal{J}$ consists of two operations O_{j1} and O_{j2}. The operation O_{jk} corresponds to the execution of task j on machine k. For task $i \in \mathcal{J}$ we define: p_{ik} – operation execution time O_{ik}, d_i – desired due date, and w_i – weight of the profit cost function. Each task must be performed on both machines, and they must be the following restrictions are met:

(a) each task must be completed on the first and then on the second machine,
(b) tasks cannot be interrupted,
(c) a task can only be executed on one machine at a time,
(d) a machine cannot perform more than one task at a time,
(e) an order of execution of tasks on both machines must be the same.

A feasible solution may be any order of task execution that meets constraints (a)–(e). It can be represented by a certain permutation of elements (tasks) from the set $\mathcal{J}$. Let Φ be the set of all such permutations.

For the permutation $\pi \in \Phi$ (fixed order of execution of tasks on machines), let $S_{\pi(i),j}$ will be the starting moment (time) of the operation $O_{\pi(i),j}$ ($i \in \mathcal{J}$, $j = 1, 2$). Constraints (b) and (c) imply that $C_{\pi(i),j} = S_{\pi(i),j} + p_{\pi(i),j}$ is the moment of completion of the operation $O_{\pi(i),j}$. These moments can be determined from the following relationships recursively:

$$C_{\pi(i),j} = \max\{C_{\pi(i-1),j},\ C_{\pi(i),j-1}\} + p_{\pi(i),j}, \quad i = 1, 2, \ldots, n, \quad j = 1, 2, \tag{1}$$

with initial conditions:

$$C_{\pi(0),j} = 0, \quad j = 1, 2 \text{ i } C_{\pi(i),0} = 0, \quad i = 1, 2, \ldots, n, \tag{2}$$

or non-recursively

$$\mathcal{C}_{\pi(k)} = C_{\pi(k),2} = \max\left\{\sum_{i=1}^{k-s} p_{\pi(i),1} + \sum_{i=k-s}^{k} p_{\pi(i),2} : s = 0, 1, \ldots, k-1\right\}, \tag{3}$$

for $k = 1, 2, \ldots, n$. By $\mathcal{C}_{\pi(k)} = C_{\pi(k),2}$ we denote the deadline for completing the task $\pi(k)$, i.e. the operation $O_{\pi(k),2}$. Then

$$U_{\pi(i)} = \begin{cases} 0 \text{ if } \mathcal{C}_{\pi(i)} \leq d_{\pi(i)}, \\ 1 \text{ if } \mathcal{C}_{\pi(i)} > d_{\pi(i)}. \end{cases} \tag{4}$$

is the *binary tardiness* of task $\pi(i)$, and $w_{\pi(i)} \cdot (1 - U_{\pi(i)})$ *profit* for being $\pi(i)$ on time. Profit of performing all tasks in order π is

$$\mathcal{F}(\pi) = \sum_{i=1}^{n} w_{\pi(i)} \cdot (1 - U_{\pi(i)}). \tag{5}$$

In the problem under consideration, the order of tasks execution must be determined which maximizes the total profit of completing tasks on time, i.e., an optimal permutation $\pi^* \in \Phi$ for which

$$\mathcal{F}(\pi^*) = \min\{\mathcal{F}(\pi) : \ \pi \in \Phi\}. \tag{6}$$

The problems of task scheduling with sum-cost criteria have been considered in the literature for many years. The first work by Rinnoy Kan et al. [15] from 1975 was dedicated to a single-machine NP-hard problem. An exact algorithm was included based on the branch and bound method and computational results for small examples. Multi-machine problems were mainly considered with minimizing the number of late tasks $\sum w_i U_i$ criterion. Lenstry et al. [11] proved that this is a problem for two machines $F2||\sum U_i$ is strongly NP-hard. For the multi-machine problem $F||\sum U_i$ Hariri and Potts [10] presented an exact algorithm that can, in a reasonable amount of time, solve examples with 25 tasks and 3 machines. Multi-machine problems with minimizing *the sum* of late costs turn out to be much more difficult to solve. There are few works devoted to the more frequently studied problem of minimizing the sum of penalties for untimely execution of tasks on two machines $F2||\sum w_iU_i$ and methods of solving it. Liao et al. [12] presented an algorithm based on the tabu search method. Review of methods, algorithms and related publications on multi-machine task scheduling problems with sum-cost criteria is presented in the works of: Gupta and Kumar [9], Adamu and Adewumi [1], Vallady et al. [17], Penna [14] and Chen et al. [7].

Currently, no properties are known for multi-machine task scheduling problems with sum-cost criteria enabling an indirect overview of the elements of the solution set or indicating areas with promising solutions. In the case of minimizing the completion time of tasks with the $C_{\max}$ criterion, the properties of blocks from the critical path (Nowicki and Smutnicki [13] and Grabowski and Wodecki [8]) significantly improved the effectiveness of exact algorithms and metaheuristics. Unfortunately, such properties have not been formulated yet for the objective function under consideration.

In the further part of the work, we propose three models of representation of the considered problem that allow it to be run in the D-Wave quantum computer environment.

3 Constrained Quadratic Model – CQM

In this section, we propose a constrained quadratic programming model for the considered problem. It allows the solution (or its upper bound if the optimization is not exact) to be determined using quantum annealing.

By $\mathcal{C}_i$ we mean the moment of completion of the task i on the last (second) machine. Let matrix $\mathbf{x}=[x_{ij}]_{n\times n}$ where $x_{ij} \in \{0,1\}$. We must determine

$$\max \sum_i \sum_j w_j x_{ij} \tag{7}$$

subject to

$$\mathcal{C}_i \le \sum_{j=1}^{n} d_i x_{ji}, \;\; i = 1,2,\ldots,n, \tag{8}$$

$$\sum_{i=1}^{n} x_{ij} \le 1, \; j = 1,2,\ldots,n, \tag{9}$$

$$\sum_{j=1}^{n} x_{ij} \le 1, \; i = 1,2,\ldots,n. \tag{10}$$

$$\left(\sum_{i=1}^{j}\sum_{s=1}^{n} p_{s1}x_{is}\right) + \left(\sum_{i=j}^{k}\sum_{s=1}^{n} p_{s2}x_{is}\right) \le \mathcal{C}_k, \; j = 1,2,\ldots,k, \; k = 1,2,\ldots,n, \tag{11}$$

$$\mathcal{C}_i \in \mathbb{N} \cup \{0\}, \; i = 1,2,\ldots,n, \tag{12}$$

$$x_{ij} \in \{0,1\}, \; i,j = 1,2,\ldots,n. \tag{13}$$

The matrix $\boldsymbol{x}$ is interpreted as follows: if $x_{ij} = 1$, then a task j on the position i in the schedule is on time; elsewhere, it is 0.

4 Binary Constrained Quadratic Model

Formulating the problem for the quantum annealer requires placing constraints directly in the objective function. To do this, the constraints should be in the form of qualities, and the variables should be binary. In this section, we propose a binary model with equality constraints:

$$\max \sum_i \sum_j w_j x_{ij} \tag{14}$$

subject to

$$\sum_{s=1}^{\widehat{C}} s \cdot y_{si} = \sum_{j=1}^{n} d_i x_{ji}, \;\; i = 1, 2, \ldots, n, \tag{15}$$

$$\sum_{i=1}^{n} x_{ij} = \sum_{k=0}^{1} k \cdot a_{jk} = a_{j1}, \;\; j = 1, 2, \ldots, n, \tag{16}$$

$$\sum_{j=1}^{n} x_{ij} = \sum_{k=0}^{1} k \cdot b_{ik} = b_{i1}, \;\; i = 1, 2, \ldots, n. \tag{17}$$

$$\left(\sum_{i=1}^{j} \sum_{s=1}^{n} p_{s1} x_{is}\right) + \left(\sum_{i=j}^{k} \sum_{s=1}^{n} p_{s2} x_{is}\right) = \sum_{s=1}^{\widehat{C}} s \cdot y_{sk}, \;\; j = 1, 2, \ldots, k, \;\; k = 1, 2, \ldots, n, \tag{18}$$

$$\sum_{s=1}^{\widehat{C}} y_{si} = 1, \;\; i = 1, 2, \ldots, n, \tag{19}$$

$$a_{j0} + a_{j1} = 1, \;\; j = 1, 2, \ldots, n, \tag{20}$$

$$b_{i0} + b_{i1} = 1, \;\; i = 1, 2, \ldots, n, \tag{21}$$

$$x_{ij}, a_{i0}, a_{i1}, b_{i0}, b_{i1} \in \{0, 1\}, \;\; i, j = 1, 2, \ldots, n, \tag{22}$$

$$y_{si} \in \{0, 1\}, \;\; i = 1, 2, \ldots, n, \;\; s = 1, 2, \ldots, \widehat{C}, \tag{23}$$

where $\widehat{C} = \sum_{i=1}^{n} (p_{i1} + p_{i2})$ is a constant (completing times horizon). The variables $\boldsymbol{y}$ and $\boldsymbol{a}$ and $\boldsymbol{b}$ are auxiliary, allowing us to transform the inequality (8)–(11) into the equality form (15)–(18).

5 Quadratic Unconstrained Binary Model – QUBO

Now we propose a model without constraints – they are built into the objective function:

$$\max_{\boldsymbol{x},\boldsymbol{y},\boldsymbol{a},\boldsymbol{b}} \left[\sum_i \sum_j w_j x_{ij} \right.$$

$$-M\left(\sum_{s=1}^{\widehat{C}} s\cdot y_{si} - \sum_{j=1}^{n} d_i x_{ji}\right)^2$$

$$-M\left(\sum_{i=1}^{n} x_{ij} - a_{j1}\right)^2$$

$$-M\left(\sum_{j=1}^{n} x_{ij} - b_{i1}\right)^2$$

$$-M\left(\left(\sum_{i=1}^{j}\sum_{s=1}^{n} p_{s1}x_{is}\right) + \left(\sum_{i=j}^{k}\sum_{s=1}^{n} p_{s2}x_{is}\right) - \sum_{s=1}^{\widehat{C}} s\cdot y_{sk}\right)^2$$

$$-M\left(\sum_{s=1}^{\widehat{C}} y_{si} - 1\right)^2$$

$$-M\left(a_{j0} + a_{j1} - 1\right)^2$$

$$\left. - M\left(b_{i0} + b_{i1} - 1\right)^2 \right], \tag{24}$$

$$x_{ij} \in \{0,1\},\ i,j = 1,2,\ldots,n, \tag{25}$$

$$a_{i1}, a_{i2}, b_{i1}, b_{i2} \in \{0,1\},\ i = 1,2,\ldots,n, \tag{26}$$

$$y_{si} \in \{0,1\},\ i = 1,2,\ldots,n,\ s = 1,2,\ldots,\widehat{C}, \tag{27}$$

where $M = \widehat{C}\cdot\sum_{i=1}^{n} w_i$ is a big constant. The idea is that failure to meet any of the constraints (15)–(21) results in a value of the objective function (25) lower than that of any feasible solution (objective function is maximized; if a solution is feasible than subtracted elements with big M are zeros).

6 Computational Experiments

The calculations were performed in the *D-Wave Leap* quantum cloud environment in two configurations. The first one involved using the *LeapHybridCQMSampler* solver, which uses a hybrid CPU (and GPU) and quantum QPU processors. The second one used the native QUBO (Quadratic Unconstrained Binary Optimization) approach obtained by converting the CQM (Constrained Quadratic Model) problem to BQM (Binary Quadratic Model), which allowed the use of quantum annealing.

The calculations were performed using the following environments:

(i) `hybrid_constrained_quadratic_model_version1p` solver – `LeapHybridCQM` `Sampler` class from `dimod` package, using CPU, GPU and QPU processors, as well as metaheuristics and partially quantum annealing.
(ii) `Advantage_system6.4` solver – `DwaveSampler` class from `dimod` package, performing native quantum annealing on QPU.

and run on a machine with D-Wave *Pegasus* topology type. The number of active couplers for the D-Wave annealer was 40297, and the number of active qubits was 5627.

The calculations were performed on randomly generated examples. Each $n = 4, 5, \ldots, 10$ example was run five times due to the nondeterminism of quantum machine computations. The results are included in Table 1. The individual columns contain run number, example size n, obtained objective function value $\mathcal{F}$, computation times on the QPU quantum processor t_{QPU} (in milliseconds) and total t_{RUN} (in seconds), separately for the *LeapHybridCQMSampler* and *DWaveSampler* environments.

The solution values (F column) obtained with the *LeapHybridCQMSampler* solver are generally better, but they use much longer processor time. In turn, the

Table 1. Results of computational experiments (with limited computation time)

run	n	*LeapHybridCQMSampler*			*DWaveSampler* for QUBO	
		$\mathcal{F}$	t_{QPU} [ms]	t_{RUN} [s]	$\mathcal{F}$	t_{QPU} [ms]
1	4	17	32.05	4.97	16	16.02
2	4	17	32.05	5.17	13	16.03
3	4	17	32.04	5.10	12	16.00
4	4	17	32.02	5.08	18	16.02
5	4	17	32.05	5.18	13	15.99
1	5	26	16.03	5.00	20	16.05
2	5	26	32.06	5.35	13	16.05
3	5	26	16.03	5.02	26	16.02
4	5	26	32.06	5.23	20	16.05
5	5	26	16.03	5.00	18	16.04
1	6	45	32.07	5.24	11	16.03
2	6	45	16.01	5.00	21	15.95
3	6	45	32.09	5.31	31	16.01
4	6	45	32.05	5.46	16	15.78
5	6	45	32.08	5.09	21	16.05
1	7	38	32.06	5.19	–	–
2	7	38	32.06	5.19	–	–
3	7	38	32.05	5.31	–	–
4	7	38	31.99	5.08	–	–
5	7	38	32.10	5.39	–	–

continued

Table 1. continued

run	n	*LeapHybridCQMSampler*			*DWaveSampler* for QUBO	
		$\mathcal{F}$	t_{QPU} [ms]	t_{RUN} [s]	$\mathcal{F}$	t_{QPU} [ms]
1	8	40	16.04	5.29	–	–
2	8	40	32.08	5.21	–	–
3	8	40	15.99	5.07	–	–
4	8	40	16.06	5.29	–	–
5	8	40	16.04	5.31	–	–
1	9	51	16.00	5.09	–	–
2	9	51	16.04	5.27	–	–
3	9	51	32.10	5.43	–	–
4	9	51	32.00	5.10	–	–
5	9	51	32.00	4.72	–	–
1	10	56	31.92	5.07	–	–
2	10	56	32.03	5.33	–	–
3	10	56	15.98	5.00	–	–
4	10	56	32.11	5.34	–	–
5	10	56	31.97	5.06	–	–

– instance too big (too many qubits needed) for embedding onto QPU

quantum annealing results obtained by DWaveSampler are obtained in (practically) constant time. Directly running quantum annealing (*DWaveSampler*) is of limited use due to the requirement of a large number of qubits, which limited the size of instances to $n \leq 6$ (for $n \geq 7$ D-Wave reports an embedding error).

7 Conclusions

The paper considers an NP-hard two-machine task scheduling problem with a sum-cost criterion. Two models have been proposed for the D-Wave quantum computing environment: hybrid, using CPU and QPU *LeapHybridCQMSampler* processors, and using quantum annealing on QPU *DWaveSampler*. Experiments were performed to compare the effectiveness of these approaches. Due to the rapidly growing demand for resources (qubits needed to represent the binary variables of the model), the practical use of the *DWaveSampler* environment is today only possible to a limited extent, for instances with a size no larger than 6. The advantage of the quantum environment is a very short, practically constant, computation time. In the future, when quantum computers will have a much larger number of qubits, it will be possible to solve large practical discrete optimization problems.

Acknowledgment. We gratefully acknowledge Polish high-performance computing infrastructure PLGrid (HPC Center: ACK Cyfronet AGH) for providing computer facilities and support within computational grant no. PLG/2024/017186. Calculations have been partially carried out using resources provided by the Wroclaw Centre for Networking and Supercomputing (http://wcss.pl), grant No. 96.

References

1. Adamu, M., Adewumi, A.: Minimizing the weighted number of tardy jobs on multiple machines: a review. J. Ind. Manag. Optim. **12**(4), 1465–1493 (2016)
2. Bożejko, W., Klempous R., Rozenblit J., Pempera J., Uchroński, M., Wodecki, M.: Optimal solving of a scheduling problem using quantum annealing metaheuristics on the D-Wave quantum solver. TechRxiv, Preprint (2023). https://doi.org/10.36227/techrxiv.22677721.v1
3. Bożejko, W., Burduk, A., Pempera, J., Uchroński, M., Wodecki, M.: Optimal solving of a binary knapsack problem on a D-Wave quantum machine and its implementation in production systems. Ann. Oper. Res. (2024, in press). https://doi.org/10.1007/s10479-024-06025-1
4. Bożejko, W., Pempera, J., Uchroński, M., Wodecki, M.: Quantum annealing-driven branch and bound for the single machine total weighted number of tardy jobs scheduling problem. Futur. Gener. Comput. Syst. **155**, 245–255 (2024). https://doi.org/10.1016/j.future.2024.02.016
5. Bożejko, W., Pempera, J., Uchroński, M., Wodecki, M.: Determination of the lower bounds of the goal function for a single-machine scheduling problem on D-wave quantum annealer. In: Mikyška, J., de Mulatier, C., Paszynski, M., Krzhizhanovskaya, V.V., Dongarra, J.J., Sloot, P.M. (eds.) ICCS 2023. LNCS, vol. 14077, pp. 201–208. Springer, Cham (2023). https://doi.org/10.1007/978-3-031-36030-5_16
6. Karp, R. M.: Reducibility among combinatorial problems. In: Complexity of Computer Computations (Proc. Sympos., IBM Thomas J. Watson Res. Center, Yorktown Heights, N.Y., 1972), pp. 85–103. Plenum, New York (1972)
7. Chen, X., Miao, Q., Lin, B.M.T., Sterna, M., Blazewicz, J.: Two-machine flow shop scheduling with a common due date to maximize total early work. Eur. J. Oper. Res. **300**(2), 504–511 (2022)
8. Grabowski, J., Wodecki, M.: A very fast tabu search algorithm for the permutation flow shop problem with makespan criterion. Comput. Oper. Res. **31**(11), 1891–1909 (2004)
9. Gupta, U., Kumar, S.: Minimization of weighted sum of total tardiness and make span in no wait flow shop scheduling Using different heuristic algorithm: a Review. Int. J. Adv. Eng. Sci. **5**(4), 1–10 (2015)
10. Hariri, A.M.A., Potts, C.N.: Branch and bound algorithm to minimize the number of late jobs in a permutation flowshop. Eur. J. Oper. Res. **38**, 228–237 (1989)
11. Lenstra, J.K., Rinnoy Kan, A.G.H., Brucker, Ann, P.: Complexity of machine scheduling problems. Discrete Math. **1**, 343–362 (1977)
12. Liao, C.J., Liao, L.M., Tseng, C.T.: A performance evaluation of permutation vs. non-permutation schedules in a flowshop. Int. J. Prod. Res. **44**(20), 4297–4309 (2006)
13. Nowicki, E., Smutnicki, C.: A fast tabu search algorithm for the permutation flowshop problem. Eur. J. Oper. Res. **91**(1), 160–175 (1996)

14. Penn, M., Raviv, T.: Complexity and algorithms for min cost and max profit scheduling under time-of-use electricity tariffs. J. Sched. **24**(1), 83–102 (2021). https://doi.org/10.1007/s10951-020-00674-3
15. Rinnoy Kan, A.H.G., Lageweg, B.J., Lenstra, J.K.: Minimizing total costs in one-machine scheduling. Oper. Res. **25**, 908–927 (1975)
16. Ruiz, R., Stützle, T.: A simple and effective iterated greedy algorithm for the permutation flowshop scheduling problem. Eur. J. Oper. Res. **177**(3), 2033–2049 (2007)
17. Vallada, E., Ruiz, R., Minella, G.: Minimising total tardiness in the m-machine flowshop problem: a review and evaluation of heuristics and metaheuristics. Comput. Oper. Res. **35**(4), 1350–1373 (2008)

Integrating Optimization Techniques and Live Tracking Software in Maritime Logistics

Bruno Lorenzo Arroyo-Pedraza, Sergio Leopoldo Benítez-Delgado, Airam Expósito-Márquez, Christopher Expósito-Izquierdo, and Israel López-Plata(✉)

Universidad de La Laguna, C/ Padre Herrera s/n, 38200 San Cristóbal de La Laguna, Santa Cruz de Tenerife, Spain
ilopezpl@ull.edu.es
http://www.ull.es

Abstract. The optimization of berthing operations has a significant impact on the overall performance of port infrastructures, providing various benefits such as the reduction of operational time, minimization of fuel consumption, and optimization of resource planning, among others. Berthing planning depends on the arrival of vessels at the port, which introduces a high degree of uncertainty due to its dependency on external factors. This paper presents a new decision support system aimed at managing the stay of vessels in ports. This software provides real-time tracking of vessels' positions and identifies the efficient berthing position for each incoming vessel. To determine the berthing positions, the software solves the Berth Allocation Problem (BAP), incorporating container movement costs and real-time vessel position data from the Automatic Identification System (AIS) to predict their arrival at ports. To solve this problem, the software integrates a Greedy Randomized Adaptive Search Procedure (GRASP). GRASP dynamically allocates berths, minimizing container movement expenses and orchestrating efficient vessel sequencing within port infrastructures. Results demonstrate the software's effectiveness in proactive planning, resource allocation, and congestion mitigation.

Keywords: Berth allocation problem · Greedy randomized adaptative search procedure · Vessel tracking

1 Introduction

Maritime transport is the most important mode of transport in international trade, accounting for about 80% of the overall transported volume [2]. Port infrastructures have considerably increased the number of operations performed in recent decades, making the optimization of these operations crucial for improving port performance and increasing port benefits. In particular, according to

A. Quesada-Arencibia et al. (Eds.): EUROCAST 2024, LNCS 15174, pp. 79–86, 2025.
https://doi.org/10.1007/978-3-031-83885-9_8

UNCTAD, the number of tons transported by container vessels was around 2000 million tons at the end of 2022 [10]. The optimization of vessel loading and unloading operations is highly studied in the scientific literature due to its associated benefits as well as its high complexity [1].

The Berth Allocation Problem (BAP) [4] is a logistical challenge within container port operations that seeks to assign berths to incoming vessels. The vessels arrive at the port at different time instants and use a specific space on the berthing line. In the present paper, this Berth Allocation Problem is combined with the cost of performing loading and unloading operations, with the main goal being to minimize the overall cost of transferring containers.

In this work, a Greedy Randomized Adaptive Search Procedure (GRASP) [3] is proposed to solve the BAP from an approximate point of view. This metaheuristic explores the solution space by combining exploration and exploitation, gradually refining solutions until an optimal or near-optimal solution is achieved.

Lastly, a decision support system software is proposed, whose main goal is to assist terminal managers in scheduling vessel operations. This system combines live tracking of vessel positions with optimization algorithms to create effective future berthing plans.

The remainder of this paper is organized as follows. Firstly, Sect. 2 describes the BAP proposed in this work. Section 3 details the adaptation of the GRASP to solve the proposed BAP. Section 4 describes the features provided by the created decision support system. Finally, Sect. 5 presents the main conclusions from this work and suggests several lines for further research.

2 Problem Description

This paper addresses the Berth Allocation Problem (BAP) in order to schedule the arrival of vessels at the port. A solution for this problem involves assigning vessels to specific positions along the berthing line, which influences several aspects of the loading and unloading operations, such as the number of stacking cranes assigned or the number of resources required to perform these operations. If a vessel is assigned to an occupied space in the berthing line, it must wait until the assigned space becomes available.

In the scientific literature, different variants of the BAP exist depending on whether the berthing line is divided into discrete units [4] or considered as a continuous line [6]. Other main variants of this problem are formalized according to the time instants when vessels arrive at the port. The Static BAP (SBAP) [4] assumes that all vessels to be planned have already arrived at the port. Conversely, in the Dynamic BAP (DBAP) [5], new vessels can arrive during the planning horizon. The problem solved in this work is a SBAP with a discrete berthing line.

The main goal of this problem is to minimize the cost of moving containers between vessels and storage. These movements can occur between the arrived vessels and the port (yard-berth flow) or between two different vessels (berth-berth flow). It is important to note that if a vessel is not already positioned in the berthing area, the cost of moving to or from this vessel is increased accordingly, to represent the waiting times until it becomes available. Additionally, the problem includes the following constraints:

- The berthing line is divided into discrete berths. Each berth has the capacity for one vessel.
- The berths have availability times. Outside these times, no vessel can berth.
- There are a set of prefix storage areas in the yard. The cost to move from one berth to a storage area is predefined.
- The set of container movements to be performed from/to the vessels is known in advance.
- The time during which each vessel is occupying its assigned berth is also known in advance.

Figure 1 shows an example solution for the BAP addressed in this paper, including the berth-berth flows (in blue) and yard-berth flows (in red). Additionally, the grey zones represent the times when the specific berth is not available.

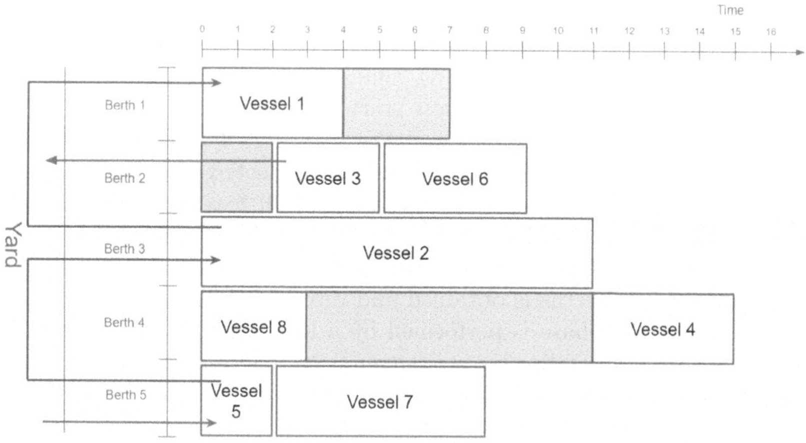

Fig. 1. Example of solution for Berth Allocation Problem (Color figure online)

3 Optimization Approach

In order to solve the BAP in Sect. 2, a Greedy Randomized Adaptive Search Procedure (GRASP) [3] is proposed. In general terms, a GRASP is an iterative metaheuristic based on two main phases: the first phase creates feasible solutions with constructive algorithms (constructive phase) while the second phase is dedicated to improving the quality of the found solutions (intensification phase). If the solution obtained after the two phases improves the best solution found, this

Algorithm 1 Constructive phase of GRASP

Input: N_v. Number of vessels
Input: *topV*. Top vessels to be selected
Input: *topS*. Top solutions to be selected
1: $orderedVessels \leftarrow$ Sort vessels by arrival time
2: $initialSolution \leftarrow$ Empty solution
3: **for** $i \leftarrow 0$ to N_v **do**
4: $\quad vessel \leftarrow randomVessel(orderedVessels, topV)$
5: $\quad possibleSolutions \leftarrow getAllFeasibleSolutions(initialSolution, vessel)$
6: $\quad initialSolution \leftarrow randomSolution(possibleSolutions, topS)$
7: **end for**
8: Return $initialSolution$

best solution is updated. The process is repeated until a specific stop criterion is met. The GRASP has demonstrated high performance when tackling a wide range of heterogeneous problems, such as those in [7,8], among others.

The constructive phase of the proposed GRASP is depicted in Algorithm 1, whose main strategy is to assign vessels to berths according to their arrival time. Firstly, the algorithm orders the list of vessels by arrival time (line 1) and, starting from an empty solution (line 2), assigns the vessels to berths iteratively. The assignment process is repeated N_n times (line 3), one iteration per vessel to be assigned. The assignment process starts by selecting one vessel from the first *topV* unassigned vessels to arrive at the port (line 4). Then, the algorithm explores all possible feasible solutions when the selected vessel is assigned to the current solution (line 5) and, from the list of all feasible solutions, selects one random solution among the *topS* solutions according to the lowest objective function value (line 6). Once the iterative process ends, a feasible solution with all vessels assigned to berths is obtained and returned (line 8).

The intensification phase is performed by a local search which explores the solution space using the following movements, considering an assignment as a pair (v_i, b_j), where vessel v_i is assigned to berth b_j:

- *Swap positions.* Trades the position of two vessels, including the assigned berth and order. So, for example, a solution composed of $r = \{(v_1, b_1), (v_2, b_2)\}$ once swapping v_1 for v_2, will result in $r = \{(v_2, b_1), (v_1, b_2)\}$.
- *Vessel reinsertion.* Puts one vessel in front of the other. For example, a solution composed of $r = \{(v_1, b_1), (v_2, b_2), (v_3, b_3)\}$, when reinserting v_1 in front of v_3 will result in $r = \{(v_2, b_2), (v_3, b_3), (v_1, b_3)\}$.

4 Decision Support System

The decision support system proposed in this work seeks to help terminal managers assign the correct berth to each incoming vessel, as well as to control and predict the arrival of new vessels at the port. Thus, the software provides the following main functionalities:

- Harnesses the wealth of real-time data from Automatic Identification System (AIS) [9] sources, allowing comprehensive monitoring of vessel positions globally.
- Forecasts vessel arrivals at the port employing predictive algorithms, enabling proactive planning and resource allocation.
- Optimizes the arrangement of vessels within port infrastructures based on predicted arrival times, particularly in the berthing line.

The use of this software maximizes port infrastructure utilization, minimizes congestion, and optimizes the overall logistical flow, ensuring smoother operations and enhanced efficiency within the complex maritime environment.

The functionalities implemented in the decision support system are divided into the following three main sections.

4.1 Live Tracker

Live tracker of the decision support system shows real-time vessel positions according to data obtained from the Automatic Identification System (AIS). This allows the terminal manager to follow the status of every vessel worldwide. Additionally, the live tracker provides its information to prediction algorithms that estimate the arrival of vessels to ports. This information is consequently used to solve the Berth Allocation Problem (see Sect. 4.3).

The tracker implements several filters to present the terminal manager with only the information relevant to its operations. The filters allow searching for vessels by name, IMO, MMSI, destination port, or navigation status, among others. The system provides users with complete information about vessels using two different and complementary controllers:

- *Display vessel positions and orientations geolocated on a map.* This map controller includes two options to enrich the map information. The first option indicates if the user wants to see all available ports, and the second option allows showing or hiding the path followed by the vessels. Additionally, if a vessel is selected on the map, the tracker focuses the information only on that vessel. Figure 2 shows an example of the live tracker using the map controller.
- *Visualize the main information of vessels using a table.* The information displayed on the table includes the vessel name, IMO, MMSI, arrival port, and estimated time of arrival (ETA) at the port. Additionally, each row includes a button that focuses the selected vessel on the map controller.

4.2 Ports and Vessels Information

This section of the decision support system provides complete information about all ports and vessels stored in the system. The information is presented in the form of a table and, like the live tracker explained in Sect. 4.1, it can be filtered according to different fields. For vessels, these fields include name, IMO,

Fig. 2. Live tracking of vessels within the decision support system

MMSI, destination port, and navigation status. For ports, the fields include name, LOCODE, country, type of port (*e.g.*, bulk, ro-ro, fishing, and more), services offered, and port capacity.

To obtain more details about specific ports or vessels, complete information is accessible if the user clicks on a row of their corresponding table. Vessel information comprises general data, navigation data, AIS information, and a vessel picture. Figure 3 shows an example of a vessel information screen.

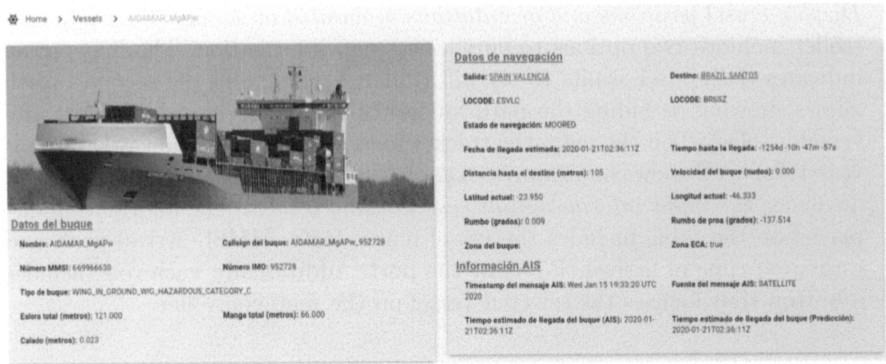

Fig. 3. Vessel information

Port information includes general data, map position, and port pictures. Besides, this section includes the following options aimed at controlling vessel traffic at the port:

- Check vessels' arrival and departure historical data.
- Create a berthing plan according to the next vessels to arrive at the port. This option is explained in detail in Sect. 4.3.
- See upcoming vessel arrivals and departures at the port, as well as the vessels currently berthed.

4.3 Berthing Management

The present section helps terminal managers create a berthing plan for vessels arriving at the port in the near future. To create this plan, the BAP explained in Sect. 2 is solved with a planning horizon of one week, using the GRASP technique explained in Sect. 3.

The berthing plan is presented as a Gantt diagram to emphasize the temporal component. Each line in the Gantt diagram represents a berth at the port, and the elements on the line represent the time a vessel occupies that berth. This view allows for easy checking of the congestion of the berthing line and detection of free spaces to be used in unforeseen circumstances. Figure 4 shows an example of the berthing plan view.

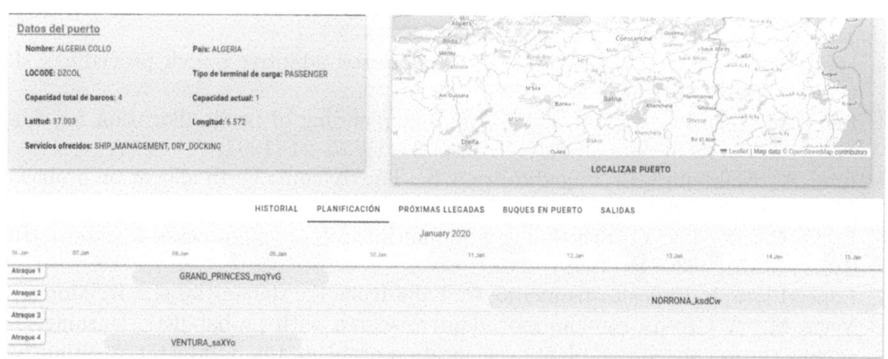

Fig. 4. Berthing plan within the decision support system

5 Conclusions and Future Work

This paper presents a decision support system focused on aiding berthing management. This system allows the control of the status of every vessel worldwide with live tracking. Additionally, it integrates advanced optimization methods to solve the Berth Allocation Problem (BAP) considering container movement costs and provides optimized berthing plans to terminal managers. The integration of these techniques into management software enhances efficiency and maximizes the utilization of port facilities.

Several promising lines remain open for further research. One is to enhance the berthing management section by including several Key Performance Indicators (KPIs) in the proposed berthing plans and enabling the option to edit those plans. Additionally, agent-based simulation techniques can be integrated into the software, allowing the testing of proposed berthing plans' performance under unexpected situations, such as delays in vessel arrival times or the unavailability of specific berths.

Acknowledgments. This work has been partially funded by the University of La Laguna through the projects headed by young researchers of its own Research Plan 2023 (accounting code 2023/2305) and the Grants for Research Projects 2023, CajaCanarias Foundation and "La Caixa" Foundation, (project 2023DIG35).

References

1. Dulebenets, M., Pasha, J., Abioye, O., Kavoosi, M.: Vessel scheduling in liner shipping: a critical literature review and future research needs. Flex. Serv. Manuf. J. **33**, 43–106 (2021)
2. Ferrari, E., Christidis, P., Bolsi, P.: The impact of rising maritime transport costs on international trade: estimation using a multi-region general equilibrium model. Transp. Res. Interdisc. Pers. **22**, 100985 (2023)
3. Feo, T.A., Resende, M.G.C.: Greedy randomized adaptive search procedures. J. Global Optim. **6**(2), 109–133 (1995)
4. Imai, A., Nagaiwa, K., Tat, C.W.: Efficient planning of berth allocation for container terminals in Asia. J. Adv. Transp. **31**(1), 75–94 (1997)
5. Imai, A., Nishimura, E., Papadimitriou, S.: The dynamic berth allocation problem for a container port. Transp. Res. Part B Methodol. **35**(4), 401–417 (2001)
6. Li, C., Cai, X., Lee, C.: Scheduling with multiple-job-on-one-processor pattern. IIE Trans. **30**(5), 433–445 (1998)
7. López-Plata, I., Expósito-Izquierdo, C., Lalla-Ruiz, E., Melián-Batista, B., Moreno-Vega, M.: A Greedy randomized adaptive search with probabilistic learning for solving the uncapacitated plant cycle location problem. Int. J. Interact. Multimedia Artif. Intell. **8**(2), 123–133 (2023)
8. Rodriguez-Molins, M., Salido, M.A., Barber, F.: A GRASP-based metaheuristic for the Berth Allocation Problem and the Quay Crane Assignment Problem by managing vessel cargo holds. Appl. Intell. **40**, 273–290 (2014)
9. Ten, K.H., et al.: Automatic identification system in accelerating decarbonization of maritime transportation: the state-of-the-art and opportunities. Ocean Eng. **289**, 116232 (2023)
10. Review of Maritime Transport 2023. UNCTAD. https://unctad.org/system/files/official-document/rmt2023_en.pdf

Incrementally Solving the Dynamic Stacking Problem

Sebastian Leitner[1,2](✉), Stefan Wagner[1,2], and Michael Affenzeller[1]

[1] Heuristic and Evolutionary Algorithms Laboratory, University of Applied Sciences Upper Austria, 4232 Hagenberg, Austria
sebastian.leitner@fh-hagenberg.at

[2] Josef Ressel Center for Adaptive Optimization in Dynamic Environments, Hagenberg, Austria

Abstract. In this paper we tackle the dynamic stacking problem by introducing a framework for incremental online optimization. The dynamic stacking problem features continuous uncertain arrival and delivery of blocks via a crane controlled by the solver. The problem is implemented as a discrete event simulation and the solver runs asynchronously. We develop a framework that can use our existing offline solver for the dynamic stacking problem and turn it into an online solver capable of incrementally updating optimized plans.

We test our framework by comparing to our previously published iterative approach as well as a rule based baseline solver on a diverse set of problem instances. Using the new framework, the solver improves our key performance indicators across the benchmark instances. We also investigate the reasons for the performance differences both in the aggregate as well as the level of individual simulation runs. The framework not only works well on this specific stacking problem, but is general enough to be used in many online dynamic optimization problems.

1 Introduction

Stacking problems are important everywhere from container terminals to steel plants. Wherever there is a gantry crane there is a desire to operate it as efficiently as possible and to minimize the relocation effort. There is no shortage of static problem variants and corresponding solvers. Sadly, these are insufficient for applications in the real world where dynamic effects and uncertainties must be considered. An overview of uncertainties and dynamic aspects in steel industry applications has been given [1] Distinguishing between (i) environmental uncertainty, (ii) implementation uncertainty, and (iii) dynamic and disruptive changes. To address these aspects, stochastic planning models and strategies on

The financial support by the Austrian Federal Ministry for Digital and Economic Affairs and the National Foundation for Research, Technology and Development and the Christian Doppler Research Association is gratefully acknowledged.

A. Quesada-Arencibia et al. (Eds.): EUROCAST 2024, LNCS 15174, pp. 87–97, 2025.
https://doi.org/10.1007/978-3-031-83885-9_9

how to handle disruptions may be required. In the context of dynamic optimization problems (DOP) the application of algorithms to decide during the simulation is called "online solving" [6], while the overall performance which is observed after consecutive applications of the online algorithms is called "offline performance" [3]. The latter is an important criterion in determining success or failure to control the dynamic problem. However, this performance is often available to an online solver only in hindsight. Thus, it must forecast its performance given a model of the uncertainties and dynamics that may arise in order to optimize for the long-term objectives and not towards short-term gains. A crucial aspect when solving DOPs is the definition of the dynamic environment, which in our case comes in the form of a discrete event simulation. A brief literature review on dynamic stacking problems respectively stacking problems with uncertainty is presented in this work. A dynamic container relocation problem (DCRP) has been introduced [3]. However, the only dynamic aspect in the DCRP is the rolling planning horizon. There are no uncertainties, and all events occurring within the planning horizon are known. The stacking problem (SP) [9] is extended by the DCRP by associating a time window (release, due) to each block. This time window describes its earliest availability at a source stack and its latest possible relocation to a handover stack. The steel stacking problem (SSP) redefines a block to be a material, i.e., slab, coil, bloom, sheet, etc., which gains additional attributes such as temperature, length, width, height, and weight that are relevant to several stacking constraints [8]. In the SSP two time windows are associated with each material as there are both, release, and due dates, for the source and the handover stack. Additionally, the SSP features non-instantaneous crane movements. Uncertainties have also been described, for instance in form of uncertain weights of containers in a port application [4]. Also, handover priorities may be uncertain, for instance, in the online block relocation problem (BRP) only the next to be retrieved block is known, while the order of all other blocks is unknown and a leveling heuristic with a known competitive ratio has been described [11]. Another work considers time windows for the handover in which trucks randomly arrive to pick up blocks [5]. In the stochastic container retrieval problem blocks are assigned to batches that have a fixed and known order, but within a batch, the order is random and determined online [2]. We published a dynamic stacking problem with uncertain arrival and retrieval time windows that can only be solved online [7]. We implemented a simulation, defined challenging benchmark instances and compared two online solvers for the problem using the relevant performance indicators. We also previously investigated the effect of increasing uncertainty about the arrival rate on the solver performance, as well as the use of different estimators for the uncertain quantities [10]. In this work, we use the same dynamic stacking problem and propose a framework for incremental optimization that can integrate the previously used iterative model-based solvers to significantly improve their performance. This is achieved by avoiding reoptimizing whenever possible.

2 Dynamic Stacking Problem

The dynamic stacking problem that we tackle in this work is composed of one crane and three types of stacks at which blocks may be placed one on top of another. The crane can only load a single block at a time and can only access the topmost block of each stack. Blocks have a certain and known due date and a certain but unknown ready date that precedes the due date. Every block must stay in the system until their respective ready date and should leave the system before their due date.

- *Arrival stack:* This single stack is where new blocks enter the system. The upstream process adds blocks to the bottom and thus the arrival stack is a first-in-first-out (FIFO) queue. If the arrival stack is full, the next block is lost and the upstream process is suspended.
- *Handover stack:* This single stack is filled by the crane and cleared by the downstream process. It can only hold one block and thus, the clearing decision is made immediately upon dropping off a block there, which is also called a delivery. Such a delivery takes some time after which the handover stack is ready again.
- *Buffer stacks:* These stacks act as a buffer between the arrival and the handover stack. Each block consumes one unit of height and there is a maximum height per stack - here it is the same among all buffer stacks.

This problem is described in the form of a simulation model that is implemented using the Sim# simulation framework Beham et al. (2014). Sim# is a process-based discrete-event simulation framework, where a process is simply a C# method that manipulates its local state as well as the simulation's state. The dynamic stacking problem is implemented using a pseudo-realtime simulation environment, meaning that the advancement of the simulation time may incur a real-world delay. This is useful when the solver interacting with this dynamic stacking problem should be tested in a real-world like scenario, i.e., the solver process runs concurrently to the simulation. However, the pseudo-realtime simulation may also run in virtual time, i.e., as fast as possible, in which case a synchronous interaction between simulation and solver may be achieved. Still, the availability of the decision within the simulation can be simulated by accounting for a delay that is equal to the solver's runtime.

2.1 Processes

The processes within this simulation govern the change of the system state. In this dynamic stacking problem, there are four processes that we describe here.

1. An upstream process produces new blocks at the arrival stack.
2. A block process determines the block's readiness.
3. A crane process executes the crane movements.
4. A downstream process that clears and readies the handover stack.

Upstream: This process adds new blocks at the bottom of the arrival stack in random intervals. If the arrival stack is observed to be full when the block should arrive, that block is considered to be "waste" and the arrival process is suspended. The arrival process is resumed after the crane picks up a block from the arrival stack and thus creates room for a new block, which is spawned again according to a log-normal distributed arrival rate. The solvers may observe the last 100 sampled inter-arrival times which it can use to generate an estimate of the uncertainty.

Block: The block process is initiated when a new block is created and marks the block ready when its ready date has passed. An important parameter is the mean customer required lead time DUE and the mean relative time span RDY after which it becomes ready. The customer-required lead time will be sampled from a log-normal distribution with mean DUE and the relative readiness time will be sampled from a uniform distribution with mean RDY. The actual readiness time is not disclosed and thus unknown to a solver.

Crane: The crane process is initiated by the solver. In this process, the moves will be performed according to a schedule specified by the solver. Before a move is performed it is checked for validity. When an invalid move is encountered, the crane process skips it and continues with the next valid move. Moves may become invalid for several reasons, such as forbidden destinations, i.e., relocation to the arrival stack, violating the height restrictions, and more. When a new schedule is sent, the crane will abort its current schedule after completing the move that is currently in progress. The crane takes some time to move horizontally between stacks and some time to lower and raise the hoist to pick up or drop off a block. The longer the distance, the longer it takes for both directions. The actual time to perform a single move in one of those directions is described by parameters HOR and VER for the mean horizontal movement (crane) and the mean vertical movement (hoist)respectively. Both HOR and VER are described by log-normal distributions in this work. Again, solvers may observe the last 100 relocation times and estimate the uncertainty.

Downstream: The downstream process is initiated when the crane drops-off a block at the handover stack. The handover stack then becomes unavailable until it is cleared. During this time no new blocks may be delivered. Similar to the above processes, data about the last 100 clearing intervals are available to the solver for uncertainty estimation. The stochastic variable HND describes the average handover time.

2.2 Performance Measurement

The performance of the described dynamic stacking problem is described in several dimensions. We describe some of these in more detail and derive a lexicographic objective function from some of these performances that closely match with the priorities observed in a comparable real-world scenario. The following key performance indicators (KPIs) are updated live as the simulation is running. Thus, the KPIs represent the performance of the system up to the current simulated time.

Blocked arrival time (BAT) counts the total time that the arrival process was suspended. The higher this time, the worse the performance as blocking the upstream processes may have severe consequences. For instance, when continuously casting steel, blocking the caster is highly undesirable as there are long setup and potentially cleaning operations necessary when restarting.

Total blocks on time (TBT) counts all blocks that have been delivered before their due date, as well as those that are not overdue and still at a stack. The more blocks that have been delivered on time, the better the performance.

Crane manipulations (CM) count the total number of block relocations performed by the crane. Picking up and dropping off blocks is a critical process where accidents are more likely to occur. Thus, the less manipulations are necessary, the better.

For comparing solvers, we chose a lexicographic objective that includes the first three KPIs: (1) minimize BAT, (2) maximize TBT, (3) minimize CM. This objective function represents the priorities that we have observed in real-world cases in steel stacking where it is of utmost importance to avoid stalling the continuous casting process. Furthermore, it is important to adhere to the due times as much as possible and deliver as much as possible in terms of the total quantity. Third, excessive restacking should be avoided to minimize the probability of accidents and conserve energy and thus crane manipulations are also to be minimized. Our implementation of this problem is available as open source at https://github.com/dynstack/dynstack.

3 Solving the Dynamic Stacking Problem

When solving any online DOP there is a fundamental trade-off between trying to find the best solution possible and finding a feasible solution as fast as possible. While trying to find the optimal solution at every point in time might seem like a reasonable approach it can easily backfire because by the time the solution is found the situation may have changed in a way that it is no longer optimal or even infeasible. Additionally, any time the crane spends waiting for orders from the optimizer is unproductive and can prevent clearing the arrival or delivering a block in time. The previously published model-based solver was simply applied to the current state every time the crane needs new orders. The current world state is translated into a model and a tree-search algorithm searches for the best choice of moves to clear the arrival and deliver the next couple of blocks. From these optimized crane moves we pick the first up to three moves and send them to the simulation to serve as the new schedule. Limiting the length of the schedule is important to avoid executing moves that are no longer good based on newly revealed information.

This is wasteful as the world states produced by the simulation are not independent of each other and the previously optimized crane movements might still be useful. To determine whether this is the case we can no longer rely on a single snapshot of the world instead, we propose the architecture shown in Fig. 1. In this new architecture, the optimizer is made up of three parts with distinct responsibilities. The stacking optimizer is the same as in the previously described iterative model-based optimizer. It is responsible for building a model of the current state and using this model to find a sequence of crane moves that optimizes for the KPIs described in Sect. 2. This sequence of moves is then used to construct a plan for the next few moves the crane should perform. To know if a previously optimized sequence of moves is still applicable to the current state of the system, we need to know what changed since the optimizer generated it. The change detection is responsible for comparing two snapshots and determining all the changes that occurred between them. It uses seven types of changes that signal different state changes for a given block and or stack. StackTake and StackPut events are issued if the crane takes a block from or puts one back onto a stack, respectively. BlockArrive and BlockDelivered events are produced by blocks entering and leaving the system. BlockReady, BlockLate and Handover-Ready signal that a block can and should be put on the handover stack. Given two arbitrary world states it is not possible to guarantee that the list of changes the change detector produces is in the correct order or even complete. The completeness of observed changes depends primarily on the time between the two snapshots so when using the change events resilience in the face of missing information is important.

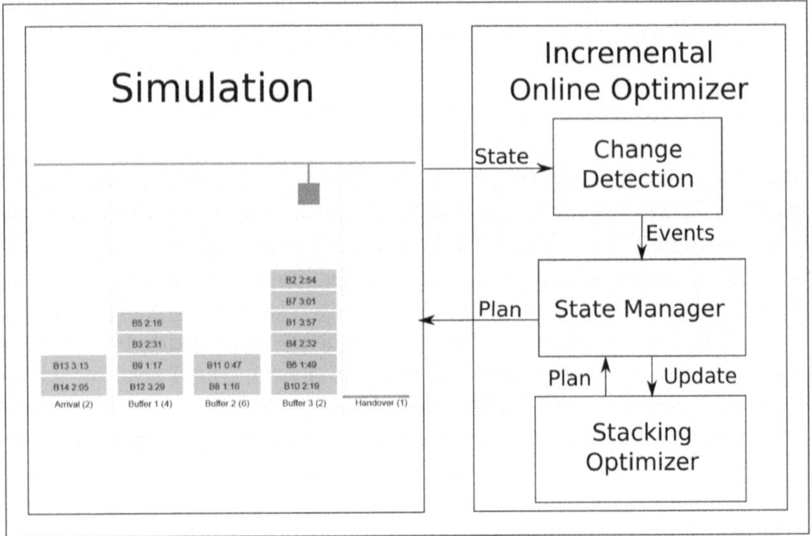

Fig. 1. Framework for incremental optimization.

The central piece of our incremental online optimizer is the so-called State Manager it is responsible for keeping track of three kinds of state. The known state of the world in the present and past, our plans, and our predictions for uncertain events in the future. The first kind is the easiest to handle as the current world state comes directly from the simulation and only the previously received state needs to be stored as well. With the current and previous state, we generate a list of change events using the change detection. These changes are then used to update our predictions on the arrival of the next block, the availability of the handover stack and when each block will be ready. Finally, we determine if the existing plan is still valid by checking which moves have been executed and if our predictions where close enough to be acceptable. If the current plan is still valid, we use it to generate a crane schedule from it and send it to the simulation. If not, we pass the current state as well as our updated predictions to the stacking optimizer which then generate a new plan. After fully processing a new world state the state manager can have five different results SendNewPlan, SendUpdatedPlan, FollowPlan, NoChanges, NoMovesFound. The first two indicate that a crane schedule was send to the simulation while in the latter three cases there is no action required or possible. FollowPlan occurs when the crane is currently executing a planned move. When the crane currently has no moves and the current plan necessitates waiting on a event like a block becoming ready or the handover becoming available we see NoChanges as an outcome until the event happens. NoMovesFound signifies that we started the stacking optimizer but were unable to find a valid solution. This can happen when there is not enough space for the blocks we would need to relocate to reach a ready block to put on the handover.

4 Experiments

For our experiments we used four different classes of instances called A, B, C and D of two different sizes. The smaller instances feature 6 buffer stacks and the larger ones 9. For every combination of class and size we evaluate ten instances with random seeds from 0 to 10 for a total of 80 instances each with a simulated runtime of one hour. For every instance we compare the performance of our rules based baseline, the iterative online optimizer and the incremental online optimizer. The problem configurations are called HS/GECCO2021 and can be found in the GitHub repository[1].

In Table 1 we use the KPIs from Sect. 2.2 to compare the simple rule-based solver to the iterative model-based solver to our new incremental model-based solver. The best result per type and KPI is in bold font. We can clearly see that the incremental solver is the best at our highest priority objective of not blocking the arrival stack on all instance types. As the incremental approach has more detailed information on the arrival- and crane move times it sometimes decides that a block cannot delivered on time without blocking the arrival stack. This leads to a slightly less TBT in some of the six stack instances. In the larger instances, the incremental solver consistently outperforms in this metric for two reasons. The incremental solver can reuse the existing plan between 50 and 60%

[1] github.com/dynstack/dynstack/tree/main/simulation/settings/HS/GECCO2021.

Table 1. Improvements from using incremental framework

Type	Blocked Arrival Time			Total Blocks on Time			Crane Moves		
	Rule	Iter	Incr	Rule	Iter	Incr	Rule	Iter	Incr
6A	0.7	0.3	**0.0**	244.8	**273.4**	272.3	836.5	803.9	927.9
6B	5.8	0.9	**0.0**	233.7	**304.8**	304.0	820.6	844.1	960.9
6C	21.4	1.3	**0.0**	158.6	302.7	**316.0**	784.0	870.4	960.5
6D	18.1	0.6	**0.0**	216.4	218.8	**219.0**	655.9	671.5	773.4
9A	83.1	16.4	**0.0**	214.7	248.2	**255.0**	643.9	726.3	796.4
9B	66.8	4.7	**1.9**	205.2	266.0	**278.6**	628.9	749.6	811.0
9C	62.3	44.7	**2.6**	158.6	213.2	**272.9**	587.2	756.5	793.3
9D	79.9	37.2	**1.2**	206.1	210.0	**214.8**	539.7	606.0	679.9

of the time. This leads to significantly shorter reaction times in the case of blocks becoming ready or the handover becoming available. This in turn means better utilization of the crane and the handover resulting in more blocks being delivered on time. The rule-based solver generally requires the least amount of moves simply because it is worse at BAT and TBT and therefore processes fewer blocks. The incremental solver generally uses more moves to achieve its superior performance in the primary metrics.

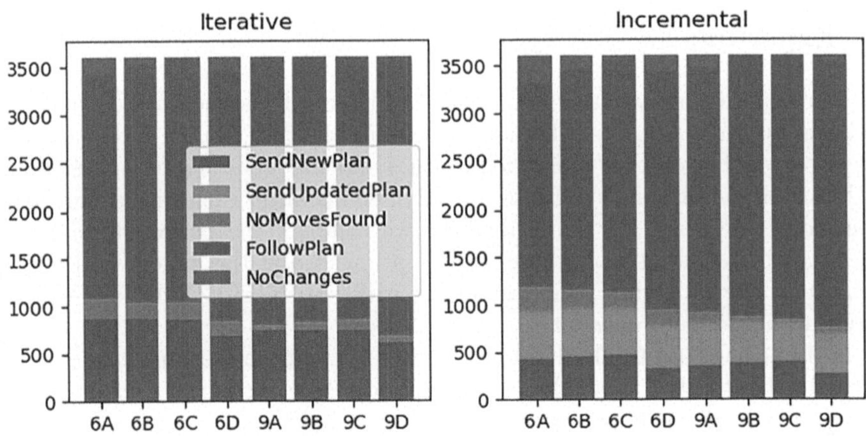

Fig. 2. Comparing state manager outcomes between the iterative and incremental approach.

Figure 2 compares the mean count of state manager outcomes, across our problem configurations, between the iterative and incremental solver. To be able to compare the outcomes results we used the incremental optimization framework and turned off the ability to update an existing plan for the iterative solver. Across both solvers, we see the different characteristics of our instance types reflected in the outcomes. Type A and D feature more waiting as seen in the higher NoChanges count. In type D instances the block due dates are significantly longer in the future and everything moves more slowly. In this environment, approximately 60% of the plans sent to the simulation are adapted from a previously found stacking solution. For the particularly hectic C instances, this goes down to 50% updated plans.

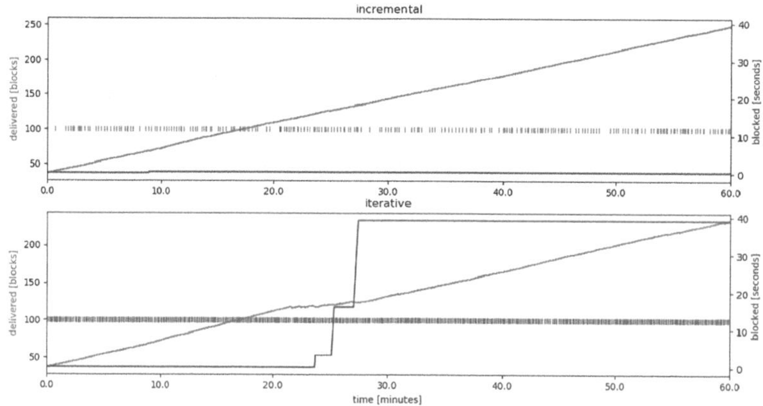

Fig. 3. Comparison iterative and incremental solver on instance 9C with seed 9.

Figure 3 shows two runs on the same challenging problem instance one using the incremental framework and the other one the old iterative approach. We can see that the iterative approach starts to fail around 25 min. At this point, all the buffer stacks are filled and the arrival stack cannot be cleared anymore because the crane utilization was just not high enough. If none of the top blocks are currently ready the solver has no choice but to wait until one becomes ready because there is no space for relocations. At some point, enough blocks become ready and the stacking problem becomes trivial but both the BAT and TBT clearly show the impact of this event. In contrast, the incremental approach just briefly blocked the arrival stack once around the nine-minute mark, because it overestimated the remaining time until the next block arrived. The vertical bars indicate when a new crane schedule was calculated, and we can see that the incremental updating means that we need to run the optimizer less frequently. When the existing crane schedule can be updated, we can save time which improves crane utilization and helps to avoid blocking the arrival stack and missing the due dates of blocks.

5 Conclusion

In this work, we have addressed the dynamic stacking problem with uncertain arrival and retrieval time windows by proposing a framework for incremental optimization that significantly improves the performance of iterative model-based solvers. The framework consists of three major components: the stacking optimizer, a change detection mechanism, and the state manager. This architecture allows for the reuse of previously optimized crane movements whenever possible, thereby reducing the frequency of re-optimization and enhancing overall efficiency.

The results from our experiments show that the incremental solver significantly outperforms both the rule-based and iterative model-based solvers on our most important metric the blocked arrival time across a wide array of problem configurations and sizes. By efficiently managing the arrival and delivery processes and minimizing unproductive crane waiting times, our incremental approach provides a more reliable and effective solution to the dynamic stacking problem.

The proposed incremental optimization framework represents a valuable advancement in managing complex, uncertain, and dynamic stacking environments and is generic enough to be transferable to other dynamic online optimization problems.

References

1. Beham, A., Raggl, S., Wagner, S., Affenzeller, M.: Uncertainty in real-world steel stacking problems. In: GECCO 2019 Companion - Proceedings of the 2019 Genetic and Evolutionary Computation Conference Companion, pp. 1438–1440 (2019). https://doi.org/10.1145/3319619.3326803
2. Galle, V., Manshadi, V.H., Boroujeni, S.B., Barnhart, C., Jaillet, P.: The stochastic container relocation problem. Transp. Sci. **52**(5), 1035–1058 (2018)
3. Hakan Akyüz, M., Lee, C.Y.: A mathematical formulation and efficient heuristics for the dynamic container relocation problem. Naval Res. Logist. (NRL) **61**(2), 101–118 (2014)
4. Kang, J., Ryu, K.R., Kim, K.H.: Deriving stacking strategies for export containers with uncertain weight information. J. Intell. Manuf. **17**, 399–410 (2006)
5. Ku, D., Arthanari, T.S.: Container relocation problem with time windows for container departure. Eur. J. Oper. Res. **252**(3), 1031–1039 (2016)
6. Nguyen, T.T., Yang, S., Branke, J.: Evolutionary dynamic optimization: a survey of the state of the art. Swarm Evol. Comput. **6**, 1–24 (2012). https://doi.org/10.1016/j.swevo.2012.05.001. https://www.sciencedirect.com/science/article/pii/S2210650212000363
7. Raggl, S., Beham, A., Wagner, S., Affenzeller, M.: Solution approaches for the dynamic stacking problem. In: Proceedings of the 2020 GECCO Conference, GECCO 2020, pp. 1652–1660. Association for Computing Machinery, New York (2020). https://doi.org/10.1145/3377929.3398111
8. Raggl, S., Beham, A., Tricoire, F., Affenzeller, M.: Solving a real world steel stacking problem. Int. J. Serv. Comput. Orient. Manuf. **3**(2) (2018). https://doi.org/10.1504/IJSCOM.2018.091621
9. Rei, R., Pedroso, J.P.: Tree search for the stacking problem. Ann. Oper. Res. **203**, 371–388 (2013)

10. Sebastian, L., Beham, A., Wagner, S., Affenzeller, M.: Effects of arrival uncertainty on solver performance in dynamic stacking problems. In: 32nd European Modeling and Simulation Symposium, EMSS 2020, pp. 193–200 (2020). https://doi.org/10.46354/i3m.2020.emss.027
11. Zehendner, E., Feillet, D., Jaillet, P.: An algorithm with performance guarantee for the online container relocation problem. Eur. J. Oper. Res. **259**(1), 48–62 (2017)

Predicting the Processing Effort for Block Relocation Problems

Roland Braune[1,2,3](✉) and Michael Raunig[2]

[1] Operations Management, University of Applied Sciences Upper Austria, Wels, Austria
roland.braune@univie.ac.at

[2] Department of Business Decisions and Analytics, University of Vienna, Vienna, Austria

[3] Josef Ressel Center for Adaptive Optimization in Dynamic Environments, University of Vienna, Vienna, Austria

Abstract. In this paper, we propose a machine learning-based prediction approach for the block relocation problem. The target concept to be captured is the minimum number of relocations needed to clear all stacks of a given configuration. Since the problem is NP-hard, an exact determination of this value is computationally expensive. Therefore, quick and precise estimates are highly valuable, especially when the problem appears in hierarchical optimization contexts as a subproblem of another optimization problem, for example. We propose a design and training concept for a convolutional neural network that is capable of achieving accurate predictions on benchmark instances from the literature. The computational results further show that it is able to outperform competitor approaches like lower bounds, alternative machine learning techniques, and fast heuristics in terms of speed and common error metrics on most instance classes.

Keywords: Block relocation problem · Deep learning · Convolutional neural network · Regression

1 Introduction

The block relocation problem (BRP) is concerned with minimizing the number of relocations needed to retrieve items from a storage yard in a predefined order. The yard is organized into bays of two-dimensional type, meaning that the stored items are organized into multiple stacks of potentially different height. This problem setting most prominently arises in container terminals, but also, for example, in steel production facilities where large quantities of steel slabs are stacked in outdoor storage yards prior to further processing such as hot rolling. The latter scenario serves as the background and motivation for the research presented in this paper. In this context, the block relocation problem occurs as a subproblem of a so-called pickup-and-delivery vehicle routing problem (PDVRP)

A. Quesada-Arencibia et al. (Eds.): EUROCAST 2024, LNCS 15174, pp. 98–106, 2025.
https://doi.org/10.1007/978-3-031-83885-9_10

(see, e.g., [2]). Roljic et al. [13] give an overview of the industrial problem setting, where the primary goal is to fulfill transportation requests for steel slabs in the most efficient manner. Hence, besides the routing aspect itself, which focuses on the minimization of the total travel time, the actual pickup of specific slabs from storage yards may consume a substantial amount of time and is, therefore, also subject to optimization. Although the block relocation problem encountered in this real-world setting differs from the academic one in that usually, only a subset of slabs have to be retrieved from a bay, the underlying goal remains the same, namely minimizing the number of necessary relocations.

The nesting of the block relocation problem within a vehicle routing problem is currently addressed in a hierarchical fashion. In fact, a large neighborhood search (LNS) [11] algorithm is employed for the VRP part of the problem. At every pickup node, the algorithm has to solve a corresponding block relocation problem to be able to get accurate timing results for the visit time window [13]. Since the LNS evaluates thousands of different solutions during its trajectory through the search space, the computation time needed to solve the embedded block relocation problems is of crucial importance. During the neighborhood evaluation phase, a quick and accurate estimate of the number of relocations needed to retrieve the slab(s) would be sufficient to assess the quality of the generated solutions quickly. To match both the swiftness and accuracy requirements, we developed an approach based on predictive analytics.

In essence, it is a regression approach, taking BRP instances as an input and yielding the estimated number of required relocations as an output. The main goal was to keep the feature engineering step as simple as possible because the regressor is called very often during the overall optimization process and, therefore, does not leave room for complex calculations and transformations. To accomplish this, we had to shift the complexity towards the regressor itself. We chose a deep neural network that is able to process a BRP instance in matrix form, its most intuitive and natural representation. Finding a proper structure of the network, including the design of an input layer that is able to cope with problem instances of different dimensions and the setup of an effective training process, represent the main contributions of this work.

The final computational study covers both the training procedure and the performance validation of the trained neural network based on benchmark instances. As far as the training is concerned, we randomly generated a few thousand BRP instances which were tackled by an exact solver to achieve the utmost accuracy with regard to the instance labels. The final performance validation and competitor analysis confirm and underpin the effectiveness of the proposed prediction concept.

This paper is based on a recently submitted Master's thesis [12], which might be consulted for further details on the presented research work.

2 Problem Statement and Related Work

Kim and Hong [8] describe the BRP in its abstract form as a given set of homogeneous items, referred to as *blocks*, stored in vertical stacks arranged in a bay, where a target block is accessible only if it is on the top of a stack. The blocks have to be retrieved according to a given priority list, with the smallest number indicating the highest priority (= urgency). Generally, one has to assume that the retrieval sequence has not been known upon storage, and consequently, the blocks are not stored in a sorted fashion. If the target block, i.e., the next block to be retrieved, is "buried" below other blocks with a lower priority, those blocks have to be removed successively (one-by-one) from the stack first. The required operations are called *relocations*. A relocated block can only be placed on other stacks of the same bay; hence, a new stack cannot be opened.

The state of a BRP, referred to as a *configuration*, can be described by an $N \times S$ matrix, where N denotes the number of blocks and S is the number of stacks. The blocks are assigned numbers $1, \ldots, N$, reflecting their priority of retrieval as described above. Caserta et al. [4] distinguish between two variants of the BRP: In the first variant, which they refer to as BRP-I, any block that is on top of a stack can be relocated, whereas in variant BRP-II, only blocks that are above the target block within the same stack are allowed to be moved. These two variants are commonly known as the restricted and the unrestricted BRP, respectively, and have both been proven to be NP-hard.

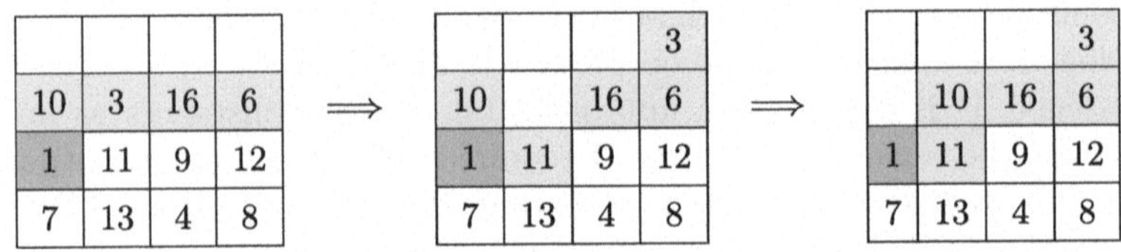

Fig. 1. Retrieving item #1 in an unrestricted block relocation problem

Figure 1 shows a series of relocation moves for an example of an unrestricted BRP, which is the variant that we consider in this paper. Block #1 is the target block but cannot be retrieved immediately. Note that it would be sufficient to relocate block #10 from the same stack to be able to retrieve the target block. However, with regard to future retrievals, it is more effective to first relocate block #3 to the rightmost stack and move block #10 to the second stack. Otherwise, block #10 will have to be moved at least a second time. From a general point of view, the unrestricted BRP offers more potential with regard to a look-ahead kind of optimization, but it clearly also has a larger solution space than its restricted counterpart.

For the BRP in both variants, a broad spectrum of exact and heuristic solution approaches appeared in the literature over the years. Chronologically, the most important and frequently cited ones can be summarized as follows. The first branch-and-bound (B&B) algorithm dates back to 2006 [8], followed by the look-ahead heuristic of Caserta et al. [3]. Seminal work in mixed-integer programming (MIP) formulations was done by Caserta et al. [4]. Petering et al. [10] proposed a more compact MIP formulation and an extended look-ahead heuristic. Strong lower bounds and further exact approaches were devised by Tanaka

0	0	0	0	0	0	0	0	0
0	0	0	0	0	0	0	0	0
0	10	3	16	6	0	0	0	0
0	1	11	9	12	0	0	0	0
0	7	13	4	8	0	0	0	0
0	5	15	2	14	0	0	0	0
0	0	0	0	0	0	0	0	0

Fig. 2. CNN input matrix (5×7) plus padding

and Takii [14] (B&B), Tricoire et al. [15] (B&B), and recently by Liu et al. [9] (iterative MIP).

Expectedly, techniques from machine learning have grown in importance also for the BRP in the more recent past. Research work in this area that is close to our approach shall briefly be stated here. Zhang et al. [18], for example, include a classification approach into their branch-and-bound algorithm to prune parts of the search tree. A conceptually similar approach is adopted by Hottung et al. [7], who rely on two deep neural networks (DNNs) to guide a heuristic tree search algorithm for the container pre-marshalling problem. One of these DNNs is used to predict lower bounds on the number of remaining moves required at a particular state of the solution process. The basic idea is, hence, analogous to the one presented in this paper. The underlying problem, on the other hand, is related but structurally different with regard to the solution process. Ye et al. [17] propose a multi-class classification approach for predicting the number of relocations based on specifically extracted and engineered features. However, the scope of their approach is limited with regard to bay configurations and problem scale, and is suitable primarily for the restricted version of the BRP.

3 A Deep-Learning-Based Prediction Approach

The main idea of our approach is to provide the configuration of the bay to a regressor *as is*. This means that, for example, the BRP shown in Fig. 1 is directly taken in its (natural) matrix representation and handed over to the prediction facility. This way of input processing captures the BRP as if it were an image. It is known from the field of image processing, in particular image recognition, that deep neural networks [6] are well-suited for this purpose. For the research presented in this paper, we employed a *convolutional neural network* (CNN).

The input layer provides support for BRPs up to 5×7 in size, as shown in Fig. 2. The 5×7 base matrix is surrounded by so-called *padding* elements. This helps prevent the loss of information, especially within the matrix boundaries. In case a BRP instance is smaller, it is placed within the inner 5×7 matrix such that its lower left corner is aligned with the lower left corner of the accommodating matrix. All remaining elements within the base input matrix and also the

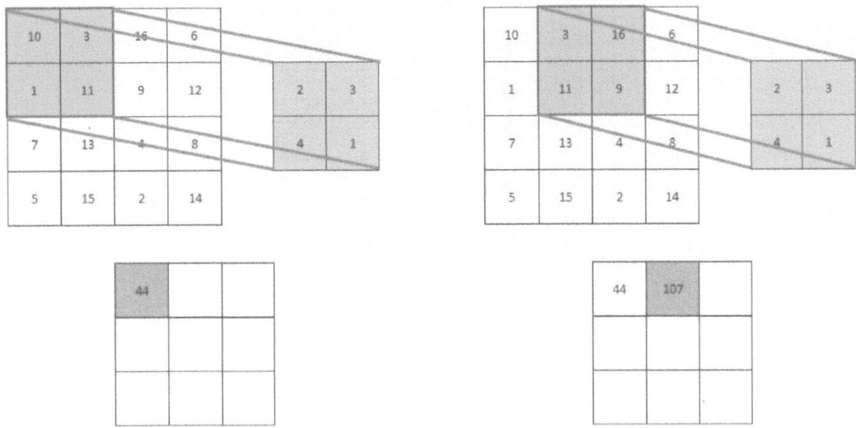

Fig. 3. Stepwise convolution of the input matrix in groups of 2×2 elements

padding elements are simply set to zero. The convolution step itself is based on 2×2 sub-matrices, as shown in Fig. 3.

Table 1. Layer configuration of the applied convolutional neural network

Layer	Dimensions	Output Channels
Input	5×7	1
Convolutional 1	6×8	16
Convolutional 2	5×7	32
Convolutional 3	4×6	64
Convolutional 4	4×6	128
Fully connected	3×5	–

Besides the input layer, our CNN is made up of 4 convolutional layers (ReLU-activated) and one fully connected layer. The actual layer configuration is summarized in Table 1. The stochastic gradient descent principle, in combination with the mean squared error (MSE) as a loss function, was applied for training the network over 10 epochs in total. All parameter settings were obtained through manual experimentation. Further details can be found in [12].

Finally, it has to be remarked that the number of relocations required for a given configuration is not sensitive to the actual order of the stacks within the bay. Clearly, this might raise symmetry issues. Fortunately, given the theoretically possible number of *unique* BRP instances, it still allows for the generation of a sufficiently large training set. On the other hand, dedicated preliminary experiments showed that our CNN turned out to be fairly robust against those symmetry issues, making potentially sophisticated countermeasures unnecessary.

4 Experimental Setup

To provide enough training instances for the CNN described in Sect. 3, we randomly generated greater amounts of data. Mimicking the bay layouts used by Caserta et al. [5] for their benchmark instances, the following configurations were produced by our generator: $3 \times S$, with $S \in \{3, 4, 5, 6\}$, 4×4, and 4×5, where the first figure represents the number of blocks and the second one the number of stacks (see Sect. 2). The main reason for this very choice was the solvability of instances by the MIP approach that we used for calculating the instance labels, i.e., the exact number of relocations needed to clear the bay. For this purpose, we decided to rely on the iterative MIP-based algorithm proposed by Liu et al. [9], which is known to perform well also for the larger Caserta instances. Nevertheless, the rate of achieved optimal solutions drops sharply for the layouts 4×6 and 4×7. In order to avoid generating excessive amounts of BRP instances, 4×5 is the largest size considered in this paper. Note that the average time to optimality required by the iterative MIP algorithm ranged between 0.2 and 1917 s for the smallest (3×3) and the largest (4×5) layout, respectively.

We finally generated 750 instances per layout, resulting in 6750 instances in total. The problem generator was implemented in the C# programming language, whereas for the MIP approach, we used OPL, as provided by IBM ILOG CPLEX Optimization Studio (version 22.1.0). Python's PyTorch library [1] served as the environment for the neural network implementation. Training and testing activities took place on a Windows 10 workstation equipped with an Intel Core i5-9300 CPU (max. 4.1 GHz) and 8 GB RAM. Parts of the MIP runs were conducted on a cluster machine providing 2× Intel Xeon 6226R CPUs per node.

5 Computational Results

As mentioned in Sect. 4, our deep neural network was trained using randomly generated instances of different sizes. In the final computational experiments, we used the well-known and widely used benchmark instances originally created by Caserta et al. [5] to evaluate the prediction performance of our CNN and to compare it against other approaches from the literature. The reference values for the required number of relocation moves for each of those instances were obtained by running our re-implementation of the iterative MIP approach initially proposed by Liu et al. [9].

As competitors with regard to the predictive power, i.e., the ability to provide close estimates for the true number of relocation moves, we chose approaches of different kinds involving lower bounds, other regression techniques, and heuristics. All of these are designed to deliver bounds or predictions for the target value with relatively low computational effort. Hence, a rigorous analysis concerning both accuracy and efficiency was a central aspect of our computational evaluation.

Table 2. Scores for different error metrics obtained by lower bounds, linear regression, and the CNN-based prediction approach.

Class	LB_3 [15]			Linear regression				CNN			
	MSE	MAE	R^2	MSE	MAE	R^2	Max Error	MSE	MAE	R^2	Max Error
3×3	1.69	1.01	0.76	1.83	1.04	0.42	4.41	0.57	0.62	0.82	1.98
3×4	1.38	0.92	0.80	0.70	1.00	0.64	2.69	0.98	0.80	0.65	2.49
3×5	1.50	0.96	0.81	0.83	0.70	0.72	2.21	0.51	0.55	0.83	1.95
3×6	1.21	0.85	0.86	1.22	0.89	0.66	2.45	0.98	0.81	0.73	2.72
3×7	0.99	0.69	0.85	1.17	0.88	0.55	2.88	0.87	0.75	0.66	2.04
4×4	4.53	1.86	0.72	1.35	0.94	0.57	2.97	1.31	0.89	0.59	2.60
4×5	2.47	1.21	0.73	2.18	1.18	0.16	4.01	1.19	0.89	0.54	2.75
All	1.97	1.07	0.79	1.37	0.90	0.80	4.41	0.91	0.75	0.87	2.75

First, we compared our CNN against a simple linear regression approach and the BRP lower bound established by Tricoire et al. [15] (denoted as LB_3), focusing on classical error metrics used in the machine learning context. Table 2 gives an overview of the scores obtained for selected classes of the Caserta benchmark instances. From an overall perspective, it becomes apparent that the CNN is able to achieve the highest R^2 values among the tested approaches. On the other hand, it yields the lowest mean squared and mean absolute errors. Compared to linear regression, the maximum (absolute) error is also smaller. Note that other lower bounds were also tested, but LB_3 delivered the best performance among them, and it can still be quickly computed.

Table 3. Performance comparison between selected approaches to the BRP and the CNN-based prediction approach.

Class	KH [8]	DH [16]	CM [5]	PH [10]		BRP-CNN		MIP
	Reloc.	Reloc.	Reloc.	Reloc.	Time (s)	Reloc.	Time (s)	Reloc.
3×3	7.1	5.6	5.4	5.1	<1	4.91	<0.001	5.15
3×4	10.7	7.3	6.5	6.3	<1	5.5	<0.001	6.2
3×5	14.5	8.0	7.3	7.0	<1	6.99	<0.001	6.93
3×6	18.1	10.2	7.9	8.4	<1	8.16	<0.001	8.25
3×7	20.1	11.3	8.6	9.2	<1	8.81	<0.001	8.95
4×4	16	12.2	9.9	10.4	<1	9.27	<0.001	9.72
4×5	23.4	15.7	16.5	13.0	<1	11.19	<0.001	11.45

Another facet of the performance analysis was the comparison with effective heuristic approaches known from the BRP literature. Table 3 displays the associated results, where KH denotes the heuristic proposed by Kim and Hong [8],

DH the "difference heuristic" developed by Ünlüyurt and Aydin, and CM the heuristic according to Caserta et al. [5]. The acronym PH stands for the look-ahead approach proposed by Petering and Hussein [10]. The reported figures are the average number of relocations for each instance class. The reference values are provided by our implementation of the iterative MIP approach of Liu et al. [9]. Computation times could only be retrieved for the PH heuristic since the other references do not report timing results. Note that the "computation" times stated for our CNN refer to the application of the already trained network. The table reveals that Petering and Hussein's PH heuristic is obviously our strongest competitor with regard to both accuracy and speed. However, it loses ground for the larger instances (3×7 and above), where our deep neural network is still able to provide the closest estimates. Besides that, it has to be emphasized that once trained, this kind of regressor is able to deliver predictions within extremely short time frames, i.e., in under a millisecond.

6 Conclusion and Outlook

We have proposed and successfully implemented a deep neural network-based approach for predicting the number of relocations required to clear all stacks of an arbitrary block relocation problem as long as it is within the maximum size bounds which it was trained for. One of the main advantages of the employed convolutional neural network is the fact that feature engineering is not necessary at all since the instance configuration can directly be fed into the network in its natural matrix representation. Though the training process is also relatively simple, the linchpin of reliable predictions is still the availability of accurate labels. This means that the training instances have to be solved to optimality for this purpose. For the computational experiments described in this paper, this was accomplished by using a MIP-based algorithm. The trained network was then applied to common benchmark instances from the literature and outperformed other approaches, including lower/upper bounding techniques as well as alternative regressors, with regard to various error metrics.

Our future research in this area will focus on the embedding of the devised prediction technique into the superordinate pickup-and-delivery algorithm to boost its performance. To enable a successful integration, we will have to (1) transfer our prediction method to the restricted version of the BRP because both variants can occur in the real-world scenario, and (2) enable predictions on "partial" BRPs since only particular blocks might have to be retrieved from a bay.

Acknowledgments. The financial support by the Austrian Federal Ministry for Digital and Economic Affairs, the National Foundation for Research, Technology and Development, and the Christian Doppler Research Association is gratefully acknowledged.

References

1. PyTorch documentation. https://pytorch.org/docs/stable/index.html. Accessed 8 June 2023
2. Battarra, M., Cordeau, J.F., Iori, M.: Pickup-and-Delivery Problems for Goods Transportation, chap. 6, pp. 161–191. SIAM (2014). https://doi.org/10.1137/1.9781611973594.ch6
3. Caserta, M., Schwarze, S., Voß, S.: A new binary description of the blocks relocation problem and benefits in a look ahead heuristic. In: Cotta, C., Cowling, P. (eds.) EvoCOP 2009. LNCS, vol. 5482, pp. 37–48. Springer, Heidelberg (2009). https://doi.org/10.1007/978-3-642-01009-5_4
4. Caserta, M., Schwarze, S., Voß, S.: A mathematical formulation and complexity considerations for the blocks relocation problem. Eur. J. Oper. Res. **219**(1), 96–104 (2012)
5. Caserta, M., Voß, S., Sniedovich, M.: Applying the corridor method to a blocks relocation problem. OR Spectrum **33**(4), 915–929 (2011)
6. Goodfellow, I., Bengio, Y., Courville, A.: Deep Learning. Adaptive Computation and Machine Learning. The MIT Press, Cambridge (2016)
7. Hottung, A., Tanaka, S., Tierney, K.: Deep learning assisted heuristic tree search for the container pre-marshalling problem. Comput. Oper. Res. **113**, 104781 (2020). https://doi.org/10.1016/j.cor.2019.104781
8. Kim, K.H., Hong, G.P.: A heuristic rule for relocating blocks. Comput. Oper. Res. **33**(4), 940–954 (2006)
9. Liu, S., Liu, S., Lu, C.: An integer programming formulation and iterative scheme algorithm for the block relocation problem. J. Control Decis. **10**, 1–10 (2022)
10. Petering, M.E., Hussein, M.I.: A new mixed integer program and extended look-ahead heuristic algorithm for the block relocation problem. Eur. J. Oper. Res. **231**(1), 120–130 (2013)
11. Pisinger, D., Ropke, S.: Large Neighborhood Search, pp. 399–419. Springer, Boston (2010). https://doi.org/10.1007/978-1-4419-1665-5_13
12. Raunig, M.: Using deep learning to make predictions about the block relocation problem (2023)
13. Roljic, B., Leitner, S., Doerner, K.F.: Stacking and transporting steel slabs using high-capacity vehicles. Procedia Comput. Sci. **180**, 843–851 (2021). https://doi.org/10.1016/j.procs.2021.01.334. Proceedings of the 2nd International Conference on Industry 4.0 and Smart Manufacturing (ISM 2020)
14. Tanaka, S., Takii, K.: A faster branch-and-bound algorithm for the block relocation problem. IEEE Trans. Autom. Sci. Eng. **13**(1), 181–190 (2016)
15. Tricoire, F., Scagnetti, J., Beham, A.: New insights on the block relocation problem. Comput. Oper. Res. **89**, 127–139 (2018)
16. Ünlüyurt, T., Aydin, C.: Improved rehandling strategies for the container retrieval process: advances in transportation analysis. J. Adv. Transp. **46**(4), 378–393 (2012)
17. Ye, R., Ye, R., Zheng, S.: Machine learning guides the solution of blocks relocation problem in container terminals. Transp. Res. Rec. **2677**(3), 721–737 (2023). https://doi.org/10.1177/03611981221117157
18. Zhang, C., Guan, H., Yuan, Y., Chen, W., Wu, T.: Machine learning-driven algorithms for the container relocation problem. Transp. Res. Part B Methodol. **139**, 102–131 (2020)

Modelling Electric Vehicle Routing Problem with Heterogeneous Fleet for Simultaneous Pickup and Delivery

Prateek Gupta[1(✉)], Devanand[1], Antonio Ken Iannillo[1], Jorge Augusto Meira[1], Radu State[1], and Danilo D'Aversa[2]

[1] SnT, University of Luxembourg, 29 Av. John F. Kennedy, 1855 Luxembourg City, Luxembourg
{prateek.gupta,devanand.devanand,antonioken.iannillo,jorge.meira, radu.state}@uni.lu

[2] Gulliver Luxembourg S.à r.l., Luxembourg City, Luxembourg
danilo.daversa@gullivernet.lu

Abstract. Vehicles that run on fossil fuel emit numerous air pollutants, and transitioning from conventional vehicles to their electric counterparts within a transportation fleet significantly reduces overall emissions. Electric vehicles are now an economically viable mode of transportation with decreasing cost of batteries, increasing power output, and rapid expansion of charging infrastructure. Electric vehicle routing problem (EVRP) aims to create routing plans for customers using a fleet of electric vehicles with diverse battery constraints. This paper proposes a new mathematical model for solving simultaneous pickup and delivery vehicle routing using a heterogeneous electric and fossil fuel vehicle fleet. The model is tested on logistics partner data using a standard CPLEX solver.

Keywords: simultaneous pickup and delivery · EVRP · transportation · heterogeneous fleet

1 Introduction

There is growing interest in the logistics sector to adopt electric vehicles (EVs) for transportation, driven by incentives promoting green technologies and reducing reliance on fossil-fuel-based vehicles [9,10]. The long-term cost-effectiveness of EVs is also becoming more attractive due to improved battery performance and reduced maintenance requirements. However, EVs have high initial costs and limited driving ranges, which are exacerbated by the need for frequent charging. Furthermore, they are susceptible to battery degradation following prolonged usage and experience significant battery drainage when driven at maximum speed. As a result, instead of a complete replacement with EVs, a gradual transition from fossil-fuel-based vehicles to EVs is necessary. This necessitates addressing the complexities of standard operating behavior for EV batteries in a heterogeneous

A. Quesada-Arencibia et al. (Eds.): EUROCAST 2024, LNCS 15174, pp. 107–116, 2025.
https://doi.org/10.1007/978-3-031-83885-9_11

fleet that includes both fossil-fuel-based vehicles and EVs. In this paper, we focus on one of the logistic complexities, the vehicle routing problem (VRP), where the objective is to obtain an ideal routing plan for both fleets. VRP is a classic combinatorial optimization problem, first introduced by Dantzig and Ramstedt [4]. They formulated the truck dispatching problem as a mixed integer programming problem. VRP aims to create a set of routes for a fleet of vehicles to meet customer demands while minimizing the overall cost of distance traveled. The vehicles are subject to constraints such as origin and endpoints and the number of visits to each customer. The heterogeneous vehicle routing problem (HVRP) is an extension of the classical VRP, which requires consideration of the specific capacity of each vehicle. The Fleet Size and Mix Vehicle Routing Problem [8] introduced by Golden et al. focuses on determining the optimal mix of vehicles and their routes to minimize costs. Vehicle Routing Problem with simultaneous pickup and delivery (VRPSD) is a variant of VRP, where customers can request both pickup and delivery of goods. Min's paper [14] is one of the earliest works to address the problem of routing multiple vehicles to handle both deliveries and pickups simultaneously.

Electric vehicle routing problem (EVRP) is another generalization of VRP, minimizing the cost while considering the charging capacity and operational constraints of EVs. Erdogan [5] addresses the unique challenges posed by EVs in routing. Schneider [16] formulated the EVRP with time windows and explicitly incorporated recharging stations into the routing problem. Conrad [3] introduced recharging vehicle routing problem (RVRP), where vehicles with limited range are allowed to recharge at customer locations mid-tour. Keskin and Çatay [11] extended the problem to include fast charging capability of the available equipment in the station. Prior papers [7,13] have highlighted that refueling can serve as a bottleneck and impacts logistics efficiency, which can be extended to recharging in the case of EVs. We refer the reader to [12] for further related work on EVRPs.

Heterogeneous vehicle routing problem with simultaneous pickup and delivery (HVRPSPD) is a variant of HVRP that includes mixed fleet vehicles and the requirement for simultaneous pickup and delivery. This problem is well-suited to modeling real-world logistics operations due to its ability to capture the intricate complexities and demands of practical and operational logistics. The simultaneous pickup and delivery requirement, combined with the use of a mixed fleet of vehicles, creates a problem that closely mirrors the challenges faced by logistics companies in their daily operations. Goel's paper [7] provides a comprehensive assessment of hours of service (HOS) regulations across different countries and their impact on road freight transport, including the constraint that drivers cannot drive more than a certain number of hours. While there is extensive research on heterogeneous fleets comprising fossil-fuel vehicles, there is a limited body of research on heterogeneous fleets that include EVs. Our paper centers on the practical scenario of full charge starts for EVs and full tank starts for fossil fuel vehicles, allowing for intraday delivery distances without the need for mid-route refueling. This approach simplifies the problem by eliminating the complexity of mid-route charging or refueling, making it more manageable and realistic for logistics operations. Our research modifies the HVRPSPD to accurately capture the distinct characteristics of mixed vehicle fleets when incorporating EVs, as well as the inherent complexity of logistics operations that require simultaneous pickup and delivery services. Papers closely related to our work focus on the impact of load on energy consumption [6] and allowing partial recharging by multiple chargers [15].

The rest of the paper is organized as follows: Section 2 summarizes existing mathematical models of heterogeneous and EVRP models, and their challenges and our contribution to the extensions. Section 3 presents computational results and compares the performance with a baseline heuristic. Section 4 lists the conclusion and future work.

2 Mathematical Model

2.1 Existing Models and Their Challenges

The mathematical formulation by Avci et al. [2] models the heterogeneous vehicle routing problem with simultaneous pickup and delivery. The objective function of the model minimizes the total cost (distance travelled by the trucks).

$$\text{Minimize: } Z = \min \sum_{k=1}^{T} \sum_{i=0}^{n} \sum_{j=0}^{n} x_{k,ij} \cdot cost_{ij} \tag{1}$$

$$\text{Subject to: } \sum_{k=1}^{T} y_{i,k} = 1, \quad \forall i \in N \tag{2}$$

$$\sum_{j \in V} x_{k,ij} = \sum_{i \in V} x_{k,ij} = y_{i,k}, \quad \forall i \in V, k = 1, \ldots, T \tag{3}$$

$$\sum_{i \in V} \sum_{k \in \{1,\ldots,T\}} pvar_{k,ji} - \sum_{i \in V} \sum_{k \in \{1,\ldots,T\}} pvar_{k,ij} = pd_j, \quad \forall j \in N \tag{4}$$

$$\sum_{i \in V} \sum_{k \in \{1,\ldots,T\}} dvar_{k,ij} - \sum_{i \in V} \sum_{k \in \{1,\ldots,T\}} dvar_{k,ji} = dd_j, \quad \forall j \in N \tag{5}$$

$$\sum_{i \in N} \sum_{k \in \{1,\ldots,T\}} pvar_{k,0i} = 0 \tag{6}$$

$$\sum_{i \in N} \sum_{k \in \{1,\ldots,T\}} dvar_{k,i0} = 0 \tag{7}$$

$$pvar_{k,ij} + dvar_{k,ij} \leq v_k x_{k,ij}, \quad \forall i, j \in A, k \in \{1, \ldots, T\} \tag{8}$$

Constraint 2 and 3 guarantee the uniqueness of visits that each customer is visited only once by a single vehicle. Constraint 4 preserves the flow of delivery load for each vehicle, ensuring that it decreases monotonically throughout the journey. Constraint 5 maintains the flow of pickup load for each vehicle, ensuring that it increases monotonically throughout the journey. Constraint 6 ensures that the pickup load at the start of journey is 0. Constraint 7 ensures that the delivery load at the start of journey is 0. Constraint 8 ensures that the vehicle capacity is not exceeded at any point during the journey, tying the variables pvar and dvar to the vehicle capacity. This constraint is also useful for subtour elimination. A summary of the symbols used in Avci's formulation is presented in Table 1.

Table 1. Symbols Used in the Avci's Formulation

Symbol	Definition
$cost_{ij}$	Distance between nodes i and j
dd_i	Delivery demand for customer i
pd_i	Pickup demand for customer i
v_k	Capacity of vehicle k
$x_{k,ij}$	1 if vehicle k is used to visit customer j from customer i, else 0
$y_{i,k}$	1 if vehicle k is used to visit customer i
$pvar_{k,ij}$	Total load picked up by vehicle k during the journey when traveling from i to j
$dvar_{k,ij}$	Total load delivered by vehicle k during the journey when traveling from i to j

Amiri et al. [1] presented a bi-objective programming model that aimed to minimize the total cost of transportation and fuel consumption for diesel trucks, thereby reducing greenhouse gas (GHG) emissions. In addition to the traditional VRP constraints, Amiri also considers constraints for time windows, flow of discharge when visiting nodes to account for consumption and amount of charging possible at recharging stations. A summary of the symbols used in Amiri's formulation is presented in Table 2

$$\text{Minimize: } Z_2 = \sum_{k\in K_c}\sum_{\forall i\in N_0}\sum_{j\in N_{n+1}, i\neq j} (W_v\rho\sigma_{ij}d_{ij} + fIEt_{ij} + \epsilon\rho d_{ij}\left(\frac{d_{ij}}{t_{ij}}\right)^2)\lambda x_{ij}^k + \sum_{k\in K_c}\sum_{\forall i\in N_0}\sum_{j\in N_{n+1}, i\neq j} \rho\sigma_{ij}\lambda d_{ij}q_{ij}^k \tag{9}$$

Table 2. Symbols Used in the Amiri's Formulation

Symbol	Definition
K_c	Set of available Fossul Fuel Vehicles
N_0	Set of customers, departure depot, charging stations, and their copies
N_{n+1}	Set of customers, arrival depot, charging stations, and their copies
σ_{ij}	factor or coefficient between vertices i and j
d_{ij}	Distance between vertex i and vertex j
t_{ij}	Travel time from vertex i to vertex j
W_v	Curb Weight of vehicle v including a full tank of fuel
ρ	Factor affecting fuel consumption
f	Engine friction factor
I	Engine speed
E	Engine displacement
ϵ	Efficiency parameter for diesel engines
λ	Factor affecting fuel consumption
x_{ij}^k	1 if vehicle k travels arc (i, j), 0 otherwise
q_{ij}^k	The flow of load carried from vertex i to vertex j by vehicle k

2.2 Our Model

Building upon previous research, we propose a novel formulation for the Heterogeneous Vehicle Routing Problem with Simultaneous Pickup and Delivery. This formulation addresses key limitations in existing models, including:

1. Avci's formulation, which focused solely on simultaneous pickup and delivery, whereas our model extends this scope to also minimize GHG emissions
2. Amiri's formulation, which considered GHG emissions, but it did not fully capture the complexities of a heterogeneous fleet, which is a critical aspect of real-world logistics operations

Our formulation takes into account various constraints, including:

1. Speed and capacity limitations for each vehicle
2. Adherence to government regulations, including restrictions on overall journey time and distance for a driver
3. Changes in traffic during rainfall and peak hours

To address the complexities of managing EVs in a logistics setting, we introduce decision variables that enable fine-tuning of EV performance, which can deteriorate over time. Additionally, we allow for adjustments to be made to the maximum travel time and distance thresholds to optimize operations in accordance with regulatory requirements. We assume that EVs are fully charged at the depot before the start of the journey and a buffer time for charging is included.

This formulation is designed to accommodate capacity and speed constraints, as well as incorporate the possibility of extending the green energy-based objective functions, as proposed by Amiri et al., to further reduce the environmental impact of the logistics operations. A summary of the symbols used in Avci's formulation is presented in Table 3.

Table 3. Symbols Used in the Updated Formulation

Symbol	Definition
$x_{k,ij}$	1 if vehicle k is used to visit customer j from customer i, else 0
m_k	Maximum allowable journey time for vehicle k
s_k	Average speed of vehicle k
d_{ij}	Distance between nodes i and j
D_k	Maximum distance that vehicle k can travel

The planner can exploit the intrinsic relationship between speed and charge to optimize the distance traveled by EVs, thereby maximizing their utilization. This flexibility is particularly useful when one or more parameters are unknown and only an upper bound is provided.

$$\sum_{\{i,j\}\in A} d_{ij}x_{k,ij} \leq D_k, \quad \forall k \in \{1,\ldots,T\} \tag{10}$$

$$\sum_{\{i,j\}\in A} d_{ij}x_{k,ij} \leq s_k m_k, \quad \forall k \in \{1,\ldots,T\} \tag{11}$$

Constraint 10 offers flexibility in constraining each vehicle by the total journey distance, allowing the planner to set a specific limit for each vehicle. Constraint 11 provides an additional layer of flexibility, enabling the planner to fine-tune the distance traveled by the EV based on its current battery degradation. By leveraging Constraints 10 and 11, the logistics company planner can generate feasible and practical results.

3 Computational Results

Computational experiments were carried out on an Apple M1 computer with 16 GB of memory, running the Sonoma 14.0 operating system. The programming language used was Python 3.10.12, in conjunction with the industry-standard CPLEX 22.1.1.0 solver.

To assess the performance of the model, a diverse set of synthetic data was generated. A 100x1 rectangle was used to randomly select locations, while the average speed for the vehicles was randomly generated between 0–100 km/h. The duration of each route was randomly assigned between 4–8 h. Customer load were randomly generated between 5–10 kg. The capacity of each truck was randomly selected between 10 kg and the sum of the maximum pickup and delivery load from all customers.

To assess the performance of the model on real world data, a collaboration was established with a logistics company, which provided actual data from their day-to-day operations over a three-month period. The data received included location coordinates of customers and depot locations. The average speed of the company's vehicles was estimated to be 50 km/h for fossil fuel-powered trucks and 40 km/h for EVs, as per the provided data. The journey time for fossil fuel vehicles was capped at 8 h, while EVs had a shorter 6-h window. The capacities for the 16 fossil fuel trucks ranged between 700 kg to 14,000 kg, and the 2 EVs had capacities between 610 kg and 620 kg, respectively.

The logistics partner relied on a basic heuristic algorithm to use in their operations. Our implementation of this heuristic algorithm works as follows: the algorithm begins by selecting the heaviest vehicle available. It then searches for the nearest deliveries without pickups and selects them. Next, it identifies points with both pickups and deliveries and adds them to the route. Once it is no longer possible to take on additional customers, the algorithm selects customers with only pickups. Finally, if the vehicle reaches its maximum capacity, it returns to the depot and the next heaviest vehicle is selected to continue the route. This process is illustrated in Fig. 1 below.

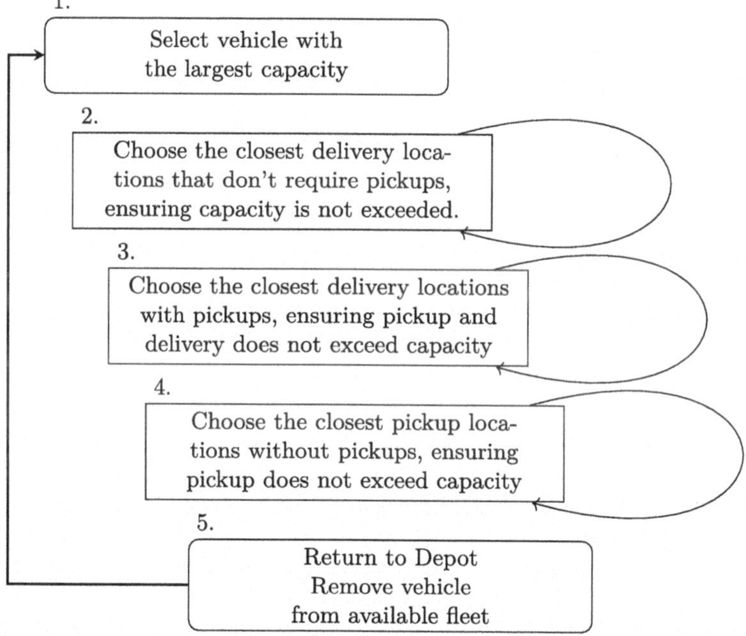

Fig. 1. Flowchart depicting the existing heuristic.

Table 4. Performance Comparison between Exact and Heuristic Method on Simulated Data

	Exact (3600 sec timeout)			Existing Heuristics		
#Instances	Time(sec)	Cost (kms)	#Vehicles	Time(sec)	Cost (kms)	#Vehicles
5	0.17	122	2	0.071	142	2
10	1.68	172	2	0.002	218	3
15	372.20	278	4	0.003	291	4
20	Timeout	360	5	0.005	717	8
25	Timeout	535	7	0.012	589	6

Table 5. Performance Comparison between Exact and Heuristic Method on Logistics Partner Data

	Exact (3600 sec timeout)			Existing Heuristics		
#Instances	Time(sec)	Cost (kms)	#Vehicles	Time(sec)	Cost (kms)	#Vehicles
5	0.31	1	1	0.004	1	1
10	3.33	14	1	0.005	29	2
15	1,360.02	16	3	0.011	30	2
20	Timeout	17	4	0.009	33	3
25	Timeout	20	6	0.011	36	4

To simulate a realistic day-to-day scenario, the CPLEX solver was configured to utilize a time limit of 3600 s, as specified by the "timelimit" parameter. This parameter enables the solver to terminate its search for an optimal solution if the computation exceeds the allotted time frame. In such instances, the solver will return a feasible solution.

In Table 4, a comparative analysis of the results for customers of varying sizes (5, 10, 15, 20, and 25) is presented, examining the performance of heuristic and exact methods. Notably, the exact method consistently outperforms the heuristic approach in terms of distance and the number of vehicles utilized for all instances. Specifically, as illustrated in the Table 4, for customer sizes of 20, the exact method generates routes with a distance of 360 kms and 5 vehicles, whereas the existing heuristics produce a route of 717 kms with 8 vehicles. In Table 5, a comparative analysis is conducted on real-world logistic partner data, demonstrating that the exact method yields feasible solutions that utilize fewer vehicles and reduce distance travelled compared to the heuristics for all instances. Furthermore, the heuristics fail to find a feasible solution when used with more than 10 nodes, highlighting the limitations of the greedy nature of the heuristic approach.

4 Conclusion and Future Work

This study presents a novel formulation for the VRP that incorporates EVs into a heterogeneous fleet, scalable for the operations of a logistics company. Our work makes a significant contribution to the existing literature on VRP by introducing new parameters and levers for the logistics planner that enable the minimization of air pollution and the optimization of fleet performance in the long run. Unlike previous studies, our approach considers these factors in a day-to-day operational manner, highlighting the potential of optimization techniques to drive sustainable and efficient operations in the logistics industry.

Future extensions to this formulation could include time windows, split deliveries, allowing multiple attempts, and mid-route refueling or recharging for longer journeys.

In this study, we have modeled electric vehicles in the formulation, but it is not necessary for the solver to pickup the electric vehicles in the final solution as the objective function solely focuses on minimizing the total distance traveled by the vehicles. To further enhance the formulation, we propose incorporating CO_2 emissions and real-time traffic information as multi-objectives. This would enable the solver to prioritize electric vehicles, optimizing the overall efficiency and sustainability of the logistics operations.

Acknowledgments. This research is funded by a collaboration project between the University of Luxembourg and Gulliver Luxembourg s.a r.l.

Disclosure of Interests. The authors have no competing interests to declare that are relevant to the content of this article.

References

1. Amiri, A., Amin, S.H., Zolfagharinia, H.: A bi-objective green vehicle routing problem with a mixed fleet of conventional and electric trucks: considering charging power and density of stations. Expert Syst. Appl. **213**, 119228 (2023)
2. Avci, M., Topaloglu, S.: A hybrid metaheuristic algorithm for heterogeneous vehicle routing problem with simultaneous pickup and delivery. Expert Syst. Appl. **53**, 160–171 (2016)
3. Conrad, R.G., Figliozzi, M.A.: The recharging vehicle routing problem (2011)
4. Dantzig, G., Fulkerson, R., Johnson, S.: Solution of a large-scale traveling-salesman problem. J. Oper. Res. Soc. Am. **2**(4), 393–410 (1954)
5. Erdoğan, S., Miller-Hooks, E.: A green vehicle routing problem. Transp. Res. Part E Logist. Transp. Rev. **48**(1), 100–114 (2012)
6. Goeke, D., Schneider, M.: Routing a mixed fleet of electric and conventional vehicles. Eur. J. Oper. Res. **245**(1) (2015)
7. Goel, A., Vidal, T.: Hours of service regulations in road freight transport: an optimization-based international assessment. Transp. Sci. **48**(3), 391–412 (2014)
8. Golden, B., Assad, A., Levy, L., Gheysens, F.: The fleet size and mix vehicle routing problem. Comput. Oper. Res. **11**(1), 49–66 (1984)

9. Günther, H.O., Kannegiesser, M., Autenrieb, N.: The role of electric vehicles for supply chain sustainability in the automotive industry. J. Clean. Prod. **90**, 220–233 (2015)
10. Juan, A.A., Mendez, C.A., Faulin, J., De Armas, J., Grasman, S.E.: Electric vehicles in logistics and transportation: a survey on emerging environmental, strategic, and operational challenges. Energies **9**, 86 (2016)
11. Keskin, M., Çatay, B.: A matheuristic method for the electric vehicle routing problem with time windows and fast chargers. Comput. Oper. Res. **100**, 172–188 (2018)
12. Kucukoglu, I., Dewil, R., Cattrysse, D.: The electric vehicle routing problem and its variations: a literature review. Comput. Ind. Eng. **161** (2021)
13. Laporte, G., Osman, I.H.: Routing problems: a bibliography. Ann. Oper. Res. **61**(1), 227–262 (1995)
14. Min, H.: The multiple vehicle routing problem with simultaneous delivery and pick-up points. Transp. Res. Part A Gen. **23**(5), 377–386 (1989)
15. Sassi, O., Cherif, W.R., Oulamara, A.: Vehicle routing problem with mixed fleet of conventional and heterogenous electric vehicles and time dependent charging costs (2014)
16. Schneider, M., Stenger, A., Goeke, D.: The electric vehicle-routing problem with time windows and recharging stations. Transp. Sci. **48**(4), 500–520 (2014)

“Green AI” and SW-Tools for Sustainable Energy and Materials Consumption

A Predictive Maintenance Concept for Sustainable Lubricant Oil Usage Based on Federated Learning

Hadi Ghaeni[1], Ferdinand Heinrich[2], Florian Rieger[2], Franz Wenninger[2], Tim Egger[1], and Benjamin Kormann[1](✉)

[1] Munich University of Applied Sciences, Lothstraße 64, 80335 München, Germany
{hghaeni,tegger,kormann}@hm.edu

[2] Fraunhofer-Institut für Elektronische Mikrosysteme und Festkörper-Technologien (EMFT), München, Germany
{ferdinand.heinrich,franz.wenninger}@emft.fraunhofer.de

Abstract. The SmartGear research project is working on a predictive maintenance concept for the sustainable use of lubricant oil. The core idea of this concept is to estimate laboratory quality measurements from real-time sensor data with a machine learning regression model. This work focuses on the estimation of the water content from sensor data. The federated learning approach is chosen to increase data security and to reduce network traffic, given the nature of the data, which is distributed across multiple sources, such as multiple machines within a factory or across different companies. This article presents the architecture of the federated learning environment. And to test the feasibility of the architecture, a dataset recorded on a laboratory test rig is split by experiments so that each client in the simulation contains a unique feature and target distribution. Exemplary the results of 4 different federated learning strategies are compared with a model trained on the same data in a centralised fashion. The centrally trained model achieves a coefficient of determination of 0.9 on the test set, while the best federated server model achieves a coefficient of determination of 0.79. The beast mean coefficient of determination of all clients on the validation set is 0.80. The investigation of a federated learning environment with real-world time series data shows accurate results for real-time condition monitoring while respecting data privacy and provides a reliable basis for predicting the remaining life of lubricant oil.

Keywords: federated learning · predictive maintenance · condition monitoring · machine learning · lubricant oil · federated strategies

1 Introduction

Effective machine lubrication is essential for smooth operation in production environments. Timely lubricant analysis can detect early signs of potential

H. Ghaeni and F. Heinrich—These authors contributed equally to this work.

A. Quesada-Arencibia et al. (Eds.): EUROCAST 2024, LNCS 15174, pp. 119–131, 2025.
https://doi.org/10.1007/978-3-031-83885-9_12

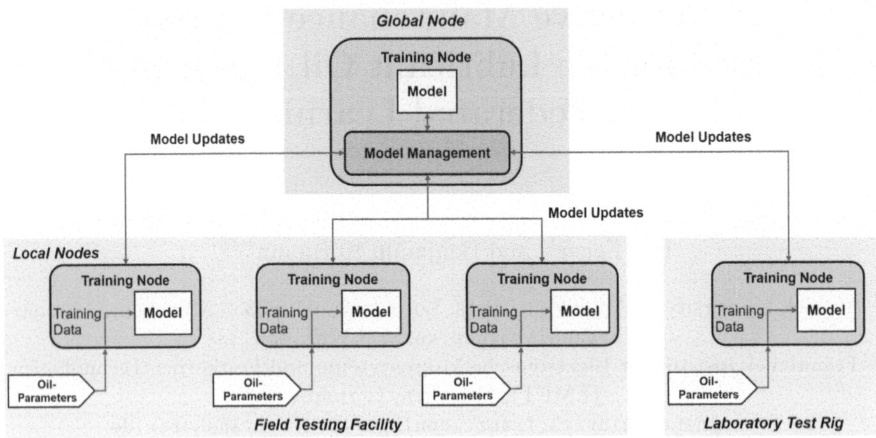

Fig. 1. The setup of distributed training nodes in the SmartGear project. With federated learning the global model collects model updates from local nodes in the field and form the laboratory test rig.

machine malfunction. Such problems can be caused either by normal ageing of the oil as it approaches the end of its useful life, or by sudden changes within the tribological system. Implementing on-line sensors to monitor the tribological system can be instrumental in detecting component failures. In addition, tracking typical ageing processes such as additive degradation or lubricant oxidation helps to estimate the remaining life of the lubricant and provides information on the optimum timing for oil changes.

The SmartGear project adopts an innovative strategy that integrates sensor technology with machine learning to move towards a predictive maintenance model. By analysing sensor data in real time, the project aims to continuously assess the condition of the oil and predict its remaining useful life. This will facilitate the creation of efficient maintenance schedules.

As the sensor data is acquired at multiple local nodes the network shown in Fig. 1 results. There are two sources of data. Part of the data comes from a laboratory test rig where experiments are performed according to a design of experiments to provide a data base for a machine learning model of oil ageing. In addition, raw data is collected locally at several industrial sites in the field. Both raw data sources can be labelled with the gold standard in oil quality assessment, a lubricant condition laboratory analysis. The raw oil sensor data can indirectly contain sensitive information, for example, oil temperature can be used to infer machine running time, which correlates with capacity utilisation. In order to provide a solution that does not require the transfer of raw data and therefore enables data security, Federated Learning (FL) is used. In addition, each industrial plant in the field is unique in terms of working environment and service history, and in a FL environment it is possible to deploy personalised machine learning models at each local node. Network traffic can also be reduced because only model updates are transferred, not raw data.

The natural ageing of lubricating oil occurs during the operation of machinery and our hypothesis is that it can be monitored by sensor units that measure various physical values. This multivariate time series data is the input to a machine learning model. The task is to find a regression model that can estimate the laboratory data from these input features (see Fig. 2). Laboratory analyses are performed on oil samples to evaluate and determine target values that act as ground truth for our regression objectives, such as viscosity and water content. By analysing these values, we can assess the condition of the oil and determine its current state.

This paper focuses on the effect of external contaminants, more specifically the water content in the oil. The methods described hereafter can be transferred to any other numerical regression target in the lubricant condition analysis.

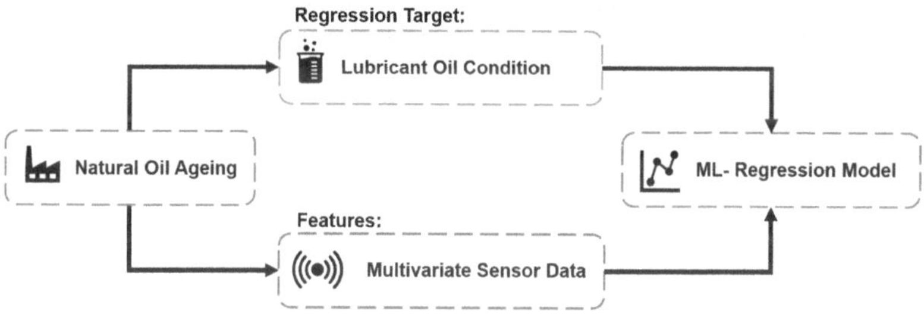

Fig. 2. Natural ageing of oil is traditionally monitored by laboratory measurements, which are used to estimate the condition of the oil. The SmartGear project builds a machine learning regression model that estimates this oil condition from real-time sensor data. This model is then deployed at each local node (see Fig. 1).

2 State of the Art

2.1 Condition Monitoring and Predictive Maintenance for Lubricant Oil

The traditional method of oil condition monitoring is a time-consuming process that requires manual labour and the use of expensive laboratory equipment. Analysing samples in a laboratory through several stages provides high quality data, which is considered the gold standard for assessing oil condition. To enable a predictive maintenance solution, the condition monitoring must first be automated. In the literature, this is done by estimating the condition of the lubricant oil based on real-time sensor data gathered on site. Based on this real-time condition, an estimate of the remaining useful life is required to enable predictive maintenance. This would enable more accurate and timely predictions of oil life and service requirements, helping to conserve resources.

In the literature, sensors are used in combination with empirical formulae or machine learning to estimate the current condition of lubricant oil. Conway et al. [4] present a sensor platform that uses mid-infrared spectroscopy to assess oil degradation at the molecular level. They claim to apply the same analytical techniques in real time at the point of oil use as would normally be done in a laboratory. Kimpl et al. [8] have developed a method for monitoring gearbox condition, which incorporates oil quality assessment based on a three-part system. The first element assesses the condition of the gearbox in terms of load, operating speed and vibration. The second monitors lubrication levels to prevent damage caused by inadequate oil supply or lubrication. The last and most important aspect in this scenario is to determine the condition of the oil by estimating its quality. Using empirical formulae, they estimate oil ageing based on a combination of real-time sensor data measured in the field and laboratory data.

Other publications use test benches to simulate fault conditions in systems and use sensors combined with machine learning to classify fault conditions. Helwig et al. [6] presented the condition monitoring of a complex hydraulic test rig, which allows to simulate fault conditions for components such as a cooler, a valve and a pump. The test rig is equipped with various sensors that measure different parameters such as temperature, air pressure and drive voltage at different times of each work cycle. The approach was to analyse the data in the time and frequency domain and, after feature selection, apply supervised learning. Different machine learning models such as Linear Discriminant Analysis (LDA), Artificial Neural Network (ANN) and Support Vector Machine (SVM) were trained to classify the fault conditions.

2.2 Federated Learning

Federated learning (FL) is a machine learning method where the training of a model is performed across multiple training nodes that hold local data samples without sharing them. Therefore, the model must be learned collaboratively across the network. In a turn-based learning scheme, the global server model aggregates the local models by aggregating the parameters, such as the weights of a neural network, or the gradients of the local training. The global model is then updated and the updated model is sent back to the local nodes. As no raw data is shared, privacy can be maintained and the need to transfer large amounts of data is reduced [2,10].

Federated Learning Architecture. According to the survey by Nguyen et al. [18], the architecture of FL can be divided into two main categories: a centralised and a decentralised FL network structure. In a centralised FL architecture, a global server model aggregates the information from local client models. In a decentralised FL, the model is only exchanged between local clients. The centralised FL architectures are further subdivided by Nguyen et al. [18] according to the characteristics of the sample and feature space in the dataset, as well as the communication and data exchange between the local training nodes. In the horizontal FL architecture, which is the focus of this paper, all local training nodes have the same feature space to train their local model, but different samples. The central training node aggregates and updates the model parameters from each local training node, and there is no communication between the local training nodes.

The work of Guendouzi et al. [5] outlines the evolution of Fl with respect to challenges such as communication overhead and data heterogeneity. A review of various aggregation techniques for the purpose of improving FL is presented. Additionally, the paper reviews the tools and frameworks available for the development of FL, as well as the metrics for evaluating FL algorithms.

One framework for FL is Flower [1]. It is designed to work with a wide range of edge devices, despite their inherent heterogeneity. The framework operates through three main server-side components: the FL loop, the RPC server based on the RPC/gRPC protocol [11], and a policy component that dictates the aggregation of model parameters. Importantly, Flower is framework agnostic and can work with any other ML framework for the training process. With Flower, model training can be facilitated across different client platforms and implementations without the need to know client specifics. It also supports on-device training in multiple programming languages, which is essential for mobile and embedded platforms that may not support Python. Flower's language-independent approach is enabled by the Flower protocol, which defines server-client interactions for model training and evaluation, complete with customisable metadata to control device-specific training details.

Marthur et al. [15] implemented and evaluated a FL setup using the Flower framework. They evaluated model accuracy, convergence time and energy consumption for object recognition tasks with up to 10 Android-based devices as clients.

Pruckovskaja et al. [19] evaluated the efficiency of FL in a predictive maintenance scenario with a focus on quality inspection in industrial applications. The efficacy of distinct FL aggregation strategies was assessed and contrasted with that of centralised and localised training approaches. The study was based on three public datasets and one newly published dataset. The findings indicated that the efficacy of FL is significantly influenced by the nature and distribution of the data across clients.

Strategies. The strategy is a cyclical process of training, updating, aggregating and distributing the local models over the network that is repeated through numerous iterations until the performance of the global model is optimised and a sufficiently accurate level of confidence is achieved. Moshawrab et al. [17] provide a comprehensive review of aggregation algorithms.

The research perspective differs depending on whether the focus is on achieving better results on the client side or on having a robust and universally valid global model with high confidence. In the SmartGear project, the focus is on client performance because ultimately the oil condition estimate at each individual client is the basis for all maintenance decisions.

One of the most challenging aspects of FL is that the data is often unbalanced and the local datasets are not independent and identically distributed (IID). Different clients contribute different amounts of data, and features may have different distributions. As a result, the local models can be very different, so server aggregation techniques and strategies are needed to overcome this challenge. The following strategies are relevant to this application [7,21].

- Federated Averaging (FedAvg) [16]:
  In the FedAvg strategy, each client locally performs gradient descent on the current model using its local data. The server model is then updated with a weighted average of the resulting models. The strategy is controlled by three hyperparameters: the fraction of randomly selected clients to perform computation in each round, the number of epochs or training passes each client performs on its local data set, and the local minibatch size used.
- Federated Averaging with Extensions (FedAvgM [7] and qFedAvg [13]):
  Federated Averaging with Server Momentum (FedAvgM) extends the FedAvg method with a server-side momentum to smooth the learning process from inherently different gradients obtained from local client models trained on non-IID data. Q-Fair FL (qFedAvg) aims to increase the fairness or uniformity of client model performance while maintaining average performance. To achieve this, the method gives higher weights to devices with poor performance. This increases their influence on the global model, resulting in a more even distribution of accuracies across the network.
- Robust Aggregation Methods (e.g., FedMedian and Trimmed Mean [22]):
  In the approach proposed by Yin et al. [22], there are two robust decentralised machine learning algorithms that use the median and trimmed mean methods to combine data, which can be used as a FL aggregation strategy. The FedMedian is an alternative aggregation mechanism aimed at enhancing robustness to adversarial attacks and reducing the impact of outliers in federated learning. Unlike traditional averaging methods, FedMedian involves clients computing their local model updates and then sending these updates to a server. Instead of averaging these updates, the server computes the element-wise median of the received model parameters. This model update strategy is particularly valuable in scenarios where some clients might contribute highly skewed or malicious updates, which could significantly degrade the performance of the global model if not mitigated. The trimmed mean method removes the highest and lowest values and averages the rest. These methods are tested on different loss functions and show strong performance, especially for highly convex losses.
- Federated XGBoost with Learnable Learning Rates (FedXG-Bllr [14]):
  Ma et al. [14] developed federated learning for gradient boosting trees that does not rely on sharing gradients and hessians, further improving data security. By making the learning rates learnable they claim that the network traffic is reduced in comparison with other FL strategies.

- Secure Aggregation Techniques (e.g., Salvia based on SecAgg(+)):
  In some use cases, privacy and data protection are more important. The Secure Aggregation set focuses on the different FL aggregation architectures that ensure high data security and use methods such as quantization and weighted aggregation to train a global model [3,12].

3 Methods

3.1 Federated Learning

In this paper, several state-of-the-art FL strategies are evaluated to test the applicability of an oil condition regression model in a FL use case as shown in Fig. 1.

Architecture. In the SmartGear project, it is proposed that in a future application, each local node in the field will utilise the same sensor set that was used at the laboratory test rig to build the oil condition regression model. Consequently, all local nodes share the same feature domain. Given the distinct operational conditions and service histories of each local node in the field, it is inevitable that the distribution of features, namely the raw sensor data, and the regression targets, namely the laboratory results, will differ between each node. The decision to take laboratory samples at a local node can be determined by the confidence of a local model. In order to aggregate the information from both the local nodes in the field and the laboratory test rig, a FL strategy is required. It is not intended that the local models will communicate with each other. This results in a horizontal server-client FL architecture.

The technical implementation of a local node is based on a programmable logic controller (PLC) device, which serves as a local data collector and gateway. The connection to the cloud or server is based on an MQTT [20] protocol derivation using LTE infrastructure.

Strategy Evaluation. The results presented in this work are based on a simulation performed with the FL framework Flower [1]. A number of strategies are tested and evaluated for the SmartGear dataset. A reliable baseline for the SmartGear dataset is the FedAvg method. The various extensions of FedAvg, such as server-side FedAvg with momentum (FedAvgM) and q-fair FedAvg (qFedAvg), as well as FedMedian, provide valuable experiments for comparing and analysing model performance.

3.2 Oil Condition Regression Model

The regression model is a small, densely connected neural network. It has two hidden layers of 64 neurons each, uses a leaky rectified linear unit as the activation function, and employs dropout regularisation during training. The output layer uses a Tangens Hyperbolicus activation function. The loss used is the mean absolute error and an ADAM [9] optimiser with a learning rate of 0.001 is used.

A laboratory evaluation test bed was used to conduct 17 experiments with fresh, used and artificially aged oil. The test plan defines different temperatures and water contents to simulate different operating environments. A set of sensors collects multivariate time series data of 12 features, including oil temperature, humidity, electrical conductivity, permittivity and calculated values, which sensor manufacturers claim can be used to assess oil quality. The regression targets are laboratory measurements. In this work, we present the results for the measured water content of the oil. The methodology described here could be applied to any other numerical laboratory measurement.

In order to test a FL setup for this use case, it is necessary to split the data into individual clients. The method of data splitting is illustrated in Fig. 3. Given the relatively small size of the data set, it is only possible to simulate a setup with three clients. Each client is assigned a unique set of experiments. As each experiment is distinct in terms of the combination of test plan and oil condition, the distribution of targets and features is inherently different for each client. The distribution of water content per client is illustrated in Fig. 4. In particular, client 1 exhibits a significantly different target distribution, with all target values being less than 0.4.

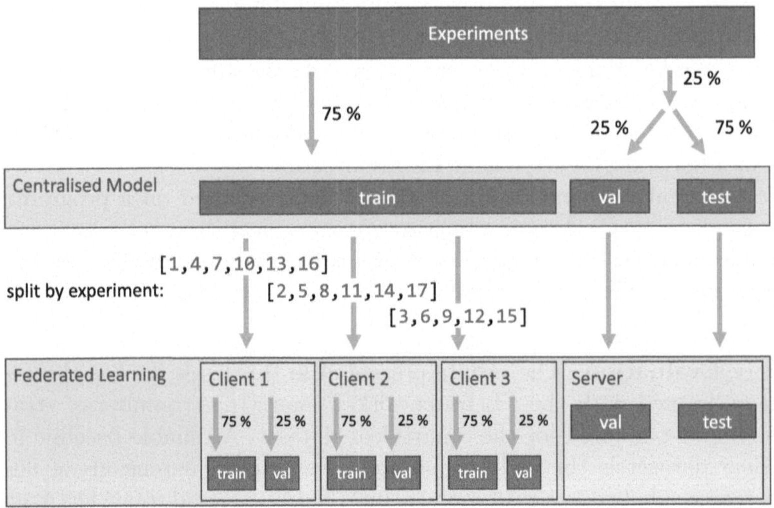

Fig. 3. Method of splitting data into individual clients to simulate a FL setup. Each client is allocated a unique set of experimental data.

Training. During each FL server round all three clients are fitted for two epochs. The best model is chosen with respect to the server validation error. A model trained on the entire dataset is used as a performance benchmark and is referred to as the centralised model in the following.

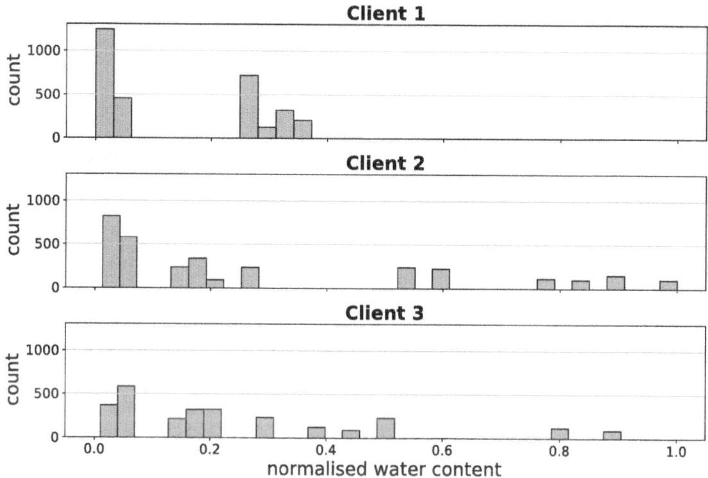

Fig. 4. The distribution of the normalised water content, i.e. the regression target, in the training data. Each client has a unique target distribution.

4 Results

Figure 5 shows the learning curves of the federated model training for the FedAvg and FedMedian methods for 300 server rounds. For FedAvg, the learning curve of the clients shows improvements for two clients, while the regression performance of client 1 actually decreases initially and then increases again later. This could be due to the fact that the regression target distribution of client 1 is different from that of the other clients, as it contains only smaller values (see Fig. 4). Therefore, updating with a global model that generalises across the entire regression target range will not necessarily improve local performance on a small regression target range. The FedMedian method achieves a similar coefficient of determination on the server validation data set, while the learning curves of the individual clients show a more diverse development. This may be due to the fact that the server-side momentum allows the hypothesis space of the model to be explored more efficiently.

Table 1 summarises the achieved performance metrics of the different FL strategies. Interestingly, the best-performing mean values of the client and server metrics are very similar. The coefficient of determination of the server on the test dataset is between 0.77 and 0.79, while the mean coefficient of determination of the clients on the validation dataset is between 0.78 and 0.80. The centrally trained model achieves a coefficient of determination of 0.90 on the test dataset.

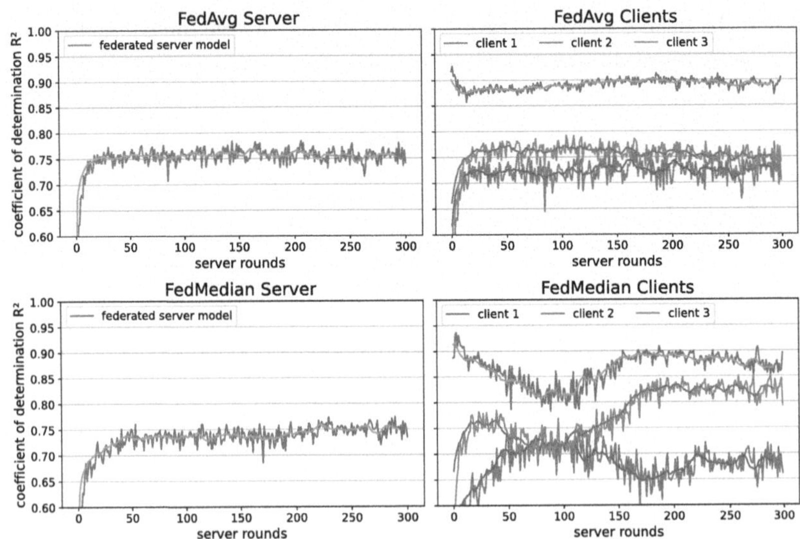

Fig. 5. Learning curve of the federated server model and clients for the FedAvg and FedMedian methods. Shown here is the coefficient of determination obtained on the validation data sets.

For the different FL strategies, the difference in performance between clients is also very similar for all methods, with a standard deviation between 0.06 and 0.08. Since the maintenance decision is based on the oil condition estimate at the local node, the local performance of the federated models is more important than the server performance. Therefore, the FedMedian and QFedAvg methods with a coefficient of determination of 0.80 can be considered as the best performing methods, but the margin is unlikely to be significant.

Table 1. Coefficient of determination of the different FL strategies and the centralised model.

performance metric: coefficient of determination R^2									
	clients						server		
strategy	client 1	client 2	client 3	mean	std	rank	val	test	rank
FedAvg	0.89	0.75	0.74	0.79	0.07	2	0.78	0.79	1
FedAvgM	0.89	0.71	0.75	0.78	0.08	3	0.78	0.79	1
FedMedian	0.89	0.70	0.81	0.80	0.08	1	0.77	0.78	2
QFedAvg	0.89	0.75	0.77	0.80	0.06	1	0.77	0.77	3

centralised model	0.90

Figure 6 compares the models with the lowest validation error of both the centrally trained model and the FedMedian server model. In both settings, the models appear to underestimate the higher normalised water content values and show a tendency to predict the regression target even close to zero. For the federated model this tendency is even greater and this may explain to some extent the difference in the coefficient of determination between the centralised model and the FedMedian server model. To overcome this problem, it may be necessary to adjust the model or the error function.

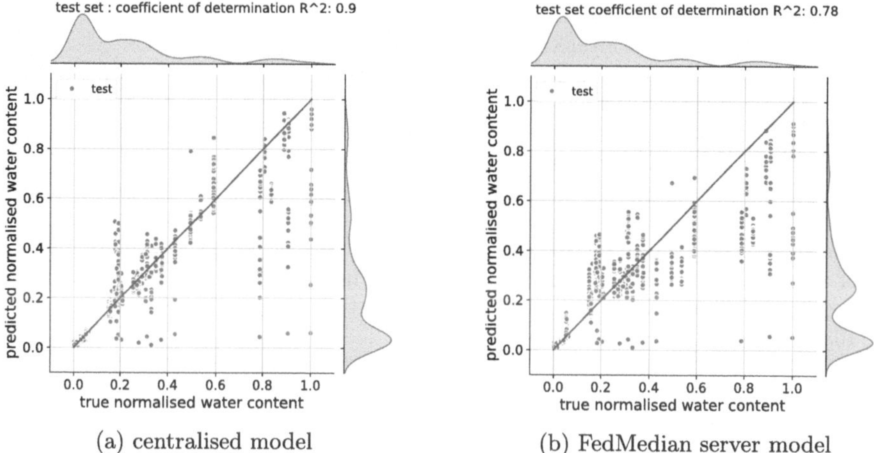

(a) centralised model

(b) FedMedian server model

Fig. 6. Test set regression performance of the centralised and the FedMedian server model.

5 Summary

To enable a privacy preserving method for real-time condition monitoring of lubricant oils, a horizontal FL architecture is simulated by splitting experimental data into a dataset with 3 clients. Each client has a unique distribution of raw sensor data as features and laboratory results representing the current condition of the oil as regression targets. In this research, the experiments were conducted with the measured water content in the lubricant oil as the regression target. The simulation of the FL shows promising results, as the federated models achieve a mean coefficient of determination of the clients of 0.78–0.80, which is relatively close to the performance of a centrally trained model with a coefficient of determination of 0.90. As the FL strategies all achieved very similar results, it is not possible to determine which strategy fits the problem best. The only way to test which method fits the problem best is to collect more data, simulate more clients and perform extensive hyper-parameter optimisation. In future research, it is also very interesting to test methods that implement a personalised model per client or methods that focus even more on privacy and data protection, such as the secure aggregation set. In addition, the current condition monitoring approach needs to be extended to include an estimate of the remaining useful life of the oil to enable a true predictive maintenance solution.

Acknowledgements. This research was funded by the Bavarian Research Foundation as part of the SmartGear project under grant number AZ-1523-21.

References

1. Beutel, D.J., et al.: Flower: a friendly federated learning research framework. https://doi.org/10.48550/arXiv.2007.14390
2. Bonawitz, K., et al.: Towards federated learning at scale: system design. http://arxiv.org/pdf/1902.01046v2
3. Bonawitz, K., et al.: Practical secure aggregation for federated learning on user-held data. https://doi.org/10.48550/arXiv.1611.04482
4. Conway, N., Giebeler, C.: 24/7 real-time oil condition monitoring. Tribol. Schmierungstech. **69**(7), 4–8 (2022)
5. Guendouzi, B.S., Ouchani, S., EL Assaad, H., EL Zaher, M.: A systematic review of federated learning: challenges, aggregation methods, and development tools. J. Netw. Comput. Appl. **220**, 103714 (2023). https://doi.org/10.1016/j.jnca.2023.103714
6. Helwig, N., Pignanelli, E., Schutze, A.: Condition monitoring of a complex hydraulic system using multivariate statistics. In: 2015 IEEE International Instrumentation and Measurement Technology Conference (I2MTC) Proceedings, pp. 210–215. IEEE (2015). https://doi.org/10.1109/I2MTC.2015.7151267
7. Hsu, T.M.H., Qi, H., Brown, M.: Measuring the effects of non-identical data distribution for federated visual classification. http://arxiv.org/pdf/1909.06335
8. Kimpl, E., Stroi, M.: The 3 columns of gear condition monitoring. In: OilDoc Conference (2019)
9. Kingma, D.P., Ba, J.: Adam: a method for stochastic optimization. https://doi.org/paper. https://arxiv.org/pdf/1412.6980
10. Konečný, J., McMahan, H.B., Ramage, D., Richtárik, P.: Federated optimization: distributed machine learning for on-device intelligence. http://arxiv.org/pdf/1610.02527v1
11. Lee, C.S., Lee, K.H., Lee, J.K.: A group RPC protocol for distributed systems. In: Proceedings of ICICS, 1997 International Conference on Information, Communications and Signal Processing, Theme: Trends in Information Systems Engineering and Wireless Multimedia Communications (Cat. No. 97TH8237), pp. 805–809. IEEE (1997). https://doi.org/10.1109/ICICS.1997.652090
12. Li, K.H., de Gusmão, P.P.B., Beutel, D.J., Lane, N.D.: Secure aggregation for federated learning in flower. In: Proceedings of the 2nd ACM International Workshop on Distributed Machine Learning, pp. 8–14. ACM, New York, NY, USA (2021). https://doi.org/10.1145/3488659.3493776
13. Li, T., Sanjabi, M., Beirami, A., Smith, V.: Fair resource allocation in federated learning. https://doi.org/ICLR. http://arxiv.org/pdf/1905.10497
14. Ma, C., Qiu, X., Beutel, D., Lane, N.: Gradient-less federated gradient boosting tree with learnable learning rates. In: Yoneki, E., Nardi, L. (eds.) Proceedings of the 3rd Workshop on Machine Learning and Systems, pp. 56–63. ACM, New York, NY, USA (2023). https://doi.org/10.1145/3578356.3592579
15. Mathur, A., et al.: On-device federated learning with flower (2021). https://doi.org/10.48550/arXiv.2104.03042

16. McMahan, H.B., Moore, E., Ramage, D., Hampson, S., Arcas, B.A.Y.: Communication-efficient learning of deep networks from decentralized data (2016). https://doi.org/10.48550/arXiv.1602.05629
17. Moshawrab, M., Adda, M., Bouzouane, A., Ibrahim, H., Raad, A.: Reviewing federated learning aggregation algorithms; strategies, contributions, limitations and future perspectives. Electronics **12**(10), 2287 (2023). https://doi.org/10.3390/electronics12102287
18. Nguyen, D.C., Ding, M., Pathirana, P.N., Seneviratne, A., Li, J., Poor, H.V.: Federated learning for internet of things: a comprehensive survey (2021). https://doi.org/10.48550/arXiv.2104.07914
19. Pruckovskaja, V., et al.: Federated learning for predictive maintenance and quality inspection in industrial applications. http://arxiv.org/pdf/2304.11101v1
20. Quincozes, S., Emilio, T., Kazienko, J.: MQTT protocol: fundamentals, tools and future directions. IEEE Lat. Am. Trans. **17**(09), 1439–1448 (2019). https://doi.org/10.1109/TLA.2019.8931137
21. Reddi, S., et al.: Adaptive federated optimization. http://arxiv.org/pdf/2003.00295v5
22. Yin, D., Chen, Y., Ramchandran, K., Bartlett, P.: Byzantine-robust distributed learning: towards optimal statistical rates. http://arxiv.org/pdf/1803.01498v2

Introduction to Circular System Design and First Use Cases for Sustainable Product Development in Smart Meter Remanufacturing and Robotics

Nathanael Nafz[1], Bernhard Höfig[1(✉)], Markus Glück[1], and Niclas-Alexander Mauß[2]

[1] Aalen University of Applied Sciences, Beethovenstr. 1, 73430 Aalen, Germany
bernhard.hoefig@hs-aalen.de

[2] CIRCULAR REPUBLIC/UnternehmerTUM GmbH, Freddie-Mercury-Str. 5, 80797 Munich, Germany

Abstract. Product design has a major, often under-estimated impact on sustainability. This article describes the process of a new sustainable product design aiming for integrating circular engineering and social aspects as an integral part of the design process. A methodology is presented that enables a holistic, systematic approach to product development with the product design goal of a 'Circular System' with three subordinates but interdependent key elements: the 'Product', its 'Life Cycle System' and the related 'Context System'. Social and ecological responsibility is integrated into product design from the beginning, ending up in a cyclic 'Convergent Creation Model'. The associated methodology can be understood as a valuable opportunity to structure and control the complexity of sustainable product design for circularity. Two representative use cases - an established high-volume circular product (smart water metering unit) and a strategic design and R&D perspective on "green" robots, contributing as sustainably engineered production systems to zero emission production – are discussed. Both demonstrators for the general applicability of the proposed 'Circular System Design' approach underline the potential of the methodology for advanced sustainable systems engineering in different phases of product design and circular production.

Keywords: Sustainable Design · System Thinking · Circular Economy · Product Development · Systems Engineering

1 Introduction

The impact of human activity on the environment has become obvious since the intensified discussion about the scarcity of raw materials, human-related global warming and the naming of a new geological era as the 'Anthropocene' [1–3]. One of the reasons for these far-reaching interventions is the so-called 'linear economy', which can also be described as a 'take-make-dispose' model [4]. According to a World Bank report, the

A. Quesada-Arencibia et al. (Eds.): EUROCAST 2024, LNCS 15174, pp. 132–146, 2025.
https://doi.org/10.1007/978-3-031-83885-9_13

amount of waste which is generated every year will increase dramatically by 2050 [5]. Additionally, a 2023 report by the International Labour Organisation states the fact that for the majority of workers, work does not always guarantee a decent living neither social justice [6]. Ecological, ethical and social aspects are so far not sufficiently considered in product design and development.

Therefore, a paradigm shift, both in methodologies and in the mind of developers, is needed. New ways to create products that systematically incorporate social and ecological in addition to economic aspects from the very beginning are required.

A promising solution is circular economy and the circular thinking that goes with it [7, 8]. A transformation from purely linear to circular processes and products is distinctly necessary. This has also been concluded previously in numerous publications such as the 'Circular Economy Roadmap for Germany', the 'Standardization Roadmap Circular Economy' and the 'Circular Economy Action Plan' of the European Union for instance, respectively [9–11]. There, the need for a 'circular design' is explicitly postulated.

In the following, we present our holistic concept for Circular System Design. It is a new system-oriented approach for sustainable product design and development supported with an iterative agile and cyclic methodology (Convergent Creation Model) which is targeted on a corresponding newly oriented circular ecosystem (Circular System). With this approach, we want to offer a new view on product design and engineering, which gives a consistent guideline towards circular economy.

2 Methodical Approaches in Product Design

Numerous methodologies for the design and development of new products have already been proposed. A selection with relevance to our considerations is provided in the following:

At the beginning of the 1990s, Cooper's Stage-Gate approach triggered a transformation from purely design methodology-oriented linear processes to business and management-oriented product development processes [12]. The central design criterion is the subdivision of subsequent activities into phases and the early review of relevant work package results at stage gates. This type of model is supported by the assumption that product innovation and the development of new products is a controllable, linear process. Subsequently, the stage-gate model was adapted to current needs in three generations [13]. Further improvements to the stage-gate process have been proposed by the Verein der Deutschen Ingenieure (VDI). The guideline for the development of technical products, VDI 2221, was developed. It is based, among other things, on Cooper's methodology and is still commonly used in science and industrial practice [14].

The VDI 2206 guideline - Development of mechatronic and cyber-physical systems - describes an extended methodological framework for the modular development of complex technical systems with the V-model as a basis [15]. It specifically addresses the close interaction of mechanical and electronic systems with computer sciences in close integration on a functional carrier.

The integrated product development model (iPeM) proposed by Albers et al. in [16] is also based on the stage-gate approach. Unlike other methods, it considers the development of product generations and incorporates existing knowledge from previous developments in product innovation. It is the basis for the method and process research of the Karlsruhe School of Product Development.

With the help of Scrum, an iterative, strongly stakeholder-oriented development framework has been established in recent years, originally used for advanced software engineering. It describes roles and working rules in an agile manner, that makes it possible to adapt work packages very quickly to changes in requirements and customer expectations. It is a cyclic process for the accelerated development of products with enhanced flexibility and special focus on the iterative development of minimum viable products for immediate prototype testing [17].

In Eco Design, ecological aspects receive increased attention. The designer consequently mediates development goals between technology, consumers, the environment and the economy. This primarily involves the integration of environmental aspects into various planning processes and ecological requirements. Key performance indicators (KPI) are introduced in order to better control and optimize the type and quantity of materials used, the waste produced, energy consumption and intensity of use, or minimising emissions [18].

Many of the new development methods are designed for more flexibility and closer stakeholder integration. However, they pay insufficient attention to ecological (i.e. in the sense of circularity) and social aspects. The need for a new or at least revised product development methodology follows from the previously analysed methodologies and was also proposed by Hollander et al. [19].

3 Definition of the Circular System

Before introducing the definitions of the term 'Circular System' and its key elements, it is important to understand the design objectives that have so far been in the primary focus when designing new products: for satisfying customers' needs and functional requirements [20]. Consequently, social and ecological goals recede into the background. Even later they only receive attention as a 'megatrend' [21].

This does not result in a fundamental consideration and consistent concretisation of sustainability aspects in product design and systems engineering. It is therefore necessary to change the major goal of product design and development: From the beginning, it must be clearly defined which holistic objectives exist in economic terms as well as in ecological and social terms. Developers must seek for technical solutions that are in harmony with society and our living space.

The following quote illustrates why a new term must also be generated for this new objective. "[Language] can serve as a medium through which we create new understandings and new realities as we begin to talk about them. In fact, we don't talk about what we see; we see only what we can talk about. […] To reshape the measurement and communication systems of a [society] is to reshape all potential interactions at the most fundamental level. Language […] as articulation of reality is more primordial than strategy, structure, or […] culture." [22].

We therefore propose to move away from the pure focus on a product and introduce the new term Circular System. It represents a model comprising three key elements: the 'Product', the 'Life Cycle System' and the 'Context System' (Fig. 1). They are to be regarded as equivalent and interdependent. The interactions between the Product, the Life Cycle System and the Context System must not be neglected, as only the interaction of all elements can lead to a functioning overall system. Figure 1 shows the correlation of the individual elements of the Circular System. Interactions of the elements arranged in the triangle are indicated by arrows. An ellipse summarises the three key elements and their interactions. This is intended to make clear that all three fall under the concept of the Circular System. The over-all concept of the Circular System consequently merges the systematic emergence of a holistic, sustainable system and enables a thought process on different levels (see Sect. 4, Fig. 4).

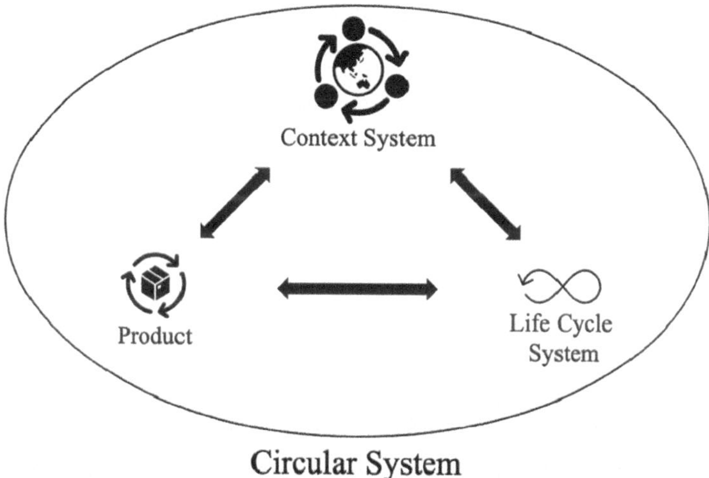

Fig. 1. Components of the Circular System

The Context System influences both, the Product and the Life Cycle System. In terms of sustainability, the Product and the Life Cycle System must fit into the Context System like pieces of a puzzle and must not have any negative effects on it. This must be considered for all three dimensions of sustainability (economic, ecological and social). Boundary conditions are created by direct and indirect specifications from the Context System. They are of political, ecological and economical in origin. It is important to recognise, that all inputs and outputs, without exception, flow into and out the Context System. Examples of this would be political restrictions, but also a lack of resources, triggered by the linear economy.

The Product and the Life Cycle System are also directly correlated. For example, the element of use contained in the Life Cycle System influences the Product. But other elements, such as production or recycling, also interact directly with the Product. The three elements of the Circular System are described in more detail below.

3.1 Product

A Product is the result of human labour and serves to satisfy needs and creates value [20]. Therefore, the Product is an elementary component of the superordinate Circular System.

In the early phases of task clarification and functional definition, the classical systems engineering approach considers the flows of energy, material and information turnover (cf. [23].) in a linear manner. The aim is to make the unknown function, initially presented as a 'black box', more concrete. The 'black box' is gradually supplemented with details and thus becomes a 'white box'. The development task is to transfer the identified functions into technical solutions in order to be able to create a Product at the end. In the conceptual world of the Circular System, this representation is extended by additional feedbacks (see Fig. 2). They have to be considered from the beginning to create an awareness of cycles. Depending on the Product, however, the loops are pronounced differently.

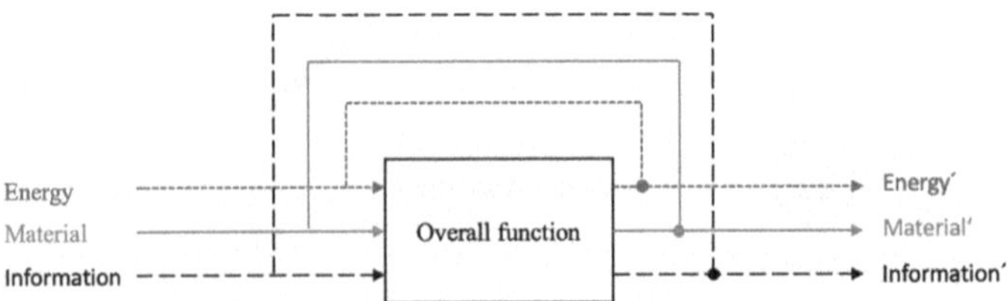

Fig. 2. Product "black box" based on [23]

3.2 Life Cycle System

Based on the system diagram, shown in Fig. 2 [23] and the butterfly diagram, proposed by the Ellen McArthur Foundation [4], a general representation of the Life Cycle System was developed (Fig. 3). The special aspect is, that the Product described above is also part of the Life Cycle System. Through the material flow, but also the product flow, it is possible to understand and further develop the respective interdependencies between the individual elements. The necessary technical solutions must be sought for the respective functions in accordance with the requirements of the Product and the Context System. The inner product/substance cycles are to be prioritized [4]. This means, for example, that the repair cycle should have priority over product recycling.

Looking at the energy flow, it is possible to see the life cycle in a different context. Energy can also possibly be traced back. In addition, it is important to challenge the overall system behaviour in the context of energy and resources consumption to optimize sustainability as well as circularity. It should be noted, that secondary materials can have an energy advantage compared to primary materials. Recycling, for example, takes on a different weighting when it is expanded to include this aspect. For example, recycling aluminium saves about 95% of the energy compared to primary production [24].

The energy and product/substance cycles are supported by the flow of information. Only when the required information is transferred correctly, an effective circular system performance is achieved. For example, recycling needs information about disassembly or the materials, that have been used.

All input and output flows must be seen in the relationship of the Context System. If, for example, water leaves the Life Cycle System during production, it must be analysed what happens in the Context System as a result. It may affect the ecology or the society living there. A comprehensive flow of information is also important here and ensures cross-system networking and transparency.

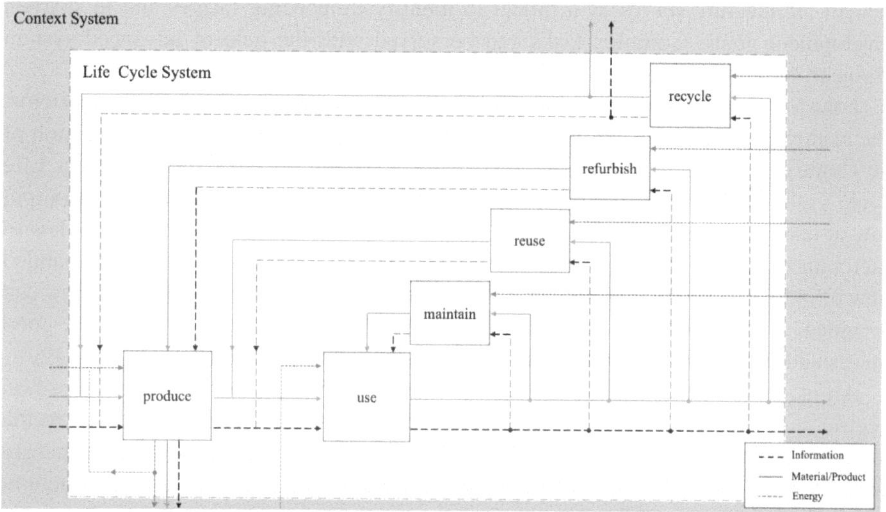

Fig. 3. Basic structure of the Life Cycle System

In the sense of the butterfly diagram [4], special attention must be paid to the technical and biological cycle. Among other things, these environmental aspects are to be considered in combination with the Context System.

3.3 Context System

The Context System describes the ecosystem in which the Product and the Life Cycle System interact. Its application is diverse and contains ecological, social and economic subsystems, depending on the development project [25]. Sociotechnical and socioecological systems are a way of systematically identifying ecological and social interactions. A sociotechnical system is understood as the interaction between people and technology [26]. Here, among other things, the inclusion of social systems is important. It is recommended to consider the basic structure of the Life Cycle System and the elements contained therein (see Fig. 3) from the point of view of social aspects. One way of doing this is to consider the suppliers, the structure in one's own company, but also the conditions under which recycling takes place.

In addition, socioecological systems must be taken into account [27]. It is consequently necessary to make developers aware of their social and ethical responsibility. There must be a balance between locality and globality.

As development progresses, the Context System becomes more elaborated and refined. This refinement is necessary in order to be able to make long-term decisions on the development path to follow. The continuous iterative rethinking of the Context System in generations therefore plays an important role.

Different disciplines are involved in detailing the Context System and holistically mapping its relationships to the Life Cycle System and the Product. These essentially include the engineering sciences, bionics, circular engineering, computer sciences, business administration, sociology and labour and economic sciences [21]. The Context System architecture serves as a model to identify influencing factors and to sharpen development goals. Complex tasks can be solved with the help of advanced system engineering.

For a fully intact habitat, it is a prerequisite to create coherent and networked systems. The example of industrial symbioses can be used to describe the diverse application of the Context System. A Life Cycle System for a specific Product supports other Life Cycle Systems [28]. Based on nature, completely new potentials are created. The output flow of one system is the input to another. Mechatronic systems use information flow to interconnect systems and transform them into cyber-physical systems. In the expanded view of industrial symbioses, the interdependencies of the energy and material flow can be added. The focus here is on adapting and imitating systems from nature. A good understanding of ecological processes and systems is a fundamental prerequisite [29].

An example of the Circular System is the development, production and use of an electric car. The development of the vehicle as a Product requires, in addition to the purely basic function of "driving electrically", additional products and processes that are assigned to the Life Cycle System. These are processes that are adapted to the production, use, maintenance, reuse, repair and recycling of the respective components. Examples are: recycling of rare earth elements from batteries and motors or the use of materials like copper and aluminium with substantial content of recycled material contributions instead of using new materials from primary resources. In the Context System of electromobility, other aspects must also be taken into account, such as legal constraints for CO2 emissions or the development of a charging infrastructure, ethically justifiable resilient supply chains, the acceptance of new ideas and alternative mobility concepts by society, and the interaction of all subsystems with the over-all traffic ecosystem. This overview reflects only a few of the many aspects that contribute to the Circular System.

4 Convergent Creation Model – Circular System Design

The 'Convergent Creation Model' (Fig. 4) aims to integrate sustainability into product design and development from the very beginning. Unlike the commonly used methodologies for product creation, it does not describe the process of creating a product, but the general process of creating the Circular System. We call this process 'Circular System Design' (CSD). The term 'creation', based on VDI2221, refers to the planning, design (i.e. development) and implementation of the circular system [14]. The term 'convergence' was chosen, because the process model aims to iteratively approach the ideal state of a comprehensive, sustainably balanced circularity. Each cycle corresponds to a generation. When a new development process begins, it builds on previous circular systems. The consideration of generations in the creation process is fundamental, because "[...] products are developed in generations" [16].

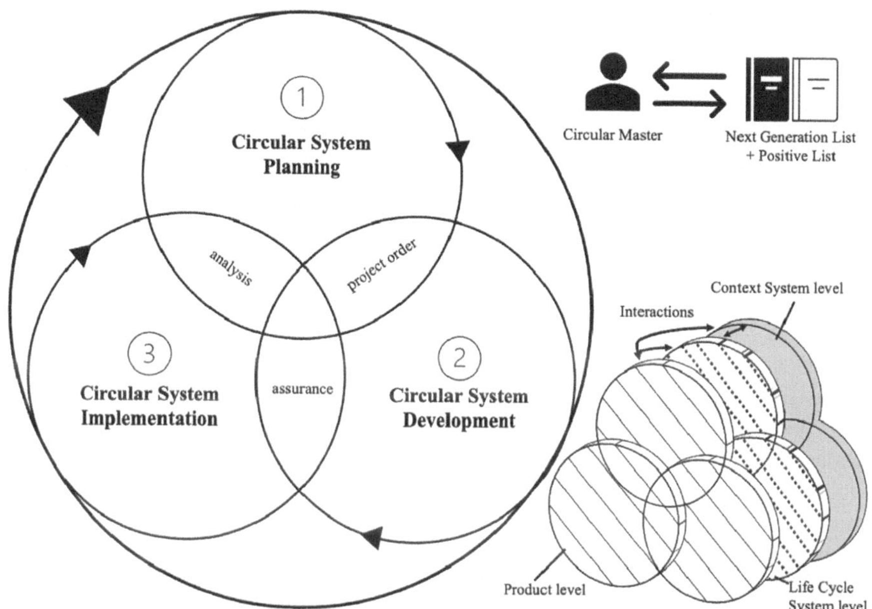

Fig. 4. The Convergent Creation Model of the Circular System

Based on the good experiences from 'Scrum', the inner cycles and the 'Circular Master', as a new key role, ensure agility and personal commitment. The inner cycles show that it is necessary to subject them to several iterations or 'sprints' in order to adapt them to customer requirements and changes in market requests, but also to new insights and requirements from related circular developments. The inner cycle must be defined in terms of time and can be supplemented by further inner cycles in the form of daily consultations, such as stand-up meetings known from 'Scrum' [17]. The Circular Master is like a 'sprint master' or 'product owner' in agile organisations - a dedicated person who specialises in the Circular System and the associated creation processes. He coordinates and owns the consideration of the three elements of the Circular System.

In the Convergent Creation Model for the Circular System, the iteration steps of planning, development and implementation are cycled with special attention to three elements (Product, Life Cycle System and Context System) in order to holistically consider the interactions between the elements. Bottom right in Fig. 4, these elements are therefore shown in three levels to graphically illustrate the permanent occurrence of the individual creation steps for all elements. Throughout the creation process, the interactions between each other must be considered. This will lead to new requirements as well as valuable new insights.

For this process model to remain applicable in practice, the Circular Master is free to make decisions that are against circularity through agreements within a certain framework. This may be necessary, for example, if the safety of a system can only be guaranteed with non-circular materials. However, the overall goal of circularity remains intact, as the decisions are only made under the condition of solving the problem in future generations of the circular system. For this purpose, the so-called 'Next Generation List' is introduced. It summarizes the decisions taken in a comprehensive way. This gap list must stay under priority review and has to be worked through stepwise in the sense of convergence. In combination with the 'Positive List' of proven solutions, the Circular System Design can be further accelerated. It summarises circular substances, suppliers and materials that are sensible and proven for the company in a focussed guideline or a special knowledge management database [30].

4.1 Circular System Planning

The first step in Circular System Design is the planning phase. The goal of the planning phase is the creation of the project order. According to relevant design standards, a project order must contain at least the following contents: Objective, expected results, boundary conditions, responsibilities, planned resources, concurring declaration of intent by the customer and the person responsible for the project (Trans. by author.) [31]. In addition, the assignment should include the three levels. This can be done, for example, by naming particularly important interactions. A possible focus on the interaction 'repair' in relation to Context System and Product is one of many possibilities. However, the major task should be to consider all interactions. The concept of convergent iterations across generations helps to approach this goal step by step.

Once the planning has been concretised to such an extent that development can take place, the project order for the Circular System is handed over to the development team. It contains all the information necessary for the start of the development process. The handover of the project order does not represent the end of the planning phase. It serves to define the goal and the realization path for the development to lead the way. A change of the content based on consultation is always possible and should be clarified by the inner, overlapping circles of the Convergent Creation Model.

4.2 Circular System Development

Based on the requirements in the project order, the development of the Circular System begins. The task of 'Circular System Development' is to identify problems and address them with technical solutions on all levels of the Circular System. Like the planning process, the development process is iterative in cycles and - as in the 'Scrum' method - characterised by regular consultations with the planning department and potential end-users. An additional iterative connection exists with the Circular System Implementation. It documents the real (trial, test) and/or virtual (calculations, simulation) assurance (validation and verification) of the results [14]. Assurance takes place at all levels. A variety of well-known and proven process models supports the specific activities during the development iterations.

The development of complex cyber-physical systems can be carried out with the help of the V-Modell, as specified in VDI 2206. On this basis, for example, the V-Modell can be further developed and extended with the concepts of Circular System Design.

4.3 Circular System Implementation

The third phase of Circular System Design describes the implementation, i.e. the specific realisation of the entire Circular System. This includes the embedding of the Life Cycle System in the Context System, the actual production of the Product, its use, reuse and recycling. The process of implementation is iterative and is linked to development in the Convergent Creation Model. Emerging knowledge about the system during implementation may require further development efforts. It is also conceivable to plan again based on previous implementations of a Circular System, with new focal points and goals. The main goal of a fundamentally sustainable Circular System can thus be achieved gradually, in the sense of convergence.

5 Use Case Studies

In this section, we describe two representative use case studies to illustrate the application of the concepts and terms presented. It is intended to underline the applicability of Circular System Design in two types and stages of a development effort and to draw some initial conclusions.

5.1 Circular Production of Smart Water Metering Units

The first case study describes the successful introduction of a circular business model based on the remanufacturing of water metering units. The company Lorenz GmbH & Co. KG from Schelklingen-Ingstetten specializes in water and radio water meters. The "Smart Water Metering" Product is used to record water consumption and must, among other things, comply with legal requirements in terms of accuracy (verified by regular calibration). The product essentially consists of a hydraulic component (made of brass), a plastic counter and an electronic circuit board for intelligent data acquisition and communication.

In contrast to its competitors, Lorenz decided to develop the product for a holistic, sustainable use and to establish a circular business model innovation [9]. In our methodology, this first essential step is located in the Circular System Planning phase of the Convergent Creation Model (see Fig. 4). The chosen process was to focus on material savings based on remanufacturing. Remanufacturing, i.e. the processing of the used product through various process steps so that at least the quality level of a new product is achieved, serves as the basis for circularity. The customer can use the remanufactured product like a new product without any difference in quality.

At the end of their service life, the water metering units are returned to the supplier. As an incentive, the customer receives a credit note for the returned products. Automated dismantling, cleaning, testing, reconditioning, reassembly and quality testing are carried out at the factory. Here, we find the results of the Circular System Development and

Implementation phases for the Life Cycle System. This circular business model has enabled the company to achieve continuous growth in a saturated market, while at the same time significantly reducing its environmental impact compared to new production [32].

This example clearly shows that successful circular product development must be understood as a holistic task that considers and designs the Product, the Life Cycle System and the Context System from the outset. Circular System Design as a holistic development methodology makes it possible to describe and relate the various development steps and their dependencies.

Within the Circular System Development phase the Product "Smart Water Metering Unit" is developed from the outset with the requirements for a modular, easily dismantled assembly. The components are designed for a long service life, the memory modules are dimensioned larger (despite higher initial costs) in order to be prepared for future software updates. These product requirements result from the Life Cycle System of the remanufacturing process.

In addition to pure product development, it is also necessary to develop the remanufacturing process as a Life Cycle System. This includes, for example, issues relating to take-back (collection, logistics and storage areas) and the materials used (raw material criticality) for components and spare parts. Furthermore, Lorenz has developed its own automation solutions for the efficient processing of the returned products.

In the Context System, we will allocate for example, the requirements with regard to the legal framework and the economic viability of the circular business model. In addition, social (job security, single-shift operation) and ecological aspects (climate-neutral production, industrial symbioses, enriching ecosystems) are considered and designed here.

In this example, the role of the Circular Master was taken over by the management of Lorenz. Here, the strategic decisions for the remanufacturing process were made for all three key elements of the Circular System and the necessary resources were provided for their implementation. Future developments and proven solutions for the product, the remanufacturing process and the circular business model are collected in a Next Generation List and Positive List in order to further improve the degree of circularity.

With the help of the Circular System Design approach, the complex development process with its various stakeholders and tasks can be structured very well. The concept of "Product", "Life Cycle System" and "Context System" allows development tasks to be divided into modularized projects in the sense of systems engineering. The mutual dependencies can thus be taken into account at an early stage in the requirements for product design and engineering. The proposed Convergent Creation Model with is agile circular phases of Circular System Planning, Development and Implementation guides the development team through the whole design process. The overarching goal of a sustainable circular product and business model is consistently in focus.

5.2 Application in Modern Automation Processes – Green Robotics

The second use case describes the application of the Circular System Design approach for industrial robots, which are at risk of becoming a quickly interchangeable commodity product.

Following the Circular System Design approach, it is first and foremost necessary to develop a completely different 'non linear' view on the product lifecycle and its perspective. State of the art industrial robots as Products according to the new terminology are increasingly providing levers to relieve people from physically and mentally demanding work [33]. Most of them are used in high-volume series production, e.g. in automotive industry, operating as key components in automated handling, dispensing or welding applications [34]. Their primary function is to support the assembly of car bodies at highest speed. Robots are not at all used as isolated components in single applications. In contrary, most robots are an integral part of interconnected process and supply chains consuming a lot of energy. Today, approximately 60% of the energy consumption in car body assembly is caused by robots.

A clear vision of the product needs to be established by placing its long-term and future functionalities into the center of the long-term product concept. It leads to the Life Cycle System: State of the art industrial robots are in most cases not yet optimized with respect to sustainability aspects. The potential for extending their life cycle and improving their resource-efficiency is still underestimated [35]. The current life cycle of a robot is correlated with a typical 7-year life cycle of automotive production. Robot designs must be prepared for circular economy by increasing the reuse, refurbish and recycling potentials in future equipment set-up.

In addition, the Context System must be analysed: Industrial robots definitely need to undergo a profound transformation process towards "green" robotics as the automotive industry is legally enforced to substantially decrease CO2 emission. The prosecuted primary goal is climate neutrality in production, following a distinct zero emission strategy in society. Another target is strengthening the resilience of supply chains. Robots offer an opportunity to restore production activities from distant countries. This reduces logistics efforts and minimizes the ecological footprint attributed to logistics. In addition to these important global targets, further direct environmental impacts (e.g. land and water use, toxicity) of the Life Cycle System have to be considered. Also, the design of possible industrial symbioses falls within the scope of the Context System.

The complex transformation towards "green" robotics can only be achieved by a revolutionary new modular robot design that is ideally developed following the guidelines of Circular System Design based on the frame conditions of the Life Cycle System and the Context System - a paradigm shift!

During the initial Circular System Planning phase, not only system parameters like cycle times need to be derived. All internal components have to be categorized according to their maintenance, reuse, refurbish, and recycling potential. In parallel, the supplier base needs to be evaluated for ethical risks. All contributions to minimize energy consumption and CO2 emissions during robot production and subsequent system operation need to be systematically identified. For example, lightweight construction of arms must become part of the Circular System Development efforts in agile processes. Also, the reuse of key components and energy recuperation must be considered to increase the resource efficiency and enhance motion control. From the Context System, an attractive business process innovation was deduced. The provision of energy from renewable resources by the robot supplier as a new additional customer service is currently under investigation.

6 Conclusions

This article proposes Circular System Design as an advanced new sustainable methodology for circular product design and systems engineering. It serves to structure the individual development tasks and to visualize interdependencies between the different areas of Product, Life Cycle System and Context System. It transforms the traditional linear view on a product development into a wider context of sustainable ecosystem design. In addition to economic interests, ecological as well as social requirements are anchored as an integral part of future product design.

It is evident, that the development of sustainable and circular systems is characterized by a higher degree of complexity. Circular System Design provides a valuable guideline to structure and control this complexity. Advanced systems engineering and agile product development provide the appropriate toolset to accelerate innovation under joint review with relevant stakeholders.

Circular System Design has proven its general applicability in two representative use cases targeting the visions of "green robotics" and "circular production of smart water metering units". In both cases, the related system and design complexity has to be managed in a holistic manner. The Circular System Design approach revealed to be a powerful agile methodology to manage complex ecosystems and associated development tasks.

The need for early visualization of all related efforts and related interdependencies in a Product, a Life Cycle System and a Context System helps to identify and prioritize development goals as well as product definition and planning efforts. Consequently, the realization speed can significantly be accelerated by setting up and following the iterative Convergent Creation Model cycle in an agile manner.

Future work will be dedicated to derive lean recommendations for practical implementation of Circular System Design in daily engineering business in addition to the conceptual guideline presented in this paper. The new approach for sustainable product design and systems engineering must be supported by suitable software tools, e.g. digital twins or databases adopted from Product Lifecycle Management (PLM). For data analysis and design, it may be helpful to benefit from the use of AI-based methods.

References

1. Meadows, D.H., Club of Rome (eds.): The Limits to Growth: A Report for the Club of Rome's Project on the Predicament of Mankind. Universe Books, New York (1972)
2. Intergovernmental Panel on Climate Change: Climate Change 2021 – The Physical Science Basis: Working Group I Contribution to the Sixth Assessment Report of the Intergovernmental Panel on Climate Change, 1st ed. Cambridge University Press (2023). https://doi.org/10.1017/9781009157896
3. Crutzen, P.J.: The "Anthropocene". In: Ehlers, E., Krafft, T. (eds.) Earth System Science in the Anthropocene, pp. 13–18. Springer, Heidelberg (2006). https://doi.org/10.1007/3-540-26590-2_3
4. Ellen MacArthur Foundation: Towards the circular economy Vol. 1: an economic and business rationale for an accelerated transition (2013). Accessed 17 May 2023. https://ellenmacarthurfoundation.org/towards-the-circular-economy-vol-1-an-economic-and-business-rationale-for-an

5. Kaza, S., et al.: What a waste 2.0: a global snapshot of solid waste management to 2050. In: Urban Development Series. World Bank Group, Washington, DC, USA (2018). https://doi.org/10.1596/9781464813290
6. Samaan, D., et al.: World Employment and Social Outlook: Trends 2023. ILO, Geneva (2023). https://doi.org/10.54394/SNCP1637
7. Bijleveld, M., Bergsma, G., Nusselder, S.: The circular economy as a key instrument for reducing climate change (2016)
8. European Commission, Cambridge Econometrics, Trinomics, and ICF: Impacts of circular economy policies on the labour market: final report and annexes. Publications Office, LU (2018). Accessed 16 May 2023. https://data.europa.eu/doi/10.2779/574719
9. Kadner, S., et al.: Circular economy roadmap für Deutschland. Acatech - Deutsche Akademie der Technikwissenschaften (2021). https://doi.org/10.48669/CEID_2021-3
10. DIN e.V.: DKE German Commission for Electrical, Electronic & Information Technologies, and VDI – The Association of German Engineers (eds.) 'Standardization Roadmap Circular Economy', January 2023
11. European Commission, 'Circular economy action plan' (2020). Accessed 4 Jan 2023. https://environment.ec.europa.eu/strategy/circular-economy-action-plan_en
12. Cooper, R.G.: Stage-gate systems: a new tool for managing new products. Bus. Horiz. **33**(3), 44–54 (1990). https://doi.org/10.1016/0007-6813(90)90040-I
13. Cooper, R.G.: Third-generation new product processes. J. Prod. Innov. Manag. **11**(1), 3–14 (1994). https://doi.org/10.1111/1540-5885.1110003
14. Verein Deutscher Ingenieure e.V (ed.): VDI-Richtline 2221, Blatt1, Entwicklung technischer Produkte und Systeme Modell der Produktentwicklung, November 2019
15. Verein Deutscher Ingenieure e.V: VDI 2206, Entwicklung mechatronischer und cyber-physischer Systeme, November 2021
16. Albers, A., Reiss, N., Bursac, N., Richter, T.: IPeM – integrated product engineering model in context of product generation engineering. Procedia CIRP **50**, 100–105 (2016). https://doi.org/10.1016/j.procir.2016.04.168
17. Rupp, C. (ed.): Requirements-Engineering und -Management: aus der Praxis von klassisch bis agil, 6., Aktualisierte und erw. Aufl. München: Hanser (2014)
18. Alber-Laukant, B.: Handbuch Konstruktion, 2, Aktualisierte Hanser, München (2018)
19. Den Hollander, M.C., Bakker, C.A., Hultink, E.J.: Product design in a circular economy: development of a typology of key concepts and terms: key concepts and terms for circular product design. J. Ind. Ecol. **21**(3), 517–525 (2017). https://doi.org/10.1111/jiec.12610
20. Voigt, P.D.K.-I.: Definition: Produkt. https://wirtschaftslexikon.gabler.de/definition/produkt-42902. https://wirtschaftslexikon.gabler.de/definition/produkt-42902/version-266242. Accessed 19 Jan 2023
21. Dumitrescu, R., Albers, A., Riedel, O., Stark, R., Gausemeier, J.: Engineering in Deutschland - Status quo in Wirtschaft und Wissenschaft. Ein Beitrag zum Advanced Systems Engineering, Paderborn (2021)
22. Kofman, F.: Double-loop accounting: a language for the learning organization. Syst. Think. **3**(1) (1992)
23. Bender, B., Gericke, K., Pahl, G., Beitz, W. (eds.): Pahl/Beitz Konstruktionslehre: Methoden und Anwendung erfolgreicher Produktentwicklung, 9. Auflage. Springer, Heidelberg (2021)
24. Green, J.A.S. (ed.): Aluminum Recycling and Processing for Energy Conservation and Sustainability. ASM International, Materials Park, Ohio (2007)
25. Van Doorsselaer, K., Koopmans, R.J.: Ecodesign: A Life Cycle Approach for a Sustainable Future. Carl Hanser Verlag GmbH & Co. KG, München (2020). https://doi.org/10.3139/9781569908624
26. Ropohl, G.: Allgemeine Technologie: eine Systemtheorie der Technik, 3, Überarb Universitätsverlag, Karlsruhe (2009)

27. Fischer, J., et al.: Advancing sustainability through mainstreaming a social–ecological systems perspective. Curr. Opin. Environ. Sustain. **14**, 144–149 (2015). https://doi.org/10.1016/j.cosust.2015.06.002
28. SPIRAX-SARCO Limited: Applying the principles of industrial symbiosis for more sustainable manufacturing, CORDIS | European Commission. Accessed 24 Aug 2023. https://cordis.europa.eu/article/id/257676-applying-the-principles-of-industrial-symbiosis-for-more-sustainable-manufacturing
29. Hehenberger, P., Habib, M., Bradley, D. (eds.): EcoMechatronics: Challenges for Evolution, Development and Sustainability. Springer, Cham (2022). https://doi.org/10.1007/978-3-031-07555-1
30. McDonough, W., Braungart, M.: Cradle to Cradle: Remaking the Way We Make Things, 1st edn. North Point Press, New York (2002)
31. DIN 69901-5:2009-01: Projektmanagement – Projektmanagementsysteme. Deutsches Institut für Normung e.V, January 2009
32. Herrmann, C., Vetter, O.: Ökologische und ökonomische Bewertung des Ressourcenaufwands – Remanufacturing von Produkten. VDI Zentrum Ressourceneffizienz GmbH (VDI ZRE) (2021). https://www.ressource-deutschland.de/service/publikationen/detailseite/studie-remanufacturing/
33. Glück, M.: Mensch-Roboter-Kooperation erfolgreich einführen: Grundlagen, Leitfaden, Applikationen. Springer Fachmedien Wiesbaden, Wiesbaden (2022). https://doi.org/10.1007/978-3-658-37612-3
34. Müller, C.: World Robotics 2023 – Industrial Robots. International Federation of Robotics (IFR), IFR Statistical Department, VDMA Services GmbH, Frankfurt (Main) (2023)
35. Carabin, G., Wehrle, E., Vidoni, R.: A review on energy-saving optimization methods for robotic and automatic systems. Robotics **6**(4), 39 (2017). https://doi.org/10.3390/robotics6040039

Elegant Architectures: Sustainability in Information Technology

Enrique Ismael Mendoza Robaina(✉), José María Silva Bravo, Alberto García Cabrera, and Diego Ambite Varona

IBM Global Services España, Madrid, Spain
{enrique.ismael.mendoza.robaina,josem.silva, diego.ambite}@ibm.com
https://www.ibm.com

Abstract. This paper aims to analyze and compare several technologies to measure their energy efficiency, with the goal of defining sustainable software design and architectural patterns. The study presents a methodology designed for assessing and optimizing energy consumption in IT systems and demonstrates how it contributes to sustainable development within the industry.

Keywords: Green IT · Sustainability · Energy Consumption · IT Architecture

1 Introduction

1.1 Context

Information Technologies has become an important piece of all human activities, increasing exponentially their energy consumption in every technology revolution. In the global need for a more sustainable world, the need for energy-efficient IT solutions has never been more critical. As data centers and IT infrastructures continue to grow, so does their impact on global energy consumption and carbon emissions. This study introduces an innovative method to measure and analyze the energy efficiency of various technological solutions. By focusing on different databases, programming languages, and communication protocols, we aim to provide a comprehensive approach to quantifying energy usage, guiding decisions towards more sustainable IT practices.

1.2 Background and Motivation

With IT energy consumption potentially accounting for 1.5–5% of global demand, and data centers alone expected to contribute 3.2% of global emissions by 2025, the urgency for sustainable solutions is clear. The increasing adoption of artificial intelligence (AI) and other advanced technologies further exacerbates this issue, as their power consumption grows exponentially (it's estimated that AI power consumption doubles every 3 months). Our motivation stems from the need to identify and promote energy-efficient technologies that can help mitigate these impacts while supporting the growth and evolution of IT services.

A. Quesada-Arencibia et al. (Eds.): EUROCAST 2024, LNCS 15174, pp. 147–153, 2025.
https://doi.org/10.1007/978-3-031-83885-9_14

1.3 Expected Benefits

The anticipated benefits of our research are multifold. Primarily, it aims to provide a deeper understanding of the energy implications of different technological choices. By identifying more energy-efficient technologies, organizations can reduce their carbon footprint and align with global sustainability goals. Additionally, our findings are expected to aid in cost reduction through energy savings and improve overall system performance, offering a dual advantage of environmental and economic sustainability.

2 Methodology

Our methodology involves a systematic approach to measuring and optimizing IT energy consumption. The process includes:

- **Establishing a baseline**: Measuring the energy usage of various IT components allowing to know actual situation to be able to compare.
- **Measurement**: Evaluating the energy efficiency of the different technologies involved in the IT system.
- **Action and Optimization**: Implementing strategies to reduce energy consumption.
- **Observability**: Continuous monitoring of IT system behavior allowing to detect trends and deviations to implement a continuous improvement process.

We conducted a series of experiments to compare the energy consumption across different databases, programming languages, and communication protocols. Each experiment was designed to isolate the impact of specific technological choices on energy usage.

2.1 Application Optimization

To optimize applications and services, we have developed a method that allows us to replicate measurement and optimization actions. This methodology (see Fig. 1) ensures both new and existing applications are developed and maintained with a focus on sustainability and energy efficiency. The process includes categorization, containerization, individual consumption measurement, and stress consumption measurement, all aimed at establishing a comprehensive baseline for energy usage.

Following the baseline calculation, we conduct static source code analysis to identify inefficiencies and areas for improvement. Recommendations are made to optimize the code for better energy efficiency. This step ensures that the applications are scrutinized at the code level, allowing for targeted improvements that reduce energy consumption. In parallel, we execute the application (both isolated and under stress situation) to measure the real energy consumption and detecting any improvement areas.

Finally, based on the analysis and recommendations, source code optimization is performed. Necessary changes are implemented to the application's codebase to enhance energy efficiency, and corrective actions are taken to address any issues. This structured approach ensures that applications not only meet performance requirements but also contribute to broader sustainability goals.

For the static source code analysis, we rely on the utilization of commercial tools that implement that functionality.

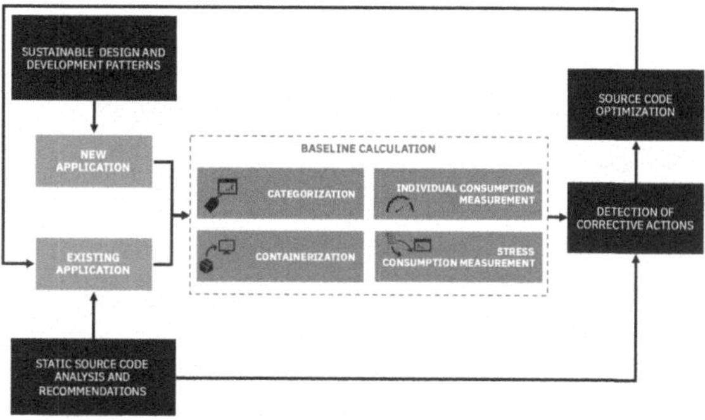

Fig. 1. Application methodology for power consumption optimization

2.2 Experimental Setup

For our experiments, we utilized a consistent testing environment to ensure that the results were comparable across different technologies. The infrastructure (see Fig. 2) included virtual machines running Linux, with applications containerized to isolate their execution environments. We employed the PowerTop tool for measuring power consumption, which provided detailed insights into the energy usage of different processes.

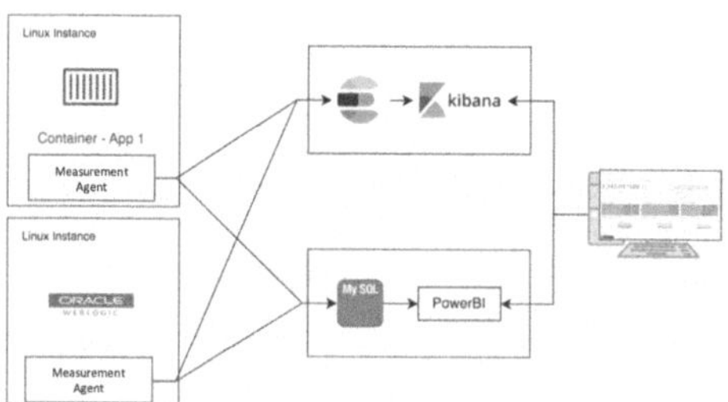

Fig. 2. Technical solution architecture to deploy experiments

3 Experiments and Results

3.1 Database Comparison

Objective: Compare the energy consumption of relational (SQL) and non-relational (NoSQL) databases.

Method: Deployed MySQL and MongoDB databases with identical data sets on the same infrastructure. Measured energy consumption using PowerTop.

Findings: NoSQL databases, particularly MongoDB, consumed significantly less energy than SQL databases. This suggests that the choice of database type can substantially impact the carbon footprint of IT architectures (Table 1).

Table 1. Average power consumption per component/technology in w/s

Type	Component	Microservice	Database	Total
Database 3	NoSQL	412.88	177.74	590.62
Database 1	SQL	713.72	1,065.32	1,779.04
Database 2	SQL	783.00	1,858.14	2,641.14

The significant difference in power consumption can be attributed to the architectural differences between SQL and NoSQL databases. SQL databases often require complex queries and transactions that consume more computational resources, whereas NoSQL databases, designed for flexibility and scalability, handle data operations more efficiently.

3.2 Programming Languages

Objective: Evaluate the energy efficiency of different programming languages used in microservices.

Method: Developed identical microservices in Java (Spring Boot), NodeJS (Express), and Python (Flask). Measured energy consumption during identical workloads.

Findings: Python was the most energy-efficient, followed by NodeJS, and then Java, highlighting significant differences in the energy efficiency of programming languages (Tables 2, 3, 4, and 5).

Table 2. Average power consumption in w/s for Java with Spring Boot

Type	Microservice	Database	Total
NoSQL	412.88	177.74	590.62
SQL	713.72	1,065.32	1,779.04

Table 3. Average power consumption in w/s for NodeJS with Express

Type	Microservice	Database	Total
NoSQL	333.37	130.57	463.94
SQL	313.79	503.00	816.79

The differences in energy consumption among programming languages can be explained by their runtime characteristics and how they handle resource management. Python, known for its simplicity and ease of use, shows the lowest energy consumption. NodeJS, optimized for I/O operations, also demonstrates good energy efficiency. Java, although powerful and widely used in enterprise environments, consumes more energy due to its more complex runtime environment.

Table 4. Average power consumption in w/s for Python with Flask

Type	Microservice	Database	Total
NoSQL	218.26	131.07	349.62
SQL	8.04	564.69	572.73

Table 5. Comparison of average power consumption per programming language

Type	Average
Java with Spring Boot	~2,369 w/s
NodeJS with Express	~1,279 w/s
Python with Flask	~921 w/s

3.3 Communication Protocols

Objective: Compare the energy consumption of GRPC and HTTP/REST communication protocols.

Method: Implemented microservices using both GRPC and HTTP/REST. Conducted tests with 100 concurrent users to simulate real-world usage.

Findings: GRPC was much more energy-efficient compared to HTTP/REST, especially in multi-tier scenarios. This highlights the importance of protocol choice in developing energy-efficient IT architectures (Table 6).

Table 6. Average power consumption per component/technology in w/s

Type	Microservice 1	Microservice 2	Total
REST	80.00	465.96	545.96
GRPC	59.19	57.79	116.97

The higher efficiency of GRPC can be attributed to its use of HTTP/2 and Protocol Buffers for serialization, which are both optimized for low latency and reduced resource consumption. In contrast, HTTP/REST, using JSON for data interchange, incurs higher overhead due to text parsing and larger payload sizes.

4 Discussion

The results from our experiments indicate clear advantages in selecting certain technologies for sustainable IT practices. NoSQL databases and GRPC communication protocols demonstrated substantial energy savings. Python emerged as the most efficient programming language, followed by NodeJS and Java. These differences underscore the need for careful consideration in technology selection.

These findings are crucial for organizations aiming to reduce their carbon footprint and align with global sustainability goals. By adopting more energy-efficient technologies, businesses can achieve significant cost savings and improve overall system performance.

4.1 Implications for IT Management

For IT managers and architects, these results provide actionable insights into how different technology choices can impact energy consumption. Implementing NoSQL databases for data storage, choosing GRPC for microservice communication, and developing applications in Python can lead to more sustainable and cost-effective IT operations.

4.2 Broader Impact on Sustainability

The broader impact of these findings extends beyond individual organizations. As the IT industry collectively adopts more energy-efficient technologies, the cumulative reduction in energy consumption can significantly contribute to global efforts to combat climate change. This research supports the development of industry-wide standards and best practices for sustainable IT.

5 Future Work

Our research will expand to include a broader range of technologies and scenarios. Future work will focus on:

- **Benchmarking Framework**: Developing a comprehensive framework for evaluating the energy efficiency of emerging technologies.
- **AI and Machine Learning**: Integrating these techniques to predict and optimize energy consumption.
- **Cloud-Native Environments**: Exploring the energy efficiency of different cloud architectures and services.
- **Hybrid Architectures**: Evaluating the impact of hybrid cloud and on-premises solutions on energy consumption.
- **User Behavior**: Studying how different user interactions and usage patterns affect energy efficiency.

6 Conclusions

This study provides a detailed analysis of the energy consumption of different IT components, offering insights that can guide sustainable practices in the industry. The results demonstrate significant variations in energy efficiency across databases, programming languages, and communication protocols. By adopting the most efficient technologies, organizations can reduce their environmental impact and achieve economic benefits.

The key takeaways from this research are:

- **Database Selection**: NoSQL databases are more energy-efficient than SQL databases.
- **Programming Languages**: Python is the most energy-efficient language for developing microservices.
- **Communication Protocols**: GRPC significantly reduces energy consumption compared to HTTP/REST.

These insights can help organizations make informed decisions about their IT infrastructure, contributing to both sustainability and operational efficiency.

Acknowledgments. All authors are employed by IBM Consulting Spain, and the research presented in this paper was conducted as part of our professional responsibilities at IBM. The study was funded by IBM Consulting Spain, which provided financial support and access to necessary technologies, tools, and infrastructure.

Disclosure of Interests. The authors have conducted the research impartially and reported the findings accurately, without undue influence from commercial or financial interests. The primary goal of this research is to advance the understanding of sustainable IT practices and contribute to the broader field of energy-efficient technology development. The authors affirm that the presented work adheres to the ethical standards of the research community and that any potential conflicts of interest have been disclosed and addressed to ensure the integrity of the research.

References

1. Cormenzana, B., Marinescu, M.-C., Marrero, M., Mendoza, S., Rueda, S., Uceda-Sosa, R.: Models for sustainability. In: 2015 IEEE First International Smart Cities Conference (ISC2), pp. 1–6 (2015). https://doi.org/10.1109/ISC2.2015.7366221
2. Calero, C., Platinni, M.: Green in Software Engineering. Springer, Castilla-La Mancha (2015) ISBN: 978-3-319-08580-7
3. Silva, J.M.: Journey to Cloud Tales IV: Arquitecturas elegantes como paradigma GreenIT. https://www.muycomputerpro.com/2023/01/30/cloud-tales-greenit. Accessed 10 Apr 2023
4. How to Architect for Sustainability in a Cloud Native Environment. https://www.contino.io/insights/cloud-native-sustainability. Accessed 11 Dec 2022
5. Achieve Green Computing with Open Hybrid Cloud. https://www.ibm.com/cloud/blog/achieve-green-computing-with-open-hybrid-cloud. Accessed 30 May 2024
6. Climate change is a major challenge for insurers, but AI and cloud can help. https://www.ibm.com/thought-leadership/institute-business-value/blog/climate-change-insurers-ai-cloud. Accessed 30 May 2024

Surrogates for Fair-Weather Photovoltaic Module Output

Dominik Falkner[1,2(✉)], Michael Bögl[1], Ines Langthallner[1], Jan Zenisek[2,3], and Michael Affenzeller[2,3]

[1] RISC Software GmbH, Hagenberg, Austria
dominik.falkner@risc-software.at
[2] Institute for Formal Models and Verification, Johannes Kepler University, Linz, Austria
[3] University of Applied Sciences Upper Austria, Hagenberg, Austria

Abstract. In the field of time series analysis, the scarcity of comprehensive datasets poses a significant challenge for the development of reliable predictive models. This study addresses the difficulties in forecasting solar module outputs and enhancing data accessibility for modeling, especially in residential sectors. We propose a general method to establish a distribution of photovoltaic module parameters across a country and, from this, generate a synthetic dataset for simulation and modeling pv module output. This approach integrates multiple freely available data sources. The study is focused on Germany, utilizing the Marktstammdatenregister as its main source for the module parameter distribution. The data is then enriched using publically available data. Based upon this, a crawler is developed to gather fair-weather module outputs from the Photovoltaic Geographical Information System for training, testing, and benchmarking purposes. One benchmark has fixed locations and the second one has fixed module parameters. Additionally, we provide a data loader with artificial degradation for all datasets. In the last step we test multiple state of the art models on the dataset and show that the proposed forecasting task is not trivial. All the code and data is publically available.

Keywords: photovoltaic · pvgis · machine learning · distributions · surrogate

1 Motivation

The success of the energy transition and the future stability of energy networks are closely linked to the output of renewable energy sources such as photovoltaic (PV) modules. According to the International Renewable Energy Agency, there is a pressing need for a rapid increase in the deployment of renewables to meet the 1.5 °C climate goal, with predictions indicating a seven-fold increase by 2030 [7]. The federal association for PVs in Austria projects that PVs will produce 15% of the total energy consumption by 2030 [2].

As PVs become more integral to the energy mix, their impact on the power grid's balance becomes increasingly significant, particularly for energy providers.

A. Quesada-Arencibia et al. (Eds.): EUROCAST 2024, LNCS 15174, pp. 154–166, 2025.
https://doi.org/10.1007/978-3-031-83885-9_15

Moreover, the growing number of small, privately-owned PV systems, compared to large PV power plants, results in greater installation diversity per kilowatt produced. Consequently, there is a need to develop tools capable of simulating PV module output across a wide range of parameters.

To address this need, we provide a method for constructing a distribution of PV module parameters for Germany. This distribution is then used to create a benchmark dataset aimed at people modeling and simulating energy grids or providing estimations for privately owned PV modules.

2 Related Work

In the past, extensive research has been dedicated to estimating the solar potential for cities. For instance, Singh et al. presented a method to estimate the solar potential for a given city [13]. In recent years, the focus has shifted towards predicting the output of solar modules with two primary objectives: estimating the impact on the energy grid and designing optimally parameterized PV modules for private households. For example, Rajagukguk et al. conducted a study comparing different deep learning methods and highlighted the necessity for more data (from a single module) to achieve accurate predictions [12].

Another relevant project, Deep Solar for Germany, aims to detect the presence of PV modules using aerial images. It provides various parameters for PV modules across all German states. However, this project relies on 3D building data, which is not available for every country [10].

Additionally, research into the degradation of solar modules is an adjacent area of interest. Jordan et al. measured the degradation rates of solar modules in Northern California, Colorado, Switzerland, and Italy [4]. Degradation is a particularly interesting and challenging variable to control in real-world data. Future considerations should take into account the impact of degradation on the model's accuracy.

3 The Search for PV Module Data

Data availability and quality on solar installations within the European Union are significantly constrained. No centralized repository exists for aggregating data from electricians or installation companies, leading to fragmented and incomplete datasets. Available data frequently lacks details, often providing either module output for short periods without technical parameters or parameters devoid of corresponding module outputs. Furthermore, business reports on solar installations typically lack the granularity required for accurate regional modeling. Most comprehensive datasets are proprietary, held by large PV producers and not publicly accessible. Nevertheless, the following provides an overview of used data sources.

3.1 Data Sources

The following specifies which data sources where employed in this paper. It also describes how the data was gathered and some constraints.

Marktstammdatenregister (MaStR) is a comprehensive database maintained by the German Federal Network Agency (Bundesnetzagentur) that records detailed information about all electricity and gas market entities in Germany. Its primary purpose is to enhance transparency, efficiency, and regulatory oversight in the energy markets [6].

This paper mainly employs the solar source for determining a parameter distribution. As of accessing the data it contains around 2 million entries. The data filtering and fusion is described in Sect. 3.2.

License: The data has been both accessed and used in accordance with the terms of the Open Data License Germany - Namensnennung 2.0. The data is publicly available and can be accessed at http://www.govdata.de/dl-de/by-2-0.

PVOutput.org is an online platform that allows PV system owners to upload, share, and compare data regarding their solar energy production and consumption. It serves as a community-driven, open tool that enables users to track their PV system's performance in real-time. The data mainly encompasses energy generation or energy consumption (if available). Additionally, users can add information about their PV system's configuration, such as the number of panels, tilt angle, orientation, and inverter details [16].

The platform provides an API that allows users to access their data programmatically. However, the free tier of the API has strict rate limits. The data in this paper has been obtained using the donation tier of the API.

Photovoltaic Geographical Information System (PVGIS) is an online tool developed by the European Commission's Joint Research Centre. It is designed to estimate the produced solar energy for different geographical locations primarily in Europe, Africa, and South-West Asia. The PVGIS allows users to calculate the expected performance of PV systems based on various geographical and technical input parameters [8].

PVGIS includes data on solar radiation and temperature derived from satellite and ground measurements. Users can specify parameters such as the location, type of solar panel, installation angle, and orientation to receive estimates of hourly, monthly and annual fair-weather energy production. All the module data in this paper has been attained using the PVGIS using the freely available API.

3.2 Constructing a Module Parameter Distribution for Germany

In the process of data preparation for the analysis, the initial MaStR dataset comprising approximately 2 million entries is systematically filtrede to around 1 million rows. These steps are essential for selecting relevant data, focusing specifically on typical household installation characteristics. The following list details each of the filtering steps applied, explaining their rationale and impact on the dataset.

1. **Column Filtering:** The dataset initially contains a wide range of variables, many of which are not relevant for residential solar installations. Such columns are identified and removed. This reduction not only declutters the dataset but also decreases the overall size.
2. **Installation Placement Limitations:** To tailor the dataset for residential analysis, entries are filtered to include only those installations located on building structures, specifically roofs and walls. This excludes ground-mounted and other non-building related installations, which are less common in residential settings and avoids misleading results.
3. **Exclusion of Sun-Tracking Systems:** This step simplifies the data to reflect the more commonly used fixed-panel installations in residential settings, thus maintaining the focus on typical homeowner scenarios.
4. **Orientation Filter:** Installations with an east-west orientation are omitted from the analysis. This decision is based on the limitations of the PVGIS, which does not support these orientations. By excluding these data points, the dataset remains compatible with the analytical tools used.
5. **Residential Focus:** The dataset is further refined to focus exclusively on residential installations. This aligning it with the study's aim to generate insights that are directly applicable to residential solar panel planning and policy-making.
6. **Outlier Removal:** The kilowatt peak (kWp) was filtered because it contains outliers. All data points below and above the 1 and 99% are removed. This translates to installations, which are between 1 kWp and 50 kWp.

Through these filtering steps, the dataset is effectively reduced to approximately 1 million rows. However, the module tilt angle is only available in coarse buckets, which limits the granularity of the analysis. Currently the dataset contains the following parameters:

- **kWp:** Represents the maximum power capacity of the installation kilowatt.
- **Tilt:** Denotes the inclination angle of the installation, expressed in degree ranges (e.g., 0–20°, 20–40°, etc.).
- **Orientation:** Refers to the direction of the installation, measured in degrees.
- **Location:** The location is not available in MaStR dataset, to avoid privacy issues.

3.3 Enriching the Distribution

The tilt of solar modules is a critical factor that significantly influences the system's behavior and energy yield. However, MaStR provides the data on module tilt in bins, which makes it impossible to employ the PVGIS, which requires the tilt to be exact. To address this issue, two approaches can be implemented to refine the tilt data. The first one is to assume a uniform distribution for each bucket. This method assumes that within each bin, the tilt of modules is evenly distributed across the possible range. The second solution is to utilize a different data source from the same population. Most roofs in Germany have a set tilt angle, and it is unlikely that the tilt is uniformly distributed. Therefore, we decided to use the latter approach.

As described in Sect. 3.1, PVOutput contains exact angles of the module tilt. Fusing the data involves matching the coarse tilt categories from MaStR with corresponding bins in PVOutput. Once the data is binned accordingly, the next step involves matching the orientation of the modules, grouping them by orientation and coarse tilt. For each sample, a tilt value is then randomly selected based on the matching group. The PVOutput data contains only around usable 1000 observations for households but is the best approximation for the exact tilt.

The last missing information is the location of the modules. To overcome this, we randomly sample locations in Germany. This step is kept simple as we do not have enough data to build an estimate how likely it is for a given point, in Germany, to contain a PV module.

The result in summarized in Fig. 1a. It shows the parameter distributions of all the available data. There are two interesting things to note. One is that the tilt seems to be concentrated around specific degrees. The other is that the parameter kWp peaks around 10 kWp, which is a common size for household installations. The orientation is as expected, with most installations being oriented towards the south (0° denotes South, −90° denotes East and 90° represents West).

Based on the distribution parameters identified in Sect. 3.2, a crawler is implemented to optimize future data collection efforts. For this purpose, the crawler acquires fair-weather output data from the PVGIS. Each set of data collected is stored in individual files, accompanied by additional JSON files that detail the exact parameters used in data retrieval. The total size of the data is around 50 Gigabytes, containing thousands of modules. For retrieval, the crawler draws data from the distribution and combines it with necessary API parameters. Listing 1.1 shows an example of the JSON parameters used for the data retrieval.

```
{
    // parameters from the distribution
    "lat":49.826447039945144, "lon":10.658869563405087,
    "peakpower":9.57, "angle":45.0, "aspect":-90.0,
    // fixed parameters
    "outputformat":"json", "mounting":"building",
    "startyear":2005, "endyear":2020,
    "usehorizon":1, "pvcalculation":1,
    "fixed":1, "pvtechchoice":"crystSi" "loss":14.0,
}
```

Listing 1.1. JSON Parameters Data Retrieval, The second part of the parameters are fixed for all modules. Additionally, the orientation is translated to degrees according to the PVGIS documentation.

4 Gathering Fair-Weather Photovoltaic Datasets

The following sections first defines the datasets, which are obtained using the PVGIS service, and provides a preliminary view of it. In total around 50 Gigabytes of data is downloaded.

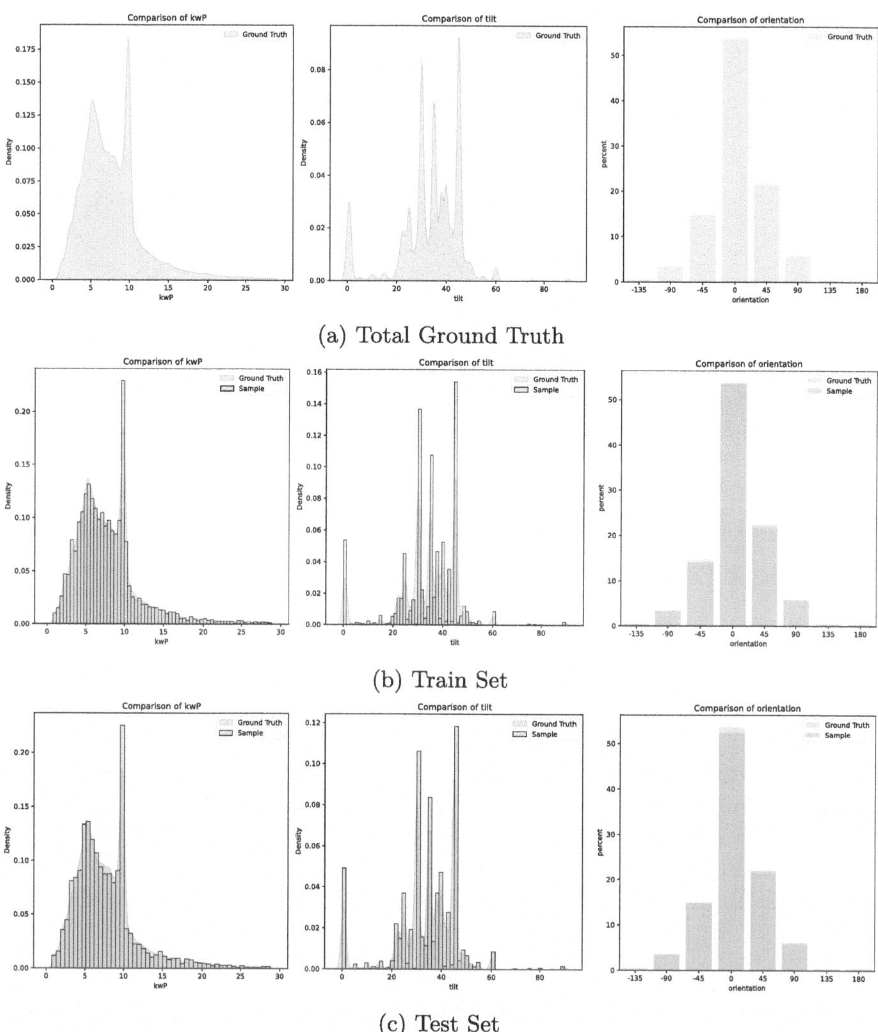

Fig. 1. This figure presents the distributions of three parameters: kWp (in watts), tilt (in degrees), and orientation (in degrees) across the total dataset, train and test datasets, which consist of approximately 1,000,000, 10,000, and 5,000 entries, respectively. Each parameter is visualized in a separate subplot, organized vertically. The test and train distribution has been sampled randomly from the ground truth. Histograms are normalized to match the kernel density plot of the ground truth. The tilt is clearly concentrated around a few specific values, which is expected. The kWp histograms shows a peak around 10 kWp. 10 kWp is a common size for household installations. Following this peak, the number of installations declines. The most common orientation is towards the south (0°). This might change in the future as people start to optimize how they install their modules.

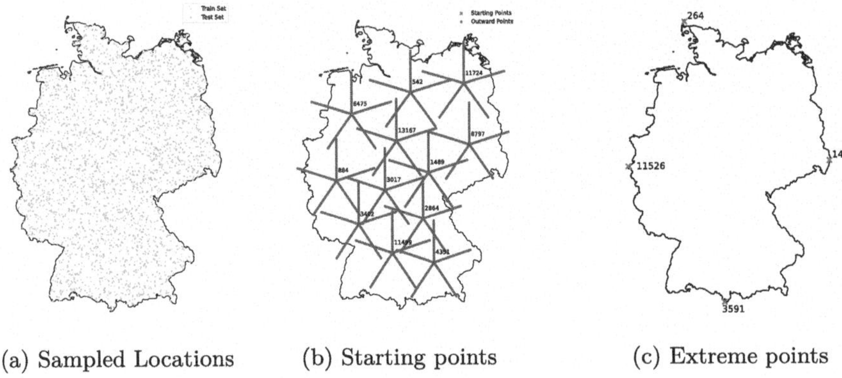

(a) Sampled Locations (b) Starting points (c) Extreme points

Fig. 2. This figure shows interesting points for the dataset. (a) shows the randomly selected points for the dataset shown in Sect. 4.1. (b) shows the center of the outward points dataset as well as the points spread around the initial location in blue. (c) shows the most extreme module locations based on latitude and longitude.

4.1 Dataset Definitions

In total the crawler downloads three datasets derived from the initial parameters. Additionally, we provide a package which add yearly degredation in a linear fashion to each dataset. The following explains them in more detail.

Random Sample: The main dataset contains around 15000 modules. It is split into a train set with around 10000 modules and a test set with around 5000 modules. The parameters have been drawn randomly based on the obtained distribution. Figure 1b and Fig. 1c show a visual representation of the sampled parameters. As mentioned the exact locations are drawn randomly, as shown in Fig. 2a.

Fixed Location Benchmark: This dataset reuses the test set defined in the previous section, but it employs a fixed location for all modules. Thus, the modules only vary in their other parameters. This dataset is utilized to estimate the impact of changing parameters on the model's accuracy.

Outward Points Benchmark: In this benchmark all parameters are fixed but the location is varied. For the location a few points have been chosen in Germany with no overlapping regions. The module distance, from the central points, is then varried across 5 bearings. The distance to the central point is increased by 5 km each step. Figure 2b depicts this process. This dataset is used to estimate the impact of changing locations on the model's accuracy.

Download Errors: Some of the data points could not be downloaded because they are too close to the ocean. The access layer provided in **`pv-surrogate-data`** *package skips these automatically. They are kept in the data package for completeness sake. For example, the random sample dataset contains 18 errors out of 15000 modules.*

4.2 A Peak into the Data

Figure 3 shows the daily aggregated data, where it can be observed that the fair-weather data is noisy, yet a clear seasonality is evident. It's also clear that the data does not contain degredation.

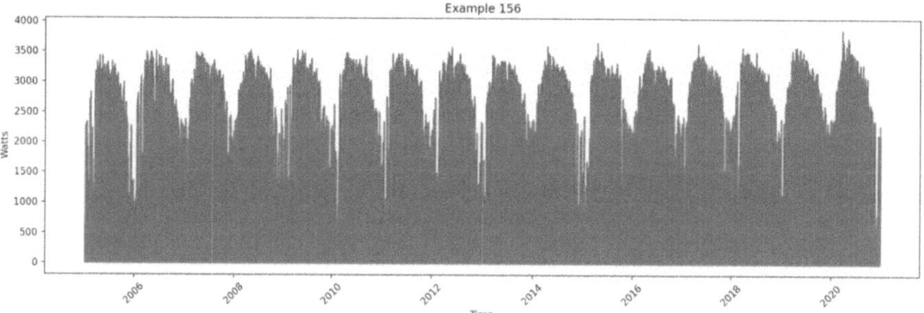

(a) Hourly data directly obtained from the PVGIS.

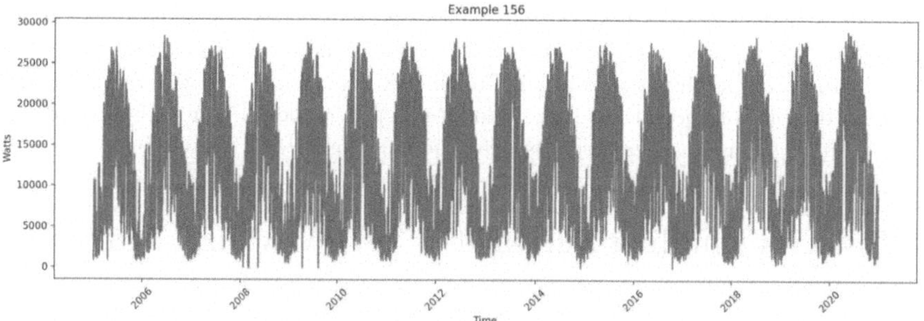

(b) Daily data, aggregated from the hourly data

Fig. 3. Hourly (a) and daily (b) data from module 156. Both contain a lot of noise for fair-weather predictions. The daily data contains a few outliers where no energy is produced. This is likely due to errors in the original data.

Additionally, Fig. 4 illustrates the difference in extrema, demonstrating that even on the same day of the year, the modules produce different power profiles. The figure also shows the impact of seasonal changes. The data includes the following features per timestep: power produced by the module, global irradiance, current height of the sun, temperature at 2 m, wind speed at 10 m. Module data spans from the beginning of 2005 to the end of 2020.

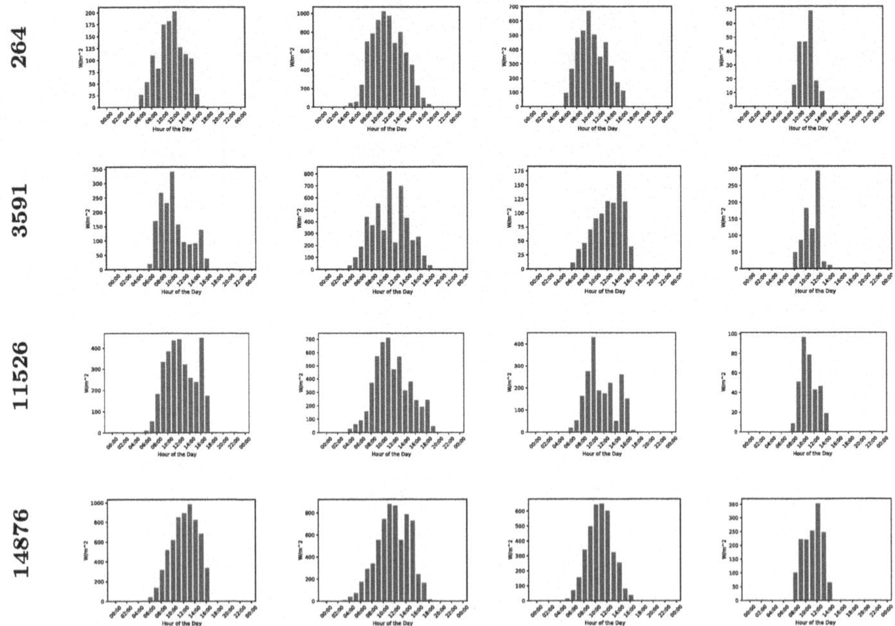

Fig. 4. PV module output of four station (rows) over the course of a year. The columns show four extrem days (columns), w.r.t. available sunlight, in a year: spring equinox, summer solstice, autumn equinox and winter solstice. The figure shows that even at the same day of the year the modules produce a different profile for power on an hourly level. Additionally, the figure shows the start/end of a module output shifting between different ranges, depending on which day of the year is shown. Other difference can be attributed to noise or specific module parameters. Differences in longitude and latitude are likely more pronounced on regions near the equator or over larger distances.

5 Towards Building Surrogates for PV Module Output

The following sections define how surrogates are built and evaluated. The goal is to show how well the models can predict the output of different modules.

5.1 Forecasting Task

Initially, the task involved making hourly forecasts for the following day, but most models did not produce valuable results due to the presence of zeros in the data before sunrise and after sunset. The models only began to improve after incorporating features accounting for sunrise and sunset times. To simplify, we decided to focus solely on daily output from the module, providing a manageable yet challenging starting point.

All models were provided with information regarding the module's parameters and location. They were trained using daily data to forecast the subsequent day. NHITS, MLP and PatchTST received the previous day as input. All models were assessed using test and benchmark datasets, which were not utilized during the training phase. Symbolic regression did not receive any past data.

5.2 Error Metric

The Symmetric Mean Absolute Percentage Error (SMAPE) is a commonly used error metric for evaluating the accuracy of forecasts. It is an improvement over the traditional Mean Absolute Percentage Error (MAPE) as it addresses some of the limitations associated with MAPE [9]. The formula for SMAPE is:

$$\text{sMAPE}(\mathbf{y}_\tau, \hat{\mathbf{y}}_\tau) = \frac{1}{H} \sum_{\tau=t+1}^{t+H} \frac{|y_\tau - \hat{y}_\tau|}{|y_\tau| + |\hat{y}_\tau|} \tag{1}$$

where:

- $\hat{y}_\tau$ is the forecasted value at time τ,
- y_τ is the actual value at time τ,
- H is the number of observations in y and $\hat{y}$.

SMAPE has several advantages. Firstly, it offers symmetry by treating over-forecasting and under-forecasting equally, unlike MAPE, which can be skewed by large positive errors. Additionally, Lastly, SMAPE is bounded between 0 and 2, providing a consistent and interpretable range for error assessment.

Despite its benefits, SMAPE has some downsides. One major issue is the division by zero problem, which occurs when both actual and forecasted values are zero, making SMAPE undefined or problematic. This is addressed manually by excluding days with no energy production from the calculation. Additionally, it can result in higher values compared to MAPE.

5.3 Considered Models

The following is a quick overview of models which were considered for the task. Training was done only on the train set and evaluation was done on the test and benchmark datasets. Every model was pretrained on the train set using the root mean squared error as a loss function. Symbolic regression worked with the data as it is, the other models received the data normalized using standard scaling.

Multilayer Perception (MLP). Taud et al. gives an overview of the MLP. They are a type of artificial neural network known for their simplicity and effectiveness in a wide range of machine learning tasks. They consist of at least three layers: an input layer, one or more hidden layers, and an output layer. Each layer is made up of neurons that use nonlinear activation functions, except for the input nodes [15].

Neural Hierarchical Interpolation for Time Series (NHITS). Challu et al. introduces the NHITS architecture. They use hierarchical interpolation and multi-rate data sampling techniques, which help in assembling predictions sequentially across different frequencies and scales [3].

PatchTST. Yuqi et al. introduces an innovative design for Transformer-based models tailored for multivariate time series forecasting and self-supervised representation learning. The design leverages two main strategies: segmenting time series into subseries-level patches as input tokens, and maintaining channel independence across multiple univariate time series using shared embeddings and Transformer weights [11]. This model received as input the previous day.

SymReg. Symbolic regression is a modeling technique that excels in creating detailed, understandable models from complex data. It uses genetic programming to evolve mathematical expressions that describe the relationship between input and output data [1].

5.4 Results

The daily forecasting task was evaluated using all models by first pretraining the model on the training set. In a second step the models were evaluated on 10 different modules over a year. The results are shown in Table 1. The results show that no model can not quite capture the relationships in the data well.

Table 1. Performance comparison of different models on the datasets described in Sect. 4.1 onwards.

Dataset	MLP	NHITs	PatchTST	SymReg	SymReg*
Test	1.999	1.869	0.882	0.751	0.597
Fixed Location	1.999	1.873	0.769	0.737	0.585
Outward Points	1.999	1.877	0.763	0.720	0.553

The surrogate step is considered preliminary, as many of the models have yet to be sufficiently tuned to yield conclusive results, due to limitations mentioned later. To sum it up, it shows that the MLP does not perform well on this task. NHITS starts to show improvements, however, it is not able to capture the relationships in the data. PatchTST better results which is likely due to the previous value it receives and the attention mechanism. The last model SymReg* received additional features (day, week and month of the year as a number) and shows a big improvement.

Limitation of Experiments: To limit the amount of computation, the evaluation and training is limited. Training was done on around 100 modules and evaluation was done with 10 models. Only the first year of a given module is used. This results in 36500 training samples and 3650 evaluation samples.

6 Conclusion

This research introduces a technique for generating parameter distributions independently of additional data, which is not available in all countries. It also presents a comprehensive dataset that can serve as a foundation for pretraining models focused on PV or for simulation purposes, contributing to the limited number of available datasets in the time series domain. Moreover, the study proposes several benchmarks to help identify issues within models and includes an extra challenge dataset that adds degradation to encourage further research in this area.

The surrogates can be improved by incorporating more data or by using of additional features. Nevertheless, this phase demonstrates that the task of modeling in this context is not trivial. The SymReg* model shows that additional features can improve the model's performance and that symbolic regression might be a good choice for selecting such features for larger and more computational expensive models, because domain experts can validate the output.

Future research can build on the findings of this study by addressing several key areas. One improvement could involve the selection of locations to increase the correctness of the parameter distribution, for example by using density based on housing [14]. Additionally, future work should consider incorporating the ability to model east-west orientation. Lastly, the study indicates that time series with numerous zeros pose a challenge for models to generate accurate forecasts.

Data Access. The data can be accessed via the internet archive[1] (`ID: pv-surrogate-data_dfalkner`) or zenodo [5]. We advise everyone to download the data using a torrent. Additionally, we provide a Python access layer as a package (`pv-surrogate-data`)[2]. The full code for generating the distribution is available on GitHub[3].

Data Validity. The project focused on Germany. The parameter distribution might not be applicable for other countries/regions.

Acknowledgments. The work was done within the project "Secure Prescriptive Analytics", funded by the state of Upper Austria as part of the research program "#upperVISION2030".

Disclosure of Interests. The authors have no competing interests to declare that are relevant to the content of this article.

1 https://archive.org/details/pv-surrogate-data_dfalkner.
2 https://pypi.org/project/pv-surrogate-data/.
3 https://github.com/prescriptiveanalytics/paper_pv_surrogate_eurocast.

References

1. Affenzeller, M., Winkler, S.M., Kronberger, G., Kommenda, M., Burlacu, B., Wagner, S.: Gaining deeper insights in symbolic regression. In: Riolo, R., Moore, J.H., Kotanchek, M. (eds.) Genetic Programming Theory and Practice XI. GEC, pp. 175–190. Springer, New York (2014). https://doi.org/10.1007/978-1-4939-0375-7_10
2. Bundesverband Photovoltaic Austria: Die Österreichische Photovoltaic und Speicherbranche 2022. https://pvaustria.at/wp-content/uploads/2023_Fact_Sheet_PV_Branche.pdf. Visited 23 Oct 2023
3. Challu, C., Olivares, K.G., Oreshkin, B.N., Garza, F., Mergenthaler-Canseco, M., Dubrawski, A.: N-HITS: neural hierarchical interpolation for time series forecasting (2022). https://doi.org/10.1609/aaai.v37i6.25854
4. Dirk, J.C., Kurtz, S.R., VanSant, K., Newmiller, J.: Compendium of photovoltaic degradation rates. Prog. Photovoltaics Res. Appl. **24**(7), 978–989 (2016). https://doi.org/10.1002/pip.2744
5. Falkner, D., Bögl, M., Langthallner, I., Zenisek, J., Affenzeller, M.: Photovoltaic power data (2024). https://doi.org/10.5281/zenodo.11503147. Accessed 6 Aug 2024
6. Hülk, L., Pleßmann, G., Muschner, C., Kotthoff, F., Tepe, D.: open-MaStR, April 2024. https://github.com/OpenEnergyPlatform/open-MaStR/
7. International Renewable Energy Agency: World Energy Transitions Outlook 1.5C Pathway 2022 edition. IRENA (2022). ISBN: 978-92-9260-429-5
8. Joint Research Centre: Photovoltaic geographical information system PVGIS. http://re.jrc.ec.europa.eu/pvgis. Visited 23 Oct 2023
9. Makridakis, S.: Accuracy measures: theoretical and practical concerns. Int. J. Forecast. **9**(4), 527–529 (1993). https://doi.org/10.1016/0169-2070(93)90079-3. https://www.sciencedirect.com/science/article/pii/0169207093900793
10. Mayer, K., et al.: 3D-PV-locator: large-scale detection of rooftop-mounted photovoltaic systems in 3D. Appl. Energy **310**, 118469 (2022). https://doi.org/10.1016/j.apenergy.2021.118469. https://www.sciencedirect.com/science/article/pii/S0306261921016937
11. Nie, Y., Nguyen, N.H., Sinthong, P., Kalagnanam, J.: A time series is worth 64 words: long-term forecasting with transformers. In: International Conference on Learning Representations (2023). https://doi.org/10.48550/arXiv.2211.14730
12. Rajagukguk, R.A., Ramadhan, R.A.A., Lee, H.J.: A review on deep learning models for forecasting time series data of solar irradiance and photovoltaic power. Energies **13**(24), 6623 (2020). https://doi.org/10.3390/en13246623
13. Singh, R., Banerjee, R.: Estimation of rooftop solar photovoltaic potential of a city. Sol. Energy **115**, 589–602 (2015). https://doi.org/10.1016/j.solener.2015.03.016
14. Statistisches Bundesamt (Destatis): Bautätigkeit und Wohnungen: Bestand an Wohnungen. Fachserie 5 Reihe 3, pp. 1–120, July 2022. https://www.destatis.de/fachserien
15. Taud, H., Mas, J.: Multilayer perceptron (MLP). In: Camacho Olmedo, M., Paegelow, M., Mas, J.F., Escobar, F. (eds.) Geomatic Approaches for Modeling Land Change Scenarios. LNGC, pp. 451–455. Springer, Cham (2018). https://doi.org/10.1007/978-3-319-60801-3_27
16. PVOutput Team: PVOutput — pvoutput.org. https://pvoutput.org. Accessed 27 Dec 2023

How Digital Twins Can Help to Accelerate the Transition to a Carbon-Neutral System

Tobias Rodemann[1(✉)] and Christiane Attig[2]

[1] Honda Research Institute Europe, Offenbach am Main, Germany
tobias.rodemann@honda-ri.de
[2] University of Lübeck, Lübeck, Germany
christiane.attig@uni-luebeck.de

Abstract. In this article we report about our efforts to employ detailed physical simulation models (so called digital twins) and advanced optimization algorithms to identify optimal investment decisions into renewable energy systems to reduce energy costs and carbon emissions. From our own experience and discussions with several energy consultants, we learned that even when presented with very good investment options, decision makers are very often hesitant to act quickly. In this work we argue that to tackle this problem, the psychological aspects of the optimization and decision making process need to be addressed explicitly. We review some of the main insights from psychology of decision making and propose trust as the key factor with transparency and explainability as the main necessary contributors for building trust.

Keywords: Digital Twin · Optimization · Decision Making · Trust

1 Digital Twins

Climate change and increasing energy costs are motivating companies and other larger institutions to consider upgrades to their energy systems, such as the installation of renewable energy systems like Photo Voltaics (PV) or wind turbines. However, good investment decisions are challenging due to high budget requests, complex systems, and multiple objectives (e.g., investment costs, annual electricity bills, carbon emissions) to consider. Simulation models of current and potential future energy systems (so called digital twins) can help to generate a deeper understanding, better recommendations, more reliable forecasts of costs and savings, and eventually better green energy decision making. We therefore developed detailed simulation models for our research facility (see Figs. 1 and 2) using a simulation approach based on the Modelica [1] standard.

An example use case is to compute the expected reduction in annual electricity costs or CO_2 emissions for a potential new PV system with different size (and required investment). In Fig. 3 we plot the remaining annual CO_2 emissions for different financial investments levels. We observe an almost linear trend but also notice a slight knee point from where further investments provide a lower

A. Quesada-Arencibia et al. (Eds.): EUROCAST 2024, LNCS 15174, pp. 167–175, 2025.
https://doi.org/10.1007/978-3-031-83885-9_16

return on the investment (due to decreasing self-consumption rates). This type of analysis is very helpful for decision makers as it provides a good estimation of potential savings and guidelines for optimal sizing of the hardware.

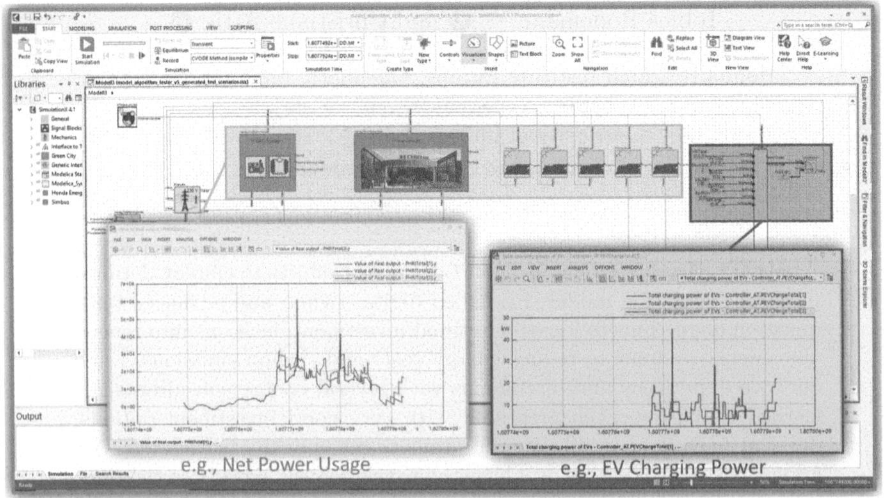

Fig. 1. Screenshot of the Digital Twin simulation environment for our facility.

1.1 Validation of Digital Twin Model

A major concern for decision makers is the precision of the simulation results. This topic is rarely discussed for complex simulation models, as there are no easy metrics to use. As our simulation tool uses a hybrid simulation approach, different aspects need to be considered.

1. As much as possible, real measured data is used, for example historical building consumption patterns or weather data. This approach not only simplifies the simulation, but also increases trust in the results.
2. For technical systems for which no measurements exist (yet), Modelica uses systems of differential equations derived from textbook knowledge. Commercial vendors provide various pre-defined modules, for instance, to simulate PV systems where only some parameters like orientation angle or peak power output need to be specified. For validation we compared the output of the simulator with real measured values and found a very high fit (few percent relative mean error between measured and simulated data).
3. Human behavior is very hard to model especially for new fields like electric mobility. Here, special local assumptions have to be made without historical data or behavioral models. This is most likely the largest source of modeling errors and a major concern for decision makers. As an example, take the

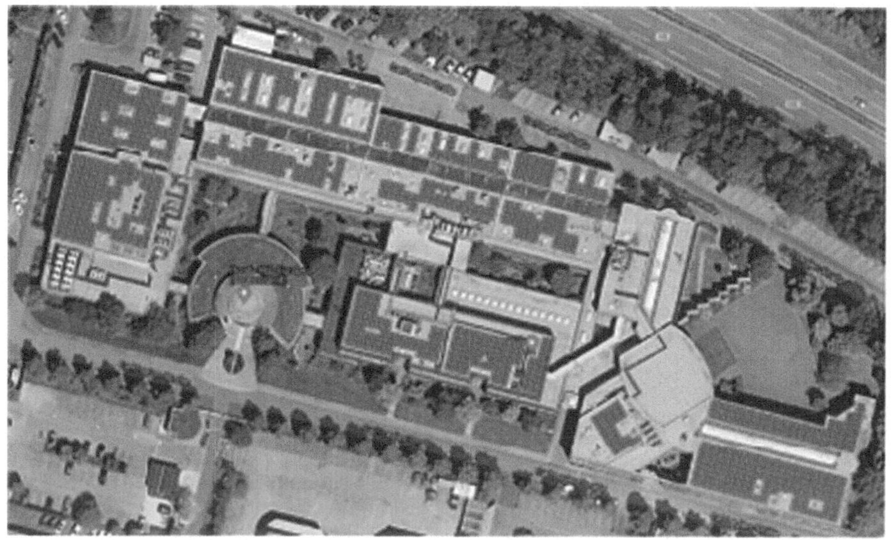

Fig. 2. Satellite view of our facility with PV array. For more information on the installed smart charging and energy management system see [22].

charging behavior of employees if the company newly offers onsite charging opportunities. Questions regarding the number of people who will have shifted to electric vehicles (EVs) or time and frequency of charging events are hard to answer in advance and potential modeling errors difficult to assess.

1.2 Optimization Methods

Another challenge is the large variety of options both on the hardware and the control system level. Numerous modules like PV system or storage battery can be installed (in different sizings) with considerable correlation between individual modules. For instance, a battery system can make use of surplus PV energy leading to potential synergies.

In order to find the optimal configuration of all investment options, we employed sophisticated many-objective optimization methods like the ones in [13,17,18]. We also used surrogates (also called meta-models) of the digital twin and were able to find optimal solutions considering several objectives, allowing decision makers to select the best option based on economic, environmental and comfort factors from a set of Pareto-optimal solutions.

We early on realized that selecting a single solution (the actual investment to be executed) from a very large set of options is extremely challenging. Therefore we increased the interaction between the optimization process and the decision maker by allowing to provide preferences to the optimizer (a preferred weighting of different objectives) and re-adjusting these preferences during the optimizer run [2].

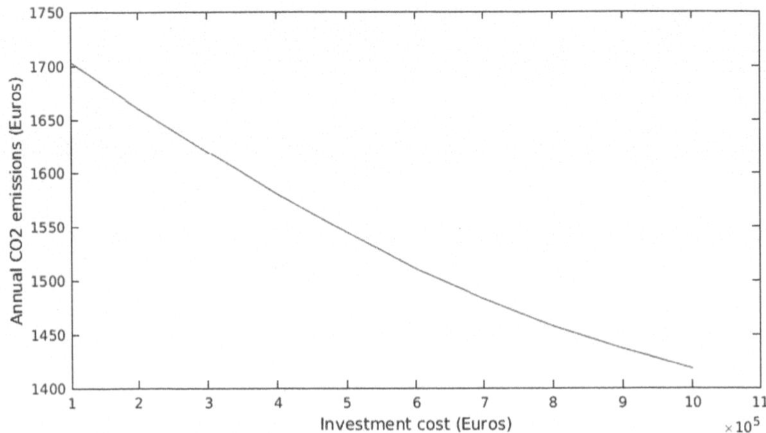

Fig. 3. Trade-off between remaining annual CO_2 emissions (in tons) and hardware investment costs for a proposed Photovoltaic system (in 10,000 Euros).

1.3 Impact

The information provided by the digital twin and the optimizer was generally considered as novel and valuable, but often did not trigger a direct action from the decision maker (i.e., no budget was invested). We heard similar experiences from different internal and externals sources (see also [5]). Even if all simulations indicate a very good return of investment and substantial reductions in CO_2 emissions, direct actions are limited. Rather additional meetings are scheduled, decisions are deferred or transferred to somebody else. This unfortunately delays the green energy transition producing substantial avoidable CO_2 emissions.

2 The Role of User Psychology in Green Energy Decisions

2.1 Insights from Psychology of Decision Making Under Uncertainty and Risk

From a behavioral economics perspective, the use of simulation models to facilitate energy efficiency decision making can be understood as a means of reducing uncertainty (i.e., ambiguity in the probability distributions of different outcomes; [11]) by specifying probabilities of possible outcomes with respect to certain solutions (e.g., regarding return of investment and reductions in CO_2 emissions), which transforms a situation under *uncertainty* to a situation under *risk*. These are distinct situations with specific psychological mechanisms at play [8,11,23]. However, as we will argue, even though decision makers are provided with outcome probabilities by the simulation tool and should therefore be able to estimate decision risk, they tend to remain in a state of uncertainty due to low trust in the digital twin model.

Rational choice theories focus on the assumption that humans make rational decisions under risk through cost-benefit analyses [11,16]. For instance, expected utility theory suggests that the decision maker calculates each option's *expected utility* by multiplying each options' *utility* with their respective *probability*. Consequently, the option with the biggest expected utility should be chosen [11,16]. In the case of using the digital twin model to facilitate the decision of financial investment in a PV system (see Fig. 3), this would mean that the decision maker chooses the option with the highest product of multiplying each option's trade-off between remaining annual CO_2 emissions and hardware investment cost for the PV system (i.e., each option's utility) and each option's respective probability.

Psychological research has shown that rational choice theories are valuable in a normative sense (i.e., they can provide insights into how humans should optimally decide in situations under risk). However, these approaches have several limitations when used in a descriptive sense [19]. First, information on options' utility and probability might not be taken into account adequately if the information is not trusted (e.g., when trust in the digital twin model is low). Hence, uncertainty remains strong and decision making is aggravated [6]. Second, particularly in situations with high cognitive load, the tendency for using low-effort cognitive heuristics instead of high-effort analytical thinking becomes stronger [21]. Consequently, option-irrelevant information might influence the decision-making process, which can lead to biased decisions or decision inertia [19].

One example is the *status quo bias*, which refers to the tendency to stick with the status quo even though other options are feasible and better. Research has identified loss aversion as a central driver for the status quo bias: Particularly when the stakes rise, decision makers tend to weigh losses more heavily than equal-sized gains [11]. Furthermore, affective processes can contribute to the status quo bias. The *feelings-as-information heuristic* or *affect heuristic* states that humans tend to use their affective reaction as a basis of judgment, i.e., decision makers rely on their subjective, emotional perception of options [21]. Low trust in the digital twin model can lead to negative affect ("bad feeling") about the presented options and a contrasting, more positive affect regarding the status quo.

We can conclude that real-life decision making is often not exclusively based on rational arguments based on cost-benefit analyses, which is what we also observed (see Sect. 1.3). If information is available for these analyses, but the source of this information is not trusted, then the information will not be (adequately) considered and the probability for decision inertia rises. The question now is: How can we include these psychological mechanisms into the simulation?

2.2 A Control-Theoretic Approach for Structuring User Interaction with Simulation and Optimization Tools

In the following, we introduce a conceptual framework (see Fig. 4) that might serve as a groundwork for modeling the psychological processes of a decision maker as part of the simulation and optimization process. This framework describes the interaction with the simulation and optimization tool and is based on a control-theory model of self-regulation [7], which has been applied to other areas of energy efficiency behavior in past research [4,9,14,15]. According to psychological control theory[1], behavior can be understood as resulting from a negative feedback loop that aims at diminishing any discrepancy between a goal status and the perceived status [7]. In the context of interacting with the system, this means that the user perceives the current simulated state of the energy system (i.e., input), which is compared to a pre-defined energy and/or financial goal (i.e., reference value). If the user perceives a discrepancy between the input and the goal, they can decide to execute optimization suggestions to diminish the discrepancy (i.e., output). This first feedback loop can be interpreted as the core interaction with the system; that is, using the system as it is intended. However, a second feedback loop has to be considered, which describes further psychological processes when using the system: The user also compares expected and perceived system performance of the tool itself. The result of this comparison is the user experience. Consequently, if there is a discrepancy between the perceived actual and the expected system performance, negative affect (e.g., frustration) might follow. Moreover, the perceived system performance also determines the perceived traceability of the system (i.e., transparency, understandability, predictability; [20]), which serves as a prerequisite for trust in the system.

Consider the situation that a decision maker is presented with results from the tool as in Fig. 1 and Fig. 3. The decision maker perceives these information as input data and compares them to reference values (e.g., targeted reductions in CO_2 emissions; financial budget available). If there is a fit between input and reference values, then an investment decision should be made (Feedback Loop 1). However, the input is also perceived as information regarding the system per-

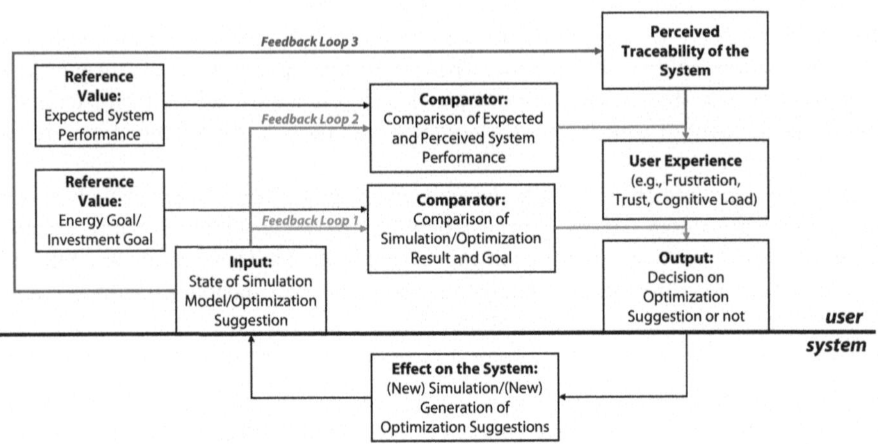

Fig. 4. Framework of the decision making process based on a control-theoretic approach of self-regulation [7].

[1] Note that control here is meant as a mental process in the decision maker, not an energy controller in the facility.

formance: For instance, if the decision maker has difficulties understanding the input because of information overload, frustration can follow (Feedback Loop 2), which can serve as a negative affect devaluating the tool and revaluating the status quo. Finally, the input is also perceived with respect to system traceability: If the decision maker is not able to grasp how the system works (e.g., if the system is not transparent regarding its functionalities and limitations) and realizes that it comes to different solutions than the decision maker expects, low system trust will emerge (Feedback Loop 3), which eventually can contribute to decision inertia.

To sum it up, even if the simulation and optimization tool suggests practicable solutions for enhancing energy efficiency, the decision to follow the system's suggestions can be impeded by aspects of user experience.

3 Summary and Outlook

In this article we have first described an advanced energy system simulation and optimization approach that combines state-of-art methods in simulation and many-objective optimization to support upgrades to building energy systems that should result in substantial cost and emission reductions.

Unfortunately, our (and probably many others') experience is that despite great results on a technical level, the necessary investments are not executed. Our main message in this publication is that the situation will probably not be improved by better simulation and optimization tools alone but a stronger focus on the decision makers and their cognitive and affective state.

Research on psychology provides ample insights into the decision making process. As a major takeaway, we want to highlight the crucial role of cognitive and affective processes in decision-making that go beyond rational reasoning. Under circumstances with high cognitive load, analytical thinking is impeded [3] and heuristics and reliance on feelings as information become more apparent in decision-making [21]. These processes can lead to biased decisions or decision inertia.

However, these cognitive shortcuts are not necessarily disadvantageous. Heuristics are often adaptive to manage complex decision-making processes under constraints of limited cognitive capacities and may lead to sufficiently good decisions [10]. Hence, a beneficial new perspective would be to incorporate knowledge about both analytic and heuristic reasoning into discussions about investments into green energy systems. For example, practical guidelines that tackle the issues as depicted in Sect. 2 could be: (1) Support the decision maker with few comprehensible, precise, and trustworthy options to choose from (goal: low cognitive load), (2) optimize simulation tools for high transparency, understandability, and predictability (goal: high system traceability), (3) let trusted experts present information and give recommendations (goal: compensate uncertainty and/or system distrust with human trust).

Empirical support for these guidelines in the specific domain of organizational or industrial green energy transition is lacking yet, but similar ideas have been stated in the past. For instance, [12] highlight the beneficial role of heuristic thinking in managerial decision making in the green energy context. The authors derived simple rules from mathematical models and tested their validity. By describing the effects of individual variables, these rules reduced the complexity of having many interacting variables (e.g., "Stationary batteries work efficiently when cheap energy can be stored and used whenever necessary", p. 5); thus, they might serve as cognitive shortcuts that support decision making [12].

Finally, to better understand sustainable decision making for fostering green energy transition, deepened empirical research on the role of system traceability and cognitive load on system trust and decision quality is needed.

Acknowledgments. We want to thank Tim Schrills for his valuable comments on the conceptual framework.

Disclosure of Interests. The authors have no competing interests to declare that are relevant to the content of this article.

References

1. Modelica association. https://modelica.org/. Accessed 22 May 2024
2. Aghaei-Pour, P., Rodemann, T., Hakanen, J., Miettinen, K.: Surrogate assisted interactive multiobjective optimization in energy system design of buildings. Optim. Eng. **23**(1), 303–327 (2022)
3. Allen, P.M., Edwards, J.A., Snyder, F.J., Makinson, K.A., Hamby, D.M.: The effect of cognitive load on decision making with graphically displayed uncertainty information. Risk Anal. **34**(8), 1495–1505 (2014)
4. Arend, M.G., Franke, T., Stanton, N.A.: Know-how or know-why? The role of hybrid electric vehicle drivers' acquisition of eco-driving knowledge for eco-driving success. Appl. Ergon. **75**, 221–229 (2019)
5. Büscher, C., Sumpf, P.: "Trust" and "confidence" as socio-technical problems in the transformation of energy systems. Energy Sustain. Soc. **5**, 1–13 (2015)
6. Cagno, E., Worrell, E., Trianni, A., Pugliese, G.: A novel approach for barriers to industrial energy efficiency. Renew. Sustain. Energy Rev. **19**, 290–308 (2013)
7. Carver, C.S., Scheier, M.F.: On the structure of behavioral self-regulation. In: Handbook of self-regulation, pp. 41–84. Elsevier (2000)
8. De Groot, K., Thurik, R.: Disentangling risk and uncertainty: when risk-taking measures are not about risk. Front. Psychol. **9**, 342416 (2018)
9. Franke, T., Neumann, I., Bühler, F., Cocron, P., Krems, J.F.: Experiencing range in an electric vehicle: understanding psychological barriers. Appl. Psychol. **61**(3), 368–391 (2012)
10. Gigerenzer, G., Gaissmaier, W.: Heuristic decision making. Annu. Rev. Psychol. **62**, 451–482 (2011)
11. Johnson, J.G., Busemeyer, J.R.: Decision making under risk and uncertainty. Wiley Interdisc. Rev. Cogn. Sci. **1**(5), 736–749 (2010)
12. Krawinkler, A., Breitenecker, R.J., Maresch, D.: Heuristic decision-making in the green energy context: bringing together simple rules and data-driven mathematical optimization. Technol. Forecast. Soc. Chang. **180**, 121695 (2022)

13. Liu, Q., Lanfermann, F., Rodemann, T., Olhofer, M., Jin, Y.: Surrogate-assisted many-objective optimization of building energy management. IEEE Comput. Intell. Mag. **18**(4), 14–28 (2023)
14. McCalley, L., Midden, C.J.: Energy conservation through product-integrated feedback: the roles of goal-setting and social orientation. J. Econ. Psychol. **23**(5), 589–603 (2002)
15. Nielsen, K.S.: From prediction to process: a self-regulation account of environmental behavior change. J. Environ. Psychol. **51**, 189–198 (2017)
16. Platt, M.L., Huettel, S.A.: Risky business: the neuroeconomics of decision making under uncertainty. Nat. Neurosci. **11**(4), 398–403 (2008)
17. Rodemann, T.: A many-objective configuration optimization for building energy management. In: IEEE (ed.) WCCI 2018 Conference. IEEE (2018)
18. Rodemann, T.: A comparison of different many-objective optimization algorithms for energy system optimization. In: Kaufmann, P., Castillo, P. (eds.) Applications of Evolutionary Computation, pp. 1–16. LNCS, vol. 11454. Springer (2019)
19. Samuelson, W., Zeckhauser, R.: Status quo bias in decision making. J. Risk Uncertain. **1**, 7–59 (1988)
20. Schrills, T., Franke, T.: How do users experience traceability of AI systems? Examining subjective information processing awareness in automated insulin delivery (AID) systems. ACM Trans. Interact. Intell. Syst. **13**(4), 1–34 (2023)
21. Slovic, P., Finucane, M.L., Peters, E., MacGregor, D.G.: Risk as analysis and risk as feelings: some thoughts about affect, reason, risk and rationality. In: The Feeling of Risk, pp. 21–36. Routledge (2013)
22. Stadie, M., et al.: V2B vehicle to building charging manager. In: EVTeC: 5th International Electric Vehicle Technology Conference 2021. Japanese Society of Automotive Engineers (2021)
23. Volz, K.G., Gigerenzer, G.: Cognitive processes in decisions under risk are not the same as in decisions under uncertainty. Front. Neurosci. **6**, 105 (2012)

Performance and Computation Time Gains Caused by Sampling Rate Reduction in Time Series Deep Anomaly Detection

Dominik Wiesner(✉) and Frank Schirmeier

University of Applied Sciences Kempten, Bahnhofstraße 61, 87435 Kempten, Germany
{dominik.wiesner,frank.schirmeier}@hs-kempten.de

Abstract. In the face of climate change, it is a necessity to reduce the environmental impact of AI models. The pursuit of more energy-efficient AI is referred to as Green AI. A key ingredient in Green AI strategies is to reduce the amount of data used for training and inference. This is especially important for energy intensive sectors like the manufacturing industry, which is already under pressure to reduce their production-related CO_2 emissions. This study evaluates empirically the impact of sample rate reduction on time series data as a possibility to implement Green AI for manufacturers that use CNC machining. A real-world dataset is used for this research to evaluate the performance of the decimation pre-processing step for our sample application, semi-supervised deep anomaly detection (DAD). The results show that decimation has the potential to assist manufacturers to reduce resource consumption and to make advances in operational sustainability. In addition, the DAD performance is not only stable, but even improves to a certain extent in the course of the sample rate conversion. This can arguably be attributed to the beneficial effect of noise reduction. This research contributes to the ongoing discourse to develop energy efficient AI methods and is especially applicable to the field of manufacturing processes.

Keywords: Green AI · Deep Anomaly Detection · Sampling Rate Reduction · Time Series · Machining

1 Introduction

The goal of Green AI is to increase the efficiency of AI models, especially in the field of deep learning. This can be achieved by reducing the cost of the result (R) in Eq. (1) [8].

$$Cost(R) \propto E \cdot D \cdot H \tag{1}$$

The cost (R) depends on the cost of running a single training example (E), the size of the data set (D) and the number of hyperparameter experiments (H). Consequently, the efficiency of an AI model can be increased by reducing

A. Quesada-Arencibia et al. (Eds.): EUROCAST 2024, LNCS 15174, pp. 176–186, 2025.
https://doi.org/10.1007/978-3-031-83885-9_17

the time required for a training example, and also by reducing the amount of data required. This paper examines the impact of these measures in the form of data stream decimation on the performance of a deep anomaly detection. Here, decimation refers to the sample rate reduction for measured time series data. We compare different decimation increments for a certain range of DAD models and analyse the amount of decimation that is possible without deteriorating the model performance. To evaluate the potential impact on real-world processes that are relevant for the manufacturing industry, a data stream recorded in a Computerized Numerical Control (CNC) milling process is used for our empirical analysis. The results are discussed in the broader context of the research project DIONE-X [1] in which the impact of novel data reduction and obfuscation schemes on innovative data-driven business use cases in the milling industry is studied.

2 Related Work

The research area Green AI spans multiple topics, including monitoring, hyperparameter tuning, model benchmarking and deployment. Most often the focus lies on gaining energy efficiency improvements via modifications of the model architecture; approaches that analyse the data preprocessing pipeline are still rare [13]. The goal of this paper is to contribute to the data-centric Green AI research in particular in the context of time series data in industrially relevant use case scenarios like the optimization of manufacturing processes. It has already been shown that the energy consumption of machine learning models correlates with the number of data points used [12]. For instance, the energy consumption was reduced to up to 92.16% with only a small loss of accuracy [12]. Even more, under favorable conditions machine learning models are capable to perform even better with less data [14], a phenomenon that has been observed in the experiments for this paper as well. Since most studies focus on text or image data, there appears to be a lack of Green AI literature for time series data, in particular in the context of manufacturing processes. This kind of data is useful for a broad range of predictive maintenance and process monitoring applications. For instance, DAD methods are quite commonly used to implement such use cases [9].

For these reasons, reducing the amount of data needed to train DAD models on manufacturing data has the potential to considerably reduce carbon emissions in real-world use case scenarios. This paper thus investigates whether sample rate reduction is a suitable data-centric Green AI approach in the context of deep anomaly detection in manufacturing time series data.

3 Experimental Setup

3.1 Data Preprocessing

The machining data set introduced in [10] is used for the experiment. The data set covers acceleration data in the X, Y and Z directions on three CNC machines over three years in production. The data is recorded at 2000 Hz from 15 different operations with various tools and spindle speeds ranging from 75 to 250 Hz. The time series data is divided into chunks that have binary labels (OK/NOK) according to process status. To reduce the amount of training data (D), the data set is decimated by means of sampling rate conversion. For the analyses, the entire data set is reduced to four further iteration levels with 1000, 500, 250 and 125 Hz in addition to the full resolution of 2000 Hz. This halves the size of the data set with each iteration. As a result, the data volume in the last iteration stage is $\frac{1}{16}$ of the original data volume.

For the DAD models used, the recorded sensor data is segmented into windows. To capture an identical semantic context window, the temporal context of two seconds is used and maintained for each clock rate reduction stage. As a result, the number of data points within the segmented windows and thus the training and inference time for a single training example (E) is assumed to be reduced in each iteration. This design choice – in contrast to the alternative choice to keep the number of data points constant, effectively doubling the length of the temporal context in each reduction step – has been made to decouple the performance effects of the temporal context length from the effects of the decimation, for the sake of a fair comparison of models trained on differently decimated data.

The DAD models are implemented and trained in a semi-supervised manner. We chose this method as the unsupervised method is often difficult to evaluate [2,4] and requires a certain ratio of OK/NOK labelling [3]. Supervised methods, on the other hand, are often impractical due to their reliance on sufficiently labelled data sets [4]. Semi-supervised methods use only OK data as training data and OK/NOK data for evaluation [3]. The functionality of semi-supervised anomaly detection using reconstruction (see Subsect. 3.2) is illustrated in Fig. 1. The figure demonstrates the extent to which the different labels OK and NOK are used for the detection process.

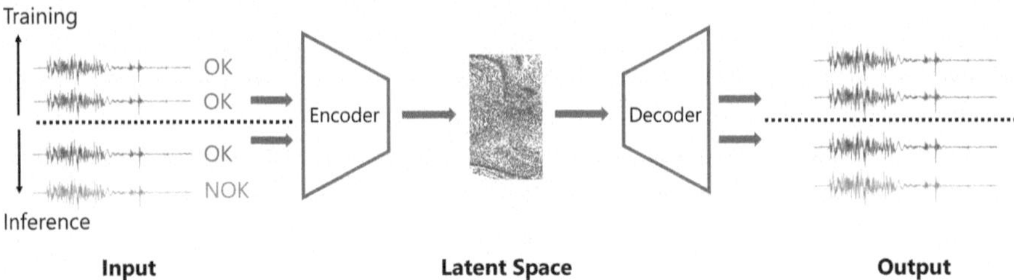

Fig. 1. Semi-supervised training of an anomaly detection model. Semi-supervised means that during training only samples labeled as OK are presented to the model. The model architecture displayed here is a reconstruction model (on 1D data). Signals are marked as anomalies if the reconstruction error after a compression and decompression stage is high.

To adjust the anomaly detection task to the process status, the data is cleansed. For this purpose, 4% are cut off at the beginning or end of a time series if a certain recurring signal that clearly does not belong to the normal production process is encountered. The data is then filtered and decimated using an FIR filter. Corresponding artifacts are removed. The data is split into a distribution per time frame following the recommendation of [10].

3.2 DAD Model Architectures

In this study, three DAD model families are considered which cover state of the art models as well as conceptually simple models: two reconstruction models and one prediction model.

- In a reconstruction model, an autoencoder is optimized to reconstruct a given time series data window which undergoes a compression in the encoder phase and a decompression in the decoder phase of the model. Due to the information bottleneck in the so-called latent space between encoder and decoder and the restricted number of model parameters, the model must sacrifice reconstruction quality for anormal data in favour of the normal data the model is trained on. The drop in reconstruction quality can then be used to label data segments as anomalies. We consider a reconstruction model architecture on the raw (1D) time series data as well as another architecture on (2D) spectrograms, in which the Fourier spectrum within small time steps is visualized.
- Prediction models, on the other hand, predict the next few data points based on the currently observed window; this prediction is then compared to the actually observed data points in order to potentially classify these as anomalies.

In our study, the reconstruction model design choices are based on domain-specific studies [6,11] where comparable models have already achieved state of the art results. An anomaly score is calculated based on the comparison of the input and output of convolutional autoencoders (CAE), which are trained on raw data (1D) and on spectrograms (2D) respectively. For the prediction models, Long Short-Term Memory (LSTM) networks are trained on the raw data. LSTM Models have been shown to be the state-of-the-art in terms of DAD performance [7]. We refer to the two reconstruction models (on 1D and 2D data) and the prediction model (the LSTM model) as *model families* that form the basis for our analysis. The model architectures used in this study can each be understood to be composed of smaller structures called *modules*. In the reconstruction models, a (encoder) module consists of a convolutional layer followed by a batch normalisation layer, a ReLU activation function and finally a max-pooling layer. In the decoder, the module structure is reversed. In the prediction models, we refer to the LSTM layers as modules.

In order to have a broad range of models with different parameter counts and therefore information processing capabilities in this evaluation – for each base model architecture – the number of modules is varied between 1 and 3, resulting in different *model extension lengths*. An exception is that the 2D reconstruction model is not implemented with three modules because the incurred reduction in latent-space dimensionality would lead to degenerate internal states. The goal of the implementation of different model extension lengths is to reduce the arbitrariness in the precise model implementation details and to make the interpretation of the results more robust. For the prediction model, we expect a monotone relationship between module count and anomaly detection performance; for the reconstruction models however, this is less obvious, as the model parameter restrictions are crucial for the separation between normal and anormal data.

3.3 Hyperparameter Search and Training Scheme

In order to minimise a distortion of the results by hyperparameters choices of the human experimenter that may not be equally optimal for different model architectures, an extensive search for an "appropriate" set of hyperparameters [2] is conducted. The computation budget for the hyperparameter search is set to a fixed amount (either 24h or 48h, depending on the training phase, on 1–2 GPUs) for each model family, each model extension length and each sample rate. It is assumed that this amount is sufficient to reach settings that are as good as settings set by a human expert. It should be noted however that complicated models (with a high model extension length) should train less quickly, implying that the random search has fewer chances to find a good optimum; this is a desired behaviour from the perspective of practical applications in which the compute budget (and experimenter patience) is limited as well.

The random search is divided into two phases: First, a rough search is conducted over a broad range of reasonable settings in order to find a good starting point comparable to the a priori knowledge of an experienced experimenter. Each DAD model trains 24 h on two GPUs for this task. Secondly, a fine search (training) is conducted focusing on a promising subspace of the hyperparameter space. For each combination of DAD model, model extension length and sample rate, 24 h on one GPU are provided.

To make the training durations comparable for different model architectures, the reconstruction models (i.e. autoencoders) train – for each model candidate – for 50 epochs on a batch size of 32 training examples, the prediction models (i.e. LSTMs) train for 30 epochs on a batch size of 256 training examples. The learning rate varies randomly between 0.001 and 0.0001. All models use as evaluation metric the mean square error (averaged over time points and 2s-windows) and ADAM as optimizer. Each model candidate is evaluated on the validation data. An Intel(R) Xeon(R) Silver 4215R, two NVIDIA GeForce RTX 3090 and 192 GB RAM and Tensorflow 2.7 and Python 3.8.10 are used to carry out the experiment. The full details w.r.t. the training scheme can be found in [5]. It should be emphasized that the goal of the training is not the search for a single final model that optimizes the anomaly detection task, but to find a collection of suitable inference models that can be used to assess the effects of sample rate reduction in a general way. The evaluation in the following section thus focuses not on the single best model, but instead the performance range of all models trained during the fine search is visualized via box plots.

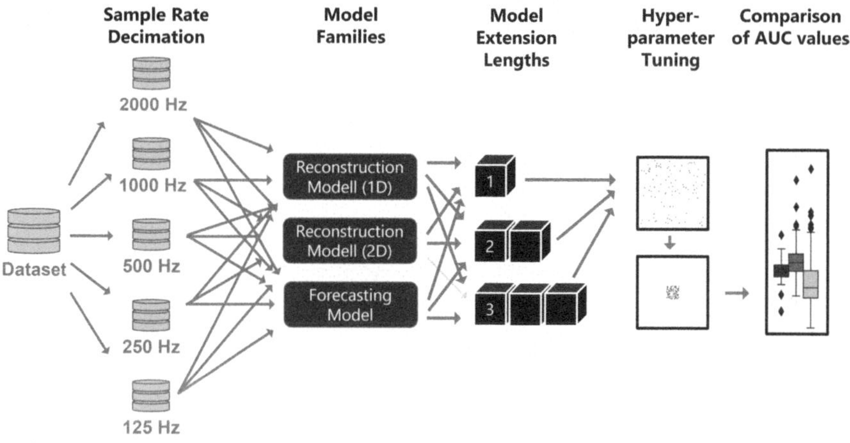

Fig. 2. Overview of the experimental setup.

3.4 Evaluation Methodology

The Area Under the Curve (AUC)-Receiver Operating Characteristic (ROC) of the respective inference models is calculated for evaluation. One challenge in calculating the AUC-ROC is the labelling of the time series in the data set used for the experiments. The time series in the data set represent entire tool operations, which last several seconds. Segmenting the data into two-second windows for the DAD models may result in section that do not represent the behavior according to the labelling of the entire tool process. Therefore, the difference between the original value and the reconstruction/prediction is calculated for each data point in each window, and the average over these mean squared errors is calculated over the entire tool operation process. If the difference exceeds a certain threshold, the entire time series is predicted as NOK. Gradually increasing the threshold yields the AUC-ROC. Figure 2 depicts the experimental setup.

4 Result

The results of the three deep learning methods trained with five sampling rates (2000, 1000, 500, 250, and 125 Hz) are presented in Fig. 3. All model families show comparable performances (with the 1D reconstruction model (1D-CAE) slightly outperforming the other architectures, cf. also Table 1 for a performance comparison for the best models at 500 Hz); the goal of the extensive model selection and hyperparameter tuning to allow for generalizable assertions that are robust w.r.t. model details and parameter and hyperparameter settings has thus been reached. Therefore, the figure allows to focus on the effects of sample rate decimation and its role as a potential Green AI measure on semi-supervised anomaly detection. It can be observed that increasing the decimation strength from 2000 Hz to 500 Hz target sample rate leads to an increase of the detection performance across all model families. Arguably, this can be attributed to the beneficial effects of noise reduction. Furthermore, it can be observed that from 250 Hz onwards, most anomalies cannot be captured anymore. We argue that this implies that the anomalies in this data set are characterised by high frequencies that get lost once the decimation strength is too high.

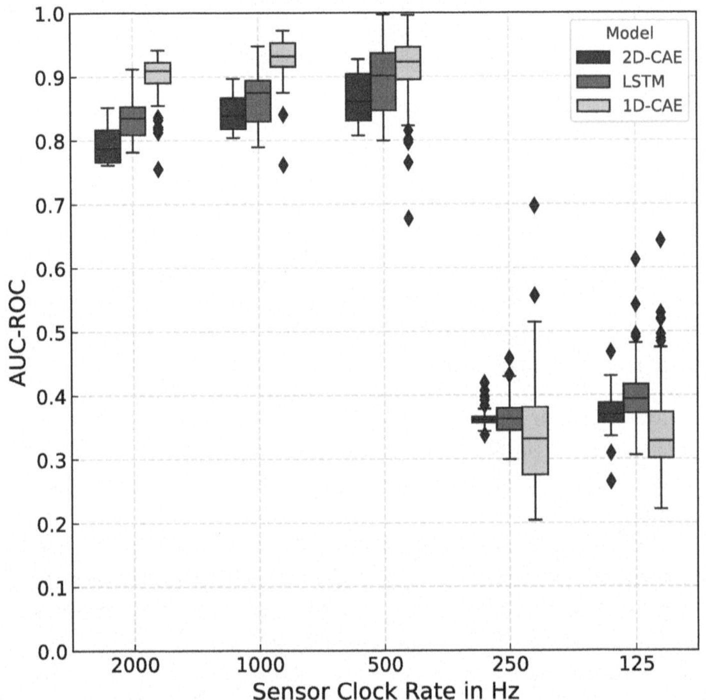

Fig. 3. Result with all architectures.

In Table 1 the 1D reconstruction model (1D-CAE) overall appears to be the best-suited architecture for this task. For the critical decimation target rate 500 Hz however it is on par with the prediction model (LSTM). The 2D reconstruction model (2D-CAE) has the lowest performance which indicates that for the given compute and parameter budget the switch to the frequency domain (i.e. the spectrograms) is not parameter-efficient.

In order to substantiate the assumption that the performance boost results from noise reduction, a bandpass filter between 75 Hz and 500 Hz is applied in a

Table 1. Maximum AUC-ROC per sampling rate.

	2000 Hz	1000 Hz	500 Hz	250 Hz	125 Hz
LSTM	0.912	0.948	0.997	0.458	0.613
1D-CAE	0.942	0.972	0.996	0.697	0.643
2D-CAE	0.852	0.897	0.927	0.419	0.468

further experiment. These numbers are derived from the lowest spindle speed of the tool operation (75 Hz) and the results of the first experiment (500 Hz). The term noise is understood here as any information that is not required for the deep anomaly detection task. This follow-up experiment is performed on the 1D convolutional autoencoder only since this is a reasonable baseline architecture.

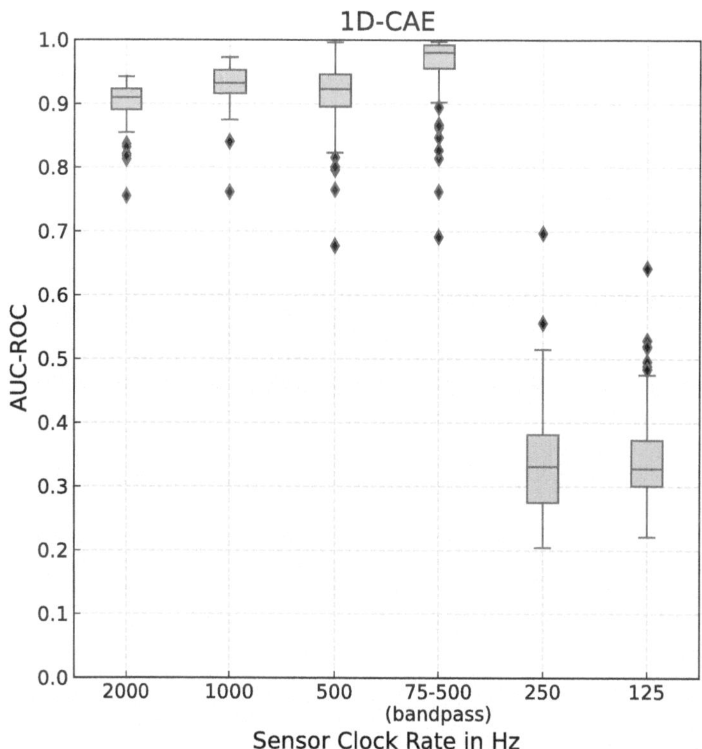

Fig. 4. Sample rate reduction with bandpass.

The results represented in Fig. 4 demonstrate that the anomaly detection performance improves as more information is discarded, even in the lower frequency range. The performance increase can arguably be attributed to a more efficient usage of the fixed parameter and compute budget. Moreover, this leads to the hypothesis that most anomalies are noticeable between 75 Hz and 500 Hz, and that discarding irrelevant information in the lower and upper frequency range allows the models to focus on the anomalous behaviour in a more parameter- and time-efficient way.

To quantify the speed-up incurred by sample rate decimation, we evaluate the 1D reconstruction models, for which the average parameter count for the 500 Hz models (approx. 71k) is comparable to the average count for the 2000 Hz models (approx. 70k). Here, the training time is approximately halved (579 instead of 261 models can be trained within a fixed time budget of 24h) while the inference time is reduced by one third (0.22 s instead of 0.32 s). For the other model families, similar speed-ups can be observed, which are however less easily interpreted due to a greater variation in the parameter count.

Finally, a noteworthy observation is that for a decimation target rate of 250 Hz or smaller, AUC-ROC < 0.5 are observed. This means that the reconstruction or prediction error on the anomalous data is in fact smaller compared to normal data. In view of the automated training and evaluation scheme, the most obvious explanations concerning mislabeled data or other mishaps can be ruled out. Instead, our explanation is as follows:

1. For lower signal strengths, the reconstruction or prediction errors are generally lower.
2. Even though the signal strength for normal and anormal data appears to be comparable overall, the DAD performance drop between decimation target rate 500 Hz and 250 Hz indicates that in anormal sequences, there are high frequencies that contribute to the signal strength.

In short, we hypothesize that filtering out these high frequencies leads to lower signal strengths, which in turn have – in tendency – lower prediction errors.

5 Conclusion

In summary, the detection performance of the models improves in initial data decimation steps (with decreasing sampling rate and thus lower data volume), while strong decimation leads to a loss of anomaly detection capability. The AUC-ROC increases in each decimation step between 2000 Hz and 500 Hz. This increase can arguably be attributed to the beneficial effect of noise smoothing. A large performance drop can be recognised between 500 Hz and 250 Hz. From 250 Hz onwards, classification is essentially indistinguishable from a random decision. These phenomena are equally recognisable in both the reconstruction and prediction methods. The results allow to minimise calculation efforts by reducing sensor data sampling rate. The smaller amount of data allows to reduce training and inference time, implying that the search for suitable hyperparameters is either faster or – when the compute budget is held constant – more extensive. In addition, less storage space and network traffic is required for the converted data set. For real-word applications like the development of predictive maintenance models for manufacturing processes, this research can help to reduce the training and inference time as well as to improve the performance for the developed model. This together with other beneficial side-effects like the desired incurred loss of sensible information in the data stream (data obfuscation) makes targeted, i.e. use case specific, sample rate decimation a valuable building block to be included in future model architectures.

Acknowledgments. This research has received funding from the German Federal Ministry of Education and Research under grant agreement 02J21D130 in the scope of the research project DIONE-X.

References

1. Dione-x (29052024). https://dione-x.de/
2. Aggarwal, C.C.: Outlier Analysis, 2nd edn. Springer International Publishing and Imprint: Springer, Cham (2017)
3. Chandola, V., Banerjee, A., Kumar, V.: Anomaly detection: a survey. ACM Comput. Surv. **41**(3) (2009). https://doi.org/10.1145/1541880.1541882
4. Darban, Z.Z., Webb, G.I., Pan, S., Aggarwal, C.C., Salehi, M.: Deep learning for time series anomaly detection: a survey (2022). http://arxiv.org/pdf/2211.05244v2
5. Wiesner, D.: Sensordatenfusion und anomaliedetektion für prozessbegleitende sensordaten in der zerspanung [unpublished master's thesis] (2023)
6. Jourdan, N., Bayer, T., Biegel, T., Metternich, J.: Handling concept drift in deep learning applications for process monitoring. In: 56th CIRP Conference on Manufacturing Systems, CIRP CMS 23, South Africa (2023)
7. Schmidl, S., Wenig, P., Papenbrock, T.: Anomaly detection in time series. Proc. VLDB Endow. **15**(9), 1779–1797 (2022). https://doi.org/10.14778/3538598.3538602
8. Schwartz, R., Dodge, J., Smith, N.A., Etzioni, O.: Green AI. arXiv e-prints arXiv:1907.10597 (2019). https://doi.org/10.48550/arXiv.1907.10597
9. Serradilla, O., Zugasti, E., Rodriguez, J., Zurutuza, U.: Deep learning models for predictive maintenance: a survey, comparison, challenges and prospects. Appl. Intell. **52**(10), 10934–10964 (2022). https://doi.org/10.1007/s10489-021-03004-y
10. Tnani, M.A., Feil, M., Diepold, K.: Smart data collection system for brownfield CNC milling machines: a new benchmark dataset for data-driven machine monitoring. Procedia CIRP **107**, 131–136 (2022). https://doi.org/10.1016/j.procir.2022.04.022. Leading manufacturing systems transformation – Proceedings of the 55th CIRP Conference on Manufacturing Systems 2022
11. Tnani, M.A., Subarnaduti, P., Diepold, K.: Efficient feature learning approach for raw industrial vibration data using two-stage learning framework. Sensors **22**(13) (2022). https://doi.org/10.3390/s22134813. https://www.mdpi.com/1424-8220/22/13/4813
12. Verdecchia, R., Cruz, L., Sallou, J., Lin, M., Wickenden, J., Hotellier, E.: Data-centric green AI an exploratory empirical study. In: Calero, C. (ed.) 2022 International Conference on ICT for Sustainability, pp. 35–45. IEEE Computer Society, Conference Publishing Services, Los Alamitos, CA (2022). https://doi.org/10.1109/ICT4S55073.2022.00015

13. Verdecchia, R., Sallou, J., Cruz, L.: A systematic review of green AI. WIREs Data Mining Knowl. Discov. **13**(4) (2023). https://doi.org/10.1002/widm.1507
14. Zogaj, F., Cambronero, J.P., Rinard, M.C., Cito, J.: Doing more with less: characterizing dataset downsampling for automl. Proc. VLDB Endow. **14**(11), 2059–2072 (2021). https://doi.org/10.14778/3476249.3476262

Exploring the Green AI Potential of Adapter Tuning for Language Models

Dennis Mustafić(✉) and Frank Schirmeier

University of Applied Sciences Kempten, Bahnhofstr. 61, 87435 Kempten, Germany
{dennis.mustafic,frank.schirmeier}@hs-kempten.de

Abstract. Large Language Models are of fundamental importance for future AI usage in industry and society. The environmental impact of training and inference of such models however is devastating, which necessitates research into more efficient model mechanisms. In the simple context of the well-established BERT architecture, this study performs a comprehensive comparison between classical fine-tuning, which involves most or all of the model weights, and parameter-efficient Adapter Tuning, in which shallow trainable layers are introduced throughout the model while the vast majority of original weights remain unchanged. A series of experiments were carried out in which the BERT$_{base}$-architecture was trained on the LexGLUE benchmark with fine-tuning and Adapter Tuning for each data set. Through extensive comparisons in the experiments, it was found that Adapter Tuning is advantageous from a green AI perspective at epoch level, supporting the claims made in the literature. However, in our experiments reaching model convergence with Adapter Tuning requires significantly more time, making this training method in total less environmentally friendly than the conventional fine-tuning method, at least for the chosen model family.

Keywords: Adapter Tuning · Parameter Efficiency · Energy Consumption · Large Language Models (LLMs)

1 Introduction and Motivation

Fine-tuning of pre-trained Transformer models is ineffective, as all weights are completely changed when adapting to a new task. This leads to parameter-inefficiency, as the pre-trained model parameters cannot be reused and therefore a completely new model is required for each task. Adapter Tuning by Houlsby et al. [1] is an alternative approach to allow for more efficient parameter training. Here, the pre-trained model is freezed, and adaptation to the downstream task occurs by training so-called Adapter modules instead, which are incorporated into the Transformer layers. By design, the theoretic efficiency is significantly increased, as the Adapter modules only comprise 0.5–8% of the original parameters and can be replaced depending on the task. GPU resources are also saved during the training process, as only a fraction of the gradients needs to be calculated during backpropagation. This means that language models can be trained

A. Quesada-Arencibia et al. (Eds.): EUROCAST 2024, LNCS 15174, pp. 187–196, 2025.
https://doi.org/10.1007/978-3-031-83885-9_18

on less powerful infrastructures and still achieve similar performance [1]. Adapter Tuning can be used alternatively or additionally to other approaches like Low Rank Adaptation [2] and derivations thereof.

The objective of this study is to assess the usability of Adapter Tuning in practice and derive conclusions about the environmental friendliness of this parameter-efficient training method. In order to evaluate the usability of Adapter Tuning in practice, this study carries out a series of tests in order to specialize the underlying BERT architecture to different downstream tasks. Four different downstream tasks as specified in the LexGLUE benchmark dataset [3] are evaluated. In these tests, the performance (evaluated by task-specific means) of classical fine-tuning serves as a base-line to which the performance of the models trained with Adapter Layers is compared. The comparison focuses on four key areas: performance, epoch durations, model convergence, and energy consumption.

2 Related Work

Prior research has addressed this topic. In their work, Rückle et al. [4] proposed a technique called AdapterDrop, which involves removing Adapter modules from lower Transformer layers during training and inference in order to achieve an efficiency increase. In this study, the authors also conducted measurements, which demonstrated that Adapter Tuning can be up to 60% faster than conventional model fine-tuning per epoch. Similarly, to the approach proposed by Rückle et al. [4], Mahabadi et al. [5] have developed an alternative training method called Compacter. This method was evaluated in terms of its per-epoch efficiency gains when using Adapter Tuning. Both of these works demonstrate that Adapter Tuning has a higher efficiency per epoch. However, they do not account for the slower model convergence when performing model adaption with Adapter modules.

The studies by Ding et al. and Mundra et al. [6,7] examine various alternative training methods. Ding et al. covers multiple PEFT methods, while Mundra et al. focuses specifically on Adapter Tuning. Ding et al. also show that the per epoch speed of Adapter Tuning can be faster. However, the findings of [6,7] indicate that alternative methods, including Adapter Tuning, exhibit a slower convergence rate compared to the baseline fine-tuning approach. This slower convergence rate has implications for training times and environmental impact.

As our work focuses on energy consumption, the work of Wang et al. [8] is of importance, in which a novel fine-tuning method, Recurrent Adaptation of Large Transformers (READ) is proposed. The article also included the measurement of energy for a range of training methods, including Adapter Tuning and fine-tuning. These measurements were conducted on a T5_{base}-model. The results demonstrated that Adapter Tuning exhibited a higher energy efficiency than fine-tuning. In contrast, our findings for the BERT_{base}-model indicate that due to the extended time required for model convergence, adaptation using Adapter modules consumes more energy.

3 Experiment

The overarching objective of the experiment is to conduct a comprehensive comparison between fine-tuning and Adapter Tuning, with a particular focus on convergence speed and energy consumption of the two training methods. The training and measurements were conducted on a single NVIDIA H100 80 GBs GPU.

Data. The comparison is conducted using the LexGLUE benchmark from Chalkidis et al. [3], which comprises seven datasets with three different task types: multi-label classification, multi-class classification and multiple choice question answering. The dataset includes a wide range of legal texts from Terms of Services (ToS), EU laws to US court decisions. This experiment uses a subset of four datasets (CaseHOLD, SCOTUS, UNFAIR-ToS, EUR-LEX) due to simpler comparability. Nevertheless, the data sets used in this experiment exhibit a high degree of variability, considering different characteristics.

Model. BERT_{base}-uncased with 110 million parameters [9] was used as the model in this experiment. BERT_{base} was chosen because of its simple and well-understood architecture and because of the readily available reference performance metrics for the LexGLUE-Benchmark.

Hyperparameter. For this experiment, we adopted hyperparameters based on the series of experiments conducted by Chalkidis et al. [3]. These hyperparameters were then combined with the corresponding Adapter parameters during Adapter Tuning. As in the original paper on Adapter Tuning by Houlsby et al. [1], we employed bottleneck adapters. To ensure comparability, both training procedures used identical hyperparameters and seed values for weight initialization. The detailed hyperparameter settings can be found in Appendix A, while the Adapter module parameters are provided in Appendix B.

Methodology. Due to the different loss magnitudes generated by the two training methods, as shown in Fig. 1, a user-defined callback was developed in addition to early stopping, which enables time-controlled training. With early stopping, the optimal model state is determined by comparing training and evaluation losses. However, this creates a challenge as different loss values are generated depending on the selected training method. Using the same patience parameters in early stopping may result in errors. For this reason, time-dependent training was introduced as a precaution measure, in which the models are trained with both methods over a period of 12 h and compared afterwards, in addition to the early stopping models. This minimizes the variability in the comparison since the convergence criterion is no longer solely based on the loss magnitudes. Nevertheless, the models determined by early stopping are also saved and used for evaluation, as these are of great importance in practical applications and a comparison is therefore essential.

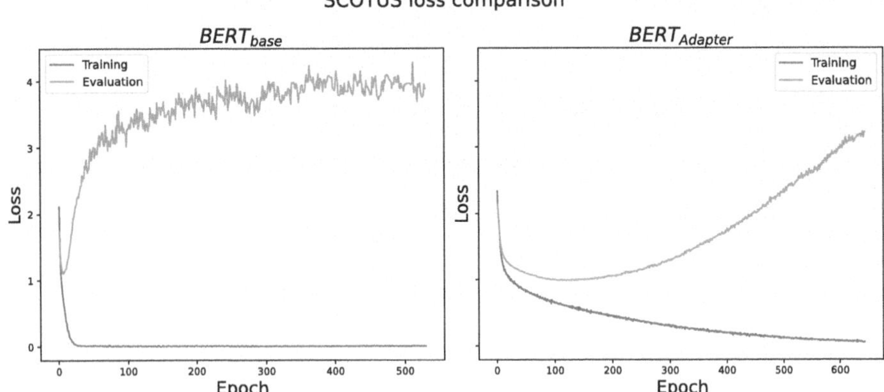

Fig. 1. Comparison of the loss curves for SCOTUS. Both training methods yield different loss structures, with fine-tuning tending towards stronger overfitting. In contrast, Adapter Tuning produces a smoother curve through the use of skip connections.

4 Results

4.1 Performance

This experiment uses the μ-F1 (micro) as the main performance metric, given that the data sets exhibit class imbalances. Chalkidis et al. calculated additionally the m-F1 (macro) in their original experiment in [3]. These results were also obtained in this experiment and can be found in the Appendix C.

Early Stopping. In all cases in which the early stopping procedure is applied, the Adapter Tuning method exhibits a slight decline in performance compared to conventional fine-tuning, due to limitations in their capacity for learning finer details of the given data. Nevertheless, the observed performance differences are relatively minor, indicating that the selected hyperparameter configuration for both training methods is suitable for further comparison.

12 Hours. The 12-hour results are comparable to the early stopping results, with the exception of CaseHOLD, where adaptation through Adapters exhibits a marginal improvement. This exception from the general rule is likely linked to fluctuations resulting from differing weight initialization. The overall performance comparison indicate that both training methods achieved similar performances. Therefore, an evaluation of both training methods from a green AI perspective is meaningful from a practical point of view (Table 1).

Table 1. Results for the μ-F1 metric for models with early stopping and those trained for 12 h.

	Early-Stopping				12 h			
	CaseHOLD	SCOTUS	UNFAIR-ToS	EUR-LEX	CaseHOLD	SCOTUS	UNFAIR-ToS	EUR-LEX
Adapter	0.6994	0.6557	0.9402	0.6925	0.6994	0.6564	0.9503	0.7019
Base	0.7169	0.6750	0.9512	0.6969	0.6766	0.6928	0.9540	0.7033
Difference	−0.0475	−0.0193	−0.0110	−0.0044	+0.0228	−0.0364	−0.0037	−0.0014

4.2 Epoch Durations

Figure 2 depicts the required times for completing an epoch for each data set, as illustrated by the violin plot. This plot reveals a significant difference between the two training methods, with Adapter Tuning requiring less time to complete a single training epoch. This is not surprising, given that Adapter Tuning only needs to calculate a fraction of parameters, compared to fine-tuning in the backpropagation step. These results confirm the conclusions of previous studies, including those by Mahabadi et al. [5] and Rückle et al. [4], which indicate that, per epoch, Adapter Tuning is more efficient. Furthermore, the low spread of the violins indicates that the time measurements are relatively consistent.

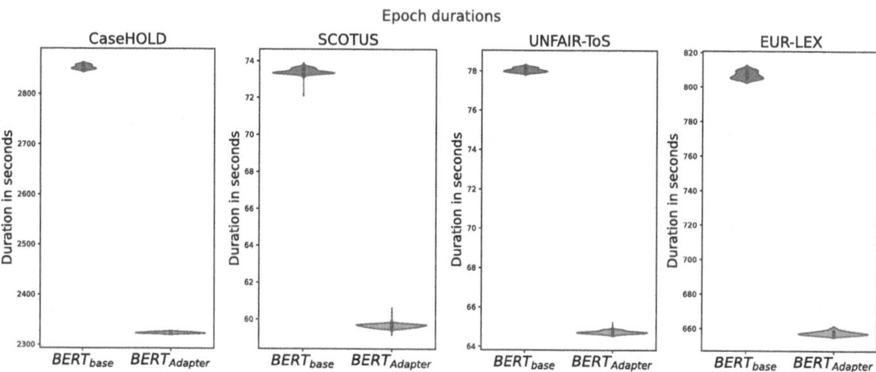

Fig. 2. Epoch durations for each dataset.

Figure 3 provides a clearer view of the relative efficiency gains per epoch. These percentages, derived from differences in individual epoch durations, bring the results to a comparable scale for different datasets and tasks. Here we compare the mean epoch times in both methods. This figure demonstrates a steady trend in the per-epoch efficiency increase of Adapter Tuning, with an average around 17%.

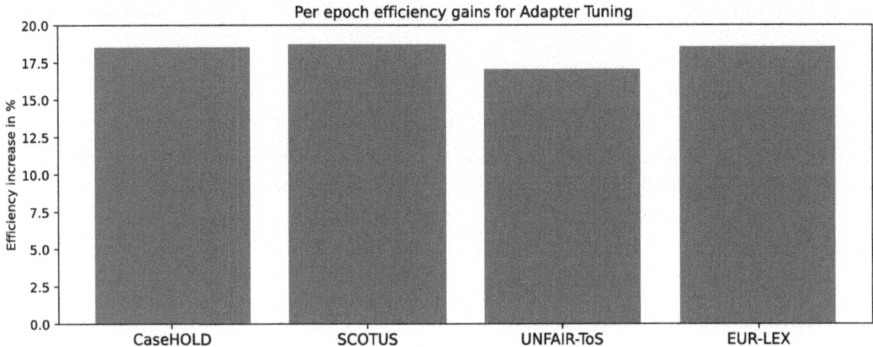

Fig. 3. Illustration of epoch time efficiency gains in percent when using Adapter Tuning.

4.3 Model Convergence

It is not necessarily the case that shorter epoch durations result in accelerated model convergence, as the Adapter modules restrict the model capacity. Consequently, one of the primary objectives of this experiment is to determine the model convergence speed by measuring the number of epochs as well as the absolute amount of time until the early stopping criterion is met.

The left side of Fig. 4 illustrates that, in all cases, $\text{BERT}_{Adapter}$ requires additional epochs to trigger early stopping. This is expected because of the fewer number of trainable parameters. However, the right side of Fig. 4 shows that Adapter Tuning also requires a longer training duration in terms of absolute time differences for the model to reach convergence compared to the baseline fine-tuning method.

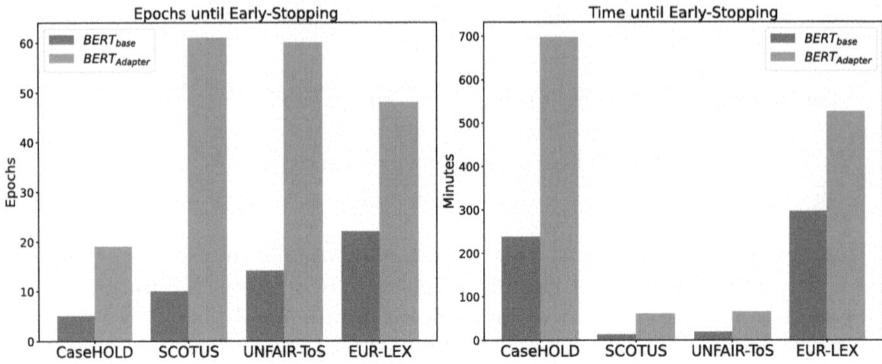

Fig. 4. Comparison of training epochs until early stopping triggers (left) and time taken (right) for both training methods.

4.4 Energy Consumption

The methodology outlined in [8] was adopted in this experiment to quantify the energy consumed, whereby the energy was calculated by the graphics card utilization. In a second experiment, energy measurements were conducted for the respective downstream training over a 12-hour period. Wang et al. assume that there is a linear relationship between the GPU utilization and its power consumption when calculating the corresponding energy consumption. The calculation of the energy consumption, E, in kWh, is as follows:

$$E = \int_0^H \frac{u(t)}{100} \cdot p_0 \, dt \,, \tag{1}$$

where H is the number of hours of training, p_0 is the power consumption in kW, and $u(t)$ is the GPU utilization in percent. In our case, the approximation of formula (1) is such that utilization u_i is measured after each batch - referred to as a step - and S denotes the total number of steps:

$$E = H \cdot \frac{\sum_{i=1}^{S} u_i}{S} \cdot \frac{p_0}{100} \tag{2}$$

In our study, we consider a constant power of 350 W (p_0) for the GPU (according to its specifications). The initial measurement period (H) is set to 12 h. However, the number of steps (S) varies for each downstream training for different datasets and training methods. In this particular instance, we observed that the energy consumption was higher for fine-tuning within the 12-hour period, as shown in the left part of Fig. 5. This is primarily because the GPU is more utilized during the training process.

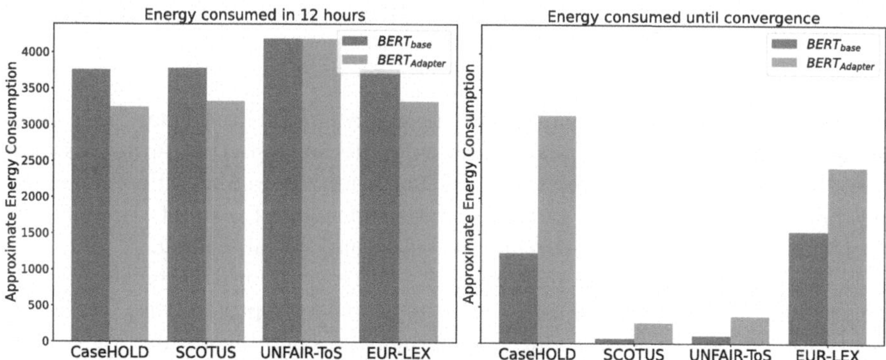

Fig. 5. Comparison of energy consumption for different timescales: fixed duration of 12 h (left) and model convergence (right).

Our primary interest however lies in the energy consumption until the early stopping criterion is met, which is the relevant quantity from a practical point of view. Combining the utilization measurements with the model convergence times from Subsect. 4.3, we find that the total energy consumption for Adapter Tuning is actually higher (see the right part of Fig. 5). This increase can be attributed to the extended training time required until the early stop criterion; the decrease in GPU power utilization is thus not sufficient to make Adapter Tuning beneficial from the vantage point of energy consumption.

5 Discussion

It can be criticized that the full potential of the GPU was not utilized in our experiments, thereby not fully exploiting the parallelization power offered by Adapter Tuning, since we used a fixed batch size for both experiments. This is particularly relevant as the batch size can be increased when using Adapter Tuning because fewer parameters need to be trained. To investigate this, we repeated the experiment with the maximum possible batch sizes for one dataset (UNFAIR-ToS, considered as representative) to determine the effect of increasing batch sizes. In the initial experiment with a batch size of 8, the training time (until early stopping) for Adapter Tuning was found to be 255% longer compared to full fine-tuning. When the batch sizes were maximized (to 120 for fine-tuning and to 145 for Adapter Tuning), the training time overhead for Adapter Tuning was reduced to 169%. Despite this reduction, Adapter Tuning still required a longer time to converge, and the overall power consumption is still larger.

It is unclear whether the contradicting results compared to Wang et al. [8] are caused by the model architecture, the benchmark dataset or the experimental setting including the hardware specifications. In Wang et al., the Adapter tuned model needed fewer epochs until the convergence criterion was reached compared to the baseline model. This is in contrast do the results of Ding et al., Mundra et al. and our findings, which hints that the results are problem-specific and generalizations should be formulated with care.

Limitations. The time measurements are highly specific to the hardware used, the model employed, and the data analyzed. This suggests that future research should aim to include a wider variety of hardware, as well as different models and data sizes. Additionally, further investigation should take into account the effect of randomness in the experimental setup and initial seeding.

In our setup, long time measurements (12 h and until early stopping is reached) and GPU utilization measurements have been separated into two experiments for practical reasons. Our measurement of energy consumption is thus based on indirect methods and should be seen as approximative results. It is however assumed that energy consumption remains consistent across both experiments, given that the only modification is the additional GPU utilization measurement. To enhance the precision of our calculations, we suggest that future research should incorporate the measurement of GPU utilization within the same experiment together with all other metrics.

6 Conclusion

Section 4.1 demonstrated that Adapter Tuning is capable of achieving comparable performances in the downstream tasks. This shows that the comparison of durations and energy consumptions in the two training methods is meaningful from a practical point of view. Subsequently, Sect. 4.2 demonstrated that the use of Adapter modules can result in time savings at epoch level. Taking in Sect. 4.3 into account that more epochs are needed to reach convergence however leads to a significant increase of computation times for Adapter Tuning. By measuring the GPU utilization, calculating the energy consumption, and combining this with the results from the previous section, it can be concluded that Adapter Tuning consumes more energy than baseline fine-tuning. This results in a greater production of CO_2 during training, making this training method appear – from a green AI perspective – less environmentally friendly.

A Hyperparameter

Table 2. The list of hyperparameters used in the experiment series, which are utilized by both training methods.

Parameter	Selected
Checkpoint	bert-base-uncased
Batch-Size	8
Optimizer	Adam
Learning rate	3^{-6}
Early stopping patience	3
Sequence length	512
Padding	True

B Adapter Parameters

Table 3. Utilized parameters for Adapter Tuning.

Parameter	Selected
Multi-head Adapter	True
Output Adapter	True
Non-linearity	ReLU
Reduction factor	16

C Macro-F1 Results

Table 4. Results for the m-F1 metric for models with early stopping and those trained for 12 h.

	Early-Stopping				12 h			
	CaseHOLD	SCOTUS	UNFAIR-ToS	EUR-LEX	CaseHOLD	SCOTUS	UNFAIR-ToS	EUR-LEX
Adapter	0.6993	0.4615	0.6977	0.4755	0.6993	0.5638	0.7984	0.5044
Base	0.7169	0.4097	0.7581	0.4712	0.6766	0.5768	0.7833	0.5396
Difference	−0.0476	+0.0518	−0.0884	+0.0043	−0.0073	−0.0130	+0.0151	−0.0352

References

1. Houlsby, N., et al.: Parameter-efficient transfer learning for NLP. In: International Conference on Machine Learning, pp. 2790–2799. PMLR (2019)
2. Hu, E.J., et al.: LoRA: Low-Rank Adaptation of Large Language Models. arXiv preprint arXiv:2106.09685 (2021)
3. Chalkidis, I., et al.: LexGLUE: a benchmark dataset for legal language understanding in English. arXiv preprint arXiv:2110.00976 (2021)
4. Rücklé, A., et al.: AdapterDrop: On the Efficiency of Adapters in Transformers. arXiv prepreprint arXiv:2010.11918 (2021)
5. Karimi Mahabadi, R., Henderson, J., Ruder, S.: Compacter: efficient low-rank hypercomplex adapter layers. In: Ranzato, M., Beygelzimer, A., Dauphin, Y., Liang, P.S., Wortman Vaughan, J. (eds.) Advances in Neural Information Processing Systems (NeurIPS), vol. 34, pp. 1022–1035. Curran Associates, Inc. (2021)
6. Ding, N., et al.: Delta tuning: a comprehensive study of parameter efficient methods for pre-trained language models. arXiv preprint arXiv:2203.06904 (2022)
7. Mundra, N., Doddapaneni, S., Dabre, R., Kunchukuttan, A., Puduppully, R., Khapra, M.M.: A comprehensive analysis of adapter efficiency. In: Proceedings of the 7th Joint International Conference on Data Science and Management of Data (11th ACM IKDD CODS and 29th COMAD), pp. 136–154 (2024)
8. Wang, S., Nguyen, J., Li, K., Wu, C.-J.: Read: recurrent adaptation of large transformers. arXiv preprint arXiv:2305.15348 (2023)
9. Devlin, J., Chang, M.-W., Lee, K., Toutanova, K.: BERT: Pre-training of Deep Bidirectional Transformers for Language Understanding. CoRR, abs/1810.04805 (2018)

Stochastic Models, Statistical Methods, and Applied Systems Simulations

Disease Incidence in a Stochastic SVIRS Model with Waning Immunity

M. J. Lopez-Herrero(✉) and D. Taipe

Complutense University of Madrid, Madrid, Spain
{lherrero,dtaipe}@ucm.es

Abstract. This paper deals with the long-term behaviour and incidence of a vaccine-preventable contact disease, under the assumption that both vaccine protection and immunity after recovery are not lifelong. The mathematical model is developed in a stochastic markovian framework. The evolution of the disease in a finite population is thus represented by a three-dimensional continuous-time Markov chain, which is versatile enough to be able to compensate for the loss of protection by including vaccination before the onset of the outbreak and also during the course of the epidemics.

Keywords: Epidemic model · Temporary immunity · Vaccine failures

1 Introduction

An essential tool to represent the evolution of an infectious process through a population is mathematical modeling. Many epidemic models involve a compartmental division of individuals which take into account their health status with respect to the infection. It is also a common assumption that individuals are randomly in contact with each other and have no preferences for relationship.

The fundamental compartmental model for studying an infectious disease that confers immunity is the SIR proposed by Kermack & McKendrick [1], which can be modified to take into account the control of disease spread (e.g., vaccination [2–4]) or the effects of loss of immunity [2,3,5].

In this paper, we consider an infectious disease taking place in a finite and isolated population. We assume that the disease is transmitted by direct contact with an infectious individual. After recovery, individuals show temporary immunity. In addition, we assume that the disease is a vaccine-preventable infection, but vaccinated individuals are not lifelong fully protected, either because of vaccine failures or because of waning immunity. Given the latter fact, re-vaccination of susceptible individuals is planned as the epidemic progresses.

Consequently, the involved compartmental model divides the population in four classes: Susceptible to the infection (S), vaccine protected (V), infectious (I) and recovered-temporary immune individuals (R). Once the temporary immunity is lost, individuals become susceptible to the disease again. Figure 1 shows

A. Quesada-Arencibia et al. (Eds.): EUROCAST 2024, LNCS 15174, pp. 199–212, 2025.
https://doi.org/10.1007/978-3-031-83885-9_19

the movement of individuals between the four compartments involved in the mathematical model.

Our research will focus on the study of the evolution of a communicable disease by incorporating vaccination and loss of immunity into the epidemiological model, considering both waning vaccine effects and temporary immunity after recovery. In particular, we consider a Markovian model to represent the spread of the pathogen that causes the disease in a finite population of constant size N.

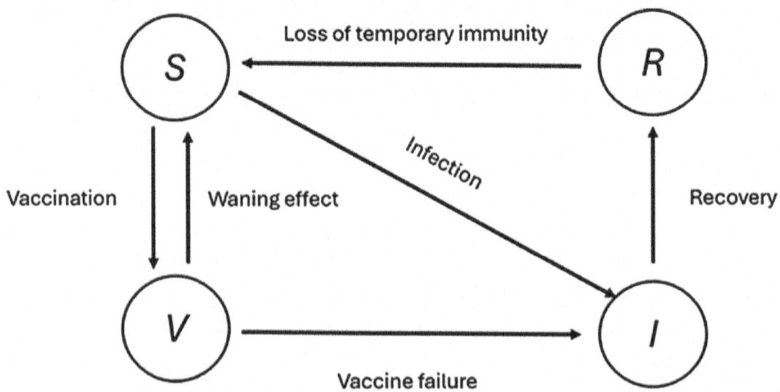

Fig. 1. Epidemic compartmental diagram

The aim of this research is, firstly, to observe the long-term behaviour of the Markov chain and thus of the epidemic process itself. Secondly, to study the total number of infections that occur during an outbreak (i.e., the period from the appearance of the first case to the time when there are not infectious individuals in the population).

Theoretical derivations related to the stationary distribution and the probabilistic description of the disease incidence during an outbreak will result from the application of the first-step methodology [6,7].

2 Model Description

Mathematical description involves a continuous-time Markov chain (CTMC), which provides the evolution of the disease in terms of the number of individuals present in each compartment at any time t. Hence, we record the number of unprotected susceptible, $S(t)$, vaccinated, $V(t)$, infected, $I(t)$, and recovered-temporary immune individuals, $R(t)$. The hypothesis of constant size for the population gives, for any $t \geq 0$, the following relationship among the sizes of the allowed compartments: $N = S(t) + V(t) + I(t) + R(t)$. In consequence, the evolution of the epidemics is represented by a three-dimensional CTMC

$$\mathcal{X} = \{(I(t), S(t), V(t)) : t \geq 0\}$$

with state space $\mathcal{S} = \{(i, s, v) : 0 \le i, s, v \le N, 0 \le i + s + v \le N\}$, containing a possibly large number of $(N+1)(N+2)(N+3)/6$ states.

We assume that individuals have no relationship preferences, so that any individual can be in contact with any other inhabitant of the population.

The pathogenic agent is transmitted to susceptible population by direct contact with an infectious individual, at time point of a time-homogeneous Poisson process with the usual bilinear mass action form $\beta(i, s) = \beta is$, depending on infectious and susceptible individuals, where β represents the effective contact rate. Since the vaccine administered is not perfect, we assume that there is a probability, h, that it fails in protecting vaccinated individuals. Hence, the pathogen can be transmitted to vaccinated individuals when they are in touch with the infectious ones. The transmission function in the vaccinated class is $\eta(i, v) = h\beta iv$, that depends on the existing infectious and vaccinated individuals, and also on the probability of vaccine failure.

Infectious periods of different infected individuals are represented by independent exponentially distributed random variables, with rate γ. Each recovered individual, no matter if he was previously vaccinated or not, develops a temporal immunity. The length of the immunity periods of the recovered individuals are independent and also exponentially distributed with rate ϵ. When temporal immunity disappears, recovered individuals become susceptible to the disease. To prevent the spread of the disease, susceptible individuals can receive the available vaccine. The vaccination process is scheduled at time points of a time-homogeneous Poisson process with rate ρ. Finally, for each vaccinated individual, vaccine protection is assumed to last for an exponentially distributed random time with rate θ.

According to the above description, transitions between states in $\mathcal{S}$ are consequence of one of the following events:

a_1 : New infection of a susceptible individual
a_2 : New infection of a vaccinated individual, due to vaccine failure
a_3 : Recovery of one of the existing infectious individuals
a_4 : Vaccination of a susceptible individual
a_5 : A vaccinated person loses vaccine protection
a_6 : A recovered individual loses temporary immunity

Given an initial state $(i, s, v) \in \mathcal{S}$, Table 1 displays information about possible transitions from the initial state, providing the final states and rates associated with each of the events $a_1 - a_6$.

Sojourn times at each state in $\mathcal{S}$ are independent and exponentially distributed random variables, with rate

$$q_{(i,v,s)} = \beta i(s + hv) + \gamma i + \rho s + \theta v + \epsilon(N - i - s - v). \tag{1}$$

Since we assume that the population is isolated, part of the states in $\mathcal{S}$ - those corresponding to situations where there are neither infectious nor recovered individuals - are absorbing. Let us denote by $\mathcal{S}_A = \{(0, s, N - s) : 0 \le s \le N\}$ the irreducible set of absorbing states. On the other hand, the set of transient states is $\mathcal{S}_T = \mathcal{S} - \mathcal{S}_A$, which is reducible and finite.

Table 1. Transitions and rates for each effective event.

Effective event	Final state	Rate
a_1	$(i+1, s-1, v)$	βis
a_2	$(i+1, s, v-1)$	$h\beta iv$
a_3	$(i-1, s, v)$	γi
a_4	$(i, s-1, v+1)$	ρs
a_5	$(i, s+1, v-1)$	θv
a_6	$(i, s+1, v)$	$\epsilon(N-i-s-v)$

2.1 Long-term Behaviour

As $\mathcal{X}$ is a finite state CTMC, the absorption into $\mathcal{S}_A$ is certain and it occurs in a finite expected time. Moreover, since the absorbing set is a single class of communicating states, the stationary distribution assigns mass to every state in $\mathcal{S}_A$. We notice that our model is a special case of a finite birth-death process (see, for instance [8], Chap. 6), whose stationary distribution is well known. Focusing on the number of susceptible individuals at time t, a birth corresponds to the end of vaccine protection, due to waning immunity; a death corresponds to the vaccination of a susceptible individual. Thus, given that the process $\{S(t) : t > 0\}$ is in state s, the birth and death rates correspond to $\theta(N-s)$ and ρs, respectively. After some algebra we derive its stationary distribution, $\{p_s : 0 \leq s \leq N\}$, which is given by a binomial law

$$p_s = \binom{N}{s}(\frac{1}{1+\rho/\theta})^s(\frac{\rho/\theta}{1+\rho/\theta})^{N-s}, \text{ for } 0 \leq s \leq N.$$

Hence, we got for any state $(i, s, v) \in \mathcal{S}$ that

$$lim_{t\to\infty}P\{I(t) = i, S(t) = s, V(t) = v\} = \delta_{i,0}\delta_{v,N-s}\binom{N}{s}(\frac{\theta}{\theta+\rho})^s(\frac{\rho}{\theta+\rho})^v,$$

where symbol $\delta_{a,b}$ is the Kronecker's delta function, defined as 1 when $a = b$ and by 0 otherwise.

3 Incidence of the Disease During an Outbreak

This section examines the number of infections that occur during an outbreak of the disease. According to the model description, the epidemic stops as soon as there are not infectious cases in the population. We will then consider that outbreaks last while infectious individuals are present in the population and we assume that the outbreaks start from a single infectious individual.

To study the incidence of cases of infection during an outbreak, we will partition the whole state space in levels according to the number of infectious individuals in the population:

$$\mathcal{S} = \bigcup_{i=0}^{N} \mathcal{S}(i),$$

where, for $0 \leq i \leq N$, each set $\mathcal{S}(i) = \{(i,s,v) \in \mathcal{S} : 0 \leq s+v \leq N-i\}$ contains $c_i = \binom{N-i+2}{2}$ states.

For later use, the above partition of $\mathcal{S}$ by levels,as well as the transition rates among them yield a block-tridiagonal structure for the infinitesimal generator of $\mathcal{X}$ that look as follows:

$$\mathbf{Q} = \begin{pmatrix} \mathbf{A}_{0,0} & \mathbf{A}_{0,1} & & & \\ \mathbf{A}_{1,0} & \mathbf{A}_{1,1} & \mathbf{A}_{1,2} & & \\ & \ddots & \ddots & \ddots & \\ & & \mathbf{A}_{N-1,N-2} & \mathbf{A}_{N-1,N-1} & \mathbf{A}_{N-1,N} \\ & & & \mathbf{A}_{N,N-1} & \mathbf{A}_{N,N} \end{pmatrix} \quad (2)$$

where sub-matrices $\mathbf{A}_{i,i^*}$ refer to the transition rates from states in the level $S(i)$ to states in the level $S(i^*)$. The diagonal entries correspond to $-q(i,s,v)$, defined in Eq. (1), and the remaining rates are summarised in Table 1.

In terms of the CTMC describing the evolution of the epidemics, the outbreak starts from a state $(1, s_0, v_0)$ and ends when the chain enters into the set $\mathcal{S}(0)$.

Let us denote by L, the random variable that records the cases of infection observed during the outbreak. We will describe its probabilistic behaviour with the help of a set of auxiliary variables, namely $\{L_{(i,s,v)} : (i,s,v) \in \mathcal{S}\}$. Where each auxiliary variable $L_{(i,s,v)}$ is defined as the number of new infections that occur during the remaining part of the outbreak, given that the current state of the Markov chain is (i,s,v).

To analyze the total incidence during the outbreak we take into account the following relationship:

$$L = 1 + L_{(1,s_0,v_0)}. \quad (3)$$

Next, we introduce some notation regarding mass and generating functions, and factorial moments of the auxiliary variables, conditioned to a specific state $(i,s,v) \in \mathcal{S}$.

$$y^j_{(i,s,v)} = P\{L_{(i,s,v)} = j\}, \text{ for } j \geq 0,$$

$$\varphi_{(i,s,v)}(z) = E[z^{L_{(i,s,v)}}] = \sum_{j=0}^{\infty} z^j y^j_{(i,s,v)}, \text{ for } |z| \leq 1,$$

$$m^k_{(i,s,v)} = \begin{cases} \sum_{j=0}^{\infty} y^j_{(i,s,v)}, & \text{for } k = 0, \\ E[\prod_{j=0}^{k-1}(L_{(i,s,v)} - j)], & \text{for } k \geq 1. \end{cases}$$

We notice that for states $(0,s,v) \in \mathcal{S}(0)$ no additional infections are possible. So, we get

$$y^j_{(0,s,v)} = \delta_{0,j}, \text{ for } j \geq 0. \quad (4)$$

Consequently,

$$\varphi_{(0,s,v)}(z) = 1, \text{ for } |z| \leq 1, \tag{5}$$

$$m^k_{(0,s,v)} = \delta_{0,k}, \text{ for } k \geq 0, \tag{6}$$

where the result in (6) comes from Eq. (5) and the relationship $m^k_{(i,s,v)} = \frac{\partial^k \varphi_{(i,s,v)}(z)}{\partial z^k}|_{z=1}$, for $(i, s, v) \in \mathcal{S}$ and $k \geq 0$.

For the remaining group of states $(i, s, v) \in \mathcal{S} - \mathcal{S}(0)$ we will find recursive results to determine probabilities, generating functions and moments.

To study the mass distribution of L, we assume that the outbreak starts from the state $(1, s_0, v_0)$, where $1 + s_0 + v_0 = N$.

Given a non-negative integer k and a state $(i, s, v) \in \mathcal{S}$, we introduce the tail probability $x^k_{(i,s,v)} = P\{L_{(i,s,v)} \geq k\}$, which represent the probability of having at least k new contagions in the rest of the outbreak, given that the current state of the population is (i, s, v).

Then, we have from Eq. (3) that

$$P\{L \geq k\} = P\{L_{(1,s_0,v_0)} \geq k - 1\} = x^{k-1}_{(1,s_0,v_0)}, \text{ for } k \geq 1. \tag{7}$$

As all the epidemic outbreaks start from a single infectious individual, the event $\{L \geq 1\}$ (or equivalently, $\{L_{(1,s_0,v_0)} \geq 0\}$) occurs almost surely. So, the tail probabilities of 0 additional infections in the outbreak are $x^0_{(1,s_0,v_0)} = P\{L \geq 1\} = P\{L_{(1,s_0,v_0)} \geq 0\} = 1$.

We can extend trivially the above result for tail probabilities of 0 additional infections conditioned to any state $(i, s, v) \in \mathcal{S}$. That is,

$$x^0_{(i,s,v)} = 1. \tag{8}$$

On the other hand, as the outbreak ends when the chain $\mathcal{X}$ reaches any state in $\mathcal{S}(0)$, for states in this level we have that

$$x^k_{(0,s,v)} = 0, \text{ for } k \geq 1. \tag{9}$$

Given $k \geq 0$, let us denote by $\mathbf{x}^k_i$ the c_i-dimensional vector whose components are the tail probability of k additional infections related to states in the level $\mathcal{S}(i)$. That is, $\mathbf{x}^k_i = (x^k_{(i,s,v)} : (i, s, v) \in \mathcal{S}(i))'$, where the symbol $'$ means transpose.

Moreover, in what follows $\mathbf{1}_a$ and $\mathbf{0}_a$ represent the all ones and all zeros vectors of dimension a, respectively, and the empty products, appearing in theoretical derivations, are an identity matrix of the appropriate dimension.

The following theorem provides a scheme to determine the tail probabilities recursively.

Theorem 1. *For a given integer $k \geq 1$, the tail probability vectors $\mathbf{x}^k_i$ are recursively determined from $\mathbf{x}^{k-1}_i$ through the following equations*

$$\mathbf{x}^0_i = \mathbf{1}_{c_i}, \text{ for } 0 \leq i \leq N, \tag{10}$$

$$\mathbf{x}^k_0 = \mathbf{0}_{c_0}, \text{ for } k \geq 1, \tag{11}$$

$$\mathbf{x}^k_i = -\mathbf{A}^{-1}_{i,i} \sum_{m=1}^{i} \left(\prod_{j=m}^{i-1} \mathbf{A}_{j+1,j}(-\mathbf{A}^{-1}_{j,j}) \right) \mathbf{d}^k_m, \text{ for } 1 \leq i \leq N, \tag{12}$$

where $\mathbf{d}_m^k = -(1-\delta_{i,N})\mathbf{A}_{m,m+1}^{-1}\mathbf{x}_{m+1}^{k-1}$, *for* $1 \leq m \leq N$.

Proof. First, note that the results in Eqs. (10) and (11) are the matrix form expressions of results given in Eqs. (8) and (9).

Next, for states in $\mathcal{S}(i), 1 \leq i \leq N$, and $k \geq 1$, we determine tail probabilities using a first-step argument. Thus, for a fixed integer $k \geq 1$ and a given state $(i,s,v) \in \mathcal{S}(i)$, with $1 \leq i \leq N$, we condition on the first transition out of the initial state and we derive the following relations:

$$\begin{aligned}
x_{(i,s,v)}^k &= \frac{\beta is}{q_{(i,s,v)}} x_{(i+1,s-1,v)}^{k-1} + \frac{h\beta iv}{q_{(i,s,v)}} x_{(i+1,s,v-1)}^{k-1} \\
&+ \frac{\gamma i}{q_{(i,s,v)}} x_{(i-1,s,v)}^k + \frac{\rho s}{q_{(i,s,v)}} x_{(i,s-1,v+1)}^k \\
&+ \frac{\theta v}{q_{(i,s,v)}} x_{(i,s+1,v-1)}^k + \frac{\epsilon(N-i-s-v)}{q_{(i,s,v)}} x_{(i,s+1,v)}^k, \text{ for } 1 \leq i \leq N-1, \\
x_{(N,0,0)}^k &= \frac{\gamma N}{q_{(N,0,0)}} x_{(N-1,0,0)}^k.
\end{aligned}$$

which are equivalent to

$$\begin{aligned}
-\gamma i x_{(i-1,s,v)}^k - \rho s x_{(i,s-1,v+1)}^k &+ q_{(i,s,v)} x_{(i,s,v)}^k \\
-\theta v x_{(i,s+1,v-1)}^k &- \epsilon(N-i-s-v) x_{(i,s+1,v)}^k \\
= \beta is x_{(i+1,s-1,v)}^{k-1} &+ h\beta iv x_{(i+1,s,v-1)}^{k-1}, \text{ for } 1 \leq i \leq N-1,
\end{aligned} \tag{13}$$

$$-\gamma N x_{(N-1,0,0)}^k + q_{(N,0,0)} x_{(N,0,0)}^k = 0. \tag{14}$$

For each level i, $1 \leq i \leq N$, we can express Eqs. (13) and (14) in matrix form as follows

$$-\mathbf{A}_{i,i-1}\mathbf{x}_{i-1}^k - \mathbf{A}_{i,i}\mathbf{x}_i^k = (1-\delta_{i,N})\mathbf{A}_{i,i+1}\mathbf{x}_{i+1}^{k-1}. \tag{15}$$

Recalling the definition of $\mathbf{d}_m^k$ given in the statement of the theorem, Eq. (15) is

$$-\mathbf{A}_{i,i-1}\mathbf{x}_{i-1}^k - \mathbf{A}_{i,i}\mathbf{x}_i^k = \mathbf{d}_i^k, \text{ for } 1 \leq i \leq N \text{ and } k \geq 1.$$

Finally, a standard forward elimination-backward substitution procedure drives to expression (12).

Since neither the variable number of cases of infection, L, nor the auxiliary variables are bounded, we cannot determine their moments directly from their mass distribution functions. Instead, we will derive recursive schemes for computing means, variances, and any other higher-order moment.

First, we introduce some notation. Given $k \geq 0$ we denote by $\mathbf{m}_i^k$ the c_i−dimensional vector containing the factorial moments of order k related to states in $\mathcal{S}(i)$. That is, $\mathbf{m}_i^k = (m_{(i,s,v)}^k : (i,s,v) \in \mathcal{S}(i))'$.

Following result shows the scheme to compute the factorial moments of auxiliary variables $L_{(i,s,v)}$, for any state $(i,s,v) \in \mathcal{S}$, in a recursive way starting from the explicit values of the order zero moments.

Theorem 2. *Given a non-negative integer k, factorial moments of order k, $\mathbf{m}_i^k$ are computed as follows*

$$\mathbf{m}_i^0 = \mathbf{1}_{c_i}, \ \textit{for } 0 \leq i \leq N \tag{16}$$
$$\mathbf{m}_0^k = \mathbf{0}_{c_0}, \ \textit{for } k \geq 1 \tag{17}$$
$$\mathbf{m}_N^k = -\mathbf{B}_{N,N}^{-1}\mathbf{C}_N^k, \ \textit{for } k \geq 1 \tag{18}$$
$$\mathbf{m}_i^k = -\mathbf{B}_{i,i}^{-1}(\mathbf{A}_{i,i+1}\mathbf{m}_{i+1}^k + \mathbf{C}_i^k), \ \textit{for } k \geq 1 \textit{ and } 1 \leq i \leq N-1, \tag{19}$$

where matrices $\mathbf{B}_{i,i}$ and $\mathbf{C}_i^k$ are recursively determined from

$$\mathbf{B}_{i,i} = \delta_{1,i}\mathbf{A}_{1,1} + (1-\delta_{1,i})(\mathbf{D}_i^k - \mathbf{A}_{i,i-1}\mathbf{B}_{i-1,i-1}^{-1}\mathbf{A}_{i-1,i})$$
$$\mathbf{C}_i^k = \delta_{1,i}\mathbf{D}_1^k + (1-\delta_{1,i})\left(\mathbf{D}_i^k - \mathbf{A}_{i,i-1}\mathbf{B}_{i-1,i-1}^{-1}\mathbf{C}_{i-1}^k\right)$$

with $\mathbf{D}_i^k = (1-\delta_{i,N})k\mathbf{A}_{i,i+1}\mathbf{m}_{i+1}^{k-1}$, *for* $1 \leq i \leq N$.

Proof. For states $(0,s,v) \in \mathcal{S}(0)$, the results shown in Eqs. (16) and (17) come from Eq. (6).

For remaining states, a first-step argument, conditioning on the first transition out of a fixed state $(i,s,v) \in \bigcup_{i=1}^N \mathcal{S}(i)$, gives that generating functions $\varphi_{(i,s,v)}(z)$ satisfy the following system of linear equations:

$$\begin{aligned}\varphi_{(i,s,v)}(z) &= \frac{\beta is}{q_{(i,s,v)}} z\varphi_{(i+1,s-1,v)}(z) + \frac{h\beta iv}{q_{(i,s,v)}} z\varphi_{(i+1,s,v-1)}(z) \\ &+ \frac{\gamma i}{q_{(i,s,v)}}\varphi_{(i-1,s,v)}(z) + \frac{\rho s}{q_{(i,s,v)}}\varphi_{(i,s-1,v+1)}(z) \\ &+ \frac{\theta v}{q_{(i,s,v)}}\varphi_{(i,s+1,v-1)}(z) + \frac{\epsilon(N-i-s-v)}{q_{(i,s,v)}}\varphi_{(i,s+1,v)}(z),\end{aligned}$$

which are equivalent to

$$\begin{aligned}&-\gamma i\varphi_{(i-1,s,v)}(z) - \rho s\varphi_{(i,s-1,v+1)}(z) + q_{(i,s,v)}\varphi_{(i,s,v)}(z) - \theta v\varphi_{(i,s+1,v-1)}(z) \\ &-\epsilon(N-i-s-v)\varphi_{(i,s+1,v)}(z) = \beta isz\varphi_{(i+1,s-1,v)}(z) + h\beta ivz\varphi_{(i+1,s,v-1)}(z)\end{aligned} \tag{20}$$

We observe that, when $(i,s,v) \in \bigcup_{i=1}^N \mathcal{S}(i)$, the system of equations given by (20) is strictly diagonally dominant. Therefore, for each $|z| \leq 1$ there is a unique solution of the system. In particular, for $z=1$ we have that the trivial choice $\varphi_{(i,s,v)}(1) = 1$, for all $(i,s,v) \in \bigcup_{i=1}^N \mathcal{S}(i)$, is the solution of the above system of equations. Then,

$$m_{(i,s,v)}^0 = \varphi_{(i,s,v)}(1) = 1, \ \text{for } (i,s,v) \in \bigcup_{i=1}^N \mathcal{S}(i),$$

which proves result in Eq. (16), for $1 \leq i \leq N$.

Next, by differentiating Eq. (20) regarding z repeatedly k times and evaluating at $z = 1$ we get a new system of equations involving factorial moments that look as follows:

$$\begin{aligned}
&-\gamma i m^k_{(i-1,s,v)} - \rho s m^k_{(i,s-1,v+1)} + q_{(i,s,v)} m^k_{(i,s,v)}(z)\\
&\quad - \theta v m^k_{(i,s+1,v-1)} - \epsilon(N-i-s-v) m^k_{(i,s+1,v)}(z)\\
&\quad = \beta i s\big(m^k_{(i+1,s-1,v)} + k m^{k-1}_{(i+1,s-1,v)}\big) + h\beta i v\big(m^k_{(i+1,s,v-1)} + k m^{k-1}_{(i+1,s,v-1)}\big),
\end{aligned}$$

which can be expressed in matrix form with the help of the block description of the infinitesimal generator appearing in the expression (2). Hence, for $k \geq 1$ and $1 \leq i \leq N$, we have

$$-\mathbf{A}_{i,i-1}\mathbf{m}^k_{i-1} - \mathbf{A}_{\mathbf{i},\mathbf{i}}\mathbf{m}^k_i - (1-\delta_{i,N})\mathbf{A}_{i,i+1}\mathbf{m}^k_{i+1} = (1-\delta_{i,N})k\mathbf{A}_{i,i+1}\mathbf{m}^{k-1}_{i+1}. \quad (21)$$

Note that the right-hand side term of Eq. (21) agrees with the definition of $\mathbf{D}^k_i$ in the statement of Theorem 2.

Finally, a standard forward elimination backward substitution procedure gives the expressions (18) and (19).

4 Numerical Results

In this section we present some numerical illustrations of the theoretical results. In all the experiments, we consider an isolated population of $N = 100$ individuals and we set the recovery rate $\gamma = 1.0$, so that the unit time corresponds to the mean time to recovery from the contact disease.

Let us begin by showing results and applications coming from the stationary distribution. We recall that as time goes on, the population tends towards a pathogen-free situation, where individuals only fluctuate between susceptible and vaccinated compartments. As we stated in Sect. 2.1, the stationary distribution describes the chance of finding s susceptible and $N - s$ vaccinated individuals, in terms of a Binomial distribution. If we focus on the number of vaccinated individuals in the population in the long run, this random variable behaves like a Binomial distribution of N trials and probability of success given by $\frac{\rho}{\rho+\theta} = \frac{\rho/\theta}{1+\rho/\theta}$. Therefore, the probability of success remains constant when the booster rate and the waning rate have a constant ratio.

The Fig. 2 shows the binomial form of the stationary distribution of the number of vaccinated individuals in a population of $N = 100$ individuals. We display results for $\frac{\rho}{\theta} \in \{0.5, 1.0, 2.0\}$; that is, when the mean time between booster doses is double, equal to or half the expected duration of vaccine protection. As would be expected, the higher the quotient, the greater the chance that a larger number of vaccinated individuals will be found in the population.

For a general population of N individuals, in the long run, it is expected to find $E[V] = N\frac{\rho/\theta}{1+\rho/\theta}$ vaccinated individuals in average. This explicit and simple result may be used to state a criterion for setting an adequate value for the vaccination rate parameter ρ, whose inverse value represents the mean time between

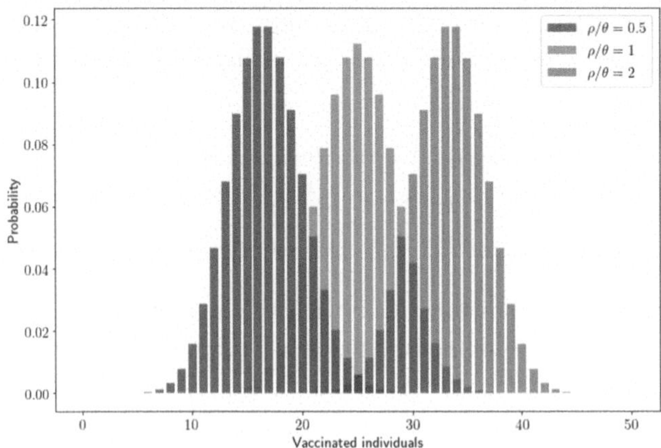

Fig. 2. Stationary distribution of V, as a function of $\frac{\rho}{\theta}$

booster doses of the vaccine. Our criterion will provide protection to susceptible individuals by maintaining a sufficient group of vaccinated individuals, taking into account the characteristics of the disease (basic reproductive number R_0) and the characteristics of the vaccine (efficacy and waning effect). Our idea is to choose the booster rate of the vaccine so that, in the long run, the expected number of vaccinated individuals is greater than the vaccination coverage that provides population herd immunity.

The term herd immunity threshold refers to the critical proportion of immune individuals required to interrupt epidemic transmission in a population. There is a simple relationship between herd immunity and R_0. For a vaccine-preventable contact disease, if a perfect vaccine is available and a fraction f of the population is vaccinated, then the disease will not spread if $(1-f)R_0 < 1$. In general, the quality of a vaccine is represented by its probability of failure $h \in [0,1]$, where $h = 0$ indicates a perfect vaccine and $h = 1$ indicates a useless one.

For imperfect but not useless vaccines, critical coverage is related to the quotient $(1-1/R_0)/(1-h)$ and is the result of a reduction in virus transmission caused by the removal of protected individuals from the susceptible class. The critical coverage, f, gives the herd-immunity threshold based on the control reproduction number $R_c = R_0(1-(1-h)f)$, which guarantees that $R_c < 1$. More precisely, starting from the basic reproductive number of the analogous deterministic model, $R_0 = \beta/N\gamma$, the coverage is chosen to satisfy $f > (R_0 - 1)/R_0(1-h))$.

Using the explicit value of $E[V]$ along with the waning rate of the vaccine, for a given contact disease and an appropriate vaccination coverage $v_c = Nf$, our criterion provides the booster rate ρ such that $E[V] \geq v_c$. That is,

$$\rho \geq \frac{v_c}{N - v_c}\theta.$$

In the Table 2, we show the vaccination coverage and the ratio between the booster rate and the waning rate as we vary the probability of vaccine failure $h \in \{0.05, 0.1, 0.2\}$, for diseases with a basic reproduction ratio $R_0 \in \{1.2, 2.5, 4.2\}$. The results in Table 2 for v_c are intuitively correct, showing that we must increase coverage for less effective vaccines (i.e.; as vaccine failure probability increases) and for increasing values of R_0. On the other hand, for increasing values of the probability of vaccine failure and also for increasing values of R_0, the ratio θ/ρ decreases.

Table 2. Vaccination coverage and relation between booster and waning vaccine rates

v_c || θ/ρ	$h = 0.05$	$h = 0.1$	$h = 0.2$
$R_0 = 1.2$	18 || **4.55**	19 || **4.26**	21 || **3.76**
$R_0 = 2.5$	64 || **0.56**	67 || **0.49**	75 || **0.32**
$R_0 = 4.2$	81 || **0.23**	85 || **0.17**	96 || **0.04**

For example, for the Ebola virus, the transmission R_0 is around 1.2. Vaccines have only recently been introduced and there is not yet enough information on the waning effects, but their efficacy varies from 75% to 100%. So, in an isolated population of 100 people, we need to keep at least 18 vaccinated if the vaccine is 95% effective, or at least 21 if the vaccine is 80% effective. Correspondingly, to maintain the herd protection level in the long-term, the ratio between booster doses and waning time is 4.55 (i.e.; the mean time between booster doses, $1/\rho$, is at most 4.55 the expected duration of vaccine protection, $1/\theta$). For a disease with basic reproduction number R_0 close to 4.2, such as diphtheria, if we administer a 95% effective vaccine, we observe that $v_c = 81$ and $\theta/\rho = 0.23$. Therefore, if we fix the number of vaccine protected individuals to be at least 81 in the long run, the mean time between booster doses should be approximately the fourth part of the expected duration of vaccine protection.

We will now present results that deal with L, the incidence of the infection or the total number of cases of infection that are observed in an outbreak. We consider a population of 100 individuals, the contact rate β and the loss of protection rate ϵ are fixed at 0.04. Finally, the probability of failure is set at 0.1.

The Table 3 shows results for the expected and standard deviation of the incidence L. We choose $(\theta, \rho) \in \{(0.5, 1.0), (1.0, 1.0), (1.0, 0.5)\}$, and three different proportions of susceptible and vaccinated individuals as initial situations. More precisely, the initial number of vaccinated individuals is the half, equal to and twice the number of susceptible individuals.

It can be seen that the expected incidence of the infection is reduced when we increase the initial proportion of vaccinated individuals relative to the susceptible ones. For the standard deviation, $SD[L]$, we find that the concentration of the incidence L around its expected value is slightly affected by the initial number of vaccinated individuals.

If we look at the influence of the quotient between the waning rate and the booster rate, θ/ρ, numerical results show that the mean and standard deviation of L are not constant when both rates have a constant ratio. For our particular choice of values of the pair (θ, ρ), we find that an increase in its quotient increases both the expected incidence of cases of infection and the variability around this value.

Table 3. Mean and standard deviation for the total number of cases of infection.

			$(\theta,\rho)=(0.5,1.0)$	$(\theta,\rho)=(1.0,1.0)$	$(\theta,\rho)=(1.0,0.5)$
(i_0,s_0,v_0)	$(1,66,33)$	$E[L]$	31.7604	51.0289	62.4891
		$SD[L]$	33.1116	43.7637	47.1506
	$(1,49,50)$	$E[L]$	27.2026	46.8978	57.9486
		$SD[L]$	32.0267	44.0196	48.0731
	$(1,33,66)$	$E[L]$	23.0980	42.8589	53.2856
		$SD[L]$	30.6280	43.9308	48.5877

5 Conclusions

In this paper we consider a stochastic SIVRS model with imperfect vaccine and loss of protection. The mathematical model used to describe how the epidemic evolves is a compartmental stochastic model involving a three-dimensional CTMC. The finite size and isolation of the population guarantees that the pathogen will disappear as time goes on. And the stationary distribution gives chance to situations where only vaccinated and susceptible individuals exist in the population. The form of this distribution is binomial of N trials and probability of success depending on the quotient between the waning effect rate and the vaccination rate.

Apart from that, our aim in this paper is to analyze the probabilistic nature of L, the number of infections observed during an outbreak of the disease. With the help of some auxiliary variables, we derive stable recursive schemes to compute the mass distribution and moments of the random variable L.

To represent more realistic situations, our model can be extended to non-isolated populations by considering transmission functions $\beta(i,s)$ and $\eta(i,v)$ that are not zero when $\imath = 0$. In this situation, the disease may disappear for a short time (i.e.; while $I(t) = 0$), but through external contacts, the infection is reintroduced later [9].

The research in this paper can be extended to measure the spread of disease in the population by focusing on the infectiousness of each resident to the whole group [10–12] or just to the vaccinated pool of individuals [13]. It will also be interesting to analyse the time taken to reach a threshold in the number of infections. This can be interpreted as a first passage time of the underlying process describing the evolution of epidemics (see e.g. [14,15]).

Acknowledgments. This research was supported by the Ministry of Science and Innovation (Government of Spain) through project PID2021-125871NB-I00. The second author also acknowledges the support of Banco Santander and the Complutense University of Madrid, Pre-doctoral Researcher Contract CT63/19-CT64/19.

References

1. Kermack, W.O., McKendrick, A.G.: A contribution to the mathematical theory of epidemics. Proc. R. Soc. Lon. A **115**, 700–721 (1927). https://doi.org/10.1098/rspa.1927.0118
2. Angelov, G., Kovacevic, R., Stilianakis, N.I., Veliov, V.M.: An immuno-epidemiological model with waning immunity after infection or vaccination. J. Math. Biol. **88**, 71 (2024). https://doi.org/10.1007/s00285-024-02090-z
3. Turkyilmazoglu, M.: An extended epidemic model with vaccination: weak-immune SIRVI. Physica A. **598**, 127429 (2022). https://doi.org/10.1016/j.physa.2022.127429
4. Zhou, A., Sattayatham, P., Jiao, J.: Dynamics of an SIR epidemic model with stage structure and pulse vaccination. Adv. Difference Equ. **2016**, 140 (2016). https://doi.org/10.1186/s13662-016-0853-z
5. Batistela, C.M., Correa, D.P.F., Bueno, Á.M., Piqueira , J.R.C.: SIRSi compartmental model for COVID-19 pandemic with immunity loss. Chaos Soliton Frac. **142**, 110388 (2021). https://doi.org/10.1016/j.chaos.2020.110388
6. Artalejo, J.R., Lopez-Herrero, M.J.: Stochastic epidemic models: new behavioral indicators of the disease spreading. Appl. Math. Model. **38**, 4371–4387 (2014). https://doi.org/10.1016/j.apm.2014.02.017
7. Amador, J., Lopez-Herrero, M.J.: Cumulative and maximum epidemic sizes for a nonlinear SEIR stochastic model with limited resources. Discrete Contin. Dyn. Syst. Ser. B. **23**, 3137–3157 (2018). https://doi.org/10.3934/dcdsb.2017211
8. Ross, S.: Introduction to Probability Models, 12th edn. Academic Press an imprint of Elsevier (2019). ISBN 978-0-443-18761-2
9. Gamboa, M., Lopez-Herrero, M.J.: Measuring infection transmission in a stochastic SIV model with infection reintroduction and imperfect vaccine. Acta. Biotheor. **68**, 395–420 (2020). https://doi.org/10.1007/s10441-019-09373-9
10. Artalejo, J.R., Lopez-Herrero, M.J.: On the exact measure of disease spread in stochastic epidemic models. Bull. Math. Biol. **75**, 1031–1050 (2013). https://doi.org/10.1007/s11538-013-9836-3
11. López-García, M.: Stochastic descriptors in an SIR epidemic model for heterogeneous individuals in small networks. Math. Biosci. **271**, 42–61 (2016). https://doi.org/10.1016/j.mbs.2015.10.010
12. Lopez-Herrero, M.J.: Epidemic transmission on SEIR stochastic models with nonlinear incidence rate. Math. Method. Appl. Sci. **40**, 2532–2541 (2017). https://doi.org/10.1002/mma.4179
13. Gamboa, M., López- García, M., Lopez-Herrero, M.J.: On the exact and population bi-dimensional reproduction numbers in a stochastic SVIR model with imperfect vaccine. Appl. Math. Comput. **468**, 128526 (2024). https://doi.org/10.1016/j.amc.2023.128526

14. Gamboa, M., Lopez-Herrero, M.J.: The effect of setting a warning vaccination level on a stochastic SIVS model with imperfect vaccine. Mathematics **8**, 1136 (2020). https://doi.org/10.3390/math8071136
15. Gómez-Corral, A., López- García, M., Lopez-Herrero, M.J., Taipe, D.: On first-passage times and sojourn times in finite QBD processes and their applications in epidemics. Mathematics **8**, 1718 (2020). https://doi.org/10.3390/math8101718

A Spreaders-Ignorants-Skeptics Model for the Spreading of Fake News and a Related Finite Birth-Death Process

Paola Paraggio and Serena Spina(✉)

University of Salerno, Via Giovanni Paolo II, 132, Fisciano, Italy
{pparaggio,sspina}@unisa.it

Abstract. In the present work, we consider a compartmental model to mimic the temporal diffusion of fake news. The three compartments in which the population is divided are represented by spreaders, ignorants and skeptics. The spreaders are individuals that know the fake news and transmit it among the population. The ignorants do not know the rumor and when contacted by a spreader they become spreaders too. The skeptics are individuals able to discover the evidence of the received fake news and thus they persuade the spreader to not transmit it anymore. Firstly, the model is studied from a deterministic point of view. In particular, we determine the asymptotic behavior of the compartments and the maximum number of spreaders and we evaluate its transient evolution through numerical evaluation. Then, a stochastic counterpart is presented. More specifically, we define a two-dimensional time-homogeneous birth-death process specifying its state space and the Kolmogorov equations for the transition probabilities. We use the probability generating function approach that leads to the partial differential equation for such function that unfortunately cannot be solved analitically. However, we obtain the system of differential equations solved by the means of the categories, coinciding with the deterministic case. Finally, we present an algorithm to simulate the paths of the compartments to perform a qualitative study of the process and of the absorbing time.

Keywords: Rumor spread · Two-dimensional stochastic process · Birth-death process · Probability generating function

1 Introduction

The attention on mathematical models for the propagation of fake news in social networks is increasing nowadays, since it is becoming a crucial topic for information security. Some recent papers in this area have been devoted to construct discrete-time stochastic models for the spreading of fake news in a community (see Mahmoud [15], Esmaeeli *et al.* [7]). Other approaches are finalized to describe the growth of the number of individuals reached by rumors through deterministic or stochastic models (cf., for instance, San Martín *et al.* [20], Di Crescenzo *et al.* [6]).

A. Quesada-Arencibia et al. (Eds.): EUROCAST 2024, LNCS 15174, pp. 213–227, 2025.
https://doi.org/10.1007/978-3-031-83885-9_20

It is worth emphasizing that the models for the phenomenon of fake news diffusion share significant similarities with epidemiological models used to describe the evolution of a disease. Although the application context of these models is vastly different, they share some aspects such as:

(i) Diffusion on social networks: epidemiological models study how diseases spread through individual contacts, while models for the diffusion of fake news analyze how information spreads through social interactions.
(ii) Definition of different compartments: in simpler epidemiological models, individuals can be classified as susceptible, infected, or recovered. Similarly, in models for the diffusion of fake news, people can be considered as susceptible (informable), infected (exposed to fake news), or recovered (those who have stopped believing in the news).
(iii) Mitigation interventions: epidemiological models can be used to assess the effectiveness of interventions such as vaccinations or control measures. Similarly, models for fake news can be used to evaluate the impact of strategies such as public education to raise user awareness or technological tools to recognize false or manipulated news.

Therefore, these models can provide useful insights for understanding and managing the diffusion of complex phenomena within communities of individuals.

The analysis of multi-dimensional stochastic processes is common in various fields of applications, not only in epidemiology (see for instance Billard [1] and Griffiths and Greenhalgh [11]) and fake news diffusion (cf. De Martino and Spina [3], Di Crescenzo and Paraggio [5] and Kapsikar [12]), but also for queueing systems (see for instance Di Crescenzo and Martinucci [4]), politics (cf. Mobilia [16]), service systems (Krishna-Kumar *et al.* [14]). The most of these processes are quite hard to study theoretically, therefore they are analyzed through numerical procedures (as done in Servi [21], Brandwajn [2], Fayolle *et al.* [8], Remiche [19] and Møller and Berthelsen [17]).

Fake news are false or misleading news, deliberately and intentionally spread to deceive the public or influence public opinion on certain topics. This phenomenon has become increasingly widespread with the advent of social media and online platforms, where information can be rapidly disseminated without being carefully verified. Fake news can be created for a variety of reasons, including political, financial purposes, or simply to generate clicks and online traffic. The consequences of fake news can be serious, as they can fuel misinformation, undermine trust in information sources, and influence political and social decisions. Therefore, the aim of our study is to consider a model able to take under control the spreading of fake news. Indeed, in addition to the classical considered categories, i.e. spreaders and ignorants, we introduce the compartment of the skeptics. The spreaders are individuals that know the fake news and transmit it among the population. The ignorants do not know the rumor and when contacted by a spreader they become spreaders too. The skeptics are individuals able to discover the evidence of the received fake news and thus they persuade the spreader to not transmit it anymore. The considered dynamics ensure that as $t \to \infty$ all spreaders become skeptics, thus stopping the spread of fake news.

In Sect. 2, the deterministic model is introduced, consisting in a system of ordinary differential equations. We solve numerically such system, we analyze the asymptotic behavior of the three categories and the maximum number of spreaders. The corresponding stochastic model, consisting in a two-dimensional and temporally homogeneous birth-death process is presented in Sect. 3. For the aforementioned process, we determine the state space and its cardinality, the Kolmogorov equations for transition probabilities, and the partial differential equation solved by the probability generating function. From the latter, the differential equations solved by the means of spreaders and ignorants are derived, noting a complete correspondence with the previously described deterministic model. The resulting stochastic process is not easily tractable; therefore, attention is shifted to the presentation of a simulation algorithm, written in the `R` programming language, which is used to obtain simulated sample-paths of the process and histograms of the absorbing times, i.e. the times in which the spreaders become 0.

2 The Deterministic Model

We denote respectively with $X(t), Y(t), Z(t)$ the percentage of spreaders, ignorants and skeptics at time $t \geq 0$, such that $X(t), Y(t), Z(t) \geq 0$ with

$$X(t) + Y(t) + Z(t) = 1. \tag{1}$$

A spreader is a person that knows the fake news and transmits it when he/she meets an ignorant or a skeptic. An ignorant is a person who does not know the rumor and then, when he/she is contacted by a spreader, becomes a spreader. A skeptic, when contacted by a spreader, is able to discover the evidence of the received fake news and thus persuades the spreader to not transmit it anymore. We assume that the rate of contacts between a spreader and an ignorant is $\lambda > 0$, and between a spreader and a skeptic is $\xi > 0$. Following the described rules of the rumor spread we obtain the following system of ordinary differential equations, for $t \geq 0$:

$$\begin{cases} \dfrac{dX(t)}{dt} = X(t)\left(\lambda Y(t) - \xi \left(N - X(t) - Y(t)\right)\right), \\ \dfrac{dY(t)}{dt} = -\lambda X(t) Y(t), \\ \dfrac{dZ(t)}{dt} = \xi X(t) Z(t), \end{cases} \tag{2}$$

where $Z(t) = 1 - X(t) - Y(t)$, $\forall t \geq 0$, due to Eq. (1). We remark that a similar model has been studied in Giorno and Spina [10]. The initial conditions are

$$X(0) = x_0 \in (0,1), \quad Y(0) = y_0 \in [0,1), \quad Z(0) = z_0 \in (0,1), \tag{3}$$

with $x_0 + y_0 + z_0 = 1$. Note that it is not possible to find the solution of (2) in a closed form, but from the second and the third equations of (2) one has:

$$Y(t) = y_0\, e^{-\lambda \int_0^t X(\theta) d\theta}, \qquad Z(t) = (1 - x_0 - y_0)\, e^{\xi \int_0^t X(\theta) d\theta}. \tag{4}$$

Thanks to Eq. (1), it is easy to note that the dynamical system (2) can be written as follows

$$\begin{cases} \dfrac{\mathrm{d}X(t)}{\mathrm{d}t} = \lambda X(t)Y(t) - \xi X(t) + \xi[X(t)]^2 + \xi X(t)Y(t) \\ \dfrac{\mathrm{d}Y(t)}{\mathrm{d}t} = -\lambda X(t)Y(t). \end{cases} \tag{5}$$

The trapping region of (5) is given by the triangle

$$T_r = \left\{(x, y) \in \mathbb{R}^2 :\ 0 \le x \le 1,\, 0 \le y \le 1 - x\right\}.$$

Hence, from the second equation of (4) it follows that

$$\int_0^{+\infty} X(\theta) d\theta < \frac{1}{\xi}\left|\log\left(1 - x_0 - y_0\right)\right|. \tag{6}$$

In Fig. 1, the solutions of system (2) are represented for some choices of the parameters.

2.1 Asymptotic Behaviour

Let us define the asymptotic percentage of spreaders, ignorants and skeptics, respectively, as follows:

$$X := \lim_{t \to +\infty} X(t), \qquad Y := \lim_{t \to +\infty} Y(t), \qquad Z := \lim_{t \to +\infty} Z(t).$$

Proposition 1. *The set*

$$A := \{(0, k) : 0 \le k \le 1\}, \tag{7}$$

contains the stable equilibrium points of (2).

Proof. For $t \to +\infty$, system (2) becomes:

$$\begin{cases} \lambda XY - \xi X(1 - X - Y) = 0, \\ -\lambda XY = 0, \end{cases} \tag{8}$$

with $Z = 1 - X - Y$. The solutions of (8) are $(0, k)$ with $k \ge 0$ and $(1, 0)$. Recalling the initial conditions (3), the solution $(1, 0)$ is not acceptable because there is at least one skeptic that does not allow to obtain the asymptotic percentage of spreaders $X = 1$. Hence, the set of acceptable equilibrium points of (2) is given by (7). Note that all the elements of A are stable equilibrium points.

Note that, from the definition of the set A given in (7), there are no spreaders asymptotically. In particular $(0,0)$ represents the situation for that all the elements of the population become skeptics (i.e. all individuals know the news and stopped it becoming skeptics), whereas $(0,k)$, $k>0$ means that there is a percentage k of the population that does not know the news and a percentage $1-k$ that is skeptic.

Now we are interested in computing the final percentage of ignorants

$$k = Y = \lim_{t\to+\infty} Y(t) = y_0\, e^{-\lambda \int_0^{+\infty} X(\theta)d\theta} > 0;$$

in particular we focus on the relative number of ignorants over their initial value, i.e.

$$w := \frac{y_0}{Y} = e^{\lambda \int_0^{+\infty} X(\theta)d\theta},$$

so that

$$k = Y = \frac{y_0}{w}. \tag{9}$$

Note that due to (6) and $Y < y_0$ (because the ignorants can only decrease) one has

$$1 < w < \left(\frac{1}{1-x_0-y_0}\right)^{\rho}. \tag{10}$$

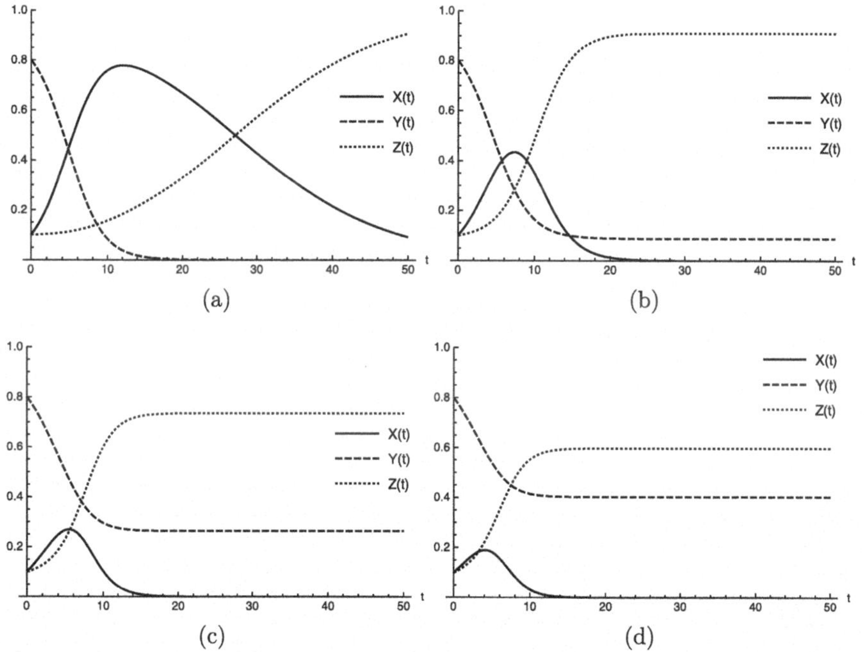

Fig. 1. The solutions of system (2) for $x_0 = 0.1$, $y_0 = 0.8$, $\lambda = 0.5$ and $\xi = 0.1,\ 0.5,\ 0.9,\ 1.3$ from (a) to (d).

Proposition 2. *The equation*

$$(1 - x_0 - y_0)w^{1+\frac{1}{\rho}} - w + y_0 = 0, \tag{11}$$

has a unique solution in the interval

$$\left[\max\left\{1, \left(\frac{1}{1 - x_0 - y_0}\right)^\rho \left(\frac{\rho}{\rho + 1}\right)^\rho\right\}, \left(\frac{1}{1 - x_0 - y_0}\right)^\rho\right[, \tag{12}$$

with

$$\rho = \frac{\lambda}{\xi}. \tag{13}$$

In particular, if $\rho = 1$*, one has*

$$w = \frac{1 + \sqrt{(2y_0 - 1)^2 + 4x_0 y_0}}{2(1 - x_0 - y_0)}. \tag{14}$$

Proof. Starting from (4) and considering (1) for $t \to +\infty$, one obtains:

$$y_0\, e^{-\lambda \int_0^{+\infty} X(\theta)d\theta} + (1 - x_0 - y_0)\, e^{\xi \int_0^{+\infty} X(\theta)d\theta} = 1,$$

that is equivalent to (11). Let us consider the continuous function

$$f(w) = (1 - x_0 - y_0)w^{1+\frac{1}{\rho}} - w + y_0, \tag{15}$$

for w specified in Eq. (10). For the function f in (15), one has

$$\lim_{w \to 1^+} f(w) = -x_0 < 0, \qquad f\left(\frac{1}{1 - x_0 - y_0}\right) = y_0 > 0,$$

so that there is a solution of Eq. (11) in $\left]1, \left(\frac{1}{1-x_0-y_0}\right)^\rho\right[$ due to the Bolzano's theorem. Now we observe that the function f defined in (15) is increasing in $\left]\left(\frac{1}{1-x_0-y_0}\right)^\rho \left(\frac{\rho}{\rho+1}\right)^\rho, \left(\frac{1}{1-x_0-y_0}\right)^\rho\right[$, by studying its first derivative.

If $\left(\frac{1}{1-x_0-y_0}\right)^\rho \left(\frac{\rho}{\rho+1}\right)^\rho < 1$, the solution of (11) is obviously unique, however this also holds if $\left(\frac{1}{1-x_0-y_0}\right)^\rho \left(\frac{\rho}{\rho+1}\right)^\rho > 1$ because the function f evaluated in $\left(\frac{1}{1-x_0-y_0}\right)^\rho \left(\frac{\rho}{\rho+1}\right)^\rho$ is negative. Therefore, the first part of the proposition is proved.

The explicit solution (14) can be obtained by solving Eq. (11) with $\rho = 1$; indeed, one has $w = \frac{1 \pm \sqrt{(2y_0-1)^2 + 4x_0y_0}}{2(1-x_0-y_0)}$. Hence, the solution in (14) is the unique acceptable solution, by virtue of (12).

In Fig. 2, we show some plots of the final percentage k of Eq. (9) as a function of ρ, x_0 and y_0. Note that k turns out to be an increasing function with respect to ρ and x_0 and increasing with respecto to y_0.

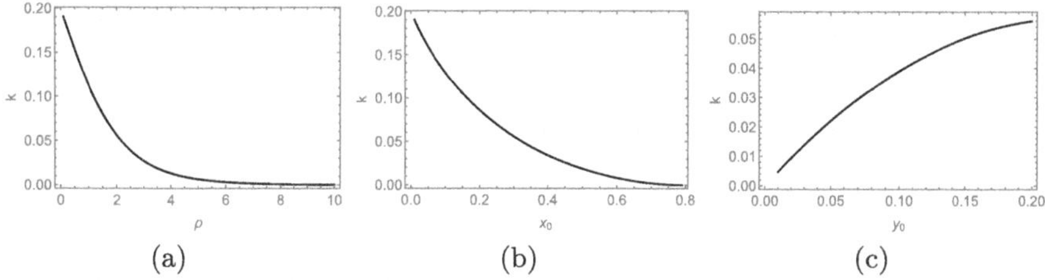

Fig. 2. The final percentage of ignorants given in Eq. (9) as a function of ρ with $x_0 = 0.3$ and $y_0 = 0.3$ in (a), as a function of x_0 with $y_0 = 0.2$ and $\rho = 2$ in (b) and as a function of y_0 with $x_0 = 0.3$ and $\rho = 2$ in (c).

As an example, we compute numerically the percentage Y when $\rho \neq 1$ ($\lambda \neq \xi$), and exactly when $\lambda = \xi$ for the same choices of Fig. 2, fixed $x_0 = 0.1$, $y_0 = 0.8$, $\lambda = 0.5$:

$$Y = \begin{cases} 8 \cdot 10^{-6}, \text{ if } \xi = 0.1, \\ 8 \cdot 10^{-2}, \text{ if } \xi = 0.5, \\ 2 \cdot 10^{-1}, \text{ if } \xi = 0.9. \end{cases} \tag{16}$$

One can observe that the final percentage of ignorants is increasing with ξ, when the other parameters are fixed. Indeed, when the contact rate between spreaders and skeptics increases, more ignorants are not reached from the fake news.

2.2 Maximum Number of Spreaders

In this Section, we focus on the maximum number of spreaders, depending on the parameter of the model, in order to analyze how the spreading of a fake news can be controlled. Note that the number of spreaders can be always decreasing if there are no interactions between spreaders and ignorants. In the following proposition, we consider the case in which there is at least an interaction between spreaders and ignorants.

Proposition 3. *Let us consider a time $t_* > 0$ such that:*

$$x_* := X(t_*) = 1 - (\rho + 1)\, y_0 \left[\frac{1 - x_0 - y_0}{\rho\, y_0} \right]^{1 - \frac{1}{\rho+1}}. \tag{17}$$

If $\rho > \frac{1 - x_0 - y_0}{y_0}$, hence the function $X(t)$ has a maximum given in (17), otherwise the maximum of $X(t)$ is x_0.

Proof. From the first equation in (2), one has that the critical points of $X(t)$ are solution of:

$$X(t)[\rho Y(t) - Z(t)] = 0, \tag{18}$$

with ρ given in (13). The solution $X(t) = 0$ of (18) is not acceptable since $X(0) = x_0 > 0$, then we focus only on $\rho Y(t) - Z(t)$, i.e.

$$X(t) = 1 - (1 + \rho) Y(t), \tag{19}$$

because $Z(t) = 1 - Y(t) - X(t)$. Hence, if the function $X(t)$ has a maximum in $t_* > 0$, it results, from (19) and (1),

$$X(t_*) + (1+\rho)Y(t_*) = 1 = X(t_*) + Y(t_*) + Z(t_*).$$

Consequently, one has:

$$Y(t_*) = \frac{1}{\rho} Z(t_*). \tag{20}$$

From (4), the expression (20) allows to obtain:

$$e^{\int_0^{t_*} X(\theta) d\theta} = \left(\frac{1 - x_0 - y_0}{\rho y_0} \right)^{-\frac{1}{\lambda+\xi}}. \tag{21}$$

By substituting Eq. (21) in the first of (4), Eq. (19) leads to $X(t_*)$ in (17). It follows that for $X(t_*)$ given in (17), t_* is a maximum point since $X''(t)$ for $t = t_*$ is negative.

Now, we consider x_* as a function of ρ, and we note that x_* attains its minimum value, i.e. x_0, when $\rho = \frac{1-x_0-y_0}{y_0}$. Hence, when $\rho < \frac{1-x_0-y_0}{y_0}$, then $x_* < x_0$, otherwise $x_* > x_0$. Considering Eq. (21), it is not hard to notice that if $\rho < \frac{1-x_0-y_0}{y_0}$ then $t_* < 0$. Hence, since t_* is non negative, when $\rho < \frac{1-x_0-y_0}{y_0}$ the maximum value of $X(t)$ is given by x_0. Indeed, in this case $X(t)$ can only decrease from the initial value x_0.

We compute the maximum number of spreaders from (17) for the same choices of Fig. 1, for fixed $x_0 = 0.1$, $y_0 = 0.8$, $\lambda = 0.5$:

$$X(t_*) = \begin{cases} 0.778083, \text{ if } \xi = 0.1, \\ 0.434315, \text{ if } \xi = 0.5, \\ 0.269514, \text{ if } \xi = 0.9. \end{cases}$$

As we expect, $X(t_*)$ is decreasing when ξ increases. By considering again the same choices, i.e. $x_0 = 0.1$, $y_0 = 0.8$, $\lambda = 0.5$, we have that for $\xi > 4$, $X(t_*) = x_0 = 0.1$ since $\rho < \frac{1-x_0-y_0}{y_0}$.

3 The Related Two-Dimensional Finite Birth-Death Process

In this Section we consider the stochastic counterpart of the model, as done in many similar researches (see, for instance, Giorno and Nobile [9]). In the following we denote by $\mathbb{N}$ the set of positive integers and with $\mathbb{N}_0 := \mathbb{N} \cup \{0\}$.

Let $\{(X(t), Y(t), Z(t)); t \geq 0\}$ be a three-dimensional time homogeneous birth-death process, where $X(t)$ represents the number of spreaders, $Y(t)$ represents the number of ignorants and $Z(t)$ represents the number of skeptics at time $t \geq 0$. We suppose that the diffusion of the fake news regards a finite population of size $N \in \mathbb{N}$, hence $X(t) + Y(t) + Z(t) = N$, $t \geq 0$. For this reason, we now focus on the two-dimensional time-homogeneous birth-death process

$\{(X(t), Y(t)); t \geq 0\}$. The dynamic of the process is governed by the following rules:

$$\begin{aligned}
&\mathsf{P}\left(\begin{matrix} X(t+\Delta t)=n+1 \\ Y(t+\Delta t)=m-1 \end{matrix} \middle| \begin{matrix} X(t)=n \\ Y(t)=m \end{matrix}\right) = \lambda n m \Delta t + o(\Delta t), \quad n, m \in \mathbb{N} \\
&\mathsf{P}\left(\begin{matrix} X(t+\Delta t)=n-1 \\ Y(t+\Delta t)=m \end{matrix} \middle| \begin{matrix} X(t)=n \\ Y(t)=m \end{matrix}\right) = \xi n(N-n-m)\Delta t + o(\Delta t), \; n \in \mathbb{N}, \; m \in \mathbb{N}_0 \\
&\mathsf{P}\left(\begin{matrix} X(t+\Delta t)=0 \\ Y(t+\Delta t)=m \end{matrix} \middle| \begin{matrix} X(t)=0 \\ Y(t)=m \end{matrix}\right) = 1, \quad m \in \mathbb{N}_0,
\end{aligned} \tag{22}$$

where $\lambda > 0$ denotes the intensity of the meeting between a spreader and an ignorant, $\xi > 0$ denotes the intensity of the meeting between a spreader and a skeptic. Note that such dynamic is in agreement with Eq. (2). We remark that, from Eq. (22), the set of absorbing states is given by

$$A = \{(0, k); k \in \mathbb{N}_0\}$$

in analogy with Eq. (7). Indeed, for the corresponding deterministic case, the set A, defined in Eq. (7), contains all the acceptable equilibrium points.

According to the dynamics described by Eq. (22), the state-space of the two-dimensional finite birth-death process is represented by

$$S := \{(n, m) : 0 \leq n \leq x_0 + y_0, \quad 0 \leq m \leq \min\{y_0, x_0 + y_0 - n\}\}.$$

A plot of the state-space S is given in Fig. 3. It is possible also to compute its cardinality $\#S$, i.e. the number of points contained in S included the edge. Note that S is made up of the lattice points of a rectangle R having vertices $(0,0)$, $(0, y_0)$, $(x_0, 0)$ and (x_0, y_0) and a triangle T having vertices $(x_0+1, 0)$, (x_0+1, y_0-1) and $(x_0+y_0, 0)$. Hence the cardinality of S is given by

$$\#S = \#R + \#T = (x_0+1)(y_0+1) + \frac{y_0(y_0+1)}{2}.$$

Note that the knowledge of the cardinality of the state-space S can be very useful from a modeling perspective. In fact, even if the mean-field approach, which considers a complete graph, is sufficient to describe the spreading of news or epidemics, the spatial heterogeneity could be included. Therefore studying the spreading of news on graphs could be useful to properly represent the transmission system (see, for example, Naldi and Patané [18]). By setting

$$p_{n,m}(t) := \mathsf{P}[X(t) = n, Y(t) = m], \qquad t \geq 0, \quad n, m \in \mathbb{N}_0, \tag{23}$$

the following proposition provides the Chapman-Kolmogorov equations for the transition probabilities (23) of the process $(X(t), Y(t))$.

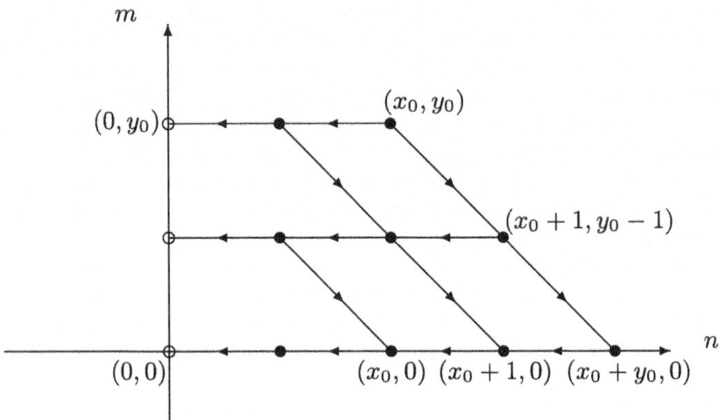

Fig. 3. Representation of the state-space for $(x_0, y_0) = (2, 2)$. The hollow dots indicate the absorbing states, whereas the vectors represent all the admissible transitions.

Proposition 4. *The transition probabilities of the two-dimensional birth-death process* $(X(t), Y(t))$, $t \geq 0$, *satisfy the following system of differential equations*

$$\frac{d}{dt}p_{0,m}(t) = p_{1,m}(t)\xi\left(N-1-m\right), \qquad 0 \leq m \leq y_0$$

$$\frac{d}{dt}p_{1,m}(t) = 2\xi\left(N-2-m\right)p_{2,m} - p_{1,m}(t)\left(\lambda m + \xi\left(N-1-m\right)\right), \; 0 \leq m \leq y_0$$

$$\frac{d}{dt}p_{n,m}(t) = \lambda(n-1)(m+1)p_{n-1,m+1} + \xi(n+1)(N-n-1-m)p_{n+1,m}(t)$$
$$- n\left(\lambda m + \xi(N-n-m)\right)p_{n,m}(t), \quad n \geq 2, 0 \leq m < y_0, n+m \neq x_0+y_0$$

$$\frac{d}{dt}p_{n,y_0}(t) = \xi(n+1)(N-n-1-y_0)p_{n+1,y_0}(t)$$
$$- \xi n(N-n-y_0)p_{n,y_0}(t), \quad 2 \leq n < x_0,$$
$$\frac{d}{dt}p_{n,x_0+y_0-n}(t) = \lambda(n-1)(x_0+y_0-n+1)p_{n-1,x_0+y_0-n+1}(t)$$
$$- \lambda n(x_0+y_0-n)p_{n,x_0+y_0-n}(t) - \xi n(N-x_0-y_0)p_{n,x_0+y_0-n}, \quad x_0 < n \leq x_0+y_0$$
$$\frac{d}{dt}p_{x_0,y_0}(t) = \lambda x_0 \cdot y_0 p_{x_0,y_0}(t) - \xi x_0(N-x_0-y_0)p_{x_0,y_0},$$

with the initial condition given by

$$p_{n,m}(0) = \delta_{n,x_0} \cdot \delta_{m,y_0} \tag{24}$$

where $n, m \in \mathbb{N}$, *being* $\delta_{i,j}$ *the Kronecker symbol.*

Proof. The differential equations for the probabilities (23) follow by considering all the possible transitions of the process given in Eq. (22).

It turns out to be complicated to express equations given in Proposition 4 in matrix form. In the remainder of the paper, we denote by E_{x_0,y_0} and

Var_{x_0,y_0}, respectively, the mean and the variance conditional on the initial state $(X(0), Y(0)) = (x_0, y_0)$. In order to study the characteristics of $(X(t), Y(t))$, we provide the partial differential equation solved by the corresponding probability generating function. More in detail, let us consider the probability generating function $G_{x_0,y_0}(u, v, t)$ of the two-dimensional process $(X(t), Y(t))$ defined as follows

$$G_{x_0,y_0}(u, v, t) := \mathsf{E}_{x_0,y_0}\left[u^{X(t)} v^{Y(t)}\right] = \sum_{n=0}^{x_0+y_0} \sum_{m=0}^{\min\{y_0, x_0+y_0-n\}} u^n v^m p_{n,m}(t), \quad (25)$$

with $|u| \leq 1$, $|v| \leq 1$, $t \geq 0$.

Proposition 5. *The probability generating function $G(u, v, t)$ defined in Eq. (25) solves the following partial differential equation*

$$\begin{aligned} \frac{\partial}{\partial t} G(u, v, t) &= \xi(N-1)(1-u) \frac{\partial}{\partial u} G(u, v, t) + \xi u(u-1) \frac{\partial^2}{\partial u^2} G(u, v, t) \\ &\quad + \left(-\xi v + \xi u v + \lambda u^2 - \lambda u v\right) \frac{\partial^2}{\partial u \partial v} G(u, v, t), \quad t \geq 0, \end{aligned} \quad (26)$$

with initial condition given by $G(u, v, 0) = u^{x_0} v^{y_0}$.

Proof. Equation (26) follows by considering the differential equations given in Proposition 4. The initial condition is an immediate consequence of Eq. (24).

We point out that from the partial differential Eq. (26) it is not possible to derive explicit expressions of the transition probabilities and of the means of the components of the two-dimensional process $(X(t), Y(t))$. Indeed, by deriving Eq. (26) with respect to the variable u (or v), we obtain the differential equation solved by the mean of the spreaders $X(t)$ (or the mean of the ignorants $Y(t)$) but it involves also the mixed moment of the process. Indeed, denoting by $m_X(t) := \mathsf{E}_{x_0,y_0}(X(t))$, $m_Y(t) := \mathsf{E}_{x_0,y_0}(Y(t))$, $m_{X^2}(t) := \mathsf{E}_{x_0,y_0}\left(X^2(t)\right)$ and $m_{X \cdot Y}(t) := \mathsf{E}_{x_0,y_0}(X(t) \cdot Y(t))$, we have

$$\begin{aligned} &\frac{\mathrm{d}}{\mathrm{d}t} m_X(t) = \xi m_{X^2}(t) + (\lambda + \xi) m_{X \cdot Y}(t) - \xi N m_X(t), \qquad m_X(0) = x_0, \\ &\frac{\mathrm{d}}{\mathrm{d}t} m_Y(t) = -\lambda m_{X \cdot Y}(t), \qquad m_Y(0) = y_0. \end{aligned} \quad (27)$$

We remark that Eqs. (27) are in complete agreement with the deterministic model, provided in Eq. (5). Hence, in order to analyse the process' evolution we construct a simulating algorithm.

In Fig. 4 we provide 50 simulated sample paths of the number of spreaders, i.e. $X(t)$, the number of ignorants, i.e. $Y(t)$, and the number of skeptics, i.e. $N - X(t) - Y(t)$ obtained by using the code given above. As can be noticed, the simulated sample-paths of $X(t)$ are increasing for small t and decreasing for large t, the simulated sample-paths of $Y(t)$ are decreasing with respect to the time, and the simulated sample-paths of $N - X(t) - Y(t)$ are increasing. We also observe that the number of spreaders is maximum when the number of ignorants is 0 in agreement with the dynamics driving the process, according to which the number of spreaders can increase only for a meeting between spreaders and ignorants. Moreover, we note that at the end of the diffusion the number of skeptics is maximum. The sample-paths produced by means of the simulation algorithm can be employed to develop a simulation-based approach for addressing the problem of the absorbing time and that of the determination of the final number of ignorants. The absorbing time is defined as the random variable representing the time instant in which the process $(X(t), Y(t))$ reaches an absorbing state or equivalently the first-time-instant in which the number of spreaders become 0, i.e.

$$\tau_A := \inf\{t \geq 0 : X(t) = 0\}.$$

Specifically, some estimates of the probability density function of the absorbing time can be obtained using histogtams derived from extensive simulations (in this case we use 10^4 simulated sample paths). As an example we examine two different case studies. The corresponding histograms are given in Fig. 5. Note that the support of the probability density function is larger when $\lambda > \xi$. In Fig. 5, we also provide the histograms related to the final number of ignorants. It is worth to notice that the final number of ignorants is larger when $\lambda < \xi$. Moreover, we remark that the results obtained by means of the simultation study are in agreement with the corresponding deterministic ones (cf. Sect. 2.1). As an example, considering the case (b) of Fig. 5, the mean of the final number of ignorants obtained through the simultation study is given by $k \simeq 26.65$ and it corresponds to the deterministic value of Y given in Eq. (16).

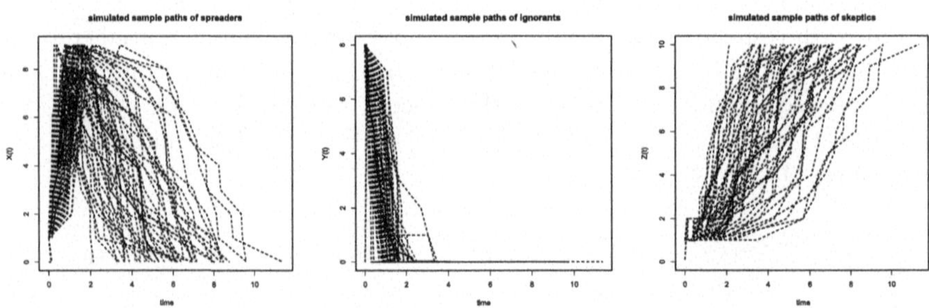

Fig. 4. 50 simulated sample paths of $X(t)$, $Y(t)$ and $Z(t) := N - X(t) - Y(t)$ with $\lambda = 0.5$, $\xi = 0.1$, $x_0 = 1$, $y_0 = 8$ and $N = 10$. The black lines represent the mean.

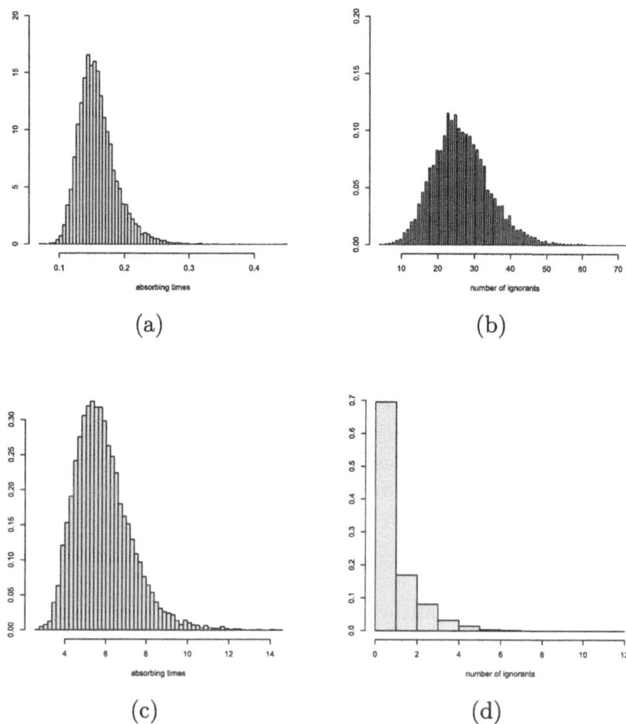

Fig. 5. Histograms of simulated absorbing times of the process $(X(t), Y(t))$, on the left, and of the corresponding final number of ignorants, on the right, with $N = 100$ and (a-b) $x_0 = 10$, $y_0 = 80$, $\lambda = 0.5$, $\xi = 0.9$; (c-d) $x_0 = 20$, $y_0 = 30$, $\lambda = 0.05$, $\xi = 0.01$.

4 Conclusions

In this work, we considered a compartmental model to describe the temporal spread of fake news. The model consists of three compartments: spreaders, who disseminate the news whenever they come into contact with an ignorant person; ignorants, who have not yet been reached by the news; and skeptics, who persuade spreaders of the falsity of the news. The model was firstly studied from a deterministic perspective, with particular attention to the asymptotic behavior and the maximum number of spreaders. Specifically, two possible asymptotic equilibrium situations are identified: one where the entire population eventually becomes skeptics, and another where there is a residual percentage of ignorants and a complementary percentage of skeptics. Regarding the number of spreaders, it was observed that it always reaches a maximum value at least equal to the initial percentage of spreaders. Moreover, we considered a stochastic counterpart of the model represented by a two-dimensional birth-death process. We analyzed its state space, focusing on its cardinality, the corresponding Chapman-Kolmogorov equations, the differential equations for the probability generating function and for the means. Concerning the differential equations for the means, we noticed a complete correspondence with the deterministic model. However, due to the intractability of the stochastic model, we constructed a simulation algorithm by using R software. The simulations have been employed to construct hsitograms of absorbing times and of the final number of ignorants. As a future development, we could include the spatial heterogeneity in the model, in order to take into account the nature of connections, particularly properties such as symmetry and transitivity, which together provide measures of social cohesion. In this sense, the review Keeling and Eames [13] provides a variety of methods that allow the mixing network, or an approximation to the network, to be ascertained in future works.

Acknowledgments. The authors are members of the research group GNCS of INdAM (Istituto Nazionale di Alta Matematica). This work is partially supported by INdAM-GNCS, project: Metodi analitici e computazionali per processi stocastici multidimensionali ed applicazioni (CUP E53C23001670001) and by the 'European Union – Next Generation EU' through MUR-PRIN 2022, project 2022XZSAFN, and MUR-PRIN 2022 PNRR, project P2022XSF5H.

Disclosure of Interests. The authors have no competing interests to declare that are relevant to the content of this article.

References

1. Billard, L.: Generalized two-dimensional bounded birth and death processes and some applications. J. Appl. Probab. **18**, 335–347 (1981). https://doi.org/10.2307/3213281
2. Brandwajn, A.: An iterative solution of two-dimensional birth and death processes. Oper. Res. **27**, 595–605 (1979). https://doi.org/10.1287/opre.27.3.595
3. De Martino, G., Spina, S.: Exploiting the time-dynamics of news diffusion on the Internet through a generalized Susceptible-Infected model. Phys. A **438**, 634–644 (2015). https://doi.org/10.1016/j.physa.2015.07.022
4. Di Crescenzo, A., Martinucci, B.: A first-passage-time problem for symmetric and similar two-dimensional birth-death processes. Stochastic Models **24**(3), 451–469 (2008). https://doi.org/10.1080/15326340802232293
5. Di Crescenzo, A., Paraggio, P. : Modeling the random spreading of fake news through a two-dimensional time-inhomogeneous birth-death process. Math. Methods Appl. Sci. **47**(18), 13621–13650 (2024)
6. Di Crescenzo, A., Paraggio, P., Spina, S.: Stochastic growth models for the spreading of fake news. Mathematics **11**(16), 3597 (2023)
7. Esmaeeli, N., Sajadi, F.: On the probability of rumour survival among sceptics. J. Appl. Probab. **60**(3), 1096–1111 (2023)
8. Fayolle, G., King, P.J.B., Mitrani, I.: The solution of certain two-dimensional Markov models. Adv. Appl. Prob. **14**, 295–308 (1982). https://doi.org/10.1145/1009375.806175
9. Giorno, V., Nobile, A.: Time-inhomogeneous finite birth processes with applications in epidemic models. Mathematics **11**(21), 4521 (2023)

10. Giorno, V., Spina, S.: Rumor spreading models with random denials. Phys. A **461**, 569–576 (2016)
11. Griffiths, M., Greenhalgh, D.: The probability of extinction in a bovine respiratory syncytial virus epidemic model. Math. Biosci. **231**, 144–158 (2011). https://doi.org/10.1016/j.mbs.2011.02.011
12. Kapsikar, S., Saha, I., Agarwal, K., Kavitha, V., Zhu, Q.: Controlling fake news by collective tagging: a branching process analysis. IEEE Control Syst. Lett. **5**(6), 2108–2113 (2021). Article 9296289. https://doi.org/10.1109/LCSYS.2020.3045299
13. Keeling, M.J., Eames, T.D.: Networks and epidemic models. J. R. Soc. Interface **2**, 295–307 (2005)
14. Krishna Kumar, B., Sankar, R., Navaneetha Krishnan, R., Rukmani, R.: Multi-server call center retrial queue under Bernoulli vacation schedule with two-way communication and orbital search. Telecommun. Syst. **84**, 23–51 (2023). https://doi.org/10.1007/s11235-023-01025-1
15. Mahmoud, H.: A model for the spreading of fake news. J. Appl. Probab. **57**(1), 332–342 (2020)
16. Mobilia, M.: Commitment versus persuasion in the three-party constrained voter model. J. Stat. Phys. **151**, 69–91 (2013). https://doi.org/10.1007/s10955-012-0656-x
17. Møller, J., Berthelsen, K.K.: Transforming spatial point processes into Poisson processes using random superposition. Adv. Appl. Probab. (SGSA) **44**, 42–62 (2012). https://doi.org/10.1239/aap/1331216644
18. Naldi, G., Patané, G.: A Graph-Based Modelling of Epidemics: Properties, Simulation, and Continuum Limit. arXiv:2208.07559 [math.NA] (2023)
19. Remiche, M.A.: Time to congestion in homogeneous quasi-birth-and-death processes. Opsearch **35**, 169–192 (1998). https://doi.org/10.1145/1009375.806175
20. San Martín, J., Drubi, F., Rodríguez Pérez, D.: Uncritical polarized groups: the impact of spreading fake news as fact in social networks. Math. Comput. Simul. **178**, 192–206 (2020)
21. Servi, L.D.: Algorithmic solutions to two-dimensional birth-death processes with application to capacity planning. Telecommun. Syst. **21**(2–4), 205–212 (2002). https://doi.org/10.1023/A:1020942430425

Comparing Some Simulation Strategies for First Passage Times of Time-Changed Brownian Motion

Luigia Caputo[1], Maria Francesca Carfora[2(✉)], and Enrica Pirozzi[3]

[1] Dipartimento di Matematica e Applicazioni "Renato Caccioppoli", Università degli Studi di Napoli Federico II, Napoli, Italy
luigia.caputo@unina.it

[2] Consiglio Nazionale delle Ricerche, Istituto per le Applicazioni del Calcolo "Mauro Picone", Napoli, Italy
mariafrancesca.carfora@cnr.it

[3] Dipartimento di Matematica e Fisica, Università degli Studi della Campania "Luigi Vanvitelli", Caserta, Italy
enrica.pirozzi@unicampania.it

Abstract. The first passage time of a time-changed Brownian motion through a given boundary is investigated by means of three simulation methods. The time-changed process is constructed by composing the Brownian motion with the inverse of an α-stable subordinator process. We implement a path simulation algorithm and two variants of the hazard rate simulation algorithm. The two variants are based on different expressions for the hazard rate of the time-changed process. Results obtained by applying the different strategies are graphically compared and discussed.

Keywords: First passage problem · Subordinator · Path simulation · Hazard rate method

1 Introduction

The recent growing interest in time-changed processes (see, for instance, [12,13]) stems from the understanding that many real-world phenomena, from finance to physics and biology, can be modeled as dynamics of diffusing particles that evolve according to the stochastic occurrence of other events playing the role of a stochastic clock. For this reason, their dynamics is stochastically time-changed. Such anomalous diffusions are often observed in real data, indeed they manifest in asymmetric densities, heavy tails, sharp peaks, different spreading rates. Moreover, the probability for these diffusing particles to reach a given state for the first time can be expressed as the First Passage Time (FPT) of a stochastic

M.F. Carfora and E. Pirozzi are members of the Gruppo Nazionale Calcolo Scientifico - Istituto Nazionale di Alta Matematica (GNCS-INdAM).

A. Quesada-Arencibia et al. (Eds.): EUROCAST 2024, LNCS 15174, pp. 228–242, 2025.
https://doi.org/10.1007/978-3-031-83885-9_21

process through an assigned boundary, and it is of great interest in the modeling context, even if it is more challenging than the classical case.

These anomalous diffusions are also called fractional diffusions because the corresponding probability law solves the fractional diffusion equation obtained by replacing one or both derivatives with their fractional analogues. In particular, we consider the following time-fractional diffusion equation [14]

$$\frac{\partial^\alpha p(x,t)}{\partial t} = \frac{\partial^2 p(x,t)}{\partial x^2}$$

that governs the limit of a random walk with waiting times between jumps: the n-th particle jump is preceded by a waiting time τ_n with a power law probability distribution [13], i.e.

$$\mathbb{P}(\tau_n > t) \approx t^{-\alpha}, \qquad 0 < \alpha < 1,\, t > 0.$$

This random walk model converges to a Brownian motion with the time index replaced by a random time E_t. The resulting process $B(E_t)$ is sub-diffusive, spreading at a slower power rate $\alpha/2$ than the usual rate $1/2$ for a traditional Brownian motion. Solutions to the time-fractional diffusion equation are useful to model diffusive phenomena in which particles rest for long periods between movements. Together fractional time-changed processes, fractional operators and, in particular, fractional time derivatives are able to capture some specific memory effects, which lead to the corresponding power-law relaxation time. Their non-local nature can also be useful to investigate non local phenomena. For these reasons, fractional processes and fractional differential equations have been used in different domains to model subdiffusive phenomena. Along with these differential models, fractional calculus provides extremely useful and new stochastic models.

This work is motivated by the need to develop simulation algorithms for the First Passage Time of time-changed Diffusions such as Gauss-Markov (GM) Processes [12]. In particular, as it was already done for GM processes [8], our purpose is to propose suitable modifications of the hazard rate simulation algorithm. In order to follow such idea, many attempts were made; here, we present results of our investigations and comparisons with the results provided by the classical path simulation algorithm, whose computational cost can be extremely high.

As a first step, our study is focused on the time-changed Brownian motion (TCBM), due to the central role of Brownian motion for Gaussian diffusions. Indeed, the proposed methods and algorithms can be adapted also to the general time-changed Gauss-Markov processes and fractional diffusions, in the same way the Brownian motion can be generalized to GM processes.

In summary, in Sect. 2 we recall the path simulation strategy and the hazard rate simulation algorithm for FPT of GM processes. In Sect. 3 we give the essential definitions about subordinators, inverse subordinators and time-changed processes. In Sect. 4 we describe the specialized path simulation algorithm and two versions of the modified hazard rate simulation algorithm for the TCBM, where closed form results [12] can be exploited, in order to test the reliability of our estimates. In Sect. 5 we compare and discuss the numerical results, also providing details on the implementation of the algorithms. Main conclusions are finally given.

2 Simulation Strategies for FPTs of Gauss-Markov Processes

2.1 About the FPT of a Brownian Motion

The well-known standard Brownian motion $\{B(t)\}_{t\geq 0}$ is a GM stochastic process with stationary, independent and Gaussian increments, such that $\forall t \geq 0, h > 0$, $B(t+h) - B(t) \sim \mathcal{N}(0, h)$. Here, we refer to the continuous version of the Brownian motion, or specifically to the *canonical* Brownian motion, as defined at page 53 in [4]. Its transition probability density function (pdf), here denoted by $p(x,t) := p(x_0, t_0; x, t_0 + t)$ for given (x_0, t_0) is such that for all Borel set A,

$$\int_A p(y,t)dy = \mathbb{P}(B(t) \in A), \quad \forall t \geq 0,$$

under the conditioning that $\mathbb{P}(B(t_0) = x_0) = 1$, with $x_0 \in \mathbb{R}$. It is also well-known that it is the solution of the Fokker-Planck equation:

$$\frac{\partial p(x,t)}{\partial t} = \frac{1}{2}\frac{\partial^2 p(x,t)}{\partial x^2}, \qquad \text{with } \lim_{t\to t_0} p(x,t) = \delta(x - x_0).$$

The FPT of the Brownian motion through a continuous time-varying boundary $S(t)$ is defined as the absolutely continuous stopping time:

$$T = \inf\{t \geq 0 : B(t) > S(t)\},$$

with pdf:

$$g[t|x_0, t_0] = \frac{d\mathbb{P}(T \leq t)}{dt}.$$

Despite the FPT density of a Brownian motion through a linear boundary is known analytically (see [1], and references therein), results about general boundaries are very scarce and fragmentary. For this reason, simulation methods are often adopted for the estimation of FPT densities.

The Path Simulation Algorithm. By recalling the Donsker invariance principle [10], and successive extensions, the Brownian motion is the limit in distribution of suitable re-scaled random walks. By applying this result to the stochastic simulation (see, for instance, [11]), Brownian trajectories can be approximated (i.e. simulated) by random walks with independent and identically distributed (iid) $\mathcal{N}(0, \Delta t)$ steps at times $t_n = t_0 + n\Delta t$ with a very small time-step Δt. Consequentially, the FPT distribution for the Brownian motion can be estimated by simulating a large number of trajectories of the process and by recording the FPT for each of them through a given boundary in the state space. In such a way, samples of FPTs can be obtained. However, this procedure is generally very time-consuming and sensitive to the chosen time discretization. Moreover, even if the paths simulation strategy is very commonly used, its main drawback is that the FPT is anyway overestimated, due to the fact that for each simulated trajectory the FPT can also occur during the time intervals of duration Δt between the successive time steps of the random walks. In such a way, unseen FPTs can occur, they are not recorded and can affect the reliability of estimates derived from the simulated FPTs. Some papers are specifically devoted to this problem, providing estimates of the error (see, for instance, [17]).

2.2 About the FPT of Gauss-Markov Processes

The FPT problem for GM processes has also been investigated and analytical results on the related FPT distribution are provided by means of suitable time-space transformations of already known results for the Brownian motion. Indeed, from [9] we recall that a Gauss-Markov process $X(t)$ with mean value $m(t)$ and covariance $Cov(X(s), X(t)) = u(s)v(t)$, for any couple of time instants $s \leq t$, is defined by the following formula in terms of a standard Brownian motion:

$$X(t) = m(t) + v(t)B(r(t)), \quad \forall t \geq 0,$$

with $r(t) = u(t)/v(t)$ positive monotone increasing $C^1(\mathbb{R}^+)$-function and $v(t) \neq 0\, \forall t \geq 0$. Under some regularity assumptions (see [4,6]), Gauss-Markov processes are also called Gaussian diffusions. The path simulation algorithm, described above for the Brownian motion, can be suitably adapted to a general GM process to obtain simulated samples of its FPT. Similar algorithms, such as those based on the Euler discretization method, can be found, e.g., in [4,17]. Here, we propose hazard rate based algorithms as an alternative.

The Hazard Rate Simulation Algorithm. In [9] it was proved that the FPT density of a Gauss-Markov process solves a non-singular second-kind Volterra integral equation. Such result allows to obtain accurate numerical approximations of the FPT density. Successively, starting from these numerical approximations of FPT density, in [7] a very efficient strategy was devised for the estimation of the FPT density of a Gaussian diffusion; this procedure was also implemented in the R package GaDiFPT [8]. Here we briefly outline its main points.

For a continuous GM stochastic process $X(t)$, whose FPT T through a given boundary $S(t)$ admits density $g[t|x_0, t_0]$ and distribution function $G[t|x_0, t_0]$, it is possible to define the hazard rate function $\lambda(t)$ such that $\lambda(t)dt = \mathbb{P}(t < T < t + dt | T > \text{ t})$ as it follows

$$\lambda(t) = \frac{g[t|x_0, t_0]}{1 - G[t|x_0, t_0]}, \qquad t \geq t_0. \tag{1}$$

In case $\lambda(t)$ is bounded, i.e. there exists a positive real number Λ such that $\lambda(t) \leq \Lambda$, and $\int_0^\infty \lambda(t)dt = \infty$, the hazard rate method [16] allows one to obtain realizations of T by simulating a Poisson process having rate Λ and then accepting the time of occurrence of each event with probability $\lambda(t)/\Lambda$: these occurrence times are instances (realizations) of T.

By focusing on the Brownian motion, as a specific GM process, the general form of the probability distribution of the FPT is the well known inverse Gaussian distribution. In particular, if we assume $x_0 = 1$ and a constant threshold $S(t) = 0$, the FPT density $g[t|x_0, 0] = g[S(t), t|x_0, 0]$ has the closed form expression:

$$g[0, t|1, 0] = \frac{1}{\sqrt{2\pi}t^{3/2}} \exp\left(-\frac{1}{2t}\right), \tag{2}$$

from which the distribution function $G[0, t|1, 0]$ and the hazard rate function can be numerically evaluated. (Note that (2) coincides with $g[1, t|0, 0]$ for time-space homogeneity properties of the BM). Finally, a large number of FPTs can be simulated with no high computational costs, and, consequently, the FPT density can be estimated.

3 Time-Changed Processes

A time-changed process [3] is the composition of two independent processes: the outer process (also called the parent process) and a stochastic process with suitable properties (i.e. positive, non decreasing,...) in order to work as a stochastic time . Under suitable assumptions on the time-change process, it can be proved that the composed time-changed process is characterized by continuous sample paths if the outer process has continuous paths, even preserving Hölder continuity properties [3]. Here, we consider the Brownian motion as the outer process and we choose the inverse of an α-stable subordinator process for the time-change (see, for instance, [12]) with $\alpha \in (0, 1)$.

We briefly recall some definitions and state some notations, taking into account those of [2,5,14].

Subordinators and Inverse Processes. A stochastic process $\{Y(t)\}_{t\geq 0}$ is an α-stable Lévy motion (cfr [2,13,14]) if

- $Y(0) = 0$ a. s.;
- Y has stationary and independent increments;
- Y is stochastically continuous, i.e., for all $t \geq 0$ and $\epsilon > 0$,

$$\lim_{s\to t} \mathbb{P}(|Y(t) - Y(s)| > \epsilon) = 0;$$

- there exist $\alpha \in (0, 2]$, $\beta \in [-1, 1]$, and $\gamma > 0$ such that $Y(t)-Y(s) \sim \mathcal{S}^\alpha(\beta, \gamma(t-s)^{1/\alpha}, 0)$.

Here, $\mathcal{S}^\alpha$ denotes an α-stable distribution whose characteristic function ϕ is completely described by the four parameters α (stability order), β (skewness), γ (scale), δ (location) and it is such that

$$\log(\phi(z)) = \begin{cases} -\gamma^\alpha|z|^\alpha[1 - i\beta(\text{sign}(z)\tan(\frac{\pi\alpha}{2})] + i\delta z, & \alpha \neq 1 \\ -\gamma|z|[1 + \frac{2i\beta}{\pi}(\text{sign}(z)\log(|z|)] + i\delta z, & \alpha = 1. \end{cases}$$

An α-stable subordinator is an α-stable Lévy motion with $\alpha \in (0, 1)$ and $\beta = 1$, with càdlàg paths. In the following, as in [13], we also assume $\gamma = (\cos \frac{\pi\alpha}{2})^{1/\alpha}$ and simply denote by D^α the corresponding α-stable subordinator.

As an example [15], let $\{B(t)\}_{t\geq 0}$ be a standard Brownian motion, and let $\tau(a)$ be the first passage time to the level $a > 0$, that is,

$$\tau(a) = \inf\{t : B(t) > a\}.$$

Then the process $\{\tau(a)\}_{a\geq 0}$ is a stable subordinator with $\alpha = 1/2$.

Given an α-stable subordinator $D^\alpha(t)$ we consider the inverse α-stable subordinator $E^\alpha(t)$, i.e.

$$E^\alpha(t) = \inf\{u > 0 : D^\alpha(u) > t\}.$$

The trajectories of E^α are a.s. continuous and no decreasing, since D^α is a.s. strictly increasing. Note that for all $t > 0$ $E^\alpha(t)$ is the time at which the trajectory $D^\alpha(u)$ exceeds t. In practice, the state of E^α is a time for the α-stable subordinator D^α. Moreover, the time variable t in E^α represents a lower bound on the position of D^α. This is explained by the relation

$$\mathbb{P}(E^\alpha(t) \leq x) = \mathbb{P}(D^\alpha(x) \geq t), \quad \forall t, x > 0.$$

$E^\alpha(t)$ is a self-similar process, indeed for $c > 0$,

$$c^{-\alpha} E^\alpha(ct) = E^\alpha(t), \quad \forall t \geq 0.$$

Moreover, if we denote by $\gamma_\alpha(x)$ the pdf of $D^\alpha(1)$ and by $\nu_\alpha(x, t)$ the pdf of $E^\alpha(t)$, it holds [14]

$$\nu_\alpha(x, t) = \frac{t}{\alpha} x^{-1-\frac{1}{\alpha}} \gamma_\alpha(t x^{-\frac{1}{\alpha}}), \qquad x \geq 0, t > 0. \tag{3}$$

The Time-Changed Brownian Motion. Consider a Brownian motion $\{B(t)\}_{t\geq 0}$ and $E^\alpha(t) = \inf\{s > 0 : D^\alpha(s) > t\}$ that is the right-continuous inverse of an α-stable (with $\alpha \in (0, 1]$) subordinator process $\{D^\alpha(s)\}_{s\geq 0}$, i.e. $E^\alpha(t) = \inf\{s > 0 : D^\alpha(s) > t\}$. The TCBM is the stochastic process obtained by composing such processes, i.e.

$$B_\alpha(t) := B(E^\alpha(t)).$$

The new process is neither Gaussian nor Markovian. Its pdf $f_\alpha(x, t)$ is:

$$f_\alpha(x, t) = \int_0^\infty f(x, s) \nu_\alpha(s, t) ds, \qquad \forall t \in I \subset \mathbb{R}^+,$$

where $\nu_\alpha(s, t)$ is the pdf of $E^\alpha(t)$ given in (3).

The time-changed Brownian motion $B_\alpha(t)$ has a *subordinated (non Markov) transition pdf* for $0 < \tau < t$

$$f_\alpha(x, t|y, \tau) = \int_0^\infty f(x, s|y, \tau) \nu_\alpha(s, t) ds, \qquad x, y \in \mathbb{R},$$

where $f(x, t|y, s)$ is the transition function of $B(t)$. As shown in [12], $f_\alpha(x, t|y, \tau)$ satisfies the following *fractional Fokker-Planck* equation:

$$ {}^C D_t^\alpha f_\alpha(x, t|y, \tau) = \frac{1}{2} \frac{\partial^2}{\partial x^2} f_\alpha(x, t|y, \tau) $$

with

$$ \lim_{t \downarrow \tau} f_\alpha(x, t|y, \tau) = \delta(x - y) $$

and

$$ {}^C D_t^\alpha f(t) = \frac{1}{\Gamma(1-\alpha)} \int_0^t f'(\tau)(t-\tau)^{-\alpha} d\tau $$

is the Caputo fractional derivative of order α. For this reason, the time-changed processes are also called fractional time-changed processes (Fig. 1).

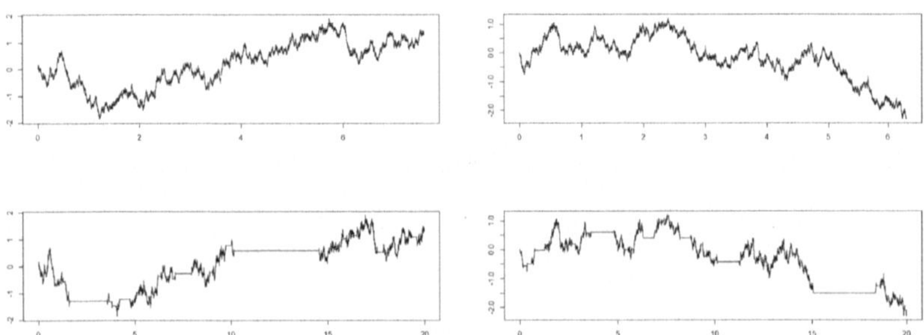

Fig. 1. Simulations of time-changed Brownian motion paths for $\alpha = 0.95$ (left) and $\alpha = 0.9$ (right) from $t = 0$ to $t = 20$. In the first row the horizontal axis represents the transformed time $E^\alpha(t)$, while in the second row it shows the time t.

4 The FPT of a Time-Changed Brownian Motion

In [12], for the TCBM $B_\alpha(t)$, when the parent process $B(t)$ evolves in presence of a linear boundary $S(t) = at + b$, with $b > x_0$ and for all $t \geq t_0$, the authors characterized the First Passage Time by means of the *subordinated* FPT density

$$ g_\alpha[at + b, t|x_0, t_0] = \int_0^\infty g[as + b, s|x_0, t_0] \nu_\alpha(s, t) ds \tag{4} $$

that, by using the closed form expression of $g[as + b, s|x_0, t_0]$, becomes

$$ g_\alpha[at + b, t|x_0, t_0] = \frac{1}{\sqrt{2\pi}} \int_0^\infty \frac{|at_0 + b - x_0|}{(s - t_0)^{3/2}} \exp\left\{ -\frac{(as + b - x_0)^2}{2(s - t_0)} \right\} \nu_\alpha(s, t) ds, \tag{5} $$

with $\nu_\alpha(s, t)$ defined in (3). Such subordinated FPT pdf is particularly useful for a constant boundary $S(t) \equiv S$, for which we denote it as $g_\alpha(S, t|x_0, t_0)$. Figure 2 shows some examples of subordinated FPT densities for different values of α.

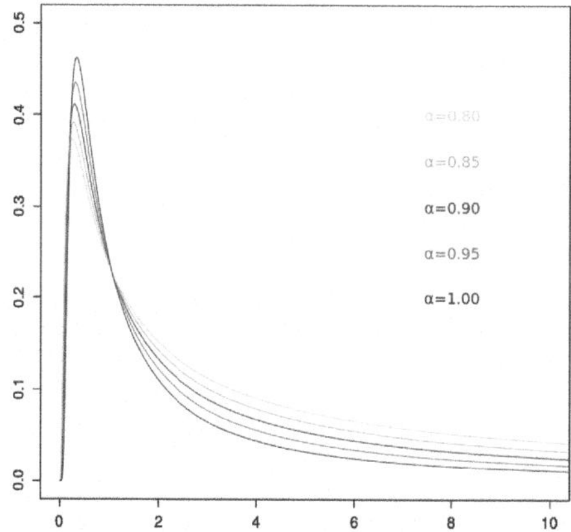

Fig. 2. Plot of FPT subordinated densities $g_\alpha(S, t|x_0, 0)$ of the time–changed Brownian motion for $\alpha = 0.8$ (cyan), $\alpha = 0.85$ (green), $\alpha = 0.9$ (blue) and $\alpha = 0.95$ (red) evaluated for $x_0 = 1$ and $S = 0$. The FPT density for the standard Brownian motion is shown for comparison (black). (Color figure online)

4.1 FPT Estimation Strategies for a TCBM

As seen for the Brownian motion, the FPTs distribution of a time-changed Brownian motion can be estimated by simulating a large number of trajectories of the process and by registering their FPT. This procedure, relying on the simulation of stable distributions, is generally very time-consuming and sensitive to the chosen time discretization; moreover, the simulation time is strongly affected by the value of α. Nevertheless, we consider this simulation strategy (Algorithm 1 in the following) as a baseline to investigate and compare other simulation methods, whose details are given in the next Section. We propose two different strategies for the estimation of the FPT distribution of a TCBM through a constant boundary by two variants of the hazard rate method.

The Modified Hazard Rate Method: Variant a (Algorithm 2a). We denote by T_α the FPT of the process $B_\alpha(t)$ through the boundary S. The associated subordinated pdf, from (4) and (5), is

$$\begin{aligned} g_\alpha[S, t|x_0, t_0] &= \int_0^\infty g[S, u|x_0, t_0]\nu_\alpha(u, t)du \\ &= \frac{1}{\sqrt{2\pi}} \int_0^\infty \frac{|S - x_0|}{(u - t_0)^{3/2}} \exp\left\{-\frac{(S - x_0)^2}{2(u - t_0)}\right\} \nu_\alpha(u, t)du. \end{aligned}$$

The hazard rate method allows one to obtain realizations of the random variable T_α having bounded hazard rate function $\lambda_\alpha(t)$ with

$$\int_0^\infty \lambda_\alpha(t)dt = \infty.$$

Given a constant value Λ such that $\lambda_\alpha(t) \leq \Lambda$, for all $t \geq t_0$, we simulate a Poisson process having rate Λ; the time of occurrence of each event will be then accepted with probability $\lambda_\alpha(t)/\Lambda$. The occurrence times are the simulated instances (realizations) of T_α.

In this case, similarly to Eq.(1), we adopt the hazard rate function $\lambda_\alpha(t)$ defined as

$$\lambda_\alpha(t) = \frac{g_\alpha(t)}{1 - \mathcal{G}_\alpha(t)}, \qquad t \geq t_0$$

where $g_\alpha(t)$ stands for $g_\alpha[S, t|x_0, t_0]$, whereas $\mathcal{G}_\alpha(t) = \mathcal{G}_\alpha[S, t|x_0, t_0]$ is defined as the Riemann-Liouville fractional integral (see [3]) of order α of $g_\alpha(t)$:

$$\mathcal{G}_\alpha(t) = \frac{1}{\Gamma(\alpha)} \int_0^t \frac{g_\alpha(\tau)}{(t-\tau)^{1-\alpha}} d\tau. \tag{6}$$

In this approach, we substantially follow the classic hazard rate method by substituting in the definition of $\lambda_\alpha(t)$ the transition density $g[S, t|x_0, t_0]$ and the transition distribution function $G[S, t|x_0, t_0]$ with $g_\alpha(t)$ and $\mathcal{G}_\alpha(t)$, respectively.

The Modified Hazard Rate Method: Variant b (Algorithm 2b). An alternative approach is to define $\lambda_\alpha(t)$ as the *subordinated* hazard rate function:

$$\lambda_\alpha^{\text{sub}}(t) = \int_0^\infty \lambda(s)\nu_\alpha(s,t)ds, \tag{7}$$

where $\lambda(t)$ is the hazard rate of the Brownian motion. Then, the algorithm proceeds by applying the classical hazard rate method with this hazard rate function. The different time behavior of $\lambda_\alpha(t)$ and $\lambda_\alpha^{\text{sub}}(t)$, for some values of α, is evident in Fig. 3.

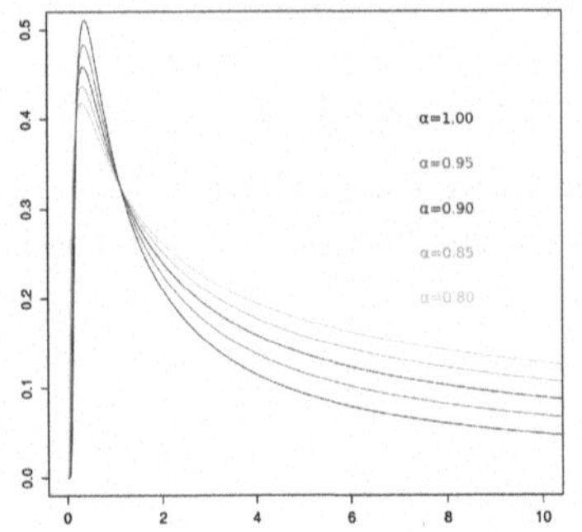

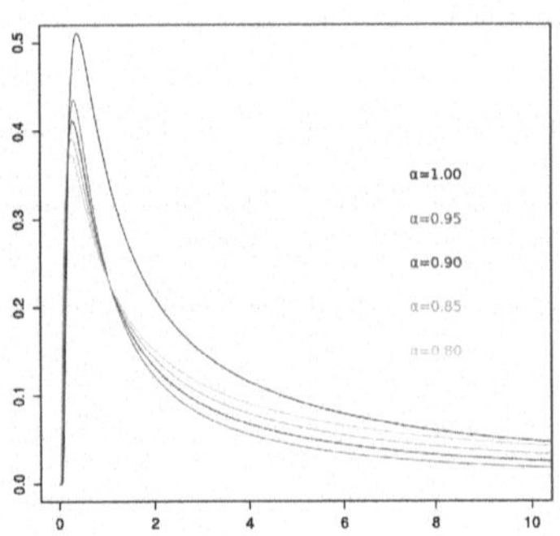

Fig. 3. Plot of hazard rate functions $\lambda_\alpha(t)$ (left) and $\lambda_\alpha^{\text{sub}}(t)$ (right) for the time-changed Brownian motion for different values of α with initial condition $x_0 = 1$ and constant threshold $S(t) = 0$. The hazard rate function for the standard Brownian motion with the same initial condition and threshold is shown for comparison (black).(Color figure online)

5 Numerical Simulations: Implementation Details and Results

Before showing the results on the simulation of FPTs for the TCBM, we provide a quantitative assessment of the proposed methodology: in the simplest case of Brownian motion, we checked that the distribution of FPTs retrieved by the hazard method is coherent with the one obtained by path simulations. Specifically, we compared the empirical distribution obtained by 10000 trajectory simulations with the one retrieved by the generation of 10000 FPT through the hazard rate method. Two-sample bootstrapped tests based on Kolmogorov-Smirnov, Anderson-Darling and Cramer-von Mises statistics confirm the equivalence of the two empirical distributions (p-value > 0.10) when paths are simulated with a sufficiently small timestep (10^{-3} or lower).

Then, we give some details on the path simulation algorithm we developed for the time-changed Brownian motion. A sketch of the algorithm is reported in Algorithm 1. To simulate paths of the time-changed process, relying on the R package `stabledist` [18], we simulate the stable subordinator D^α in the interval [0,T] as a sequence of steps for each of the subintervals $[t_{i-1}, t_i]$, with $t_0 = 0$, $t_N = T$ and we register the number of steps n_k that are needed to reach $t_k = k\Delta t$. The corresponding value of E^α is then $n_k \Delta t$ (recall that E^α can be seen as a FPT for D^α). The time-changed Brownian motion trajectory is finally obtained as a Brownian motion in the changed timesteps $n_1\Delta t, n_2\Delta t, \ldots, n_N\Delta t$.

Algorithm 1: Algorithm for estimating the FPT of a TCBM by trajectory simulation. $t_0 = 0$, $x_0 > S$.

```
function FPTpath (α, dt, Tmax, x0, S);
Input  : The stability order α, the timestep dt, the final simulation time
         Tmax; the starting point x0, the threshold S.
Output: a single FPT
time = 0;
xold = xnew = x0;
tchange=0;
sumstab=0;
i=0;
while (xnew > S) and (tchange < Tmax) do
    tchangeold = tchange;
    xold = xnew;
    time = time + 1;
    while sumstab < time do
        i = i+1;
        step = rstable(α) ;          /* random value from α-stable dist. */
        sumstab = sumstab + step;
    end
    tchange = i * dt;
    dtch = tchange - tchangeold;
    xstep = rnorm(0, dtch^(1/2)) ;   /* random value from N(0,dtch) */
    xnew = xold + xstep;
end
FPT = time * dt;
return FPT
```

The modified hazard methods, in both variants 2a and 2b, requires a previous estimate of the rate $\lambda_\alpha(t)$ or $\lambda_\alpha^{\text{sub}}(t)$, respectively. We rely again on the R package `stabledist` [18] to numerically evaluate $\nu_\alpha(x,t)$ and obtain g_α, $\mathcal{G}_\alpha$, λ_α by numerical quadrature of (5),(6) and (7), respectively. This is a fixed computational cost, because the quadrature is performed just once, independently of the number of FPTs to be simulated. Then, FPTs are generated as described in Algorithm 2, with hazard rate corresponding to Algorithm 2a or 2b. Table 1 shows the computational cost of the three methods when M=10000 FPTs are generated for different values of α on a Ubuntu workstation equipped with AMD Ryzen 7 2700x eight-core processor, 64 GiB RAM. As expected, the cost of Algorithm 1 is highly dependent on α and on the simulation timestep; on the contrary, the cost of Algorithm 2 is almost constant, and essentially due to the numerical quadrature, since the cost for generating the FPTs is irrelevant (about 0.2 s for M=10000).

Algorithm 2: Algorithm for generating M values of FPT of a TCBM by hazard method. $t_0 = 0$, $x_0 > S$.

```
function FPThazard (α, dt, lambda, M);
Input  : The stability order α, the timestep dt, the rate vector lambda, the
         number M of FPT to be generated.
Output: a vector FPT
N = length(lambda); Tmax=(N-1)*dt; lamax = 1.01*max(lambda);
FPT = numeric(M); nreject = 0; tol = 10^-4;
for i in 1:M do
    Tcurr = 0;
    repeat
        Tcurr = Tcurr - log(runif(1))/lamax ;        /* exp. time interval */
        lambdacurr = lambda[Nmax];
        if Tcurr < Tmax then
            icurr = min(floor((Tcurr-t0)/deltat+1.001),(Nmax-1));
            lambdacurr = lambda[icurr]+(lambda[icurr+1]-
              lambda[icurr])*(Tcurr-tempi[icurr])/dt;
        end
        u2 <- runif(1);
        lacheck <- abs(lambdacurr/lamax - u2) ; /* accept if lambda/lamax
          > u2 */
        if lacheck <= tol then
            nreject = nreject + 1 ;
            Tcurr =0;
        end
    until (lacheck > tol) and (lambdacurr/lamax ≥ u2);
    FPT[i] <- Tcurr
end
return FPT
```

Finally, we present some results of all the compared algorithms. In the following Figs. 4, 5, 6 and 7 the empirical FPT pdfs, as estimated with the three algorithms, are superimposed to the subordinated FPT pdf g_α for different values of α. For all methods, the agreement between the empirical and theoretical curves worsens as α decreases. Moreover, the hazard algorithms seems to better estimate the peak of the subordinated density $g_\alpha(t)$, while on the tail all of the methods appear to underestimate and their behavior is very similar.

Table 1. Computational cost (minutes) of the compared algorithms for generating 10000 FPTs.

Algorithm	$\alpha = 0.95$	$\alpha = 0.9$	$\alpha = 0.85$	$\alpha = 0.8$
1 (dt=0.01)	6.42	9.89	16.16	53.19
1 (dt=0.001)	67.15	99.84	192.79	789.30
2a	37.58	37.80	37.54	37.67
2b	36.85	36.92	36.74	36.81

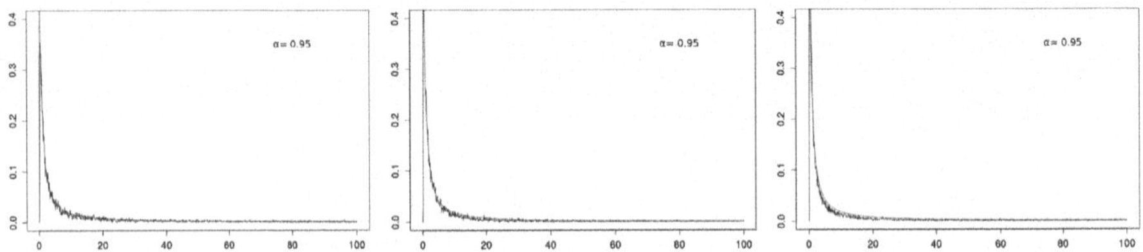

Fig. 4. Graphical comparison of the empirical FPT densities as retrieved through the FPTs of simulated TCBM paths - Algorithm 1 (left), by the hazard rate Algorithm 2a with rates $\lambda_\alpha(t)$ (center) and by the hazard rate Algorithm 2b with $\lambda_\alpha^{\text{sub}}(t)$ (right) for $\alpha = 0.95$; the red line represent the subordinated FPT density $g_{0.95}(0, t|1, 0)$. (Color figure online)

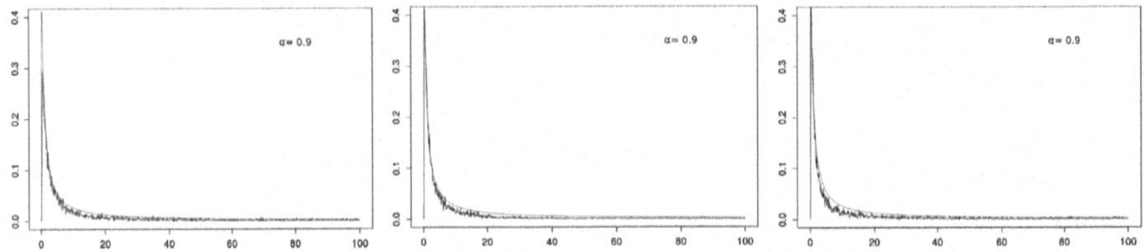

Fig. 5. Graphical comparison of the empirical FPT densities as retrieved through the FPTs of simulated TCBM paths - Algorithm 1 (left), by the hazard rate Algorithm 2a with rates $\lambda_\alpha(t)$ (center) and by the hazard rate Algorithm 2b with $\lambda_\alpha^{\text{sub}}(t)$ (right) for $\alpha = 0.9$; the red line represent the subordinated FPT density $g_{0.9}(0, t|1, 0)$. (Color figure online)

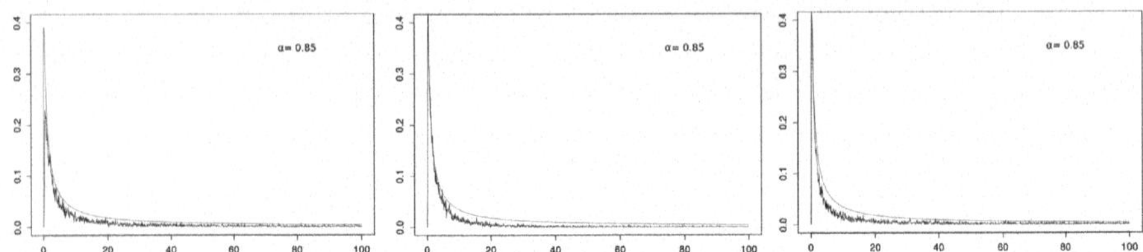

Fig. 6. Graphical comparison of the empirical FPT densities as retrieved through the FPTs of simulated TCBM paths - Algorithm 1 (left), by the hazard rate Algorithm 2a with rates $\lambda_\alpha(t)$ (center) and by the hazard rate Algorithm 2b with $\lambda_\alpha^{\text{sub}}(t)$ (right) for $\alpha = 0.85$; the red line represent the subordinated FPT density $g_{0.85}(0, t|1, 0)$. (Color figure online)

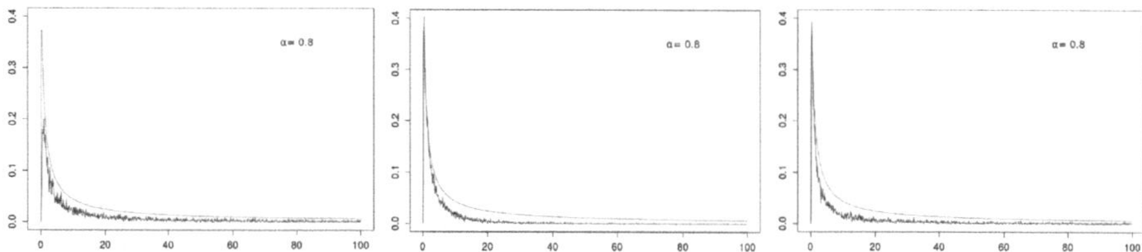

Fig. 7. Graphical comparison of the empirical FPT densities as retrieved through the FPTs of simulated TCBM paths - Algorithm 1 (left), by the hazard rate Algorithm 2a with rates $\lambda_\alpha(t)$ (center) and by the hazard rate Algorithm 2b with $\lambda_\alpha^{\mathrm{sub}}(t)$ (right) for $\alpha = 0.8$; the red line represent the subordinated FPT density $g_{0.8}(0, t|1, 0)$.

6 Conclusions

We investigated the simulation of FPTs for time-changed Brownian motion and propose three numerical strategies. Our main findings are:

- FPT obtained through paths simulations confirm the expected heavy tails but the distribution peak is quite overdamped. Moreover the simulation is very time-consuming and sensitive to both the chosen timestep and the fractional index α;
- the modified hazard Rate algorithm, in both variants, is faster and seems to better reproduce the first part of the distribution, but its estimate of the tail is still inaccurate; the expression we adopted for the fractional rate has to be further validated;
- the information provided by the subordinated FPT density $g_\alpha(t)$ is just qualitative; our main objective in future work is to improve the estimates for the fractional FPT pdf and to consolidate the theoretical justification of the related simulation methods.

Acknowledgments. This study was partially funded by the projects PRIN2022-MUR 2022XZSAFN, PRIN-PNRR P2022XSF5H and by the H2020-ICT-48 TAILOR Network (GA 952215).

Disclosure of Interests. The authors have no competing interests to declare that are relevant to the content of this article.

References

1. Abundo, M.: Some results about boundary crossing for Brownian motion. Ric. Mat. **50**(2), 283–301 (2001)
2. Applebaum, D.: Lévy processes-from probability to finance and quantum groups. Not. Am. Math. Soc. **51**(11), 1336–1347 (2004)
3. Ascione, G., Mishura, Y., Pirozzi, E.: Fractional Deterministic and Stochastic Calculus. De Gruyter, Berlin, Boston (2024)

4. Baldi, P.: Stochastic Calculus. Universitext. Springer, Cham (2024)
5. Bertoin, J.: Subordinators: examples and applications. In: Bernard, P. (ed.) Lectures on Probability Theory and Statistics. LNM, vol. 1717, pp. 1–91. Springer, Heidelberg (1999). https://doi.org/10.1007/978-3-540-48115-7_1
6. Buonocore, A., Caputo, L., Pirozzi, E., Ricciardi, L.M.: The first passage time problem for Gauss-diffusion processes: algorithmic approaches and applications to LIF neuronal model. Methodol. Comput. Appl. Probab. **13**(1), 29–57 (2011)
7. Buonocore, A., Caputo, L., Pirozzi, E., Carfora, M.F.: A simple algorithm to generate firing times for leaky integrate-and-fire neuronal model. Math. Biosci. Eng. MBE **11**(1), 1–10 (2014)
8. Buonocore, A., Carfora, M.F.: GaDiFPT: first passage time simulation for gaussian diffusion processes (2015). http://cran.nexr.com/web/packages/GaDiFPT
9. Di Nardo, E., Nobile, A.G., Pirozzi, E., Ricciardi, L.M.: A computational approach to first-passage-time problems for Gauss-Markov processes. Adv. Appl. Probab. **33**(2), 453–482 (2001)
10. Donsker, M.D.: An invariance principle for certain probability limit theorems. Memoirs Am. Math. Soc. **6**, 12 (1951)
11. Étoré, P., Lejay, A.: A Donsker theorem to simulate one-dimensional processes with measurable coefficients. ESAIM: Prob. Stat. **11**, 301–326 (2007)
12. Leonenko, N., Pirozzi, E.: First passage times for some classes of fractional time-changed diffusions. Stoch. Anal. Appl. **40**(4), 735–763 (2022)
13. Meerschaert, M.M., Sikorskii, A.: Stochastic models for fractional calculus. De Gruyter Studium (2019)
14. Meerschaert, M.M., Straka, P.: Inverse stable subordinators. Math. Model. Nat. Phenom. **8**(2), 1–16 (2013)
15. Nolan, J.P.: Univariate Stable Distributions. SSORFE, Springer, Cham (2020). https://doi.org/10.1007/978-3-030-52915-4
16. Ross, S. M.: Introduction to Probability Models. 10th edn. Academic Press (2010)
17. Taillefumier, T., Magnasco, M.O.: A fast algorithm for the first-passage times of gauss-markov processes with Hölder continuous boundaries. J. Stat. Phys. **140**, 1130–1156 (2010)
18. Wuertz, D. Maechler, M.: stabledist: Stable distribution functions (2016). https://cran.r-project.org/package=stabledist

Numerical Evaluations for Fractional Stochastic Differential Equations in Neuronal Dynamics

Enrica Pirozzi(✉)

Dipartimento di Matematica e Fisica, Università degli Studi della Campania "Luigi Vanvitelli", Caserta, Italy
enrica.pirozzi@unicampania.it

Abstract. We consider two coupled fractional stochastic differential equations useful to model activity of the neuronal membrane voltage subject to a correlated input. We give the explicit expression of the solution processes. In particular, we develop the calculation of the covariance of the neuronal process and we provide numerical evaluations for different values of specified parameters. We show that the different time-scales adopted for the involved dynamics and the correlation in the input process affect the behavior of the covariance of the resulting process. In this sense, the proposed model is able to preserve memory effects.

Keywords: Fractional Caputo derivative · Fractional differential equations · Covariance · Leaky Integrate-and-fire neuronal model

1 Introduction

The fractional version of the stochastic Leake Integrate-and-Fire (sLIF) model for neuronal dynamics ([7,18]) is considered by substituting the well-known fractional Caputo-derivative to the classical derivative. The main advantage of a such mathematical generalization of the sLIF model is that it makes possible to adopt a different time-scale. Indeed, the fractional derivative depends of an fractional order $\alpha \in (0, 1]$: for $\alpha = 1$, we recover the classical (integer) case; for positive α but less than 1, we will be integrate the process on a finer time-scale or equivalently on a dilation of the time, in some sense. By means of statistical techniques applied to available data, it is possible to obtain useful estimates for tuning the values of fractional order α. As an addition feature of a such approach, we remark also that the non-local fractional derivative constitutes the suitable differential operator for describing dynamics with memory effects.

Furthermore, we consider the phenomenological requirement to insert a correlated input in the neuronal model. This was consider previously ([6,13]) by

E. Pirozzi is member of the Gruppo Nazionale Calcolo Scientifico - Istituto Nazionale di Alta Matematica (GNCS-INdAM).

A. Quesada-Arencibia et al. (Eds.): EUROCAST 2024, LNCS 15174, pp. 243–251, 2025.
https://doi.org/10.1007/978-3-031-83885-9_22

substituting a "colored"noise in place of the usual delta-correlated white noise. Moreover, a fractional stochastic correlated input can also be considered.

Specifically, as in [15], we consider the two following stochastic equations for the stochastic process $V(t)$ describing the membrane voltage of the neuron and for the stochastic input $\eta(t), \forall t > 0$:

$$\mathcal{D}^{\alpha}V(t) = F(t, V(t), V_L) + \sigma\eta(t), \qquad V(0) = V_0, \tag{1}$$

$$\mathcal{D}^{\beta}\eta(t) = G(t, \eta, I) \quad + \gamma dW(t), \qquad \eta(0) = \eta_0, \tag{2}$$

with $\alpha, \beta \in (0, 1]$. Here, $\mathcal{D}^{\nu}$ is the fractional Caputo derivative ([3,17]) with $\nu = \alpha, \beta \in (0, 1]$, respectively. Here, V_L stand for the resting value of V, and I is the term of a synaptic or other injected current.

Such a model allows to describe the neuronal dynamics by means of an α-fractional stochastic process $V(t)$ obtained as the fractional integral of a β-fractional stochastic correlated input $\eta(t)$.

Such approach was born in [14] and it was developed in [15]. In the previous works, mathematical assumptions under which the existence of solutions is guaranteed ([2]) was verified.

Here, we focus on the fractional neuronal model based on Eqs. (1)-(2) with $\alpha \in (0, 1]$ and $\beta = 1$. For this specific model we determine an more explicit expression for the covariance of the modeling process and we give numerical evaluations of such covariance in order to show its graphical behavior, suitable to be studied and compared by varying some involved parameters. In the last section devoted to the numerical evaluations we show some graphical results and we give comparative comments.

We finally remark that the proposed model and its detailed study allows to adopt some existing simulation techniques (like those in [1,10]), but also to specialize other algorithms based on Euler-Maruyama schemes for stochastic fractional differential equation (as in [8]). The simulations of such processes is mainly oriented to provide estimations of the firing times (first passage times through a given boundary) that is the mechanism triggering the information transmission between neurons. (This work will be the object of a future paper.)

2 The Fractional Stochastic Differential Model

We essentially focus on the system of two fractional SDEs as in the model (1)-(2), for $\alpha \in (0, 1)$ and $\beta = 1$. Specifically, we set in (1) and in (2)

$$F(t, V(t), V_L) = -\frac{g_L}{C_m}[V(t) - V_L], \quad \sigma = 1/C_m,$$

$$G(t, \eta, I) = -\frac{\eta(t) - I}{\tau}, \quad \gamma = \varsigma/\tau,$$

respectively. This is the case of a neuronal model with the so-called leakage, similarly to the classical a LIF model. Hence, we have to study the following system:

$$\mathcal{D}^{\alpha}V(t) = -\frac{g_L}{C_m}[V(t) - V_L] + \frac{\eta(t)}{C_m}, \quad V(0) = V_0 \tag{3}$$

$$d\eta(t) = -\frac{\eta(t) - I}{\tau}dt + \frac{\varsigma}{\tau}dW(t), \quad \eta(0) = \eta_0. \tag{4}$$

This can be viewed as a generalization of *the classical stochastic LIF model* based on the stochastic Langevin equation ([7]):

$$dV(t) = -\frac{g_L}{C_m}[V(t) - V_L]dt + \frac{1}{C_m}dW, \qquad V(0) = V_0, \forall t > 0, \tag{5}$$

in which the fractional Caputo derivative takes the place of the classical one (see, also [18]) at the LHS of (5) and the process $\eta(t)$ is in place of dW. The last change implies that a fractional integral of the process $\eta(t)$ will have considered in place of the Itô integral, in order to determine the solution process. Moreover, the process $\eta(t)$, solution of the Eq. (4), is a stochastic model for a correlated input.

The stochastic process $V(t)$ models the voltage of the neuronal membrane, in correspondence to the following functions and parameters and their physical meanings: C_m the membrane capacitance, g_L the leak conductance, V_L the "resting" value of potential, $dW(t)$ the white noise (with $W(t)$ a standard Brownian motion (BM)), ς the intensity (or amplitude) of the noise and τ is related to the characteristic decaying time of the process towards its asymptotic mean.

About the Mathematical Resolution of the Involved Equations. In particular, for the specified involved functions, we note that Eq. (3) is a stochastic version of no-homogeneous linear fractional differential equation (FDe) on the bounded interval $[0, T]$:

$$\mathcal{D}^{\alpha}y(t) = Ay(t) + B(t), \quad y(0) = y_0 \tag{6}$$

where $T > 0$ is a positive real number, $y(t)$ a function of $C^1([0, T])$, A, $B(t)$ measurable and bounded real-valued functions on $[0, T]$ and $\mathcal{D}^{\alpha}$ is the Caputo derivative ([3,16]), i.e. for $\alpha \in (0, 1)$, $\mathcal{D}^{\alpha}$, for all $f \in C^1$, it is

$$\mathcal{D}^{\alpha}(f)(t) = \frac{1}{\Gamma(1-\alpha)}\int_0^t (t-s)^{-\alpha} f'(s)ds. \tag{7}$$

Indeed, (3) is the same of (6) with

$$A = -\frac{g_L}{C_m}, \qquad B(t) = \frac{g_L V_L}{C_m} + \frac{\eta(t)}{C_m}.$$

Recalling Theorem 1 of [15], we know that the solution of (6) $\forall t$ in $[0, T]$ is:

$$y(t) = E_{\alpha}(t^{\alpha}A)y_0 + \int_0^t (t-s)^{\alpha-1}E_{\alpha,\alpha}\left((t-s)^{\alpha}A\right)B(s)ds, \tag{8}$$

with $E_{\alpha,\alpha}(z) = \sum_{k=0}^{\infty} \frac{z^k}{\Gamma(\alpha k+\alpha)}$ and $E_\alpha(z) = E_{\alpha,1}(z)$ Mittag-Leffler functions ([9]) (The proof of the cited theorem is in [12]).

We note that the case we are considering, i.e. the Eq. (3), is the stochastic version of FDe (6). Indeed, $B(t)$ is a stochastic process of a complete filtered probability space $(\Omega, \mathcal{F}, \{\mathcal{F}_t\}_{t\in[0,\infty)}, \mathbb{P})$ with a.s. Hölder continuous paths: $B(t)$ involves the $\eta(t)$ process, solution of (4).

About the Eq. (4) it is the integer version of (2), i.e. with $\beta = 1$, and it is a classical stochastic differential equation (SDE).

2.1 The Correlated Input Process

We firstly specify that $\eta(t)$, from the well-known SDE (4), is a non-stationary Gauss-Markov (GM) Ornstein-Uhlenbeck (OU) process ([7]). The process $\eta(t)$ has the following mean function

$$m(t) = I + e^{-t/\tau}(\eta_0 - I) \tag{9}$$

and covariance function

$$c(s,t) = \frac{\varsigma^2}{2\tau}\left(e^{-(t-s)/\tau} - e^{-(s+t)/\tau}\right), \; 0 \le s \le t. \tag{10}$$

Furthermore, it can be written as a Gauss-Markov process in terms of a standard BM process $W(t)$ with the transformed time $r(t)$, i.e.

$$\eta(t) = m(t) + h(t)W(r(t)) \tag{11}$$

with the positive increasing function $r(t) = \frac{k(t)}{h(t)}$, and functions $k(s)$, $h(t)$ are such that the covariance (10) can be factorized as $c(s,t) = k(s)h(t)$, due the Markov property. Hence, from (10), we have

$$k(t) = \frac{\varsigma}{2}\left(e^{t/\tau} - e^{-t/\tau}\right), \; h(t) = \frac{\varsigma}{\tau}e^{-t/\tau}. \tag{12}$$

Finally, an explicit form of $\eta(t)$ ([1,14]) is:

$$\eta(t) = I + e^{-t/\tau}(\eta_0 - I) + \frac{\varsigma}{\tau}e^{-t/\tau}W\left(\frac{1}{\tau}(e^{2t/\tau} - 1)\right) \tag{13}$$

from which it is possible to understand how the stochastic input process $\eta(t)$ depends, in particular, on its initial value and on the constant input current term I.

3 The Voltage Process $V(t)$

We apply Theorem 1 of [15] to Eq. (3) and by referring to [9,11,14,16], the process $V(t)$ can be specified as follows:

$$\begin{aligned} V(t) &= V_0 t^{\alpha-1} E_{\alpha,\alpha}\left(-\frac{g_L t^\alpha}{C_m}\right) \\ &+ \int_0^t \left[\frac{g_L V_L}{C_m} + \frac{\eta(s)}{C_m}\right](t-s)^{\alpha-1} E_{\alpha,\alpha}\left(-\frac{g_L (t-s)^\alpha}{C_m}\right) ds. \end{aligned} \tag{14}$$

The Eq. (14) is substantially obtained by applying a fractional integration involving a Mittag-Leffler function and the input process $\eta(t)$. Hence, from the explicit expression of $\eta(t)$ in (13), and setting $V_0 = 0$, we have a more explicit form of $V(t)$

$$V(t) = \int_0^t \left[\frac{g_L V_L}{C_m}\right] (t-s)^{\alpha-1} E_{\alpha,\alpha}\left(-\frac{g_L (t-s)^\alpha}{C_m}\right) ds \tag{15}$$

$$+\frac{1}{C_m}\int_0^t (t-s)^{\alpha-1} E_{\alpha,\alpha}\left(-\frac{g_L (t-s)^\alpha}{C_m}\right) \Big[I + e^{-s/\tau}(\eta_0 - I) + \frac{\varsigma}{\tau} e^{-s/\tau} W\left(\frac{1}{\tau}(e^{2s/\tau}-1)\right)\Big] ds. \tag{16}$$

The Gaussian process $V(t)$ (see, Theorem 4 in [5]) has mean function:

$$\begin{aligned}\mathbb{E}[V(t)] &= \frac{g_L V_L}{C_m}\int_0^t (t-s)^{\alpha-1} E_{\alpha,\alpha}\left(-\frac{g_L (t-s)^\alpha}{C_m}\right) ds \\ &+\frac{1}{C_m}\int_0^t m(s)(t-s)^{\alpha-1} E_{\alpha,\alpha}\left(-\frac{g_L (t-s)^\alpha}{C_m}\right) ds\end{aligned} \tag{17}$$

where $m(t)$ is the mean of $\eta(t)$ as specified in (9), from which the final explicit expression of the mean as function of the input is:

$$\begin{aligned}\mathbb{E}[V(t)] = \frac{g_L V_L}{C_m}\int_0^t (t-s)^{\alpha-1} E_{\alpha,\alpha}\left(-\frac{g_L (t-s)^\alpha}{C_m}\right) ds \\ +\frac{1}{C_m}\int_0^t \Big[I + e^{-s/\tau}(\eta_0 - I)\Big](t-s)^{\alpha-1} E_{\alpha,\alpha}\left(-\frac{g_L (t-s)^\alpha}{C_m}\right) ds.\end{aligned} \tag{18}$$

In the last provided expression for the mean function of $V(t)$ it is evident the dependence on the magnitude of the input current term I and also on the decaying time parameter τ whose value is directly involved in the long/short effect in time of the input process.

3.1 The Covariance of $V(t)$

From (14) we understand that the covariance function of $V(t)$

$$Cov[V(u), V(t)]$$

is obtained from

$$\begin{aligned}\mathbb{E}\Big\{\Big[\textstyle\int_0^u \left[\frac{\eta(s)}{C_m}\right] (u-s)^{\alpha-1} E_{\alpha,\alpha}\left(-\frac{g_L (u-s)^\alpha}{C_m}\right) ds\Big] \\ \times \Big[\textstyle\int_0^t \left[\frac{\eta(v)}{C_m}\right] (t-v)^{\alpha-1} E_{\alpha,\alpha}\left(-\frac{g_L (t-v)^\alpha}{C_m}\right) dv\Big]\Big\}.\end{aligned} \tag{19}$$

Moreover, from (16) we can put in evidence the stochastic terms that contributes to the calculus of the covariance of $V(t)$, that are specifically due to the Brownian motion terms in a transformed time. Indeed, (11) with $r(t) = \frac{1}{\tau}(e^{2t/\tau} - 1)$, we have that

$$\eta(t) = m(t) + \left[\frac{\varsigma}{\tau}e^{-t/\tau}\right] W\left(\frac{1}{\tau}(e^{2t/\tau} - 1)\right) \tag{20}$$

that, by substituting it in (19), allows us to write, for $0 \leq u \leq t$,

$$\begin{aligned} &Cov[V(u), V(t)] \\ &= \frac{\varsigma^2}{\tau^2 C_m^2} \mathbb{E}\left\{\left[\int_0^u (u-s)^{\alpha-1} E_{\alpha,\alpha}\left(-\frac{g_L(u-s)^\alpha}{C_m}\right) e^{-s/\tau} W\left(\frac{1}{\tau}(e^{2s/\tau} - 1)\right) ds\right]\right. \\ &\times \left.\left[\int_0^t (t-v)^{\alpha-1} E_{\alpha,\alpha}\left(-\frac{g_L(t-v)^\alpha}{C_m}\right) e^{-v/\tau} W\left(\frac{1}{\tau}(e^{2v/\tau} - 1)\right) dv\right]\right\}. \end{aligned} \tag{21}$$

By proceeding in the calculation of the covariance, by taking into account that the covariance of the Brownian motion is such that $cov(W(s)W(v)) = \min\{s, v\}$, and by denoting

$$\hat{E}_{\alpha,\alpha}(x, y) = E_{\alpha,\alpha}\left(-\frac{g_L(x-y)^\alpha}{C_m}\right),$$

we have that the covariance can be written as the sum involving the following three terms:

$$\begin{aligned} I_1 &= \int_0^u ds \int_0^s dv (u-s)^{\alpha-1}(t-v)^{\alpha-1}\hat{E}_{\alpha,\alpha}(u,s)\hat{E}_{\alpha,\alpha}(t,v)e^{-s/\tau}\tfrac{1}{\tau}(e^{v/\tau} - e^{-v/\tau}) \\ I_2 &= \int_0^u ds \int_s^u dv (u-s)^{\alpha-1}(t-v)^{\alpha-1}\hat{E}_{\alpha,\alpha}(u,s)\hat{E}_{\alpha,\alpha}(t,v)e^{-v/\tau}\tfrac{1}{\tau}(e^{s/\tau} - e^{-s/\tau}) \\ I_3 &= \int_0^u ds \int_u^t dv (u-s)^{\alpha-1}(t-v)^{\alpha-1}\hat{E}_{\alpha,\alpha}(u,s)\hat{E}_{\alpha,\alpha}(t,v)e^{-v/\tau}\tfrac{1}{\tau}(e^{s/\tau} - e^{-s/\tau}). \end{aligned} \tag{22}$$

Hence, finally one has

$$Cov[V(u), V(t)] = \frac{\varsigma^2}{\tau^2 C_m^2}(I_1 + I_2 + I_3). \tag{23}$$

3.2 Numerical Evaluations

In order to study the behavior of the covariance by varying the the fractional order α of the modeling process V and by varying the τ parameter of the input process η, we numerically evaluate the covariance (23) by means of the integrals (22) and we plot the obtained results for graphical comparisons.
Similarly in [4,15], we adopt the following choices for parameters:
and we choose different values for α, as done in Figs. 1 and 2. Then, we choose different values for τ when we set $\alpha = 0.7$ and $\alpha = 0.99$, as done in Fig. 3, on left and on right, respectively.

Membrane capacitance:	$C_m = 1\mu\text{F}$
Resting membrane potential:	$V_L = -0.1\,\text{mV}$
Initial membrane potential:	$V_0 = 0\,\text{mV}$
Leak conductance:	$g_L = 0.1\,\text{mS}$
Characteristic time of the membrane:	$C_m/g_L = 10\,\text{ms}$
Initial input value:	$\eta_0 = 0\,\text{nA}$
Input characteristic time:	$\tau = 5\,\text{ms}$
Constant current:	$I = 0.01\,\text{nA}$
Intensity parameter:	$\varsigma^2 = 1\,\text{nA}^2\text{ms}$
Fractional order for the input:	$\beta = 1$

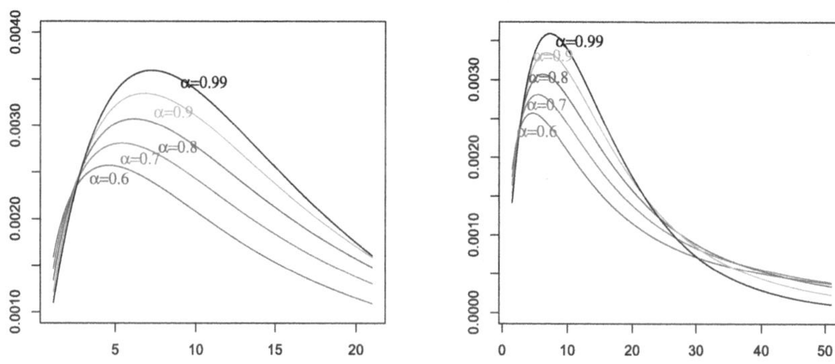

Fig. 1. Plot of covariance (23) for different values of α as indicated in the figure. Here, $u = 1$ and $t > u$. On the left $t \in (u, 20)$, on the right $t \in (u, 50)$. All other parameters are set as specified in the text.

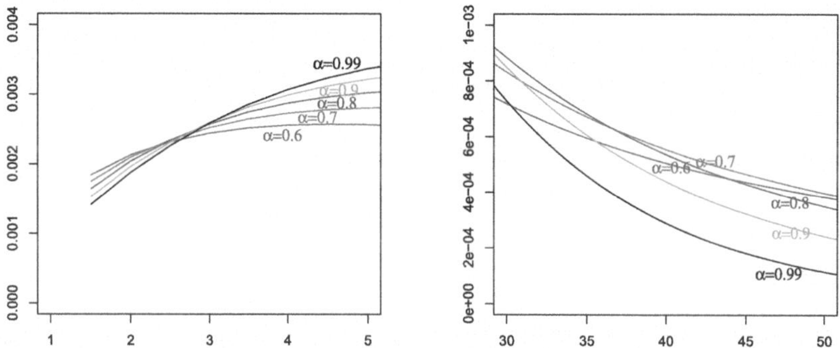

Fig. 2. Zoom of the plot of the covariance (23) as in Fig. 1, with $u = 1$ and $t > u$. On the left $t \in (u, 5)$, on the right $t \in (30, 50)$. All other parameters are set as specified in the text.

By focusing on left of Fig. 1, we can see the higher value of α the higher the value of covariance function. We plot also the numerical evaluation R-code for long times, as in the right of Fig. 1. After a careful study, we understand that the increasing values of the covariance corresponding to increasing values of α appear only in a specific period of time, because we note that initially (see Fig. 2 left) and also for large times (on the tails of the covariances, see Fig. 2 right) an opposite behavior appears. Indeed, we can say that a long-range dependence of the covariance function of $V(t)$ turns out more and more evident as α decreases.

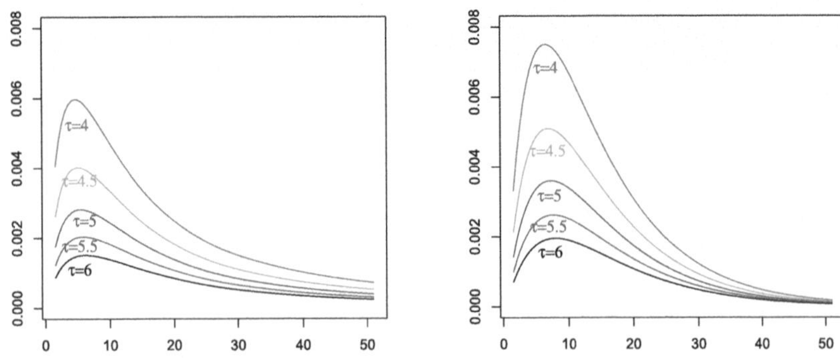

Fig. 3. Plot of the covariance (23) for different values of τ, with $u = 1$ and $t > u$. On the left $\alpha = 0.7$, on the right $\alpha = 0.99$. All other parameters are set as specified in the text.

In Fig. 3 the sensitivity of the covariance to the value of τ appears evident. The covariance shows high values in correspondence to low values of τ. This happens for different values of α, even if the heavy tails are visible for $\alpha = 0.7$ (on the left of Fig. 3), whereas they disappear for $\alpha = 0.99$ (on the right of Fig. 3).

Acknowledgments. This study was partially funded by the projects PRIN2022-MUR 2022XZSAFN and PRIN-PNRR P2022XSF5H.

Disclosure of Interests. The author has no competing interests to declare that are relevant to the content of this article.

References

1. Abundo M., Pirozzi E., Abundo, M., Pirozzi, E.: Fractionally integrated Gauss-Markov processes and applications. Commun. Nonlinear Sci. Num. Simul. **101**, 105862 (2021). ISSN 1007-5704
2. Anh, P.T., Doan, T.S., Huong, P.T.: A variation of constant formula for Caputo fractional stochastic differential equations. Statist. Probab. Lett. **145**, 351–358 (2019)
3. Ascione, G., Mishura, Y., Pirozzi. E.: Fractional Deterministic and Stochastic Calculus. De Gruyter (2024)
4. Ascione, G., Pirozzi, E.: On a stochastic neuronal model integrating correlated inputs. Math. Biosci. Eng. **16**(5), 5206–5225 (2019)

5. Ascione, G., Pirozzi, E.: Generalized fractional calculus for Gompertz-type models. Mathematics **9**, 2140 (2021)
6. Bazzani, A., Bassi, G., Turchetti, G.: Diffusion and memory effects for stochastic processes and fractional Langevin equations. Phys. A Stat. Mech. Appl. **324**, 530–550 (2003)
7. Burkitt, A.N.: A review of the integrate-and-fire neuron model: I. Homogeneous synaptic input, Biol. Cybern. (2006). https://doi.org/10.1007/s00422-006-0068-6
8. Doan, T.S., Huong, P.T., Kloeden, P.E., Vu, A.M.: Euler-maruyama scheme for Caputo stochastic fractional differential equations. J. Comput. Appl. Math. **380**, 112989 (2020)
9. Garrappa, R., Kaslik, E., Popolizio, M.: Evaluation of fractional integrals and derivatives of elementary functions: overview and tutorial. Mathematics **7**, 407 (2019). https://doi.org/10.3390/math7050407
10. Haugh, M.: Generating Random Variables and Stochastic Processes. Columbia University, Monte Carlo Simulation (2017)
11. Kazem S.: Exact solution of some linear fractional differential equation by laplace transform. Int. J. Nonlinear Sci. **16**(1), 3–11 (2013)
12. Li, K., Peng, J.: Laplace transform and fractional differential equations. Appl. Math. Lett. **24**, 2019–2023 (2011)
13. Pirozzi, E.: Colored noise and a stochastic fractional model for correlated inputs and adaptation in neuronal firing. Biol. Cybern. **112**(1–2), 25–39 (2018)
14. Pirozzi, E.: On the integration of fractional neuronal dynamics driven by correlated processes. In: Moreno-Díaz, R., Pichler, F., Quesada-Arencibia, A. (eds.) EUROCAST 2019. LNCS, vol. 12013, pp. 211–219. Springer, Cham (2020). https://doi.org/10.1007/978-3-030-45093-9_26
15. Pirozzi, E.: Some fractional stochastic models for neuronal activity with different time-scales and correlated inputs. Fractal Fract. **8**, 57 (2024). https://doi.org/10.3390/fractalfract8010057
16. Podlubny, I.: Fractional Differential Equations. Academic Press, New York (1999)
17. Samko S.G., Kilbas A.A., Marichev O.I.: Fractional Integrals and Derivatives: Theory and Applications, Gordon and Breach Science Publishers (1993)
18. Teka W., Marinov T.M., Santamaria F.: Neuronal spike timing adaptation described with a fractional leaky integrate-and-fire model. PLoS Comput. Biol. **10**, e1003526 (2014)

Handling Uncertainties on the Right-Hand Side of a Classical Transportation Model by Stochastic Optimisation and a Matheuristic Approach

Abtin Nourmohammadzadeh[1(✉)] and Stefan Voß[1,2]

[1] Institute of Information Systems, University of Hamburg, Hamburg, Germany
{abtin.nourmohammadzadeh,stefan.voss}@uni-hamburg.de
[2] Escuela de Ingenieria Industrial, Pontificia Universidad Católica de Valparaíso, Valparaíso, Chile
stefan.voss@pucv.cl

Abstract. The classical transportation problem (TP), which entails the allocation of a (set of) product (products) from multiple origins to multiple destinations at the minimal feasible expense, encompasses a broad spectrum of significant transportation and industrial problems in reality. Within real-world scenarios, the supply capacities of goods at origins and the demands of goods at destinations are subject to variability and may be influenced by various internal and external factors. In this study, we develop a stochastic optimisation model for the classical TP that accounts for multiple types of products and uncertainty in both supply and demand quantities. This model includes uncertainties located on the right-hand side (RHS), making it a special type of stochastic models. To address this ensuing intricate problem, a matheuristic algorithm is constructed, composed of ideas from variable neighbourhood search (VNS), fixed set search (FSS), and partial mathematical optimisation. This algorithm demonstrates notable efficiency when compared to some alternative methodologies.

Keywords: Berth and Quay Crane Assignment · Robust Optimisation · Right-Hand-Side Uncertainty · Matheuristics · Variable Neighbourhood Search · Fixed Set Search

1 Introduction

The classical transportation problem (TP) is a cornerstone of operational research, dealing with the optimal distribution of products from multiple sources to various destinations at the minimum possible cost. The fundamental elements of the TP include sources, where goods are produced (e.g., factories); destinations, where goods are needed (e.g., warehouses); and costs, the expense of transporting goods from any source to any destination.

A. Quesada-Arencibia et al. (Eds.): EUROCAST 2024, LNCS 15174, pp. 252–267, 2025.
https://doi.org/10.1007/978-3-031-83885-9_23

Figure 1 illustrates a simple transportation network existing in the TP. In this network, sources S_1 and S_2 produce goods that need to be transported to destinations D_1 and D_2. The costs c_{ij} represent the transportation costs from source S_i to destination D_j.

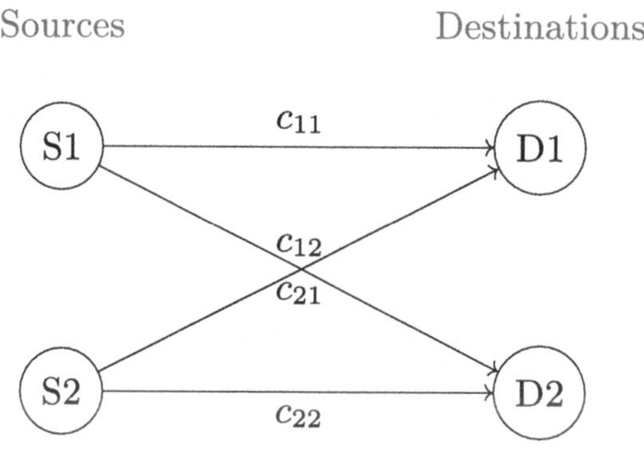

Fig. 1. TP network

Researching this problem is critical due to its wide range of real-world applications, including logistics management, supply chain optimisation, resource distribution in disaster management, and workforce allocation. In logistics management, for example, efficient transportation strategies can significantly reduce costs and improve service levels. In supply chain optimisation, the TP helps in minimising the total operational cost while ensuring timely delivery of goods. Resource distribution in disaster management relies on efficient allocation to ensure that aid reaches the affected areas swiftly and efficiently. Workforce allocation similarly benefits from optimised distribution to meet varying demands across locations.

The classical TP with one product and deterministic parameters can be formulated as a linear programming (LP) problem. Solving this using exact solvers such as CPLEX or GUROBI is feasible and typically has polynomial-time complexity relative to the size of the network. However, real-world scenarios often involve uncertainties. Production capacities at sources and demands at destinations can fluctuate due to numerous factors, such as economic conditions, natural disasters, and market demands.

When dealing with multiple products and stochastic supply and demand, the problem complexity increases significantly. This version of the TP includes a larger number of variables and constraint blocks, various possible scenarios and their combinations, and the objective to minimise not just the cost but also to consider risk or uncertainty in the decisions. This elevated complexity makes the solution of TPs impossible by an available exact solver within a practical timeframe. Some examples of challenges with intricacies of stochastic TPs are addressed in [5,25] and [22].

The extended TP addressed in this paper incorporates uncertainties in the right-hand side (RHS) of some constraints, where parameters are not fixed but have possible scenarios or values with a probability corresponding to each. This stochastic model has not been extensively studied in the literature, yet our main contribution is to delve deeper into the characteristics of RHS uncertainty in the TP. The importance of researching RHS uncertainty includes ensuring feasibility under different scenarios, enhancing flexibility to adapt to unexpected changes, improving cost efficiency by planning for contingencies, and supporting better decision making by factoring in risk and providing a range of options.

To manage these uncertainties, various optimisation methods can be employed, including:

- Stochastic Programming [26]: Utilises probability distributions for RHS parameters to generate solutions that are optimal on average.
- Chance-Constrained Programming [20]: Ensures constraints are satisfied with a certain probability, thus guaranteeing reliability.
- Robust Optimisation [3]: Develops solutions that are resilient to uncertainty within predefined limits, without relying on probabilistic information.

In our approach, we use stochastic optimisation due to its ability to handle scenarios based on corresponding probabilities, acknowledging that some values for uncertain parameters are more likely than others. We aim to minimise the average objective value across all scenarios. Given the complexity of this problem, we employ a matheuristic optimisation approach combining ideas from variable neighbourhood search (VNS) [8], fixed set search (FSS) [13], and partial mathematical optimisation. VNS and FSS are adept at exploring and improving solutions, avoiding local optima, while mathematical programming optimises parts of the solution, leveraging exact solvers where solving the entire problem directly is impractical.

Our algorithm is benchmarked against various metaheuristic and matheuristic alternatives and a state-of-art method from the literature which has been proved to be superior to some commonly used conventional methods.

The remainder of this paper is organised as follows: Sect. 2 provides a background on the TP and optimisation under RHS uncertainty. Section 3 describes the problem and its stochastic modelling. The solution approach is detailed in Sect. 4. Section 5 presents the results from extensive computational experiments and comparisons. Finally, Sect. 6 draws overall conclusions and suggests potential directions for future research.

2 Background

The classical transportation problem (TP) is a fundamental optimisation issue in operational research, initially formulated by [10] and later refined by [15].

[12] discusses the impact of variations in requirements and prices on TPs, and similarly, [2] addresses the challenges of performing sensitivity analysis on TPs by introducing a parametric analysis approach. A stochastic TP is discussed

in [25] and suggests a method to handle it by a transformation into a more manageable mathematical optimisation framework. [16] identifies shortcomings in existing methods for solving unbalanced fully fuzzy TPs and proposes two new methods that use LR flat fuzzy numbers to achieve exact fuzzy optimal solutions, demonstrating their superiority through comparative problem-solving examples.

Several recent significant contributions have shaped the landscape of research and practice. [1] explores various alternative algorithms for solving the classical TP, providing easy-to-understand reformulations and comparisons that yield either close-to-optimal or optimal solutions directly through illustrative examples. In [11], an amendment to Vogel's approximation method (VAM) for finding the initial basic feasible solution of the TP is suggested, which is iterative and provides results close to or equal to an optimal solution, demonstrating superior efficiency and effectiveness through numerical comparisons with classical methods. [27] introduces a technique tailored to maximise objectives, surpassing the performance of three established classical methods.

It should be noted that the classical TP is "easy". However, to the best of our knowledge, the application of RHS uncertainty in the classical TP has remained unexplored and makes the problem more complex. Its significance has been noted in various practical scenarios of importance. A study by [19] introduces a robust optimisation framework incorporating RHS uncertainties for the bus driver rostering problem. This framework is further tackled using a matheuristic approach inspired by the concept of partial metaheuristic optimisation under special intensification conditions (POPMUSIC) [23]. The work of [14] delves into maximising monotone sub-modular functions within the realm of an uncertain knapsack problem. Meanwhile, [21] directs attention towards a bi-level knapsack problem involving stochastic RHSs, employing mathematical modelling methodologies. Within the domain of optimisation under RHS uncertainty, seminal contributions are made by [17] and [18], focusing on the investigation of 2-stage robust linear programming issues with RHS uncertainty and examining the intricacies and practical implications of the same, respectively. Nevertheless, current research on this topic is scarce and even modern generative artificial intelligence tools have difficulties to find further entries [24].

In summary, an analysis of the two fields reveals a promising avenue for addressing the research gap pertaining to the absence of studies on a TP involving multiple goods and uncertain supplies and demands.

3 Problem Description and Modelling

The classical transportation problem is a linear programming problem used to minimise the cost of transporting a certain quantity of some products (P is the set of products) from multiple suppliers (I is the set of suppliers) to multiple consumers (J is the set of consumers). $x_{pij} \geq 0$ is the quantity of product p to be transported from supplier i to consumer j. c_{pij} is the cost of transporting one unit of product p from supplier i to consumer j. s_{pi} is the supply capacity of supplier i for product p and d_{jp} is the demand of consumer j for product p. The mathematical model of the problem is as follows:

$$Z = \sum_{p \in P} \sum_{i \in I} \sum_{j \in J} c_{pij} x_{pij} \tag{1}$$

$$\sum_{j \in J} x_{pij} \leq \boldsymbol{s_{pi}} \qquad \forall p \in P; i \in I \tag{2}$$

$$\sum_{i \in I} x_{pij} \geq \boldsymbol{d_{pj}} \qquad \forall p \in P; j \in J \tag{3}$$

$$x_{pij} \geq 0 \qquad \forall p \in P; i, j \in J \tag{4}$$

(1) is the objective function, which seeks to minimise the total transportation costs pertaining to the delivery of all product units from their suppliers to their consumers. Constraint (2) ensures that the total amount of each product supplied from each supplier does not exceed its capacity. Consequently, constraint (3) guarantees that the total consumer demand for each product is satisfied. The feasible domain of decision variables x_{pij} is implied by (4).

In reality, the capacity of suppliers may fluctuate due to production or product availability issues, and consumer demand can vary for various reasons. Therefore, we treat these two RHS parameters, i.e. s_{pi} and d_{pj} (highlighted in bold), for all products, suppliers and consumers as non-deterministic. For each of these parameters, we consider several possible values with their corresponding probability and use a stochastic optimisation approach. The probabilities are distributed such that the highest probability is found at the median, with probabilities decreasing as we move away from it in both directions.

To integrate the RHS uncertainties into the model, the approach involves solving the model for each potential scenario, accounting for all combinations of the possible s_{pi} and d_{pj} values. In order to incorporate the likelihood of each scenario, the objective function considers the probabilities linked to every possible value of s_{pi} and d_{pi}. Given that the problem is framed as minimisation, scenarios with higher probabilities should enhance the objective outcome, while those with lower probabilities should deteriorate it. Hence, the probability of a scenario exerts an opposing influence on the objective function value. In the context of stochastic programming, the aim is to find a comprehensive solution that minimises the objective value across all scenarios and their associated probabilities. Each specific scenario $scen$ involves solving a model, called $Model_{scen}$, where $Scen$ is the set of all scenarios:

$\boldsymbol{Model_{scen}} \qquad scen \in Scen$

$$\min Z_{scen} = \sum_{i=1}^{m}\sum_{j=1}^{n} R_{s_{pi(scen)}} R_{d_{pj(scen)}} c_{pij} x_{pij} \tag{5}$$

$$\sum_{j=1}^{n} x_{pij} \leq s_{pi(scen)} \qquad \forall i \in I \tag{6}$$

$$\sum_{j=1}^{n} x_{pij} \geq d_{pi(scen)} \qquad \forall j \in J \tag{7}$$

$$R_{s_{pi(scen)}} = \frac{1 - Pr_{s_{pi(scen)}}}{\sum_{s_{pi(se)}, se \in Scen} 1 - Pr_{s_{pi(se)}}} \tag{8}$$

$$R_{d_{pj(scen)}} = \frac{1 - Pr_{d_{pj(scen)}}}{\sum_{d_{pj(se)}, se \in Scen} 1 - Pr_{d_{pj(se)}}} \tag{9}$$

The objective function 5 operates to minimise the overall stochastic transportation costs by weighing them based on the inverse impact of the scenario's probability. Constraints 6 and 7 mirror their deterministic counterparts in the previous model, but now include the supply and demand values associated with *scen* on the RHS, denoted as $s_{pi(scen)}$ and $d_{pj(scen)}$, respectively. Equations 8 and 9 quantify the inverse effect of the probabilities corresponding to the specific supply and demand values in the scenario *scen*. $Pr_{s_{pi(scen)}}$ and $Pr_{d_{pj(scen)}}$ are the probabilities of the values $s_{pi(scen)}$ and $d_{pj(scen)}$ for the corresponding supply and demand.

After solving all the models, the optimal solution with the lowest objective value across all models is chosen as the most favourable outcome of this stochastic optimisation. In essence, a solution corresponding to $min_{se \in Scen} Z_{se}$ is the target.

4 Solution Approach

A matheuristic is formulated to address the issue at hand. Matheuristics combine (meta-)heuristics with mathematical programming methodologies, allowing for the utilisation of the advantages of both exact and heuristic approaches while maintaining a balance between solution quality and computational effectiveness. Matheuristics have the capability to discover high-quality solutions for combinatorial optimisation problems and are versatile in their applicability to a diverse array of optimisation problems, particularly those where conventional exact methods encounter difficulties.

The representation of a solution for our transportation problem involves an assortment of strings, each corresponding to a s_{pi}. An instance of a basic string for a specific $s_{pi} = 5$ is depicted in Fig. 2. In addition to the blue balls representing individual product units, (Nb. of consumers-1) red balls are included to distribute the resources among consumers (clients or destinations). Another crucial aspect of our problem concerns the fulfilment of demand constraints, which are managed by incorporating a penalty function that sums up the violations and multiplies the total amount by a substantial M value to the overall objective.

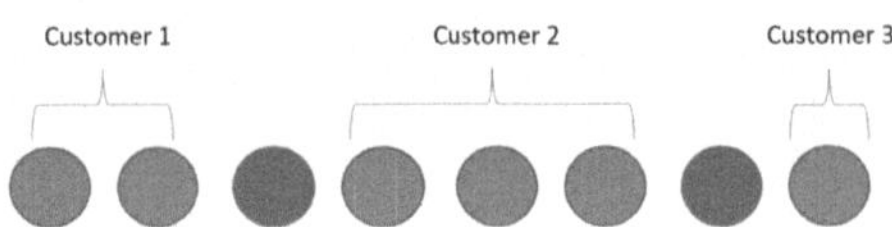

Fig. 2. Solution representation

At the onset of our algorithm, a stochastic population of PS solutions is generated randomly. Subsequently, the variable neighbourhood search (VNS) commences by conducting local explorations around each solution using 2-opt and 3-opt operators as illustrated in Fig. 3 and Fig. 4, respectively. The likelihood of either operator being applied is equivalent. In the 2-opt scenario, two segments of equal size within the solution are selected and their contents are interchanged, while in the 3-opt, three segments are chosen with content exchanges occurring between any pair of them. If an improved neighbouring solution (based on the objective function) is identified at any point, it replaces the current solution, and exploration continues from that new solution. Conversely, if no enhancements are observed after a series of local searches, a substantial portion of the solution is selected and substituted with another random permutation of its components (represented by blue or red balls). A simple instance of this process, which corresponds to the shaking phase in VNS, is depicted in Fig. 5.

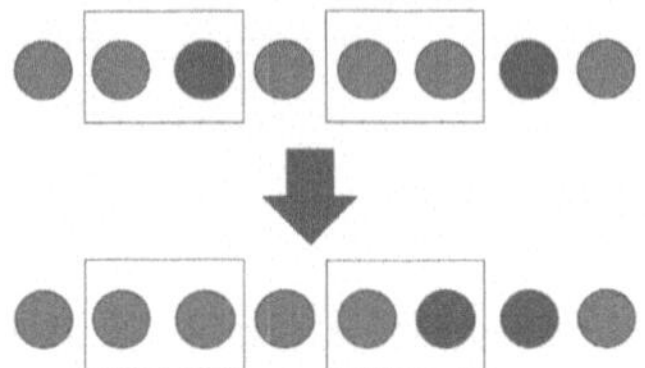

Fig. 3. 2-opt

From this point onwards, an idea motivated by the fixed set search (FSS) component of the algorithm is implemented. Within the FSS framework, a fixed-sized set (referred to as FS) of the best solutions is selected. These solutions

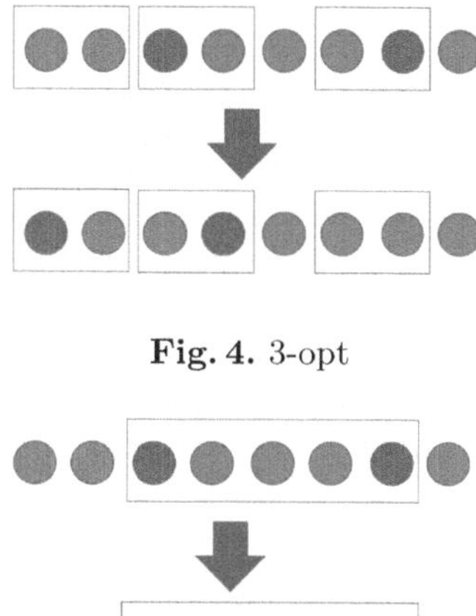

Fig. 4. 3-opt

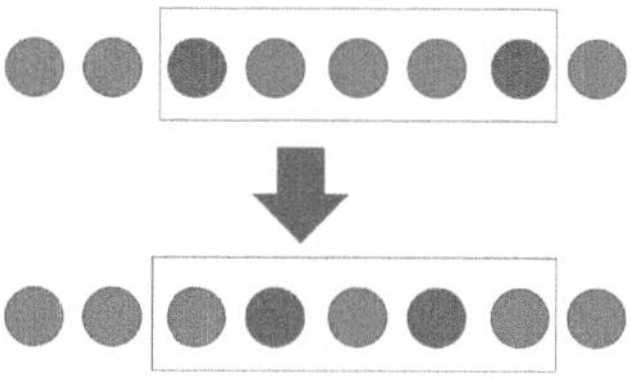

Fig. 5. Shaking

undergo pairwise crossovers (like in genetic algorithms [9]) as illustrated in Fig. 6. An integral aspect of our algorithm involves the random selection of certain solutions, with a quantity (ES) of decision variables being refined within the mathematical model by the solver. Given that the mathematical programming (MP) is restricted to a portion of the problem, the difficulties faced by the exact solver are considerably reduced, resulting in significantly shorter computational times compared to solving the entire model using the same approach. At the conclusion of each FSS iteration, the newly generated solutions from crossovers and mathematical programming are incorporated into the set, while inferior solutions are eliminated to maintain a consistent set size. With a constant set size always in place, the memory demands remain fixed, offering a distinct advantage that renders FSS suitable for addressing large-scale problems. Should no

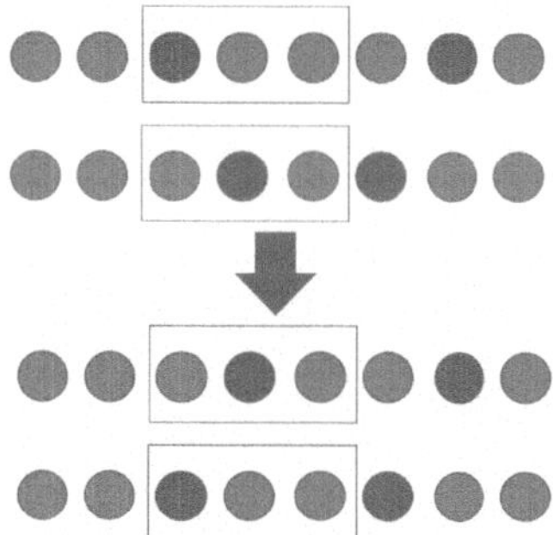

Fig. 6. Crossover

enhancements be observed following a series of successive iterations within FSS, this phase concludes, and the algorithm progresses to the subsequent iteration.

This matheuristic algorithm has several hyper-parameters in its VNS, FSS and MP part, which significantly effect its performance. These parameters are set in the beginning of its implementation by the response surface method (RSM). The algorithm persists in its iterative fashion until a specified limit on the number of consecutive iterations with no improvement in the objective value (stagnant iterations) is reached. Upon reaching this threshold, the algorithm ceases and the ultimate best solution is presented. The pseudocode outlining this algorithm is depicted in Algorithm 1.

Algorithm 1: Our Matheuristic Algorithm

```
Initialise the values of the algorithm's parameters by RSM.
Initialise a population of (PS) random solutions.
while The maximum number of stagnant consecutive iterations (ESIT) is not
  exceeded do
    Evaluate the solutions based on the objective value.
    Sort the solutions based on the objective value.
    Perform neighbourhood searches based on the two techniques.
    if The neighbouring solution has a lower objective value then
        Replace the current solution with the neighbouring solution.
    end
    if No better solution is found around a solution after a number of
      consecutive neighbour search attempts (NST) then
        Choose a large segment of the solution randomly and change the
        contents of that segment to other feasible values (shaking).
    end
    Choose a number (FS) of best solutions and put them into a fixed set.
    while The maximum number of stagnant consecutive iterations (FSIT) is
      not exceeded do
        Apply pairwise crossovers to a randomly chosen subset of the fixed set.
        Select some random solutions from the fixed set and optimise a random
        section comprising ES variables of them by mathematical programming.
        if The objective value is not improved after a number of consecutive
          mathematical optimisation attempts then
            Finish this action for that solution.
        end
    end
    Merge all generated solutions with the original population.
end
Report the final best solution.
```

5 Results

30 instances consisting of 3 to 15 suppliers, 10 to 200 consumers, and 1 to 10 products are randomly generated. Each instance is represented by three hyphen-separated values: Number of suppliers - Number of consumers - Number of products (product types). For example, 10-150-6 represents the instance with 10 suppliers, 150 consumers, and 6 products.

Within these instances, the variable c_{pij} is uniformly created within the range of 1 to 20. A total of 10 potential values are taken into account for s_{pi}, d_{pj} with a probability distribution illustrated in Fig. 7. This entails that a median value a is randomly generated for each parameter, with possible values spanning from $0.55a$ to $1.45a$, where the probabilities peak around the median and diminish as the distance from the median increases. The instances are categorised into small, medium, and large groups. Each group contains 10 instances.

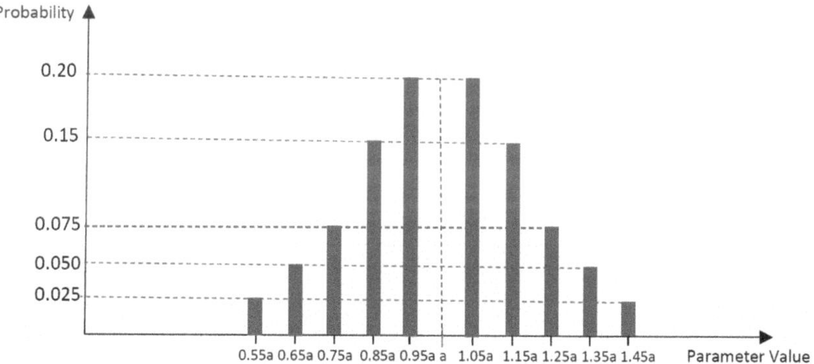

Fig. 7. The probability distribution of possible scenarios

In addition to the described matheuristic (denoted as OMM), we employ a pure mathematical programming (PMP), a pure genetic algorithm (PGA), a pure VNS (PVNS), and a genetic algorithm incorporating the same FSS as the MP (GAM). Pure means here that no other algorithm or component is combined with the method. The rationale behind comparing these algorithms with ours is to assess the efficiency and effectiveness of the components of our algorithm. This enables us to scrutinise the implications of removing or substituting a component with an alternative. In a final comparative assessment, our matheuristic is tested against a state-of-the-art method from the literature.

The parameter configuration is specifically tailored for small, medium, and large instances on a representative instance from the middle of each group.

The experiments are conducted on computers equipped with a Core(TM) i7 processor, 3.10 GHz CPU, and 16 GB of RAM. Python is utilised as the programming language, and Gurobi 11.0.1 [7] is employed as a standard exact solver. A time limit of 5 h is set for each run. Regarding metaheuristic and matheuristic approaches, 5 runs are performed for each instance, and their average outcome is considered, given the stochastic nature of these methods and the potential variability in results across runs.

Figures 8, 9, and 10 display the average objective values achieved by PMP, PGA, PVNS, GAM, and OMM (our matheuristic) algorithms depicted as bar charts for small, medium, and large instances, respectively. For the small instances, PMP provides the best average results. It is due to the fact that the Gurobi solver is able to find optimal or good-quality results in many cases. However, as the size of the problem increases, metaheuristics and matheuristics become more effective. Both metaheuristic approaches (PGA and PVNS) and matheuristic methods (GAM and OMM) exhibit superior performance than the pure MP (PMP). This disparity of PMP arises from the exact solver's inability to finish with optimal outcomes within the specified long time limit, leading to considerably weaker results. It is apparent that our algorithm demonstrates the lowest average objective value across all instances of the medium and large category. Notably, the VNS algorithm outperforms GA, whether utilised solely or within the matheuristic paradigm. This is evident from the superior outcomes of PVNS compared to PGA, as well as OMM vs. GAM. Additionally, the impact of the FSS and MP components becomes apparent when contrasting OMM with PVNS.

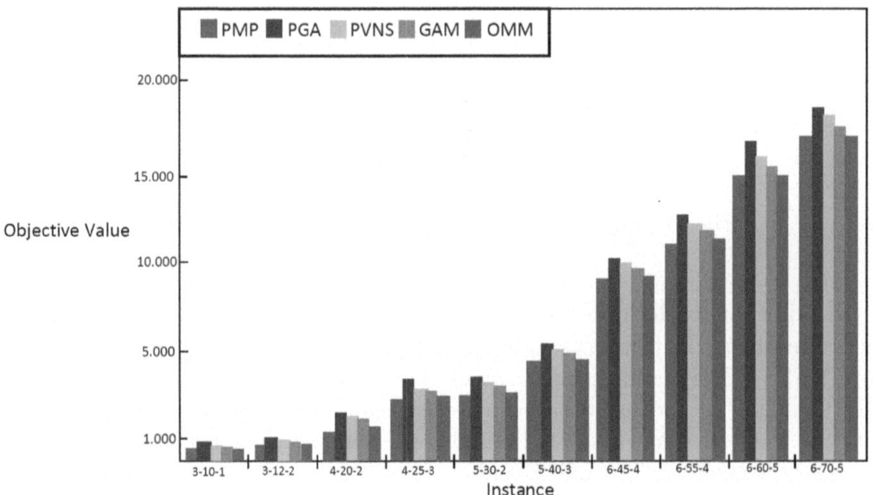

Fig. 8. The average objective values of the examined algorithms for small instances

Figure 11 illustrates the average execution times of the algorithms on all 30 instances collectively represented in a line graph. Owing to the lack of space, the instances are here denoted numerically from 1 to 30. Specifically, 1 corresponds to instance "3-10-1", 2 denotes "3-12-2", and so forth until 30, which signifies the

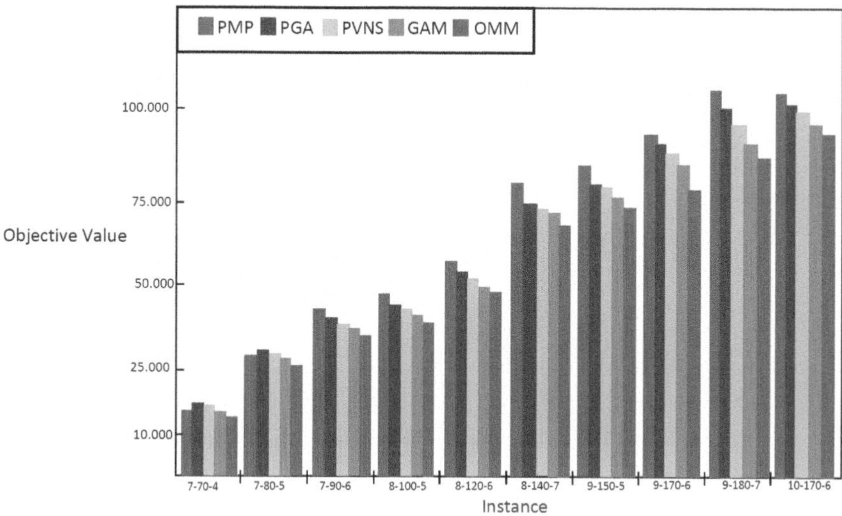

Fig. 9. The average objective values of the examined algorithms for medium instances

largest instance or "15-200-10". It is evident that the PMP cannot complete its optimisation process within the stipulated time from the 11th instance onwards (for medium and large instances). Therefore, its corresponding line stays constant on 5 h or 18,000 s (the predetermined time limit) from the 11th to the last instance. Notably, metaheuristics such as PGA and PVNS exhibit the shortest average execution times. Integrating MP into the metaheuristic to form a matheuristic is anticipated to lead to an increase in the respective average execution times. Nevertheless, this increment does not bother us, and the times remain practical. Furthermore, our matheuristic with VNS demonstrates a slight improvement in speed compared to its counterpart, which utilises a GA.

In the subsequent phase, our matheuristic is juxtaposed with a recent technique introduced in [27] (here referred to as STA), which works based on finding an appropriate initial solution. The assertion by the authors demonstrates the superiority of their methodology over several commonly used methods like the north-west corner method, least cost method, and Vogel's approximation method. This comparative analysis offers valuable insights into the performance of our matheuristic in relation to these aforementioned methods. While STA is specifically tailored for a type of TP with a maximisation objective in [27], there is an anticipation of its efficacy in addressing a classical type of TP with a minimisation objective. We have also undertaken the re-implementation of this methodology in Python. The graphical representation of this comparison pertaining to the mean objective values is depicted in Fig. 12.

Evidently, except for initial instances with limited scale, the average objective values achieved by our methodology surpasses those of STA. This observation

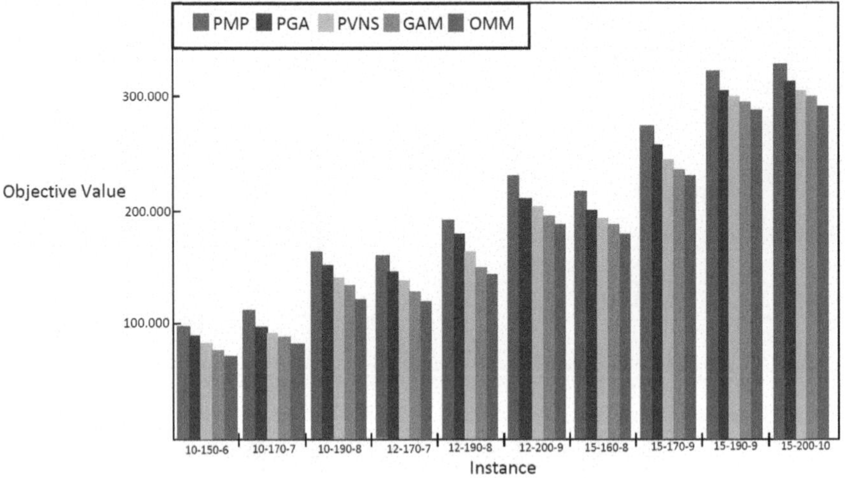

Fig. 10. The average objective values of the examined algorithms for large instances

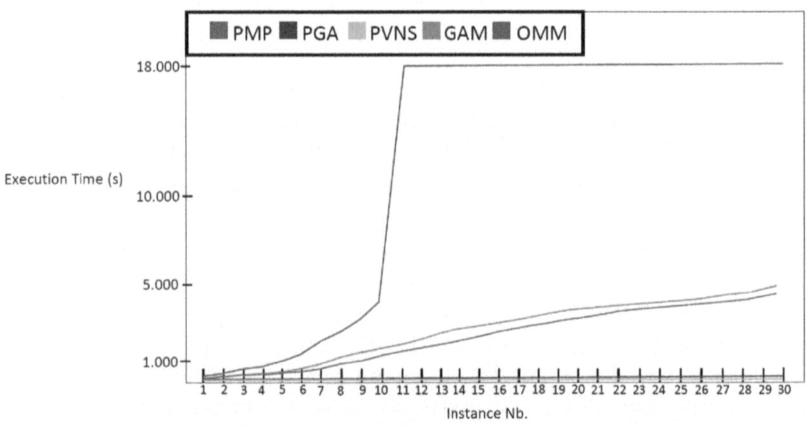

Fig. 11. The average execution time for instances

signifies the superior performance of our matheuristic compared to this recent method and the traditional approaches that it has already surpassed.

In the final phase of our computational investigation, a comprehensive comparison is conducted among the means of the objective values of the methodologies using a non-parametric Friedman test followed by the Bergmann-Hommel post-hoc procedure [4], a highly recommended approach for comparing multiple groups [6]. The notably low p-values resulting from the pairwise comparisons across all techniques lead to the rejection of the null hypothesis of equality at a significance level of $\alpha = 0.0001$. This unequivocally indicates the presence of statistically significant disparities in the average objective values between any pair of the methodologies.

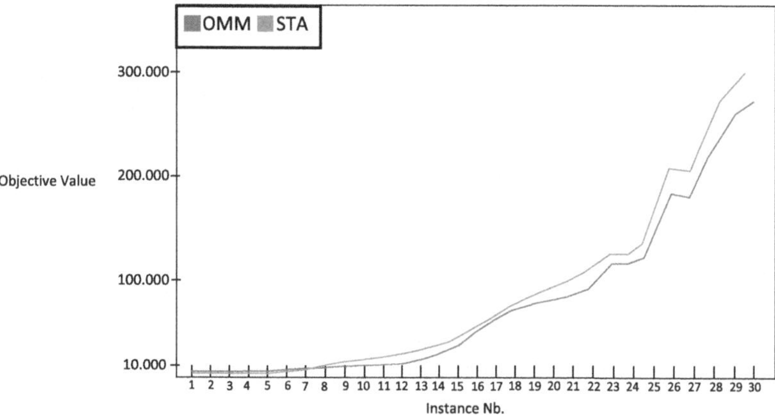

Fig. 12. The comparison of our approach to a state-of-the-art method from [27] (STA)

6 Conclusions

In this study, the classical transportation problem (TP) is examined in light of the actual presence of multiple types of products and variations in the quantities of supply and demand. The presented pragmatic model also incorporates uncertainties in its right hand side (RHS). Thus, this research delves into a significant classical problem within the field of operational research, characterised by uncertainties in the RHS and proposes an effective approach for obtaining good solutions. Additionally, our methodology can be extended to a broad range of real-world problems stemming from the TP.

Hence, a potential future research avenue can involve the application of our approach to analogous problems that may encompass a larger number of elements and possess increased complexity. The uncertainty related to cost values can also be examined concurrently with RHS uncertainties. Furthermore, exploring additional matheuristic principles is also a viable consideration.

Acknowledgments. This research is funded by dtec.bw – Digitisation and Technology Research Centre of the Bundeswehr. dtec.bw is funded by the European Union – NextGenerationEU.

References

1. Abdelati, M.H., Khalil, M.I., Abdelgawwad, K.A., Rabie, M.: Alternative algorithms for solving classical transportation problems. J. Adv. Eng. Trends **39**(1), 13–21 (2020). https://doi.org/10.21608/jaet.2020.73323
2. Arsham, H., Kahn, A.: A refined simplex algorithm for the classical transportation problem with application to parametric analysis. Math. Comput. Model. **12**(8), 1035–1044 (1989). https://doi.org/10.1016/0895-7177(89)90209-4

3. Ben-Tal, A., Nemirovski, A.: Robust solutions of uncertain linear programs. Oper. Res. Lett. **25**(1), 1–13 (1999). https://doi.org/10.1016/s0167-6377(99)00016-4
4. Bergmann, B., Hommel, G.: Improvements of general multiple test procedures for redundant systems of hypotheses. In: Bauer, P., Hommel, G., Sonnemann, E. (eds.) Multiple Hypothesenprüfung / Multiple Hypotheses Testing, pp. 100–115. Springer, Berlin, Heidelberg (1988). https://doi.org/10.1007/978-3-642-52307-6_8
5. Chen, A., Kim, J., Lee, S., Kim, Y.: Stochastic multi-objective models for network design problem. Expert Syst. Appl. **37**(2), 1608–1619 (2010). https://doi.org/10.1016/j.eswa.2009.06.048
6. Derrac, J., García, S., Molina, D., Herrera, F.: A practical tutorial on the use of nonparametric statistical tests as a methodology for comparing evolutionary and swarm intelligence algorithms. Swarm Evol. Comput. **1**(1), 3–18 (2011). https://doi.org/10.1016/j.swevo.2011.02.002
7. Gurobi Optimization, LLC: Gurobi Optimizer Reference Manual (2021). https://www.gurobi.com/?s=optimizer+reference+manual
8. Hansen, P., Mladenović, N., Pérez, J.: Variable neighbourhood search: methods and applications. 4OR **6**(4), 319–360 (2008). https://doi.org/10.1007/s10288-008-0089-1
9. Haupt, R.L., Haupt, S.E.: Practical Genetic Algorithms. Wiley (2003). https://doi.org/10.1002/0471671746
10. Hitchcock, F.L.: The distribution of a product from several sources to numerous localities. J. Math. Phys. **20**(1–4), 224–230 (1941). https://doi.org/10.1002/sapm1941201224
11. Hussein, H.A., Shiker, M.A.K., Zabiba, M.S.M.: A new revised efficient of VAM to find the initial solution for the transportation problem. J. Phys: Conf. Ser. **1591**(1), 012032 (2020). https://doi.org/10.1088/1742-6596/1591/1/012032
12. Intrator, J., Paroush, J.: Sensitivity analysis of the classical transportation problem. A combinatorial approach. Comput. Oper. Res. **4**(3), 213–226 (1977). https://doi.org/10.1016/0305-0548(77)90016-8
13. Jovanovic, R., Tuba, M., Voß, S.: Fixed set search applied to the traveling salesman problem. In: Blesa Aguilera, M.J., Blum, C., Gambini Santos, H., Pinacho-Davidson, P., Godoy del Campo, J. (eds.) HM 2019. LNCS, vol. 11299, pp. 63–77. Springer, Cham (2019). https://doi.org/10.1007/978-3-030-05983-5_5
14. Kawase, Y., Sumita, H., Fukunaga, T.: Submodular maximization with uncertain knapsack capacity. SIAM J. Discret. Math. **33**(3), 1121–1145 (2019). https://doi.org/10.1137/18m1174428
15. Koopmans, T.C.: Optimum utilization of the transportation system. Econometrica **17**, 136–146 (1949). https://doi.org/10.2307/1907301
16. Kumar, A., Kaur, A.: Application of classical transportation methods to find the fuzzy optimal solution of fuzzy transportation problems. Fuzzy Inf. Eng. **3**(1), 81–99 (2011). https://doi.org/10.1007/s12543-011-0068-7
17. Minoux, M.: On 2-stage robust LP with RHS uncertainty: complexity results and applications. J. Global Optim. **49**(3), 521–537 (2011). https://doi.org/10.1007/s10898-010-9645-2
18. Minoux, M.: Two-stage robust LP with ellipsoidal right-hand side uncertainty is NP-hard. Optim. Lett. **6**(7), 1463–1475 (2011). https://doi.org/10.1007/s11590-011-0341-z
19. Nourmohammadzadeh, A., Voß, S.: An effective matheuristic approach for robust bus driver rostering with uncertain daily working hours. In: LNCS, vol. 14239, pp. 365–380. Springer, Cham (2023). https://doi.org/10.1007/978-3-031-43612-3_23

20. Olson, D.L., Wu, D.: Chance constrained programming. In: Enterprise risk management models, pp. 143–157. Springer, Heidelberg (2010). https://doi.org/10.1007/978-3-642-11474-8_11
21. Özaltın, O.Y., Prokopyev, O.A., Schaefer, A.J.: The bilevel knapsack problem with stochastic right-hand sides. Oper. Res. Lett. **38**(4), 328–333 (2010). https://doi.org/10.1016/j.orl.2010.04.005
22. Singh, S., Pradhan, A., Biswal, M.P.: Computation of some stochastic transportation problems using Essen inequality. Int. J. Appl. Comput. Math. **7**(6), 1–26 (2021). https://doi.org/10.1007/s40819-021-01131-1
23. Taillard, É.D., Voss, S.: POPMUSIC — partial optimization metaheuristic under special intensification conditions. In: Ribeiro, C., Hansen, P. (eds.) Essays and Surveys in Metaheuristics, pp. 613–629. Springer, Boston (2002). https://doi.org/10.1007/978-1-4615-1507-4_27
24. Voß, S.: Successfully using ChatGPT in logistics: are we there yet? Lect. Notes Comput. Sci. **14239**, 3–17 (2023). https://doi.org/10.1007/978-3-031-43612-3_1
25. Williams, A.C.: A stochastic transportation problem. Oper. Res. **11**(5), 759–770 (1963). https://doi.org/10.1287/opre.11.5.759
26. Wilson, J.M.: Introduction to stochastic programming. J. Oper. Res. Soc. **49**(8), 897–898 (1998). https://doi.org/10.1057/palgrave.jors.2600031
27. Zabiba, M.S.M., Al-Dallal, H.A.H., Hashim, K.H., Mahdi, M.M., Shiker, M.A.K.: A new technique to solve the maximization of the transportation problems. In: AIP Conference Proceedings, vol. 2414, p. 040042. AIP Publishing (2023). https://doi.org/10.1063/5.0114806

Unified Formulations of Entropy and Extropy

Maria Longobardi(✉)

Università di Napoli Federico II, Naples, Italy
malongob@unina.it

Abstract. In the last decades the measures of uncertainty are of growing interest. Since there are many versions of entropy and of its dual version, unified formulations for entropy and extropy have been introduced to study their properties and to compare them.

Keywords: Shannon entropy · Dempster-Shafer Theory · Tsallis entropy · Fractional entropy · Extropy

1 A Unified Definition of Entropy in the Classical Theory

Let X be a discrete random variable with support S of cardinality N and with probability vector $(p_1, \ldots, p_N)$. Shannon [9] introduced a measure of uncertainty on X, known as Shannon entropy:

$$H(X) = -\sum_{i=1}^{N} p_i \log p_i, \tag{1}$$

where log denotes the natural logarithm. In the literature the paper of Shannon is a pioneering one: several papers have been written about measures of information in various contexts. Another well-known generalization of the Shannon entropy, is the Tsallis entropy defined in [10] as

$$S_\alpha(X) = \frac{1}{\alpha - 1}\left(1 - \sum_{i=1}^{N} p_i^\alpha\right), \tag{2}$$

where α is a parameter greater than 0 and different from 1. It is clear that $\lim_{\alpha\to 1} S_\alpha(X) = H(X)$. The study of the measures of uncertainty has been recently extended to the fractional calculus: the fractional entropy (see Ubriaco [11]) is, for $0 < q \leq 1$,

$$H_q(X) = \sum_{i=1}^{N} p_i[-\log p_i]^q, \tag{3}$$

For $q = 0$ it reduces to 1 due to the normalization condition; for $q = 1$ it reduces to the Shannon entropy, i.e., $H_1(X) = H(X)$.

A. Quesada-Arencibia et al. (Eds.): EUROCAST 2024, LNCS 15174, pp. 268–276, 2025.
https://doi.org/10.1007/978-3-031-83885-9_24

Recently, it was proposed by Balakrishnan et al. [1] a new definition given with the purpose of unifying the definitions of Shannon entropy, Tsallis entropy and fractional entropy. We refer to this definition as fractional Tsallis entropy, or unified formulation of entropy, and it is given as

$$S_{\alpha}^{q}(X) = \frac{1}{\alpha - 1} \sum_{i=1}^{N} p_i (1 - p_i^{\alpha-1})(-\log p_i)^{q-1}, \tag{4}$$

where $\alpha > 0$, $\alpha \neq 1$ and $0 < q \leq 1$. We can summarize the relations among these measures in the Fig. 1.

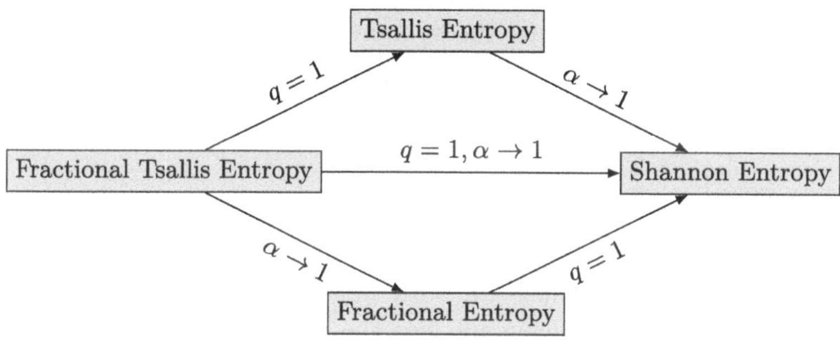

Fig. 1. Relationships among different entropies in classical probability theory.

2 A Unified Definition of Entropy in Dempster-Shafer Theory of Evidence

The study of the measures of uncertainty has been extended to the Dempster-Shafer theory of evidence [4,8]. It is a generalization of the classical probability theory which allows to manage more uncertainty. More precisely, the discrete probability distributions are replaced by the mass functions which can give a weight, a sort of degree of belief, towards all the subsets of the space of the events. An uncertain event with a finite number of alternatives is considered, and a mass function over the power set of the alternatives, that is a degree of confidence to all of its subsets, is defined. If we give positive mass only to singletons, we recover a discrete probability distribution. By the DST it is possible to describe situations in which there is less specific information.

A frame of discernment (FOD) X is a set of mutually exclusive and collectively exhaustive events indicated by $X = \{\theta_1, \theta_2, \ldots, \theta_{|X|}\}$. The power set of X is denoted by 2^X with cardinality $2^{|X|}$. A function $m : 2^X \to [0, 1]$ is called a mass function or a basic probability assignment (BPA) if $m(\emptyset) = 0$ and $\sum_{A \in 2^X} m(A) = 1$. If $m(A) \neq 0$ implies $|A| = 1$ then m is also a probability mass function, i.e., BPAs generalize discrete random variables. Moreover, the elements A such that $m(A) > 0$, are called focal elements.

One of the most important measures of discrimination in the DST context is Deng entropy, introduced in [5] for a BPA m as

$$ED(m) = - \sum_{A \subseteq X : m(A) > 0} m(A) \log_2 \left(\frac{m(A)}{2^{|A|} - 1} \right). \quad (5)$$

This entropy is similar to Shannon entropy and they coincide if the BPA is also a probability mass function. The term $2^{|A|} - 1$ represents the potential number of states in A. For a fixed value of $m(A)$, as the cardinality of A increases, $2^{|A|} - 1$ increases and then also Deng entropy does. The fractional version of Deng entropy was proposed and studied by Kazemi et al. [6]. Based on these measures, Balakrishnan et al. [1] defined a unified formulation of entropy also in the context of Dempster-Shafer theory named fractional Tsallis-Deng entropy and defined by

$$SD_{\alpha}^{q}(m) = \frac{1}{\alpha - 1} \sum_{A \subseteq X : m(A) > 0} m(A_i) \left[1 - \left(\frac{m(A_i)}{2^{|A_i|} - 1} \right)^{\alpha - 1} \right] \left(- \log \frac{m(A_i)}{2^{|A_i|} - 1} \right)^{q-1}, \quad (6)$$

where $\alpha > 0$, $\alpha \neq 1$, $0 < q \leq 1$. It is a general expression of entropy as it includes several versions of entropy measure both in the context of DST and in the classical probability theory viewpoint. For the relations among these measures see the Fig. 2.

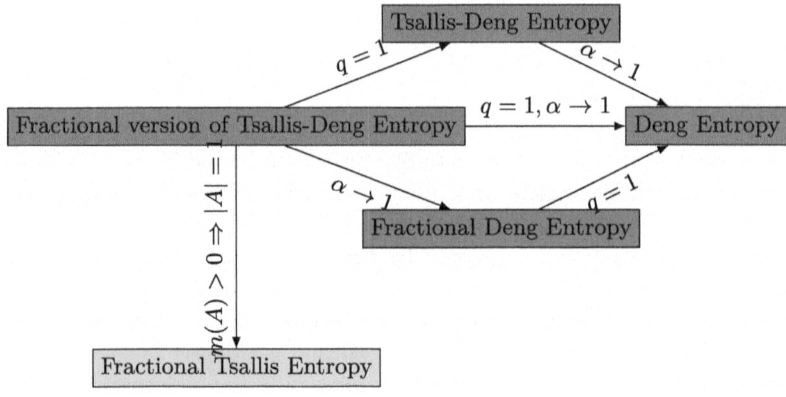

Fig. 2. Relationships among different entropies in DST and in classical probability theory.

3 A Unified Definition of Extropy in the Classical Theory: Fractional Tsallis Extropy

Recently, the introduction of the extropy as a measure of uncertainty dual of Shannon entropy opened up interest in new aspects of the subject (see [7]). Its definition is

$$J(X) = -\sum_{i=1}^{N}(1-p_i)\log(1-p_i).$$

In this section, we introduce the unified formulation of extropy in the context of classical probability theory. We refer to this formulation as fractional Tsallis extropy and, for a discrete random variable X, it is defined as

$$JS_{\alpha}^{q}(X) = \frac{1}{\alpha-1}\sum_{i=1}^{N}(1-p_i)[1-(1-p_i)^{\alpha-1}][-\log(1-p_i)]^{q-1}, \qquad (7)$$

where $\alpha > 0$, $\alpha \neq 1$ and $0 < q \leq 1$.

Remark 1. The fractional Tsallis extropy is non-negative for any discrete random variable. In fact the term $1-(1-p_i)^{\alpha-1}$ is positive for $\alpha > 1$ and negative for $0 < \alpha < 1$, so that the sum in (7) has a definite sign and it is the same of $\alpha - 1$.

As mentioned above, the purpose of giving this definition is based on the fact that this expression includes the classical extropy, Tsallis extropy and fractional extropy all as special cases. These other definitions of extropy are given in the following remarks:

Remark 2. If in (7) we take $q = 1$, then we obtain

$$JS_{\alpha}^{1}(X) = \frac{1}{\alpha-1}\sum_{i=1}^{N}(1-p_i)[1-(1-p_i)^{\alpha-1}] = JS_{\alpha}(X),$$

so that the fractional Tsallis extropy coincides with the Tsallis extropy.

Remark 3. The fractional Tsallis extropy converges to the fractional extropy as α goes to 1. By taking the limit for α to 1 in (7) and by applying L'Hôpital's rule, we obtain

$$\begin{aligned}
\lim_{\alpha\to 1} JS_{\alpha}^{q}(X) &= \lim_{\alpha\to 1}\frac{1}{\alpha-1}\sum_{i=1}^{N}(1-p_i)[1-(1-p_i)^{\alpha-1}][-\log(1-p_i)]^{q-1} \\
&= \lim_{\alpha\to 1}\sum_{i=1}^{N}(1-p_i)[-(1-p_i)^{\alpha-1}]\log(1-p_i)[-\log(1-p_i)]^{q-1} \\
&= \lim_{\alpha\to 1}\sum_{i=1}^{N}(1-p_i)^{\alpha}[-\log(1-p_i)]^{q} = \sum_{i=1}^{N}(1-p_i)[-\log(1-p_i)]^{q} \\
&= J_q(X).
\end{aligned}$$

Remark 4. If both parameters of the fractional Tsallis extropy go to 1, then it converges to the classical extropy,

$$\lim_{\alpha,q\to 1} JS_\alpha^q(X) = J(X).$$

Moreover, also the unified formulation of extropy is analyzed in the context of Dempster-Shafer theory of evidence.

In analogy with the relation between Shannon entropy and extropy, Buono and Longobardi [3] defined the Deng extropy as a measure of uncertainty dual of Deng entropy. The definition was given in order to satisfy the invariant property about the sum of entropy and extropy. For a BPA m over a FOD X, the Deng extropy is defined by

$$JD(m) = -\sum_{A\subset X:m(A)>0} (1-m(A))\log\left(\frac{1-m(A)}{2^{|A^c|}-1}\right), \tag{8}$$

where A^c is the complementary set of A in X and $|A^c| = |X|-|A|$. In addition, in the context of fractional calculus, Kazemi et al. [6] defined the fractional version of Deng extropy as

$$JD^q(m) = \sum_{A\subset X:m(A)>0} (1-m(A))\left[-\log\left(\frac{1-m(A)}{2^{|A^c|}-1}\right)\right]^q, \quad 0<q\leq 1. \tag{9}$$

The corresponding measure related to the Tsallis entropy, named as Tsallis-Deng extropy, is defined by

$$JD_\alpha(m) = \frac{1}{\alpha-1}\sum_{A\subset X:m(A)>0} (1-m(A))\left[1-\left(\frac{1-m(A)}{2^{|A^c|}-1}\right)^{\alpha-1}\right], \quad \alpha>0,\alpha\neq 1. \tag{10}$$

The results given are summarized in Fig. 3 in the form of a schematic diagram by displaying the relationships among different kinds of extropy.

In the following remark, we show that the fractional Tsallis entropy and the fractional Tsallis extropy satisfy a classical property of entropy and extropy related to their sum.

Remark 5. Let X be a discrete random variable with finite support S and with corresponding probability vector $\mathbf{p}$. Then,

$$S_\alpha^q(X) + JS_\alpha^q(X) = \sum_{i=1}^N S_\alpha^q(p_i, 1-p_i) = \sum_{i=1}^N JS_\alpha^q(p_i, 1-p_i), \tag{11}$$

where $S_\alpha^q(p_i, 1-p_i)$ and $JS_\alpha^q(p_i, 1-p_i)$ are the fractional Tsallis entropy and extropy of a discrete random variable taking on two values with corresponding probabilities $(p_i, 1-p_i)$.

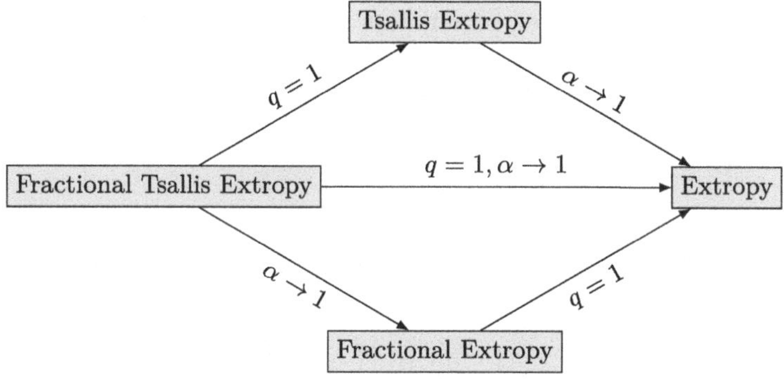

Fig. 3. Relationships among different versions of extropy in classical probability theory.

Table 1. Values of the fractional Tsallis extropy for the discrete uniform distribution as a function of N, for different choices of q and α.

N	$\alpha = 0.5,\ q = 0.2$	$\alpha = 0.5,\ q = 0.5$	$\alpha = 0.5,\ q = 0.75$	$\alpha = 5,\ q = 0.2$	$\alpha = 5,\ q = 0.5$	$\alpha = 5,\ q = 0.75$
5	3.1349	1.9990	1.3739	1.9601	1.2498	0.8590
10	5.8921	2.9997	1.7090	4.6824	2.3838	1.3581
15	8.3445	3.7415	1.9175	7.1670	3.2135	1.6470
20	10.6254	4.3588	2.0743	9.4836	3.8904	1.8514
25	12.7888	4.8989	2.2020	11.6792	4.4739	2.0110
30	14.8637	5.3851	2.3107	13.7825	4.9934	2.1426
35	16.8683	5.8309	2.4060	15.8120	5.4657	2.2553
40	18.8149	6.2450	2.4911	17.7805	5.9016	2.3541
45	20.7122	6.6332	2.5683	19.6975	6.3082	2.4424
50	22.5670	7.0000	2.6391	21.5699	6.6907	2.5225

4 A Unified Formulation of Extropy in DST

We introduce a unified formulation of extropy also in the context of Dempster-Shafer theory of evidence as

$$JD^q_\alpha(m) = \frac{1}{\alpha - 1} \sum_{A \subset X : m(A) > 0} (1 - m(A)) \left[1 - \left(\frac{1 - m(A)}{2^{|A^c|} - 1}\right)^{\alpha - 1}\right] \left(-\log \frac{1 - m(A)}{2^{|A^c|} - 1}\right)^{q-1} \quad (12)$$

where $\alpha > 0$, $\alpha \neq 1$, $0 < q \leq 1$, (see for details [2]). In analogy with the fractional Tsallis extropy, it is a general formulation as it includes several versions of extropy measure both in the context of DST and in the classical probability theory.

Remark 6. In analogy with Remark 1, the unified formulation of extropy (12) is non-negative too.

Remark 7. If $q = 1$, the unified formulation of extropy in (12) is equal to Tsallis-Deng extropy in (10). In fact

$$JD^1_\alpha(m) = \frac{1}{\alpha - 1} \sum_{A \subset X: m(A)>0} (1 - m(A)) \left[1 - \left(\frac{1 - m(A)}{2^{|A^c|} - 1}\right)^{\alpha - 1}\right] = JD_\alpha(m),$$

As α goes to 1, (12) converges to the fractional Deng extropy (9). By taking the limit for α which goes to 1 in (12), and by using L'Hôpital's rule, it follows

$$\begin{aligned}\lim_{\alpha \to 1} JD^q_\alpha(m) &= \lim_{\alpha \to 1} \sum_{A \subset X: m(A)>0} (1 - m(A)) \left[\left(\frac{1 - m(A)}{2^{|A^c|} - 1}\right)^{\alpha - 1}\right] \left(-\log \frac{1 - m(A)}{2^{|A^c|} - 1}\right)^q \\ &= \sum_{A \subset X: m(A)>0} (1 - m(A)) \left(-\log \frac{1 - m(A)}{2^{|A^c|} - 1}\right)^q = JD^q(m).\end{aligned}$$

When both the parameters α and q in (12) tend to 1, (12) converges to Deng extropy (8), i.e.,

$$\lim_{\alpha, q \to 1} JD^q_\alpha(m) = JD(m).$$

Remark 8. If the BPA m is such that for each focal element $|A| = n - 1$, then in the expression of the unified formulation of extropy $|A^c| = 1$ for each addend in the sum. Hence, the unified formulation of extropy reduces to

$$\begin{aligned}JD^q_\alpha(m) &= \frac{1}{\alpha - 1} \sum_{A \subset X: m(A)>0} (1 - m(A)) \left[1 - (1 - m(A))^{\alpha - 1}\right] [-\log(1 - m(A))]^{q-1} \\ &= JS^q_\alpha(Y),\end{aligned}$$

where Y is a discrete random variable with support $X = \{\theta_1, \ldots, \theta_n\}$ such that $p_i = \mathbb{P}(\theta_i) = m(X \setminus \{\theta_i\})$.

To summarize the results given above, the relationships among different formulations of extropies are depicted in the form of a schematic diagram, in Fig. 4.

Example 1. Let X be a frame of discernment with cardinality four and consider the BPA m^* such that

$$m^*(A) = \frac{2^{|A|} - 1}{\sum_{B \subseteq X} (2^{|B|} - 1)}, \quad A \subseteq X.$$

It is a well-known BPA which gives the same mass to all the subsets with the same cardinality. More precisely, with $|X| = 4$, we have four subsets with cardinality one and mass $1/65$, six subsets with cardinality two and mass $3/65$, four subsets with cardinality three and mass $7/65$ and one subset with cardinality four and mass $15/65$. Remember that the last one, that is the entire frame of discernment X, is not involved in the evaluation of the unified formulation of extropy.

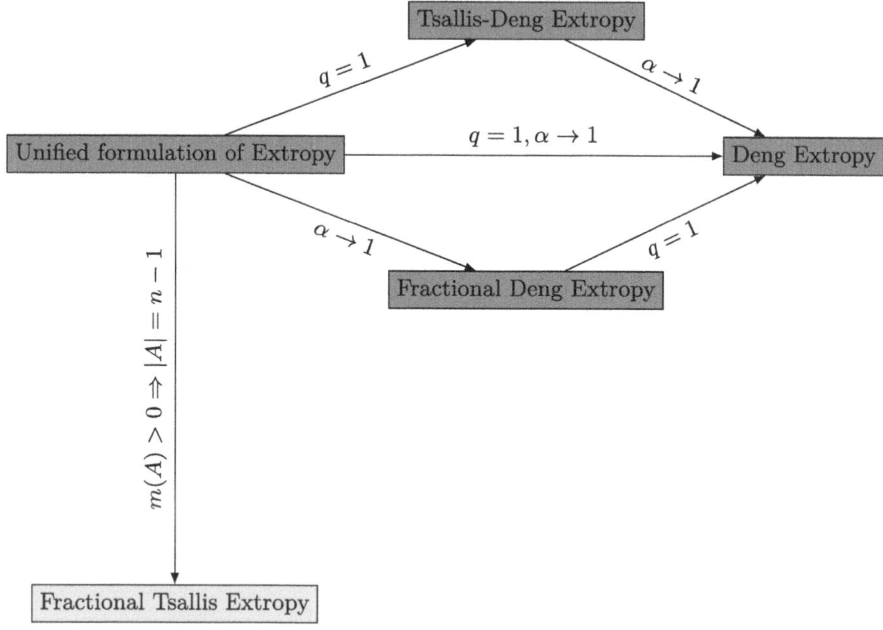

Fig. 4. Relationships among different entropies in DST theory (blue) and in classical probability theory (yellow). (Color figure online)

Acknowledgments. Maria Longobardi is member of the research group GNAMPA of INdAM (Istituto Nazionale di Alta Matematica) and is partially supported by MIUR - PRIN

References

1. Balakrishnan, N., Buono, F., Longobardi, M.: A unified formulation of entropy and its application. Phys. A **596**, 127214 (2022)
2. Balakrishnan, N., Buono, F., Longobardi, M.: On Tsallis extropy with an application to pattern recognition. Stat. Prob. Lett. **180**, 109241 (2022)
3. Buono, F., Longobardi, M.: A dual measure of uncertainty: the Deng extropy. Entropy **22**, 582 (2020)
4. Dempster, A.P.: Upper and lower probabilities induced by a multivalued mapping. Ann. Math. Stat. **38**, 325–339 (1967)
5. Deng, Y.: Deng entropy. Chaos, Solitons Fractals **91**, 549–553 (2016)
6. Kazemi, M.R., Tahmasebi, S., Buono, F., Longobardi, M.: Fractional Deng entropy and extropy and some applications. Entropy **23**, 623 (2021)
7. Lad, F., Sanfilippo, G., Agrò, G.: Extropy: complementary dual of entropy. Stat. Sci. **30**, 40–58 (2015)
8. Shafer, G.: A Mathematical Theory of Evidence. Princeton University Press, Princeton, NJ, USA (1976)

9. Shannon, C.E.: A mathematical theory of communication. Bell Syst. Tech. J. **27**, 379–423 (1948)
10. Tsallis, C.: Possible generalization of Boltzmann-Gibbs statistic. J. Stat. Phys. **52**, 479–487 (1988)
11. Ubriaco, M.R.: Entropies based on fractional calculus. Phys. Lett. A **373**, 2516–19 (2009)

Time-Inhomogeneous Diffusion Process for the SI Epidemic Model

Virginia Giorno(✉) and Amelia G. Nobile

Dipartimento di Informatica, Università di Salerno, Via Giovanni Paolo II, No. 132, 84084 Fisciano, (SA), Italy
{giorno,nobile}@unisa.it

Abstract. We consider a time-inhomogeneous diffusion process useful to model the evolution of the infected population in the susceptible-infectious epidemic model in a random environment. We assume that there are no removals, no immunes, and no recoveries from infection. The susceptible individuals become infected through contact with infectious individuals. A such model is suitable for describing some classes of micro-parasitic infections to which individuals never acquire a long lasting immunity and over the course of the epidemic everyone eventually becomes infected. We determine the expression of the transition probability density function and of its conditional moments. Particular attention is dedicated to the first-passage time problem, by deriving closed form results for the first-passage time density through a constant boundary. For the time-homogeneous process, the behavior of the mean and of the variance of the first-passage time is analyzed and some comparisons between the deterministic model and the obtained diffusion process are provided.

Keywords: Population dynamics · Transition density · First-passage time problem

1 Introduction

Deterministic and stochastic epidemic models are used in the literature to analyze the behaviors of biological diseases and how they spread (cf. Allen [1,2], Bailey [3]). The simplest epidemic models assume that an individual can be in one of only two states, either susceptible (S) or infectious (I). For $t \geq t_0$, we denote by $S(t)$ the number of susceptible individuals, by $I(t)$ the number of individuals infected and by N the total population size, where $N = S(t) + I(t)$ is constant. In Giorno and Nobile [4], several time-inhomogeneous deterministic models, useful to describe the evolution of a finite population constituted by susceptible and infectious individuals have been considered. Moreover, stochastic models based on finite birth processes have been also analyzed. For these processes, we have determined the explicit expression of the transition probabilities and of the first-passage time densities. Furthermore, particular attention

A. Quesada-Arencibia et al. (Eds.): EUROCAST 2024, LNCS 15174, pp. 277–285, 2025.
https://doi.org/10.1007/978-3-031-83885-9_25

has been dedicated to the SI model and its counterpart stochastic based on finite birth processes.

In the deterministic SI model, the population dynamics of the infected $I(t)$ can be described by the Pearl-Verhulst logistic growth differential equation:

$$\frac{dI(t)}{dt} = \frac{\lambda(t)}{N}[N - I(t)]\, I(t), \qquad t > t_0, \tag{1}$$

where the transmission intensity function $\lambda(t)$ is a positive, bounded and continuous function of t. The solution of (1) is

$$I(t) = \frac{N\, I(t_0)}{I(t_0) + [N - I(t_0)]\, e^{-\Lambda(t|t_0)}}, \qquad t \geq t_0, \tag{2}$$

with

$$\Lambda(t|t_0) = \int_{t_0}^{t} \lambda(\theta)\, d\theta. \tag{3}$$

The time until the infected population size reaches N is infinite because N is asymptotically approached. To obtain an estimate of the time required T_k^* until k individuals of population are infected, we solve the equation $I(T_k^*) = k$. In particular, if $\lambda(t) = \lambda$, from (2) one has

$$T_k^* = t_0 + \frac{1}{\lambda}\, \ln\Big\{\frac{[N - I(t_0)]\, k}{I(t_0)}\Big\}, \qquad I(t_0) < k < N. \tag{4}$$

In [4], we have considered the SI birth process $\{M(t), t \geq t_0\}$ by assuming that the births at time t occur with intensity functions given by $\lambda_n(t) = \lambda(t) n(N - n)/N$ for $n = j, j+1, \ldots, N$.

The aim of the present paper is to build a time-inhomogeneous diffusion process to model the size of the infected population as an alternative to the SI birth process $M(t)$ considered in [4].

2 The SI Diffusion Model

Under the assumption of random environment, we denote with $\{X(t), t \geq t_0\}$ the stochastic process describing the size of the infected population at time t and we interpret $\Lambda(t|t_0)$ as the mean of a time-inhomogeneous Wiener process $\{Z(t), t \geq t_0\}$, described by the stochastic equation

$$Z(t) = \Lambda(t|t_0) + W\big[V(t|t_0)\big], \qquad t \geq t_0, \tag{5}$$

where $W(t)$ is the standard Wiener process and

$$V(t|t_0) = \int_{t_0}^{t} \sigma^2(\theta)\, d\vartheta, \qquad t \geq t_0, \tag{6}$$

with $\sigma(t)$ positive, bounded and continuous function of t. From (2), one can derive the stochastic equation:

$$\ln\Big[\frac{X(t+\Delta t)}{N-X(t+\Delta t)}\Big]-\ln\Big[\frac{X(t)}{N-X(t)}\Big]=Z(t+\Delta t)-Z(t), \tag{7}$$

from which for $n=1,2,\ldots$ one obtains:

$$\mathrm{E}\Big\{\Big(\ln\Big[\frac{X(t+\Delta t)}{N-X(t+\Delta t)}\Big]-\ln\Big[\frac{X(t)}{N-X(t)}\Big]\Big)^n\Big|X(t)=x\Big\}=\mathrm{E}\big\{[Z(t+\Delta t)-Z(t)]^n\big\}. \tag{8}$$

Expanding the left side of Eq. (8) in a Taylor series, one is led to

$$\begin{aligned}&\sum_{k_1=1}^{+\infty}\frac{1}{k_1}\Big[\frac{1}{(N-x)^{k_1}}+\frac{(-1)^{k_1-1}}{x^{k_1}}\Big]\sum_{k_2=1}^{+\infty}\frac{1}{k_2}\Big[\frac{1}{(N-x)^{k_2}}+\frac{(-1)^{k_2-1}}{x^{k_2}}\Big]\times\cdots\\&\times\sum_{k_n=1}^{+\infty}\frac{1}{k_n}\Big[\frac{1}{(N-x)^{k_n}}+\frac{(-1)^{k_n-1}}{x^{k_n}}\Big]\mathrm{E}\Big\{[X(t+\Delta t)-X(t)]^{k_1+k_2+\ldots+k_n}\Big|X(t)=x\Big\}\\&\qquad=\mathrm{E}\big\{[Z(t+\Delta t)-Z(t)]^n\big\}.\end{aligned} \tag{9}$$

We note that for $k=0,1,\ldots$ one has

$$\begin{aligned}&\mathrm{E}\big\{[Z(t+\Delta t)-Z(t)]^{2k}\big\}=(2k)!\sum_{r=0}^{k}\frac{\big[\Lambda(t+\Delta t|t)\big]^{2r}\big[V(t+\Delta t|t)\big]^{k-r}}{2^{k-r}(k-r)!\,(2r)!},\\&\mathrm{E}\big\{[Z(t+\Delta t)-Z(t)]^{2k+1}\big\}=(2k+1)!\sum_{r=0}^{k}\frac{\big[\Lambda(t+\Delta t|t)\big]^{2r+1}\big[V(t+\Delta t|t)\big]^{k-r}}{2^{k-r}(k-r)!\,(2r+1)!},\end{aligned} \tag{10}$$

so that

$$\begin{aligned}&\lim_{\Delta t\downarrow 0}\frac{\mathrm{E}\{Z(t+\Delta t)-Z(t)\}}{\Delta t}=\lambda(t),\quad \lim_{\Delta t\downarrow 0}\frac{\mathrm{E}\{[Z(t+\Delta t)-Z(t)]^2\}}{\Delta t}=\sigma^2(t),\\&\lim_{\Delta t\downarrow 0}\frac{\mathrm{E}\{[Z(t+\Delta t)-Z(t)]^n\}}{\Delta t}=0,\qquad n=3,4,\ldots\end{aligned} \tag{11}$$

Let

$$A_n(x,t)=\lim_{\Delta t\downarrow 0}\frac{\mathrm{E}\{[X(t+\Delta t)-X(t)]^n|X(t)=x\}}{\Delta t},\qquad n=1,2,\ldots, \tag{12}$$

be the infinitesimal moments of $X(t)$. Dividing both sides of (9) by Δt and proceeding to the limit as $\Delta t\downarrow 0$, by virtue of (11) one obtains:

$$A_1(x,t)=\frac{\lambda(t)}{N}(N-x)x+\frac{1}{4}\frac{\partial A_2(x,t)}{\partial x},\qquad A_2(x,t)=\sigma^2(t)\,\frac{(N-x)^2x^2}{N^2} \tag{13}$$

and $A_n(x,t)=0$ for $n=3,4,\ldots$. Therefore, $X(t)$ is a time-inhomogeneous diffusion process, having infinitesimal drift and infinitesimal variance given (13) with the state-space $(0,N)$, being 0 and N unattainable end-points.

3 Description of the SI Diffusion Model

In this section, we determine the transition probability density function (pdf) of $X(t)$ and we analyze the first-passage time (FPT) problem through a constant boundary. We note that the time-homogeneous case, in which $\lambda(t) = \lambda$ and $\sigma^2(t) = \sigma^2$, is also considered in Tuckwell [5].

3.1 Transition Pdf and Related Moments

The transition pdf $f_X(x,t|x_0,t_0)$ of $X(t)$ is solution of the Kolmogorov equation

$$\frac{\partial f_X(x,t|x_0,t_0)}{\partial t_0} + A_1(x_0,t_0)\,\frac{\partial f_X(x,t|x_0,t_0)}{\partial x_0} + \frac{A_2(x_0,t_0)}{2}\,\frac{\partial^2 f_X(x,t|x_0,t_0)}{\partial x_0^2} = 0, \tag{14}$$

to solve with the delta initial condition $\lim_{t_0\uparrow t} f_X(x,t|x_0,t_0) = \delta(x-x_0)$. Making use of the transformations

$$y = \int_u^x \frac{N\,dz}{z(N-z)} = \ln\Big(\frac{x(N-u)}{u(N-x)}\Big), \quad y_0 = \int_u^{x_0} \frac{N\,dz}{z(N-z)} = \ln\Big(\frac{x_0(N-u)}{u(N-x_0)}\Big)$$

$$f_Y(y,t|y_0,t_0) = \frac{x(N-x)}{N}\, f_X(x,t|x_0,t_0), \tag{15}$$

with $u \in (0,N)$, Eq. (14) leads to:

$$\frac{\partial f_Y(y,t|y_0,t_0)}{\partial t_0} + \lambda(t_0)\,\frac{\partial f_Y(y,t|y_0,t_0)}{\partial y_0} + \frac{\sigma^2(t_0)}{2}\,\frac{\partial^2 f_Y(y,t|y_0,t_0)}{\partial y_0^2} = 0, \tag{16}$$

with the delta initial condition $\lim_{t_0\uparrow t} f_Y(y,t|y_0,t_0) = \delta(y-y_0)$. Equation (16) is the Kolmogorov equation of a time-inhomogeneous Wiener process with infinitesimal drift $B_1(t) = \lambda(t)$ and infinitesimal variance $B_2(t) = \sigma^2(t)$. Since

$$\lim_{x\downarrow 0} \ln\Big(\frac{x(N-u)}{u(N-x)}\Big) = -\infty, \qquad \lim_{x\uparrow N} \ln\Big(\frac{x(N-u)}{u(N-x)}\Big) = +\infty,$$

the state-space of $Y(t)$ is $\mathbb{R}$. Therefore, $f_Y(y,t|y_0,t_0)$ is the normal density:

$$f_Y(y,t|y_0,t_0) = \frac{1}{\sqrt{2\pi\,V(t|t_0)}}\,\exp\Big\{-\frac{[y-y_0-\Lambda(t|t_0)]^2}{2\,V(t|t_0)}\Big\}, \qquad y,y_0 \in \mathbb{R}, \tag{17}$$

with $\Lambda(t|t_0)$ and $V(t|t_0)$ given in (3) and (6), respectively. Making use of (15), for $x, x_0 \in (0,N)$ one has:

$$f_X(x,t|x_0,t_0) = \frac{N}{x(N-x)}\,\frac{1}{\sqrt{2\pi\,V(t|t_0)}}\,\exp\Big\{-\frac{\big[\ln\big(\frac{x(N-x_0)}{x_0(N-x)}\big) - \Lambda(t|t_0)\big]^2}{2\,V(t|t_0)}\Big\}. \tag{18}$$

Moreover, the transition distribution function of $X(t)$ is

$$F_X(x,t|x_0,t_0) = \frac{1}{2}\Big\{1+\mathrm{Erf}\Big[\frac{\ln\big(\frac{x(N-x_0)}{x_0(N-x)}\big) - \Lambda(t|t_0)}{\sqrt{2\,V(t|t_0)}}\Big]\Big\}, \qquad x, x_0 \in (0,N). \tag{19}$$

The conditional median $\mu[X(t)|X(t_0)=x_0]$ of the process $X(t)$ can be obtained from (19) by imposing that $F_X(x,t|x_0,t_0)=1/2$ for $t\geq t_0$, so that

$$\mu[X(t)|X(t_0)=x_0]=\frac{N\,x_0}{x_0+(N-x_0)\,e^{-\Lambda(t|t_0)}},\qquad t\geq t_0. \tag{20}$$

By comparing (2) and (20), we note that the conditional median of $X(t)$ identifies with the deterministic solution of Eq. (1) for $I(t_0)=x_0$. Hence, the conditional median of $X(t)$ does not depend on the environmental variability expressed by $\sigma^2(t)$. Moreover, if $\lim_{t\to+\infty}\Lambda(t|t_0)=+\infty$, from (20) one has $\lim_{t\to+\infty}\mu[X(t)|X(t_0)=x_0]=N$.

For $x_0\in(0,N)$ and $k=1,2,\ldots$, the k-th conditional moment of $X(t)$ is:

$$\begin{aligned}
\mathrm{E}[X^k(t)|X(t_0)=x_0]&=\int_0^N x^k\,f_X(x,t|x_0,t_0)\,dx\\
&=\frac{N^k}{\sqrt{2\pi\,V(t|t_0)}}\int_{-\infty}^{+\infty}\Big(\frac{1}{1+e^{-y}}\Big)^k\exp\Big\{-\frac{\big[y-\ln\big(\frac{x_0}{N-x_0}\big)-\Lambda(t|t_0)\big]^2}{2\,V(t|t_0)}\Big\}\,dy\\
&=\frac{N^k}{\sqrt{\pi}}\int_{-\infty}^{+\infty}\Big(1+\frac{N-x_0}{x_0}\exp\Big\{-z\sqrt{2V(t|t_0)}-\Lambda(t|t_0)\Big\}\Big)^{-k}e^{-z^2}\,dz, \qquad (21)
\end{aligned}$$

where (18) has been used and the change of variable $y=\ln\big(\frac{x}{N-x}\big)$ has been applied. Furthermore, if $\lim_{t\to+\infty}\Lambda(t|t_0)=+\infty$, from (21) one has

$$\lim_{t\to+\infty}\mathrm{E}[X^k(t)|X(t_0)=x_0]=N^k,\qquad k=1,2,\ldots.$$

In Fig. 1 we plot the median, the mean and the coefficient of variation as

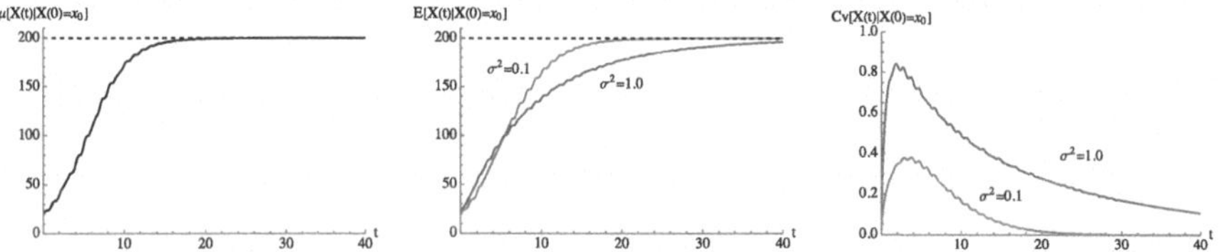

Fig. 1. Median, mean and coefficient of variation of the diffusion process $X(t)$ for $x_0=20$, $N=200$, $\lambda(t)=0.4\,[1+0.9\cos(2\pi\,t)]$ and $\sigma^2(t)=\sigma^2$ as function of t.

function of t for the SI diffusion process (13) by choosing $t_0=0$, $x_0=20$, $N=200$, $\lambda(t)=0.4\,[1+0.9\cos(2\pi\,t)]$ and $\sigma^2(t)=\sigma^2$, with $\sigma^2=0.1,1.0$.

3.2 FPT Problem for the SI Diffusion Process

Let

$$\mathcal{T}_X(S|x_0,t_0)=\begin{cases}\inf_{t\geq t_0}\{t:X(t)\geq S\}, & x_0<S,\\ \inf_{t\geq t_0}\{t:X(t)\leq S\}, & S<x_0,\end{cases}\qquad x_0,S\in(0,N),$$

be the random variable that describes the FPT of $X(t)$ through S starting from $X(t_0)=x_0\neq S$. We denote by $g_X(S,t|x_0,t_0)=dP\{T_X(S|x_0,t_0)\leq t\}/dt$ the FPT density. The transition pdf and the FPT density are related from the following renewal equation

$$f_X(x,t|x_0,t_0)=\int_{t_0}^{t} g_X(S,\theta|x_0,t_0)\, f_X(x,t|S,\theta)\, d\theta,$$
$$[x_0<S\leq x] \text{ or } [x\leq S<x_0], \qquad (22)$$

with $x_0,x\in(0,N)$. Making use of the transformations (15), for $u,x_0,S\in(0,N)$ one has:

$$g_X(S,t|x_0,t_0)=g_Y\Big(\ln\Big[\frac{S(N-u)}{u(N-S)}\Big],t\Big|\ln\Big[\frac{x_0(N-u)}{u(N-x_0)}\Big],t_0\Big), \qquad x_0\neq S, \quad (23)$$

where $g_Y(y,t|y_0,t_0)$ is the FPT density of the Wiener process $Y(t)$ with infinitesimal drift $B_1(t)=\lambda(t)$ and infinitesimal variance $B_2(t)=\sigma^2(t)$. In the sequel, we consider the FPT problem in two cases: *(i)* $X(t)$ is a time-homogeneous diffusion process with $\lambda(t)=\lambda$, $\sigma^2(t)=\sigma^2$ in (13) and *(ii)* $X(t)$ is a time-inhomogeneous diffusion process having $\lambda(t)=\alpha\,\sigma^2(t)$ in (13), with $\alpha>0$.

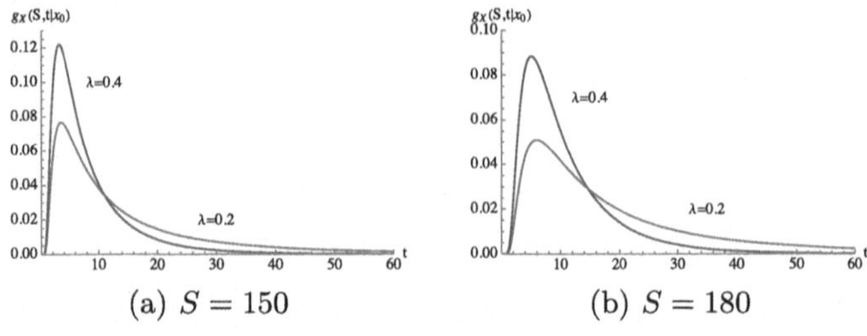

Fig. 2. FPT density as function of t for $X(t)$ with $x_0=20$, $N=200$, $\lambda(t)=0.4$ and $\sigma^2(t)=1.0$.

Case (i): Time-homogeneous SI process By setting $\lambda(t)=\lambda$ and $\sigma^2(t)=\sigma^2$ in (13), $X(t)$ has infinitesimal moments:

$$A_1(x)=\frac{(N-x)x}{N}\Big(\lambda+\frac{\sigma^2}{2}-\frac{\sigma^2\,x}{N}\Big)\qquad A_2(x)=\sigma^2\,\frac{(N-x)^2x^2}{N^2}, \qquad (24)$$

with $x\in(0,N)$. In this case, by setting $t_0=0$ in (23), for $x_0,S\in(0,N)$, with $x_0\neq S$, one obtains:

$$g_X(S,t|x_0)=\frac{\Big|\ln\Big(\frac{S(N-x_0)}{x_0(N-S)}\Big)\Big|}{\sqrt{2\pi\sigma^2\,t^3}}\exp\Big\{-\frac{\Big[\ln\Big(\frac{S(N-x_0)}{x_0(N-S)}\Big)-\lambda\,t\Big]^2}{2\sigma^2\,t}\Big\}. \qquad (25)$$

Moreover, the ultimate FPT probability is

$$P_X(S|x_0) = \int_0^{+\infty} g_X(S,t|x_0)\,dt = \begin{cases} 1, & S > x_0, \\ \left[\frac{S(N-x_0)}{x_0(N-S)}\right]^{2\lambda/\sigma^2}, & S < x_0, \end{cases} \qquad x_0, S \in (0,N).$$

In Fig. 2 we plot the FPT density (25) as function of t for $x_0 = 20$, $N = 200$, $\lambda(t) = 0.4$, $\sigma^2(t) = 1.0$ and $S = 150, 180$. In these cases the first passage is a sure event. Recalling (23), for $0 < x_0 < S < N$ one has (cf. Giorno and Nobile [6]):

$$t_n(S|x_0) = \int_0^{+\infty} t^n\, g_X(S,t|x_0)\,dt = \frac{2\ln\Big(\frac{S(N-x_0)}{x_0(N-S)}\Big)}{\sigma\sqrt{2\pi}} \Big\{\frac{1}{\lambda}\ln\Big(\frac{S(N-x_0)}{x_0(N-S)}\Big)\Big\}^{n-1/2}$$
$$\times\Big[\frac{S(N-x_0)}{x_0(N-S)}\Big]^{\lambda/\sigma^2} K_{n-1/2}\Big[\frac{\lambda}{\sigma^2}\ln\Big(\frac{S(N-x_0)}{x_0(N-S}\Big)\Big], \qquad n = 1, 2, \ldots \quad (26)$$

where $K_\nu(z)$ denotes the modified Bessel function of third kind, which can be expressed in terms of the modified Bessel function of first kind $I_\nu(z)$:

$$K_\nu(z) = \frac{\pi}{2}\,\frac{I_{-\nu}(z) - I_\nu(z)}{\sin(\nu\,\pi)}, \qquad I_\nu(z) = \sum_{k=0}^{+\infty} \frac{1}{k!\,\Gamma(\nu+k+1)}\Big(\frac{z}{2}\Big)^{2k+\nu}, \quad (27)$$

where $\Gamma(\nu) = \int_0^{+\infty} y^{\nu-1}\,e^{-y}\,dy$, with $\mathrm{Re}\,\nu > 0$, is the Euler gamma function. In particular, for $0 < x_0 < S < N$ from (26) one obtains the FPT mean and variance:

$$t_1(S|x_0) = \frac{1}{\lambda}\ln\Big(\frac{S(N-x_0)}{x_0(N-S)}\Big), \quad \mathrm{Var}(S|x_0) = \frac{\sigma^2}{\lambda^3}\ln\Big(\frac{S(N-x_0)}{x_0(N-S)}\Big). \quad (28)$$

In Table 1 we list the mean, the variance and the coefficient of variation of the FPT for $x_0 = 20$, $N = 200$, $\lambda = 0.4$ and $\sigma^2 = 0.1, 1.0$. By comparing (4) for $t_0 = 0$ and $I(t_0) = x_0$ with the first of (28) for $S = k$, we have $T_k^* = t_1(k|x_0)$ for $x_0 < k < N$. Hence, the time required until k individuals of population are infected in the deterministic model coincides with the FPT mean through $S = k$ in the SI diffusion model.

Case (ii): Time-inhomogeneous SI process with proportional intensity functions
By setting $\lambda(t) = \alpha\,\sigma^2(t)$, with $\alpha > 0$, in (13), $X(t)$ has infinitesimal moments:

$$A_1(x,t) = \lambda(t)\,\frac{(N-x)x}{N}\Big(1 + \frac{1}{2\alpha} - \frac{x}{\alpha N}\Big), \quad A_2(x,t) = \frac{\lambda(t)}{\alpha}\,\frac{(N-x)^2x^2}{N^2}, \quad (29)$$

with $x \in (0,N)$. From (23) for $x_0, S \in (0,N)$, with $x_0 \neq S$, one obtains:

$$g_X(S,t|x_0,t_0) = \frac{\lambda(t)\,\sqrt{\alpha}\,\Big|\ln\Big(\frac{S(N-x_0)}{x_0(N-S)}\Big)\Big|}{\sqrt{2\pi[\Lambda(t|t_0)]^3}}\exp\Big\{-\frac{\alpha\left[\ln\Big(\frac{S(N-x_0)}{x_0(N-S)}\Big) - \Lambda(t|t_0)\right]^2}{2\,\Lambda(t|t_0)}\Big\}. \quad (30)$$

Moreover, if $\lim_{t\to+\infty}\Lambda(t|t_0) = +\infty$, for $x_0, S \in (0,N)$ one has:

Table 1. For the SI diffusion process the mean, the variance and the coefficient of variation of the FPT are listed for $x_0 = 20$, $N = 200$, $\lambda = 0.4$ and various values of S.

		$\sigma^2 = 0.1$		$\sigma^2 = 1.0$	
S	$t_1(S\|x_0)$	$\mathrm{Var}(S\|x_0)$	$\mathrm{Cv}(S\|x_0)$	$\mathrm{Var}(S\|x_0)$	$\mathrm{Cv}(S\|x_0)$
40	2.02733	1.26708	0.555237	12.6708	1.75581
60	3.37482	2.10926	0.430343	21.0926	1.36086
80	4.47940	2.79962	0.373534	27.9962	1.18122
100	5.49306	3.43316	0.337313	34.3316	1.06668
120	6.50672	4.06670	0.309927	40.6670	0.980074
140	7.61131	4.75707	0.286557	47.5707	0.906172
160	8.95880	5.59925	0.264128	55.9925	0.835247
180	10.9861	6.86633	0.238516	68.6633	0.754254

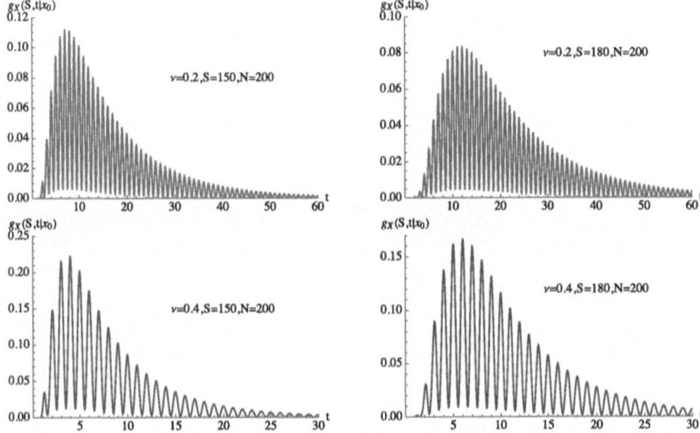

Fig. 3. FPT density as function of t for the diffusion process $X(t)$ with $x_0 = 20$, $N = 200$, $\lambda(t) = \nu\,[1 + 0.9\cos(2\pi\, t)]$ and $\sigma^2(t) = 2\,\lambda(t)$.

$$P_X(S|x_0,t_0) = \int_{t_0}^{+\infty} g_X(S,t|x_0,t_0)\,dt = \begin{cases} 1, & S > x_0, \\ \left[\frac{S(N-x_0)}{x_0(N-S)}\right]^{2\alpha}, & S < x_0. \end{cases}$$

In Fig. 3 we plot the FPT density (30) as function of t for $x_0 = 20$, $N = 200$, $\alpha = 0.5$, $\lambda(t) = \nu\,[1 + 0.9\cos(2\pi\, t)]$ with $\nu = 0.2, 0.4$ and $S = 150, 180$. In these cases, the first passage is a sure event and the FPT densities exhibit damped oscillations having the same period of the intensity functions.

Acknowledgments. This research is partially supported by MUR-PRIN 2022, project 2022XZSAFN "Anomalous Phenomena on Regular and Irregular Domains: Approximating Complexity for the Applied Sciences", and MUR-PRIN 2022 PNRR, project P2022XSF5H "Stochastic Models in Biomathematics and Applications". The authors are members of the GNCS-INdAM.

References

1. Allen, L.J.S.: An Introduction to Stochastic Processes with Applications to Biology. Chapman and Hall/CRC, Lubbock, Texas, USA (2010)
2. Allen, L.J.S.: Stochastic Population and Epidemic Models. MBILS, vol. 1.3. Springer, Cham (2015). https://doi.org/10.1007/978-3-319-21554-9 Springer International Publishing, Switzerland (2015)
3. Bailey, N.T.J.: The Elements of Stochastic Processes with Applications to the Natural Sciences. Wiley, New York (1964)
4. Giorno, V., Nobile A.G.: Time-inhomogeneous finite birth processes with applications in epidemic models. Mathematics **11**, 4521 (2023)
5. Tuckwell, H.C.: A study of some diffusion models of population growth. Theor. Popul. Biol. **5**, 345–357 (1974)
6. Giorno, V., Nobile A.G.: On the absorbing problems for Wiener, Ornstein–Uhlenbeck, and Feller diffusion processes: similarities and differences. Fractal Fract. **7**, 11 (2023)

A Vasicek-Type Model with Structural Breaks in the Drift

Giuseppina Albano[1(✉)] and Virginia Giorno[2]

[1] Dipartimento di Studi Politici e Sociali, Università degli Studi di Salerno, Via Giovanni Paolo II n. 132, 84084 Fisciano, SA, Italy
pialbano@unisa.it

[2] Dipartimento di Informatica, Università degli Studi di Salerno, Via Giovanni Paolo II n. 132, 84084 Fisciano, SA, Italy
giorno@unisa.it

Abstract. We consider a time inhomogeneous diffusion process with piece-wise linear drift and infinitesimal variance generally depending on time. Such a process is able to model the dynamics of phenomena in which structural breaks occur at fixed times due to sudden changes.

The probability distribution of such process is analyzed by obtaining its transition probability density function and the related moments.

Moreover, we focus on the statistical analysis of the process. In particular, starting from a discrete sampling, an inference procedure based on the maximum likelihood estimation and the generalized method of moments is provided to address the estimation of the drift and of the infinitesimal variance.

Finally, a simulation study is made to evaluate the performance of the provided procedure. In such simulation study, by means of a suitable statistical test we also discuss the presence of structural breaks in the drift parameters.

Keyword: Non homogeneous process · Inference · Tests for structural breaks

1 Introduction and Background

The Ornstein Uhlenbeck (OU) process, originally introduced by Langevin in 1908, to describe the velocity of a particle moving in a fluid, has also used in biological context as model of a single neurons' activity. Further, it is widely used in economics and in financial literature under the name of Vasicek model to describe interest rates and commodity prices (see, for example, [1] and references therein).

The OU process is described by the following stochastic differential equation (SDE):

$$dY(t) = [-\alpha Y(t) + \beta]dt + \sigma dW(t), \qquad Y(t_0) = y_0,$$

where $W(t)$ is a standard Wiener process and $\alpha, \beta, y_0 \in \mathbb{R}$, $\sigma > 0$, $t_0 \geq 0$. For $\alpha > 0$ the process $X(t)$ is mean reverting, so it tends to oscillate around

A. Quesada-Arencibia et al. (Eds.): EUROCAST 2024, LNCS 15174, pp. 286–294, 2025.
https://doi.org/10.1007/978-3-031-83885-9_26

the equilibrium state β/α. It is also ergodic and the stationary distribution is $N(\beta/\alpha, \sigma^2/2\alpha)$. Further, the conditional distribution of $Y(t+\Delta)$ given $Y(t)$ is normal with mean $\beta(1-e^{-\alpha\Delta})/\alpha + Y(t)e^{-\alpha\Delta}$ and variance $\sigma^2(1-e^{-2\alpha\Delta})/(2\alpha)$, from which the Maximum Likelihood (ML) Estimator can be explicitly obtained as shown in [2,3].

In [4] a non-homogeneous OU-type process was considered and a statistical procedure to fit the constant parameters and the time-dependent functions involved in the model was provided. Such methodology is based on two steps: the first one is able to estimate the constant parameters, while the second one fits the non-homogeneous terms of the process. Then, in [5], for the same process, the inference was provided by means of an iterative procedure that, in each step, combines the classical maximum likelihood estimation and a generalized method of moments (GMM).

In this paper, we consider a generalization of the classical OU process by including in the infinitesimal moments suitable deterministic time dependent functions and some discontinuities to describe the presence of structural breaks in the dynamics. In [6] some examples of phenomena in which the underlying process shows several structural breaks in the trend are shown in the context of air quality during Covid pandemics, essentially due to lockdown restrictions. In similar cases, the problem of estimating the drift and the infinitesimal variance of the process becomes of interest both of theoretical and practical contexts.

The paper is organized as follows. Section 2 presents the theoretical model, while in Sect. 3 the inference is provided. Finally in Sect. 4, a simulation experiment is performed and some conclusions close the paper.

2 The Model

Let $\{X(t),\ t \geq \tau_0\}$ be a stochastic process defined in $\mathbb{R}$ described by the following stochastic differential equation (SDE):

$$dX(t) = \left[-\alpha(t)X(t) + \beta(t)\right]dt + \sigma(t)dW(t), \qquad X(\tau_0) = x_0, \tag{1}$$

where $\beta(t)$ and $\sigma(t) > 0$ are real continuous functions. The function $\alpha(t)$ is a piecewise constant function, that has a finite number L of pieces, i.e.

$$\alpha(t) = \sum_{k=1}^{L} \alpha_k I_k(t) \tag{2}$$

with

$$I_k(t) = \begin{cases} 1, & \tau_{k-1} \leq t < \tau_k, \\ 0, & otherwise \end{cases} \qquad k = 1, 2, \dots,\ \mathrm{L} \tag{3}$$

denoting the indicator function of the interval $[\tau_{k-1}, \tau_k)$. Here, τ_k is a point of discontinuity of the function $\alpha(t)$ and it describes the time in which a structural break occurs. The process $X(t)$ is a time inhomogeneous OU process with drift and infinitesimal variance $A_1(x,t) = -\alpha(t)x(t) + \beta(t)$, $A_2(t) = \sigma^2(t)$. We note that $\tau_0, \tau_1, \tau_2, \ldots, \tau_L$ are times in which the observations exhibit some types of anomalies similar to structural breaks. After a structural break the process restarts according a different law. Specifically, after the time τ_{k-1} the process restarts from $X(\tau_{k-1})$ with a drift $A_1^{(k)}(x,t) = -\alpha_k x + \beta(t)$ and infinitesimal variance $A_2(t)$ until the next break occurs. We point out that the sample-paths of $X(t)$ are not discontinuous in the points τ_k, but they present trend variations in such points.

One can prove that the transition probability density function of $X(t)$ is normal:

$$f(x,t|x_0,\tau_0) = \frac{1}{\sqrt{2\pi V(t|\tau_0)}} \exp\Big\{-\frac{[x - M(t|x_0,\tau_0)]^2}{2V(t|\tau_0)}\Big\}$$

with conditional mean and conditional variance given by:

$$M(t|x_0,\tau_0) = \mathbb{E}[X(t)|X(\tau_0) = x_0] = e^{-A(t|\tau_0)}\left[x_0 + \int_{\tau_0}^{t} \beta(\theta) e^{A(\theta|\tau_0)} d\theta\right] \tag{4}$$

$$V(t|x_0,\tau_0) = Var[X(t)|X(\tau_0) = x_0] = e^{-2A(t|\tau_0)} \int_{\tau_0}^{t} \sigma^2(\theta) e^{2A(\theta|\tau_0)} d\theta \tag{5}$$

where

$$A(t|\tau_0) = \int_{\tau_0}^{t} \alpha(\theta)\, d\theta = \alpha_{l+1}(t - \tau_l) + [1 - I_1(t)] \sum_{k=1}^{l} \alpha_k(\tau_k - \tau_{k-1}), \tag{6}$$

with

$$l = \begin{cases} \sup\{k-1 \,:\, \tau_{k-1} \le t < \tau_k\} & t < \tau_L. \\ L-1 & t \ge \tau_L, \end{cases} \tag{7}$$

We note that the conditional moments of $X(t)$ can be obtained making use of the following moments generating function:

$$G_{X(t)|X(\tau_0)=x_0}(s) = \exp\Big\{-M(t|x_0,\tau_0)s + \frac{V(t|\tau_0)s^2}{2}\Big\}, \qquad s \in \mathbb{R}.$$

Note that both $M(t|y,\tau)$ and $V(t|y,\tau)$, as well as all the conditional moments, involve integrals depending on the functions $\alpha(t), \beta(t)$ and $\sigma^2(t)$.

3 The Inference

In order to provide a procedure for simultaneously estimating the parameters $\alpha_1, \ldots, \alpha_L$ and the functions $\beta(t)$ and $\sigma(t)$, we note that from (4) and (5) we have:

$$\beta(t) = \alpha(t)\, M(t|y,\tau) + \frac{dM(t|y,\tau)}{dt} = \sum_{k=1}^{L} \alpha_k I_k(t)\, M(t|y,\tau) + \frac{dM(t|y,\tau)}{dt}, \tag{8}$$

$$\sigma^2(t) = 2\alpha(t) V(t|\tau) + \frac{dV(t|\tau)}{dt} = 2\sum_{k=1}^{L} \alpha_k I_k(t)\, V(t|\tau) + \frac{dV(t|\tau)}{dt}. \tag{9}$$

To illustrate the suggested procedure, we firstly consider two simpler cases:

Case 1. The parameters $\alpha_1, \ldots, \alpha_L$ have to be estimated, while the functions $\beta(t)$ and $\sigma^2(t)$ are known or previously estimated.

Case 2. The parameters $\alpha_1, \ldots, \alpha_L$ are known or previously estimated whereas the functions $\beta(t)$ and $\sigma^2(t)$ have to be estimated.

Our procedure consists in a combination of the two methodologies used to solve Case 1 and Case 2, respectively.

We point out that the use of the inference procedure requires the knowledge of the times τ_i in which the structural breaks occur. They can be detected by means of several tests (see, for example, [6,7]) as shown in our simulation study proposed in the next section.

In the following, we consider a discrete sampling of the process $X(t)$ based on d sample paths observed at the times t_j, with $j = 1, \ldots, n$, and we assume that $t_1 = \tau_0$. For $i = 1, \ldots, d$ and $j = 1, \ldots, n$, let x_{ij} be the observed values at time instants t_j. Further, for $k = 1, 2, \ldots, L$ let n_k be the number of observations in the interval $[\tau_{k-1}, \tau_k)$. Clearly, $n_1 + \cdots + n_L = n$.

Case 1. We assume that the functions $\beta(t)$ and $\sigma^2(t)$ are known whereas $\alpha_1, \ldots, \alpha_L$ are unknown. In order to estimate the parameters $\alpha_1, \ldots, \alpha_L$ we consider the conditioned likelihood function:

$$\mathbb{L}(\boldsymbol{\alpha}) = \mathbb{L}(\alpha_1, \ldots, \alpha_L) = \prod_{i=1}^{d} \prod_{j=2}^{n} f(x_{i\,j}, t_j \mid x_{i\,j-1}, t_{j-1}),$$

so the log-likelihood function is

$$\begin{aligned}\ln \mathbb{L}(\boldsymbol{\alpha}) = &-\frac{1}{2} \sum_{i=1}^{d} \sum_{j=2}^{n} \ln(2\,\pi) - \frac{1}{2} \sum_{i=1}^{d} \sum_{j=2}^{n} \ln\left(\int_{t_{j-1}}^{t_j} \sigma^2(\vartheta)\, e^{-2A(\vartheta|t_{j-1})}\, d\vartheta \right) \\ &- \sum_{i=1}^{d} \sum_{j=2}^{n} \frac{\left[x_{i\,j} - x_{i\,j-1}\, e^{-A(t_j|t_{j-1})} - \int_{t_{j-1}}^{t_j} \beta(\vartheta)\, e^{-A(\vartheta|t_{j-1})}\, d\vartheta \right]^2}{2 \int_{t_{j-1}}^{t_j} \sigma^2(\vartheta)\, e^{-2\,A(\vartheta|t_{j-1})}\, d\vartheta},\end{aligned}$$

with $A(\cdot|t_{j-1})$ given in (6). For $t_j - t_{j-1} = \Delta$, we consider the following approximation for the integral terms

$$\int_a^b g(\vartheta) d\vartheta \simeq g(a)(b-a),$$

so that, by setting the score function equal to zero, we obtain:

$$C_{1k}\gamma_k^2 - C_{2k}\gamma_k - C_{3k} = 0, \qquad (k = 1, 2, \ldots, L) \tag{10}$$

with $\gamma_k = e^{\alpha_k \Delta}$ and

$$C_{1k} = \sum_{i=1}^{d} \sum_{j=2}^{n_k} \frac{x_{ij}^2}{\sigma^2(t_{j-1})} I_k(t_{j-1}),$$

$$C_{2k} = \sum_{i=1}^{d} \sum_{j=2}^{n_k} \frac{x_{ij} x_{ij-1} + x_{ij} b(t_{j-1}) \Delta}{\sigma^2(t_{j-1})} I_k(t_{j-1}),$$

$$C_{3k} = d(n_k - 1)\Delta.$$

The solutions of (10) are

$$\gamma_k^{(1),(2)} = \frac{C_{2k} \pm \sqrt{C_{2k}^2 + 4C_{1k}C_{3k}}}{2C_{1k}} \qquad \gamma_k^{(2)} < 0 < \gamma_k^{(1)}.$$

Since $\gamma_k = e^{\alpha_k \Delta}$, we consider the positive solution $\gamma_k^{(1)}$, so

$$\widehat{\alpha}_k = \frac{\ln \gamma_k^{(1)}}{\Delta} \qquad (k = 1, 2, \ldots, L).$$

Case 2. Let us assume that the parameters $\alpha_1, \ldots, \alpha_L$ are known and the functions $\beta(t)$ and $\sigma^2(t)$ are unknown and need to estimate.

In this case, from (8) and (9) we suggest the following procedure to estimate $\beta(t)$ and $\sigma^2(t)$:

- From the data $\{x_{ij}\}$, $i = 1, \ldots, d$, and $j = 1, \ldots, n$, obtain the sample mean μ_j and the sample variance ν_j:

$$\mu_j = \frac{1}{d} \sum_{i=1}^{d} x_{ij}, \quad \nu_j = \frac{1}{d-1} \sum_{i=1}^{d} (x_{ij} - \mu_j)^2.$$

- Interpolate the values μ_j and ν_j. Let $\widehat{M}(t)$ and $\widehat{V}(t)$ be the obtained functions.
- Evaluate the derivatives of $\widehat{M}(t)$ and $\widehat{V}(t)$.
- Obtain the estimate of $\beta(t)$ and $\sigma^2(t)$ as follows:

$$\widehat{\beta}(t) = \sum_{k=1}^{L} \alpha_k I_k(t)\, \widehat{M}(t) + \frac{d\widehat{M}(t)}{dt}, \quad \widehat{\sigma}^2(t) = 2 \sum_{k=1}^{L} \alpha_k I_k(t)\, \widehat{V}(t) + \frac{d\widehat{V}(t)}{dt}.$$

The Iterative Procedure. We propose an iterative procedure in which in each iteration the functions $\alpha(t)$, $\beta(t)$ and $\sigma^2(t)$ in (1) are estimated by applying in sequence the algorithms for the Case 1 and Case 2. Precisely, let m be the index of current iteration and $h^{(m)}$ the estimation of h obtained at the m-th iteration. For a fixed precision level ε one has:

- $\mathbf{m = 1}$: By MLE we estimate $\alpha_1^{(m)}, \ldots, \alpha_L^{(m)}$ by using the observations in each interval and by assuming $\beta(t) = \beta$ and $\sigma^2(t) = \sigma^2$;

– **repeat** $\Big\{$ **m = m + 1.**

- Estimate $[\beta(t)]^{(m)}$ and $[\sigma^2(t)]^{(m)}$ via the procedure for Case 2.
- Evaluate

$$C_{1k}^{(m)} = \sum_{i=1}^{d}\sum_{j=2}^{n_k} \frac{x_{i\,j}^2}{[\sigma^2(t_{j-1})]^{(m)}} I_k(t_{j-1}),$$

$$C_{2k}^{(m)} = \sum_{i=1}^{d}\sum_{j=2}^{n_k} \frac{x_{i\,j}x_{i\,j-1} + x_{i\,j}[\beta(t_{j-1})]^{(m)}\Delta}{[\sigma^2(t_{j-1})]^{(m)}} I_k(t_{j-1}),$$

$$C_{3k}^{(m)} = d(n_k - 1)\Delta,$$

$$\gamma_k^{(m)} = \frac{C_{2k}^{(m)} + \sqrt{(C_{2k}^{(m)})^2 + 4C_{1k}^{(m)}C_{3k}^{(m)}}}{2C_{1k}^{(m)}}.$$

- Obtain $\alpha_k^{(m)} = \frac{\ln \gamma_k^{(m)}}{\Delta}, \quad k = 1, \ldots, L. \Big\}$ **until** $\max_k |\alpha_k^{(m)} - \alpha_k^{(m-1)}| < \varepsilon.$

We note that the proposed methodology combines at each iteration a ML-type estimate with GMM. Moreover, a preliminary interpolation of the points μ_j and ν_j is made. Hence, the consistence of the proposed estimators derives from the consistence of the ML and GMM estimators in addition to the uniform convergence of the used interpolation method (for example cubic spline interpolation). Further, the estimators are asymptotically normally distributed.

4 A Simulation Experiment

In order to evaluate the goodness of the proposed procedure, we now consider a simulation experiment for the Case 1, in which it is assumed that the functions $\beta(t)$ and $\sigma^2(t)$ are known and we need to estimate $\alpha(t)$ in (1). Further, we suppose that one structural break occurs in the middle of the observations interval $[0, T]$. Precisely, we set $T = 50$,

$$\beta(t) = 3[1 + \sin(t)], \quad \sigma(t) = 0.25$$

and the break point occurs at time $\tau_1 = 25$, changing the parameter $\alpha_1 = 1$ into $\alpha_2 = 0.5$. Let x_{ij} be the observed values at time instants t_j for $j = 1, \ldots, n$. Here, we assume that the observations are equally spaced with step $\Delta = 0.1$ and we fix the number of sample paths as $d = 50$ and the sample size as $n = 500$, so the sample sizes in the two subintervals $[0, 25]$ and $(25, 50]$ are both equal to 250. In order to show the trend of the process, on the left of Fig. 1 we plot one sample path of $X(t)$ to show the presence of oscillations due to the sinusoidal function in the drift and the changing trend in the center of the observations interval due to the structural break. Moreover, on the right of Fig. 1, we plot the results obtained by applying the Binary Segmentation method to identify change-points in our observations. This is made by using the function *cpt.mean* implemented in the *R*-package *changepoint* choosing a Bayesian Information Criterion penalty. A break is detected at time $\widehat{\tau}_1 = 26.09$ with significance level $\alpha = 0.01$.

In Fig. 2 the results, based on 5000 simulations, for the estimation of the parameter α_1 are shown. We can see that the estimation interval is between 0.95 and 0.98 and the empirical distribution is quite normal. The same encouraging results are obtained for the parameter α_2, as shown in Fig. 3. Finally, in Fig. 4 a simulated (blue curve) and an estimated (red curve) paths of $X(t)$ are plotted, showing that the estimated functions well fit the simulated ones. The red curve is obtained by plugging the mean of the 5000 estimates for $alpha_1$ and α_2 and by considering as the time in which the break occurs $\widehat{\tau}_1 = 26.09$.

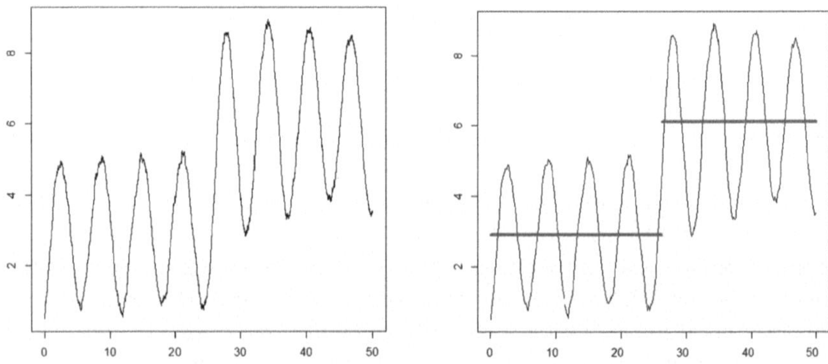

Fig. 1. A sample path of the simulated process $X(t)$ with $\alpha_1 = 1, \alpha_2 = 0.5$ and $\tau_1 = 25$ (on the left) and the result of the Binary Segmentation test for the simulated experiment (on the right).

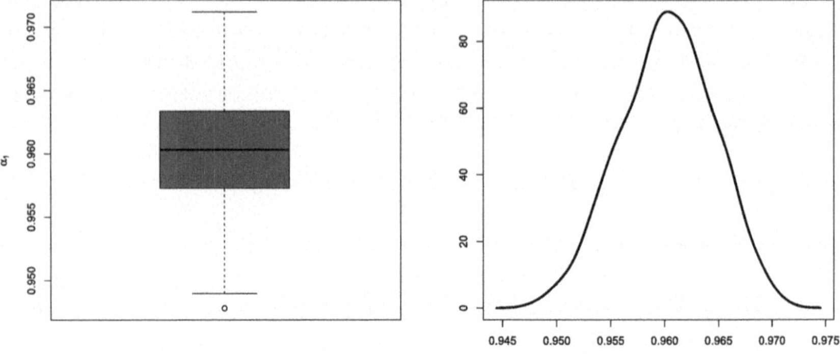

Fig. 2. Results, based on 5000 simulations, for the estimation of the parameter α_1.

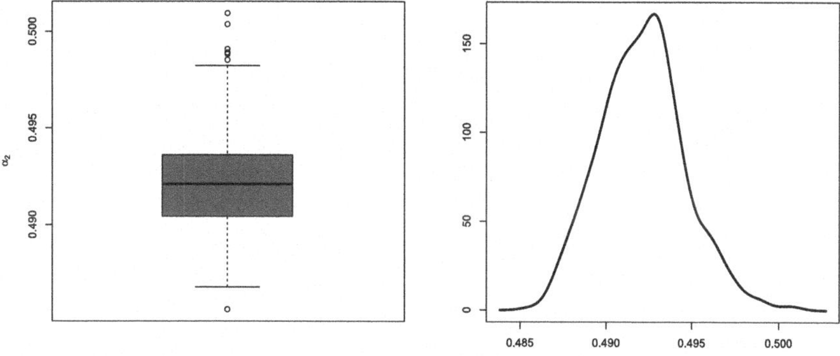

Fig. 3. Results, based on 5000 simulations, for the estimation of the parameter α_2.

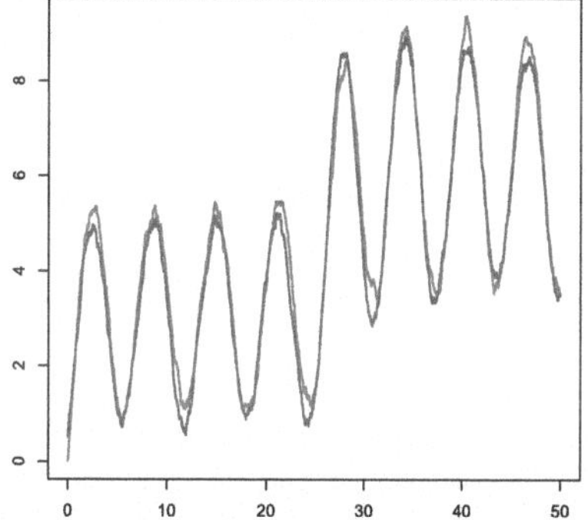

Fig. 4. Simulated (blue curve) and estimated paths (red curve) of $X(t)$. (Color figure online)

5 Conclusions

We considered a time inhomogeneous process in which the drift includes a piecewise linear function and the infinitesimal variance generally depends on time. In particular we focused on the inference for such process. In this direction, a prior analytical study of the probability distribution of the process was performed in order to look at the involved log-likelihood. Following [5], we provided an iterative estimation procedure based on the maximum likelihood estimation and the GMM. A simple simulation study was made in which one break occurs in the middle of the observations interval. A suitable test was preliminary implemented to detect the point of the structural break, and only then the proposed procedure was applied by using the estimated break. The results seem to fit very well the simulated sample paths and they encourage to follow this direction for future studies such as further simulations and investigations on the role of the preliminary tests to check for the breakpoints. Finally, it would be interesting to investigate the Kullback-Leibler divergence as an instrument for checking the underlying model, in particular it could be used as a test statistic to support the hypothesis of the presence of structural break in the diffusion processes.

Acknowledgments. This paper is partially supported by MUR-PRIN 2022, project 2022XZSAFN " Anomalous Phenomena on Regular and Irregular Domains: Approximating Complexity for the Applied Sciences", and MUR-PRIN 2022 PNRR, project P2022XSF5H "Stochastic Models in Biomathematics and Applications". The authors are members of the GNCS-INdAM.

References

1. Leung, T., Li, X.: Optimal Mean-Reversion Trading: Mathematical Analysis and Practical Applications. World Scientific Publishing Co. ISBN 978-9814725910 (2016)
2. Tang, C.Y., Chen, S.X.: Parameter estimation and bias correction for diffusion processes. J. Econometrics **149**(1), 65–81 (2009)
3. Albano, G., La Rocca, M., Perna, C.: Small sample properties of ML estimator in vasicek and CIR models: a simulation experiment. Decis. Econ. Finance **42**(1), 5–19 (2019)
4. Albano, G., Giorno, V.: Inferring time non-homogeneous Ornstein Uhlenbeck type stochastic process. Comput. Stat. Data Anal. **150**, 107008 (2020)
5. Albano, G., Giorno, V.: Inference on the effect of non homogeneous inputs in Ornstein-Uhlenbeck neuronal modeling. Math. Biosci. Eng. **19**(1), 328–348 (2020)
6. Albano, G.: Detecting time-changes in PM10 during Covid pandemic by means of an Ornstein Uhlenbeck type process. Math. Biosci. Eng. **18**(1), 888–903 (2020)
7. Lee, S., Nishiyama, Y., Yoshida, N.: Test for parameter change in diffusion processes by cusum statistics based on one-step estimators. Ann. Inst. Stat. Math. **58**, 211–222 (2006)

Estimating a Time-Inhomogeneous Hyperlogistic Diffusion Process

G. Albano[1], A. Barrera[2,5(✉)], V. Giorno[3], and F. Torres-Ruiz[4,5]

[1] Department of Political and Social Studies, University of Salerno, Salerno, Italy
pialbano@unisa.it

[2] Department of Mathematical Analysis, Statistics and Operations Research and Applied Mathematics, University of Málaga, Málaga, Spain
antonio.barrera@uma.es

[3] Dipartimento di Informatica, Università degli Studi di Salerno, Salerno, Italy
giorno@unisa.it

[4] Department of Statistics and Operations Research, University of Granada, Granada, Spain
fdeasis@ugr.es

[5] Institute of Mathematics of the University of Granada (IMAG), Granada, Spain

Abstract. We consider a stochastic model for the hyperlogistic curve, a general growth curve that includes well known models, such as Malthus, logistic and Bertalanffy. The problem of the estimation of the parameters is addressed by means of the maximum likelihood method. Due to the complexity of the resulting system of equations, the solution is approximated via metaheuristic procedures, concretely the Moth-Flame Optimization (MFO) algorithm.

Keywords: Growth curves · Inference in diffusion processes · Metaheuristic procedures

1 Introduction

Mathematical models to describe dynamic phenomena associated with growth curves are topics that have caught the eyes of many researchers. The introduction of regulatory effect into the Malthusian model gave rise to classical models such as based on the logistic or the Gompertz curves. In order to obtain curves with greater flexibility, various generalizations have been proposed. To do this, several techniques have been used, among which we can cite the introduction of suitable parameters and the use of functions with flexible behaviors. Moreover, the fact that deterministic models cannot control the variability of the phenomena has then motivated the use of randomization procedures into the ordinary differential equations that govern such models. This led to the consideration of stochastic differential equations, whose solutions are, under certain conditions, diffusion processes (see, for instance, [1–3]).

A. Quesada-Arencibia et al. (Eds.): EUROCAST 2024, LNCS 15174, pp. 295–303, 2025.
https://doi.org/10.1007/978-3-031-83885-9_27

In this paper we focus on an interesting particular case of the general growth curve described in [4,5], whose functional expression is given by

$$x(t) = x_0 \frac{g(t_0)}{g(t)}, \qquad t \geq t_0, \; x_0 > 0, \tag{1}$$

where

$$g(t) = \left(\eta + \left(1 + \eta^{1-p}(1-p)\, t \, \log\alpha\right)^{\frac{1}{1-p}}\right)^{1/n}, \tag{2}$$

being η a positive real number, $0 < \alpha < 1$, $n > 0$ and $1 < p < 1 + 1/n$.

It is important to note that curve (1) verifies a Malthusian-type differential equation, concretely

$$\frac{dx}{dt} = h(t)\, x(t), \tag{3}$$

where

$$h(t) = -\frac{\eta^{1-p} \ln\alpha \,[1 + \eta^{1-p} \ln\alpha\,(1-p)\, t]^{p/(1-p)}}{n\,[g(t)]^n}, \tag{4}$$

represents a time dependent fertility rate.

Within this broad family of curves, below we focus our attention on the particular case $n = 1$. This is an important case since it corresponds to the hyperlogistic curve, that is widely used in literature for describing real dynamics of phenomena ranging from economics to biology (see, for example, [6,7] and references therein). Further, we point out that for different choices of the parameter p, we can distinguish three kinds of behaviors of $x(t)$ (see [4]): (a) $1 < p < 2$, (b) $p = 1$, (c) $0 < p < 1$.

In cases (a) and (b) the curve is defined in $[t_0, \infty)$ and it has a sigmoidal shape. In the third case, $x(t)$ exhibits different behaviors depending on the following conditions on the ratio $m = \frac{1}{1-p}$: (c1) m even, (c2) m odd, (c3) $m \notin \mathbb{N}$. In case (c1), $x(t)$ is bell-shaped and a plateau is highlighted whose amplitude increases as p increases. In case (c2), $x(t)$ explodes in a finite time. Further, also in this case, $x(t)$ presents a plateau, whose amplitude increases as p increases, after that $x(t)$ presents an exponential behavior. Finally, in case (c3) $x(t)$ is defined in a finite time interval $[t_0, t_2)$, whose amplitude decreases for increasing p; moreover, $\lim_{t \to t_2} x(t) < \infty$, so the population reaches its carrying capacity in a finite time interval. Cases (a), (c1) and (c2) seem particularly interesting for modeling different kinds of real phenomena, so in this paper we focus on such cases, even if the theoretical results hold for all the values of p.

The introduction of a multiplicative noise in (3) gives rise to the model considered here, that is a nonhomogeneous lognormal diffusion process. The application of such stochastic models relies on the determination of their parameters, that may lead to scenarios where the estimation is hard or even impossible to accomplish. For this reason, the study of the deterministic model, trying to understand the connection between its parameters, allows us to consider bounded parametric regions in order to apply different metaheuristic approaches.

The outline of the paper is the following. In Sect. 2 we derive a stochastic process related to the hyperlogistic curve and we study its probability distribution. In Sect. 3 we analyze the estimation problem and we discuss the use of a metaheuristic optimization method. In Sect. 4 several simulation studies are provided and finally, some conclusions close the paper in Sect. 5.

2 The Hyperlogistic Diffusion Process

The hyperlogistic diffusion process, associated with the particular case of curve (1) when $n = 1$, is obtained from the deterministic growth equation (3) after introducing in it a multiplicative noise. Precisely, the fertility rate $h(t)$, given by (4), is replaced by $h(t) + \varphi(t)$, where $\varphi(t)$ is a white noise with variance σ^2. In this way, the deterministic equation (3) is generalized to the stochastic differential equation:

$$dX(t) = h(t)X(t)\,dt + \sigma\,X(t)\,dW(t), \quad t \geq t_0, \tag{5}$$

where the initial condition $X(t_0) = X_0$ is set to be independent of $W(t)$ for $t \geq t_0$. The solution of (5) is a nonhomogeneous lognormal diffusion process, characterized by drift $h(t)x$ and diffusion coefficient $\sigma^2 x^2$ (see [10] and references therein for details). The solution has the following closed-form expression:

$$X(t) = X_0 \exp\left[H(t_0, t) + \sigma\left(W(t) - W(t_0)\right)\right], \tag{6}$$

with

$$H(s,t) = \int_s^t h(u)du - \frac{\sigma^2}{2}(t-s) = \log\frac{g(s)}{g(t)} - \frac{\sigma^2}{2}(t-s),$$

with $g(t)$ defined in (2).

If the initial distribution is lognormal, i.e. $X_0 \sim \Lambda_1\left(\mu_0, \sigma_0^2\right)$ for some parameters μ_0 and σ_0^2, or degenerate at a point x_0, the finite-dimensional distributions of the process are lognormal. Concretely, $\forall n \in \mathbb{N}$ and $t_1 < \cdots < t_n$, vector $(X(t_1), \ldots, X(t_n))^T$ has a n-dimensional lognormal distribution $\Lambda_n[\boldsymbol{\varepsilon}, \boldsymbol{\Sigma}]$, where the components of the vector $\boldsymbol{\varepsilon}$ and of the matrix $\boldsymbol{\Sigma}$ are

$$\varepsilon_i = \mu_0 + H(t_0, t_i), \; i = 1, \ldots, n; \quad \sigma_{ij} = \sigma_0^2 + \sigma^2[min(t_i, t_j) - t_0], \; i, j = 1, \ldots, n,$$

respectively. The transition probability density function can be obtained from the distribution of $X(s), X(t))^T$, $s < t$, being

$$f(x, t|y, s) = \frac{1}{x\sqrt{2\pi\sigma^2(t-s)}} \exp\left(-\frac{\left[\ln(x/y) - H(s,t)\right]^2}{2\sigma^2(t-s)}\right),$$

that is, $X(t)|X(s) = y$ follows a lognormal distribution

$$X(t) \mid X(s) = y \rightsquigarrow \Lambda_1\left(\ln y + H(s,t), \sigma^2(t-s)\right), \quad s < t.$$

It is worth noting that, due to the procedure used to build the stochastic process, the mean behavior of the sample paths is given by the curve (1). Indeed, from the one-dimensional distributions and the transition distributions we find that the mean function and the conditioned mean function are, respectively,

$$E[X(t)] = E[X_0]\,\frac{g(t_0)}{g(t)} \quad \text{and} \quad E[X(t)|X(t_0) = x_0] = x(t).$$

3 Inference

In this section we will deal with the estimation of the parameters of the process by maximum likelihood. Let $\theta = (\eta, \alpha, p, \sigma)^T$ the vector containing the parameters of the process. We consider a discrete sampling of the process based on d sample paths observed at the times t_{ij}, with $i = 1, \ldots, d$ and $j = 1, \ldots, n$, and we assume that $t_{i1} = t_1$ for $i = 1, \cdots, d$. Let x_{ij} be the observed values at time instants t_{ij}, $i = 1, \ldots, d$ and $j = 1, \cdots, n$. For the sake of simplicity, we consider a degenerate initial distribution. In this way, the log-likelihood function is

$$L(\theta) = -\frac{d(n-1)}{2}\log\sigma^2 - \frac{1}{2\sigma^2}\sum_{i=1}^{d}\sum_{j=2}^{n_i}\frac{1}{\Delta_{ij}}\left(Q_{ij} - T_{ij} + \frac{\sigma^2}{2}\Delta_{ij}\right)^2 \tag{7}$$

with $\Delta_{ij} = t_{ij} - t_{ij-1}$, $Q_{ij} = \log\dfrac{x_{ij}}{x_{ij-1}}$ and $T_{ij} = \log\dfrac{g_\theta(t_{ij-1})}{g(t_{ij})}$.

The estimation of the parameters requires to solve a complex system of equations without an explicit solution. Therefore, we propose the use of metaheuristic algorithms that try to find the solution of an optimization problem by iterative procedures in which the current solution must be better than the previous one. In particular, we focus on the MFO method that is a population based algorithm inspired by the navigation of the moths around flames. Specifically, every moth moves around a flame which represents a good fit of the objective function. At each iteration, flames are sorted and reduced in number. At the final stage, the moths are flying around the best flame, which marks the point that maximize the objective function (in our case, (7)). We point out that the use of such approach requires the preliminary limitation of the parametric space that we realize by means of the study of the deterministic model (see, for example, [8,9]).

4 A Simulation Study

In order to evaluate the goodness of the proposed procedure, we perform a simulation study in which we consider three different behaviors of the process $X(t)$, related to cases (a), (c1) and (c2) described in the first Section. Such choice seems reasonable since in [4] it is shown that, for the deterministic model $x(t)$, they correspond to realistic dynamics. In particular, case (a) corresponds to the sigmoidal growth; case (c1) shows an initial growth, followed by a quite constant size and a final decrease of the population size; case (c2) differs from case (c1) in the last part where it grows indefinitely.

For all simulations, we consider $\eta = 0.0025$, $\alpha = 0.606$, $\sigma = 0.025$ and $x_0 = 0.2$. For each case, 50 simulated paths, each with $n = 501$ equally spaced points, have been simulated from $t_0 = 0$ to $T = 50$, using (6). The version of the MFO algorithm used is the one implemented in the *metaheuristicOpt* R package. In each case, 500 iterations of the algorithm has been considered. Figure 1 shows the simulated sample paths for several values of p in case (a). We can observe that the inflection point of the sample paths become more and more close to $t_0 = 0$ as p increases. This result is in accordance with the study provided for the deterministic equation (1) in [4]. Table 1 shows the results of the estimates produced by the MFO algorithm. The Mean Relative Error (MRE) is also shown in order to give a measure of the goodness of fit.

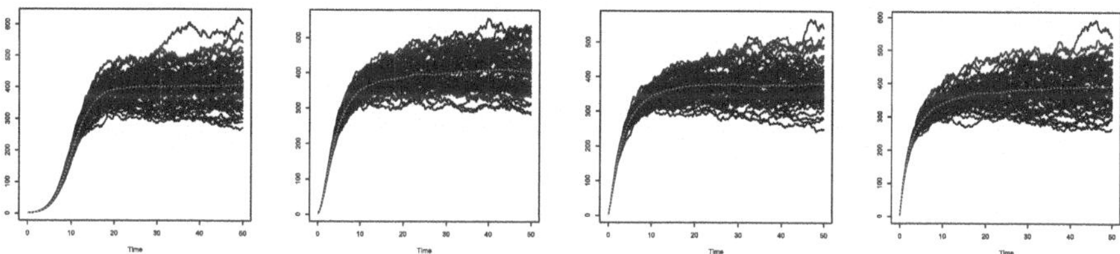

Fig. 1. Case (a): Sample paths of the process. $p = 1.1, 1.5, 1.7, 1.9$ (left to right).

Table 1. Case (a): MFO estimates of the parameters. $p = 1.1, 1.5, 1.7, 1.9$.

Id.	Type	η	α	p	σ	MRE
1	Original	0.0025	0.606	1.1	0.025	
	Estimated	0.0024	0.657	1.1117	0.025	0.0294
2	Original	0.0025	0.606	1.5	0.025	
	Estimated	0.0025	0.609	1.5019	0.0249	0.0029
3	Original	0.0025	0.606	1.7	0.025	
	Estimated	0.0025	0.6031	1.7003	0.025	0.0045
4	Original	0.0025	0.606	1.9	0.025	
	Estimated	0.0025	0.6073	1.9008	0.025	0.0012

In Fig. 2 the convergence of the MFO algorithm is plotted for the case $p = 1.1$. We can observe that the procedure reaches the final estimates in almost 100 iterations. In Fig. 3 the sample paths for case (c1) are plotted for $p = 1/2, 3/4, 5/6, 7/8$, i.e. $m = 2, 4, 6, 8$. We can observe that by increasing p, the width of the plateau of each sample path increases, showing that such model is able to describe different phenomena related, for example, to epidemics.

In Table 2 the results of MFO estimates are shown for the same values of p in Fig. 3. In this case the MRE's are bigger than the previous case, due to the worst estimation of the parameter p. Anymore, the convergence of the procedure is reached in less than 100 iterations.

Case (c2) is shown in Fig. 4 where the sample paths of the process $X(t)$ are plotted for $p = 2/3, 4/5, 6/7, 8/9$. Also in this case, when p increases, the plateau of $X(t)$ becomes larger. Table 3 shows that the estimates present a MRE's lower than the previous case, so the estimates fit well the simulated values.

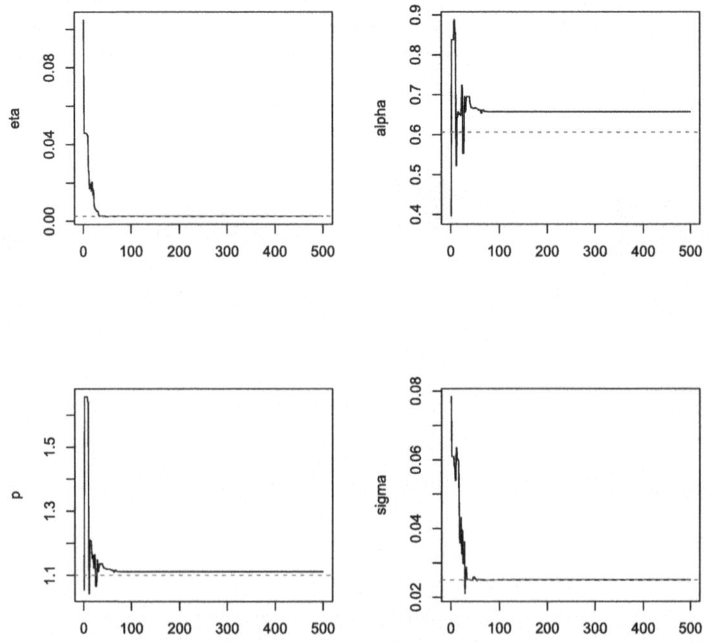

Fig. 2. Case (a): Convergence of MFO algorithm for each parameter. $p = 1.1$.

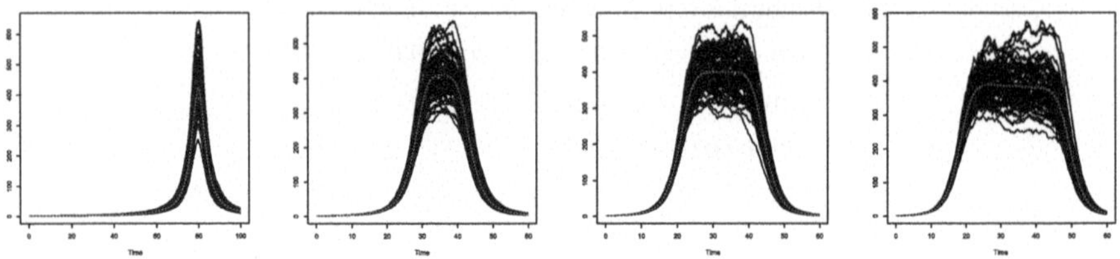

Fig. 3. Case (c1): Sample paths of the process. $p = 1/2, 3/4, 5/6, 7/8$ (left to right).

Table 2. Case (c1): MFO estimates of the parameters. $p = 1/2, 3/4, 5/6, 7/8$.

Id.	Type	η	α	p	σ	MRE	
1	Original	0.0025	0.606	0.5	0.025		$m = 2$
	Estimated	0.0017	0.8443	0.8105	0.0395	0.4794	
2	Original	0.0025	0.606	0.75	0.025		$m = 4$
	Estimated	0.0015	0.7289	0.8962	0.0495	0.4458	
3	Original	0.0025	0.606	0.83	0.025		$m = 6$
	Estimated	0.0017	0.6924	0.9284	0.05	0.3907	
4	Original	0.0025	0.606	0.875	0.025		$m = 8$
	Estimated	0.002	0.6674	0.94	0.05	0.3466	

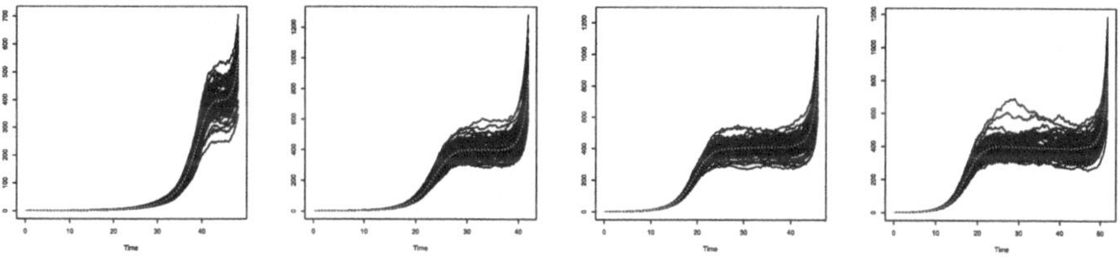

Fig. 4. Case (c2): Sample paths of the process. $p = 2/3, 4/5, 6/7, 8/9$ (left to right).

Table 3. Case (c2): MFO estimates of the parameters. $p = 2/3, 4/5, 6/7, 8/9$.

Id.	Type	η	α	p	σ	MRE	
1	Original	0.0025	0.606	0.6667	0.025		$m = 3$
	Estimated	0.0018	0.6613	0.739	0.0275	0.1419	
2	Original	0.0025	0.606	0.8	0.025		$m = 5$
	Estimated	0.0021	0.6664	0.8631	0.0351	0.1869	
3	Original	0.0025	0.606	0.8571429	0.025		$m = 7$
	Estimated	0.002	0.6543	0.9094	0.034	0.1757	
4	Original	0.0025	0.606	0.8889	0.025		$m = 9$
	Estimated	0.0021	0.6476	0.9327	0.0335	0.1542	

5 Conclusions

We consider a stochastic generalization of the hyperlogistic growth curve, given in (5). In particular, we consider a multiplicative white noise in (5), obtaining a non homogeneous lognormal process in which the parameters are η, α, p and σ. By looking at the maximum likelihood estimation, we obtain a system of equations that is impossible to analytically and also numerically solve. To the aim of finding the maximum likelihood estimates, we propose a MFO algorithm, that is a metaheuristic algorithm. This method presupposes a limitation of the parameter space which is carried out here by looking at the study of the deterministic equation (1). A simulation study shows the goodness of the proposed estimating procedure.

The present work paves the way for future works in which inference procedures in the general case of the model proposed in [5]. Further, other ways of introducing stochasticity into growth equations can also be investigated, for example by introducing an additive noise. It therefore becomes interesting to find inference procedures suitable for the various stochastic resulting processes. Finally, the comparison between several metaheuristic procedures available in literature for the inference is a field to investigate. These topics will be the subject of future research.

Acknowledgments. Work supported in part by PID2020-1187879GB-100 and CEX2020-001105-M grants, funded by MCIN/AEI/10.13039/501100011033, Spain and by PRIN 2022, the project "Anomalous Phenomena on Regular and Irregular Domains: Approximating Complexity for the Applied Sciences", and PRIN 2022 PNRR, the project "Stochastic Models in Biomathematics and Applications". The authors G.A. and V.G. are members of the research group GNCS of INdAM.

References

1. Albano, G., Giorno, V., Román-Román, P., Román-Román, S., Serrano-Peréz, J.J., Torres-Ruiz, F.: Inference on an heteroscedastic Gompertz tumor growth model. Math. Biosci. **328**, 108428 (2020). https://doi.org/10.1016/j.mbs.2020.108428
2. Barrera, A., Román-Román, P., Serrano-Peréz, J.J., Torres-Ruiz, F.: Two multi-sigmoidal diffusion models for the study of the evolution of the COVID-19 pandemic. Mathematics **9**, 2409 (2021). https://doi.org/10.3390/math9192409
3. Lo, C.F.: A modified stochastic Gompertz model for tumour cell growth. Comput. Math. Methods Med. **11**(1), 3–11 (2010). https://doi.org/10.1080/17486700802545543
4. Albano, G., Giorno, V., Román-Román, P., Torres-Ruiz, F.: Study of a general growth model. Commun. Nonlinear Sci. Numer. Simul. **107**, 106100 (2022). https://doi.org/10.1016/j.cnsns.2021.106100
5. Albano, G., Barrera, A., Giorno, V., Román-Román, P., Torres-Ruiz, F.: First Passage and First Exit Times for diffusion processes related to a general growth curve. Commun. Nonlinear Sci. Numer. Simul. **126**, 107494–107509 (2023). https://doi.org/10.1016/j.cnsns.2023.107494
6. Kyurkchiev, N.: Investigations on a hyper-logistic model. Some applications. Dynamic Systems and Applications **28**(2), 351–369 (2019). https://doi.org/10.12732/dsa.v28i2.9
7. Windarto, W., Eridani, E., Utami, D.P.: A new modified logistic growth model for empirical use. Commun. Biomathematical Sci. **1**(2), 122–131 (2018). https://doi.org/10.5614/cbms.2018.1.2.5
8. Barrera, A., Román-Román, P., Torres-Ruiz, F.: A hyperbolastic type-I diffusion process: Parameter estimation by means of the firefly algorithm. Biosystems **163**, 11–22 (2018). https://doi.org/10.1016/j.biosystems.2017.11.001

9. Barrera, A., Román-Román, P., Torres-Ruiz, F.: T-growth stochastic model: Simulation and inference via metaheuristic algorithms. Mathematics **9**(9), 959 (2021). https://doi.org/10.3390/math9090959
10. Román-Román, P., Román-Román, S., Serrano-Pérez, J.J., Torres-Ruiz, F.: Some Notes about inference for the lognormal diffusion process with exogenous factors. Mathematics **6**, 85 (2018). https://doi.org/10.3390/math6050085

Systems Cybersecurity Technologies and Quantum Approaches Potentials

A Federated Learning-Based Android Malware Detector Through Differential Privacy

Christian Peluso[2], Giovanni Ciaramella[1,2], Francesco Mercaldo[2,3](✉), Antonella Santone[3], and Fabio Martinelli[4]

[1] IMT School for Advanced Studies Lucca, Lucca, Italy
giovanni.ciaramella@imtlucca.it

[2] Institute for Informatics and Telematics, National Research Council of Italy, Pisa, Italy
{christian.peluso,giovanni.ciaramella,francesco.mercaldo, fabio.martinelli}@iit.cnr.it

[3] Department of Medicine and Health Sciences "Vincenzo Tiberio", University of Molise, Campobasso, Italy
{francesco.mercaldo,antonella.santone}@unimol.it

[4] Institute for High Performance Computing and Networking, National Research Council of Italy (CNR), Rende, Italy
fabio.martinelli@icar.cnr.it

Abstract. Discerning malware from trustworthy applications in Android has become imperative due to the increasing occurrence of fraud losses in this market area. To comply with General Data Protection Regulation, we propose an Android malware detector by exploiting federated learning to train a shared model, incorporating an additional layer of privacy preservation using a differential privacy aggregator. In this way, the trained model not only gathers all the characteristics of the models trained on locally preserved datasets but also ensures that the aggregation of these models is robust against sniffing attacks by malicious users. Specifically, we tested our model, built on top of the MobileNetV3 architecture, with default and differential privacy aggregators to analyze the properties of these techniques and their effect on the model's performance and generalization capabilities. Additionally, to simulate a real-world scenario as closely as possible, we distributed the dataset into Independent and Identically Distributed and non-Independent and Identically Distributed settings, reduced the training parameters of the model, and compressed the size of the dataset to ensure compatibility with the majority of smartphones' CPUs and RAM available in the today market. The results demonstrate that a trade-off between privacy and classification capabilities is possible with an accuracy of 84.1%.

Keywords: Deep Learning · Federated Machine Learning · Mobile · Malware · Android · Security

A. Quesada-Arencibia et al. (Eds.): EUROCAST 2024, LNCS 15174, pp. 307–319, 2025.
https://doi.org/10.1007/978-3-031-83885-9_28

1 Introduction

The paramount challenge for malware classifiers today is to balance the ever-evolving threats posed by ransomware, worms, and general viruses, and the odds are not in our favor. Data is increasingly decentralized and generated directly by users, often without sufficient awareness of the risks associated with device misuse. Research by Zimperium, a Google partner working with Malware Mitigation[1], reveals a growing number of sophisticated cybercriminals exploiting these vulnerabilities. Adding to the problem, security budgets and staffing levels have remained stagnant, leaving many security sectors without adequate countermeasures. For instance, losses from online payment fraud reached $41 billion in 2023 and are projected to rise to $48 billion in 2024. Additionally, a staggering 70% of digital fraud now targets mobile devices [1].

However, considering the increasing availability of robust and pre-trained models compatible with the range of devices on the market, in this paper we propose a deep learning classifier that can learn malware features and correctly flag them as malicious, thus defending mobile users. To achieve this, we can leverage the federated learning technique, which allows us to fit the model on local user data while respecting their privacy. This boosts the capabilities of the architecture by generalizing the training data and continuously learning new patterns. Moreover, this method would be compatible with the new General Data Protection Regulation (GDPR) of the EU.

A potential threat could be posed by a sniffer positioned between the server and the federated collaborators. This could recreate the training data owned by the user by analyzing the client's gradient updates. Although such events are particularly rare, they represent a significant security threat to current federated solutions. To prevent this possibility, we added a second layer of privacy using a differential privacy (DP) aggregator. We compare and analyze the trade-offs between it with the default aggregator, in terms of generalization and accuracy.

The upcoming sections will provide the methodology on which the proposal is based in Sect. 2. This will also include the experiments conducted to verify the properties of the problem, which will be illustrated in Sect. 3. However, to understand the magnitude of the results proposed by the literature in the same area of expertise, references from other authors will be reported in Sect. 4. The paper concludes with the conclusions and future developments in Sect. 5.

2 The Method

In this section, we will delve into the technicalities of the proposed Android malware detector, illustrated in Fig. 1. This includes the architecture customization in Sect. 2.1, conversion of *.apk* files to *.png* files in Sect. 2.2, the composition and division of the dataset in Sect. 2.3, and the properties and characteristics of the federated learning method in Sect. 2.4. Concluding the methodology, we will illustrate how the experiments were conducted to analyze and tackle the problem in Sect. 2.5.

[1] https://appdefensealliance.dev/malware-mitigation.

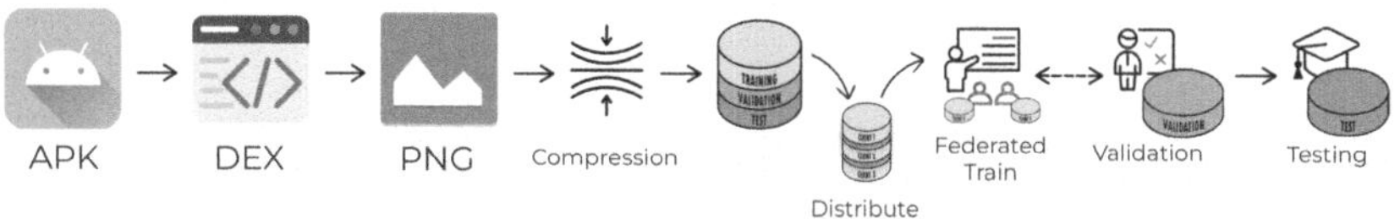

Fig. 1. The proposed Android malware detector involves the conversion and extraction of the application's DEX instructions to construct the images, the latter are compressed and organized to form the dataset. This dataset is then distributed to ensure compatibility with the federated training and validation phases. Finally, the model is tested and deployed.

2.1 Design Rationale and Architectural Variations

It's common practice to convert applications into images for use with convolutional classifiers to extract features from APKs and classify them as either malicious or trustworthy. However, our choice in this regard isn't solely due to the simplicity of the process, but also influenced by the availability of well-designed architectures that are lightweight and efficient in image feature extraction. This consideration is crucial for employing federated learning, especially since not all devices on the market can handle the intensive training demands of deep learning models, particularly when dealing with datasets as comprehensive as those from Android applications.

Instead, our architecture prioritizes compatibility with smartphones, leading us to select MobileNetV3. This model was chosen for its capabilities inherited from previous versions, including depthwise and pointwise convolutions, an inverted residual structure with linear bottlenecks, and lightweight attention modules based on squeeze-and-excitation within the bottleneck structure of the final block. These features enable significant computational savings without sacrificing performance.

To facilitate the federated training phase, we pre-trained this model to generate latent spatial features. Subsequently, we froze this component to utilize it as an embedding model, creating a vector that encapsulates all image characteristics. This vector can then be easily classified using a conventional dense neural network (NN). Essentially, collaborators need only train this final NN, thereby reducing computational costs substantially, which were incurred during the pre-training phase conducted comfortably using conventional centralized learning techniques.

Finally, we decided to vary the model's normalization technique by opting for Group Normalization (GN) due to its invariance to batch size. This is particularly important in the federated procedure, as batch sizes are not guaranteed to be homogeneous across all collaborators. The reasons together with details will be discussed in Sect. 2.4. To ensure consistency in the type of hidden spatial features, we pre-trained the custom architecture with the CIFAR-10 dataset. This dataset is open source and relatively small, allowing for reproducibility and facilitating the pre-training phase.

2.2 Image Generation

To delve into the intricate workings of Android applications and distinguish between their trustworthiness and potential malicious intent, a meticulous process unfolds. Initially, the APK file undergoes a transformation: its extension is changed from .apk to .zip, granting access to its inner components.

Once unzipped, attention turns to the classes.dex file nestled within. This file holds the application's core logic, representing its functionality in a compact yet complex manner.

To make sense of this code, it undergoes a conversion to valorize the instructions into a comprehensible structure. Each instruction is meticulously mapped to an ASCII code, a process that involves algorithms and hash functions to ensure each instruction is uniquely represented. This mapping lays the foundation for visualizing the application's complexity in a tangible form.

An image is then generated where every pixel corresponds to an ASCII code derived from a bytecode instruction. This visual representation encapsulates the nuances of the application's Dex code, providing a unique fingerprint of its inner workings.

2.3 Dataset

Once the images were formed, we grouped them under the correct label, identified through the use of VirusTotal[2] to verify whether the applications contain payloads or not. Consequently, the dataset formed was binary. However, it is important to mention that within the malware label, there are 72 different families of malware to ensure diversity during the training phase. Furthermore, the dataset consists of over 40,000 samples, resulting in the images' cumulative size composing an extraordinarily large dataset, totaling over 160GB.

Therefore, it was necessary to compress the images to be compatible with a realistic simulation of the federated approach, avoiding saturation of mobile device RAM. This compression reduced the dataset's size to approximately 2GB in total, significantly decreasing both experiment times and the carbon footprint of this study.

2.4 Federated Learning

The ever-growing necessity of mobile phones to access services transformed to the digital world has created a new trend: data are generated by users' fingertips on their smartphones. These data are regulated by GDPR, as they include sensitive information about the user. Thankfully, organizations and digital companies don't have access to this data unless they use methodologies that preserve user privacy.

Federated Learning (FL) emerged from Google's need to understand users' keystrokes to construct words, aiding in word prediction from personalized

[2] https://www.virustotal.com/.

vocabularies on Android devices. Transferring such sensitive information to a server would be impractical, as it could potentially recreate a user's chat history. Instead, with FL, not the data but the model is moved, along with the training phase, which starts whenever the smartphone is connected to an unmetered network and is charging, ensuring the user retains the full capabilities of their smartphone.

Over the years, various proposals have refined federated training to be more robust against skewed data, sniffing attacks, and high communication costs, or to save computation by using different algorithms, aggregators, or by reiterating different local epochs before communicating gradient updates. In our case, we use the Federated Average algorithm together with the differential private aggregator.

Private Adaptive Quantile Clipping incorporates differential privacy mechanisms into the aggregation process, ensuring that the adapted quantile-clipped value computed on the gradients and used as a threshold to aggregate the model update does not reveal sensitive information about any individual client's data. By adding carefully calibrated Gaussian noise to the private clipping threshold, this aggregator protects against privacy breaches while still boosting model training across distributed data sources. Differential Private Aggregation, using the precedent algorithm, permits the public release of model parameters with strong guarantees that adversaries are severely limited in what they can learn about the original training data based on analyzing the model's parameters, even with access to arbitrary side information. This aggregator aims to train a model satisfying differential privacy fundamentals with respect to user-adjacent datasets, ensuring that the presence or absence of any specific user's data has an imperceptible impact on the model parameters. Differential privacy rules out the memorization of sensitive information in a strong information-theoretic sense. The aggregator includes the technique for securing the adapted quantile clipping threshold with differential privacy procedures, maintaining a fixed L2 norm for the gradients and allowing Gaussian noise to be added to the gradient updates within a bound on the total privacy cost in terms of accuracy.

Our simulation considers both IID and non-IID data distributions, reflecting real-world scenarios where the likelihood of homogeneous data across all clients is nearly zero. Users have different personalities, hobbies, and jobs, leading to diverse data accumulation on their smartphones. To model this, we use the Dirichlet distribution, assigning each label a value in the range $[0, 1]$. This value is conditioned by the α_D parameter, which, when close to 0, decreases the probability, but all of the events probabilities have still to sum 1, consequently one label will have a peak of probability, creating a heterogeneous distribution. Finally, the probability assigned to each label is multiplied by the number of samples per label, distributing the dataset across clients.

Moreover, our experiments involve a pool of M clients, from which $S^{(T)}$ clients are randomly selected each round to simulate the scenario where not all clients are available simultaneously. This approach helps us analyze the robustness and effectiveness of the federated learning process in realistic settings.

2.5 Experiments

For the parameterization of the training phase, we opted for a random search, as the space of variables was too extensive to perform an exhaustive search of all the hyperparameters as depicted in [4]. For the actual problem, we adapted these parameters with the aggregator module, following the line search methodology of the authors. Thus, the Differential Private aggregator involves the noise multiplier (ϵ_{DP}) and the zeroing boolean aggregator.

To analyze and comprehend the properties of the task, we generated all combinations of IID and non-IID distributions, types of aggregators, and model pretraining. Indeed, the results illustrated in the following section will include 12 combinations, plus the centralized classical training, to provide a basis for comparison.

3 Results

Regarding the dataset it is composed in balanced manner between malware and trusted applications for a total of 46 867 samples. We performed a split with a 70-20-10 ratio, as reported in Table 1. Given the dataset's size, testing with 10% of the total samples is more than sufficient to verify the properties of the central model.

Table 1. Number of samples per label and relative subdivision.

Class Name	# Training	# Validation	# Test
Malware	16 402	4687	2345
Trusted	16 402	4687	2344
Total	32 804	9374	4689

The training data is distributed among the clients to initiate the federated simulation. The dynamics of the default and dirichlet processes for the dataset are illustrated by the example distributions across $M = 40$ clients in Figs. 2a and 2b, respectively. As observed from the graphs, the order of magnitude of the dataset belonging to each local client is approximately the same. This consistency is necessary because clients require a minimum amount of data to perform proper updates, and with the larger dataset, we can simulate more extensive distributions.

In our setup, we employ two optimizers: one designated for the server ($_S$) and another replicated for each client ($_C$), along with their respective models. While it's possible to customize the optimizer for the server and clients separately, we opted for Stochastic Gradient Descent with Momentum (SGDM) for both. Consequently, we have the learning rates η_S and η_C, as well as the momentums β_S and β_C. The client's optimizer operates at each local epoch (τ), whereas

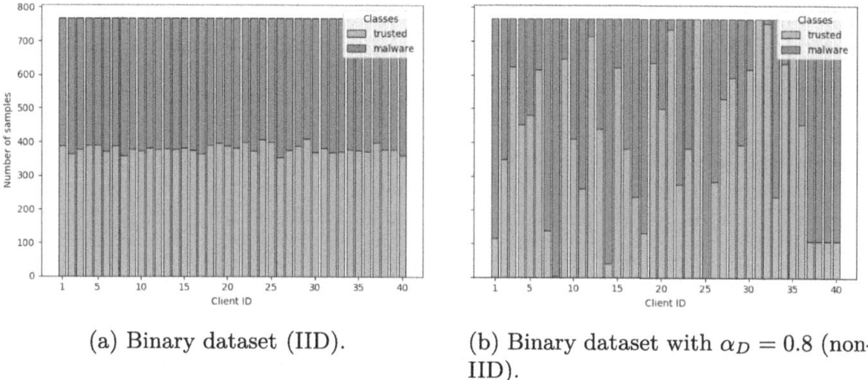

(a) Binary dataset (IID).

(b) Binary dataset with $\alpha_D = 0.8$ (non-IID).

Fig. 2. Distribution experimented based on the dataset and method applied.

the server optimizer only engages when it needs to aggregate the collaborators' updates occurring at the end of each round (T). This aspect is important because the optimizer belonging to each client has personalized momentum, following the gradients coming from each local batch.

With the introduction of schedulers, we used symbols to represent their variables: υ denotes the minimum learning rate, while ϕ correspond to the decay steps.

For the DP aggregator, a small value $\epsilon_{\text{DP}} = 6e - 3$ was chosen, as a higher noise value would affect the important clients' gradients, preventing the model from converging.

In order to understand the parameters involved in the experiments here, for brevity Table 2 indicates the meaning of each parameter, the group below the horizontal line denotes the optional parameters used.

Table 2. Here are all the hyperparameters chosen for the refitting phase.

Legend					
τ	Local Epochs	T	Global Rounds	M	Fed Population
$\mathcal{S}^{(T)}$	Cohort Size	η_S	Server LR	η_C	Clients LR
β_S	Server Mom.	β_C	Client Mom.	υ	Sched *min* LR
ϕ	Sched Decay Steps	p	Dropout		
$\epsilon_{(DP)}$	DP Noise Mult.	α_D	Dirichlet param.		

LR: Learning Rate; **Mom:** Momentum; **CFCE:** Categorical Focal Cross Entropy; **Clip:** Differential Private Clipping; **DP:** Differential Privacy.

Following the same reasoning as above, we initiated the training phase and subsequent analysis of the results. The training phase comprised $\tau = 5$ local epochs and $T = 30$ rounds, employing the FedAvg algorithm and the CosineDecay (COS) scheduler, with a population of $M = 40$ clients and a cohort size $\mathcal{S}^{(T)} = 36$ at each round.

Table 3. Here are all the hyperparameters chosen for the refitting phase of the model for the binary-classification task. We recall that α_D is used when the Dirichlet distribution method is applied since it signifies the identicalness between the distributed datasets.

Hyperparameters			
τ	3	T	20
M	40	$\mathcal{S}^{(T)}$	36
s	160	p	0.2
η_S	0.99	η_C	8e-4
β_S	0.99	β_C	0.99
ϕ	3000	υ	7e-6
$\epsilon_{(DP)}$	6e-3	α_D	0.8

In Table 4 and in Fig. 3, we can analyze the convergence trends for the binary task. In the table, it is evident that the model is able to classify the malwares even though it is almost completely frozen. Moreover, we can affirm that the Differential Approach provides more stability in the training process, acting as a normalization method, as evidenced by the fact that the test loss and accuracy are closest to the validation and training values. Astonishingly, the results obtained with the Dirichlet distribution show that the best test accuracy is achieved by the model without GN. Nonetheless, the result yielded by the custom architecture is very close to this, actually, in the training and validation sets, the metrics indicate that the GN model is the best. It may be that in terms of accuracy, the BN model has reached better results, however, when checking the loss parameter, we can see that the best result is achieved by the pretrained model, confirming our considerations.

In Fig. 4, we can see the validation results yielded by the model. Conversely, the best results have been achieved with the default aggregation module, unlike the test accuracy. This confirms that the Differential Private approach has normalization properties, enhancing the generalization capabilities during the training phase. The model with the best metrics has been used to create a Confusion Matrix in Fig. 5.

4 Related Works

In order to correctly evaluate our results and draw conclusions, we need to acknowledge our self on other solutions proposed on the android environment.

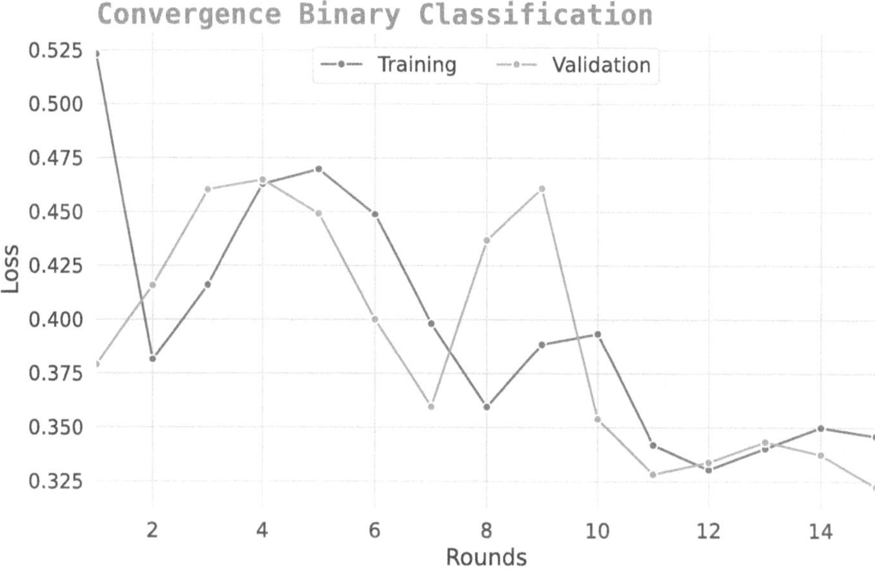

Fig. 3. Loss trend during the training and validation phases.

Table 4. These are the results obtained from the experiments conducted using the original MobileNetV3 architecture with Batch Normalization, and the custom architecture with Group Normalization.

Centralized								
Norm.	Agg.	$\mathcal{L}$(TR)	$\mathcal{A}$(TR)	$\mathcal{L}$(VA)	$\mathcal{A}$(VA)	$\mathcal{L}$(TS)	$\mathcal{A}$(TS)	Ex. Time HH:mm:ss
BN	**NA**	**0.245**	**0.896**	**0.242**	**0.899**	**0.247**	**0.895**	**00:33:34**
GN	NA	0.286	0.882	0.287	0.881	0.296	0.883	00:34:00
Default Distribution								
Norm.	Agg.	$\mathcal{L}(p_{(\mathrm{TR})})$	$\mathcal{A}(p_{(\mathrm{TR})})$	$\mathcal{L}$(VA)	$\mathcal{A}$(VA)	$\mathcal{L}$(TS)	$\mathcal{A}$(TS)	Ex. Time HH:mm:ss
BN	None	0.424	0.840	0.485	0.837	0.572	0.744	04:09:51
	DP	0.429	0.841	0.490	0.835	0.499	0.819	03:10:29
GN	**None**	**0.346**	**0.863**	**0.322**	**0.866**	**0.332**	**0.866**	**04:58:56**
	DP	0.419	0.863	0.510	0.855	0.511	0.838	03:11:11
Dirichlet Distribution								
Norm.	Agg.	$\mathcal{L}(p_{(\mathrm{TR})})$	$\mathcal{A}(p_{(\mathrm{TR})})$	$\mathcal{L}$(VA)	$\mathcal{A}$(VA)	$\mathcal{L}$(TS)	$\mathcal{A}$(TS)	Ex. Time HH:mm:ss
BN	None	0.348	0.854	0.471	0.834	0.572	0.730	4:33:49
	DP	**0.3491**	**0.855**	**0.424**	**0.839**	**0.495**	**0.841**	**3:30:27**
GN	None	0.334	0.868	0.444	0.853	0.562	0.773	4:32:21
	DP	0.324	0.872	0.391	0.842	0.397	0.820	3:26:55

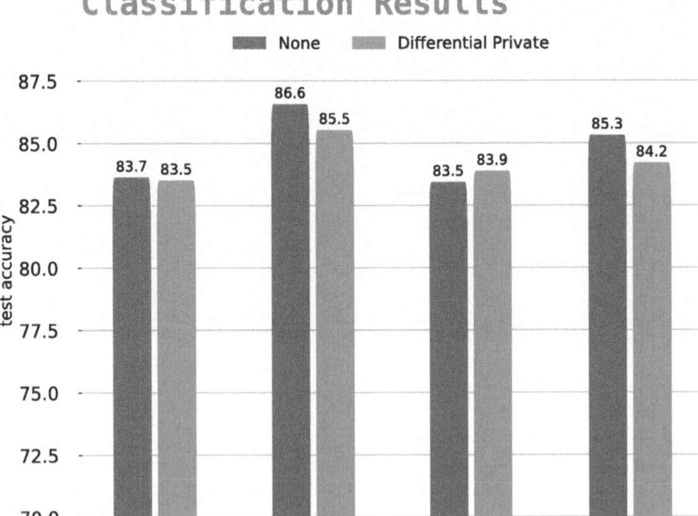

Fig. 4. Comparison between model, aggregation and distribution method.

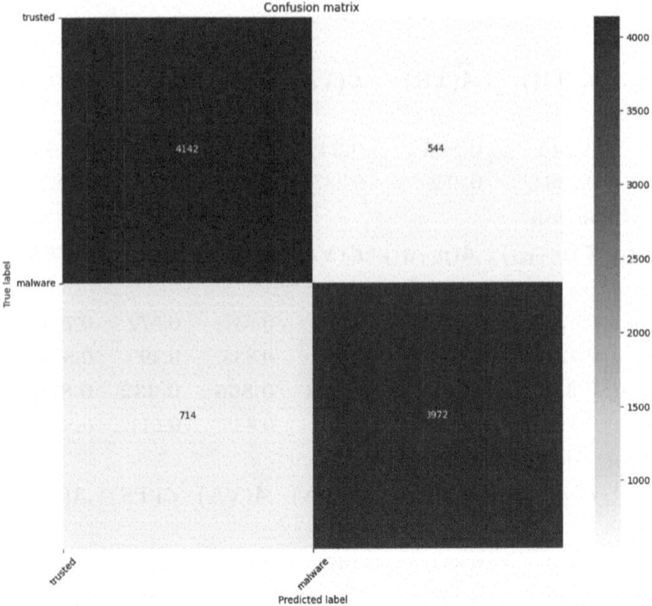

Fig. 5. Confusion matrix obtained with the classification on the validation set.

For the sick of transparency we took into consideration only federated works of the literature.

The article by [6] presents FEDriod, a comprehensive Android malware detection framework based on federated learning architecture. The framework aims to protect against the proliferation of Android malware and its emerging variants by employing a federated learning approach that respects data privacy and avoids centralized data aggregation. The authors propose a genetic evolution strategy to simulate the evolution of Android malware, creating potential malware variants for model training. They also customize an Android malware detection model based on residual neural networks to achieve high detection accuracy. The performance of FEDriod is evaluated on authoritative datasets like CIC, Drebin, and Contagio. The results show that the local model outperforms baseline classifiers, and in a federated scenario, FEDriod surpasses state-of-the-art detection methods with an F1 score of 98.53% in cross-dataset evaluation6. The method also demonstrates the ability to detect Android malware variants effectively.

The article [7] presents PE-FedAvg, a privacy-enhanced federated learning system designed for distributed Android malware detection. The main purpose is to protect user privacy while ensuring effective malware detection. The system achieves this by adding Gaussian noise to client-uploaded data and using an improved homomorphic encryption algorithm to secure gradient weight information exchange. Demonstrates high accuracy rates of 98.61% and 99.3% on the Drebin and Malgenome datasets, respectively. The results highlight the system's ability to enhance security and effectively detect Android malware without compromising user privacy.

The article [8] presents an approach to Android malware classification using Perm-Maps, which are special features combining Android permissions with their severity levels. The authors propose a federated architecture to enhance the training process of a CNN. Their experimental results demonstrate an improvement in accuracy compared to traditional classifiers like J48 trees and Naive Bayes, particularly when dealing with unbalanced datasets. The approach also reduces computational efforts, making it a promising method for classifying different malware families on Android platforms.

The author Gianni D'Angelo, cited in the previous reference, continues his research in malware classification and proposes a federated learning approach using Markov chains to classify malware in Android-based IoT devices while preserving user privacy in [5]. The methodology involves clients processing application execution data independently and sending extracted information to a central server for model building. The results show an average accuracy of 99% on a dataset of about 50,000 Android applications with various malware families, outperforming existing methods. The architecture effectively addresses privacy concerns and data leakage threats. Additionally, Markov chain-based detectors have proven resistant to evasion efforts, as they consider the sequence of API calls to model application-related behavior as a graph where each node represents a unique API and each edge represents the transition probability between two

APIs. These results demonstrate the significant advancements and achievements in evolving technologies and efforts in this field.

5 Conclusion and Future Works

As we have noticed from the experimental analysis results, our work seems to achieve the lowest results in accuracy; however, we are convinced that our method is also one of the lightest, allowing the federated training of only the final dense part. Moreover, we have tried to make the simulation as realistic as possible by compressing the data and distributing it in a non-IID manner. Additionally, in our case, the dataset is customized and created from online research of malicious applications, which does not allow for comparison with other literature articles. In future work, we aim to evaluate our method with an open-source dataset and extract metrics such as APIs and actions to evaluate applications from multiple aspects and achieve a more comprehensive classification, while always maintaining simplicity and client-side privacy. We can consider ourselves satisfied with the results obtained by adding the differential aggregation layer with an accuracy of 84.1%, and we propose to carry out works with increasingly advanced aggregators that can be more specific for security tasks in the Android environment.

Acknowledgment. This work has been partially supported by EU DUCA, EU CyberSecPro, SYNAPSE, PTR 22-24 P2.01 (Cybersecurity) and SERICS (PE00000014) under the MUR National Recovery and Resilience Plan funded by the EU - NextGenerationEU projects, by MUR - REASONING: foRmal mEthods for computAtional analySis for diagnOsis and progNosis in imagING - PRIN, e-DAI (Digital ecosystem for integrated analysis of heterogeneous health data related to high-impact diseases: innovative model of care and research), Health Operational Plan, FSC 2014-2020, PRIN-MUR-Ministry of Health, the National Plan for NRRP Complementary Investments D^3 4 Health: Digital Driven Diagnostics, prognostics and therapeutics for sustainable Health care, Progetto MolisCTe, Ministero delle Imprese e del Made in Italy, Italy, CUP: D33B22000060001, FORESEEN: FORmal mEthodS for attack dEtEction in autonomous driviNg systems CUP N.P2022WYAEW and ALOHA: a framework for monitoring the physical and psychological health status of the Worker through Object detection and federated machine learning, Call for Collaborative Research BRiC -2024, INAIL.

Disclosure of Interests. The authors have no competing interests.

References

1. Mittal, S., Paterson, J., Taylor, J., Chiaraviglio, N., Vishnubholta, K.: Global Mobile Threat Report. Zimperium, Texas (2024)
2. Andrew, G., Thakkar, O., Brendan McMahan, H., Ramaswamy, S.: Differentially Private Learning with Adaptive Clipping, arXiv, 1905.03871 (2022)
3. Brendan McMahan, H., Ramage , D., Talwar, K., Zhang, L.: Learning Differentially Private Recurrent Language Models, 1710.06963 (2018)

4. Ciaramella, G., Martinelli, F., Mercaldo, F., Peluso, C., Santone, A.: An Approach for Privacy-Preserving Mobile Malware Detection Through Federated Machine Learning, Scitepress, 127306/127306 (2024)
5. D'Angelo, G., Farsimadan, E., Ficco, M., Palmieri, F., Robustelli, A.: Privacy-preserving malware detection in Android-based IoT devices through federated Markov chains, Future Generation Computer Systems (2023). https://doi.org/10.1016/j.future.2023.05.021
6. Fang, W., et al.: Comprehensive android malware detection based on federated learning architecture. IEEE Trans. Inf. Forensics Secur. (2023). https://api.semanticscholar.org/CorpusID:259364987
7. Tang, J., et al.: PE-FedAvg: a privacy-enhanced federated learning for distributed android malware detection. In: 2023 IEEE Intl Conf on Parallel & Distributed Processing with Applications (2023). https://api.semanticscholar.org/CorpusID:269090337
8. Gianni , D., Francesco, P., Antonio, R.: Cluster Computing. In: 2023 IEEE Intl Conf on Parallel & Distributed Processing with Applications (2022). https://doi.org/10.1007/s10586-021-03490-2

A Generative Model Based Honeypot for Industrial OPC UA Communication

Olaf Sassnick[1,2,3(✉)], Georg Schäfer[1,2,3], Thomas Rosenstatter[1,2], and Stefan Huber[1,2]

[1] Josef Ressel Centre for Intelligent and Secure Industrial Automation, Salzburg, Austria
olaf.sassnick@fh-salzburg.ac.at
[2] Salzburg University of Applied Sciences, Salzburg, Austria
[3] Paris Lodron University of Salzburg, Salzburg, Austria

Abstract. Industrial Operational Technology (OT) systems are increasingly targeted by cyber-attacks due to their integration with Information Technology (IT) systems in the Industry 4.0 era. Besides intrusion detection systems, honeypots can effectively detect these attacks. However, creating realistic honeypots for brownfield systems is particularly challenging. This paper introduces a generative model-based honeypot designed to mimic industrial OPC UA communication. Utilizing a Long Short-Term Memory (LSTM) network, the honeypot learns the characteristics of a highly dynamic mechatronic system from recorded state space trajectories. Our contributions are twofold: first, we present a proof-of-concept for a honeypot based on generative machine-learning models, and second, we publish a dataset for a cyclic industrial process. The results demonstrate that a generative model-based honeypot can feasibly replicate a cyclic industrial process via OPC UA communication. In the short-term, the generative model indicates a stable and plausible trajectory generation, while deviations occur over extended periods. The proposed honeypot implementation operates efficiently on constrained hardware, requiring low computational resources. Future work will focus on improving model accuracy, interaction capabilities, and extending the dataset for broader applications.

Keywords: Operational Technology · Industrial Control System · Cyber Physical System · OPC UA · Security · Honeypot · Dataset

1 Introduction

Operational Technologies (OTs) in industrial production environments are increasingly targeted by cyber attacks [11]. In the past, OT systems remained completely isolated from public networks and were specifically designed for production processes. This gradually changed with the Industry 4.0 era to enable data-based decisions, improving the efficiency of the overall production process.

A. Quesada-Arencibia et al. (Eds.): EUROCAST 2024, LNCS 15174, pp. 320–334, 2025.
https://doi.org/10.1007/978-3-031-83885-9_29

Two design principles for modern Industry 4.0 applications are the interconnection and information transparency [9], resulting in a convergence of OT and traditional Information Technology (IT) [5]. The increased interconnection between devices and systems, however, results in more sophisticated software and hardware technologies. As such, the vulnerability against cyber attacks increases in a sector where availability and reliability is of utmost importance. Consequently, advanced network security measures are required to keep the risks of a cyber attack at a manageable level.

In this context, a honeypot can serve as a decoy and warning system. The focus of this work is put on the creation of a honeypot that authentically mimics an actual industrial process. Regarding the industrial process [8], one can distinguish between continuous industrial processes and discrete automation processes. For example, a chemical plant implements a continuous industrial process, where a product is produced as a continuous stream. In contrast, a discrete automation process is typically characterized by the assembly of units or products via a sequence of discrete steps. Most existing datasets and testbeds for security research in the OT domain focus on continuous industrial processes [6]. For this work our focus is on a discrete automation process with fast dynamics, like it is given for a piece-wise production of goods.

Most publications on honeypots for Cyber-Physical Systems (CPSs) rely on parametrized simulations. Franco *et al.* [7] found in their survey on honeypots in 2021 only one single approach [3] that employed machine-learning algorithms out of the 44 CPS-related studies reviewed. Setting up a honeypot for a brownfield OT installation by means of a simulation, however, is a challenging task, as physical system characteristics and corresponding parameters need to be determined beforehand.

The recent advances in machine-learning enable us to replace conventional simulations with self-learning models, potentially resulting in a more widespread use. In this work, we explore a generative model approach utilizing a Long Short-Term Memory (LSTM) network to learn the characteristics of a highly dynamic mechatronic system from recorded state space trajectories. Consequently it can mimic the mechatronic system via an Open Platform Communications Unified Architecture (OPC UA) interface. OP UA is used, because it is an established communication standard in the automation industry, enabling different manufacturers to operate seamlessly together.

The contribution of this work is two-fold: Firstly, we propose a proof-of-concept for a honeypot of a CPS based on generative machine-learning models with OP UA communication. Secondly, we introduce and publish a dataset for a highly-dynamic cyclic process, which can be used to train generative models.

The remaining work is organized as follows: In Sect. 2 the concept of a honeypot and its deployment variants are briefly introduced and research questions are presented. Consequently the CPS, which is being studied is introduced in Sect. 3, at first the physical hardware, and secondly the its cyber representation, namely the OP UA information model. In the following Sect. 4 the recorded data from the CPS is described, which represents a cyclic procedure, continuously carried out by the CPS. With the data, the generative model is trained, and an overview on the employed network structure is therefore given in Sect. 5. Finally, the results of the generative model are discussed in Sect. 6 and conclusions are given in Sect. 7.

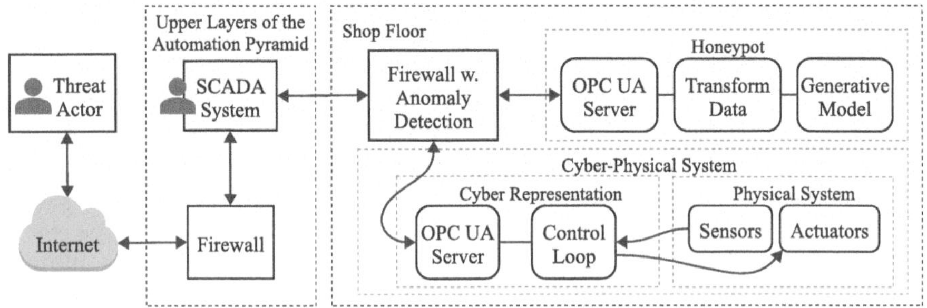

Fig. 1. Cyber-physical system architecture with a honeypot for security, where the threat actor gained access to the SCADA system.

2 Approach

In our approach, we assume a scenario as shown in Fig. 1. A threat actor is attacking a production environment remotely via the Internet. By exploiting a system vulnerability or through social engineering tactics, the threat actor gains control of the Supervisory Control and Data Acquisition (SCADA) system. Consequently, the intruder can interact with the CPS located on the shop floor, communicating via the firewall. The CPS itself implements an OP UA server and a control loop, while it has sensors and actuators interacting with the environment on a physical level. The honeypot is able to replicate the OP UA server of the CPS, including all relevant variables and their trajectories over time. For the deployment of the honeypot, we propose two variants:

Variant 1: permanently. In the traditional way, matching its original definition, the honeypot can be deployed permanently. As such, it must lure the attacker into interaction and therefore is placed easily noticeable for the attacker. For example, it could communicate only with a reduced set of security measures. Any kind of interaction with the honeypot is suspicious and will trigger an alarm.

Variant 2: on-demand For the second variant, the honeypot is only created once an intruder has been detected. At first the intruder interacts with the actual CPS, however is being detected by the Intrusion Detection System (IDS) based on introduced anomalies. Instead of ceasing the communication channel, the intruder is forwarded to an on-demand honeypot, which is set up with the initial state of the CPS, isolated from the network in the production environment. Consequently, all actions and observations by the intruder are performed on the honeypot instead of the real CPS. As such, the interaction with the honeypot exposes information regarding the attackers behavior, which in return can be utilized to strengthen the system's security.

While **variant 1** mainly extends the available intrusion detection capabilities, **variant 2** can be considered as a form of an automated threat detection and response.

The remaining work is guided by the following three research questions:

RQ1. Can a generative model-based industrial honeypot be realized by replicating a cycling process via OP UA communication?
RQ2. What long-term characteristics can be expected from a generative model?
RQ3. What hardware resources are required for the deployment of a generative-model-based industrial honeypot?

To address **RQ1**, we first introduce an appropriate CPS in Sect. 3, and subsequently record a corresponding dataset (Sect. 4). The next step involves presenting a proof-of-concept for a generative model in Sect. 5, capable of replicating the dataset's trajectories. Following this, we discuss the necessary implementation steps to deploy the generative model integrated with an OP UA server, thereby completing the honeypot. To answer **RQ2**, we examine the long-term characteristics in Sect. 6 by evaluating the Root Mean Squared Error (RMSE) for multiple generated trajectories over an extended period. Additionally, **RQ3** is addressed in Sect. 6, by providing the specifications of the deployed system hardware and presenting runtime performance metrics for comparison.

3 Cyber-Physical System

The CPS in this work is represented by a demonstrator with two fans mounted on a balancing beam, manufactured by Quanser. It has two Degree of Freedoms (DoFs), namely the pitch Ψ and the jaw Θ, as shown in Fig. 2. By controlling the airflow of two fans, configurable target angles for both yaw and pitch can be maintained.

This demonstrator was selected for multiple reasons: First, it provides system characteristics with a high dynamic range and small physical time constants, as typically found in industrial discrete automation for piecewise goods production [2]. Secondly, when compared to a typical industrial robotic arm with 6 to 7 DoFs, the two DoFs make it a good starting candidate to explore generative model-based approaches for honeypots.

System Description. The demonstrator is equipped with two actuators, specifically two DC-motors, each with a fan directly coupled to its output shaft. The speed of each motor can be adjusted by varying the supply voltage between -24 to 24 V. An optical incremental encoder mounted on the opposite side of each

DC-motor provides speed feedback. Additional sensory input is provided by two incremental encoders, one on the pitch axis and the other on the jaw axis. A control loop maintains a configurable target yaw and pitch by adjusting the airflow generated by the fans, implemented using a state-space-based Linear-Quadratic Regulator (LQR).

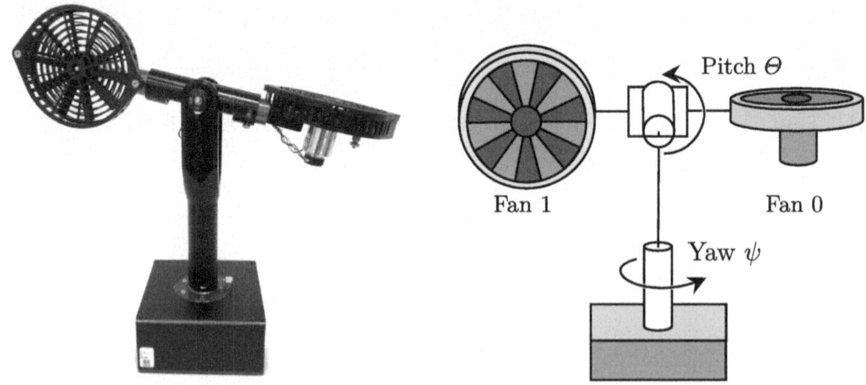

Fig. 2. The Quanser Aero 2 (left) and its schematic representation (right) in a 2-DoF configuration.

OPC UA Information Model. The OP UA information model provides an abstract definition framework for organizing and structuring data of a system. A root node serves as the entry point to the model, with the objects node containing instances of various types. In the context of the used CPS, the "Fan"-type and "Target"-type are defined within this model, as shown in Fig. 3. While the "Fan"-type is solely set readable, the "Target"-type supports read-write access.

4 Dataset

Using the CPS introduced in Sect. 3 a dataset is created. By commanding target yaw Ψ_T and pitch Θ_T angles over time, different device poses are repeatedly realized. The resulting cyclic process resembles a pick-and-place operation. The cyclic process itself consists of four different sequences, as visualized in Fig. 4, which are repeatedly being carried out. The duration of each sequence is as well given in Fig. 4.

While running the cyclic process, data is sampled at a rate of 500 Hz over a total duration of 2 h. The resulting dataset is in CSV-format and stores twelve different variables[1]. These variables include motor voltages (U_0, U_1), actual yaw

[1] The dataset is available under https://www.github.com/JRC-ISIA/paper-2024-eurocast-honeypot.

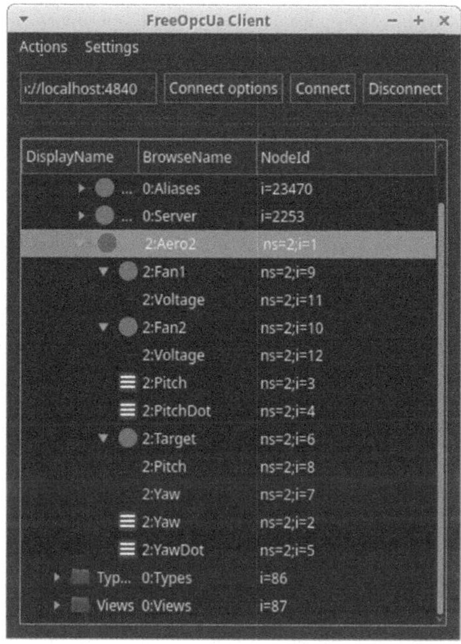

Fig. 3. OPC UA Server Interface for the CPS queried with the `opcua-client-gui` [4]https://github.com/FreeOpcUa/opcua-client-gui .

Table 1. Description of variables in the published CSV data file.

Col.	Name	Description	Type	Symbol	Unit
0	Time	Elapsed time since measurement start	–	t	s
1	Voltage0	DC-motor 0 voltage	output	U_0	V
2	Voltage1	DC-motor 1 voltage	output	U_1	V
3	Current0	DC-motor 0 current	measured	I_0	A
4	Current1	DC-motor 1 current	measured	I_1	A
5	MotorSpeed0	Rotational speed of fan 0	measured	s_0	rpm
6	MotorSpeed1	Rotational speed of fan 1	measured	s_1	rpm
7	Yaw	Actual yaw angle	measured	Ψ	rad
8	Pitch	Actual pitch angle	measured	Θ	rad
9	TargetYaw	Target yaw angle	input	Ψ_T	rad
10	TargetPitch	Target pitch angle	input	Θ_T	rad
11	YawDot	Yaw, angular velocity	estimated	$\dot{\Psi}$	rad/s
12	PitchDot	Pitch, angular velocity	estimated	$\dot{\Theta}$	rad/s

and pitch angles (Θ, Ψ), actual yaw and pitch angular velocities ($\dot{\Theta}$, $\dot{\Psi}$), and target yaw and pitch angles (Θ_T, Ψ_T). A detailed listing of each variable is given in Table 1 while in Fig. 5 selected trajectories of the second sequence are shown.

5 Generative Model

In the machine-learning domain, the relevant subdomain is time-series forecasting or prediction. For this particular application, multiple variables over a longer time period are to be predicted, a task known as multivariate multi-step forecasting.

Different forecasting strategies can be used for multi-step forecasts, most commonly used is a recursive strategy with single-step forecasts or multi-step

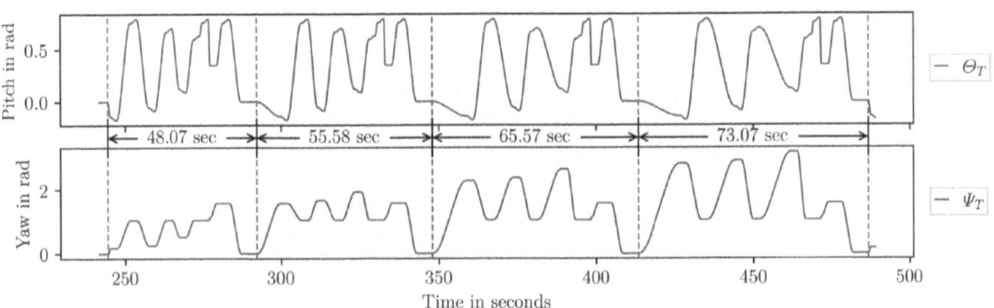

Fig. 4. The target yaw Ψ_T and pitch Θ_T angles of the CPS over time, realizing four sequences repeated in the same order multiple times. The duration of each sequence is annotated in seconds.

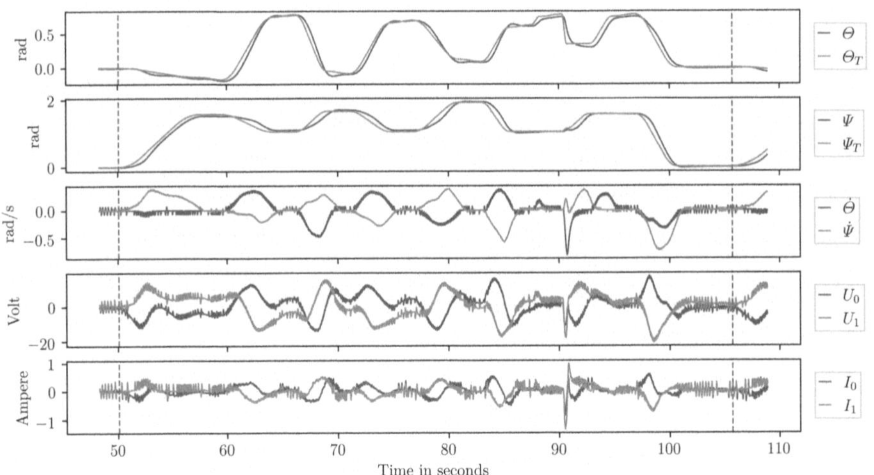

Fig. 5. The second sequence of the cyclic process with start and end marked by dashed vertical lines. Showing motor voltages (U_0, U_1), currents (I_0, I_1), angular velocities ($\dot{\Theta}$, $\dot{\Psi}$), actual pitch and yaw (Θ, Ψ), and target pitch and yaw (Θ_T, Ψ_T). The actual pitch and yaw are slightly dragging behind their targets.

forecasts [1]. As in our experiments, single-step forecasts resulted in a poor performance with multiple recursions, it was opted to use multi-step forecasts. In the end a look-back of 4 s and look-ahead of 0.4 s is used, as such the generative model uses the last 4 s (2000 samples) to generate the next 0.4 s (200 samples). To reduce the complexity for this proof-of-concept, current and speed of the DC-motors are not replicated, resulting in 8 variables, of which trajectories are to be generated. For data normalization a min-max scaler was used for all 8 variables.

For this proof-of-concept, the focus is put on LSTM, as they are reported to be overall well suited for prediction tasks [4]. The specific subtype employed is known as Encoder-Decoder LSTM. In initial experiments a single ED-LSTM with the final decoder-stage outputting all 8 variables was used. This however turned out to be challenging to train. Instead, the final approach involves using multiple smaller single-output models, which are trained individually. This method required less tuning and provides more stable results. Overall, the training is performed using the Adam optimizer with a default learning rate of 1e-3 and a default Mean Squared Error (MSE) loss function. As shown in Fig. 6, the individually trained models are joined, outputting the multi-step forecasts for the 8 variables. As such, one resulting large model can be deployed to the GPU.

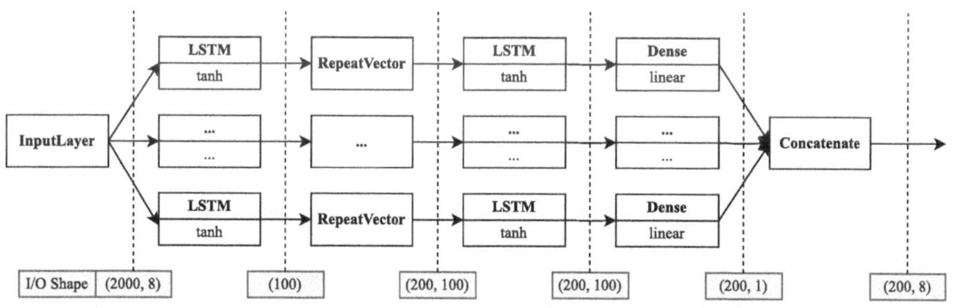

Fig. 6. Structure of the employed generative model: individually trained ED-LSTM, each for a single variable, are concatenated to build a multi-variate generative model.

In Fig. 7 the training progress of the model is visualized, showing the MSE over training epochs. Variables with higher frequency components, such as Voltage and Angular Velocities, are more challenging. These high-frequency components are harder to model accurately, which results in a slower reduction of the MSE and higher final MSE values compared to variables with lower frequency spectra.

5.1 Implementation

With the generative model defined in Sect. 5, the next step is to implement it as part of an OP UA server. The implementation is Python-based and follows the Producer/Consumer Pattern, resulting in two CPU threads working in parallel.

Figure 8 provides an overview of the implementation. In the initialization phase, the initial look-back and state for the variables is received, either directly from the real CPS or via an aggregation service as described in [10]. Afterwards, the producer thread oversees the execution of the generative model, which itself is deployed to a GPU. Once a single forecast is finished, a batch of new values is appended to a thread-safe queue at a 2.5 Hz rate. Meanwhile, the consumer thread operates the OP UA server, publishing updates of the variables at a 500 Hz rate. By doing so, it removes the values from the thread-safe queue one by one.

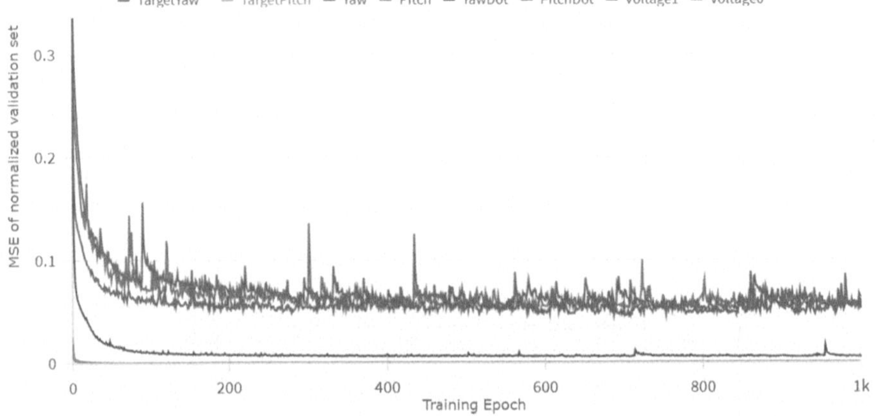

Fig. 7. Training of the generative model over 1000 epochs.

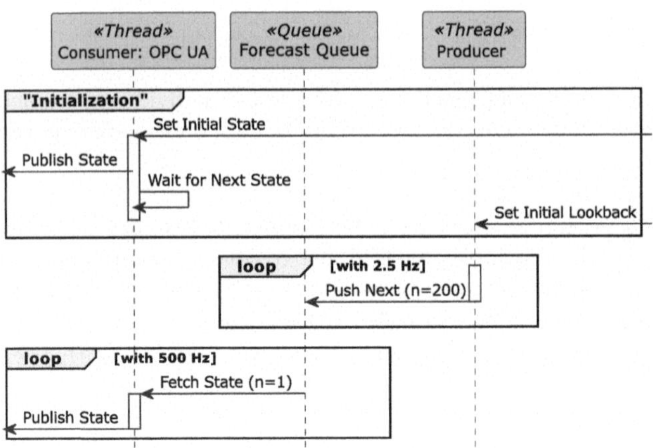

Fig. 8. Sequence diagram of the honeypot implementation.

6 Results

This section summarizes the findings from our experiments regarding the evaluation of the proposed generative model (see Sect. 5) with the newly created dataset (see Sect. 4). Besides the model performance metrics, the required hardware resources are noted as well.

6.1 Performance Evaluation

The performance of the generative model is evaluated by comparing the generated trajectories to existing trajectories from the dataset. Figure 9 shows a forecast of 6.4 s, with the time axis starting at 22 s. Up to the time of 26 s, the trajectories are used as input (look-back) for the generative model. Based on this input, the next 0.4 s are produced (look-ahead). Each look-ahead segment is indicated by a vertical dashed line in the figure. Since the generative model is operating isolated from the real CPS, every look-ahead segment becomes part of the next look-back for the generative model. Therefore, in Fig. 9, at a time of 30 s, the input for the generative model solely consists of previously generated segments. Ideally, this process can continue indefinitely, with the model generating trajectories based on a single initial input.

Following the target pitch trajectory Ψ_T in Fig. 9 more closely, discontinuities are evident in the estimated trajectory at the beginning of each look-ahead segment. Regarding ripple, while observed in the trajectories for the voltages U_0 and U_1, the replicated trajectories notably lack these features. In similar fashion, this holds true for the trajectories of the angular velocities $\dot{\Psi}$ and $\dot{\Theta}$. However it must be noted, that compared to $\dot{\Theta}$, only a lower ripple is present for $\dot{\Psi}$ on the yaw axis. There are multiple reasons for this. The lower joint, which allows for rotation around the yaw-axis, has a higher mechanical moment of inertia, therefore better mechanically dampening higher-frequency components. Additionally, the bearing of the lower joint is of a larger diameter, and it includes a slip-ring for electrical connections, together resulting in higher friction. Combined, these mechanical constraints explain well the observed lower ripple for $\dot{\Psi}$. Referring back to Fig. 7, the amount of ripple in the trajectories also correlates with the MSE in the training results.

A longer replicated trajectory of 13.2 s is shown in Fig. 10. Due to the recursive forecast strategy, errors accumulate and the generated trajectories start to deviate. For example, at 32 s, the generated trajectory is no longer in sync, instead it is slightly shifted to the right on the time-axis. This also can be observed at a time of 35 s for the voltages U_0 and U_1. Towards the end around a time of 37 s in Fig. 10, all the generated trajectories clearly deviate, seemingly resulting in unstable drifting trajectories.

In Fig. 12, the trajectories are replicated for over 8 min, in total consisting of 1200 generated segments. While clearly diverging from the original trajectories of the dataset, the generative model exhibits a seemingly stable behavior and continues to generate patterns present in the original dataset with each variable remaining within its limit.

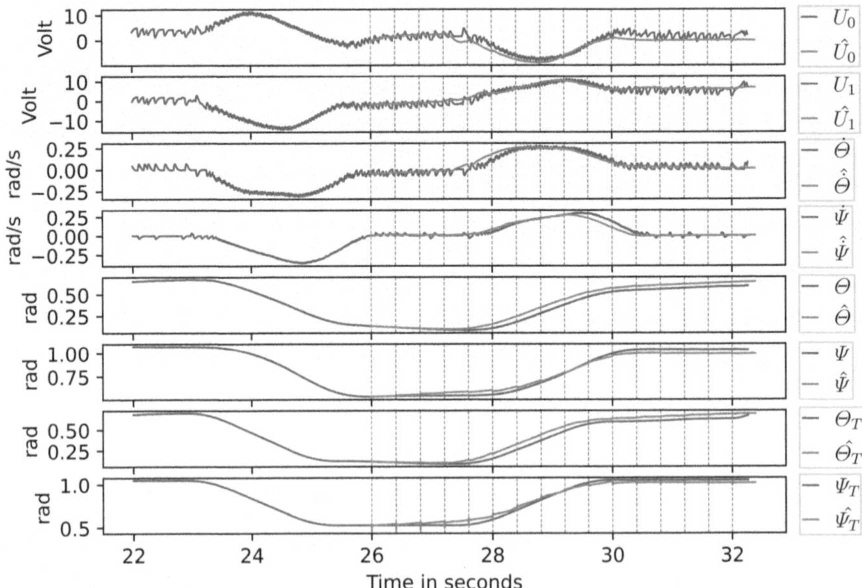

Fig. 9. The initial four seconds of data are used as input for the generative model, with a forecast of 6.4 s (16 steps) representing the state space of the trajectory. Each computation step is indicated by a vertical dashed line.

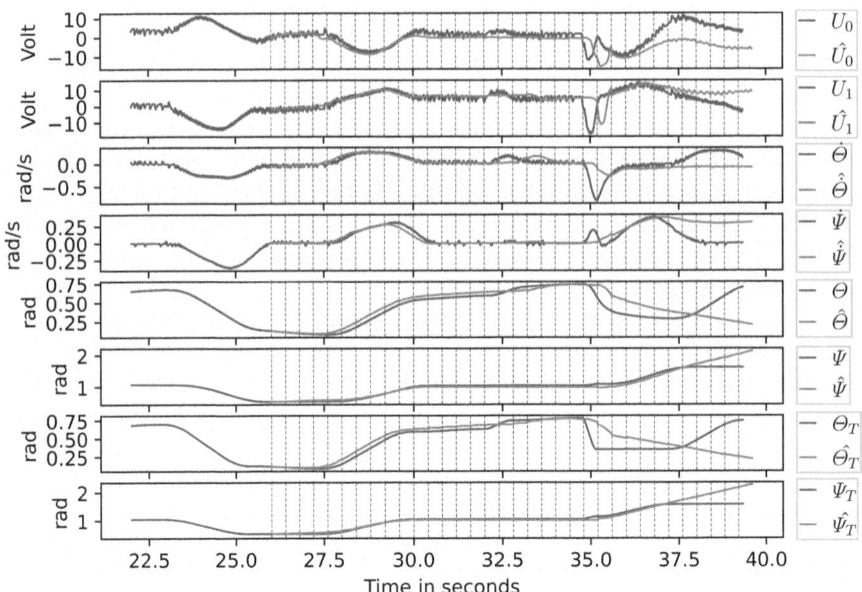

Fig. 10. Similar to Fig. 10, but with a forecast of 13.2 s (33 steps).

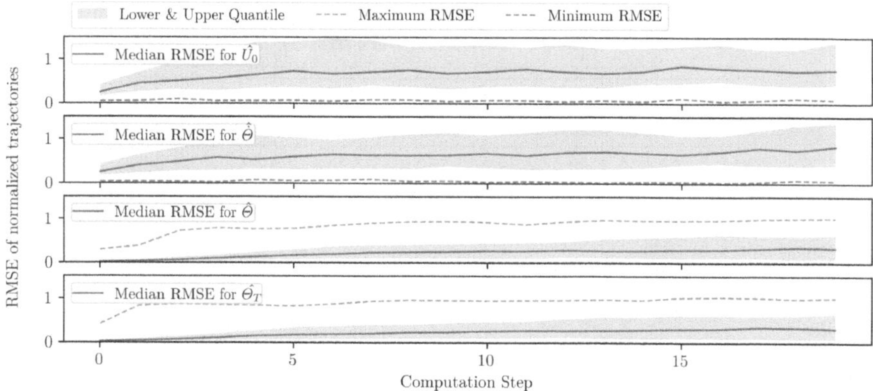

Fig. 11. Root Mean Squared Error (RMSE) of normalized values across computation steps of 301 trajectories. The solid blue line indicates the median RMSE, and the light-blue shaded area represents the range between the lower and upper quantiles. The units on the y-axis are normalized based on the min-max scaling procedure of the ML model. (Color figure online)

To evaluate the generative model statistically, 301 different trajectories are randomly selected from the validation dataset, serving as initial look-back data for the generative model. Consequently, for each input data, the model generated a trajectory consisting of 20 segments with eight variables, each made up of 200 data samples. The error of each generated segment can be computed by comparing it to the actual trajectory using the RMSE. In the following, the distribution of the 301 * 20 obtained RMSE values is examined to provide information regarding the stability of the generative model. The results are shown in Fig. 11 for the motor voltage $\hat{U_0}$, angular velocity $\hat{\dot{\Theta}}$, target pitch $\hat{\Theta_T}$, and actual pitch $\hat{\Theta}$ in this context. The unit of the y-axis is normalized based on the min-max scaling procedure of the ML model to maintain a comparable magnitude for each of the target quantities. In line with the observations of the sample trajectory shown in Fig. 10, the error of the generated trajectories generally accumulates over time. Additionally, the large shaded areas representing the lower and upper quantiles indicate that the quality of the predictions strongly depends on the initially provided input data. The proposed generative model is not able to generate trajectories equally well based on all initial look-back data. For the voltages $\hat{U_0}$ and $\hat{\dot{\Theta}}$, the results are less meaningful, as higher frequency components are missing in the replicated trajectories, therefore causing a higher RMSE.

6.2 Required Hardware Resources

The proposed implementation from Sect. 5.1 is deployed on a relatively constrained system. The system consists of an Intel Core i5 6400 series CPU, which was released in 2015, and a low profile NVIDIA A2000 GPU with a power consumption of up to 75 W. Performance measurements shown in Fig. 13 indicate

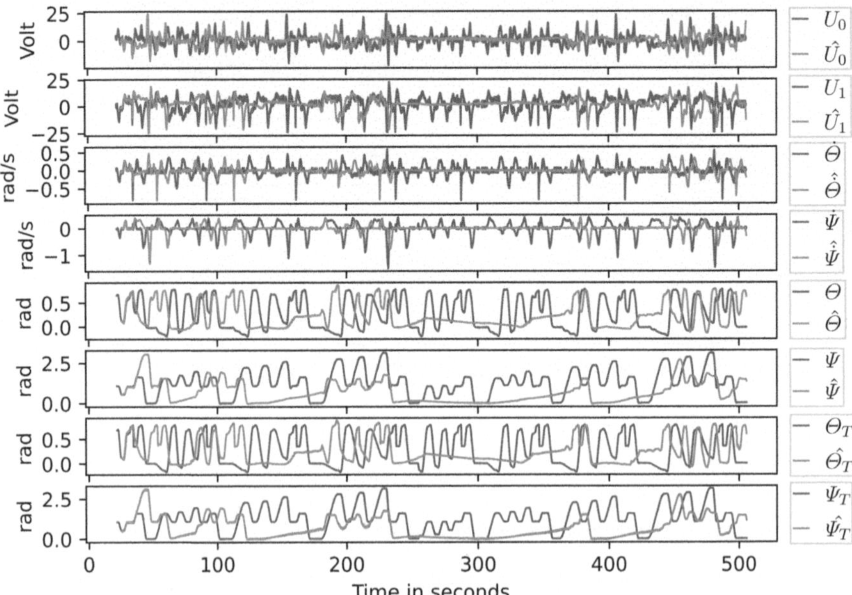

Fig. 12. Long-term forecast of 8 min (1200 Steps) representing the state space of the trajectory.

that the minimum computation time for the producer thread is 0.244 s, while the average computation time is about 0.250 s. The maximum computation time recorded is 0.261 s. Therefore, the system's performance allows to maintain an update rate of 2.5 Hz for the producer thread, enabling the consumer thread to publish updates at a rate of 500 Hz.

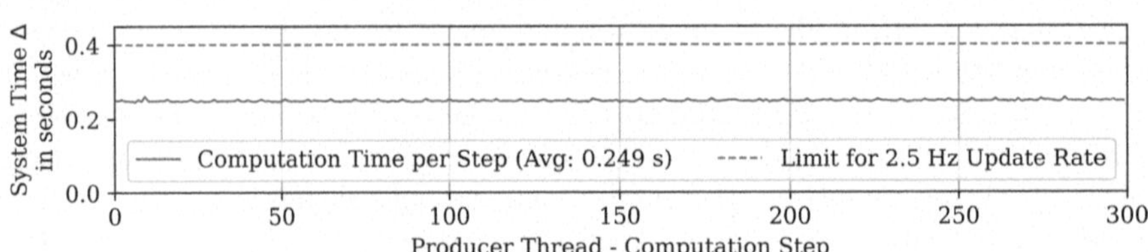

Fig. 13. Required computation time of the producer thread monitored over $n = 300$ steps.

7 Conclusion

This study demonstrates the successful deployment of an OP UA and generative model-based honeypot, giving a first glimpse of its potential for cyber security applications. The proposed implementation has managed a high sampling rate output, as typically required for discrete automation. The internal generative model is based on a LSTM network, which exhibits interesting long-term forecasting characteristics. While deviating from the actual trajectories over time, it maintains the trained variable ranges and continues to produce plausible patterns, which were observed during training. Besides the successful deployment of the generative model-based honeypot, a dataset is presented, enabling further research in which the current results can serve as an initial baseline.

As for future work, several aspects need further attention. The performance and scalability of different generative models need to be compared to improve the generative model, explore different structures, and utilize physics-based optimizers and loss functions. Modeling artificial ripple and noise is required. While it is not desirable for forecasts as it indicates over-fitting, it is necessary for a plausible trajectory replication. Then again, a highly accurate replication might not be desirable, a controllable degree of realism is required, to find a balance to generate plausible trajectories without revealing sensitive information. Also, focus can be put on the system understanding that the generative model acquires. Ideally, the generative model will gain a deeper system understanding, generalizing the training data, providing adequate responses for untrained scenarios. Finally, the current implementation only allows the intruder to observe. As such, providing a higher level of interaction for the intruder is a necessary enhancement.

Acknowledgment. The financial support by the Christian Doppler Research Association, the Austrian Federal Ministry for Digital and Economic Affairs and the Federal State of Salzburg is gratefully acknowledged.

References

1. Bontempi, G., Ben Taieb, S., Le Borgne, Y.-A.: Machine learning strategies for time series forecasting. In: Aufaure, M.-A., Zimányi, E. (eds.) eBISS 2012. LNBIP, vol. 138, pp. 62–77. Springer, Heidelberg (2013). https://doi.org/10.1007/978-3-642-36318-4_3
2. Candell Jr., R., Zimmerman, T.A., Stouffer, K.A.: An Industrial Control System Cybersecurity Performance Testbed. Technical report. NIST IR 8089, National Institute of Standards and Technology (2015). https://doi.org/10.6028/NIST.IR.8089
3. Cao, J., Li, W., Li, J., Li, B.: DiPot: a distributed industrial honeypot system. In: Qiu, M. (ed.) SmartCom 2017. LNCS, vol. 10699, pp. 300–309. Springer, Cham (2018). https://doi.org/10.1007/978-3-319-73830-7_30
4. Chandra, R., Goyal, S., Gupta, R.: Evaluation of deep learning models for multi-step ahead time series prediction. IEEE Access **9**, 83105–83123 (2021). https://doi.org/10.1109/ACCESS.2021.3085085
5. Chemudupati, A., Kaulen, S., Mertens, M., Zimmermann, S.: The convergence of IT and operational technology, pp. 3–16. Atos Scientific Community (2012)
6. Conti, M., Donadel, D., Turrin, F.: A survey on industrial control system testbeds and datasets for security research. IEEE Commu. Surv. Tutor. **23**(4), 2248–2294 (2021). https://doi.org/10.1109/COMST.2021.3094360

7. Franco, J., Aris, A., Canberk, B., Uluagac, A.S.: A survey of honeypots and honeynets for internet of things, industrial internet of things, and cyber-physical systems. IEEE Commun. Surv. Tutor. **23**(4), 2351–2383 (2021). https://doi.org/10.1109/COMST.2021.3106669
8. Groover, M.P.: Automation, production systems, and computer-integrated manufacturing. Prentice Hall, Upper Saddle River, N.J, 3rd ed edn. (2008). oCLC: ocn171536635
9. Hermann, M., Pentek, T., Otto, B.: Design Principles for Industrie 4.0 scenarios. In: 2016 49th Hawaii International Conference on System Sciences (HICSS), Koloa, HI, USA, pp. 3928–3937. IEEE (2016). https://doi.org/10.1109/HICSS.2016.488
10. Hirsch, E., Hoher, S., Huber, S.: An OPC UA-based industrial Big Data architecture. In: 2023 IEEE 21st International Conference on Industrial Informatics (INDIN), Lemgo, Germany, pp. 1–7. IEEE (2023). https://doi.org/10.1109/INDIN51400.2023.10217899
11. Makrakis, G.M., Kolias, C., Kambourakis, G., Rieger, C., Benjamin, J.: Industrial and critical infrastructure security: technical analysis of real-life security incidents. IEEE Access **9**, 165295–165325 (2021). https://doi.org/10.1109/ACCESS.2021.3133348

Theoretical Approach to Backdoor Attack on CRYSTALS-Dilithium

É. Pérez-Ramos and P. Caballero-Gil(✉)

Department of Computer Engineering and Systems, University of La Laguna, 38271 La Laguna, Tenerife, Spain
{alu0101207667,pcaballe}@ull.edu.es

Abstract. Post-quantum cryptography has recently witnessed the emergence of new and prominent representatives, such as the new standard for quantum-safe digital signatures, called CRYSTALS-Dilithium. This work presents a theoretical approach backdoor attack on that algorithm. It provides several details of the attack, which demonstrate the feasibility of leaking the original message during the signing phase.

Keywords: Post-Quantum Cryptography · Kleptography · Backdoor · Lattices · CRYSTALS-Dilithium

1 Introduction

Digital signatures play a crucial role in online security and authentication systems as they enable the verification of both authenticity and integrity of digital documents, ensuring they originate from a trusted origin and have not undergone alterations. However, with the emergence and threat of quantum computing, cryptographic algorithms employed in traditional electronic signature methods, such as RSA signature and Elliptic Curve Digital Signature Algorithm, prove to be vulnerable. Therefore, it is imperative to replace these schemes with new digital signatures that are resistant to quantum computing.

The National Institute of Standards and Technology (NIST) has recently dedicated several years of effort to the pursuit of standardizing algorithms capable of withstanding the challenges posed by quantum computing. In 2022, the four finalists of this comprehensive process were unveiled, featuring prominent algorithms such as CRYSTALS-Kyber, [1], designed for encryption, and CRYSTALS-Dilithium, [2], intended for digital signatures.

Since then, numerous efforts have been dedicated to verifying the strength of these schemes, given the importance they will take on in the coming years. In particular, NIST has recently developed the corresponding drafts of Federal Information Processing Standards (FIPS), FIPS 203 [6] and FIPS 204 [5], which specify the Module-Lattice Key-Encapsulation Mechanism (ML-KEM) and the Module-Lattice Digital Signature Algorithm (ML-DSA), derived from CRYSTALS-Kyber and CRYSTALS-Dilithium, respectively.

A. Quesada-Arencibia et al. (Eds.): EUROCAST 2024, LNCS 15174, pp. 335–343, 2025.
https://doi.org/10.1007/978-3-031-83885-9_30

In line with the research line of [3] on CRYSTALS-Kyber, the aim of this work is to establish a connection between backdoor usage, kleptography and CRYSTALS-Dilithium. Surprisingly, despite the abundance of research related to kleptographic attacks on various public key cryptography systems like RSA and elliptic curve cryptography, there is a noticeable lack of information concerning attacks on such attacks against digital signature schemes. Therefore, this study introduces a set of novel contributions aimed at addressing this knowledge gap.

This work is structured as follows. Section 2 provides essential background information for a better understanding of the attack. Section 3 gives an overview of the proposed backdoor attack. Section 4 closes the paper with some conclusions and open questions.

2 Background

Before introducing the concepts that form the basis for the message theft procedure, some preliminary terms are introduced below.

A backdoor is a hidden or secret access point that allows remote users access to a victim system. A backdoor can reach a victim system through various means: they can be pre-installed in the system, downloaded via infected files and applications through phishing, or exploited by cybercriminals through system vulnerabilities.

Kleptography is a branch of cryptography that focuses on studying methods and techniques to steal secret information or encryption keys from a cryptographic system without detection by the legitimate user or system owner.

Unlike conventional cryptanalysis, where the goal is to break a cryptographic system, kleptography aims to subvert the system to gain unauthorized access to confidential information. Some examples of kleptographic attacks may include manipulating cryptographic hardware or software to unintentionally leak secret information, introducing malicious components into the cryptographic system, or using interference signals to reveal secret information.

Kleptography can be said to explore how adversaries can potentially implant covert backdoors to compromise cryptographic systems. Therefore, according to [4], a kleptographic attack typically contains in its core an efficient algorithm called Secretly Embedded Trapdoor with Universal Protection (SETUP). This algorithm can be integrated within a cryptosystem to covertly leak secret information through the output of the cryptosystem.

Several researchers have demonstrated the theoretical feasibility and potential dangers of kleptographic attacks against certain digital signatures, such as those based on discrete logarithm [8]. Regarding CRYSTALS-Dilithium, to the best of our knowledge, the only bibliographic reference to a similar attack is [7], which is a survey on attack approaches based on subliminal channels against different NIST post-quantum signature schemes.

For the next definitions, the following notation is used. Let $q, m, n, k \in \mathbb{Z}$. If the ring of integers modulo a prime q is denoted $\mathbb{Z}_q$, let $b = (b_1, ..., b_m)$ with $b_i \in \mathbb{Z}_q$, $\forall i \in \{1, ..., m\}$. If the set of n-vectors over $\mathbb{Z}_q$ is denoted $\mathbb{Z}_q^n$, let $A =$

$(a_1, ..., a_m)$ be a $m \times n$ matrix with $a_i \in \mathbb{Z}_q^n \; \forall i \in \{1, ..., m\}$, and $s \in \mathbb{Z}_q^n$. If the polynomial ring $\mathbb{Z}_q(x)/\phi(x)$ over $\mathbb{Z}_q$ with reduction polynomial $\phi(x)$ is denoted $\mathcal{R}_q$, let $r \in \mathcal{R}_q^k$ be a *module* of dimension k.

Definition 1. *The Learning With Errors (LWE) is a search problem that consists of solving a system of m equations with errors, by finding* $s \in \mathbb{Z}_q^n$ *such that* $A \cdot s + e = b \bmod q$, *where* $e \in \mathbb{Z}_q^m$ *denotes the error.*

In other words, the definition of the LWE problem consists of hiding the value of a secret s through the introduction of noise.

Definition 2. *The Module-Learning With Errors (MLWE) is a search problem defined through many LWE instances on the polynomial ring* $\mathcal{R}_q = \mathbb{Z}_q(x)/\phi(x)$, *where* $\phi(x) = x^n + 1$, *with* $q = 2^{23} - 2^{13} + 1$ *and* $n = 256$ *so that, given a matrix* $A \in \mathcal{R}_q^{m \times n}$ *and a vector* $b = A \cdot s + e$ *where* $s \in \mathcal{R}_q^n$ *is some secret vector and* $e \in \mathcal{R}_q^m$ *is an error vector, the MLWE search problem asks to find the secret* s.

The difference between MLWE and LWE is that instead of working with Z_q, the ring $\mathbb{Z}_q(x)/x^n + 1$ is used in the MLWE. Therefore, all variables used in relation with MLWE are polynomials of some ring.

The post-quantum signature scheme called CRYSTALS-Dilithium, composed of the three algorithms shown below: Algorithm 1 KeyGen, Algorithm 2 Sign, and Algorithm 3 Verify, derives its security from the hardness of the MLWE problem.

The key generation algorithm first generates the first part of the public key, which is a matrix A. Then, it samples random secret key vectors s_1 and s_2, which are the private key. Then, the second part of the public key is computed with $t = As_1 + s_2$.

The signing algorithm first generates a vector of polynomials y. Then, the signer computes Ay and sets w_1 to be the "high-order" bits of the coefficients in this vector, and the challenge c is created as the hash of the message and w_1. After that, a potential signature is computed as $z = y + cs_1$, which is modified to prevent the secret key from being leaked from it.

The verifier first computes w_1' to be the high-order bits of $Az - ct$, and then accepts the signature if all the coefficients of z are low enough and c is the hash of the message and w_1'.

For a more in-depth understanding of this scheme, readers may refer to [2].

Algorithm 1. KeyGen

Ensure: pk, sk

1: $A \leftarrow \mathcal{R}_q^{k \times l}$
2: $(s_1, s_2) \leftarrow \mathcal{S}_\mu^k \times \mathcal{S}_\mu^k$
3: $t := As_1 + s_2$
4: return $(pk = (A, t),\; sk = (A, t, s_1, s_2))$

Algorithm 2. Sign

Require: sk, M, τ
Ensure: $\sigma = (z, c)$

$z := \perp$
while $z = \perp$ **do**
    $y \leftarrow \mathcal{S}^{l}_{\gamma_1 - 1}$
    $w_1 :=$ **HighBits**$(Ay, 2\gamma_2)$
    $c \in \mathcal{B}_\tau :=$ **H**(M, w_1)
    $z := y + cs_1$
    if $\| z \|_\infty \geq \gamma_1 - \beta$ or $\|$ **LowBits**$(Ay - cs_2, 2\gamma_2) \|_\infty \geq \gamma_2 - \beta$ **then**
        $z := \perp$
    end if
end while
return $\sigma = (z, c)$

Algorithm 3. Verify

Require: $pk, M, \sigma = (z, c)$

$w_1' :=$ **HighBits**$(Az - ct, 2\gamma_2)$
if $\| z \|_\infty < \gamma_1 - \beta$ **and** $c =$ **H**$(M \| w_1')$ **then**
    return True
else
    return False
end if

3 Backdoor Attack on Dilithium

The proposed attack against CRYSTALS-Dilithium are based on a black-box cryptographic module that introduces a backdoor into Dilithium's Sign procedure in order to obtain information about the message. As in [3], the attacker only requires access to the public outputs of the algorithm, with no other type of interaction or access required. Another assumption is that the attacker knows both the user's public key *pk* and the user's secret key *sk*.

In the proposed attack, the attacker manages to discover the original binary message M from the output of the signature scheme $Sign(sk, M) = \sigma(z, c)$. An example of application of this attack could be the following. Suppose that, during the signature creation process, the attacker installs a backdoor. Then, it is assumed that the attacked user sends the encrypted signed document or message through one channel and the digital signature through another channel. Then, the attacker proceeds by intercepting the signature, and managing to extract the document from it.

The Attack

The attack consists of hiding the message encoded in M bits within the first part of the z signature. The main concept of this attack is to hide M_{bits} in z, using a seed ρ and an XOR operation and randomly assigning 0 bits to even (or odd) numbers and 1 bits to odd (or even) numbers, as depicted in Fig. 1.

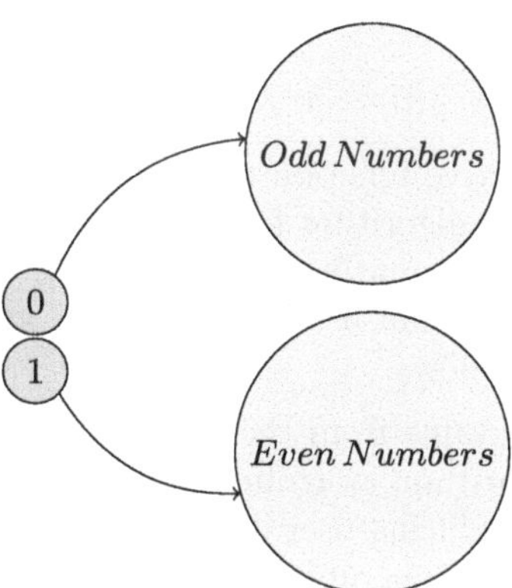

Fig. 1. Idea of the second attack

The form of z is:

$$z = \begin{pmatrix} p_1 \\ p_2 \\ \vdots \\ p_k \end{pmatrix}, \quad p_i \in \mathcal{R}_q, \quad \forall i \in \{1, 2, \ldots, k\} \tag{1}$$

Indeed, $256 \cdot k$ coefficients $p_{i,j} \in \mathbb{Z}_q$ exist such that:

$$z = \begin{pmatrix} p_{1,1} & p_{1,2} & \cdots & p_{1,256} \\ p_{2,1} & \alpha_{2,2} & \cdots & p_{2,256} \\ \vdots & \vdots & \ddots & \vdots \\ p_{k,1} & p_{k,2} & \cdots & p_{k,256} \end{pmatrix} \cdot (X^k)^t, \quad X = \begin{pmatrix} 1 \\ x \\ x^2 \\ \vdots \\ x^{255} \end{pmatrix} \tag{2}$$

In order to establish a bidirectional relationship that enables both message encoding and retrieval, it is essential to lay the mathematical foundations. To do so, the following equivalence relation is defined. Set $x, y \in \mathbb{Z}$, then:

$$x \sim_A y \iff x \wedge y \text{ are even} \tag{3}$$

Then, the quotient set is:

$$A = \mathbb{Z} \setminus \sim_A \; = \; \{[x], [y] : x \text{ is odd and } y \text{ is even (or vice versa)}\} \tag{4}$$

The equality $|A| = 2$ is evident. Additionally, considering $M_{bit} = \{0, 1\}$ leads to $|M_{bit}| = 2$. Subsequently, a bijective mapping is established as follows:

$$\varphi\colon M_{bit} \longrightarrow A$$
$$x \longmapsto a,$$
$$\varphi(0) = [0], \ \ \varphi(1) = [1]$$

This establishes a bijective function facilitating both encoding and retrieval of M_{bits}. Subsequently, the algorithm forming the basis of the proposed attack is presented, situated in the signature creation phase.

Observations from Algorithm 5 (the first three) and Algorithm 6 (the last two) can be discussed as follows:

1. Initial assignment of a value from the set $\{0, 1\}$ to the variable $x$introduces randomness to the algorithm, assigning even numbers if $x = 0$ and odd numbers if $x = 1$, thereby reducing user detectability.
2. In this step, the seed ρ is generated and undergoes the XOR operation with M_{bits}. This process yields M_ρ, establishing a secure foundation for subsequent operations.
3. During the intermediate phase of the algorithm, a detailed analysis of the length of M_ρ is performed. If the value of $\theta \leq 255 \cdot k - 1$, the $Parity$ function is applied to evaluate whether noise should be introduced to meet the condition $\theta = 255 \cdot k - 1$. On the other hand, if $\theta \geq 255 \cdot k$, M_ρ is divided into two parts, M_1 and M_2. For the first one, the $Parity$ function is applied, while for M_2, a procedure similar to the one explained in the previous attack, based on *ReduceBits*, is employed.
4. Ultimately, since z consists of $256 \cdot k$ elements, it is transformed into a $k \times 1$ matrix, where each element is represented by $p_i \in \mathcal{R}_q$, thus, $z \in \mathcal{R}_q^k$.
5. Within the *for* loop, when $M_\rho[i] = 1$, an even number within the range $[0, q)$ is assigned. By adding the value of x to it yields a number that can be either even or odd. On the other hand, if $M_\rho[i] = 0$, an odd number is sampled, and once again, the variable x is added to obtain the final outcome.
6. If $\theta < 255 \cdot k - 1$, noise is introduced. Specifically, starting from position $z[\theta]$, random elements are selected from $\mathbb{Z}_q$. This approach allows us to accurately determine the stopping point in the decoding of z while introducing a random component to make it less perceptible to the user.

Example 1. *Let's assume the attacker has access to both the user's public and private keys, and its goal is to decrypt the value of M. In particular, assume that M can be represented using an 6-bit set, specifically, $M_{bits} = [0, 1, 0, 1, 1, 0]$. Based on this, three different cases for $\gamma = len(z)$ are shown below where $\gamma = 6$, $\gamma = 8$ and $\gamma = 4$.*

Let us suppose that $x = 0$, then the zero bit goes to the even numbers, and the one bit goes to the odd numbers. Furthermore, let's suppose that $[0, q) = [0, 10)$ and the seed ρ is $\rho = [1, 1, 1, 0, 0, 0]$. Then:

$$M_\rho = M_{bits} + \rho = [1, 0, 1, 1, 1, 0]$$

Algorithm 4. Kleptographic Attack on Dilithium

Require: sk, M_{bits}, τ
Ensure: $\sigma = (z, c)$
$z := \perp$
while $z = \perp$ **do**
  $y \leftarrow \mathcal{S}^{l}_{\gamma_1 - 1}$
  $w_1 :=$ **HighBits**$(Ay, 2\gamma_2)$
  $c \in \mathcal{B}_\tau :=$ **H**(M, w_1)
  $z :=$ **Parity**(M_{bits}) ▷ Here is the backdoor
  if $\| z \|_\infty \geq \gamma_1 - \beta$ or $\|$ **LowBits**$(Ay - cs_2, 2\gamma_2) \|_\infty \geq \gamma_2 - \beta$ **then**
    $z := \perp$
  end if
end while
return $\sigma = (z, c)$

Algorithm 5. Parity

Require: M_{bits}
Ensure: z, x, θ, ρ
$x \leftarrow \{0, 1\}$ ▷ Randomly choose between assigning zero to evens or odds
$\rho \leftarrow \{0, 1\}^\theta$ ▷ Where $\theta =:= len(M_{bits})$
$M_\rho = M_{bits} \oplus \rho$
if $\theta \leq 256 \cdot k$ **then**
  ParityKernel(M_ρ, θ, x)
else
  Break$(M_\rho) = (M_1, M_2)$
  $z_1, z_2 =$ **ParityKernel**(M_1, θ_{M_1}, x), **StoreIndexes**(M_2)
  $z = z_1$
end if
Rebuild(z) ▷ z is restructured as a matrix
return z, x, θ, ρ

1. $\gamma = 6$. *In this case, if the ParityKernel function is applied:*

$$z = [1, 6, 5, 9, 3, 6], \;\; \textit{but also could be,} \;\; z = [7, 2, 9, 7, 5, 4]$$

In either of the two cases, when decoding,

$$M_\rho = [1, 0, 1, 1, 1, 0]$$

$$M_{bits} = \rho + M_\rho = [1, 1, 1, 0, 0, 0] + [1, 0, 1, 1, 1, 0] = [0, 1, 0, 1, 1, 0]$$

is obtained.

2. $\gamma = 8$. *Given the knowledge that there are 8 positions to fill, and given that* $\gamma = 6$, *the introduction of two positions of noise is necessary. Therefore:*

$$z = [1, 6, 5, 9, 3, 6, \mathit{0}, \mathit{1}] \;\; \textit{but also,} \;\; z = [7, 2, 9, 7, 5, 4, \mathit{3}, \mathit{8}]$$

To recover M_{bits}, *the same procedure as in the previous case is applied.*

Algorithm 6. ParityKernel

Require: M_ρ, θ, x
Ensure: z

$z := \{0\}^{256 \cdot k}$ ▷ Initialize z to zero
for $i := 0$ to $(\theta - 1)$ **do**:
  if $M_\rho[i] = 1$ **then**
    $z[i] = sample(2\mathbb{Z}_q) + x$
  else
    $z[i] = sample(\mathbb{Z}_q \setminus 2\mathbb{Z}_q) + x$
  end if
end for
if $\theta < 256 \cdot k$ **then**
  for $i := \theta$ to $(255 \cdot k - 1)$ **do**:
    $z[i] = sample(\mathbb{Z}_q)$ ▷ Introduce some noise
  end for
end if
Rebuild(z) ▷ z is restructured as a matrix
return z

3. $\gamma = 4$. *In this case, it is necessary to split* M_{bits} *into two sets:* $M_1 = [1, 0, 1, 1]$ *and* $M_2 = [1, 0]$. *Next, the ParityKernel algorithm is applied to* M_1 *and the index of the bit* 1 *is stored in* M_2*:*

$$z = z_1 = ParityKernel(M_1) = [1, 6, 5, 9]$$

$$z_2 = StoreIndexes(M_2) = [0]$$

Finally, just to clarify, in z_2*, the index of* M_2 *is stored where there was a* 1*. To recover* M_{bits}*, the same procedure as in the first case is applied.*

4 Conclusions

This study presents the first theoretical kleptographic backdoor attacks against the CRYSTALS-Dilithium post-quantum digital signature scheme. In particular, the algorithms have been designed to extract the M message from the signature $\sigma = (z, c)$. One attack is through z and the other is through c, both based on prior knowledge of the user's private key and the attacker's intervention during the signature creation phase. Additionally, implementations have been proposed for both attacks, where necessary experiments have been conducted to ensure their proper functionality, demonstrating flawless execution of the attacks. As part of work in progress, the analysis of a further attack using dynamic intervals instead of using parity is being developed, attacking in scenarios where only one of the keys is known, and conducting experiments to evaluate the effectiveness of recovering the M message in different cases, e.g. other than signature. Besides, several options for error correction codes are being analysed.

Acknowledgments. This research is possible thanks to the agreement between Atlantis SL and the University of La Laguna, the PID2022-138933OB-I00 project, and the Cybersecurity Chair financed by NextGenerationEU and Recovery and Resilience Facility.

References

1. Avanzi, R., et al.: CRYSTALS-Kyber algorithm specifications and supporting documentation. NIST PQC Round **2**(4), 1–43 (2019)
2. Ducas, L., et al.: CRYSTALS-dilithium: algorithm specifications and supporting documentation (version 3.1). In: NIST Post-Quantum Cryptography Standardization Round vol. 3 (2021)
3. Ravi, P., Bhasin, S., Chattopadhyay, A., Roy, S.S.: Kleptographic Attacks on Lattice-based KEMs, Cryptology ePrint Archive, Backdooring Post-Quantum Cryptography (2022)
4. Young, A., Yung, M.: Kleptography: Using cryptography against cryptography. In: Advances in Cryptology—EUROCRYPT'97: International Conference on the Theory and Application of Cryptographic Techniques, Konstanz, Germany, May 11–15, 1997, Proceedings 16, pp. 62–74, Springer (1997)
5. National Institute of Standards and Technology (NIST). FIPS 204 (Draft) Module-Lattice-Based Digital Signature Standard (2023). https://nvlpubs.nist.gov/nistpubs/FIPS/NIST.FIPS.204.ipd.pdf
6. National Institute of Standards and Technology (NIST). FIPS 203 (Draft) Module-Lattice-based Key-Encapsulation Mechanism Standard (2023). https://nvlpubs.nist.gov/nistpubs/FIPS/NIST.FIPS.203.ipd.pdf
7. Galteland, H., Gjøsteen, K.: Subliminal channels in post-quantum digital signature schemes, Cryptology ePrint Archive (2019)
8. Teşeleanu, G.: Threshold kleptographic attacks on discrete logarithm based signatures. In: International Conference on Cryptology and Information Security in Latin America, pp. 401–414. Springer (2017)

An IoT Lab Dedicated to Cybersecurity – Teaching, Learning and Research

Georg Hackenberg[1] and Mario Jungwirth[2](✉)

[1] University of Applied Sciences Upper Austria, Wels Campus, Wels, Austria
[2] Research Group Smart Mechatronics Engineering, University of Applied Sciences Upper Austria, Wels Campus, Wels, Austria
mario.jungwirth@fh-wels.at

Abstract. This paper presents the establishment of an Internet of Things (IoT) Lab at the University of Applied Sciences Upper Austria, Wels Campus, focusing on cybersecurity. The lab aims to address the educational gap caused by the rapid evolution and complexity of IoT systems, which traditional curricula often struggle to keep pace with. The lab provides a platform for hands-on learning and research, integrating IoT and cybersecurity principles across various academic disciplines. It is equipped with areas dedicated to device analysis, network security, data security and privacy, and cyber-physical systems. The paper also details the practical exercises provided to students, the hardware and software configuration of the lab, and a discussion on the strengths, weaknesses, and potential improvements of the lab setup. The lab represents a significant step towards fostering an environment of innovation and learning in IoT cybersecurity.

Keywords: Internet of Things (IoT) · Cybersecurity · IoT Lab · Education · Network Security · Data Security · Cyber-Physical Systems · Interdisciplinary Learning

1 Motivation

In the era of digital transformation, the Internet of Things (IoT) has emerged as a revolutionary technology, reshaping the way we interact with the world around us. However, with this rapid evolution comes a new set of challenges, particularly in the realm of cybersecurity [1]. Recognizing the critical importance of this field, the University of Applied Sciences Upper Austria, Wels Campus, has taken a significant step forward by establishing a dedicated IoT Lab focused on cybersecurity.

The establishment of this IoT Lab signifies a commitment to addressing the complex security challenges that IoT systems present. It is a testament to the university's dedication to fostering an environment of innovation and learning, where potential security risks associated with IoT devices and networks can be understood and mitigated [2].

The lab is not just a physical space; it is a hub of intellectual exploration, staffed by faculty members with expertise in cybersecurity. It is a platform for both graduate

A. Quesada-Arencibia et al. (Eds.): EUROCAST 2024, LNCS 15174, pp. 344–358, 2025.
https://doi.org/10.1007/978-3-031-83885-9_31

and undergraduate students to engage in cutting-edge research projects, pushing the boundaries of what is currently known and understood about IoT cybersecurity.

1.1 Problem

The complexity of IoT systems, coupled with their rapid evolution, has created a gap in the current educational landscape. Traditional curricula often struggle to keep pace with the speed of technological change, leaving students potentially underprepared for the realities of the modern workforce. This is particularly evident in the field of cybersecurity, where the proliferation of IoT devices has introduced a new array of security risks and vulnerabilities.

Moreover, the interdisciplinary nature of IoT, which combines elements of computer science, engineering, data analysis, and cybersecurity, among others, necessitates a holistic approach to education. This is a challenge for many universities, which are often structured around traditional, siloed academic disciplines [3].

1.2 Contribution

To address these challenges, universities must adapt and innovate [4]. This includes the development of dedicated facilities, like the IoT Lab at the University of Applied Sciences Upper Austria, Wels Campus, which provide a platform for practical, hands-on learning and research. It also involves the integration of IoT and cybersecurity principles across a range of academic disciplines, fostering a culture of interdisciplinary learning.

The aim of the IoT lab is to close the gap between the theory of IoT and cybersecurity and the numerous challenges in practice related to different areas, as.

Device Analysis Area:
This area is equipped with various IoT devices, hardware interfaces, and debugging tools. It is used to perform hard- and software security analysis on IoT devices, including firmware reverse engineering, hardware tampering, and side-channel analysis.

Network Security Area:
This area focuses on the security of IoT networks. It includes tools and software for monitoring network traffic, performing penetration testing, and analyzing network vulnerabilities. It could also simulate different network environments to study potential security threats and mitigation techniques.

Data Security and Privacy Area:
This area focuses on the security and privacy of data generated by IoT devices. It includes tools for data encryption, anonymization, and secure data transmission and storage. It is used also to study the implications of data privacy regulations on IoT data.

Cyber-Physical Systems Area:
Given that many IoT systems interact with the physical world (e.g., industrial control systems, smart home devices, etc.), this area focuses on the security of cyber-physical

systems. It includes setups for studying and demonstrating attacks and defenses in such systems.

Typical practical challenges are recreated step by step in the IoT lab and provided to the students in clearly formulated practical exercises, as

a. **Network design or planning**, e.g. subnetting, formation of zone, securing the conduits, redundancy mechanisms.
b. **Getting started**, e.g. initial configuration of the IP address on the device or login via default IP, check the currently installed firmware and update the device firmware including verification of the download, configuration of time zone and time.
c. **Configuration**, e.g. a switch, a firewall or options for system hardening, changing default password.
d. **Diagnosis**, e.g. WebUI, log files, port mirroring, snapshot using Wireshark.
e. **Error analysis**, e.g. defective cables, loops, ARP flooding, etc.

2 Hardware and Software Configuration – The IoT Lab

As noted previously, the goal of our new IoT lab is to enable Bachelor- and Master-level teaching as well as research and development project activities on industrial computer networks, the (Industrial) Internet of Things, and computer network security (or cybersecurity). On the one hand, we want the lab to be as close as possible to real-world systems and shopfloor installations at our industrial partner companies in Upper Austria and adjacent regions. On the other hand, we want the system to be as cheap as possible, as flexible as possible, and as easy to use as possible.

To achieve the first goal, we use industry-grade hardware components from well-known vendors such as Siemens and Phoenix Contact were possible. Besides the usual Programmable Logic Controllers (PLCs) these components also include network equipment such as industrial switches, routers, and firewalls. We believe, this additional network equipment is necessary for teaching topics around computer network security (or cybersecurity). With such network equipment, topics such as Virtual Local Area Networks (VLAN) for virtual network segmentation, Network Address Translation (NAT) for packet routing between (virtual) networks, and firewall configuration for traffic analysis and selective traffic filtering can be addressed.

To achieve the second goal, we use relatively cheap Raspberry Pis for the IoT Gateways and a standard workstation as an on-premises IoT Cloud. Furthermore, we use free and open-source software where possible: On the Raspberry Pis we run a standard Linux operating system (namely Raspberry Pi OS) as well as the low-code programming environment Node-RED for developing, deploying, and running custom software logic. On the on-premises IoT Cloud workstation we run an instance of the ThingsBoard Community Edition using Docker instead. Note that ThingsBoard provides all necessary features of an IoT Cloud solution such as device management, telemetry data processing, data analysis and visualization, and firmware updates. Finally, we equip the on-premises IoT Cloud workstation with a Wi-Fi hotspot so that the Raspberry Pis can connect to it and exchange network packets.

Figure 1 provides an overview of final hardware and software configuration of the new IoT lab at the School of Engineering of the University of Applied Sciences Upper

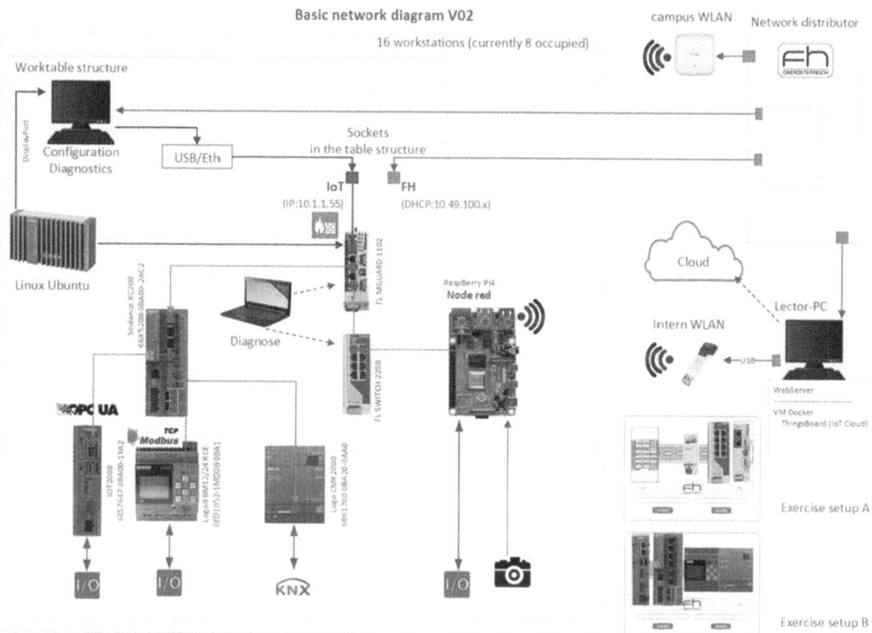

Fig. 1. Overview of the hardware and software configuration of the IoT lab.

Austria in Wels, Austria. Note that the configuration comprises **1 on-premises IoT Cloud workstation** (named *Lector-PC* and shown on the center-right of the figure) running ThingsBoard on Docker as well as **16 IoT Gateway workstations** (*big blue rectangle* on the left side of the figure). Furthermore, note that one IoT Gateway workstation is reserved for the teacher, while the remaining 15 workstations can be used by the students. Finally, each IoT Gateway workstation comprises.

- a *personal computer* with Microsoft Windows and a Web Browser as the main interface to ThingsBoard and Node-RED for teachers and students,
- one *industrial firewall* from Phoenix Contact as the top-level component in the network topology,
- one *industrial switch* from Phoenix Contact and one from Siemens both connected to the Phoenix Contact firewall,
- three *PLC-like pre-programmed components* from Siemens with OPC UA, Modbus-TCP, and KNX interfaces connected to the Siemens switch, and
- one *Rasperry Pi* running the low-code programming environment Node-RED connected to the Phoenix Contact switch.

Again, note that the Raspberry Pis communicate with the ThingsBoard workstation via Wi-Fi hotspot. Alternatively, the Raspberry Pis could use a cable-based communication path to the ThingsBoard workstation via the Phoenix Contact switch and firewall, the personal computer of the teacher or student, and a lab-wide Ethernet switch (on the top-right side of the figure), which was avoided in the first step for simplicity.

3 Practical Exercises and Solutions – The IoT Course

Our students need to work on **five different exercises** to complete the course.

- In the first exercise, the students learn how to collect and store telemetry data (see Sect. 3.1).
- In the second exercise the students learn how to visualize the collected telemetry data (see Sect. 3.2).
- In the third exercise, the students learn how to process the collected telemetry data and trigger alarms (see Sect. 3.3).
- In the fourth exercise, the students learn how remote-configure IoT devices (see Sect. 3.4).
- And in the fifth exercise, the students learn how to update IoT device firmware and software (see Sect. 3.5).

In the following, we describe each exercise in more detail.

3.1 Exercise 1: Collecting Telemetry Data

The first exercise concentrates on collection of telemetry data. Telemetry data typically represents sensor data (e.g. temperature measurements), which are recorded and stored over a longer period. For simplicity, we used a different kind of measurement in this exercise, namely the round-trip time of ICMP ping packets being between the IoT Cloud (i.e. the ThingsBoard PC) and the IoT Gateways (i.e. the Raspberry Pis).

Figure 2 shows the Node-RED flow for measuring the round-trip time on the IoT gateway in a defined interval and sending the measurements via HTTP and MQTT transports to the IoT Cloud. Note that in practice only one of the transports should be used, because otherwise the same measurement will be sent twice to the IoT Cloud causing unnecessary load.

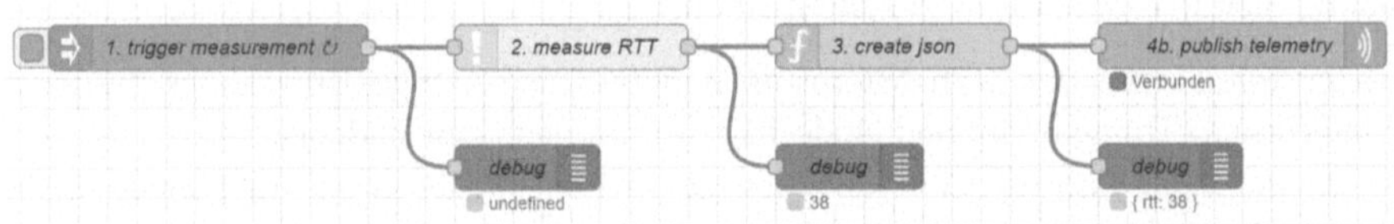

Fig. 2. Collecting measurements on the IoT gateway and sending them to the IoT Cloud.

In total, the Node-RED flow for telemetry data collection consists of four functional (i.e. none-debug) nodes and few connections between them:

1. The **inject node** *trigger measurement* triggers the round-trip time measurement in a defined interval (e.g. every 60 s).
2. The **ping node** *measure RTT* performs the actual measurement of the round-trip time using ICMP request and response messages.
3. The **function node** *create json* converts the output message of the ping node into a JSON-encoded input message for the IoT Cloud.
4. The **MQTT output node** *publish telemetry* send the JSON-encoded measurement to the IoT Cloud.

3.2 Exercise 2: Visualizing Telemetry Data

The second exercise concentrates on the visualization of telemetry data in the IoT Cloud. Typically, IoT Cloud solutions provide the concept of dashboards and widgets for this purpose. Widgets represent the actual data visualization components such as tables and charts, while dashboards arrange the widgets on the screen. Consequently, the students must configure a time series chart of the round-trip times.

Figure 3 shows a dashboard consisting of one time series chart widget showing the round-trip times measured by the IoT Gateway and sent to the IoT Cloud. Note that the chart shows the measurements of a single IoT Gateway only. In practice, the measurements of several IoT Gateways might be combined into a single chart to provide higher information density and gain better insight.

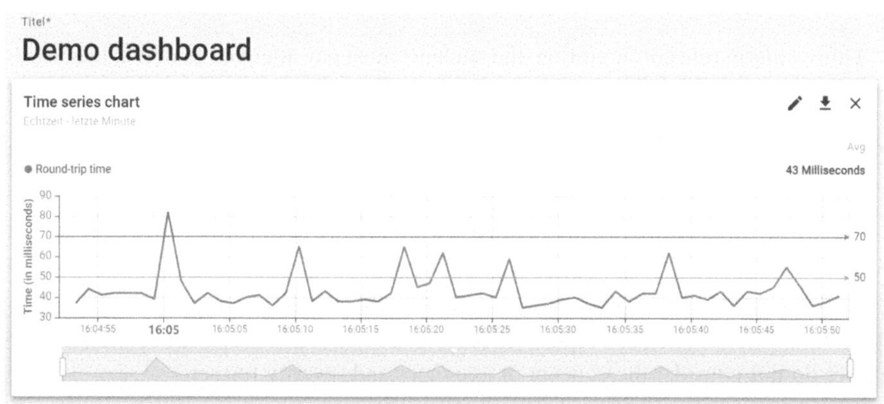

Fig. 3. Visualizing the measurements on the IoT Cloud.

The configuration of the time series chart widget comprises the following customizations, that need to be made by the students:

- The student's IoT Gateway must be selected as the **data source**.
- The round-trip time telemetry data must be added as a **series**.
- The **label of the vertical axis** must be defined to match the figure above.
- A **lower and an upper threshold** (orange and red lines) must be displayed.

3.3 Exercise 3: Processing Telemetry Data

The third exercise concentrates on the processing of the telemetry data on the IoT Cloud and on sending notifications under certain conditions. For this purpose, IoT Clouds typically provide the concept of alarm rules and alarms. Alarm rules define the conditions under which notifications are being generated. Alarms represent the actual notifications that have been sent in the past.

Figure 4 shows the alarm rules that the students must configure for their IoT Gateway. In this special use case, they must generate a warning if the measured round-trip time surpasses the lower threshold (e.g. 42 ms), and a critical alarm if the measured round-trip time surpasses the upper threshold (e.g. 45 ms; see orange and red threshold lines in time series widget of the previous section).

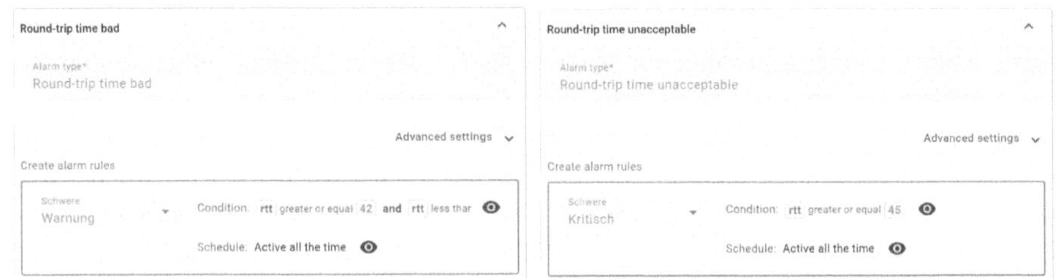

Fig. 4. Configuration of two alarm rules for warning and critical alarms.

During alarm rule configuration, the students must pay attention to define the proper conditions, under which the alarms are triggered. They must ensure that either a warning or a critical alarm are being generated, but not at the same time:

- The **value range of the warning** must include both **a lower and an upper limit** (e.g. greater than or equal to 42 and less than 45 ms).
- The **value range of the critical alarm** must include **a lower limit only** (e.g. greater than or equal to 45 ms).

Figure 5 shows actual alarms generated by the previous alarm rules. For each alarm, a timestamp, an IoT device, a type, a severity, an assignee, and a state are recorded. Note that **we do not** consider the concept of assignees and severity further.

☐	Erstellungszeit ↓	Urheber	Typ	Schwere	Assignee	Status	Details
☐	2024-05-13 14:14:12	IoT gateway 1	Round-trip time unacceptable	Kritisch	Unassigned	Nicht bestätigt aktiv	•••
☐	2024-05-13 14:12:55	IoT gateway 1	Round-trip time poor	Warnung	Unassigned	Nicht bestätigt aktiv	•••

Fig. 5. Two alarms generated by the previous alarm rules.

3.4 Exercise 4: Remote-Configuring IoT Devices

The fourth exercise focuses on remote configuration of IoT devices. IoT Cloud solutions typically provide the necessary infrastructure for managing configuration data via a public accessible Web interface and synchronizing changes to the configuration data with the IoT devices in the field. Furthermore, each application can define individually which configuration data will be used for which kind of IoT device.

ThingsBoard provides the concept of (shared) attributes for managing configuration data of IoT devices and synchronizing changes with the devices. To make remote configuration work, the students first must define a shared attribute via the ThingsBoard Web

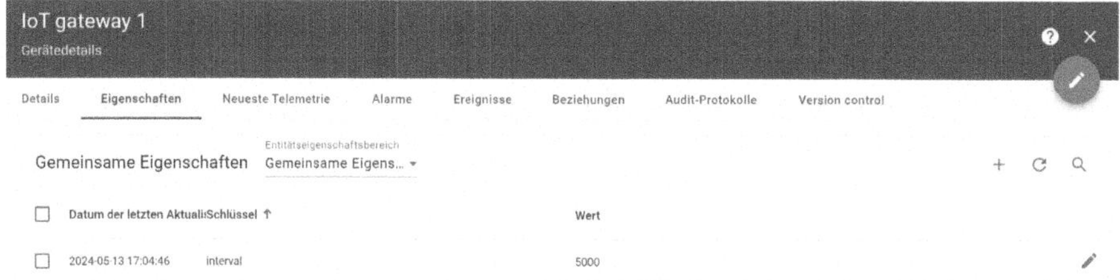

Fig. 6. Configuration of the interval for ICMP message round-trip time measurements.

interface (see Fig. 6). In this exercise, we use the interval (in milliseconds) of ICMP message round-trip time measurements as configuration variable.

After defining the configuration variable, the students must implement a Node-RED flow for requesting the current value of the variable and for subscribing to changes. Note that this functionality can be achieved both via HTTP transport and via MQTT transport. However, Fig. 7 only shows a pure MQTT-based implementation of the required IoT device behavior.

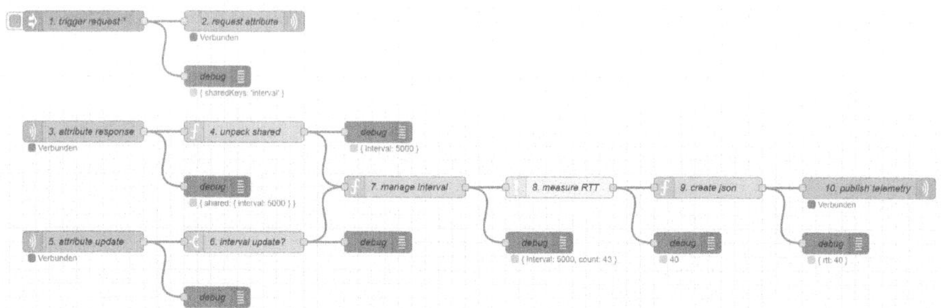

Fig. 7. Using device attributes for configuring the ping interval via the IoT Cloud.

The Node-RED flow for remote configuration of IoT devices consists of nine functional (i.e. none-debug) nodes and several connections between them:

1. The **inject node** *trigger request* makes sure the IoT devices requests the current value of the configuration variable at flow start.
2. The **MQTT output node** *request attribute* sends a request for reading the current value of the configuration variable to the IoT Cloud.
3. The **MQTT input node** *attribute response* receives the response to the previous request and forwards the response to the next node.
4. The **function node** *unpack shared* parses the forwarded response and extracts the current value of the configuration variable.
5. The **MQTT input node** *attribute update* receives changes to the value of configuration variables and forwards these new values.
6. The **switch node** *interval update?* checks where whether the interval configuration variable was updated and forwards the update only then.

7. The **function node** *manage interval* receives current values of the interval configuration variable and turns them into a trigger interval.
8. The **ping node** *measure RTT* measures the round-trip time of ICMP messages between the IoT device and the IoT Cloud.
9. The **function node** *create json* converts the round-trip time measurements into telemetry messages for the IoT Cloud.
10. The **MQTT output node** *publish elemetry* sends the telemetry messages to the IoT Cloud for storage and processing.

3.5 Exercise 5: Updating IoT Device Firmware

The fifth exercise concentrates on the full remote update of firmware and software running on IoT devices. IoT Cloud solutions typically provide the necessary infrastructure for managing firmware and software versions and notifying IoT devices about version updates. IoT devices then need to download the version update and perform the installation process themselves.

Figure 8 shows the graphical user interface of ThingsBoard for managing firmware versions. We use this feature to manage different versions of the Node-RED flows running on the IoT devices. Note that Node-RED flows can be exported to JSON format. In our case, these JSON exports represent the firmware versions of the IoT devices, which will be downloaded and installed later.

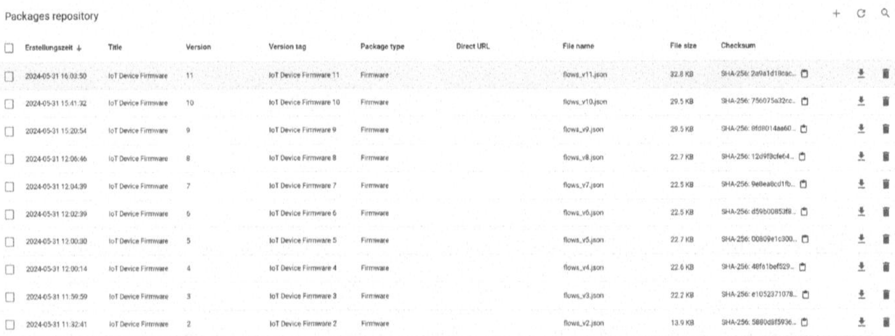

Packages repository

Erstellungszeit ↓	Title	Version	Version tag	Package type	Direct URL	File name	File size	Checksum
2024-05-31 16:03:50	IoT Device Firmware	11	IoT Device Firmware 11	Firmware		flows_v11.json	32.8 KB	SHA-256: 2a9a1d18cac...
2024-05-31 15:41:32	IoT Device Firmware	10	IoT Device Firmware 10	Firmware		flows_v10.json	29.5 KB	SHA-256: 756075a32cc...
2024-05-31 15:20:54	IoT Device Firmware	9	IoT Device Firmware 9	Firmware		flows_v9.json	29.5 KB	SHA-256: 8fd8014aa60...
2024-05-31 12:06:46	IoT Device Firmware	8	IoT Device Firmware 8	Firmware		flows_v8.json	22.7 KB	SHA-256: 12d9f8cfe64...
2024-05-31 12:04:39	IoT Device Firmware	7	IoT Device Firmware 7	Firmware		flows_v7.json	22.5 KB	SHA-256: 9e8ea8cd1fb...
2024-05-31 12:02:39	IoT Device Firmware	6	IoT Device Firmware 6	Firmware		flows_v6.json	22.5 KB	SHA-256: d59b00853f8...
2024-05-31 12:00:30	IoT Device Firmware	5	IoT Device Firmware 5	Firmware		flows_v5.json	22.7 KB	SHA-256: 00809e1c300...
2024-05-31 12:00:14	IoT Device Firmware	4	IoT Device Firmware 4	Firmware		flows_v4.json	22.6 KB	SHA-256: 48f61bef529...
2024-05-31 11:59:59	IoT Device Firmware	3	IoT Device Firmware 3	Firmware		flows_v3.json	22.2 KB	SHA-256: e1052371078...
2024-05-31 11:32:41	IoT Device Firmware	2	IoT Device Firmware 2	Firmware		flows_v2.json	13.9 KB	SHA-256: 5880d8f5936...

Fig. 8. Managing different Node-RED flows as ThingsBoard firmware versions.

ThingsBoard notifies IoT devices through (shared) attribute updates about a new firmware version. Then, IoT devices can download the new version in chunks. Each chunk must be requested independently after receiving the previous chunk. After all chunks have been transmitted, the IoT device can perform the actual installation. Figure 9 shows the implementation of this procedure in Node-RED.

The Node-RED flow of the firmware update procedure consists of fourteen functional (i.e. none-debug) nodes and various connections between them:

1. The **trigger node** *trigger request* generates an attribute request for reading the current firmware version upon flow start.

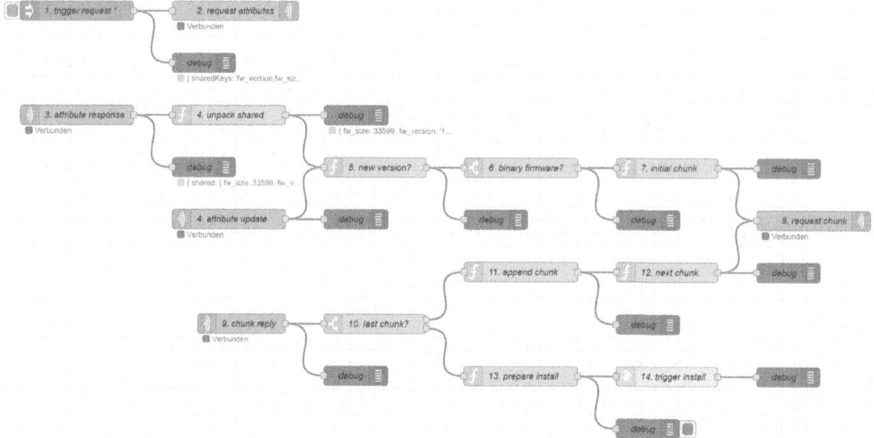

Fig.9. Downloading and installing new firmware versions with Node-RED.

2. The **MQTT output node** *request attributes* sends the previous attribute request to the IoT Cloud.
3. The **MQTT input node** *attribute response* receives and forwards the response of the IoT Cloud to the previous request.
4. The **function node** *unpack shared* unpacks the shared attributes from the MQTT payload received.
5. The **function node** *new version?* compares the version number of the requested firmware to the version number of the currently running firmware.
6. The **switch node** *binary firmware?* checks whether the new firmware can be downloaded via the ThingsBoard Device MQTT API or not.
7. The **function node** *initial chunk* prepares the request for the initial chunk of the firmware binary and initializes an internal firmware buffer.
8. The **MQTT output node** *request chunk* sends requests for chunks of firmware binaries to the IoT Cloud via the MQTT transport.
9. The **MQTT input node** *chunk reply* receives the data of previously requested chunks of firmware binaries.
10. The **switch node** *last chunk?* checks whether the last chunk was received or more chunks must be requested.
11. The **function node** *append chunk* appends the data of the received chunk to the previously initialized internal firmware buffer.
12. The **function node** *next chunk* prepares the request for the next chunk of the firmware binary after receiving and processing the previous chunk.
13. The **function node** *prepare install* parses the data of the internal firmware buffer into a proper JSON object structure.
14. The **HTTP request node** *trigger install* sends the JSON structure to the HTTP REST API of the local Node-RED instance to finish the installation.

4 Evaluation and Discussion

For evaluation, we used the previous hardware and software configuration (see Sect. 2) and exercises (see Sect. 3) in a Master-level course on the Internet of Things at the School of Engineering of the University of Applied Sciences Upper Austria. In the following, we discuss the strengths in Sect. 4.1 and weaknesses in Sect. 4.2 that we could observe during the course. Then we explain some improvements in Sect. 4.3 for the hardware and software configuration as well as the exercises that we plan to implement for the next cohort.

4.1 Strengths

We identified *four main strengths* during our Master-level course, which we explain in more detail in the following:

Strength 1 – Professional Hardware: Our hardware configuration mostly includes components from well-known vendors such as Siemens and Phoenix Contact that can be found also in factories around the world. Only maybe the Raspberry Pis represent an exception, which we use for emulating IoT Gateways running Node-RED. Note that some vendors provide industrial grade hardware components with similar features (i.e. a Linux-based operating system and a low-code programming environment). Hence, the difference of our hardware configuration to real-world hardware configurations can be considered minor.

Strength 2 – Free and Open-Source Software: We solely rely on free and open-source software for the IoT Gateways as well as the IoT Cloud. For the IoT Gateways we use a standard Linux operating system (i.e. Raspberry Pi OS) running the low-code programming environment Node-RED. For the IoT Cloud we use ThingsBoard, which provides all necessary features such as IoT device management, remote IoT device configuration, IoT device telemetry data processing, and IoT device firmware update over the air. Again, the difference to industry-grade commercial solutions based on, e.g., Microsoft Azure can be neglected.

Strength 3 – Low-Code Programming Environment: The exercises mainly concentrate on programming the IoT Gateways. In principle, any programming language and environment can be used for this purpose (e.g. C# and Microsoft.NET with Microsoft Visual Studio or Python with Microsoft Visual Studio Code). We decided to use the low-code programming environment Node-RED, which is based on the programming language JavaScript. One advantage of this choice is that the low-code approach is more accessible to newcomers. A second advantage is Node-RED comes with an integrated code editor, which reduces the maintenance effort.

Strength 4 – Internet Connection Not Required: The current hardware and software configuration can be operated entirely without Internet connection. You only must make sure, that all necessary Node-RED extensions are installed on the Raspberry Pis. Which Node-RED extensions you need depends on the exercises you want to give to the students. In our case, only the MQTT extension was required to allow Node-RED to connect to the ThingsBoard instance and send as well as receive information. In the future, we plan to add, e.g., the Modbus and OPC UA extensions for interfacing the IoT Gateways with the other industrial hardware components.

4.2 Weaknesses

Also, we could observe *seven main weaknesses* of the current hardware and software configuration as well as the exercises:

Weakness 1 – IoT Cloud Reset Every Time: For several reasons, the ThingsBoard workstation uses deep freeze to reset the system state after every reboot. While this is necessary to avoid negative long-term effects of accidental or intentional misuse, this poses a problem for the IoT course. The course is structured such that later lectures base on configuration steps performed during previous lectures. Consequently, the students must perform the necessary configuration steps again and again at each beginning of a lecture. Ideally, the ThingsBoard configuration state can be excluded from the deep freeze and preserved across system reboots.

Weakness 2 – IoT Gateway Not Reset Between Groups: On the Raspberry Pis we do not use deep freeze. Consequently, the system state is preserved across system reboots. This behavior is fine when serving only one group of students at a time. However, when serving multiple groups of students in parallel, each group has access to the Node-RED flows of all the other groups. Consequently, the solutions to the exercises can be shared easily. One solution would be to provide every student with his/her own SD-card for the Raspberry Pis. However, in the original hardware configuration the slot of the SD-card was not accessible for students easily.

Weakness 3 – JavaScript Programming Skills Required: Most of the exercises presented in Sect. 3 can be solved with little JavaScript programming skills. Only the remote configuration of the IoT Gateway requires some advanced JavaScript programming knowledge. In particular, the students should understand the concept of JavaScript interval functions. If such knowledge is not available, the students must be trained on JavaScript programming before being able to complete the exercise successfully. In some cases, this extra training might be feasible, but if time is limited, this poses a problem for the original goals of IoT courses.

Weakness 4 – Real Sensors and Actuators Not Used: So far, the exercises use "synthetic" telemetry data points. More specifically, we use the round-trip time of ICMP messages between each Raspberry Pi and the ThingsBoard workstation as sensor measurements. Consequently, we only measure the network latency and ingest these measurements into the IoT Cloud for storage, processing, and visualization. Obviously, it would be more interesting if the data of actual sensors would be collected and processed. Also, it would be more interesting if an actuator were controlled within the target IoT system.

Weakness 5 – IoT Cloud Features Not Considered: While the exercises concentrate on some key features of IoT Cloud solutions in general and ThingsBoard specifically (such as device management, telemetry data processing, and firmware update), other important features are not considered. Foremost we do not consider the problem of device provisioning, which is required for mass-deployment of IoT devices. Also, we do not consider advanced data processing features such as time-series analysis and anomaly detection. Finally, we do not consider integration capabilities with email systems or other third-party solutions.

Weakness 6 – IT Security Not Considered: Currently, we use unencrypted network traffic via HTTP and MQTT protocols during the course only. Furthermore, we do not discuss topics such as network sniffing, data encryption/decryption, certificates and certificate authorities, public key infrastructures (PKIs), IoT device tampering, and trusted platform modules (TPMs). Finally, we also do not touch the configuration of the industry-grade firewalls, which are included in the hardware configuration in principle. These elements should be considered in IoT courses focusing more on the security of computer networks and networked information systems.

Weakness 7 – Wi-Fi Hotspot via USB Stick Not Stable: Finally, we observed issues with the Wi-Fi hotspot provided by the ThingsBoard workstation for the Raspberry Pis. While the hotspot via USB stick was a cheap and easy solution for delivering IoT Gateway connectivity including Internet access, it is probably not the most stable and sustainable solution. Usually, IoT Gateway connectivity issues started occurring during the second half of the lectures. Also, if such connectivity issues occurred, they typically concerned all Raspberry Pis at the same time, but also disappeared by themselves after about half a minute.

4.3 Improvements

Based on our experiences with the previous Master-level IoT course, we plan to implement the following improvements in the future:

Improvement 1 – Cable-Based Connectivity to IoT Cloud: First, we plan to improve the stability of the connectivity between the IoT Gateways and the IoT Cloud. As explained previously, currently the connectivity is based on a Wi-Fi hotspot leading to unplanned network outages. In the future, we want to setup a cable-based solution connecting all student workplaces with the teacher's workplace and the ThingsBoard workstation. One challenge we need to solve is providing Internet access to the Raspberry Pis through the ThingsBoard workstation. Therefore, we need to configure Ethernet routing capabilities on the workstation.

Improvement 2 – IoT Gateway Programming Environment: Then, we plan to provide an additional programming environment for the IoT Gateways, which does not require JavaScript programming knowledge. Due to the alignment of our study programs, we have two primary choices, namely C# and Microsoft.NET or Python. In both cases we must think about the way changes are deployed to the IoT Gateways. One option would be to let the students edit and compile the code on the Raspberry Pis directly. Another option would be to use the firmware update feature of the ThingsBoard cloud from the beginning. We have not taken this decision yet.

Improvement 3 – Revised Exercises: As discussed before, our current exercises do not include measurement from real sensors as well as control of actuators. To make the exercises more interesting, we plan to include Modbus-TCP communication with a pre-programmed PLC in the next step. In this extension, the PLC already runs a program that collects measurements from a temperature sensor, serves these measurements via Modbus-TCP, receives control values via Modbus-TCP, and forwards the control values to a heating actuator. Based on this setup, we plan to implement the actual control logic in the IoT Cloud via the integrated rule engine.

Improvement 4 – Strengthen Focus on IT Security Topics: Finally, we plan to extend the current hardware and software configuration so that topics around IT security can be addressed more effectively. In a first step, we plan to pre-install tools for sniffing network traffic such as WireShark on the student and teacher workstations. Then, we plan to pre-configure a public key infrastructure (PKI) for managing certificates. Based on the PKI we plan to integrate certificate-based authentication of IoT Gateways including problems such as certificate expiry, certificate renewal, and certificate revocation in case of IoT Gateway compromise.

5 Conclusion

The establishment of the IoT Lab at the University of Applied Sciences Upper Austria, Wels Campus, has been a significant stride in addressing the educational gap in IoT and cybersecurity. The lab's success lies in its interdisciplinary approach, hands-on learning, and research opportunities, providing students with practical experience in device analysis, network security, data security, and cyber-physical systems.

However, the lab faced challenges, including unstable Wi-Fi connectivity and the need for advanced JavaScript programming skills for some exercises. Additionally, the lab's reliance on synthetic telemetry data and the lack of real sensors and actuators were identified as areas for improvement.

To enhance the lab's effectiveness, several improvements are planned. These include transitioning to cable-based connectivity for IoT Gateways, introducing an additional programming environment that doesn't require JavaScript knowledge, and revising exercises to include real sensors and actuators. A stronger focus on IT security topics is also planned, with the introduction of tools like Wireshark for network traffic analysis and the pre-configuration of a public key infrastructure (PKI) for managing certificates.

Future applications of the lab extend beyond the university, potentially serving external clients. For instance, the lab could fetch data from external sources like Gerstlbräu, providing students with real-world data for their exercises. The lab also plans to incorporate Modbus exercises with real data, further enhancing the practical learning experience.

In conclusion, while the IoT Lab has made significant strides in IoT and cybersecurity education, there is room for improvement and expansion. The planned enhancements and future applications promise to make the lab an even more effective and comprehensive learning environment.

Acknowledgements. We extend our heartfelt gratitude to our training partners and sponsors - Siemens AG Austria, Phoenix Contact, and B&R Industrial Automation, for their indispensable support. We also want to express our appreciation to the team from the Department of Electrical Engineering and Electronics at the University of Applied Sciences Upper Austria, Wels Campus, for their invaluable contribution in establishing the IoT laboratory.

References

1. Aman, A., Yadegaridehkordi, E., Mahmod, Z., Hassan, R., Park, Y.: A survey on trend and classification of internet of things reviews. IEEE Access. 1 (2020). https://doi.org/10.1109/ACCESS.2020.3002932
2. Anjum, A., Siddiqua, A., Sabeer, S., Kondapalli, S., Kaur, C., Rafi, K.: Analysis of security threats, attacks in the Internet of Things. Int. J. Mech. Eng. **6**(3), 2943–2946 (2021)
3. Bisri, A., Putri, A., Rosmansyah, Y.: A systematic literature review on digital transformation in higher education: revealing key success factors. Int. J. Emerg. Technol. Learn. (iJET) **18**(14), 164–187 (2023). https://doi.org/10.3991/ijet.v18i14.40201
4. Hanan, A. et al.: Internet of Things in higher education: a study on future learning. J. Phys.: Conf. Ser. **892**, 012017 (2017)

Author Index

A
Affenzeller, Michael I-45, I-53, I-122, I-140, I-172, I-272, III-3, III-38, III-87, III-154
Ahmeti, Liron II-54
Akbay, Mehmet Anıl I-90
Albano, G. III-295
Albano, Giuseppina III-286
Alberich, Ricardo I-33
Alemán-Flores, Miguel I-443
Arias-Ruiz-Esquide, Daniel II-77
Arroyo-Pedraza, Bruno Lorenzo III-79
Ascorbe, Pablo II-345
Atsushi, Ito II-103
Attenberger, Andreas II-54
Attig, Christiane III-167

B
B. de Moura Oliveira, P. II-207
Bachinger, Florian I-68, I-122, I-172
Bąk, Artur II-88, II-103, II-113
Barrera, A. III-295
Bauernfeind, Sophie II-380
Benítez-Delgado, Sergio Leopoldo III-79
Bindreiter, Oliver III-61
Blum, Christian I-90, I-236
Bögl, Michael III-154
Bonikowski, Marcin II-125
Borghoff, Uwe M. I-15, I-23
Boticario, Jesus G. I-327
Bottoni, Paolo I-23
Bożejko, Wojciech II-103, II-125, III-69
Brandstätter, Georg I-193
Braune, Roland III-50, III-98
Bravo, José María Silva III-147
Brenner, Barbara II-286
Brenner, Walter II-286
Bresich, Maria I-211
Brito, Julio I-221
Buchenrieder, Klaus II-69
Burgstaller, Michael I-283
Buur, Louise M. II-335

C
Caballero-Gil, P. III-335
Cabrera, Alberto García III-147
Campos, María S. II-345
Caputo, Luigia III-228
Cardamone, Martina I-294
Carfora, Maria Francesca III-228
Chaczko, Zenon II-88, II-103, II-125
Christie, Lee A. I-107
Ciaramella, Giovanni III-307
Clauss, Katrin II-207
Comminiello, Danilo II-19
Cruz, Nelson Alirio I-33
Cürebal, Ahmet I-181
Cyran, Achim I-15
Czemplik, Anna I-376, I-388

D
D'Aversa, Danilo III-107
Dalkilic, Mert II-380
de França, Fabrício Olivetti I-68, I-122
Devanand, III-107
Dološ, Klara II-54
Domínguez, César II-345

E
Egger, Tim III-119
Etaati, Bahareh I-53
Expósito-Izquierdo, Christopher III-79
Expósito-Márquez, Airam III-79

F
Falkner, Dominik III-154
Fellner, Robert II-197
Fernandez-Matellan, Raul I-327
Fichtl, Fabian II-157
Fiedor, Tomáš I-412

A. Quesada-Arencibia et al. (Eds.): EUROCAST 2024, LNCS 15174, pp. 359–362, 2025.
https://doi.org/10.1007/978-3-031-83885-9

Fleck, Philipp I-77, I-272, III-12
Francalanza, Emmanuel I-294
Frank, Nils II-143
Frohner, Nikolaus I-263
Fukumori, Rika I-354

G
G. Nobile, Amelia III-277
Garnica, Oscar II-367
Geiß, Manuela II-356
Ghaeni, Hadi III-119
Giorno, V. III-295
Giorno, Virginia III-277, III-286
Glück, Markus III-132
Göhner, Ulrich II-180, II-221
Gómez, David Martín I-327
González-Navasa, Cristina I-221
Grama, Lacrimioara II-27
Grama, Stefan II-27
Groesser, Stefan N. II-273
Grösser, Stefan N. II-298
Gruszecka, Katarzyna II-103
Gül-Ficici, Sebnem II-180, II-221
Gupta, Prateek III-107

H
Hackenberg, Georg III-344
Hackenberg, Rudolf II-54
Hackl, David II-3
Haghofer, Andreas II-399
Haider, Christian I-68, I-122
Halmerbauer, Gerhard II-335
Han, Kate I-107
Hangweirer, Kerstin II-399
Hänni, Marco II-298
Hanreich, Martin II-165
Heckmann, Michael III-25
Heieck, Frieder II-157
Heilig, Leonard I-181
Heinrich, Ferdinand III-119
Heras, Jónathan II-345
Hernandez-Guedes, Abian II-77
Hidalgo, J. Ignacio II-367
Hiramatsu, Yuko I-354
Hofer, Christina I-316
Höfig, Bernhard III-132
Holzinger, Florian I-68, I-172
Hrymniak, Bruno II-88
Hu, Bin I-131
Huber, Marc I-236
Huber, Stefan II-187, III-320

I
Iannillo, Antonio Ken III-107
Ito, Atsushi I-342, I-354, I-365
Iurlano, Enrico I-148

J
Jacob, Dirk I-3
Jagielski, Dariusz II-88, II-103
Janout, Hannah II-388
Jatschka, Thomas I-251
Jungwirth, Mario I-283, III-344

K
Kalayci, Can Berk I-90
Karcz-Duleba, Iwona I-376
Karder, Johannes I-140, III-25, III-38
Kastl, Christian I-316
Khan, Shahzaib II-356
Klempous, Ryszard II-88, II-103, II-113, II-125, III-69
Kluwak, Konrad II-103, II-113
Kobayashi, Nobuo I-342
Kommenda, Michael I-272
Königswieser, Tilman II-335
Kopylov, Pavel I-294
Kormann, Benjamin II-143, III-119
Kowalczyk, Hubert II-103, II-113
Krau, Tatjana II-187
Krauss, Oliver II-165, II-311, II-326
Kronberger, Gabriel I-157
Krstanovic, Sascha I-15
Kulbacki, Marek II-88, II-103, II-113, II-125
Kulbacki, Michał II-88, II-103, II-125

L
Langthallner, Ines III-154
Leitner, Sebastian I-77, III-12, III-87
Limmer, Steffen I-211
Loeffler, Andreas I-304
Longobardi, Maria III-268
López, Alfredo II-356
Lopez-Herrero, M. J. III-199
López-Plata, Israel III-79
Lüdemann-Ravit, Bernd II-157
Lunglmayr, Michael II-3, II-12

M
Mahmud, Shadman I-304
Manfredi, Karen I-294
Martinelli, Fabio III-307
Martinez-Jaramillo, Juan E. II-258
Mauß, Niclas-Alexander III-132
Mayer, Julia I-316
Mayrhuber, Elisabeth II-367
McCall, John A. W. I-107
Meira, Jorge Augusto III-107
Mercaldo, Francesco III-307
Meyer, Conrad II-54
Micheler, Matthias II-221
Miró-Julià, Margaret I-33
Moser, Bernhard II-12
Mühle, Heidrun II-311
Mustafić, Dennis III-187

N
Nafz, Nathanael III-132
Nagakura, Kota I-354
Nagao, Yoshikazu I-354
Nakano, Tomoko I-354
Neuhauser, Philipp I-77, III-12
Nezamdoust, Alireza II-19
Nguyen Duy, Du I-45
Nicoletti, Letizia I-294
Nikodem, Jan II-88, II-103, II-113
Nikzad-Langerodi, Ramin I-45
Nitzl, Christian I-15
Nourmohammadzadeh, Abtin III-252

O
Orsolits, Horst II-197, II-207
Otani, Yukitoshi I-354
Otsuka, Ami I-365
Ott, Stefan Ch. II-239

P
Padovano, Antonio I-294
Pal, Ramandeep II-197
Panejko, Anna II-103
Paraggio, Paola III-213
Pareschi, Remo I-23
Parra, Daniel II-367
Pavela, Jiří I-412
Paz Suárez Araujo, Carmen II-125
Peluso, Christian III-307
Pendl, Klaus I-316
Pérez, José Andrés Moreno I-221
Pérez, Magdalena II-345
Pérez-Ramos, É. III-335
Petz, Phillip I-429
Piñero, Francisco Cordero I-33
Pirozzi, Enrica III-228, III-243
Pitzer, Erik I-172
Ponweiser, Wolfgang I-193
Prandtstetter, Matthias I-193
Praschl, Christoph II-43, II-380
Puertas-Ramirez, David I-327
Radojičić, Nina I-181

R
Radwan, Yousef A. I-157
Raidl, Günther R. I-148, I-202, I-211, I-236, I-263
Raidl, Günther I-251
Rajab, Tabarka II-356
Raunig, Michael III-98
Reinthaler, Martin I-131
Reyes-Cabrera, Jose Juan II-77
Rieger, Florian III-119
Ritzinger, Ulrike I-131
Robaina, Enrique Ismael Mendoza III-147
Rodemann, Tobias I-202, I-251, III-167
Rodriguez-Florido, Miguel Angel II-77
Rogalewicz, Adam I-412
Rosenstatter, Thomas III-320
Rozenblit, Jerzy II-88, II-103, II-113
Ruiz-Miró, Monica J. I-33
Runte, Frederick I-316
Rusu, Corneliu II-27

S
Sandler, Simone II-311, II-326
Sandner, Georg II-399
Santone, Antonella III-307
Sasaki, Akira I-342, I-365
Sassnick, Olaf III-320
Schachner, Clara II-356
Schäfer, Georg II-187, III-320
Schaffernicht, Martin F. G. II-273
Scharinger, Josef II-399
Schedl, David C. II-43
Schichl, Thomas I-283
Schimbäck, Erwin I-316
Schirl, Maximilian II-187
Schirmeier, Frank III-176, III-187

Schlechter, Thomas I-294, I-304
Schneider, Ralf II-286
Schuler, Stephan I-429
Schurr, Jonas II-399
Schwaninger, Markus II-239
Segen, Jakub II-88, II-103, II-125
Seliger, Raphael II-221
Skoczyńska, Marta II-103
Slezak, Cyrill II-388
Spiegel, Maximilian II-180
Spina, Serena III-213
Stachno, Andrzej I-402
State, Radu III-107
Steiger, Martin I-429
Stöckl, Andreas II-43, II-311, II-326
Strobl, Marina II-335
Sturm, Valentin I-316
Suyama, Shiro I-354

T
Taipe, D. III-199
Takanashi, Yoshiro I-342
Terroba-Reinares, Ana Rosa II-345
Tilebein, Meike II-258
Tomandl, Laurenz I-251
Torres-Ruiz, F. III-295
Trujillo-Pino, Agustín II-77

U
Uchroński, Mariusz III-69
Ullrich, Marco II-157
Unume, Lily I-354

V
Varga, Johannes I-148, I-202
Varona, Diego Ambite III-147
Velasco, J. Manuel II-367
Vetter, Julia II-335
Vojnar, Tomáš I-412
Voß, Stefan I-181, III-252

W
Wagner, Stefan I-53, I-77, I-140, I-172, III-12, III-25, III-38, III-61, III-87
Wakolbinger, Markus II-380
Wegen, Jule I-294
Wenninger, Franz III-119
Werth, Bernhard I-140, III-3, III-25, III-38, III-61
Wiesner, Dominik III-176
Windhager, Daniel II-12
Winkler, Jakob II-3
Winkler, Stephan M. II-335, II-367
Winkler, Stephan I-157, I-272, II-388, II-399
Wodecki, Mieczysław III-69
Wojciechowski, Konrad II-103

Y
Yamamoto, Hirosugu I-354
Yamamoto, Naoya I-342
Yang, Kaifeng III-3
Yasugi, Masaki I-354
Yoshiura, Yasutoshi I-354

Z
Zamorano-León, José J. II-367
Zăvoianu, Alexandru-Ciprian I-107
Zenisek, Jan I-122, I-172, III-154
Zwettler, Gerald A. II-380
Zwettler, Gerald II-165
Zyśko, Dorota II-88

The manufacturer's authorised representative in the EU is Springer Nature Customer Service Centre GmbH, Europaplatz 3, 69115 Heidelberg, Germany. If you have any concerns regarding our products, please contact ProductSafety@springernature.com

Printed and bound by CPI Group (UK) Ltd, Croydon, CR0 4YY

15/07/2026

02167621-0005